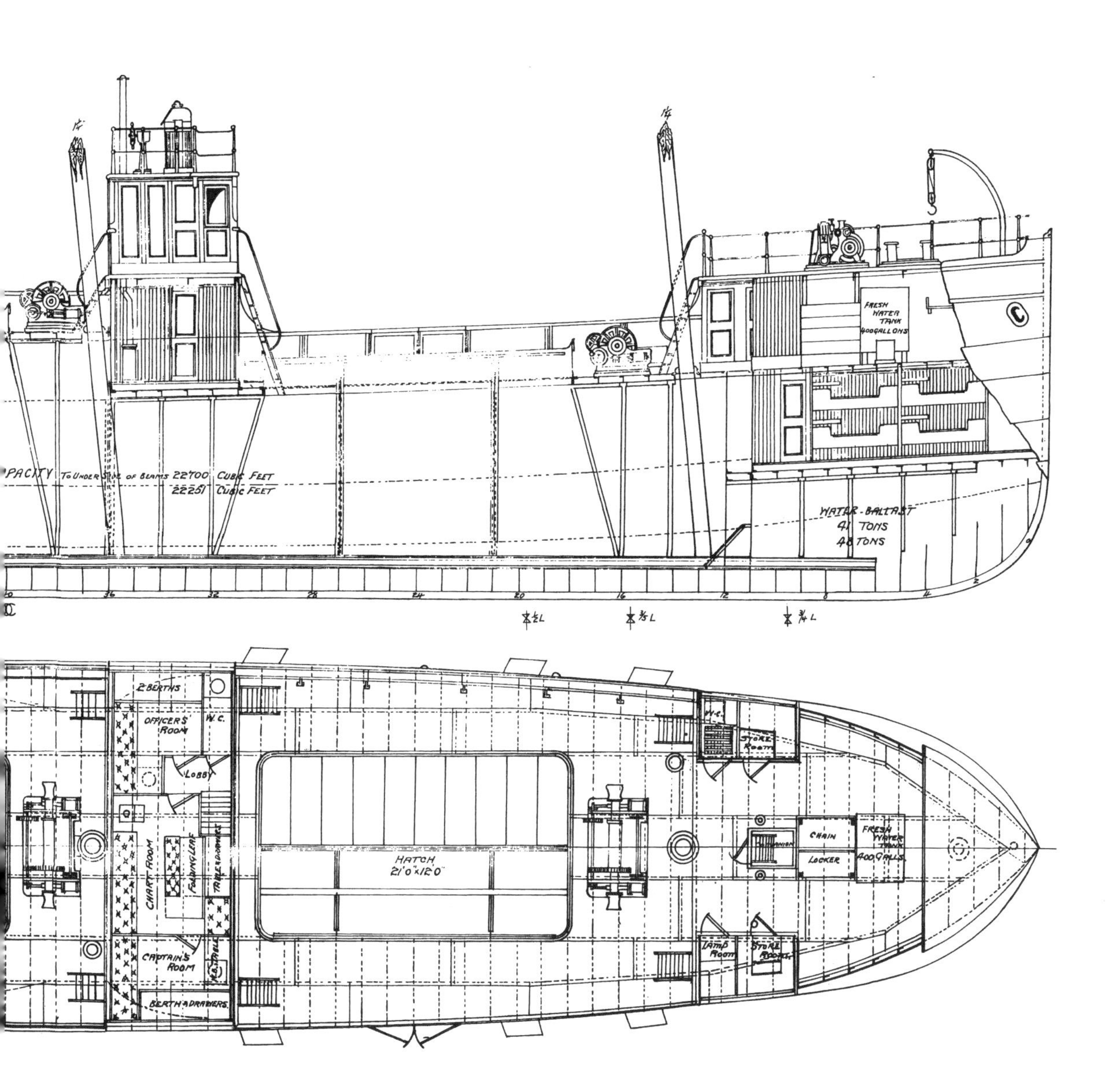
PACITY TO UNDER SIDE OF BEAMS 22700 CUBIC FEET
22251 CUBIC FEET
FRESH WATER TANK 400 GALLONS
WATER-BALLAST
41 TONS
48 TONS
2 BERTHS
OFFICERS' ROOM
W.C.
LOBBY
CHART ROOM
FOLDING LEAF
CAPTAIN'S ROOM
BERTH & DRAWERS
HATCH
21'0" x 12'0"
STORE ROOM
LAMP ROOM
CHAIN
LOCKER
FRESH WATER TANK 400 GALLS.

MERSEY ROVERS

The coastal tramp ship owners of Liverpool and the Mersey

Ashfield of the Zillah Shipping and Carrying Co. Ltd.

John Clarkson

MERSEY ROVERS

The coastal tramp ship owners of Liverpool and the Mersey

R. S. Fenton

Published by the World Ship Society
Gravesend, Kent DA12 5UB

ISBN 0 905617 84 3

CONTENTS

FOREWORD

Like a ship whose builder has more urgent calls on his time, this book has lain in frame for a number of years. It began to take shape when I realised that the amount of raw material accumulated for *Cambrian Coasters* was too much for one volume, and decided that the Liverpool-Welsh coaster owners had to await a further book. However, the keel of *Mersey Rovers* was laid over 20 years ago when I moved from the North West to London and nostalgia for home took positive shape in the form of research into the area's steam coasters.

In *Mersey Rovers* will be found many of the owners of bulk-carrying steam and motor coasters which were primarily engaged in, for want of a better word, the tramp trades. All began their shipowning careers at Liverpool or another Mersey port; several migrating from Wales to do this, others succumbing to the lure of Liverpool after a successful start at a minor port on the Mersey. Several important Liverpool owners covered in past or planned World Ship Society publications have been omitted, including the Coe, Kennaugh, Monks, and Monroe families. Also left out are owners of craft engaged largely in regular liner services and in river and estuarial trades. As the inclusions and exclusions are likely to become confusing, all the local coastal shipowners of significance have been listed in the Miscellany section. The emphasis in this book is on steam and motor coasters and, for reasons explained in *Cambrian Coasters,* sailing ships will not be found in the fleet lists, although some are referred to in the histories.

Having researched these companies over 15 years, I am all too aware of how little will ever be known about some of them. Thanks to generations of customs registrars, the record of Mersey-registered ships is comprehensive; but information on companies is neither so complete nor well preserved; whilst the oral and written testimony of family and employees of shipowners is thin and often non-existent. The historian takes what facts can be found and, with his knowledge and prejudices, weaves what he hopes is a convincing story around them. Other historians, with other facts and viewpoints, may well write different stories.

As with *Cambrian Coasters* I have attempted to examine common strands in the histories of Mersey coasters and their owners and the Introductory Survey aims to place the ports, trades, owners and ships of the river in an historical and geographical context. Writing this, I have tried to answer the question "Why did the Mersey become such a centre for coastal shipowning?" Doing this has helped me gain to a better insight into the Mersey and its large and important coastal trade, and I hope others will benefit similarly.

R.S. Fenton

Wimbledon and Hay-on-Wye

Cover illustrations: paintings of MIRIAM THOMAS and KEMPOCK by Reuben Chappell; courtesy of Ian Jones and Charles Waine.
The endpapers feature J.J. Mack's CUMBERLAND and YORKSHIRE and Henry Seddon's TREVOR.

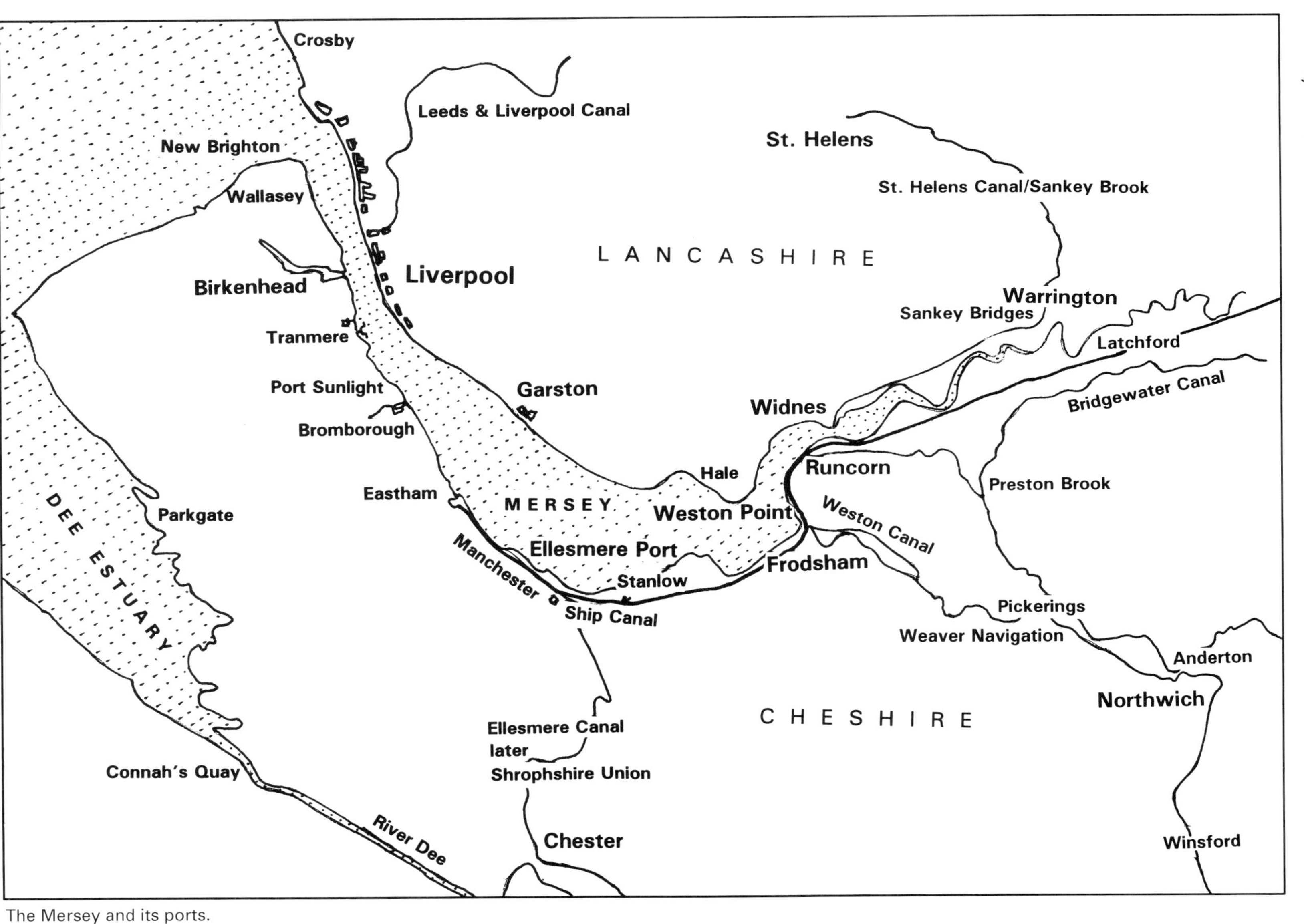

The Mersey and its ports.

INTRODUCTORY SURVEY

This survey of each of the Mersey's ports provides a geographical and historical background to the individual company histories. It will also help to explain why the Mersey nurtured so many coastal shipowners, where they came from, what kind of ships they owned and where they built them. There are books aplenty on Liverpool and the Mersey, although few bother themselves with its important coastal trades. Those readers seeking more geography and history are directed to the Bibliography.

The rise of Liverpool

Liverpool's recorded history began when advisors to King John recommended the small creek known as the Lever or Liver Pool as a base to supplement Chester for a proposed expedition to Ireland. King John's Charter of 1207 created the free borough of Liverpul. Here his subjects were free in a sense which was very important in the Middle Ages, in that they were not villeins which were virtually the property of their feudal overlord. King John invited his subjects to take small plots on which to build their homes and trade premises, and so become burgesses. They were given other trading privileges, including the right to hold a market. This cost the King nothing, but created a settlement which slowly built up a small fleet of ships which he could call upon if the area's major port, Chester, should prove surly.

From time to time Liverpool was used to embark troops for Ireland, but for the next four hundred and fifty years it remained essentially a fishing village with a very modest level of trade with Ireland and mainland Europe. The Mersey provided a safe if exposed anchorage, but the bar off Crosby, numerous sandbanks, a large tidal range and strong currents made it anything but an easy river for ships to enter or leave. This was to remain the case for almost seven hundred years, and whatever reasons Liverpool had for becoming a great port, having a superb natural harbour was not one of them. Nevertheless, the Mersey provided what was probably the best harbour between Milford Haven and Scotland, and the realisation of this superiority is reflected in the slow but inexorable rise of Liverpool, to the detriment of the other ports in this range.

For many centuries Liverpool remained subservient to Chester, of which it was for custom's purposes technically either a member port or a creek - the two towns could never agree which. It was during the seventeenth century that the relative status of the two ports began to be reversed, reflected by the granting of custom's port status to Liverpool in 1660. Physical factors are sometimes cited, with the silting sands of the Dee indicted for strangling Chester's Irish trade to the benefit of Liverpool. However, Liverpool's trade grew rapidly even during periods when Chester's river was at its best, for example in the years following improvements completed in 1737 by the River Dee Company. In truth, neither river was that well behaved towards the ports which came to depend on it. The channels of both underwent capricious changes, at different times denying sufficient water to Chester and Parkgate in the case of the Dee, and to Runcorn on the Mersey. A more likely explanation for Liverpool's rise is its links, both natural and later man-made, to its hinterland of Cheshire, Lancashire and Staffordshire.

Cheshire has been a principal area for salt extraction since at least Roman times. Originally, brine from natural springs or pits was evaporated to produce crystalline salt, but from 1670 the industry grew as the discovery of rock salt was exploited. Brine was treated locally, and at about this period coal replaced wood for heating the salt pans. Coal was being moved into the salt district from Lancashire or Staffordshire, whilst rock salt was being taken away to be refined closer to sources of coal. Given the primitive state of local roads - little improved since the Romans built them - the easiest way to move the salt and coal was by the River Weaver, navigable for small craft in the seventeenth century to Pickerings, and thence by the Mersey into which the Weaver fed at Frodsham. The importance of the Weaver to the salt trade is apparent from two attempts made to obtain Acts of Parliament to improve the river between 1660 and 1670.

Rock salt was refined on both banks of the Mersey near the mouth of the Weaver, at Frodsham to the south and Dungeon near Hale to the north. But once the salt had reached the comparatively deep waters of the Upper Mersey it could readily be carried further and, significantly for our story, a salt refinery was established at Liverpool, close to supplies of Lancashire coal. Salt was by no means the port's only export cargo, as goods such as locally-made pottery, glass and refined sugar plus Lancashire cloth were moving out in the early part of the seventeenth century. This growth in manufacturing and trade saw Liverpool expand dramatically, its population of around 5,000 becoming 20,000 by 1750. But trade in refined and coarse salt rapidly grew in importance so that in the latter part of the eighteenth century salt became Liverpool's largest export commodity.

Salt was distributed widely: by coastal vessels to fishing ports around Great Britain, and by sea-going vessels to the Baltic, West Indies, North America for the Newfoundland fisheries, and Africa. Cheshire salt was "the nursing mother" of the port of Liverpool, in the words of John Holt, helping to nurture what was already a promising infant. The significance of salt was that it provided many of Liverpool's aspiring merchant adventurers with an outward cargo: their ships then returned filled with Baltic or Canadian timber, sugar from the West Indies, or tobacco from Virginia.

Nourished by the salt trade, the growing port of Liverpool attracted entrepreneurs in a way which the older and more staid port of Chester did not. Liverpool's spirit of enterprise was seen in a spectacular form with the building between 1709 and 1715 of the world's first enclosed commercial dock; incidentally, the only dock to be constructed in Liverpool by private capital rather than by a public body. This was the first of a number of pioneering civil engineering schemes which, by vastly improving the efficiency of transport between Liverpool and its hinterland, turned it into a major port by the latter part of eighteenth century, eclipsing most other Irish Sea ports including Dublin and even Whitehaven which, until about 1750, had led Liverpool owing to its major share of the tobacco trade.

In 1720 and 1721, Acts of Parliament were passed for the improvement of the River Douglas, which allowed coal from the Wigan area to reach the Ribble and hence Liverpool by sea; to make the rivers Mersey and Irwell navigable between Warrington and Manchester; and for the improvement of the River Weaver. In 1755 came an Act to make navigable the Sankey Brook, allowing coal mined around St. Helens to be carried much more cheaply to the Mersey and to help satisfy the fuel demands of Liverpool and the Weaver salt industry. The Sankey Brook Navigation was to be particularly important to the region's industry.

The completion of the Sankey is considered to have begun the Canal Age, and the building of longer and much more ambitious canals, which were independent of existing rivers, was to dramatically improve Liverpool's connections with the developing industry of the Midlands and the North. Thanks to the comparatively short length of the Mersey suitable for navigation, Liverpool was probably the worst-connected of England's major ports in 1770. By 1800, however, it was probably the best. In 1774 the Leeds and Liverpool Canal linked the town of Liverpool with the Douglas Navigation and the important coal mines around Wigan, although the through route to Leeds was not completed until 1816, and - incredibly - the short connection to Liverpool docks had to wait until 1846. In 1776 the Bridgewater Canal was completed to the Mersey at Runcorn, providing a new link to Manchester and the growing Lancashire textile industry. This competed with the rather senile Mersey and Irwell Navigation, which retaliated at the end of the century by digging a cut between Latchford and Runcorn to bypass one of the more difficult stretches of the Mersey. The Trent and Mersey met the Bridgewater at Preston Brook near Runcorn in 1777, crossing a major watershed to provide a route to the Potteries. The Ellesmere Canal connected the Mersey with its erstwhile rival the Dee in 1797, although a strategic connection with Birmingham and its industry had to wait until 1835. The ending of the Canal Age was signalled by another major engineering achievement involving Liverpool entrepreneurs: the completion of the Liverpool and Manchester Railway in 1830.

Although the infrastructure just described was important, it must not be forgotten that it was man that built Liverpool and its trade. The growing port was able to attract the enterprising and the unscrupulous. The notorious slave trade shows what this combination of qualities could achieve: from about 1760 Liverpool became the leading

British centre of the trade, surpassing the older port of Bristol. The contribution of the slave trade to the prosperity of Liverpool should not be exaggerated, however. Although profits could be large, so could losses, and recent estimates suggest carrying slaves was no more profitable than less reprehensible trades. Indeed, Liverpool's business did not collapse on Britain's abolition of the slave trade in 1807, as its merchants were quite capable of earning good returns in other trades. The importance of the slave trade to the port is perhaps more in the trading links it forged and which ensured that tobacco and cotton from the southern United States, sugar from the West Indies, and oils from West Africa continued to make major contributions to Liverpool's import business.

Manufacturing and processing industries in Liverpool itself were initially greatly stimulated by the port's growing trade but, with notable exceptions such as sugar refining and flour milling, went into a relative decline during the eighteenth and nineteenth centuries. One reason for this was the excellent transport infrastructure which Merseyside now possessed: manufacture could take place nearer the sources of materials, particularly coal, and other raw materials and finished products be quickly and cheaply moved to and from Liverpool by canal. Land near the water in Liverpool was so in demand for dock developments that manufacturers seeking room to expand moved out to green field sites, which rapidly became anything but green. For instance, the original Liverpool salt refinery was relocated to Garston to allow for the building of a dock which, ironically, was named the Salthouse Dock.

Salt refining was predominantly an upriver activity, and it was to help develop one of Merseyside's other major industries. Using Cheshire salt and St. Helens coal, alkali was produced for the growing textile industry of Lancashire. With improvements to the original crude processes, and growing uses being found for by-products, Merseyside became a cradle for the industrial revolution in chemicals - a revolution which was to be quite as far-reaching in its effects as the use of steam or the development of steel. Liverpool both contributed to and gained from the growth of this and other industries.

A fine view of **Glenmona** entering Liverpool docks. A typical small, single-hatch coaster of a size which could trade to the smaller ports around the Irish Sea, she was owned first in the Isle of Man and then in Whitehaven. She later became **Speke** of Edward Nicholson Ltd. *John Clarkson*

The availability of alkali made Merseyside a centre of soap production, and this was later to stimulate trade in vegetable oils from West Africa. Alkali, soap and many other chemicals provided cargoes for the port's ships. Liverpool and Lancashire's cotton industry had a similar symbiotic relationship. The proximity of a major port with excellent trading links to North America helped to nurture this industry, whilst the mushrooming need for raw cotton and the export of finished goods increased Liverpool's trade.

To return to the growth of Liverpool's communications, other railways followed the opening of the Liverpool and Manchester in 1830. They began to eat away at the trade of the canals, although in some cases the "decline" of the waterways had to be hastened by railway takeovers and the subsequent disinterest of the new proprietors. Then there was the singular case of the Manchester Ship Canal opened in 1894, a waterway promoted in competition with railways and largely succeeding for its first eighty years. And just as the narrow canals had, through neglect and vested interests, succumbed to rail competition, so too did the railways decline with twentieth century road building. Alongside these changes in Liverpool's distribution network, there were even greater changes in the port's infrastructure. The majority of the vast dock estate, on both the Liverpool and Birkenhead sides of the river, has been built since 1830; and an impressive programme of training and deepening the Mersey's approach channels since the 1890s has allowed some of the world's biggest ships, including many of today's crude carriers of up to 150,000 tons, to enter the river.

As justification for treating a century and a half of history in just one paragraph, it can be argued that, although Liverpool continued to expand mightily after 1830, by that date all the factors on which its prosperity was founded could be clearly discerned. Modest but valuable natural resources of salt and coal; the creativity of the men attracted to the town as merchants, shipowners and engineers; industrial developments in its hinterland; and almost continual improvements in its transport connections to England's manufacturing heartlands: over little more than a century these turned an obscure creek on the remote and backward western edge of Europe into one of the continent's greatest ports.

But this book is about coastal shipping and, having charted and sought to explain Liverpool's growth, it must look at what this meant for the coastal trade.

The coasting trade of Liverpool

Notwithstanding its status as a world port, the coastal trades were important to Liverpool. In the mid-nineteenth century a third of the goods handled by Liverpool were shipped in coasters, either round the coast or to and from Ireland. What did these trades comprise?

Throughout the existence of the shipowners chronicled in this book, coal was the major bulk cargo shipped from the Mersey in coastal vessels; Wigan coal in particular being in some demand. Most has gone to Ireland, and particularly to Belfast which has been Britain's only industrial city without local coal supplies. Coal has also been shipped to the mineral ports of the West Country, to Holyhead for ships' bunkers, and to the Isle of Man for domestic use. A curious anomaly of the Mersey's trade was that, alongside the export of Lancashire coal, steam coal from South Wales was being imported, as bunkers for Liverpool's growing fleet of ocean-going steamers, as a cargo for re-export, and to fuel the region's textile and engineering industries. Some coal was also arriving from the much closer but smaller North Wales coalfield.

Although having ceded its premier position to coal by the mid-nineteenth century, Cheshire salt was still an important coastal cargo shipped especially to fishing ports around the British Isles. The chemical industry which was nurtured by salt also provided a growing number of cargoes, especially soda ash and fertilisers, and required sulphur and limestone to be shipped in.

Liverpool shared with the smaller Mersey ports the handling of building materials for the expanding towns and mills of South Lancashire, including roadstone and slate from North Wales, bricks and tiles. Whilst timber from North America and the Baltic was a major factor in Liverpool's overseas trade, a certain amount also came coastwise, mainly

The stone trade was one of the Mersey's oldest: here Henry Seddon's **Trevor** loads at Llanddulas.
Clive Guthrie collection

from Scotland.

A significant bulk commodity flowing coastwise into Liverpool was iron and later steel, in the form of pig iron and cast iron from South Wales and Glasgow, railway rails from Cumberland and the Clyde, and tinplate from South Wales. Some of the iron was used locally in shipbuilding and engineering works but most was shipped overseas. This trade is an example of how Liverpool's importance as a major export port helped to develop its coastal shipping: many other commodities were brought in by coaster from smaller ports for onward shipment. The coastal trade in grain, particularly to the Solway and Irish ports, reflected Liverpool's significance as a centre for importing cereals from North America, as did cargoes of flour from the mills of Birkenhead and Ellesmere Port.

Coastwise trade in a multitude of other items, from groceries for Mid Wales to guano for the farms of South Scotland, arose because of Liverpool's status as the North West's major entrepôt, a role it had gained at the expense of smaller ports around the Irish Sea, including Chester, Whitehaven and Dublin. However, most of the coastal trade resulting from Liverpool's role as a redistribution centre, along with the enormous quantity of agricultural produce imported from Ireland, involved the regular liner traders which are outside the scope of this book.

The pattern of trade discussed above did not change in its essentials until the decline of British coastal shipping began with the First World War. Many of the bulk trades continued until after the Second World War; coal continued to be shipped to Ireland from the Mersey until the British coal mining industry was largely destroyed for political reasons in the 1980s, whilst salt, soda ash and other chemicals are still exported. The major growth in the coastal trade has been in products of the petrochemical industry, and these cargoes – carried mainly to and from the lower reaches of the Manchester Ship Canal – are now the major reason why coasters visit the Mersey.

The Mersey's minor ports

Several important raw materials arriving by coaster in the Mersey largely by-passed Liverpool. China clay from Cornish ports and flints from France came mainly to Runcorn and to a lesser extent Ellesmere Port, from where they were moved by canal boat to the Potteries. Iron ore from Ulverston and Barrow-in-Furness was similarly transferred at Ellesmere Port for the Black Country. To get a full picture of the coastal trade of the Mersey as a whole, therefore, it is essential to consider the smaller ports on the river.

By the nature of these minor ports, coastal shipping was even more important to them than it was to Liverpool. Indeed, some succeeded in capturing a much bigger share of certain bulk trades than their large neighbour: Runcorn with china clay imports and Garston with coal exports being notable examples. This narrative will therefore look at each of the minor Mersey ports in turn, to consider their development and their share in the Mersey's coastal trade. The survey is conducted in roughly chronological order of the individual port's rise to prominence.

Frodsham. Situated where the Weaver joins the Mersey, Frodsham prospered through the salt and coal trades, plus the export of Cheshire cheese and grain, and in medieval times was probably second only to Chester amongst Cheshire's ports. The unimproved Weaver was navigable as far as Pickerings when there was sufficient water, but Frodsham Bridge restricted use of the river to vessels which could lower their masts. Frodsham was therefore an important transhipment point for salt brought by river or, at times when the Weaver was low, by road out of the salt district, and for Lancashire coal inbound. The town also had its own rock salt refinery. Records of vessels owned and built at Frodsham during the early eighteenth century suggest that most were river craft, intended to work to Liverpool, to the salt refinery at Dungeon Point on the north bank of the Mersey, and on the Sankey; but there were also some larger vessels which traded to Irish Sea ports, returning with cargoes such as slate.

The improvement of navigation on the Weaver in the eighteenth century began the gradual decline of Frodsham. The opening in 1810 of the Weston Canal from Sutton Lock to Weston Point by-passed Frodsham, and dock developments at Runcorn and Weston Point eclipsed the old port, although wooden shipbuilding continued there until 1862. One of the last Frodsham-owned sailing ships was the Runcorn-built SUNBEAM (148/1883), which was wrecked off Southport in October 1918. Frodsham saw little if any trade in steam coasters, but curiously still retains some lighterage traffic in cattle feed to a riverside mill.

Warrington. Another ancient Cheshire port, Warrington was long the limit of navigation on the Upper Mersey, and the lowest point at which the river was bridged. A reason for small vessels to make the notoriously difficult and sometimes dangerous passage along the twisting and frequently changing channels of the Mersey was that Warrington was the nearest point at which goods destined for Manchester could be landed. The Mersey and Irwell Navigation Act of 1721 authorised improvements to the river above Warrington including a series of locks and cuts which allowed small sea-going vessels to reach Manchester. In 1804 the completion by the Mersey and Irwell company of the Runcorn and Latchford Canal extended these improvements below Warrington.

Its river connection ensured that Warrington developed its own industries and, in the eighteenth and nineteenth centuries, sailing flats brought grain to its mills, flints to its glassworks and barley for Greenall's Brewery. Copper ore was carried from Amlwch in Anglesey to Bank Quay for the Warrington Copper and Brass Company. Warrington's major user of the river was probably Joseph Crosfield who began manufacturing soap in 1815, and later diversified into other chemicals. His factory required salt from Cheshire; tallow, palm oil and kelp transhipped from Liverpool or later Bromborough, usually in his own small fleet of river craft; and limestone from North Wales. Crosfields' river traffic continued until 1974.

Crosfields and other Warrington owners such as iron founders Monks, Hall and Co. Ltd. had modest fleets of steam flats which might occasionally venture out to sea beyond Liverpool, but Warrington cannot claim to have owned steam coasters as defined in this book. Its sailing flats did, however, nurture two important coastal shipowners, William Savage and Joseph Monks. Both had to move to Liverpool to expand ther businesses, as by the second half of the nineteenth century the capricious channel of the Mersey led to a decline in Warrington's waterborne trade. The industries using the river were not so well placed for the Manchester Ship Canal, and the facilities which have been developed along the canal have been for new users, such as the railways who brought coal to Partington and chemical factories at Acton Grange.

Weaver ports. In 1670 a test boring at Marbury near Northwich in Cheshire failed in its purpose of finding coal, but discovered rock salt. If Cheshire rock salt was to compete with salt made in traditional ways from brine, cheap transport was needed, and that was synonymous with water transport. The answer was improvement of the River Weaver, begun in 1721 and carried on almost continually during its long existence by the Weaver Navigation Trustees, a quasi-public body whose prudent management of their waterway served as an example to many commercial canal proprietors.

The Weaver's trade in coal inwards and salt out was very much in the hands of estuarial rather than coastal craft: sailing flats and their steam successors, the Weaver packets. But progressive improvements to locks and bridges, plus increasing the depth of the Weaver itself, eventually allowed sizeable sea-going ships to navigate the river and load alongside the salt works. In 1870 a steamer is reported to have loaded salt for Dublin at Anderton, a point just outside Northwich at which the Trent and Mersey Canal runs adjacent to the Weaver, and where salt from the works around Middlewich was transferred to larger craft. Later the river- and sea-going craft of the Middlewich salt proprietor Henry Seddon would load salt here.

The Weaver eventually became a victim of the growing demand for salt, especially from the chemical works which became established at Weston Point and along the

A busy scene at Anderton on the Weaver Navigation. The coaster **Purbeck** lies alongside Seddon's steam flat **Weaver Belle** and the barge **Gowanburn**. The other Weaver flat is I.C.I.'s **Gwalia**. *Edward Paget-Tomlinson*

Weston Canal. Even water transport was not economical enough, and in the 1890s brine pipelines began to be built, much to the distress of the Weaver Trustees. But their far-sighted improvements and moderate dues stood them in good stead. The river carried a proportion of the china clay and flints for the Potteries which were transhipped to Trent and Mersey narrowboats at Anderton, and this trade together with the products of the chemical works established around Northwich virtually compensated for the decline in salt traffic.

Almost alone amongst local transport undertakings, the Weaver Trustees welcomed the Manchester Ship Canal for the improved access it would give to their river. The Weaver flowed directly into the new canal, excess water flowing out through sluices into the Mersey. Adjacent to these sluices, the Ship Canal Company built Weston Marsh Lock which gave direct access to the Weston Canal. However, most vessels bound for the Weaver ports chose to use the new ship canal rather than the unreliable River Mersey.

In the twentieth century, improvements by the Trustees were concentrated on allowing larger coasters to navigate the Weaver. The last town in Cheshire to become a seaport was Winsford, which could be reached by coasters in 1938 following the replacement of a low stone bridge at Hartford. But development was concentrated on allowing coasters to reach the chemical works at Anderton, Winnington and Wallerscote near Northwich, and by 1940 a vessel 142 feet in length had navigated the river this far. Coastal traffic in salt and chemicals outlived the purely estuarial trade, which ceased when Imperial Chemical Industries Ltd. sold their Weaver packets in 1980. Occasionally coasters can be still be seen, slightly incongruous amidst the green fields of Cheshire, on their way to load soda ash or other chemicals. But the size limitations on the Weaver and its locks are proving a disadvantage in the late 1990s, and Garston is threatening to take the river's remaining trade.

Northwich owners became better known for their river craft than for coasters, the exception being the Northwich Carrying Co. Ltd. which graduated from the former to the latter. Salt and chemical manufacturers such as the Salt Union and Brunner, Mond and Co. Ltd. of Winnington had large fleets of steamers some of which were almost 200 tons gross, but these too traded only to Liverpool. Both companies became part of Imperial Chemical Industries Ltd., which did run coasters to wharves on the Weaver. Their motorship JOLLY DAYS was one of the largest ships to trade regularly to Northwich.

Runcorn. Very little has been recorded of the history of Runcorn before the eighteenth century; indeed, it is probable that there was little to record. At a narrow point of the river – Runcorn Gap – Runcorn was little more than a crossing point for the Mersey.

Modern Runcorn was born in 1776, with the completion of the Bridgewater Canal, originally intended as an outlet to the sea for the Duke of Bridgewater's coal mines at Worsley, but quickly extended to tap the cotton traffic of Manchester. In just over a year, traffic to and from the Potteries was also passing through Runcorn with the completion of the Trent and Mersey Canal. The Bridgewater quickly built docks in Runcorn; the Tidal Basin, Coal Basin and Old Dock being in use by 1785. In response to the competition for its Manchester traffic from the Bridgewater Canal, the older Mersey and Irwell Navigation completed an extension, the Runcorn and Latchford Canal, in 1804 and developed its own terminal facilities at Old Quay Basin, Runcorn.

Although most of the Manchester cotton trade merely passed through Runcorn on its way to Liverpool, sufficient cargo was handled to make Runcorn Cheshire's major port. The most important incoming cargoes were materials for the growing pottery industry of Staffordshire, and iron or iron ore for the Midlands. Coal from the Worsley mines was transhipped for Ireland, as was some coal brought down the St. Helens Canal. The port was not so well placed for the Weaver salt trade, however; although substantial quantities of salt were brought to its docks along the Trent and Mersey Canal.

The limitation on Runcorn's growth was a physical one, and common to all the Upper Mersey ports: the fickle nature of the channel of the Mersey between Runcorn Gap and Liverpool. The channel shifted continually, partly due to differences in volumes of water flowing down the Mersey and its tributary the Weaver: for a few years it might favour Runcorn with deep water, then desert it completely. During the nineteenth century the port's fluctuations in trade, and particularly foreign trade, show a direct relationship to

National Maritime Museum P2956

Runcorn Docks with a fine array of schooners, flats and two steamers.

the size of vessels which could reach Runcorn, which in turn was determined by the state of the Mersey. Steam tugs were tried on the Upper Mersey as early as 1824. Considerable effort was put into surveying and buoying the Mersey, especially after the formation of the Upper Mersey Navigation Commission in 1876. However, none of these measures could solve the fundamental problem of insufficient water, which was to doom Runcorn to play in the minor league of ports, despite its excellent connections with England's industrial heartland.

The town's growth as a port stimulated the development of related industries and those that benefited from better shipping facilities. Ships were being built at Runcorn at least as early as 1778, and with demand for stone for dock building at Liverpool the local sandstone quarries expanded their output. With salt and coal in abundance nearby, Runcorn began to attract soap and alkali manufacturers. As their confidence and technology grew, these diversified into manufacturing other chemicals, such as sulphuric acid which required imports of pyrites. Unlikely as it now sounds, the town had something of a reputation as a spa in the mid-nineteenth century. Whatever health-giving properties Runcorn's waters might have had must surely have been negated by the unsalubrious emissions from local chemical works, which were so bad as to provoke the Government to pass one of Britain's first environmental protection acts and bring into being the Alkali Inspectorate. Certainly the Bridgewater Trustees did not welcome this pollution and for many years refused to sell or lease land alongside its canal to the chemical industry. This merely had the effect of moving the industry's centre of gravity across the river to Widnes, where it prospered mightily - and still contributed to the pollution over Runcorn.

The Bridgewater Canal bought out its old rival the Mersey and Irwell in 1844 and proceeded to neglect both the older canal and its Old Quay Basin, which had been

Richard Hughes' **Moelfre Rose** unloading china clay at Runcorn. *Edward Gray*

extended as recently as 1829. Investment was concentrated on the Bridgewater's own terminal facilities where new and improved docks were steadily opened: Francis Dock in 1843, Alfred Dock in 1860, Arnold Dock in 1870, and in 1875 Fenton Dock, named after the Chairman of the Bridgewater Navigation Company (no relation), a body which had replaced the Bridgewater Trustees in 1862.

Despite its excellent water connections, Runcorn was not linked to the rail network until the 1870s and this was to cost it some of its trade. Newly-built rail-connected ports in the North West – Fleetwood, Preston and Garston – took much of its pig-iron imports, whilst the West Bank Dock at Widnes diverted coal exports originating from the mines around St. Helens. In an effort to improve Runcorn's share of the salt trade, the Runcorn and Weston Point Canal was completed in 1860 to link the town with the mouth of the Weaver. This canal saw limited use, however, and did not deter the Weaver Navigation Trustees from developing superior dock facilities at Weston Point.

Runcorn had a number of shipowners, but the size of their ships and their fleets reflected the limitations of the port itself, and only the Brundrits and William Rowland owned sea-going steamers, and before long both had moved their businesses to Liverpool. Runcorn was an important port for steam coasters, however, particularly for Richard Hughes and William Savage who specialised in the china clay trades. Runcorn's trade probably reached its peak in the early 1890s, eclipsing that of its old rivals Preston, Whitehaven and Chester. Ironically, Runcorn's decline began when its problems with access were solved, with the completion of the Manchester Ship Canal. Runcorn was rightly suspicious of the Ship Canal, although in the early years it benefited considerably from it. Two locks were provided by the Ship Canal to give access to Runcorn from the Mersey, the Bridgewater Lock opposite the Bridgewater Docks, and Old Quay Lock. The latter was close to Old Quay, although the much decayed dock facilities there had been swept away in the construction of the Ship Canal, which was largely built on the line of the Runcorn and Latchford Canal and the Mersey and Irwell Navigation. To obtain these the Ship Canal Company had bought the Bridgewater company at enormous expense.

For the first time the Manchester Ship Canal brought large sailing ships to Runcorn: they were prevented from proceeding any further by the London and North Western Railway's bridge over the Mersey. Many smaller vessels continued to use the Mersey, navigation of which was hazardous but – unlike the Ship Canal – free. The Canal Company did offer free towage, but only on strict criteria: the vessels had to be carrying china clay from certain "traditional" ports, and to arrive in the Mersey at unfavourable states of the river.

Essentially the story of Runcorn was now one of slow decline. The Runcorn and Weston Point Canal and the Francis and Arnold Docks were filled in, locks closed, towage facilities on the Mersey withdrawn in 1948, and finally the Upper Mersey Navigation Commission wound up in 1973 just before its centenary. A number of factors played their part: the continuing decline in the small sailing ships in which Runcorn specialised, the decrease in trade on the narrow canals, and the changed ownership of the Bridgewater Docks. These docks had passed to the Manchester Ship Canal Company, to whom it mattered little if cargo was handled at its Manchester, Runcorn or Ellesmere Port facilities.

Trade at Runcorn did undergo a revival in the 1960s and, as almost two centuries before, this was stimulated by radical improvements in the local transport network. The completion of a fixed road bridge over the Mersey in 1961 made Runcorn the most convenient port for much of the industry in South Lancashire. Runcorn and Weston Point Docks also benefited from the problems Liverpool was having, with obsolete equipment and working practices which made it unreliable and expensive, particularly for smaller traders. Following improvements to the Bridgewater Docks, the 1960s and 1970s saw the port once again alive with coasters, though now only a minority were British. But alas, with the economic malaise which has seen the region's industry decline, Runcorn's trade has once more fallen off, although part of the Bridgewater Dock system has recently been deepened and remains as a tangible link with the heyday of the Upper Mersey's most interesting minor port.

Weston Point. Now part of the town of Runcorn, Weston Point's docks were developed by the Trustees of the Weaver Navigation and have always been independent of the Bridgewater and Old Quay systems. The first dock at Weston Point, which became known as Old Basin, was built contemporaneously with the Weston Canal, opened in 1810 from the Mersey to near Sutton as part of the continuing efforts by the Weaver Trustees to improve their waterway for the vast and ever-growing salt output of Cheshire. Industry was attracted to the banks of the Weston Canal, and traffic increased to such an extent that a further dock was needed, so that the New Basin was opened in 1856 with its own entrance lock from the Mersey. The Weaver Trustees combined prudent investment with a regard for the moral and spiritual needs of those who worked on their river and docks, and also built and endowed the imposing Christ Church next to the entrance lock of the Old Basin.

A towage service was inaugurated from Weston Point to Liverpool in 1863, and a year later a steamer appeared for the first time on the River Weaver. This harbinger of progress, together with news of further expansion by the Bridgewater, excited the Trustees, who pressed ahead with further improvements in the hope of attracting more steamers to Weston Point. Delamere Dock was opened in 1870 with yet another entrance lock, but this time large enough to accommodate coasters so that Weston Point could begin to compete on equal terms with Runcorn's Bridgewater Docks. The engineer was Edward Leader Williams, later to achieve fame as the engineer of the Manchester Ship Canal. Cargoes handled were predominantly salt outward, brought up the Weaver by flats or produced in the adjacent salt works, and raw materials for the Potteries inwards.

Opening of the Tollemache Dock in 1885 completed the Weston Point system. The docks could take vessels drawing fifteen feet of water, but although this gave the system a competitive edge over the Bridgewater Docks, it was not always a usable one. Leader William's successor as engineer pointed out that there were only 146 tides a year when vessels drawing fifteen feet could get up the Mersey.

Unlike their Bridgewater rivals, the docks at Weston Point benefited from the construction of the Manchester Ship Canal, as the large vessels for which they were built could now reach the docks by way of the Ship Canal on any tide. And large vessels did come: there is a photograph of Alfred Holt's NELEUS (6,685/1911) loading at the Vacuum Salt Works on the Weston Canal. Small vessels still using the Upper Mersey reached Weston Point by the Weston Mersey Lock, built by the Ship Canal Company. As at the Bridgewater Docks, the Ship Canal tolls were reduced or waived on certain cargoes deemed "traditional" to and from Weston Point.

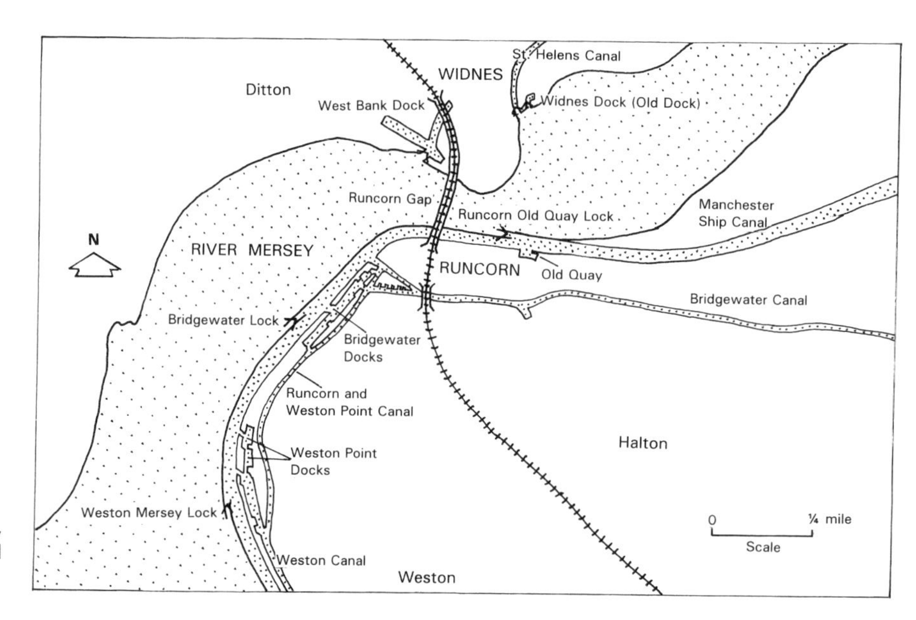

Map of Widnes, Runcorn and Weston Point.

Weston Point had at least one shipowner, Richard Clark, who was also its harbour master. It was his son, Richard Robert Clark, who went into steam, but moved to Liverpool to do this: so Weston Point cannot count as a centre for steam coaster owning.

Trade to Weston Point Docks remained at much the same level through the first forty years of the twentieth century, but was almost wiped out by the Second World War. Along with the Bridgewater Docks, Weston Point staged a dramatic come-back in the 1960s, with investment in improved facilities by the British Waterways Board: successors of the Weaver Navigation Trustees. Although trade reached more than twice its pre-war level, this was not sustained, and the docks closed in the early 1980s, only to be re-opened in 1986 but subsequently closed again. With their capacity to come back from the dead, it is hoped that Weston Point Docks may still rise again.

Widnes. In the nineteenth century Widnes grew meteorically, from a group of rural hamlets - Woodend, Ditton and Appleton - to a major base of the alkali and chemical industry, and came to be served by two busy docks. But as a port Widnes was, like Runcorn, hampered by the condition of the Mersey and as a result ultimately doomed by lack of investment from the canal and railway interests which built its docks.

Widnes can chart its rise from 1833, when the St. Helens Canal was extended from Fiddler's Ferry to a point on the Mersey opposite Runcorn known as Woodend. The original line of this canal was opened between 1757 and 1772 as the Sankey Brook Navigation, Britain's first industrial canal. An outlet for the coalfield around St. Helens, the canal's original connection with the Mersey at Fiddler's Ferry below Warrington was too far up the unreliable channel of the Mersey, hence its 1833 extension to Widnes. History was to prove that this move was insufficiently ambitious.

The St. Helens and Runcorn Gap Railway was opened to Widnes in competition with the canal earlier the same year, and a dock built adjacent both to the railway and canal termini. Known as Widnes or Old Dock, this brought Widnes its first world record (later ones being awarded for the pollution) in being the first purpose-built railway dock. Despite this, the railway suffered the unique ignominy of being beaten for the coal trade by the canal. It had seriously misjudged the ability of the Upper Mersey to take sizeable vessels, with the result that almost any vessel of a size which could reach Widnes could proceed up the St. Helens Canal and load adjacent to a colliery. Coalfield and canal prospered, however; within twenty years over half a million tons of coal was being shipped from Widnes, much of it to Liverpool and to the Weaver salt works. The railway and canal companies merged in 1845, but this was to bode ill for Widnes as a port, for the amalgamated company set its sights on a new, deep-water port for its coal shipments and began to develop Garston.

From the 1840s, coal supplies plus the availability of salt from Cheshire attracted alkali and chemical manufacturers to Widnes. Some of them moved their businesses from St. Helens in protest at the canal dues which were payable on their products but not on coal; others were chased out of Liverpool because of the smells they caused. Widnes welcomed them; emissions, effluent and all. There were seven alkali works in the town by 1855, the industry's expansion being encouraged by the cheap land available, the good rail connections which Runcorn lacked, and the refusal by the Bridgewater Trustees to lease its land in Runcorn to the chemical industry.

In response to the growth of the alkali industry, new dock facilities were opened in 1864: West Bank Dock, slightly nearer the sea than the older dock, but with no more water. West Bank Dock contributed to a further growth in the chemical industry between 1865 and 1875. Besides salt and coal the docks at Widnes also handled burnt ore from Silloth and from Dublin, pig iron from Scotland, stone from North Wales, white sand from King's Lynn and the Isle of Wight for Pilkington's glass works at St. Helens, and ore for the copper smelters of St Helens. Outgoing cargoes included bricks made in St. Helens, asbestos products, and superphosphate fertiliser.

Despite its considerable degree of trade - at the end of the nineteenth century it was claimed that sixty vessels a day left Widnes, although most were river craft - its dock facilities were primitive. The St. Helens Railway and Canal Company and its successor the London and North Western Railway were clearly reluctant to invest in its facilities, and instead developed the down-river port of Garston. Despite modest improvements made at West Bank in 1914, its entrance was always difficult for unpowered craft, and it could only accommodate smaller schooners and steamers. At neaps there was only four feet of water available over the dock sill, compared with eight feet at Runcorn and fifteen at Weston Point. The docks at Widnes remained poor cousins to those at Runcorn, and – as local waterborne traffic in coal and chemicals declined and coastal vessels grew in size – Widnes docks became less and less used. And after the opening of the Manchester Ship Canal, Runcorn benefited from guaranteed deep water.

Apart from brief upturns in activity, such as after the Second World War when West Bank was baldly but correctly advertised as a "a cheap port", Widnes's trade dwindled. West Bank Dock was formally closed in 1970 and the site became a trading estate. The St. Helens Canal was abandoned in 1963, soon after its last traffic ceased, but happily the canal's entrance and the Old Dock survive under the care of the local authority who are conscious of the site's historic importance.

In shipbuilding and shipowning, Widnes was also in the shadow of Runcorn, although the former activity prospered briefly in the 1870s as the channel of the Mersey deserted Runcorn and favoured the north bank of the Mersey. Of coastal steamship owners there was only the Cooper family, who began as general carriers but later specialised in dredging river sand (much of it destined for Pilkingtons at St. Helens), as did the other Widnes owners of estuarial craft, Abels. The coasters of Thomas Brothers Shipping Co. Ltd. and its several successors were frequently to be seen loading coal for Ireland in West Bank Dock and bringing in North Wales stone for Croft Granite.

Garston. When the St. Helens Railway and Canal Company chose Garston as the site for its access to deep water, there was already a primitive dock on the site. This dated from 1793 and had been built in association with Blackburne's saltworks, which had moved out of Liverpool.

The St. Helens company's intention was to bypass Liverpool as a port for the shipment of coal from South Lancashire, and to allow this coal to compete on more equal terms with that from around Wigan, which had enjoyed ready access to Liverpool since the opening of the Leeds and Liverpool Canal. The railway dock was opened in 1853, and was equipped with coal drops which could load ships at the rate of one hundred tons an hour – the fastest on Merseyside. Success was not won quite so easily, however. The promoters had cause to curse the waters of the Mersey yet again, as extensive dredging was needed to enlarge the approach channel for deep-sea vessels. The London and North Western Railway clearly saw an opportunity at Garston, and took over the St. Helens company and its embryo port in 1864, injecting the capital for dredging plant and for building further facilities. The Old Dock, as the 1853 facilities came to be known, was joined by the North Dock in 1875. By the end of the century Garston was estimated to have taken no less than half of Liverpool's coal trade. Garston's facilities were completed in 1910 with Stalbridge Dock, named after the Chairman of the London and North Western Railway. This new dock helped the port attract Elders and Fyffes' banana traffic from Manchester in 1912.

The London and North Western Railway had a somewhat uneasy relationship with Liverpool. As the biggest of the railways serving the port and the best provided in terms of facilities, it used its partial monopoly to squeeze as much revenue as it could out of certain lucrative traffic, especially that between Liverpool and Manchester; a cause célèbre that contributed in no little way to the building of the Manchester Ship Canal. Yet the railway in turn mistrusted Liverpool's own near-monopoly, and sought to develop its own ports at Garston and Ellesmere Port.

As elsewhere, dock facilities attracted industry which generated yet more trade, and there have been iron, steel and copper works, a tannery and a sawmill at Garston. One local manufactury owned its own steam coasters, Wilson Brothers Bobbin Co. Ltd., who entrusted their management to local broker and owner Edward W. Turner. Garston shipbrokers, including Edward Nicholson and William Darlington, have also dabbled in coaster owning.

Trades at Garston have included timber, especially for pit props, imported from Canada, the Baltic and White Sea; chemicals and ores. Regular cargo liner services have also come and gone, typically trades such as those to Iceland, the Iberian peninsula or

Garston's New Dock in September 1932. The ships which can be identified are, to the left, the C.W.S. steamer **New Pioneer,** William Robertson's **Fluor** in the centre of the dock, and a dredger to the right. *National Maritime Museum G3711*

the Eastern Mediterranean which used middle-sized ships. But coal shipments, largely to Ireland, have always dominated Garston's trade. This has brought to the port a wider variety of coasters than perhaps any other Mersey port has seen, including vessels belonging to local owners such as Zillah, and others from across the Irish Sea: Kelly, Lockington, Alliance and Dublin Consumers' Gas Co., Fishers of Newry, and the Ramsey Steamship Co. Ltd.

Thanks to its railway connections and ownership, Garston has been one of the few Upper Mersey ports which could offer serious competition to Liverpool. Its fortunes have varied, however, often inversely with those of its larger neighbour. With Liverpool suffering dock labour problems in the 1970s, Garston did relatively well, and investment in container equipment plus the neighbouring Freightliner terminal won it a daily container service to Belfast. However, a more aggressive policy by Liverpool and the ending of the Dock Labour Scheme saw this trade taken by its Seaforth Container Terminal, and with coal exports now virtually ended, Garston's trade is somewhat depressed in 1997.

Ellesmere Port. Even more than Runcorn, Ellesmere Port is a child of the canal age, and has benefited from two great canals: the Shropshire Union, as the Ellesmere Canal eventually became, and the Manchester Ship Canal. The town owes even its name to canal promoters.

The Ellesmere Canal was envisaged largely as providing an outlet to the Mersey for the produce of Shropshire and North Wales. Of particular interest to the promoters were the area around Ironbridge on the River Severn, where smelting of iron had begun and with it the industrial revolution; and the coal, iron and minerals of North Wales. But the grandiose plans of the promoters were gradually scaled down or postponed, and by the time most had been met the canal's industrial hinterland had declined in importance. One of the plans to be altered was the width of the locks on the more distant stretches of the canal, which were reduced from fourteen feet to seven feet. The Wirral Line, from the Mersey to Chester, was completed in 1795, and within a year the name Ellesmere Port was being used to refer to the area around the canal's terminal. The locks between canal and river were also known as Whitby Locks, after one of the small communities which were to be incorporated into the town of Ellesmere Port.

The decision to build a largely narrow canal turned out to be of great benefit to the infant town. It meant that cargoes had to be transferred from river- or sea-going craft to narrow boats, and hence transhipment facilities were required including basins, warehouses and cranes. Those provided initially were mostly primitive: improvement had to await the growth of canal traffic. This growth came, not as planned by the promoters of the Ellesmere Canal, but through connections made with other canals. These included the Llangollen Canal, the Trent and Mersey, and most significantly the Birmingham and Liverpool Junction Canal which in 1836 gave access to the fast-developing iron industry of the Black Country, which was beginning to earn its title "workshop of the world". New and greatly expanded terminal facilities at Ellesmere Port were necessary, and were planned by Thomas Telford and opened between 1833 and 1843. They consisted of wharves and warehouses dedicated to the expected traffic – including china clay and flints, iron ore, pottery and ironware – and a dock capable of taking sea-going ships as well as the Mersey flats which carried much of the river trade.

During 1845 and 1846, a series of amalgamations driven largely by fear of railway competition led to the Ellesmere and Chester Canal joining with its allies and a number of railway companies to form the Shropshire Union Railway and Canal Company. This was a major transport undertaking, and the equally large but more aggressive London and North Western Railway (which had itself been recently formed by an amalgamation) sought to neutralise any threat to its business by leasing the Shropshire Union. The L.N.W.R.'s other motives included acquiring dock facilities at Ellesmere Port which could compete with Liverpool, and being able to penetrate the territory of the rival Great Western Railway. For these reasons the railway did not, as others did elsewhere, run down the canal's facilities, but actually improved them, for instance by installing hydraulic power in the dock estate at Ellesmere Port in 1876. The Shropshire Union Canal prospered and with it Ellesmere Port, largely through iron ore originating in the

Mack's steamer **Lancashire** and a schooner in the lock at Ellesmere Port (above). In the lower photograph, the basin at Ellesmere Port is so crowded with canal craft as to leave little room for the steamer.

P. O'Brien collection.

Furness district being transported to the Black Country and china clay moving to the Potteries.

The next major event to affect Ellesmere Port was the coming in 1891 of the Manchester Ship Canal, which in the form finally agreed passed between the town and its docks and the Mersey. The port's protector, the London and North Western Railway, was at least partly to blame for the inception of the canal, as its punitively high freight rates between Liverpool and Manchester pursuaded the latter city that it needed its own access to the sea. During the protracted wrangling which accompanied the progress of three successive Manchester Ship Canal bills through Parliament, the railway naturally sided with Liverpool in its vehement opposition. The poor Shropshire Union was not allowed to make its own case, and the concession it received was relatively minor: small ships such as those which had formerly used the Mersey to reach Ellesmere Port could navigate the Canal free of charge. Technically, this left the docks no worse off but, in losing the battle against the Canal, the railway seems also to have lost interest in Ellesmere Port, and although there was some investment the railway's favours were mainly bestowed on its other Mersey port, Garston, where a new dock was opened in 1910.

The town of Ellesmere Port, in contrast, benefited enormously from the coming of the Ship Canal. An 1,800-foot wharf was built on the seaward side of the docks and was inaugurated in May 1892 by the Glasgow coaster PYROPE (452/1890). Ellesmere Port was now capable of berthing ocean-going ships, and in consequence it began to attract manufacturing industry, some of it relocated from inland: corrugated iron, flour milling and – most significantly – oil refining and petrochemicals. The flour milling, in particular, helped the Shropshire Union's trade, and ensured the canal and its 1843 terminal facilities did not stagnate, an arm of the canal being dug to serve the mills. Decline only began with the disruption of the First World War, when factors such as increased wage rates and the extension of the eight-hour day to boatmen began to make narrow boat traffic unprofitable. The railway's decision in 1921 to sell off the huge fleet of its Shropshire Union Canal Carrying Company, the country's largest canal carrier, and lease the docks to the Port of Manchester was the beginning of the end for Ellesmere Port as a narrow canal port. It was a long time dying, however, and regular traffic in tar from Stanlow to the Midlands continued until the 1950s, and the old dock estate was not officially closed until 1957. By the 1960s it made a fascinating if rather dangerous playground and boating pool for local schoolboys, of whom the present author was one. But it has never been satisfactorily established whether schoolboys or much older and more sinister vandals were responsible for the arson which robbed Ellesmere Port of its finest building, Telford's superb transhipment warehouse. All has not been gloom, however, as the establishment in 1976 of the estimable Boat Museum on the site has meant that the basins, locks and surviving buildings have enjoyed a renaissance.

Developments at Ellesmere Port since the First World War have been extensive, and have been due very largely to the Ship Canal. As early as 1916 the Manchester Ship Canal Company began building an oil dock at Stanlow, just above Ellesmere Port, although this was not completed until 1922. Oil refining grew steadily, and Shell's refinery on Stanlow marshes has become one of the largest in Europe. Growth in the size of tankers is considered to be a post-war phenomenon, but as early as 1927 the Manchester Ship Canal had to be deepened from Stanlow to Eastham to take vessels of 15,000 tons. The Canal Company should have known better, however, than to build an enclosed dock for tankers at the entrance to the Canal in the 1950s: growth in size of tankers meant that, by the time the Queen Elizabeth II Oil Dock was opened in 1953, crude carriers too large to enter it were being planned. Other trades have come and gone from Ellesmere Port, including container services to the Mediterranean and Ro-Ro services from the Baltic, but oil and petrochemicals have shown consistent growth, and in 1997 are the lifeblood of the town and the Manchester Ship Canal.

Ellesmere Port can claim no steam coaster owners of its own. Much of its trade before the coming of the Ship Canal was in sailing vessels, and steamers were restricted by the 100-foot Ship Lock. Coasters owned by Joseph Monks were visitors, probably bringing iron ore from Ulverston, and one of the steamers of the Manchester, Liverpool and North

Wales Steam Ship Co. Ltd. was photographed in dock amidst narrow boats and Mersey flats. A wide variety of steam and motor coasters has visited the Ship Canal wharf, and the sole surviving Liverpool coaster owner, James Fisher and Sons (Liverpool) Ltd., has tankers in the local petrochemical trade.

Bromborough and Port Sunlight. Bromborough Pool has been one of the Mersey's very minor ports, used for shipping stone from early in the nineteenth century. In 1895 William Lever built Port Sunlight Dock there to serve his soap works, but it was adequate for little more than the river craft which brought in vegetable oils from Liverpool Docks. In 1926 much larger facilities became available, when ocean-going vessels began using Bromborough Dock, also built by the soap and chemicals empire. Raw materials ranging from palm kernels to whale oil were imported through the dock, often by cargo liners serving the Mersey. Trade began to decline in the 1960s, although the dock remained full, if not busy, as a result of its becoming a base for Westminster Dredging. Bromborough Dock was closed in the 1980s, although an adjoining river wharf has since seen some coaster activity.

Manchester Ship Canal. Building the Canal between 1892 and 1894 altered the geography of the upper Mersey basin, and it merits a few lines of its own for its profound effects on the ports on the Cheshire bank of the Mersey. Some of these prospered, others withered. That precocious if unprepossessing infant Ellesmere Port did very well thank you, although in doing so it turned its back on the older canal which had given birth to and nurtured it. As befitted a river of modest ambitions, the Weaver gained moderately from the better access the Ship Canal afforded. Runcorn and Weston Point began sixty years of decline, even though the Ship Canal at last gave them guaranteed deep water access.

The construction of the Ship Canal effectively produced one dock 35 miles long, as was recognised by the creation for customs and commercial purposes of the Port of Manchester. The terminal docks were clearly the most important, but cargo handling facilities with guaranteed deep water could be readily created almost anywhere along its length, as they were at Ellesmere Port and Stanlow. Another example which is particularly relevant to the coastal trade is Partington above Warrington, where coal from

Zillah's **E. Hayward** has just entered the Manchester Ship Canal. *W.S.P.L. Brownell collection*

Lancashire, Staffordshire and Yorkshire was brought by rail for bunkering ships, and for export to Ireland and farther afield.

In the 1980s the growing size of ships, improvements in the motorway network of the North West, the decline of manufacturing industry and shift of trade from western ports to those facing Europe damaged the Ship Canal even more than they did Liverpool. With its upper reaches now moribund, the region's trade is once again largely in the hands of Liverpool, with a few minor Mersey ports squabbling over the crumbs dropped by their very big brother.

The rise of the steam coaster

The first vessels driven by steam ran uncertainly at the end of the eighteenth century. It took until the 1820s to produce a steam engine reliable enough to be trusted at sea, and the early steamers were so expensive to build and operate that they ran only as passenger vessels or tugs, where their ability to keep to a schedule or offer assistance could command premium rates. Coastal bulk carrying by steam began only after the development of effective screw propellors and water ballast tanks in the 1850s. Even then, its sole preserve was the East Coast coal trade, where the screw collier's ability to make large and regular deliveries of coal to London justified its high capital and operating costs.

Even after the Admiralty found steam colliers valuable during the Crimean War, their spread to other bulk trades was slow, and this bears some examination. A steamer was much more expensive to build than an equivalent-sized sailing ship: in the 1860s £15 would build a deadweight ton of sailing ship, but £25 to £40 would be needed for a ton of steamer. They were also more costly to operate, not only in requiring coal but also engineers and firemen to feed it into their inefficient boilers. The steamer had the advantage of being able to make more voyages in a given period than a sailing ship, but this could not always be exploited in the bulk trades. Delays in loading or unloading could quickly erode the steamer's benefits, and these were to be expected where low-value cargoes such as stone were being handled by manual labour or primitive machinery, especially when the order of loading was at the whim of the shipper. The North Wales slate quarry owners, who owned their own ports, were past masters at

Thursby of 1877: one of the earliest bulk carrying steamers owned in the North West. *John Clarkson*

manipulating shipowners to their advantage by showing preferences for one vessel over another. It is significant that some of the earliest steam coasters on the Irish Sea were owned by quarry or coal owners who could exercise some control over the despatch of their steamers. The composite steamer LLYSFAEN was built for quarrymen Raynes, Lupton and Co. in 1867; and the Fleetwood-registered iron collier THURSBY (496/1877) was ordered from Harland and Wolff for Lancashire coal owners. The widespread adoption of steam in these trades was dependent on preference being given to steamers in loading and discharge.

It was not until the 1880s that steamers began to appear in any numbers in the Irish Sea bulk trades. By then, steamers carrying passengers and high-value and perishable cargoes such as cattle and other foodstuffs were well established on coastal and short sea routes. Developments in engineering and technology were making the steamer more attractive, with high pressure boilers and compounding reducing the inefficiency of steam engines, and improvements in iron and steel production bringing down the price of building a steamer. Initially the coastal steamer had little need for the water ballast tanks fitted to East Coast colliers as it was expected to run both ways with cargo, but as trades in which return cargoes were rare - such as coal to Ireland - grew in importance, water ballast capacity was enlarged. It has to be admitted that Merseyside shipowners were not at the forefront of adopting steam. Glasgow tended to show the way, with William Robertson's AGATE (184/1878) being the forerunner of an enormous fleet of coasters primarily aimed at the Irish Sea stone and coal trades. It fell to Hume, Smith and the Mack family, and slightly later Richard Hughes, to redress the balance in favour of Liverpool.

The steam and motor coasters of the Mersey

The coasters owned on the Mersey and in other ports around the Irish Sea tended to develop along distinct lines determined by the cargoes they carried and the ports visited. There are several reasons for this uniformity.

Firstly, owners wanting a newbuilding often gave only general instructions as to length, carrying capacity and speed, and then accepted the lowest tender. They left the builder to work out details, or more likely reproduce those of the last successful ship he had built. An example is the JESSIE SUMMERFIELD, built by Ailsa for the Summerfield Steamship Co. Ltd. in 1921 to a design developed over the previous twenty years for Zillah, who had taken their business elsewhere. As owners became established and grew more experienced, they began to ask for detailed improvements in the design to suit their particular trades. They also showed considerable loyalty to one builder, but might still shop around to ensure they were getting the keenest prices from their chosen yard. Examples of this loyalty include the long sequences of vessels built for Zillah by the Ailsa and later Lytham yards.

A second factor ensuring uniformity was that a new or unusual design would require more design work and detailed discussion between builder and classification society. With an untried design, Lloyd's Register or the British Corporation would tend to play safe and demand stronger and more expensive scantlings.

The smallest steamers regularly to cross open seas were something of a speciality of Irish Sea owners. From 90 to 140 feet in length, driven by a two-cylinder compound engine, and with a single hatch and hold usually served by just one derrick, they were owned by Coopers of Widnes, Nicholsons, Henry Seddon, Thomas Brothers and Zillah. They were distinguished from estuarial craft by features to improve their seaworthiness, including high bulwarks, a raised quarterdeck aft and usually a raised forecastle; although their original open bridges suggested that protection for the crew was not a priority. Their small size was dictated by the dimensions of the ports they served, locks at Ellesmere Port and Widnes being built with small coastal sailing ships in mind. Another important factor was the relatively small consignments of cargo on offer: small coal merchants in the lesser ports of Ireland, the Isle of Man, and the south of Scotland could only afford to accept shipments of coal which were as modest as the local harbours.

Ships above 140 feet in length usually ran to two hatches separated by a navigating bridge which also housed the master and mate. The single hold tended to be

Elmfield: a typical raised quarter deck steamer. *Author's collection*

Jellicoe Rose: one of Hughes' larger ships

continuous, although movable, wooden bulkheads could be used, for instance to separate different grades of coal. The long hold was essential for carrying railway rails, a frequent cargo from the steel works at Workington. In these coasters the deck raised above the machinery space aft, the quarter deck, was usually extended forward to the bridge. This gave a deeper cargo space more or less amidships, and helped the vessel to trim well when loaded. Poor trim would make the coaster difficult to steer, and could cause difficulties getting in and out of ports with restricted draft. A good master would have the cargo loaded so that the coaster was slightly down by the stern. This made it easier to steer and meant that, as the bunker coal was burned, the ship was on an even keel by the time it arrived at its destination.

This size of coaster had at least one mast and derrick to serve each hatch, and usually had a triple expansion steam engine, although speed was no higher than the nine knots of the smaller ships. The number of such ships in Irish Sea fleets built to a length between perpendiculars of 142 feet, or about 148 feet overall, is explained by the importance of the coal trade to Ringsend Basin, Dublin where the entrance restricted ships to this size. Zillah specialised in this trade and built most of its later ships to this length. Best had his LETTY built to this size, but although she had two hatches her bridge was aft.

In busy trades with no size restrictions, such as steam coal from South Wales to Liverpool, it often paid to use larger ships, and some steam coasters up to 200 feet were built. These usually had engines amidships to facilitate trimming, but few of this type appear in this book. Richard Hughes invested heavily in large steamers during and after the First World War, partly for carrying coal from South Wales and the North East to the South East, but these were all engines-aft designs. With four hatches, ships such as LOUIE ROSE had the distinction of being some of the largest steamers running on the coast, but trade did not grow to the extent Hughes anticipated, and their high cost helped ruin him.

It will be noticed that few motor coasters were owned on the Mersey until after the Second World War. Indeed, owners like Zillah were amongst the last to cling to conventional steamers. The availability of bunker coal locally was the reason generally given for the choice of steam machinery, but more often to blame was the conservatism of the owners and their superintendents, who trusted only the machinery they had grown up with. Steam was very reliable, but motor ships had such advantages of economy (no firemen were needed), shallower draft and better carrying capacity (no space was needed for boilers) that in the harsher climate in shipping which set in about 1955, steam coasters and their owners could not compete.

Zillah's motor vessel **Fernfield**. *John Clarkson*

The coaster owners

Coastal shipowners come into the business by one of three routes: as a ship's master, as a ship broker, or as a manufacturer or merchant.

There are several examples on the Mersey of master mariners becoming owners: Richard Clark, William Rowland, William Savage who founded Zillah, and Samuel Summerfield. Owning one's own fleet could be the pinnacle of achievement for someone who had come into coastal shipping as an ordinary seaman. Indeed, one attraction of the arduous, poorly-paid, anti-social and oft times hazardous occupation of coastal seafaring was that the humblest could work his way up to master given diligence and time. A little money put by could then purchase a share or two in an older vessel, family and business contacts could be persuaded to take other shares, and given luck and buoyant trade there was a reasonable chance of the venture prospering, and the owner expanding to a fleet. William Savage was perhaps the best example of a master made good, but at the other end of the spectrum this book is littered with masters who became shipowners when they bought and skippered an old steamer, only to depart the business when the inevitable repairs swallowed up their nest egg, their under-insured vessel stranded or when freight rates fell and money just ran out.

Ship brokers and others close to the business of shipping had the advantage of having their finger on the pulse of local trade. Sensing that it was likely to quicken, they would often be tempted to float a company to acquire a coaster, and use their contacts to ensure it benefited from available cargoes. The memoranda of association of such companies invariably awarded the managers - always the vessel's brokers - a percentage of the gross freights as their fee, ensuring that they made money whether or no the ship traded at a profit. Looking into some limited companies such as those managed by Baile, Gaskell it is surprising how little of the equity the manager contributed. They probably, and rightly, considered shipowning a risky business which they would not stay in long. In contrast, other men from the shipping business like Richard Hughes saw their long-term future in shipowning, and gradually built up their personal holding by buying out the other original shareholders as the opportunity arose. Hughes began with single-ship

Calcium was built for the United Alkali Co. Ltd. in 1917, when the war had made it expensive to hire ships. *Author's collection*

companies, but as he prospered he dissolved these and vested his fleet in a company with much larger capital, much of which he subscribed himself.

The single-ship company was attractive to the aspiring coastal shipowner for several reasons. Firstly and most importantly, any claim against the company was limited to the value of its sole asset, its ship, and did not affect any other units of the fleet. A second reason which appealed to owners attempting to break into shipowning was that the capital required could be divided up into smaller units than was possible on the sixty-fourth share method which had sufficed to fund coastal sailing ships. More investors could find the £5 or £25 for a share in a company than could afford one sixty-fourth share in a steamer whose total cost was perhaps £5,000. Of course, this meant finding many more small investors, and well-known owners with established subscribers who had deep purses often set the individual share price in a new company at approximately the same level as the cost of a sixty-fourth share.

To a manufacturer reliant on ships to bring in raw materials, shipowning was attractive in a period of scarcity of ships and high freight rates, in that it helped keep costs in check. A big disadvantage was that, when rates fell to uneconomic levels, the manufacturer still had to operate the ships when chartering-in would have provided savings. The manufacturer also had the day-to-day problems of running ships, and especially of finding cargoes for voyages when his own were not being carried. The solution was to use an outsider of proven ability, as did the Garston-based bobbin manufacturers Wilson Brothers when they entrusted management to local shipbroker and ex-master, Edward Turner.

The lure of Liverpool

Of the major Liverpool coastal shipowners, few were natives of the city. Richard Hughes and William Thomas came from North Wales; whilst others began their shipowning at smaller ports and shifted it to Liverpool around 1900: William Rowland and Richard Clark from Runcorn, William Savage and Joseph Monks from Warrington, Kennaughs from Whitehaven. This they had in common with some of their illustrious ocean-going contemporaries: Brocklebanks came from Cumberland, the Harrisons from Garstang in Lancashire, Ismay from Maryport, Alfred Jones from Carmarthen, and the Holts from Rochdale.

That ambitious men like Hughes and Thomas should be attracted to a great port is not surprising, but why did relatively successful small businesses make the move? Two explanations are offered.

Firstly, Liverpool's coasting trade was well balanced between imports and exports: exceptionally so compared with other Mersey ports. A coaster arriving with one cargo could expect to leave with another, even if this did not take it right back to a port where a cargo might be lifted. Such a triangular trade might involve bringing into the Mersey a cargo of stone from a North Wales quarry jetty and then loading coal for Dublin, from where the ship would return in ballast to North Wales for more stone. A cargo of china clay from Fowey to the Mersey might be balanced by loading Lancashire coal at Garston for one of the North Cornwall mineral ports, or for Plymouth. Having an office in Liverpool put the shipowner at the centre of things, ready to respond to opportunities in Liverpool docks or elsewhere on the Mersey. Many owners were also ship brokers, and for them being in Liverpool offered more business than a minor port.

A related reason may have been the grouping in Liverpool of services which the shipowner required, particularly shipbrokers, but also including insurers, sale and purchase brokers, solicitors and banks, ship repairers, and – perhaps most important of all – those with capital to invest in shipping ventures.

The migration of shipowners and related businesses to Liverpool reflected a phenomenon seen elsewhere of trade tending to concentrate on one large port in a region. Thus Liverpool grew as an international port partly at the cost of Whitehaven and Dublin. This process tended to gain its own momentum: as Liverpool's overseas services grew in frequency, and its ships became larger and faster, it became more attractive for shippers in other ports to the detriment of services from these ports. It would be faster and more economic, for instance, for a steelworks at Workington to ship a consignment of railroad rails by coaster to Liverpool for shipment by the next cargo liner to Boston than await the less frequent and less convenient service to the U.S.A. from a nearby port. The growth of Liverpool would clearly attract shipping businesses to the growing port from the declining ones.

Steam ship building on the Mersey

The iron and steel coasters in this book were built predominantly on the Clyde and the Tyne. Why more were not built on the Mersey is not easy to explain.

As at most ports, the growth of Liverpool's trade in the eighteenth century was accompanied by an expansion of wooden shipbuilding, and over 350 shipbuilders were active at sometime during the nineteenth century. The same happened at most of the Mersey's minor ports, and small craft were built at Frodsham, Runcorn, Northwich, Widnes, Garston, Warrington, Fiddlers Ferry (below Warrington), and Sankey Bridges (on the Sankey Navigation). At Liverpool shipbuilding declined during the first half of the eighteenth century for a number of reasons, including the selfishness of shipowning interests which led to a lack of appropriate building space as dock construction demanded more of the river frontage; high rents; and high wage rates compared with other shipbuilding centres where there was less competition for labour. The growing amount of shipping in the port also diverted the available skilled shipwrights from building to repair work.

But at the time wooden shipbuilding was in decline, Merseyside was producing innovators in iron and later steel shipbuilding and marine engineering. The most illustrious examples were Jonathan Laird (his yard later became Cammell, Laird) and Alfred Holt, but the port could also boast other important builders of iron sailing and steam ships. G.R. Clover and Co. of Birkenhead, R. and J. Evans and Co., John Jones and Sons, Jones Quiggin and Co., the Liverpool Forge Co. Ltd., W.H. Potter and Son, and Thomas Royden and Son are amongst those listed in the appendix to the *Lloyd's Register* of 1898, and several of these contributed coasters to the Mersey fleet, although their output was mainly in larger ships. But with the notable exception of Lairds, who depended quite heavily on warship work, this considerable industry barely survived into the twentieth century. As other authors have pointed out, the Liverpool iron and steel shipbuilding industry and the reasons for its rise and fall are fertile grounds for research.

A look around the other Mersey ports reveals interesting if small pockets of coaster building. H. and C. Grayson Ltd. at Garston could trace their origins back to the 1750s in Liverpool. In 1911 a site for a shipyard was acquired at Garston, and the Garston Graving Dock and Shipbuilding Co. Ltd. formed. Several coasters were built, including BRITISH MONARCH and BRITISH EMPIRE for Thomas Sharp of Liverpool. Shipbuilding ended in 1922, with Grayson's decision to concentrate on the repair work which had previously been their mainstay, the company continuing as Grayson, Rollo and Clover Docks Ltd.

At Ellesmere Port a repair yard was established in October 1893, soon after the completion of the Manchester Ship Canal this far. Tyneside capital was involved in the Manchester Ship Canal Pontoons and Dry Dock Co. Ltd., the name reflecting the floating dock which was long a feature of Ellesmere Port's landscape, and was capable of docking vessels up to 350 feet. As Manchester Dry Docks Co. Ltd. (after 1906) the yard completed four small coasters for the Irish Sea trade during the early 1920s. Two of these had been ordered by The Shipping Controller during the war, and materials for a further pair ordered by the yard. The slow rate of their delivery – the last, PENSTONE, was not completed until December 1926 – reflected the depressed state of the coasting trade after 1921. The PENSTONE went to Zillah, and two of the others will be found in this book: MIA and DORIS THOMAS. The fourth, BEN SEYR (265/1921), spent its life with the Ramsey Steamship Co. Ltd.

Warrington saw an extraordinary but brief flowering of iron shipbuilding. Its first iron steamer was reputedly the WARRINGTON of 1840, built of Staffordshire iron. During the Crimean War, the coincidence of a shipbuilding boom and unusually favourable conditions in the Upper Mersey saw a number of very large sea-going iron hulls built by Tayleur and Sanderson at the Bank Quay Foundry. These included the ship TAYLEUR (1,750/1853), built for the Australian trade but lost before she left the Irish Sea on her

A product of Mersey coaster building: the **Ben Seyr**. *John Clarkson*

maiden voyage. The claims made for her - that she had the first sea-going iron hull, and was the largest merchantman built in England - were only modest exaggerations. But conditions soon became unfavourable again at Warrington, and iron shipbuilding there ceased in 1857.

It was on the Weaver that iron and steel building flourished longest. The area had a tradition of engineering, founded upon the need to construct iron pans and other equipment for the salt industry. With the Weaver's salt trade it is not surprising that attention turned to building iron and later steel river craft and coasters. The limitations of the Weaver did not restrict the outlook of its shipbuilders, who turned out craft for working in harbours and on rivers in many parts of the world. William J. Yarwood took over the Castle Dock, Northwich yard of J. Woodcock in 1896. The output of W.J. Yarwood and Co. Ltd. was prodigious and highly varied, and encompassed both hulls and engines. It included some thirty small steam coasters, including vessels for Henry Seddon and William Cooper, in which Yarwood himself took substantial shareholdings. Northwich's other shipbuilder was Isaac Pimblott Ltd., established by 1847, but few of their products feature in this book as the coasters they built were mainly for export. Yarwoods became part of the United Molasses group in 1946 and the yard closed in 1966. Pimblotts lasted until 1971.

Following the closure of Cammell, Laird as shipbuilders in the 1990s, shipbuilding on the Mersey is confined to the construction of tugs and fishing boats by McTay Marine Ltd. at Bromborough.

BAILE, GASKELL AND CO.
Liverpool

Shipbrokers are well aware of cargoes offering and of the freight rates being earned, and when business is buoyant there must be considerable temptation to enter shipowning or management and enjoy further profits. In 1896, Liverpool shipbrokers Baile, Gaskell and Co. followed this route, and became managers of and investors in the Corsair Steamship Co. Ltd. The company's small initial capital of £1,500 reflects the modest cost of the 20-year old iron steamer CORSAIR. The major shareholder was business associate and master mariner Samuel Walton, most of the other shares being taken up by Baile, Gaskell and Co. As managers, Baile, Gaskell and Co. paid themselves £200 per year plus 5% of the gross earnings, and kept any brokerage charges or commissions. Basing their income on gross earnings ensured a reasonable remuneration even when freight rates were low. CORSAIR traded widely, and as well as visiting Liverpool and ports such as Newry across the Irish Sea, she was to be seen on the East Coast at Leith, London and Rochester.

In 1898 the iron steamer NAR was acquired, and registered directly in the ownership of Baile, Gaskell and Co. Her name derived from an East Anglian river and dated from her original ownership in Kings Lynn.

At the same time as the NAR was bought the shipbrokers became involved in a more ambitious venture, rather grandly titled the Gloucester, Bantry and Liverpool Steamship Co. Ltd., and registered in Liverpool. In July 1898 Baile, Gaskell and Co. acquired the CATHERINE SUTTON, which was transferred to the company and renamed GLOUCESTER. Baile, Gaskell and Co. acted as managers to the company, jointly with Barnes and Chadborn, who were shipping contractors at Gloucester. The latter took a substantial shareholding, as did a corn merchant in Bantry, the major shareholder being a lady in Bristol, whilst there were other small investors from Worcester and Gloucester. David Baile and Harold Gaskell took just one share each, to give them a vote at shareholders meetings; their interest was in managing the ship. The company was, in fact, desperately under-capitalised, and barely a quarter of the authorised capital of £4,500 was taken up. To help finance the GLOUCESTER, a mortgage was taken out with the former owner. Gloucester had an important trade in imported corn, and with the involvement of a Bantry corn merchant GLOUCESTER would probably carry corn from Bantry, probably hoping for some general cargo from Liverpool on return voyages. Sadly, the venture does not seem to have been successful. A sign of this was GLOUCESTER straying from her intended route: in June 1900, for instance, she left Runcorn for Peterhead, no doubt with salt for the fishing industry. The company was wound up in April 1902 when freight rates had fallen in the aftermath of the Boer War, and in November GLOUCESTER was sold, only to disappear within a few months.

Meanwhile Baile, Gaskell and Co. had replaced the CORSAIR with the ST. KEVIN, but in 1902 it was decided to wind up the Corsair Steamship Co. Ltd. too. NAR was sold early in 1902, and once ST. KEVIN was disposed of in 1903 the brief career of Baile, Gaskell and Co. as shipowners and managers was at an end, and they concentrated their energies on shipbroking.

Fleet list

1. CORSAIR 1895-1900 Iron

O.N. 69405 376g 183n 160.8 x 23.2 x 12.6 feet
C. 2-cyl. by George Clark, Southwick, Sunderland.

6.9.1876: Launched by John Blumer and Co., Sunderland (Yard No. 42) for Turner, Edwards and Co., Bristol as CORSAIR. *6.10.1876:* Completed. *1885:* Sold to the London and Rotterdam Steamship Co. Ltd., London. *1889:* Sold to J. and J. Macfarlane and Co., Glasgow. *28.3.1895:* Sold to Colin Houston, Glasgow. *29.4.1895:* Sold to James Houston, Renfrew (George Milne, Glasgow, manager). *19.12.1895:* Acquired by Baile, Gaskell and Co., Liverpool. *20.7.1898:* Owners became the Corsair Steamship Co. Ltd. (Baile, Gaskell and Co., managers), Liverpool. *30.1.1900:* Sold to Louis Souchon, Port Louis, Mauritius. *25.9.1900:* Renamed SIR CELICOURT ANTELME. *8.7.1904:* Destroyed by fire off Marie Louise Island in the Seychelles whilst on a voyage from Mahé to Renic Island with general cargo. *19.9.1904:* Register closed.

2. NAR 1898-1902 Iron

O.N. 89133 299g 144n 145.0 x 22.3 x 10.5 feet
C. 2-cyl. by J. Gilmour and Co., Glasgow.

29.3.1884: Launched by Scott and Co., Bowling (Yard No. 52) for the Nar Steamship Co. Ltd. (C.E. Wise, manager), Kings Lynn as NAR. *12.5.1884:* Completed. *9.11.1891:* Manager became William Furley. *6.3.1894:* Sold to John Hay and Sons, Glasgow. *9.6.1898:* Acquired by Baile, Gaskell and Co., Liverpool. *17.12.1902:* Sold to William Thomas, Amlwch. *6.4.1903:* Sold to George Webster and Co., Glasgow. *13.12.1904:* Foundered off Kingston, Garmouth whilst on a voyage from Sunderland to Burghead with a cargo of coal.

3. GLOUCESTER 1898-1902 Steel and iron

O.N. 96112 308g 141n 150.0 x 22.6 x 9.5 feet
C. 2-cyl. by Westgarth, English and Co., Middlesbrough; 10½ knots.

5.11.1892: Launched by R. Craggs and Sons, Stockton-on-Tees (Yard No. 105) for A. Sutton and Co., Cork as CATHERINE SUTTON. *7.12.1892:* Completed. *2.4.1898:* Sold to Shipping Investments Ltd. (Charles H. Pile, manager), London. *15.7.1898:* Acquired by Baile, Gaskell and Co., Liverpool. *28.9.1898:* Owners became the Gloucester, Bantry and Liverpool Steamship Co. Ltd. (Baile, Gaskell and Co., managers), Liverpool. *4.11.1898:* Renamed GLOUCESTER. *7.11.1902:* Sold to the North Eastern Shipping Co. Ltd. (George Elsmie and Son, managers), Aberdeen. *21.2.1903:* Left Montrose for Cardiff with a cargo of oats and disappeared. She is believed to have foundered about 24.2.1903. *26.3.1903:* Register closed.

4. ST. KEVIN 1900-1903 Iron

O.N. 81446 477g 247n 178.9 x 26.2 x 12.8 feet
C. 2-cyl. by McIlwaine, Lewis and Co. Ltd., Belfast.

21.6.1883: Launched by McIlwaine, Lewis and Co. Ltd., Belfast (Yard No. 18) for John M. Inglis trading as Thomas Heiton and Co., Dublin as ST. KEVIN. *16.8.1883:* Completed. *28.9.1891:* Owners became John M. Inglis and William Hewat, Dublin. *21.6.1894:* Sold to Gregory B. Wadsworth, Goole. *4.1898:* Sold to Fredriksen and Co., Mandal, Norway. *12.3.1900:* Acquired by the Corsair Steamship Co. Ltd. (Baile, Gaskell and Co., managers), Liverpool. *13.6.1903:* Sold to William Postlethwaite, Millom. *7.1903:* Owner became George Postlethwaite, Millom. *30.5.1911:* Renamed LINDALE. *13.5.1913:* Sold to the British Phosphate Co. Ltd. (H. Freytag, manager), London. *31.5.1917:* Sold to the Anglo-Continental Guano Works Ltd. (Edward G. Martens, manager), London. *30.9.1918:* Stranded and became a total loss on the West Pier, Boulogne whilst on a voyage from Newhaven to Boulogne with a cargo of munitions. *20.12.1918:* Register closed.

THOMAS G. BEST
Liverpool

Fortune plays its part in the success or failure of any company. The Bests were a family of small Liverpool shipowners who methodically built up a fleet of coasters, keeping their investment modest and largely within the family. But of their five steamers, three were to be lost through marine hazards, and a fourth sunk although later repaired. Despite this, the business would show a handsome profit when wound-up just after the First World War.

Thomas Gardner Best was born at Hexham in Northumberland on Christmas Day 1843. Soon afterwards the family moved to Lancashire; first to Kirkham where his father had bought an iron foundry, and later to St. Helens. On his marriage in 1866 Thomas G. Best was the Liverpool representative of the Ravenhead Colliery near St. Helens, a position that would give him a useful knowledge of the port's coal trade. In 1878 he resigned and set himself up as a coal merchant and flat owner at Preeson's Row, Liverpool. Clearly Best had access to capital, perhaps inherited from his father, as he also purchased land in the Liverpool suburb of Wavertree and built two large houses.

The first vessel known to have been owned by Best was the Mersey sailing flat ANNIE (60/1835) which was registered under the ownership of Thomas Gardner Best in 1882. He is also reputed to have owned a flat called THOMAS, lost in the Mersey in December 1886, but if so it was not registered in his name. In 1889 Best bought the small wooden steamer EDITH, his first encounter with steam. It was obviously a successful encounter as, although she was soon sold, Best then ordered a new steamer from Leith.

Completed in June 1891, HERBERT was named after his youngest son, beginning a tradition of naming ships after sons and daughters; Best and his wife Martha having enough for a modest fleet. HERBERT was financed on the traditional sixty-fourth share

Herbert in the Gweebarra River, Donegal in June 1895 *Ron N. Jones*

system, of which Thomas Best took the majority. A portrait of HERBERT off Aranmore Lighthouse was painted by Edwin Brown, a Liverpool artist who married Best's elder sister Amelia. HERBERT tramped around the Irish Sea and the west of Ireland, her owners specialising in serving small ports. Indeed, in June 1895 HERBERT became the first steamer to venture up the Gweebarra River in north west Donegal.

HERBERT's visit was to deliver 240 tons of iron and steelwork for the building of a bridge over the Gweebarra. This was financed by the Congested Districts Board, and was intended to open up a remote and poor yet beautiful area and to stimulate tourism. The river had been specially buoyed, and HERBERT's voyage could only be made on the top of spring tides. The Bests seem to have extracted the maximum publicity from the occasion, as a reporter from the *Derry Journal* was invited on board to accompany Thomas and John Best and painter Edwin Brown, the ship was dressed overall, and the river was said to be lined with sightseers. On arrival HERBERT was greeted by the Lettermacaward Drum and Fife Band and a crowd estimated at two thousand, many of whom later toured the little coaster. HERBERT made two further trips from Liverpool to the Gweebarra.

HERBERT lasted only a further three years. The little steamer left Liverpool on 17th January 1898 for Galway, and met a south westerly gale in St. George's Channel. Her master, Patrick McCourt, decided to head for Belfast Lough and shelter, but the sea – now on her beam – stove in her hatches. With little hope of launching her two boats, the crew of eight waited until the HERBERT sank and the boats floated clear, although one man was lost as a boat overturned in the darkness. What followed was something of an epic of survival, as McCourt clung to an upturned boat, saw his two fellow crew men succumb to cold, and during the day watched several steamers pass without noticing him. He was eventually rescued about 3.15 a.m. the following morning by the Dinorwic slate steamer VAYNOL (233/1892) but the other boat was never found.

Herbert's crew photographed in the Gweebarra. *Ron N. Jones*

In Best's ownership, hulls seem to have been grey, but **Letty** needs a repaint. *E.N. Taylor*

HERBERT was quickly replaced, and indeed McCourt was back at sea in eight weeks. Best ordered two ships, one from each of the best respected coaster builders, Fullertons of Paisley and Williamsons of Workington. HAROLD and FRED were financed by floating single-ship companies whose capital of £6,000 covered the ship's building cost. Thomas Best took up all but six of the 600 £10 shares, in part financing this by taking out mortgages on the ships. The other six shares were distributed amongst members of the family. Thomas Best is named in the Articles of the company as manager, "for as long as he may see fit". Best's caution in using single ship companies may have arisen from the loss of HERBERT, and would mean that, in the event of an accident or financial problems, liability would be limited to the value of the ship, and legal or financial action could not affect his other interests.

HAROLD and FRED were short raised quarter deck steamers, not unlike HERBERT but a little longer. The company's trading area continued to be around the Irish Sea, and for instance FRED sailed from Liverpool to Dublin and later Carmarthen early in 1900. Occasional voyages might be slightly further afield; say, to Devon or Cornwall for clay. Best now had an office in Water Street, at the heart of Liverpool's shipping industry. The family had a substantial house in Victoria Park, Wavertree so business was obviously flourishing.

In 1908 HAROLD was lost in rather similar circumstances to HERBERT, this time off Holyhead, and was once again replaced quickly. The new steamer LETTY was financed in the same way as her predecessor, except that Thomas Best took very few of the 600 shares of the Letty Steamship Co. Ltd. The majority were registered in his wife's name, whilst sons and daughters took small holdings, including Letitia Alice Best after whom she was named. And for the first time substantial numbers of shares went to investors outside the family.

Photographs and builder's drawings of LETTY survive, showing a layout not dissimilar to that of HERBERT, but – reflecting her slightly greater length – a longer hatch ahead of her mast. Charles Waine has pointed out that the rake of her masts and funnel increases slightly fore to aft, a technique known to classical architecture and which gave the impression of parallel rake to an observer at sea level. An unusual feature clearly visible is the bunker hatch just ahead of the bridge. Placing it here rather than abaft the bridge tended to keep the after accommodation area cleaner when coal was being loaded.

When LETTY was later owned by Monroe Brothers, Captain Owen Spargo was master for a time, and he has a lot to say about her. Her accommodation for master and mate was panelled in mahogany. Such concern about the officers' surroundings when below contrasts with the open bridge with which she was built, but like most steamers she later received a closed wheelhouse. LETTY had a powerful engine which gave her a maximum speed of ten knots. At this she was heavy on coal, but her speed proved useful when she ran with market garden produce from Maasluis in Holland to London, and allowed her to arrive in time for the day's market. Like most contemporaries, she was fitted with a suit of sails when built, and in the 1930s her original mainsail was still used in moderate winds and is reckoned to have given her an extra knot.

LETTY needed careful trimming. With grain cargoes the customary procedure of loading the bulk of cargo through the main hatch meant she trimmed by the stern. The technique which Captain Spargo adopted was to load using both hatches so that the bulk of the cargo in the hold was farther forward, and to prevent the grain from shifting by piling filled sacks against each end.

LETTY also had an adventurous career. The Bests made a practice of helping out at salvage operations, and their ships were involved when the SUEVIC (12,531/1901) went ashore off the Lizard in March 1907 and when the MINNEHAHA (13,403/1900) ran aground off Scilly in April 1910. LETTY went as far as the Azores after Cunard's SLAVONIA (10,606/1903) stranded there in June 1909, and took two cargoes from her. Like many other coasters, LETTY took part in the seasonal strawberry trade from Brest to Plymouth – a trade Bests had participated in since 1900. But LETTY's biggest adventure was being sunk in collision with a Danish steamer off Southend in December 1915, fortunately without loss of life. With her valuable cargo of brass shell cases she was raised and returned to service, running Government supplies from London to France, work she was engaged in from August 1915 until April 1917.

Thomas Gardner Best, founder of the company
Ron N. Jones

Best was to suffer another loss when FRED stranded and sank near to St. David's in 1910. Again, a replacement was obtained, but this time it was a secondhand steamer. The acquisition was christened YUNGAY, breaking the tradition of christian names but still maintaining a family connection. Third son Fred Best had gone out to Chile to farm, and settled first in the town of Yungay. Rather old and built of iron, YUNGAY cost just £2,800. She was registered in the ownership of the Fred Steamship Co. Ltd.

Thomas Best died in May 1911, and his shares in the remaining companies were divided between his widow Martha and his eldest son John Joseph Best, born in 1868. John Best joined his father's business in 1886 and became the owner of the flat ANNIE in his own right in 1896. Until about 1900 he was involved in the practical side of the business, not being afraid to put on overalls and inspect engines and boilers, and later specialised in shipbroking. At this he seems to have been successful, as the small company moved into offices in the Royal Liver Buildings soon after they were completed in 1912.

John Best was less interested in running ships than his father and did not enlarge the fleet. Indeed, after a few months on Government service in 1915, YUNGAY was sold in 1916, and LETTY followed her in April 1919 - times when both would have made very much more than their modest cost prices. On the proceeds, John Best retired to a fine sandstone house near Neston on the Wirral and devoted himself to running a smallholding.

Despite considerable misfortune, the Best family most certainly did well out their modest but well-run fleet.

Fleet list

1. EDITH 1889-1890 Wood

O.N. 79662 89g 53n 82.0 x 20.2 x 8.7 feet
C. 2-cyl. by Wardhaugh and Bulmer, Newcastle-upon-Tyne.

2.1878: Launched by A.B. Gowan and Son, Berwick-on-Tweed for John H. Hedley, London as EDITH. *20.1.1879:* Completed. *1879:* Sold to Robert Cunningham, London. *1879:* Sold to William Hudson, Brighton. *2.1882:* Sold to Walter Brown, Great Yarmouth. *1887:* Sold to John T.B. Kell, Newcastle-upon-Tyne. *8.1889:* Acquired by Thomas G. Best, Liverpool. *30.7.1890:* Sold to the United Welsh Slate Co. Ltd., Manchester. *19.9.1893:* Owner became Herbert Birch, Manchester. *8.4.1894:* Burnt in Carmarthen Bay whilst on a voyage from Llanelli to Aberaeron with a cargo of burnt lime. Her crew of five was saved. *25.4.1894:* Register closed.

2. HERBERT 1891-1898

O.N. 99221 268g 112n 130.0 x 21.7 x 9.4 feet
C. 2-cyl. by Hawthorns and Co., Leith.

23.5.1891: Launched by Hawthorns and Co., Leith (Yard No. 38) for Thomas G. Best, Liverpool as HERBERT. *27.6.1891:* Completed. *18.1.1898:* Foundered in heavy weather six miles off Gunn Island, County Down whilst on a voyage from Liverpool to Galway with a cargo of wheat and mail. Seven of her crew of eight were lost. *27.1.1898:* Register closed.

3. HAROLD 1898-1908

O.N. 108776 301g 72n 140.0 x 23.1 x 9.3 feet
C. 2-cyl. by Ross and Duncan, Govan; 10 knots.

15.11.1898: Launched by John Fullerton and Co., Paisley (Yard No. 145) for Thomas G. Best, Liverpool as HAROLD. *6.12.1898:* Completed. *15.3.1899:* Owners became the Liverpool Steamship Harold Ltd. (Thomas G. Best, manager), Liverpool. *24.2.1908:* Foundered between North and South Stack, Holyhead whilst on a voyage from Teignmouth to Runcorn with a cargo of potter's clay. *21.4.1908:* Register closed.

4. FRED 1899-1910

O.N. 110560 312g 56n 141.4 x 23.1 x 9.4 feet
C. 2-cyl. by Ross and Duncan, Govan; 9$^1/_2$ knots.

28.2.1899: Launched by R. Williamson and Son, Workington (Yard No. 156) for the Fred Steamship Co. Ltd. (Thomas G. Best, manager), Liverpool as FRED. *17.3.1899:* Completed. *21.4.1910:* Stranded in Horse Ramsey Sound, near St.David's, Pembrokeshire whilst on a voyage from Cork to Llanelli via Fishguard in ballast. She floated off but sank in deep water. *5.5.1910:* Register closed.

5. LETTY 1908-1919

O.N. 127953 339g 127n 142.1 x 23.3 x 9.8 feet
C. 2-cyl. by Ross and Duncan, Govan; 10 knots.

26.11.1908: Launched by John Fullerton and Co., Paisley (Yard No. 206) for the Letty Steamship Co. Ltd. (Thomas G. Best, manager), Liverpool as LETTY. *22.12.1908:* Completed. *21.12.1915:* Sank following a collision with a Danish steamer off Southend whilst on a voyage from London to France with a cargo of brass shell cases. Her crew was saved. Later raised and returned to service. *11.3.1916:* Manager became John J. Best, Liverpool. *9.4.1919:* Sold to William A.V. James, Cardiff. *3.12.1919:* Owners became the Celyn Line Ltd. (William A. V. James, manager), Cardiff. *5.2.1923:* Owners became the Mercator Steamship Co. Ltd. (William A. V. James, manager), Cardiff. *16.3.1923:* Sold to Helen B. Monroe and Rachel E. Monroe, trading as the Letty Shipping Co. (Kenneth R. Monroe, manager), Cardiff and later Liverpool. *1.1.1931:* Owners became the Eastbrook Trading Co. (Kenneth R. Monroe, manager), Liverpool. *20.1.1931:* Owners became Monroe Brothers Ltd., Liverpool. *1.12.1936:* Owners became the Kyle Shipping Co. Ltd. (Monroe Brothers, managers), Liverpool. *22.8.1940:* Mined and sunk in Liverpool Bay whilst on a voyage from Liverpool to Buncrana with a cargo of coal. The entire crew was lost. *30.8.1941:* Register closed.

Letty in the Mersey in Monroe's ownership. The only alteration has been the fitting of a wheelhouse.
John Clarkson

6. YUNGAY 1910-1916 Iron

O.N. 89927 319g 128n 142.0 x 23.2 x 11.0 feet
C. 2-cyl. by Dunsmuir and Jackson, Govan.

4.1884: Launched by the Campbeltown Shipbuilding Co., Campbeltown (Yard No. 25) for the Jersey Steamship Co. (Alexander M. Hay, manager), Glasgow as SNIPE. *9.6.1884:* Completed. *1884:* Owners became James Hay and Sons, Glasgow. *1888:* Sold to Henry Burton, Newport. *1890:* Owners became R. Burton and Son, Newport. *20.6.1898:* Owners became R. Burton and Son Ltd., Newport. *1.6.1908:* Sold to Robert Gilchrist and Co. (Francis Johnston, manager), Liverpool. *9.7.1908:* Renamed VIRAGO. *16.6.1910:* Acquired by John J. Best, Liverpool. *21.6.1910:* Owners became the Fred Steamship Co. Ltd. (Thomas G. Best, manager), Liverpool. *15.7.1910:* Renamed YUNGAY. *21.7.1916:* Sold to the G.J. Eveson Coal and Coke Co. Ltd. (Ernest Blackburn, manager), Birmingham. *25.7.1916:* Renamed EMILY EVESON. *24.10.1916:* Owners became the Steamship Emily Eveson Co. Ltd. (Ernest Blackburn, manager), Birmingham. *12.2.1918:* Sold to the Cook Shipping Co. Ltd. (John H. Davies, manager), Swansea. *8.4.1919:* Sold to the Letricheux Line Ltd. (Letricheux and David Ltd., managers), Swansea. *21.6.1919:* Sold to William R. Barrett, Swansea. *20.5.1922:* Wrecked west of Alderney whilst on a voyage from Swansea to Rouen with a cargo of coal. *9.10.1922:* Register closed.

BRUNDRIT AND CO. LTD.
PENMAENMAWR SHIPPING CO. LTD.
Runcorn and Liverpool

The history of the Brundrit family illustrates the dynamism of which Victorian capitalists were capable. The Brundrits developed interests in quarrying, shipowning and shipbuilding and other businesses to the extent that they were a major force in the trade of Runcorn. But building on these interests they also established and developed an industry which became one of the most important in North Wales.

Dennis Brundrit was born at Stretford, Manchester in July 1796. His parents moved to Runcorn shortly afterwards, attracted by the opportunities created by the building of the Bridgewater Canal and Runcorn docks. Dennis was to profit more than most from the town's developing prosperity, and by the time he was twenty he had acquired both a druggist's shop and a wife who was the daughter of William Wright, owner of one of the town's shipyards. This yard was to pass into Dennis's hands on the death of his father-in-law. By 1823, when Brundrit entered into partnership with a Philip Whiteway as stone merchants and shipbuilders, his portfolio of investments also included the Stenhills sandstone quarry at Weston Point.

Experienced in the stone trade and with the capacity to build their own ships, Brundrit and Whiteway were quick to realise the potential of the hard igneous rock which occurs at Penmaenmawr in North Wales. The industrial towns of Lancashire and Cheshire were prosperous and expanding, and there was a growing demand for hard stone to pave their streets. Blocks of granite from quarries in Aberdeenshire had been used for paving London streets since the mid-eighteenth century and, wanting the same, the towns of the north looked for local sources of suitable stone.

The cobblestones which occurred naturally on the beach at Penmaenmawr were used as ballast by the small sailing coasters which traded between the Mersey and the North Wales coast with coal and other cargoes, and these stones grew in importance as their value for road surfacing became appreciated. Groups of local men would form small partnerships to gather together a cargo, and later they began to dress the larger boulders as roadbuilders came to favour regular rectangular setts over the irregular cobbles. Brundrit was introduced by an Edward Edwards of Conwy to the possibilities of industrialising this trade, and his first approach was to request the local men to sell him all the stone they had prepared. When this approach met with suspicion from the Welsh, Brundrit and his partner Whiteway obtained leases allowing them to collect cobblestones below the high water mark and to quarry paving and other stones at Penmaen Quarry on Penmaenmawr Mountain. From 1830 the local stone gatherers were set to work for Brundrit and Whiteway, with Edwards as foreman. Investment by the partners led to railways and inclines being built to serve the Penmaen Quarry, and jetties constructed to enable ships to be loaded with stone in comparative safety.

By the late 1850s, Brundrit and Whiteway's operations were producing annually over 50,000 tons of setts and 40,000 tons of other stone, including broken stone for use as macadam. Much of this would be shipped to Liverpool or Runcorn, the latter for transhipment to Manchester by the Bridgewater Canal. At the Runcorn yard he had inherited from his father-in-law, Brundrit and his partner built their own ships for the trade. Some thirty wooden schooners, sloops, smacks, flats and ships owned by Brundrit and his Whiteway partners have been traced, the earliest known being the schooner JOHN (62/1840). All but one of those identified were constructed at the partners' Mersey Street yard and this also built for other owners, making it one of the most important and certainly the longest lasting of the Runcorn shipyards. Two vessels built and owned by Brundrit and Whiteway, although not meant for the stone trade, were particularly notable: the ANNE CHESHYRE (413/1853) and DENNIS BRUNDRIT (462/1856). Although the largest craft ever built at Runcorn, these were considered amongst the smallest of full-rigged ships, but this did not inhibit their owners from sending them on distant voyages, and the DENNIS BRUNDRIT spent 36 years trading mostly to the Falkland Islands. In building these particularly large ships, the yard was taking

The extent of the granite workings at Penmaenmawr can be seen in this view of Brundrit's **Puffin** taking the ground at the quarry jetty. *Welsh Industrial and Maritime Museum 89.75*

advantage of a shift in the deep water channel of the Mersey which for about a decade lay immediately alongside the river's Cheshire shore.

As this diversification into larger ships suggests, the partners did not have their horizons limited by the Penmaenmawr stone trade, important though this was. They had coal and timber yards along the Mersey at Runcorn, and imported slate for the building trade and limestone for the works of Brunner, Mond and Co. Stone arrived at Runcorn in three forms: setts, curbstones or channels, all of which were dressed at their quarries for use as pavement; stone broken by hand at the quarry for use in macadam; and as large lumps known as "breakers". The last-named was broken down into pieces suitable for macadam either at Brundrit's wharf or at the point where it was to be used, sometimes by labour from a local workhouse.

The partnership between Brundrit and Whiteway ended about 1874, when the ships were transferred to the ownership of John Brundrit. The son of Dennis, John took a direct interest in the management of Penmaen Quarry, living on the site. The move from Runcorn, where his father had traded, suggests that John Brundrit intended to concentrate the family business on quarrying and transporting stone. It was under his control that the first tentative step into steam was taken with the completion of the wooden REGINALD at Runcorn in 1881. Built of wood, she would have required much the same skills from Brundrit's shipwrights as contemporary schooners. She was to be the only steamer built by the yard, although their flat PERCY of 1887 was fitted with a steam engine in 1891. The three further steamers which were to join the fleet in the decade from 1890 came from yards on the Ribble and on the Clyde which specialised in iron and steel shipbuilding. Brundrit's yard, along with the others at Runcorn, was a

Cecil arrives at Preston Dock with another stone cargo. *John Clarkson*

casualty not just of the change to iron and steel ships, but of the construction of the Manchester Ship Canal which effectively separated the town from the Mersey. Brundrit's Mersey Street yard became the town's public slipway.

The first iron steamer was the CECIL, built at Lytham in 1890 and registered under the ownership of a single-ship company. John Brundrit had the biggest single share in the Cecil Steamship Co. Ltd., but substantial holdings were taken by the Hayes and Higson families who were in the coal and stone businesses. This was to set the pattern for subsequent acquisitions, and both the steel-built TAFFY of 1894 and the PUFFIN of 1900 were registered under single-ship companies whose shares were divided amongst the Hayes, Higson and Brundrit families.

Quarry proprietor George W. Hayes had been in partnership with John Brundrit since 1886 at least and on Brundrit's death on 1st December 1896 Hayes assumed control of the business. He became the managing director of a new company registered as Brundrit and Co. Ltd. and moved the offices to Liverpool. Despite the use of their name, the Brundrit family's interests and influence began to fade. In 1898, as part of the reorganisation following John Brundrit's death, the PERCY was transferred to a new company known as the Penmaenmawr Shipping Co. Ltd. under George Hayes' management. Also transferred were the remaining sailing ships: ELLESMERE (72/1850), BERTIE (61/1859), SWIFT (66/1865) and SWALLOW (67/1868). The name Brundrit and Co.

Ltd. survived as managers of the last steamer PUFFIN, built in 1900, and the last sailing vessel acquired, SUNBEAM (148/1883).

The small fleet with which the business greeted the new century was inadequate to meet all its transport needs, as by any standards the Penmaen Quarry was now a major undertaking, employing over five hundred men and as an extractive industry second in North Wales only to the slate quarries. And unlike the latter industry, it had a bright future in supplying the increasing demand for railway ballast and roadstone. As well as the quarry workings which disfigured the huge promontory, the quarrying company was also responsible for around fifty houses built for their workforce in the towns of Penmaenmawr and Llanfairfechan.

In 1909 the decision was taken to quit shipowning and concentrate on quarrying. Most of the remaining ships – BERTIE, CECIL, PUFFIN, and SWALLOW – went to the Zillah Shipping and Carrying Co. Ltd., which company was to serve the quarries at Penmaenmawr for almost a half century. Indeed, the CECIL was the first ship to use a new jetty opened to serve the Penmaen Quarry in 1913.

In 1911 Brundrit and Co. Ltd. was liquidated and a new company incorporated which consolidated the interests that were steadily eating away the enormous headland at Penmaenmawr. The Graiglwyd Quarry was only slightly smaller in output than the Penmaen Quarry, and its management was probably more progressive in outlook, installing one of the industry's first mechanical stone crushing mills in 1888. Having passed through the ownership of Raynes, Kneeshaw and Lupton the quarry was now worked by Darbishires Ltd. Brundrits, Darbishires and the Welsh Granite Co., which worked the Eifl sett quarry at Trefor, were amalgamated as the Penmaenmawr and Welsh Granite Co. Ltd. with a capital which was little short of half a million pounds. Production expanded until well over a thousand men were employed, but the recession of the 1930s saw the end of sett production and with it a drastic fall in manpower. With the installation of modern crushing and handling machinery, Penmaenmawr concentrated on crushed roadstone production, and the quarries continue to do so today under the ownership of Kingston Minerals Ltd.

The Brundrit family had a major influence on the development of both Runcorn and the North Wales quarrying industry. But their fleet reached its peak in the days when sail was dominant in Runcorn, and the modest list of their steamers which follows does not reflect their real importance as shipowners or traders.

Fleet list

1. REGINALD 1881-1888 Wood

O.N. 83502 116g 58n 90.0 x 20.7 x 9.6 feet
C. 2-cyl. by S. Baker, Liverpool.

6.1881: Launched by Brundrit and Co., Runcorn for Brundrit and Co., Runcorn as REGINALD. *29.7.1881:* Completed. *6.1.1888:* Sold to Allen Green, Liverpool. *19.9.1899:* Owner became Mary Green, Rock Ferry. *2.1890:* Sold to J. Jörgensen, Stavanger, Norway and renamed BREMNAES. *1895:* Sold to Thomas S. Falck, Stavanger. *16.12.1901:* Destroyed by fire at Seydisfjord, Iceland whilst loading a cargo of herrings.

2. PERCY 1887-1906 Wooden steam flat

O.N. 83518 87g 38n 73.4 x 19.5 x 8.5 feet
4.1891: 2-cyl. by W.E. Bates, Northwich; 7 knots.
11.1898: C. 2-cyl. by Plenty and Sons, Newbury; 9 knots.

13.9.1887: Completed by John Brundrit, Runcorn for John Brundrit, Runcorn as the sailing flat PERCY. *18.4.1891:* Re-registered after conversion to a steamer. *1.4.1898:* Owners became the Penmaenmawr Shipping Co. Ltd. (George W. Hayes, manager), Liverpool. *11.1898:* Re-engined. *26.11.1904:* Sank in collision with the steamer PLOVER (277/1888) which was at anchor off Laird's shipyard in the Mersey whilst on a voyage from Penmaenmawr to Runcorn with a cargo of stone setts. Two of her crew were drowned. Later raised. *20.2.1905:* Owners became Thomas K. Hayes, Liverpool. *26.3.1906:* Sold to the Brandon Bay Salvage Co. Ltd., London. *3.6.1910:* Sold to Henry T. Ensor, Queenstown, Cork. *8.6.1911:* Sold to the Steam Flat Percy Co. Ltd. (Thomas J. May, manager), Liverpool. *1931:* Broken up. *7.12.1931:* Register closed.

3. CECIL 1890-1909 Iron

O.N. 97227 235g 96n 130.2 x 21.1 x 9.5 feet
C. 2-cyl. by Clayton, Goodfellow and Co., Blackburn; 10 knots.

7.10.1890: Completed by R. Smith and Co., Lytham (Yard No. 149) for John Brundrit, Runcorn as CECIL. *7.11.1890:* Owners became the Cecil Steamship Co. Ltd. (Brundrit and Co., managers), Runcorn. *7.4.1898:* Manager became George W. Hayes, Liverpool. *19.3.1909:* Sold to the Zillah Shipping and Carrying Co. Ltd. (William A. Savage, manager), Liverpool. *24.12.1915:* Stranded at the entrance to the River Somme whilst on a voyage from London to St. Valery-sur-Somme, France with a cargo of Government stores. One account suggests she had been in collision with the steamer LADY IVEAGH (2,268/1892) in the River Somme off Le Crotoy. *11.1.1917:* Register closed.

4. TAFFY 1894-1898

O.N. 102368 173g 90n 100.5 x 21.1 x 9.3 feet
C. 2-cyl. by David J. Dunlop and Co., Port Glasgow; 8 knots.

19.6.1894: Launched by David J. Dunlop and Co., Port Glasgow (Yard No. 224) for John Brundrit, Runcorn as TAFFY. *10.7.1894:* Completed. *14.4.1895:* Owners became the Taffy Steamship Co. Ltd. (Brundrit and Co., managers), Runcorn. *7.4.1898:* Manager became George W. Hayes, Liverpool. *21.12.1898:* Sold to Charles Page and Edward C. Turner, Blakeney, Norfolk. *5.8.1913:* Sold to Rix and Sons, Hull. *1.12.1914:* Sold to the Blackrock and Passage Railway, Cork. *17.11.1916:* Foundered about eight miles south of St. Govan's Head, Pembroke whilst on a voyage from Cardiff to Cork with a cargo of coal. *22.11.1916:* Register closed.

5. PUFFIN 1900-1909

O.N. 111363 404g 59n 150.0 x 25.0 x 9.9 feet
C.2-cyl. by Dunsmuir and Jackson, Govan; 11 knots.

15.3.1900: Launched by the Ailsa Shipbuilding Co., Troon (Yard No. 87) for the Puffin Steamship Co. Ltd. (Brundrit and Co. Ltd., managers), Liverpool as PUFFIN. *5.5.1900:* Completed. *19.3.1909:* Sold to the Zillah Shipping and Carrying Co. Ltd. (William A. Savage, manager), Liverpool. *1933:* Broken up during the fourth quarter. *16.7.1936:* Register closed.

Puffin. She has been fitted with a small, but well-glazed wheelhouse. Note the full set of sails in what is probably a pre-First World War view. *John Clarkson*

RICHARD R. CLARK
OVERTON STEAMSHIP CO. LTD.
Liverpool

The story of the Clark family illustrates how the commercial growth of the Mersey ports in the nineteenth century acted as a magnet to ambitious shipping men from elsewhere in the United Kingdom. During the fifty years prior to the First World War increasing industrialisation and changes in both the technology of ships and the management of shipping saw shipowning concentrated on large ports like Liverpool and Cardiff, to the detriment of smaller and once thriving seafaring communities such as those in Wales and the West Country.

Although the Clarks owned relatively few steamers, their importance to the local shipping industry was considerable, whilst their reputation spread well beyond the town of Runcorn where they first settled. Their activities encompassed ownership of both sail and steam vessels, shipbroking, ship management, towage and canal boats, and they were associated with some of the last sailing coasters to work the British coast.

Richard Clarke (the "e" was soon dropped) was born in Appledore, Devon in 1825. With his wife Ann he moved to Runcorn between 1856 and 1858, although as their first daughter was born in South Wales in 1856, they may not have come directly from the West Country. At the time of their arrival the trade of Runcorn was enjoying a period of unprecedented growth. Local industry made a substantial contribution to this seaborne trade, importing raw materials for fertiliser and alkali works, slate and roadstone for urban growth. But Runcorn owed its prosperity largely to its importance as a transhipment point for the inland waterways, as the Bridgewater Canal linked the Mersey with the mines and manufacturies of Manchester, the Trent and Mersey Canal with the Potteries. It was probably the trade in china clay which provided the connection between Runcorn and Richard Clark's birthplace. Appledore and other north Devon ports were the home and building place of many hundreds of schooners and ketches in the nineteenth century; some of which were employed carrying china clay from the southern ports of Cornwall to the Mersey. It is likely that Richard Clark, visiting Runcorn on a Devon-owned ship, realised the opportunities offered by this developing industrial town and its growing system of docks and decided to settle in Cheshire.

By 1869 he had become harbour master at Weston Point, part of Runcorn but physically and commercially separated from the town's Bridgewater Docks. Weston Point Docks developed during the 1830s at the Mersey entrance of a short canal built as far as Frodsham to improve the Weaver Navigation, down which much of Cheshire's enormous exports of salt passed. Clark's job would involve him supervising the large number of coastal sailing ships, Weaver flats and lighters which handled the salt trade and also brought in some of the immense amount of coal needed by the salt works. He lived on the job: in an imposing house known as Weaver Villa which was contemporary with the docks themselves.

The first record found of Richard Clark as a shipowner is the twelve shares he took in the locally-built steam tug SPECULATER (32/1869). It is likely that she was built to assist sailing ships bound for Weston Point through the notoriously twisting and unpredictable channels of the Upper Mersey. She probably offered a parallel service to that of the Bridgewater Trustees, who provided free towage between the Sloyne and their own docks at Runcorn. SPECULATER was sold to Spain after seven years service, but other tugs followed: the CLARISSA (92/1883) in which Clark initially took all the shares and of which he is listed as the builder (although there is no other record of this activity) and the NAVIGATOR (137/1884). Both these had engines built by Edwin Foden of Sandbach, later to be famous for his steam and diesel road vehicles. In 1875 Clark and some of those with shares in the SPECULATER considerably expanded their towage interests by floating the Weston Point Towing Co. Ltd., which eventually owned a small fleet of tugs. With its capital of £10,000 the company bought the GLADIATOR (78/1873) for £2,400, AVIATOR (66/1876) for £2,500, LIBERATOR (79/1877), and EMULATOR (106/1885) for £3,200. Clark was the largest single shareholder, a fact which explains the similarity of its naming scheme to Clark's own. The towing company survived into the 1920s, when a net loss for the year 1927 decided the owners that it should be wound up, but by then the Clark family had no financial interest in it.

As well as tugs, Richard Clark built up a fleet of sailing ships. The earliest known are the schooners FANNY (106/1872) and THE SAINT (118/1870) in which he took shares in 1875. Clark's West Country connections remained important, as although THE SAINT was registered at Runcorn, he had the FANNY re-registered at Bideford in 1878. In 1876 the yard of Thomas Cook in his home town of Appledore built for him a new schooner of 113 gross tons and with a name to celebrate his new home, WEAVER BELLE. Further ships bought secondhand were the brig COLERIDGE (211/1868) in 1879, the schooner BALLINBREICH CASTLE (111/1879) in 1880, the schooner ANN CLARK (138/1879 built as the ELIZA ANN) in 1883 and the Connecticut-built barquentine ETHIOPIAN (164/1852) in 1885. None of these wooden ships were retained long, and all had gone by 1890 when Richard Clark reached the age of 65 and sensibly decided to retire from shipowning. He was by now comfortably off, as he had invested not just in ships but also in land around Weston Point on which he built housing for the workers at the local chemical works. Known as "Clark's Backs", some of this development survives, including a Clarks Terrace. Richard Clark died in April 1897, his wife surviving him by only a few months.

The Clarks had two sons, Richard Robert born in 1863 and Frederick William in 1865, both at Weston Point. They continued the family's involvement with local shipping and transport, the latter acquiring a considerable fleet of canal boats. It was Richard R. Clark, however, who was to keep the name Clark at sea for the next half century. No doubt he had initially joined his father, who by 1887 was advertising his services as a shipbroker in Runcorn. In 1893 Richard R. Clark began in this business on his own account in partnership with George H. Grounds. The company known as Clark and Grounds became well-known, acting for many of the steamers and the surprisingly large number of sailing ships which continued to trade to Runcorn almost up until the Second World War. Clark and Grounds activities eventually encompassed shipbroking, chartering and agency work at Runcorn, Weston Point, Widnes's West Bank Dock, Garston and Ellesmere Port.

Richard R. Clark took his first tentative steps into shipowning in 1901, buying the elderly schooners ELLESMERE (72/1850) and JULIA (66/1844). Both had been built and owned by the Brundrits, who used them to carry stone from their quarries at Penmaenmawr, North Wales. In view of the next and important development in Richard R. Clark's career it is likely that these ships continued in this hard and at times dangerous trade, loading heavy cargoes at frail jetties on this exposed coast.

The year 1904 saw Clark take a far-reaching step, becoming manager of the Manchester, Liverpool and North Wales Steamship Co. Ltd., and moving into this company's offices at Albert Buildings, Liverpool. Shortly before this, Clark gives his address as Trevor, Caernarfon indicating that he was actually handling Clark and Grounds business on site at one of the major North Wales quarries. With his knowledge of local shipping and especially his experience in the stone trade, Clark was picked by the founder of this company, Rear Admiral J.P. Jones-Parry, and by Henry Seddon who became an important shareholder. The company is the subject of a separate chapter, as is the small fleet owned by Seddon himself which was also managed from Clark's Liverpool office. Stone was the most important cargo for the ships which Clark managed, but they also carried other bulk cargoes on the Irish Sea.

Clark made little distinction between the various activities he was engaged in, and both management and shipbroking were carried on from the same Liverpool office. Letters concerning ship management were sent out on Clark and Grounds' stationery and this seems to have led to the widely-held belief that this company were the managers of Clark's steam coasters. The Runcorn operation was not neglected, and shipbroking at the Top Locks office was continued under the management of Clark's son, Edgar. Clark's other son George was later to join his father in the Liverpool office. The year 1904 also saw partner George Ground develop an interest in shipowning, taking over responsibility for the JULIA from Richard Clark. After the First World War Grounds was to expand his shipowning considerably. When James Fisher of Barrow decided to abandon sail and concentrate on steamships, his schooners were bought by "Harry" Grounds who, before his death in 1932, had found some fame as the last British owner of a fleet of coastal sailing ships.

Clark took a modest financial interest in the Manchester, Liverpool and North Wales Steamship Co. Ltd. But with growing experience and capital he wanted an up-to-date fleet in which he had a greater financial interest, and from whose earnings he would be the major beneficiary. Accordingly, in 1911 he formed the Overton Steamship Co. Ltd. to own a fleet of steam coasters under his management. Clark and his family took up almost half the shares in the new company. Two steamers were delivered almost immediately: the OVERTON and the WESTDALE, the latter taking its name from Clark's home in Weston Road, Runcorn. Expansion continued with a second-hand ship, the INCHBRAYOCK, in 1913 and - from this ship's builder - the new HALTON. Her original name HEIMAT suggests that she had been intended for German account but had had her delivery prevented by the outbreak of war in August 1914.

Unlike the Manchester, Liverpool and North Wales Steamship Co. Ltd. which suffered badly from enemy action, the Overton Steamship Co. Ltd. came out of the war unscathed. Two of its ships were taken up by the Government, and served for protracted periods: HALTON from August 1915 to April 1919, and OVERTON commissioned as a Fleet Messenger from September 1915 to November 1920. Undoubtedly, Clark emerged from the war richer and ready for expansion. On the return of peace he placed an order for a 152-foot coaster with Cochranes of Selby, who were better known for their trawlers. Clark had four coasters launched in pairs, the WESTON and SUTTON on 17th June 1920 by Clark's wife Margaret or one of his daughters, and on 15th September 1920 the BEESTON and the EDERN (the latter for the Manchester, Liverpool and North Wales Steamship Co. Ltd.). Between the placing of these orders and their delivery shipping had seen the high freight rates which had ruled since the First World War go into a dramatic and irreversible fall. Indeed, it seems that completion of the later ships was delayed, probably so that Clark could put off making the final payment as long as possible. Clark paid between £28,000 and £29,000 for his steamers (other owners paid up to £38,000 for sister ships), yet values of ships fell so far and so fast that by July 1921 the builders of another coaster to the same design were begging Coppacks of Connah's Quay to take it off their hands for just £12,500. Saddled with expensive, albeit modern and well-built

Halton in the Avon Gorge. *E.N. Taylor*

steamers, the Overton Steamship Co. Ltd. would have to struggle to earn its living in the twenties and thirties when freight rates steadfastly refused to rise. Clark's involvement in shipbroking and his intimate knowledge of what cargoes were offering and where would be a major factor in keeping the fleet employed.

The Mersey now saw the company's ships less often, as they roamed widely in search of cargoes. The coal trade out of Cardiff, Newport, Swansea and Ayr was important to the company, as was East Coast coal from ports such as Goole. Some china clay continued to be delivered to Runcorn, and from Weston Point a salt cargo might well be lifted, perhaps to a fishing port on the east coast of Scotland. Lerwick saw several of Clark's steamers towards the end of the decade, arriving with Cheshire salt or perhaps coal from Blyth. During the summer of 1928, for instance, BEESTON or WESTON called at Lerwick several times each month with such cargoes, and proceeded to load "stock" - herring to be smoked at Fraserburgh, Peterhead or Stornoway. This trade continued into the 1930s; in June 1933, for instance, BEESTON brought a cargo of salt to Lerwick and sailed for Hamburg with 2,634 barrels of herring which had been salted locally.

On the East Coast of Scotland, a Clark's steamer might load Fife coal for the south, where on the Medway a cement cargo could be expected. In the early summer fruit would be carried from the Channel Islands or early vegetables from France to English Channel or Bristol Channel ports. Some of the ships, including the WESTON, were chartered by Cunard for the fruit trade. The Channel Islands would provide one of the staple cargoes of the steam coaster, stone from one of the islands' several quarries to London.

Although managed from Liverpool, the ships' connection with Runcorn was very strong, and most drew their crews from the town. John Terreta was a member of a family closely involved with the fleet. He had served on the STANLEY which Clark managed for Henry Seddon until he joined the Royal Navy during the war. On demobilisation he signed on to the new BEESTON. Such family connections could add a tragic extra dimension to casualties, however, and one of the worst of these involved the Terretas.

Towards the end of the afternoon of Friday 27th November 1925, the SUTTON left Aberystwyth for Antwerp with 260 tons of lead and zinc concentrates. This was an unusual voyage, and probably one of the last times an ore, or any other export cargo, left the Welsh port. The wind was light but freshening from the north west as she steamed out of the harbour, and by the time New Quay was abeam it had reached force 8. The ore cargo began to shift and the SUTTON foundered, taking with her the entire crew. No fewer than five members of the Terreta family were lost: Captain William H. Terreta, his wife Margaret and daughter Eleanor who frequently sailed with him, and as members of the crew his son William and son-in-law Edward Roberts. A coaster like the SUTTON would not have carried a radio and suspicions were only aroused when she failed to arrive at Antwerp the following Tuesday. Bodies and the remains of one of her boats washed ashore in Cardigan Bay confirmed her fate. It was only in recent years that her wreck was located, when Captain Eric Terreta, a former Manchester Ship Canal tug skipper, dived on the ship in which his great uncle had been lost.

In 1928 the SUTTON's place in the fleet was taken by a second-hand steamer renamed BRERETON; this replacement suggesting that trade was not wholly bad. The last addition to the Overton Steamship Company's fleet was the EDERN, transferred on the winding up of the Manchester, Liverpool and North Wales Steamship Co. Ltd.

The company's last years were to be marred by a number of accidents. In contrast to the SUTTON disaster, the first was slightly farcical. On the night of 24th February 1933 the OVERTON was anchored off St. Peter Port with a cargo of Tyne coal for Guernsey's greenhouses. In eagerness to reach harbour and shelter from a south west gale, she twice hit what were certainly rocks but which her captain euphemistically described as "submerged objects". Listing heavily, she just reached the harbour before sinking in shallow water, 200 yards short of her intended destination. Happily her crew got off in a boat and had the shortest of rows to safety. The local paper described her as lying in "a picturesque if unhappy position". Less fortunate was the short-lived BRERETON: in January 1934 she was wrecked on Carrick Rocks whilst leaving Rosslare Bay where she had spent two days sheltering from a storm.

Overton during her misadventures at St. Peter Port, Guernsey in February 1933. *D. Hocquard*

Richard Clark's last total loss was the HALTON, wrecked in the Bristol Channel in January 1940 - the winter months were cruel ones for coastal steamers. The OVERTON once again narrowly escaped her fate on 23rd August 1940 when bounced by a German aircraft off Bardsey during a ballast voyage from Bideford to the Mersey. Beached, luckily without casualties, she was refloated and dry-docked at Port Dinorwic, but as she was sold soon afterwards it is probable that she did not trade again for Clark.

Richard Clark died in 1942 and his remaining ships were quickly sold, two going to the I.C.I. Alkali Division - a near neighbour at Weston Point. It is worth noting that all the company's steamers with the exception of the EDERN met violent ends.

The disposal of the fleet was probably inevitable. The offices which the company had occupied for almost forty years had been bombed out during the Liverpool blitz. With the international situation looking grim, and shipping under strict government control, prospects for an ageing fleet of steamers must have looked poor to the family.

Although his fleet was modest, Clark had become widely known through the varied activities of Clark and Grounds and especially its schooner agency. A respected member of Liverpool's shipping community, Clark had served his term as chairman of the Liverpool Shipowner's Association. Like his father, Richard R. Clark had moved from the town of his birth when business opportunities offered elsewhere. But again like his father he had not turned his back on his old home, and although registered and managed in Liverpool, the steamers of the Overton Steamship Co. Ltd. were closely identified with Runcorn from where they drew the majority of their crews.

Richard Clark with his wife (seated centre), children and grand children.
Courtesy Mrs. Christine Evans

Fleet list

1. OVERTON 1911-1941

O.N. 131393 426g 185n 143.5 x 24.4 x 10.5 feet
C. 2-cyl. by Baird Brothers, North Shields; 9 knots.

9.10.1911: Launched by J.T. Eltringham and Co. Ltd., South Shields (Yard No. 283) for the Overton Steamship Co. Ltd. (Richard R. Clark, manager), Liverpool as OVERTON. *24.10.1911:* Completed. *24.2.1933:* Sank inside St. Peter Port harbour, Guernsey after striking a rock whilst arriving from Newcastle-upon-Tyne with a cargo of coal. *3.3.1933:* Refloated by the salvage steamer RESTORER (556/1888) and discharged her cargo. *8.3.1933:* Left in tow for Falmouth for repairs. *23.8.1940:* Beached after being damaged by a German aircraft near Bardsey whilst on a voyage from Bideford to Liverpool in ballast. There were no casualties. Later refloated. *28.8.1940:* Drydocked at Port Dinorwic for repairs. *26.8.1941:* Sold to H. Harrison (Shipping) Ltd. (William J. Ireland, manager), Liverpool. *16.9.1951:* Owners became the Thorn Line Ltd. (S. William Coe and Co. Ltd., managers), Liverpool. *7.9.1955:* Wrecked on Saddle Rock off Larne in fog whilst on a voyage from Liverpool to Larne and Coleraine with general cargo. Her crew were saved. *3.12.1955:* Register closed.

An early view of **Overton,** probably just prior to the First World War. *E.N. Taylor*

2. WESTDALE 1911-1942

O.N. 131398 424g 183n 143.5 x 24.4 x 10.5 feet
C. 2-cyl. by Baird Brothers, North Shields; 9 knots.

9.10.1911: Launched by J.T. Eltringham and Co. Ltd., South Shields (Yard No. 284) for the Overton Steamship Co. Ltd. (Richard R. Clark, manager), Liverpool as WESTDALE. *17.11.1911:* Completed. *25.7.1942:* Sold to the Ohlson Steamship Co. Ltd. (Sir Eric Ohlson, manager), Hull. *19.6.1944:* Beached in Seine Bay after being mined in position 49.24 N by 00.38 W whilst carrying a cargo of ammunition and carbide to the Normandy beaches. *28.6.1944:* Refloated. *7.7.1944:* Arrived at Southampton leaking badly and later declared a constructive total loss. *7.8.1945:* Register closed. *1945:* Sold to the Salvedor Co. Ltd. (Bauer, Philip and Co., managers), London for use as a storage hulk at Le Havre. *20.10.1949:* Allocated to T.W. Ward Ltd. for breaking up at Grays, Essex.

3. INCHBRAYOCK 1913-1920

O.N. 124459 363g 161n 140.2 x 23.7 x 11.0 feet
C. 2-cyl. by W.V.V. Lidgerwood, Coatbridge, Glasgow; 9½ knots.

6.5.1909: Launched by the Montrose Shipbuilding Co., Montrose (Yard No. 51) for the Grangemouth Steamship Co. Ltd., Grangemouth as INCHBRAYOCK. *12.6.1909:* Completed. *20.2.1913:* Acquired by the Overton

Steamship Co. Ltd. (Richard R. Clark, manager), Liverpool. *15.1.1920:* Sold to Thomas M. Collier, Bray, Wicklow. *26.6.1920:* Sold to Joseph H. Cubitt, Newcastle-upon-Tyne. *31.7.1921:* Owners became Shields Coasters Ltd. (Joseph H. Cubitt, manager), Newcastle-upon-Tyne. *22.9.1921:* Owners became the Inchbrayock Steamship Co. Ltd. (Joseph H. Cubitt, manager), Newcastle-upon-Tyne. *21.3.1924:* Managers became Park and Henderson Ltd. *3.6.1927:* Sold to Robert Taylor and Sons Ltd., Dundee. *2.8.1927:* Renamed LUNAN. *19.12.1931:* Sold to Osborn and Wallis Ltd., Bristol. *4.7.1941:* Mined and sunk off Penarth in position 51.26.48 N by 03.10.24 W whilst on a voyage from Ely Harbour to Portishead with a cargo of coal. Five of her crew of six were lost. *12.7.1941:* Register closed.

Westdale *Courtesy Mrs. Christine Evans*

Inchbrayock at Bristol in 1913 or 1914. *E.N. Taylor*

4. HALTON 1914-1940

O.N. 135598 460g 191n 150.0 x 25.2 x 10.9 feet
T. 3-cyl. by Lidgerwood Ltd., Coatbridge, Glasgow; 10¼ knots.

13.5.1914: Launched by the Montrose Shipbuilding Co., Montrose (Yard No. 59) as HEIMAT. *10.7.1914:* Completed for the Overton Steamship Co. Ltd. (Richard R. Clark, manager), Liverpool. *23.10.1914:* Renamed HALTON. *27.1.1940:* Stranded on Lundy Island whilst on a voyage from Cardiff to Brieux with a cargo of coal. Later refloated and declared a constructive total loss. *29.4.1940:* Register closed. *27.9.1940:* Arrived at Briton Ferry to be broken up by T.W. Ward Ltd.

Both **Weston** and photographer Douglas Cochrane seem to have developed a list in this shot in Preston Dock.
W.S.P.L. Cochrane collection

5. WESTON 1920-1942

O.N. 143670 485g 210n 152.0 x 25.2 x 10.8 feet
T. 3-cyl. by Charles D. Holmes and Co. Ltd., Hull; 9½ knots.

17.6.1920: Launched by Cochrane and Sons Ltd., Selby (Yard No. 743) for the Overton Steamship Co. Ltd. (Richard R. Clark, manager), Liverpool as WESTON. *16.9.1920:* Completed. 1942: Sold to Imperial Chemical Industries (Alkali Division) Ltd., Liverpool. *11.6.1945:* Owners became Imperial Chemical Industries Ltd., Liverpool. *1947:* Sold to the Coe Line Ltd., London and renamed COE-PAM. *1952:* Sold to W.N. Lindsay, Leith and renamed MISTLEY. *19.6.1957:* Sank after striking Reefdyke Rocks off North Ronaldsay whilst on a voyage from North Ronaldsay to Fair Isle with a cargo of coal.

6. SUTTON 1920-1925

O.N. 143676 485g 210n 152.0 x 25.2 x 10.8 feet
T. 3-cyl. by Charles D. Holmes and Co. Ltd., Hull; 9½ knots.

17.6.1920: Launched by Cochrane and Sons Ltd., Selby (Yard No. 744) for the Overton Steamship Co. Ltd. (Richard R. Clark, manager), Liverpool as SUTTON. *18.10.1920:* Completed. *27.11.1925:* Foundered off New Quay, Cardiganshire when her cargo of lead and zinc concentrates shifted whilst on a voyage from Aberystwyth to Antwerp. All on board were lost. *29.6.1926:* Register closed.

7. BEESTON 1921-1942

O.N. 143714 466g 192n 152.0 x 25.2 x 10.8 feet
T. 3-cyl. by Charles D. Holmes and Co. Ltd., Hull; 9½ knots.

15.9.1920: Launched by Cochrane and Sons Ltd., Selby (Yard No. 749) for the Overton Steamship Co. Ltd.

An early and tragic loss means there are few photographs of **Sutton**. *W.S.P.L.*

Beeston at Bristol. *W.S.P.L.*

(Richard R. Clark, manager), Liverpool as BEESTON. *22.2.1921:* Completed. *20.4.1942:* Sold to Imperial Chemical Industries (Alkali Division) Ltd., Liverpool. *11.6.1945:* Owners became Imperial Chemical Industries Ltd., London. *9.7.1946:* Sold to the Deeside Shipping Co. Ltd. (Thomas Rose and Co., managers), Sunderland. *21.9.1946:* Renamed DEENESS. *16.2.1951:* Wrecked in heavy weather on the Cotentin peninsula, France in position 49.38.20 N by 01.51.20 W whilst on a voyage from Guernsey to London with a cargo of granite. *5.4.1951:* Register closed.

Brereton *Gwynedd Archives XS2171/1/61*

In this view at Preston **Edern** has lost the battleaxes which were on her funnel when owned by the Manchester, Liverpool and North Wales Steamship Co. Ltd., but has not gained the blue 'O' of the Overton Steamship Co. Ltd. *W.S.P.L. Cochrane collection*

8. BRERETON 1928-1934

O.N. 144975 461g 178n 141.8 x 25.1 x 11.3 feet
T. 3-cyl. by Amos and Smith Ltd., Hull; $9\frac{1}{2}$ knots.

28.6.1921: Launched by Pitchers Ltd., Great Yarmouth (Yard No. 1) for Thomas M. Collier, Bray, Wicklow as BRAEMORE. *27.10.1921:* Completed. *25.4.1928:* Acquired by the Overton Steamship Co. Ltd. (Richard R. Clark, manager), Liverpool. *11.5.1928:* Renamed BRERETON. *18.1.1934:* Wrecked on Carrick Rocks near Rosslare whilst on a voyage from Lossiemouth to Barry with a cargo of oats. Her crew of nine was rescued by the Rosslare Lifeboat. *22.2.1934:* Register closed.

9. EDERN 1932-1942

O.N. 143710 466g 192n 152.0 x 25.2 x 10.8 feet
T. 3-cyl. by Charles D. Holmes and Co. Ltd., Hull; $9\frac{1}{2}$ knots.

15.9.1920: Launched by Cochrane and Sons, Selby (Yard No. 748) for the Manchester, Liverpool and North Wales Steamship Co. Ltd. (Richard R. Clark, managers), Liverpool as EDERN. *26.1.1921:* Completed. *29.8.1932:* Owners became the Overton Steamship Co. Ltd. (Robert R. Clark, managers), Liverpool. *16.6.1942:* Sold to the Williamstown Shipping Co. Ltd. (Comben Longstaff and Co., managers), London. *31.3.1944:* Sold to Challis, Stern and Co. Ltd. (Warren Shipping Co. Ltd., managers), London. *3.7.1946:* Renamed WARREN CHASE. *5.5.1952:* Owners became the Warren Shipping Co. Ltd., London. *15.6.1954:* Arrived at Gateshead to be broken up by J.J. King and Co. *20.10.1954:* Register closed.

Nomenclature

Richard R. Clark displayed his allegiance to the town of his birth by giving most of his coasters names taken from villages around Runcorn. He chose names ending in -ton, of which he had a wide choice: derived from the saxon *tun* meaning homestead or village, it is the most frequent element in English place-names and is particularly common in this part of Cheshire.

BEESTON — A mid-Cheshire hamlet best known for the ancient castle which occupies a romantic, rocky position nearby. The exception to the above rule, its name is old English consisting probably of a personal name and "stone".

BRERETON — The name means "village where briars grow".

HALTON — A village immediately to the east of Runcorn and now swallowed up by the expanding New Town. Judging by its proximity to the Mersey its name probably means "village by flat land near a river."

OVERTON — A settlement above Frodsham whose name means "village on a slope or ridge".

SUTTON — On the Weaver a few miles to the south – it means simply "southern village"

WESTDALE — The name of Richard R. Clark's house in Weston Point.

WESTON — Weston lies immediately south of Runcorn and gave its name to the docks at Weston Point on the Mersey. The name means "western village"

Overton *W.S.P.L.*

WILLIAM COOPER AND SONS LTD.
JAMES H. COOPER
NORTHWEST AGGREGATES LTD.
Widnes and Liverpool

William Cooper's business originated in 1850. At this time the town of Widnes, benefiting from the proximity of Cheshire salt and St. Helens' coal, was the cradle of the chemical industry, its name becoming a byword for pollution in the process. William Cooper worked as a carrier on the Mersey and its connecting waterways, his flats being involved in bringing raw materials for the Widnes chemical factories from Liverpool and Birkenhead docks, and returning with finished products for transhipment. Another important trade for his vessels was sand dredged from the Mersey for Pilkington's glass works at St. Helens, the inland terminus of the Sankey Canal which reached the Mersey at Widnes.

William Cooper and Sons Ltd. was registered in 1910. Forming a limited company reflected the growing size and diversity of Cooper's interests, although it remained very much a family business. James Henry Cooper – the head of the company in the early part of the twentieth century and presumably the founder's son – became something of a salvage expert. This was probably out of necessity, as casualties in the twisting and shifting channels of the Upper Mersey were frequent: for instance, no fewer than 13 of Cooper's river craft are recorded as sinking between 1900 and 1928. A large fleet and frequent casualties also necessitated repair facilities, and Coopers bought Gandy's shipyard at Spike Island, alongside the original Widnes Dock. Coopers themselves were based at the newer, if still rather primitive, West Bank Dock, where their office employed around ten staff.

Cooper's flats would trade outside the Mersey on occasion, but their first true steam coaster was delivered in 1909, the ASSURANCE, built and engined by Yarwoods at Northwich. In 1911 ownership passed to the Angelo Coasting Co. Ltd., of which James H. Cooper and his son Alfred were the major shareholders. When ADHERANCE was built for the Adherance Shipping Co. Ltd. in 1914 James and Alfred subscribed £1,500 each, and the owner of the yard which built her, W.J. Yarwood, provided the remaining £1,500.

The Woodend Steamship Co. Ltd. was formed in March 1918 to acquire the ALLEGIANCE, recently delivered by Yarwoods. The capital necessary to do this was £14,000; comparison with the £4,500 needed for the similar-sized ADHERANCE shows how the war had escalated shipbuilding costs. In fact, ALLEGIANCE remained in Alfred Cooper's ownership until her early sale, and the Woodend company took delivery of APPLIANCE in 1921. The Woodend investors were the same as those in the Adherance Shipping Co. Ltd. with the addition of Arthur Cooper. The Woodend company's name made a homely link with one of the rural hamlets which had originally comprised Widnes. ACCORDANCE was completed in 1923 after spending over three years fitting out – presumably due the owner's unwillingness or inability to make the final payment for her – and warranted her own company, the Accordance Shipping Co. Ltd.

The coasters were not large, they could manage around eight knots, and only the ACCORDANCE had a forecastle to improve her sea-keeping qualities. However, they served to extend Cooper's trade to the small ports of Lancashire and especially to the quarries and harbours of North Wales. They were frequently photographed at Preston, and are also known to have gone north to Barrow-in-Furness and west to Caernarfon.

The last steam coaster joined the fleet in April 1928 following a successful salvage operation, although not one carried out by Coopers themselves. On Thursday 26th January 1928 Monroe's steamer JENNIE left King's Dock, Liverpool having loaded general cargo for Dumfries. She called at Monks Ferry, Birkenhead for bunkers, but just after leaving this berth about 5.00 p.m. she was caught by a strong current and carried broadside on to the south end of landing stage for the Birkenhead ferries at Woodside. She capsized and sank under the stage's pontoons, causing considerably damage to the structure but fortunately allowing the crew of five to jump to safety. At low water the landing stage was resting on the JENNIE, crushing her upper works. The damage this was causing to the stage itself meant that salvage work was begun urgently. A camel was attached to the forepart of JENNIE on the morning of the 27th, but an attempt by four tugs to pull her out was unsuccessful. After an additional camel was brought up, JENNIE was pulled clear on 29th January, leaving damage to the landing stage estimated at between £15,000 and £20,000. JENNIE was raised the next day and beached at Tranmere where the Liverpool and Glasgow Salvage Association began to unload her cargo into flats. She was again refloated on 2nd February and taken into Albert Dock, later being declared a constructive total loss. Coopers bought the wreck in April 1928, and it was considerably rebuilt to become ASSISTANCE, losing the after mast and emerging with modified superstructure, although still retaining an open bridge.

ASSISTANCE was owned by the parent company, William Cooper and Sons Ltd., but in June 1929 she and three other ships were sold in a block to the Zillah Shipping and Carrying Co. Ltd., a sale which suggests Zillah was removing a rival from its stone trade. The sale made no difference to the ships' trade, and did not even necessitate a repaint as both Coopers and Zillah used buff funnels with black tops. Only the ASSURANCE, the pioneer coaster, was retained and survived until 1955, although she had been confined to the River Mersey since before the Second World War.

During the 1930s Coopers found their carrying business diminishing due mainly to road haulage. By the outbreak of the Second World War their core – or perhaps it should be hardcore – business was sand and gravel. This had grown out of the supply of sand to Pilkingtons, but also provided ballast to ships and supplied the construction industry, whilst in wartime it filled sandbags. The growing importance of supplying aggregates for the construction industry and the inadequacies of West Bank Dock saw the company's operations shift from Widnes to Liverpool in 1946.

After being bought as a wreck and rebuilt, **Assistance** had a very short career with Coopers, and this shot probably shows her in Zillah ownership. *John Clarkson*

What did not change was the variety and age of Cooper's fleet, which included dredgers, hoppers and barges. A financial yearbook for 1960 lists William Cooper and Sons Ltd as owning 13 vessels with an average age of 49 years. The sand and gravel fleet included several former coasters, amongst them the S.E. COOPER (660/1938) which had previously belonged to Zillah.

The introduction by Pilkingtons of a new glassmaking process which required less sand was a blow to Coopers, and this seems to have helped persuade the family to leave the business. Rather remarkably, their fleet in 1965 consisted of nothing but steamers, and they may well have been daunted by the investment required to modernise. In 1965 the company was sold to Ready Mixed Concrete Ltd., a sign that the future of the sand and gravel business lay with the construction industry. The new company was a subsidiary of William Cory and Sons Ltd., and hence Coopers had become part of the mighty Ocean Group, whose origins lay with Alfred Holt's Blue Funnel.

Outwardly, little had changed. The company name was retained, as were Cooper family names for the dredging fleet in the 1970s: the new owners even moved Cooper's operations back to Widnes. And by a strange quirk, the sale of the company led to its re-emerging as a coastal shipowner. Ready Mixed Concrete Ltd. had a quarry near Llanddulas in North Wales, and in 1973 bought a motor coaster to run stone from there to Bramley Moore Dock in Liverpool. The owners had the happy thought of christening the motorship RAYNESTONE to echo the name Raynes' Quarry (the history of this quarry is related in the chapter on Raynes, Kneeshaw and Lupton). This was a parallel to the use of the name PENSTONE by Zillah for a stone carrier almost fifty years earlier. The ship was purchased in the name of William Cooper and Sons Ltd. but was quickly transferred to the ownership of a London merchant bank, although her operation and management remained unchanged.

The name of William Cooper and Sons Ltd. survived until 1977, when the company was rechristened North West Aggregates Ltd. In Cooper's best traditions, the RAYNESTONE was kept until she was fit only for scrap, although at only 24 years old when meeting her breakers in 1982 she was a mere youngster compared to some of her steam predecessors. She was replaced by a vessel transferred from another company in the Ready Mixed Concrete empire, the suction dredger SAND SKUA, which was converted to a limestone carrier, with hatches and holds designed for easy discharging.

The sale of the SAND SKUA in 1988 was of significance in ending coastal shipowning in the one-time port of Widnes. It also closed the last chapter in the story of William Cooper, the town's only steam coaster owner.

Fleet list

1. ASSURANCE 1909-1955

O.N. 127893 203g 95n 100.0 x 22.0 x 10.0 feet
C. 2-cyl. by W.J. Yarwood and Sons Ltd., Northwich; 9 knots.

23.3.1909: Launched by W.J. Yarwood and Sons Ltd., Northwich (Yard No. 120) for James H. Cooper, Widnes as ASSURANCE. *16.6.1909:* Completed. *9.12.1911:* Owners became the Angelo Coasting Co. Ltd. (James H. Cooper, manager), Widnes. *1936:* Owners became William Cooper and Sons Ltd., Widnes and later Liverpool. *12.2.1955:* Register closed after she had been broken up.

2. ADHERANCE 1914-1929

O.N. 137387 218g 89n 99.8 x 22.3 x 10.0 feet
C. 2-cyl. by W.J. Yarwood and Sons Ltd., Northwich; 8½ knots.

31.12.1913: Launched by W.J. Yarwood and Sons Ltd., Northwich (Yard No. 206) for James H. Cooper, Widnes as ADHERANCE. *22.7.1914:* Completed. *29.4.1915:* Owners became the Adherance Shipping Co. Ltd. (James H. Cooper, manager), Widnes. *5.6.1929:* Sold to the Zillah Shipping and Carrying Co. Ltd. (William A. Savage Ltd., managers), Liverpool. *14.3.1940:* Sold to the Norwest Construction Co. Ltd. (J.S. Baucher, manager), Liverpool. *1.11.1941:* Sold to the British Iron and Steel Corporation (Salvage) Ltd. (Arthur H. Turner, manager), Glasgow. *10.12.1946:* Sold to John Lee (Isaac Stewart, manager), Belfast. *1951:* Sold to D.V. Howells and Sons Ltd., Milford Haven. *1963:* Sold to the Liverpool Derricking and Carrying Co. Ltd., Liverpool. *10.7.1963:* Arrived at Preston for breaking up by T.W. Ward Ltd. in tow of the tug HAZELGARTH (230/1963). *7.1963:* Register closed.

Assurance was the first of Cooper's small coasters, and the only one to remain in the family's ownership throughout her career, although in later life she was confined to the Mersey. *John Clarkson*

Adherance is seen, like most of the other Cooper coasters here, entering Preston with her hatches off ready to unload another stone cargo. *John Clarkson*

Allegiance in Coast Lines' colours. *W.S.P.L.*

3. ALLEGIANCE 1917-1920

O.N. 140548 171g 81n 91.5 x 21.2 x 9.2 feet
C. 2-cyl. by W.J. Yarwood and Sons Ltd., Northwich; 7 knots.

11.1.1917: Launched by W.J. Yarwood and Sons Ltd., Northwich (Yard No. 240) for Alfred Cooper, Widnes as ALLEGIANCE. *14.12.1917:* Completed. *21.1.1920:* Sold to the Hansen Shipping Co. Ltd. (Hansen Brothers Ltd., managers), Cardiff. *1921:* Sold to John Cockburn and Joseph P. Gunn, North Shields. *1925:* Sold to Coast Lines Ltd., Liverpool. *1951: S*old to Abel Barges Ltd., Liverpool and renamed WHARFEDALE. *4.1966:* Arrived at Preston to be broken up by T.W. Ward Ltd.

As both Coopers and later owners Zillah painted their funnels buff with black tops, it is not possible to identify who owned vessels in these photographs, especially as they continued to run from the stone quarries to Preston and elsewhere under Zillah ownership. This is **Appliance.** *W.S.P.L. Cochrane collection*

4. APPLIANCE 1921-1929

O.N. 143741 200g 95n 97.4 x 23.0 x 9.7 feet
C. 2-cyl. by W.J. Yarwood and Sons Ltd., Northwich.

23.12.1920: Launched by W.J. Yarwood and Sons Ltd., Northwich (Yard No. 279) for the Woodend Steamship Co. Ltd. (James H. Cooper, manager), Widnes as APPLIANCE. *2.8.1921:* Completed. *5.6.1929:* Sold to the Zillah Shipping and Carrying Co. Ltd. (William A. Savage Ltd., managers), Liverpool. *7.1949:* Sold to the Liverpool Derricking and Carrying Co. Ltd., Liverpool. *1.1963:* Register closed after being broken up.

Accordance was the last coaster built for Coopers and the only one to have a forecastle to give some protection against the weather in the Irish Sea, although she still had an open bridge. *John Clarkson*

5. ACCORDANCE 1923-1929

O.N. 147234 259g 97n 100.8 x 23.0 x 10.0 feet
C. 2-cyl. by W.J. Yarwood and Sons Ltd., Northwich; 8 knots.

23.7.1920: Launched by W.J. Yarwood and Sons Ltd., Northwich (Yard No. 284) for the Accordance Shipping Co. Ltd., Liverpool (William Cooper, Widnes, manager) as ACCORDANCE. *24.9.1923:* Completed. *5.6.1929:* Sold to the Zillah Shipping and Carrying Co. Ltd. (William A. Savage Ltd., managers), Liverpool. *22.2.1941:* Sold to the British Iron and Steel Corporation (Salvage) Ltd. (Arthur H. Turner, manager), Glasgow. *27.10.1949:* Sold to the Ministry of Transport (Arthur H. Turner, manager), London. *5.11.1949:* Sold to the Aiden Shipping Co. Ltd., Glasgow. *15.2.1951:* Breaking up commenced at Dalmuir by W.H. Arnott, Young Ltd.

6. ASSISTANCE 1928-1929

O.N. 118004 221g 86n 100.4 x 23.2 x 10.6 feet
C. 2-cyl. by Fisher and Co., Paisley.

31.1.1903: Launched by Scott and Sons, Bowling (Yard No. 160) for Joseph Monks and Co. Ltd., Liverpool as JENNIE. *20.2.1903:* Completed. *27.1.1920:* Sold to the Monroe Shipping Co. Ltd., Cardiff. *17.9.1925:* Owners became the Rena Shipping Co. Ltd. (Kenneth R. Monroe, manager), Liverpool. *20.12.1926:* Manager became Robert Monroe. *26.1.1928:* Capsized and sank after colliding with the Birkenhead Ferries' Landing Stage whilst on a voyage from Liverpool to Dumfries with general cargo. Her crew jumped clear but both the ship and the stage were damaged. *2.2.1928:* Refloated. Later declared a constructive total loss. *19.3.1928:* Register closed. *4.1928:* Acquired by William Cooper and Sons Ltd., Widnes and repaired. *29.6.1928:* Re-registered as ASSISTANCE. *5.6.1929:* Sold to the Zillah Shipping and Carrying Co. Ltd. (William A. Savage Ltd., managers), Liverpool. *14.11.1940:* Sold to the British Iron and Steel Corporation (Salvage) Ltd. (Arthur H. Turner, manager), Glasgow. *27.10.1949:* Sold to the Ministry of Transport (Arthur H. Turner, manager), London. *5.11.1949:* Sold to the Aiden Shipping Co. Ltd., Glasgow. *3.1951:* Broken up at Troon by the West of Scotland Shipbreaking Co. Ltd. *10.4.1951:* Register closed.

Raynestone *John Clarkson*

7. RAYNESTONE 1973-1982

O.N. 186662 1,334g 598n 229.3 x 35.4 x 15.1 feet
Oil engine 6-cyl. 4S.C.S.A. by Mirrlees, Bickerton and Day Ltd., Stockport; 11½ knots.

21.2.1958: Launched by Fleming and Ferguson Ltd., Paisley (Yard No. 788) for the Polar Whaling Co. Ltd. (Christian Salvesen and Co., managers), Leith as SOUTRA. *6.1958:* Completed. *1.1970:* Sold to M. and G. Shipping Ltd., Floriana, Malta (Freight Express Ltd., London, managers) and renamed MALTA FAITH. *9.1972:* Sold to Sycamore Transporters Ltd. (Stephenson Clarke Shipping Ltd., managers), London and renamed MAPLE. *8.1973:* Acquired by William Cooper and Sons Ltd., Widnes. *1.1974:* Owners became J. Henry Schroder Wagg and Co. Ltd., London (William Cooper and Sons Ltd., Widnes, managers) and renamed RAYNESTONE. *1977:* Managers became Northwest Aggregates Ltd., Widnes. *1.1982:* Breaking up began by Manor Diving and Marine Services Ltd. in the East Float, Birkenhead.

Sand Skua as a suction dredger. *W.S.P.L.*

8. SAND SKUA 1981-1988

O.N. 342230 1,168g 526n 220.3 x 41.1 x 14.5 feet
Oil engine 8-cyl. 4S.C.S.A. by English Electric Diesels Ltd., Paxman Engine Division, Colchester; 10 knots.

29.3.1971: Launched by J. Bolson and Son Ltd., Poole (Yard No. 570) for the South Coast Shipping Co. Ltd., Southampton and later Feltham, Middlesex (William Cory and Son Ltd., London) as the sand suction dredger SAND SKUA. *5.1971:* Completed. *1981:* Acquired by Northwest Aggregates Ltd., Widnes (Ready Mixed Concrete (United Kingdom) Ltd., Feltham, Middlesex) and converted to a limestone carrier. *1987:* Ultimate owners became the RMC Group plc, Feltham, Middlesex. *1988:* Sold to Trans Ocean Marine Associates, Valletta, Malta. *19.2.1990:* Arrived at Swansea for conversion to a salvage vessel, although this work was never completed. *8.1995:* Sold to Transmarine Shipping Ltd., Gibraltar, but remained at Swansea. *1996:* Sold to Northwood (Fareham) Ltd., Fareham for reconversion to a dredger. The name SOUTHLEADER was proposed. Still in existence (April 1997).

JOHN EDWARDS AND CO.
ROBERT LEESON
Liverpool

John Edwards was one of a number of Liverpool-Welsh businessmen who owned and managed ships almost as a side line to brokerage and other work. Such wide interests make the activities of Edwards and his successors more interesting than the modest size of their fleet would suggest.

Edwards was born on Anglesey in 1859, and staunchly maintained his connections with home: he was apprenticed to Anglesey's best-known shipowner William Thomas, lived in a house in Wallasey which he named 'Eilian', and encouraged many Anglesey men to take shares in his shipowning ventures.

Edwards began his own shipbroking and insurance business in 1887, and in 1891 moved into ship management when he assumed responsibility for the wooden LADY LOUISA, in which he took a single sixty-fourth share. She was sold in 1892, but this experience gave Edwards the confidence to move on to bigger and better coasters, and he began a relationship with Williamsons, the Workington shipbuilders. Their yard enjoyed an excellent reputation for building deep-water sailing vessels but – with demand for this type of ship waning fast – Williamsons were looking for new fields to conquer. They had already built a successful series of steam coasters for Whitehaven-based owners W.S. Kennaugh and Co., and – despite their yard's ability to build ships over 300 feet long – chose to concentrate on coastal steamers and barges. Edwards approached them to build an iron and steel coaster, for which he chose the name QUEEN'S CHANNEL (his telegraphic address was 'CHANNEL, LIVERPOOL'), and then set up a company to finance her, the Queen's Channel Steamship Co. Ltd. Like other builders, the Williamsons were quite prepared to put up their own money to encourage prospective owners to place orders with them, and both Richard and Robert Hardy Williamson took shares in the company. The shareholding was widespread, and within four months of the company's formation in February 1894 £5,300 of the £6,600 nominal capital had been subscribed by around one hundred individuals, mostly Liverpool and Anglesey businessmen including William Thomas of Amlwch. Edwards' company became managers of the ship in return for 2½% of its gross earnings.

In 1898 and 1899 Williamsons completed two steel steamers with similar dimensions to QUEEN'S CHANNEL, the ROCK CHANNEL and FORMBY, for the Rock Channel Steamship Co. Ltd., also managed by Edwards. Unfortunately, the ROCK CHANNEL foundered when only two months old.

Certificates of registry for QUEEN'S CHANNEL survive, and indicate that her trading was confined to the Irish Sea. She called at Liverpool, Glasgow, Barrow, Swansea, Amlwch and Caernarfon. The number of occasions on which a new master was appointed at Caernarfon suggests she was trading there regularly and that Edwards had a policy of appointing only Welshmen to command his ships. FORMBY may have traded more widely, and certainly voyaged from the Mersey to Falmouth - probably with coal out and china clay back.

In 1898 Edwards took on the management of the little steamer EMILY for Captain George Preston, an early captain-owner who bought the ship he was commanding from its Cardiff owners. Such 'owner drivers' were commonplace in sailing ships, but they appeared in steam only when older coasters became available at affordable prices. EMILY was sold after eighteen months to Coppacks of Connah's Quay, but Captain Preston was to invest in future Edward's ventures.

Edwards' letterhead describes his company as 'Steam Ship and Insurance Brokers, Freight Contractors and C.' and, more boldly, 'Brokers for Sale, Purchase and Construction of All Kinds of Shipping Property'. One of the company's activities was as agents for the Compania Mercantil Chubut of Trelew, Chubut S.A., the trading company of the Chubut Colony in Patagonia. This colony been founded in the 1860s in a wave of enthusiasm for a Welsh cultural settlement far removed from what was viewed as English oppression in Wales. Some of the earliest settlers along the Chubut river were

Welsh people who had previously emigrated to North America, but felt that even there they were threatened with assimilation by English culture. Edwards' next and most ambitious purchase, the iron steamer HINDOUSTAN (2,916/1881), was in connection with the Chubut settlement. Leaving Liverpool in July 1899, she made a leisurely passage out to Buenos Aires via Mobile - where she may have picked up more settlers - and Montevideo. She then made three trips from Argentina to South Africa, returning to Europe by way of Ceylon. Once back in Liverpool, Edwards sold the HINDOUSTAN to Japanese owners, and she left for the Far East in February 1901.

Edwards' modest fleet reached its largest extent in 1900 with the addition of the LADY MOSTYN. Surprisingly for a rather old iron steamer, she cost £8,500. This was considerably more than the last new coaster from Workington, and reflected the high freight rates ruling due to the Boer War. To raise the money Edwards floated the Lady Mostyn Steamship Co. Ltd. in July 1900. But by December only a hundred or so shares had been taken up, forty of them by Captain George Preston, and Edwards had to take out a substantial mortgage to cover her purchase price. With ship prices falling after the Boer War, LADY MOSTYN proved to be a bad investment. She was sold foreign in 1907 to pay off creditors and her insolvent owning company allowed to remain in existence until compulsorily wound up in 1915.

Not surprisingly, LADY MOSTYN was the last venture into shipowning during Edwards' lifetime, and his other ships were disposed of by 1910. On 21st April 1912 John Edwards died at the comparatively early age of 53. The agency of the Chubut Colony was taken away from his company (to be given to David Jones and Co., a Liverpool-Welsh wholesale grocery company who had fingers in many shipping pies), but John Edwards and Co. carried on in business under the direction of Robert Leeson, previously Edwards' chief clerk. It was Leeson who took it back into shipowning.

In 1913 Leeson paid a deposit on the ancient steamer KEMPOCK which was lying at Bowling on the Clyde, and sent a Captain Roberts of Anglesey to stand by her. Raising the balance of her purchase price took some months, but eventually she began trading, principally running coal for Donnelly Brothers of Dublin. In 1917 she joined a number of other coasters carrying coal to French ports from the Bristol Channel, surviving this only to succumb to submarine attack in her native Irish Sea. In April 1918 she was running potatoes from Belfast to Manchester when she met UB 85 off Copeland Light. In the ensuing gun battle both vessels were hit, the KEMPOCK being sunk but the U-boat being so badly damaged that she could not submerge and was later sunk in the North Channel by H.M.S. COREOPSIS. On the testimony of the U-boat commander, Captain Roberts was decorated in recognition of his ship's spirited fight.

Bought for a song, the KEMPOCK must have made a healthy profit, and this encouraged Robert Leeson in a much more ambitious venture. His partner was Owen Donnelly, of the Dublin coal merchants for whom KEMPOCK had traded, and who had himself owned the old slate trader DINORWIC (276/1892), which was purchased with help from Leeson. In March 1920 Leeson and Donnelly jointly bought no fewer than ten coasters, the entire existing fleet of one of the largest Liverpool coaster owners, Richard Hughes. The venture did not begin well, as within ten days the WHITE ROSE had been run down and sunk. Later in 1920, the bubble of high freight rates burst, and left Leeson and Donnelly to run expensively-purchased ships in a spectacularly depressed market. To make matters worse, the Irish Civil War hurt Donnelly's coal trade to Ireland. The National Bank to which Leeson and Donnelly had mortgaged their fleet pulled the plug on them during the summer of 1921, and in July the nine surviving ships were sold back to Richard Hughes. Donnelly was driven into bankruptcy, but in time-honoured fashion he started up again under his wife's name, and went on to own further ships, including SAMOA (320/1890) which Leeson may well have helped him run. Leeson himself was not cured of his shipowning ambitions, and in the mid-1920s he returned to the business. He now used his own name rather than that of John Edwards and Co., which disappears from local directories in the early 1920s.

The three coasters Leeson owned or managed were old, eccentric or both. KILMARNOCK was merely odd. She was the only example owned or registered in Liverpool of one of the Kil class patrol gunboats. Mostly completed for the Admiralty too late for service during the war, all but one of this large class were sold in 1920 and

Leeson's **Kilmarnock** is seen at St. John, New Brunswick, Canada in August 1931 as **Eleanor Boling**. Remarkably, she had been used as a base ship for an Antarctic expedition. *John Lochhead/SSHSA*

converted for mercantile use. Conversion normally involved removing one of the two boilers to provide the maximum of cargo space, fitting cargo gear and building up a forecastle. Straight stems replaced the rather unusual angled variety they were built with, the idea being to make both ends look similar in order to confuse German submarine commanders as to the gunboat's course. When these vessels were originally bought for conversion early in 1920, almost any cargo ship could make a good living, such was the demand for tonnage. But when the good times ended, the ships' numerous disadvantages led to most being quickly sold to overseas buyers. Their crews were quite large: KILMARNOCK needed 14. The Kils' bottoms differed from those of the typical flat-bottomed coaster in being slightly V-shaped, which improved speed but did not allow them to take the ground as was necessary at many ports. Their usefulness in the coasting trade was further restricted by a deep draft. The single boiler which remained after conversion was barely capable of supplying enough steam to the powerful engine. To make matters worse, the boiler tubes, which were of an advanced and theoretically efficient design, were difficult to clean and contributed to the engines being shy of steam. Another peculiarity was the vertical uptake tubes through which the smoke passed after leaving the horizontal boiler tubes. These uptakes often became blocked with soot, which could easily catch fire. Leeson tried having these removed on the KILMARNOCK, only to find that flames now came out of the top of the funnel.

Robert Leeson bought KILMARNOCK at the end of 1924 for about £4,000: quite a bargain considering that she had cost the British taxpayer around £20,000 to build and had then been expensively converted to a merchant ship. Owen Spargo was an able seaman in KILMARNOCK, and Leeson told him that he had recouped the purchase price on just one voyage. This involved a cargo of bunker coal from Swansea being taken to Cherbourg for the French Navy, who spent five or six weeks arguing over the quality of the coal cargo, the ship earning demurrage all the time. Making any money on this voyage was an achievement, as KILMARNOCK had had to put back into Swansea where her bunker coal – blamed for her bad steaming – was laboriously taken out and replaced.

Other voyages made by KILMARNOCK in the West Coast coal trade were from Garston and South Wales to Cork, Dublin, Waterford and Limerick, and to Falmouth where the cargo was discharged into a coal elevator. From Falmouth KILMARNOCK might go to Fowey to load china clay for Holland or for Runcorn. China clay was not a popular cargo with the crew. Not only did the holds have to be swept scrupulously clean after the previous coal cargo, but when it rained the china clay which spilled on deck during loading became very slippery, and made handling the heavy hatch covers difficult and dangerous.

KILMARNOCK was painted mainly grey, a large quantity of Admiralty grey paint having been found on board when Leeson bought her. Her funnel was initially red with a black top, but the frequent fires caused by soot igniting in the uptake tubes led to it being repainted all black, and later being treated with a mixture of oil and black lead.

The short career of KILMARNOCK under Leeson's ownership drew to an end when her furnace crowns collapsed whilst on a voyage from Limerick to Swansea, and she had to be towed into Milford Haven. Here she was laid up, and sold in November 1925. This was by no means the end of her adventures, however. When subsequently owned in Canada she was arrested by United States authorities for carrying drugs. Sold to a New York owner, she was later considered to be a suitable base ship for an Antarctic expedition: one hopes that the steaming problems which at times left her capable of only five knots had been sorted out by then. She eventually returned to cargo carrying and was lost off Cuba in 1942.

KILMARNOCK's replacement was almost as old as Edward's KEMPOCK. ADAM SMITH had been built for a regular service between Kirkcaldy and London in 1876, but was now working out her last days in the tramp trades. It is not clear how many days she did have left, as although she is reported as having been broken up in 1930 her registry was not closed until 1934. Perhaps Leeson did not get around to reporting her sale to breakers, or she had been compulsorily sold to recover harbour dues.

ADAM SMITH was neither the last nor the oldest ship in which Leeson became involved. In November 1927 he took over management of the BIRMINGHAM, owned by coal merchants in the city from which she took her name. She was 72 years old, having been built and originally owned in Hull during the dawn of the steam coaster. Her raking stem was the only part of her that looked remotely modern, but even this was due to the replacement of her original clipper bow. By 1927 her second set of engines had reached 44 years of age.

Despite her great age, **Birmingham** seems to be enjoying a race with another steamer down the Mersey.
John Clarkson

No trace of Robert Leeson as an active shipowner or manager can be found after the BIRMINGHAM and ADAM SMITH were broken up. Considering John Edwards and Robert Leeson as continuing the same business, their half century had seen the business lurch from running old coasters to building new ones and back to operating even older ones.

Fleet lists

John Edwards and Co.

1. QUEEN'S CHANNEL 1894-1907 Iron and steel

O.N. 102130 370g 128n 153.2 x 23.6 x 9.0 feet
C. 2-cyl. by Dunsmuir and Jackson, Govan; 10 knots.

24.2.1894: Completed by R. Williamson and Son, Workington (Yard No. 102) for John Edwards, Liverpool and Richard Williamson, Workington as QUEEN'S CHANNEL. *21.4.1894:* Owners became the Queen's Channel Steamship Co. Ltd. (John Edwards and Co., managers), Liverpool. *12.10.1907:* Sold to George Webster and Co., Glasgow. *12.12.1907:* Owners became the Steamship Drumalla Co. Ltd. (George Webster and Co., managers), Glasgow. *22.11.1911:* Sold to John Stewart and Walter Fulton, Glasgow. *29.11.1911:* Sold to John Emlyn Jones and Evan Williams, Cardiff. *1.2.1912:* Renamed EMLYN. *4.3.1912:* Owners became the Emlyn Line Ltd. (Emlyn, Jones and Williams, managers), Cardiff. *5.12.1916:* Managers became Emlyn Jones and Co. Ltd., Cardiff. *18.11.1919:* Sold to the British Dominions Steamship Co. Ltd. (Thomas W. Pritchard and Jonathan M. Smith, managers), Cardiff. *15.6.1920:* Sold to the Burry Port Shipping Co. (Rees G. Reynolds, John Evans and Samuel L. Greville), Burry Port. *21.6.1920:* Owners became the Pembrey Steamship Co. Ltd. (Francis J. Evans, manager), Burry Port and later renamed PEMSCO. *1.3.1922:* Left Burry Port for Dublin with a cargo of coal and disappeared. *5.4.1922:* Posted missing. *21.1.1924:* Register closed.

Queen's Channel is seen here after 1912 when owned in Cardiff as **Emlyn.** *E.N. Taylor*

2. ROCK CHANNEL 1898-1899

O.N. 110528 431g 133n 154.2 x 23.7 x 10.0 feet
C. 2-cyl. by Ross and Duncan, Govan.

15.12.1898: Launched by R. Williamson and Son, Workington (Yard No. 154) for the Rock Channel Steamship Co. Ltd. (John Edwards and Co., managers), Liverpool as ROCK CHANNEL. *30.12.1898:* Completed. *13.2.1899:* Foundered eighteen miles east north east of the North Foreland whilst on a voyage from Hull to Dublin with a cargo of barley. *21.2.1899:* Register closed.

3. FORMBY 1899-1910

O.N. 110581 430g 133n 153.7 x 23.7 x 10.0 feet
C. 2-cyl. by Ross and Duncan, Govan; 10 knots.

29.5.1899: Launched by R. Williamson and Son, Workington (Yard No. 155) for the Rock Channel Steamship Co. Ltd. (John Edwards and Co., managers), Liverpool as FORMBY. *16.6.1899:* Completed. *8.1910:* Sold to Paul Berteloot, Dunkirk, France and renamed ANTOINETTE. *11.11.1914:* Left Calais for Havre with general cargo and disappeared.

4. LADY MOSTYN 1900-1907 Iron

O.N. 84123 709g 400n 200.3 x 27.7 x 15.0 feet
C. 2-cyl. by J. Readhead and Co., South Shields; 9 knots.

6.1881: Launched by J. Readhead and Co., South Shields (Yard No. 171) for Robert Lewis and Co., Rhyl as LADY MOSTYN. *16.7.1881:* Completed. *1887:* Owners became Enoch and J. Herbert Lewis, Liverpool. *1892:* Owners became Lewis and Co., Aberdyvi. *18.6.1900:* Acquired by John Edwards and Co., Liverpool. *21.8.1900:* Owners became the Lady Mostyn Steamship Co. Ltd. (John Edwards and Co., managers), Liverpool. *6.1907:* Sold to Petzalis and Dounias, Constantinople, Turkey and renamed OLGA under the Greek flag. *1911:* Renamed CALAFAT under the Roumanian flag. *7.1915:* Taken over by the Imperial Russian Government, St. Petersburg, Russia. *4.1916:* Owner became Mehmet Fuad, Braila, Roumania and then Steana de Romana, Constanza, Roumania. *6.1916:* Owner became Mehmet Fuad, Braila, Roumania and later Istanbul, Turkey and renamed SEMRAK. *25.3.1917:* Ran aground after being mined near Agva whilst on a voyage from Istanbul to Varna with a cargo of petrol. Ten of her crew of eighteen were lost. *4.1917:* Refloated and towed to Istanbul for repair, where she was sold to Osmanli Bahriye (the Turkish Government), Istanbul. *1918:* Renamed SAHIN. *1919:* Taken over by the Turkish National Liberation Forces under Kemal Ataturk who used her as a transport between the U.S.S.R and Trabzon. *1926:* Sold for scrap after being laid up at Trabzon since 1923.

5. KEMPOCK 1913-1918 Iron

O.N. 56156 255g 104n 141.0 x 20.2 x 11.8 feet
2-cyl. by the Greenock Foundry Co., Greenock.
6.1873: C. 2-cyl. Gourlay Brothers and Co., Dundee.

9.1866: Launched by Robert Scott and Co., Greenock (Yard No. 119) for William Mories and Richard Munro, Glasgow as DENIA. *18.10.1866:* Completed. *10.1871:* Owner became William Mories, Glasgow. *1872:* Sold to Edward R. Cummings, London. *6.1873:* Fitted with new engine. *1875:* Sold to Edward D. Clarke, Plymouth. *11.1883:* Sold to G. Lennard, Swansea. *1884:* Owners became J.M. Lennard and Sons, Middlesbrough. *1890:* Sold to Robert H. Gunning, Swansea. *1891:* Owners became the Hibernia Steamship Co. Ltd. (Robert H.

Kempock *E.N. Taylor*

Gunning, manager), Swansea. *1894:* Sold to Walter B. Niven (James Hamilton, manager), Ayr. *19.2.1897:* Sold to Robert Kay, Glasgow. *9.2.1906:* Sold to Coasting Steamships Ltd. (Purdie, Glen and Millar, managers), Glasgow. *8.1906:* Renamed CORPORAL. *24.6.1909:* Sold to William J. Garscadden, Glasgow. *22.1.1910:* Sold to George L. Sweenie, East Kilbride. *14.6.1910:* Sold to the Kempock Steamship Co. Ltd. (James B. Couper, manager), Glasgow and later renamed KEMPOCK. *4.1.1913:* Acquired by John Edwards and Co., Liverpool. *30.4.1918:* Sunk by gunfire from the German submarine UB 85 six and a half miles south east of Copeland Island Light whilst on a voyage from Belfast to Manchester with a cargo of potatoes.

Managed by John Edwards and Co. for Humphrey Jones

LADY LOUISA 1891-1892 Wood

O.N. 74760 134g 73n 105.0 x 21.5 x 9.3 feet
C. 2-cyl. by J. and T. Young, Ayr.

16.6.1882: Launched by William Thomas and Co., Millom (Yard No. 4) for the Lady Kate Steamship Co. Ltd (William Postlethwaite, manager), Millom and later Amlwch as LADY LOUISA. *11.9.1882:* Completed. *5.1885:* Manager became William Thomas. *6.1886:* Sold to Georges Rodrigues, Liverpool. *1889:* Sold to John Hughes, Liverpool. *23.2.1891:* Acquired by Humphrey Jones (John Edwards and Co., managers), Liverpool. *3.3.1892:* Owners became the Steamship Lady Louisa Co. Ltd. (Humphrey Jones, manager), Liverpool. *6.11.1894:* Sold to W. Mollison and Son, Bervie, Kincardineshire. *1.7.1898:* Sold to Alexander Gray and Adam Maitland, Aberdeen. *7.5.1901:* Sold to Robert Hall, Larne. *26.2.1905:* Foundered five miles off Douglas Head, Isle of Man whilst on a voyage from Garston to Belfast with a cargo of coal. Her crew of four got off in the ship's boat. *6.3.1905:* Register closed.

Managed by John Edwards and Co. for George H. Preston

EMILY 1898-1899

O.N. 99989 227g 70n 125.2 x 20.1 x 9.5 feet
C. 2-cyl. by Ross and Duncan, Govan.

17.3.1893: Launched by John Fullerton and Co., Paisley (Yard No. 53) for William T. Symonds, Cardiff as EMILY. *4.4.1893:* Completed. *8.6.1898:* Acquired by Captain George H. Preston (John Edwards and Co., managers), Liverpool. *18.12.1899:* Sold to Thomas Coppack, Connah's Quay. *30.3.1910:* Sank following a collision with the steamer PALATINE (2,110/1882) thirty miles north of the Tuskar Rock whilst on a voyage from Point of Ayr to Rosslare with a cargo of coal. *4.5.1910:* Register closed.

Owned by Robert Leeson and Owen H. Donnelly

1. **BLUSH ROSE 1920-1921** (See Richard Hughes No.17)
2. **BRIER ROSE 1920-1921** (See Richard Hughes No.7)
3. **DUNMORE 1920-1921** (See Richard Hughes No.22)
4. **GUELDER ROSE 1920-1921** (See Richard Hughes No.18)
5. **JOFFRE ROSE 1920-1921** (See Richard Hughes No.21)
6. **MERSEY 1920-1921** (See Richard Hughes No.15)
7. **MOSS ROSE 1920-1921** (See Richard Hughes No.3)
8. **PANSY 1920-1921** (See Richard Hughes No.11)
9. **PRIMROSE 1920-1921** (See Richard Hughes No.14)
10. **WHITE ROSE 1920** (See Richard Hughes No.19)

Owned by Robert Leeson

1. KILMARNOCK 1924-1925

O.N. 143666 614g 261n 170.0 x 30.0 x 15.7 feet.
T. 3-cyl. by Smith's Dock Co. Ltd., Middlesbrough.

31.3.1919: Launched by Smith's Dock Co. Ltd., Middlesbrough (Yard No. 748) for the Admiralty as the patrol gunboat H.M.S. KILMARNOCK. *5.1919:* Completed. *14.2.1920:* Sold to L. Gueret, Cardiff for conversion to a merchant ship. *5.11.1920:* Registered under the ownership of the Kyle Transport Co. Ltd. (Alexander Bicket, manager), Liverpool as KILMARNOCK. *19.9.1923:* Sold to Henry J. Brennan, Liverpool. *24.12.1924:* Acquired by Robert Leeson, Liverpool. *5.11.1925:* Sold to James Kell, Sunderland. *15.4.1926:* Sold to Frank K. Warren, Halifax, Nova Scotia. *23.11.1926:* Sold to Kilmarnock Ltd. (William A. Shaw, manager), Halifax, Nova Scotia. *3.1927:* Seized by United States authorities for drug smuggling. *11.1927:* Sold to Richard S. Cors, New York, U.S.A. and renamed CHELSEA. *1928: S*old to the Byrd Antarctic Expedition, Boston, Massachusets, U.S.A. and renamed ELEANOR BOLING. *16.8.1930:* Registered under the ownership of Marine Agencies Ltd., St. Johns, Newfoundland as KILMARNOCK. *16.10.1930:* Renamed ELEANOR BOLING. *12.9.1930:* Sold to the Bolling Steamship Co. Ltd. (Marine Agencies Ltd., managers), St. Johns, Newfoundland. *1.1932: S*old to W.F. Parker, Miami, Florida, U.S.A. *1933:* Sold to the Vamar Steamship Co. (Hasler and Co. Inc., managers), New York and renamed VAMAR. *1941:* Sold to Sociedad Navegacion dos Oceanos Sud America (Arias Febrega y Fabrega), Panama City, Panama. *1941:* Owners became Compañia de Navegacion Bolivar-Atlantica (Maurice Benin Chartering (Canada) Ltd., managers), Panama City. *21.3.1942:* Stranded off Point Saint Joseph, Florida, U.S.A. when her timber cargo shifted in heavy seas whilst on a voyage from Tampa to Puerto Padre, Cuba. *2.9.1942:* Capsized during salvage operations.

2. ADAM SMITH 1925-1930 Iron

O.N. 62963 279g 109n 150.3 x 22.1 x 11.9 feet.
C. 2-cyl by Kincaid, Donald and Co, Greenock.

20.10.1876: Launched by H. Murray and Co. Ltd, Port Glasgow (Yard No. 82) for John T. Stocks, trading as the London and Kirkcaldy Steam Ship Co., Kirkcaldy as ADAM SMITH. *30.11.1876:* Completed. *26.12.1884: S*tranded on Long Craig Rock near Kirkcaldy while inbound from London. Later abandoned to the underwriters after salvage attempts had failed and the vessel filled with water. *3.1885:* Refloated and taken to Alloa for repair. *1.6.1885:* Re-registered under the ownership of William Wighton, Carnoustie, Fife. *13.10.1898:* Sold to James Power, London. *28.2.1899:* Sold to Thomas and John A. Steele, Ayr. *20.2.1914:* Sold to John R. Dickson junior, Ayr. *18.2.1920:* Sold to Hugh W. Lloyd and Frederick Wood, Llanelli. *29.4.1922:* Sold to Charles E. Allen, Swansea. *15.3.1924:* Sold to James O'Callaghan, New Ross, County Wexford. *11.3.1925:* Acquired by Robert Leeson, Liverpool. *4.9.1930:* Reported sold to shipbreakers at Belfast. *20.8.1934:* Register closed.

Managed by Robert Leeson for the Birmingham Steamship Co.Ltd.

BIRMINGHAM 1927-1929 Iron

O.N. 5526 323g 198n 173.2 x 21.4 x 10.8 feet
2-cyl. steam engine by C. and W. Earle, Hull.
1883: T. 3-cyl. by Earle's Shipbuilding and Engineering Co. Ltd., Hull; 8½ to 9 knots.

15.8.1855: Completed by C. and W. Earle, Hull (Yard No. 8) for John R. Ringrose, Charles L. Ringrose and T. Voase, Hull as ALERT. *5.1865:* Owners became John R. Ringrose and Charles L. Ringrose, Hull. *11.1873:* Owner became J. Ringrose, Hull. *1877:* Owners became W. Ringrose and Charles L. Ringrose, Hull. *20.3.1896:* Owners became the Hull and Netherlands Steamship Co. Ltd. (William H.H. Hutchinson and James H.N. Ringrose, managers), Hull. *23.7.1897:* Sold to Andrew Weir, Glasgow. *22.4.1899:* Sold to George Garscadden, Glasgow. *2.1.1900: S*old to George Sandford, Gravesend. *26.9.1916:* Sold to Henry Barnett, London. *20.7.1917:* Renamed BIRMINGHAM. *12.10.1917:* Sold to the Birmingham Steamship Co. Ltd. (Ernest Blackburn, manager), Birmingham. *15.11.1927:* Manager became Robert Leeson, Liverpool. *6.2.1929:* Sold to John Hornby and Son (Shipbreakers) Ltd., Bradford and broken up at Liverpool. *16.12.1929:* Register closed.

Nomenclature

FORMBY	An old, and presumably Danish, settlement on the Lancashire coast about 11 miles north of Liverpool, of which it is now a dormitory.
QUEEN'S CHANNEL	The major deep water channel from the Mersey keeps to the Lancashire bank as the Crosby Channel, and becomes the Queen's Channel further out towards the Mersey Bar.
ROCK CHANNEL	Shallower than the Queen's Channel, the Rock Channel led out of the Mersey across the top of the Wirral, and was often used by coasters bound to and from North Wales. Still marked on charts, it is no longer buoyed.

JOSEPH E. FISHER
JOSEPH W. FISHER AND CO.
WIILIAM MASON AND CO. LTD.
Liverpool

Joseph Edward Fisher was a significant figure amongst Liverpool coastal shipbrokers and shipowners, although not as well known as he merits. This is partly because the name Fisher is usually associated with the members of his family who trade from Barrow-in-Furness as James Fisher and Sons Ltd., and partly because *Lloyds Register* did not always list Joseph Fisher as the manager of ships he controlled. He operated under two other company titles, William Mason and Co. Ltd. and Joseph W. Fisher and Co. The former were shipbrokers, owned by the family of Joseph E. Fisher's mother. Joseph Fisher probably persuaded this company to go into shipowning immediately before the First World War, when it would make handsome returns on its investments, but he also speculated heavily in ships immediately after the war, when losses probably outweighed the earlier gains.

Joseph Edward Fisher was the grandson of the James Fisher who founded the long-lasting fleet at Barrow-in-Furness, but, because of the lack of application of his father, Joseph William Fisher, enjoyed a rather distant relationship with his cousins in the Furness district of Lancashire. Joseph William Fisher (1844-1901) was James' eldest son, but a preference for horse riding and the pleasures of the social life over office work saw him leave his father's company around 1887. He had taken the precaution of marrying into another shipping family, however, taking as his wife Alice Mason. Forsaking Barrow, Joseph W. moved to the booming port of Swansea in the 1880s and began business as a shipping agent as Joseph W. Fisher and Co.

Of Joseph W.'s three sons, James William Fisher (1867-1901) joined his father until both died – James tragically early – in 1901. Second son Joseph Edward Fisher – the hero of this chapter – joined his father's Swansea business, but also worked for George Shepherd and Co. where he gained experience of shipbroking which was to prove useful to him. On the death of his father and brother in 1901, he became the head of Joseph W. Fisher and Co., and found the energy to run this Swansea-based company whilst also looking for business in Liverpool. He first comes to prominence on Merseyside in 1907 when Joseph W. Fisher and Co. had entrusted to its care the management of the NICOLAS. This coaster had been built in Holland to the account of Charles Pile, a sale and purchase broker who had aspirations as a shipping speculator, building a series of steam ships in Dutch yards and selling them on to British owners, and often providing mortgages to the buyers. Owners of the NICOLAS were trading as Potter and Son of Runcorn, the controlling interest being held by Charles W. Potter, a flint merchant of Stoke-on-Trent. NICOLAS traded mainly from the china clay ports to Runcorn with occasional calls elsewhere to load return cargoes of coal.

The family of Joseph Edward Fisher's mother carried on a shipbroking business under the title William Mason and Co. Ltd. In May 1914 this company was instrumental in forming the Mason Shipping Co. Ltd., and whilst Joseph E. Fisher was not amongst the original investors he acted as manager for the company's ships. In December 1913 were ordered two coastal steamers from Fullertons of Paisley, but the outbreak of war in August 1914 meant investors were slow to take up the new company's two thousand £10 shares, and on 16th October the WILLIAM MASON ran trials under the ownership of builder John Fullerton. In addition to George Mason of William Mason and Co. Ltd., shareholders were the usual small investors and business people, but a notable inclusion was Samuel Kelly of John Kelly Ltd., Belfast; himself no mean shipowner. Joseph Edward Fisher later became the major shareholder in the Mason Shipping Co. Ltd.

The Mason company was somewhat indecisive about its naming scheme, using three different ones for its fleet of just seven ships. The first name, WILLIAM MASON, honoured the company's founder. Reflecting the prevailing mood of militarism the name BRIGADE was then chosen followed later by SQUADRON. No effort was made to rename the secondhand purchases WHINHILL and ELTHAM, but postwar newbuildings were named more peacefully as TARNWATER and ALLANWATER.

In September 1916 Joseph Edward Fisher became the manager of MASCOTA on behalf of an eponymous single ship company. With the growing shortage of ships as war losses mounted, it was obviously considered worthwhile to buy this former British-owned collier from Argentina.

The last months of 1917 saw the Mason Shipping Co. Ltd. expand its fleet, and Joseph Edward Fisher invest heavily in shipping. In October he floated a company in which he was to be the major subscriber, the Freeland Shipping Co. Ltd. Its nominal capital was £50,000 and managers were Joseph W. Fisher and Co. Shares were taken up slowly at first, but from 1918 the pace increased as inflated freight rates made coastal shipping an attractive investment. Samuel Kelly was again amongst the subscribers; he would know Fisher through the latter's shipbroking work. Fisher clearly was not short of capital and, as well as his companies' investments, he took delivery on his own account of the steamer DRAGOON in December 1917. About 18 months later DRAGOON was transferred to the ownership of the Freeland Shipping Co. Ltd. and with the ship's value inflated by wartime shortages, DRAGOON would make Fisher a handsome personal profit, although this would soon be lost.

The name of Fisher's next venture, the Pickavance Shipping Co. Ltd., can only have been suggested by the name of the converted Mersey pilot tender it was formed to acquire, a name chosen by Fisher's partner in this company, Thomas Trohear Kennaugh. The Kennaugh family were well established in the coastal shipping business at Liverpool, where they had moved from Whitehaven in 1905. Thomas Kennaugh was a consulting engineer to various shipowners, but also described himself as a naval architect when filling in forms for the Registrar of Companies. The capital of the Pickavance company, registered in January 1920, showed a further advance to £100,000, Fisher taking £2,200. Amongst small Merseyside businessmen who were about to lose serious money in this venture was Alfred Connell, met with elsewhere in this book losing money on coasters. The high capital was necessary, not just to acquire the PICKAVANCE – ageing and as doubtfully economic as any conversion – but to build new steamers. The CAMBALU arrived in November 1920 from her Southampton builders after freight rates fell catastrophically.

Despite the gloom which now fell over coastal shipping there was to be further expansion of Fisher's shipping empire. In January 1924 the GLENSIDE was bought and

Dragoon *The Ballast Trust*

Allanwater *E.N. Taylor*

registered under the ownership of a company he was to manage, the Broadlake Shipping Co. Ltd. She was soon sold to New Zealand. More significant was Fisher's investment in the Northwich Carrying Co. Ltd., described in detail in a later chapter. This company had expanded its business by buying coasters too large to reach its home port, and Fisher stepped in by offering management expertise and a Liverpool office.

With the companies which Fisher had helped float, the story was the same as for many other coaster owners which found themselves with expensively-bought ships which could not now be traded profitably or sold other than at a huge loss; a negative equity situation, in fact. There was nothing owners like Fisher could do except soldier on, meeting losses in the hope that conditions would improve, which they were not to do until the next war broke out. In the event it was the banks which had provided mortgages for the post-war steamers – and had themselves helped stoke the boom - who pulled the plug on the shipowners. Martins Bank had mortgaged the FAIRLAND, FREELAND and DRAGOON for the Freeland Shipping Co. Ltd. and the CAMBALU for the Pickavance Shipping Co. Ltd. and in 1933 foreclosed on these. The remaining ships of the Mason Shipping Co. Ltd., ALLANWATER, TARNWATER and WHINHILL, were mortgaged for a total of almost £47,000 and these too were foreclosed. Although sold by the banks, four of these ships went to James Fisher and Co. Ltd. and so stayed within the family. Perhaps the astute Barrow-in-Furness shipowners knew they were buying good ships at a very advantageous price.

With the loss of their ships Fisher's three companies ceased trading and were wound up during 1935. By then Fisher's other interest, the Northwich Carrying Co. Ltd., had also stopped carrying, and Joseph Edward Fisher returned to his original business of shipbroking. He died in 1937 at the age of 68, and probably had little to show for twenty years of shipowning. Both Joseph E. Fisher and Co. and Joseph W. Fisher and Co. were to remain in being, and like their one-time ships were taken over by James Fisher and Co. Ltd. of Barrow in 1957.

In the fleet list which follows, the ships in whose ownership Fisher had a financial interest are shown in the order in which they were acquired. The status of managed ships is accorded only to the NICOLAS, which he managed for others, and two ships he might have managed for The Shipping Controller. WAR ALNE was allocated to Fisher's management but sold before completion. Doubt surrounds the management of POLSTELL: *Lloyd's Register* credits Fisher with her management, but her registration papers do not.

Fleet list

1. WILLIAM MASON 1914-1919

O.N. 136322 425g 164n 150.1 x 23.8 x 10.4 feet
C. 2-cyl. by Fishers Ltd., Paisley; 10 knots.

8.9.1914: Launched by John Fullerton and Co., Paisley (Yard No. 235). *8.10.1914:* Completed for John Fullerton, Paisley as WILLIAM MASON. *19.10.1914:* Acquired by the Mason Shipping Co. Ltd. (William Mason and Co. Ltd., manager), Liverpool. *13.10.1919:* Sold to the Abram Steamship Co. Ltd., Glasgow. *30.12.1919:* Renamed KYLEBUTE. *2.3.1920:* Sold to the Miskin Manor Steamship Co. Ltd. (William C. Scriven and Richard S. Ridd, managers), Cardiff. It was intended to rename her MISKIN MANOR, but this was never carried out. *29.4.1924:* Renamed STANWELL. *9.10.1929:* Sold to the Portfield Steamship Co. Ltd. (William E. Hinde, manager), Cardiff. *30.1.1930:* Sold to the Stanwell Steamship Co. Ltd. (F.N. Brice, manager), Cardiff. *5.10.1934:* Foundered in position approximately 46.34 N by 07.00 W whilst on a voyage from Barry to Figueira de Foz with a cargo of coal. Her crew was rescued by the French tunnyman REVANCHE. *23.10.1934:* Register closed.

William Mason was sold in 1919 and was renamed **Kylebute,** as seen here. *E.N. Taylor*

2. BRIGADE 1914-1917

O.N. 136335 425g 164n 149.9 x 23.8 x 10.4 feet
C.2-cyl. by Fishers Ltd., Paisley; $9\frac{1}{2}$ knots.

22.10.1914: Launched by John Fullerton and Co., Paisley (Yard No. 236) for the Mason Shipping Co. Ltd. (William Mason and Co. Ltd., manager), Liverpool as BRIGADE. *19.11.1914:* Completed. *19.2.1917:* Captured by the German submarine UC 65 and sunk by gunfire twelve miles north west by half west of Cayeux Lighthouse whilst on a voyage from Hourdel to Weston Point with a cargo of flintstones. *19.3.1917:* Register closed.

3. MASCOTA 1916-1917 Iron

O.N. 87552 674g 409n 180.0 x 29.0 x 13.7 feet
T. 3-cyl. by George Clark Ltd., Sunderland; $8\frac{3}{4}$ knots.

14.4.1890: Launched by Robert Thompson and Sons, Sunderland (Yard No. 162) for Whiteway and Ball, Torquay as TORQUAY. *17.5.1890:* Completed. *3.1904:* Sold to Lloyd Bahia Blanca S.A. de Navegacion a Vapeur, Buenos Aires, Argentina and renamed MASCOTA. *1908:* Sold to the Marina Mercante Argentina, Buenos Aires. *28.9.1916:* Acquired by the Mascota Shipping Co. Ltd. (Joseph E. Fisher, manager), Liverpool. *29.3.1917:* Sunk by the German destroyers V 67 and G 95 eight miles east of Lowestoft whilst on a voyage from Tréport to the Tyne in ballast. Her crew of seven were taken prisoner. *9.8.1917:* Register closed.

4. WHINHILL 1917-1933

O.N. 133646 478g 194n 165.6 x 25.2 x 9.7 feet
T. 3-cyl. by Hall, Russell and Co. Ltd., Aberdeen; 9 1/2 knots.

15.4.1914: Launched by Hall, Russell and Co. Ltd., Aberdeen (Yard No. 548) for C.R. Davidson and Co., Aberdeen as WHINHILL. *6.5.1914:* Completed. *30.8.1917:* Acquired by the Mason Shipping Co. Ltd. (William Mason and Co. Ltd., managers), Liverpool. *28.9.1933:* Sold to Buchan and Hogg, Grangemouth. *15.10.1933:* Renamed DUNCARRON. *11.6.1941:* Owners became the Duncarron Steamship Co. Ltd. (Buchan and Hogg Ltd., managers), Grangemouth. *7.9.1941:* Torpedoed and sunk by a German E-boat three miles east of Sheringham Buoy, Norfolk whilst on a voyage from London to Lossiemouth with a cargo of cement. *30.12.1941:* Register closed.

5. DRAGOON 1917-1933

O.N. 140552 573g 258n 164.9 x 27.1 x 11.2 feet
T. 3-cyl. by John Lewis and Sons Ltd., Aberdeen; 9 1/2 knots.

13.12.1917: Completed by John Lewis and Sons Ltd., Aberdeen (Yard No. 53) for Joseph E. Fisher, Liverpool as DRAGOON. *26.4.1919:* Owners became the Freeland Shipping Co. Ltd. (Joseph E. Fisher, manager), Liverpool. *28.12.1933:* Sold to James Fisher and Sons Ltd., Barrow-in-Furness. *9.11.1934:* Renamed STRAIT FISHER. *3.1.1945:* Capsized and sank when her cargo of grain shifted three miles north of the Longships whilst on a voyage from Plymouth and Falmouth to Silloth. *22.1.1945:* Register closed.

6. SQUADRON 1918

O.N. 140572 362g 143n 135.3 x 23.6 x 10.0 feet
C. 2-cyl. by George T. Grey and Co. Ltd., South Shields; 9 knots.

26.4.1918: Completed by J. and D. Morris Ltd., Newcastle-upon-Tyne (Yard No. 64) for the Mason Shipping Co. Ltd. (William Mason and Co., managers), Liverpool as SQUADRON. *30.10.1918:* Sold to George T. Gillie, Newcastle-upon-Tyne. *7.11.1918:* Owners became the Border Shipping Co. Ltd. (G.T. Gillie and Co. Ltd., managers), Newcastle-upon-Tyne. *6.1919:* Renamed SOLWAY FIRTH. *11.12.1919:* Sold to J. Milligen and Co. Ltd., Belfast and subsequently renamed BRIDEEN. *21.7.1926:* Sold to Albert Chester and Edwin G. Tyerman, Middlesbrough, trading as the Brideen Steamship Co. *27.7.1929:* Sold to Arthur C. Reynolds, Portreath. *22.6.1938:* Sold to the Beynon Shipping Co. Ltd., Cardiff. *1.1939:* Sold to German shipbreakers. *3.2.1939:* Register closed.

7. ELTHAM 1918-1928

O.N. 136058 687g 272n 188.5 x 28.6 x 11.3 feet
T. 3-cyl. by J.G. Kincaid and Co. Ltd., Greenock; 10 knots.

3.3.1915: Launched by the Dublin Dockyard Co. Ltd., Dublin (Yard No. 87) for John Harrison Ltd., London as ELTHAM. *21.4.1915:* Completed. *26.6.1918:* Acquired by the Mason Shipping Co. Ltd. (William Mason and Co. Ltd., manager), Liverpool. *17.11.1928:* Wrecked at Chapelporth, North Cornwall whilst on a voyage from Swansea to Rouen with a cargo of coal. *31.12.1928:* Register closed.

Eltham on trials. *University of Glasgow DC101/1132*

8. FREELAND 1919-1933
O.N. 140656 574g 263n 164.8 x 27.0 x 11.1 feet
T. 3-cyl. by John Lewis and Sons Ltd., Aberdeen; 9½ knots.

24.9.1919: Completed by John Lewis and Sons Ltd., Aberdeen (Yard No. 69) for the Freeland Shipping Co. Ltd. (Joseph E. Fisher, manager), Liverpool as FREELAND. *28.12.1933:* Sold to James Fisher and Sons Ltd., Barrow-in-Furness. *29.1.1934:* Renamed FIRTH FISHER. *21.5.1940:* Mined and sunk half a mile east of Boulogne Pier whilst on a voyage from Littlehampton and Dover to Boulogne with a cargo of army stores. Seven of her crew of ten were lost. *3.6.1940:* Register closed.

Freeland *W.S.P.L.*

Bay Fisher was built for Joseph Fisher as **Tarnwater** but was sold to the Barrow-in-Furness branch of the family in 1933. *E.N. Taylor*

9. TARNWATER 1919-1933

O.N. 143599 575g 262n 164.8 x 27.0 x 11.1 feet
T. 3-cyl. by John Lewis and Sons Ltd., Aberdeen; 10 knots.

10.9.1919: Launched by John Lewis and Sons Ltd., Aberdeen (Yard No. 70) for the Mason Shipping Co. Ltd. (William Mason and Co. Ltd., manager), Liverpool as TARNWATER. *3.11.1919:* Completed. *28.12.1933:* Sold to James Fisher and Sons Ltd., Barrow-in-Furness. *19.1.1934:* Renamed BAY FISHER. 7.2.1941: Bombed and sunk by German aircraft two and a half miles and 227° from the Bell Rock whilst on a voyage from Scapa Flow to Rosyth with a cargo of government stores. Seven of her crew of eleven and one of her gunners were lost. *4.7.1941:* Register closed.

10. PICKAVANCE 1920-1928

O.N. 106814 299g 109n 128.2 x 24.1 x 13.9 feet
T. 3-cyl. by David Rowan and Son, Glasgow; 10½ knots.

25.9.1896: Launched by Murdoch and Murray, Port Glasgow (Yard No. 147) for the Mersey Docks and Harbour Board, Liverpool as FRANCIS HENDERSON. *10.1896:* Completed. *16.11.1917:* Sold to Thomas T. Kennaugh, Liverpool. *22.3.1918:* Renamed PICKAVANCE. *2.2.1920:* Acquired by the Pickavance Shipping Co. Ltd. (Joseph E. Fisher, manager), Liverpool. *5.6.1928:* Sold to John Fullerton and Co., Paisley. *20.11.1929:* Register closed after being broken up.

11. FAIRLAND 1920-1933

O.N. 143653 552g 242n 165.0 x 27.1 x 10.7 feet
T. 3-cyl. by William Beardmore and Co. Ltd., Coatbridge, Glasgow; 9 knots.

20.5.1920: Launched by the Goole Shipbuilding and Repairing Co. Ltd., Goole (Yard No. 215) for the Freeland Shipping Co. Ltd. (Joseph E. Fisher, manager), Liverpool as FAIRLAND. *14.7.1920:* Completed. *28.12.1933:* Sold to James Fisher and Sons Ltd., Barrow-in-Furness. *13.1.1934:* Renamed SEA FISHER. *8.3.1936:* Sunk in collision with the motor vessel SUTHERLAND (4,956/1935) in fog two and a half miles north west of the Shipwash Light Vessel whilst on a voyage from Blyth to Hayle with a cargo of coal. Her crew was picked up by the SUTHERLAND. *22.7.1936:* Register closed.

Fairland *A. Duncan*

Cambalu. Her funnel is black with an orange band. *A. Duncan*

12. CAMBALU 1920-1933

O.N. 143682 496g 212n 165.5 x 25.7 x 9.6 feet
T. 3-cyl. by William Beardmore and Co. Ltd., Coatbridge, Glasgow; 10 knots.

5.8.1920: Launched by Day, Summers and Co. Ltd., Southampton (Yard No. 184) for the Pickavance Shipping Co. Ltd. (Joseph E. Fisher, manager), Liverpool as CAMBALU. *19.10.1920:* Completed. *30.1.1933:* Wrecked six miles south of Hartland Point whilst on a voyage from Plymouth to the Mumbles in ballast. *17.3.1933:* Register closed.

13. ALLANWATER 1920-1933

O.N. 143702 496g 216n 165.5 x 25.7 x 9.6 feet
T. 3-cyl. by William Beardmore and Co. Ltd., Coatbridge, Glasgow; 10 knots.

14.10.1920: Launched by Day, Summers and Co. Ltd., Southampton (Yard No. 185) for the Mason Shipping Co. Ltd. (William Mason and Co. Ltd., manager), Liverpool as ALLANWATER. *13.12.1920:* Completed. *10.1.1933:*

Allanwater *John Clarkson*

Sold to A.F. Henry and Macgregor Ltd., Leith. *1.2.1933:* Renamed MARWICK HEAD. *12.12.1939:* Mined and sunk half a mile south of the North Caister Buoy whilst on a voyage from Bo'ness to London with a cargo of coal. Five of her crew were lost. *4.3.1940:* Register closed.

14. GLENSIDE 1924

O.N. 144938 554g 244n 165.0 x 27.1 x 10.7 feet
T. 3-cyl. by William Beardmore and Co. Ltd., Coatbridge, Glasgow; 9 knots.

23.3.1921: Launched by the Goole Shipbuilding and Repairing Co. Ltd., Goole (Yard No. 22) for Albert Chester, Middlesbrough as GLENSIDE. *8.1921:* Completed for the Glenside Steamship Co. Ltd. (Albert Chester, manager), Middlesbrough. *15.6.1923:* Manager became Ernest A.H. Harrison. *15.11.1923:* Sold to the Firth Shipping Co. Ltd. (G.T. Gillie Ltd., manager), Newcastle-upon-Tyne. *14.1.1924:* Acquired by the Broadlake Shipping Co. Ltd. (Joseph E. Fisher and Co., managers), Liverpool. *29.8.1924:* Sold to Richardson and Co. Ltd., Napier, New Zealand. *28.11.1924:* Renamed PARERA. *7.5.1936:* Sold to the Holm Shipping Co. Ltd. (Holm and Co. Ltd., managers), Wellington, New Zealand. *17.6.1936:* Renamed HOLMLEA. *20.12.1949:* Sold to the Lancey Steamship Pty. Ltd. (Harold R. Lancey, managers), Sydney, New South Wales. *20.1.1950:* Renamed KIAMA. *19.1.1951:* Sank after stranding on a reef near Terrigal, sixty miles north of Sydney, during a gale whilst on a voyage from Newcastle, New South Wales to Sydney with a cargo of coal. *5.2.1951:* Register closed.

Managed for Potter and Son, Runcorn

NICOLAS 1907-1926

O.N. 123707 516g 229n 159.4 x 26.2 x 11.3 feet
T. 3-cyl. by George T. Grey, South Shields; 9 knots.

28.9.1906: Completed by van Vliet and Co. Werf de Merwede, Hardinxveld, Holland (Yard No. 52) for Shipping Investments Ltd. (Charles H. Pile, manager), London as NICOLAS. *8.7.1907:* Acquired by Potter and Son, Runcorn (Joseph W. Fisher and Co., Liverpool, managers). *9.1926:* Sold to Dampskibs A/S Mallin (M. Clausen, manager), Haugesund, Norway and renamed MALLIN. *1932:* Owners became Dampskibs A/S Force (M. Clausen, manager), Haugesund and renamed FORCE. *27.5.1947:* Sold to Rederi A/B Allan (Harry Persson, manager), Landskrona, Sweden and renamed JAN. *17.8.1949:* Breaking up began by Glucksmans Metallaffar Aktiebolag at Marieholm, Gothenburg, Sweden. *19.1.1950:* Demolition completed.

Managed for The Shipping Controller

1. WAR ALNE 1919

O.N. 143297 703g 319n 180.4 x 28.0 x 12.4 feet
T. 3-cyl. by the Shields Engineering and Dry Dock Co. Ltd., North Shields.

18.6.1919: Completed by Charles Rennoldson and Co., South Shields (Yard No. 197) for the Reddington Shipping Co. Ltd. (George Traill, manager), London as CANTERBURY BELL. She had been laid down for The Shipping Controller as WAR ALNE and allocated to the management of Joseph E. Fisher. *14.7.1919:* Charles H. Pile became manager. *10.10.1919:* Sold to the Haig Shipping Co. Ltd. (King and Co. (Cardiff) Ltd., managers), Cardiff. *5.1.1922:* Capsized and sank in the Bristol Channel whilst on a voyage from Llanelli to Corcubion with a cargo of coal.

2. POLSTELL 1920-1921

O.N. 140435 1029g 729n 204.7 x 29.7 x 17.7 feet
T. 3-cyl. by Motala Mekaniska Verkstads Aktiebolag, Norrkoping, Sweden.
1900: T. 3-cyl. by W. Lindberg's Verkstads & Varfs Aktiebolag, Stockholm, Sweden.

1882: Launched by Motala Mekaniska Verkstads Aktiebolag, Norrkoping, Sweden (Yard No. 322) for Stockholms Ångfartygs Rederibolag (Ludvig Peyron, manager), Stockholm, Sweden as TELLUS. *1892:* Manager became Gustaf Brolin. *1895:* Owners became Stockholms Ångfartygs Rederiaktiebolag (Sven Ternström, manager), Stockholm. *1900:* Fitted with a new engine. *1907:* Sold to Nya Rederiaktiebolaget Svea (Hjalmar Blomberg, manager), Stockholm. *1908:* Owners became Stockholms Rederiaktiebolag Svea (Hjalmar Blomberg, manager), Stockholm. *14.9.1917:* Captured by H.M.S. RADIANT in position 52.56 N by 03.55 E whilst on a voyage from Rotterdam to Sundsvall with a cargo of coal. Taken to Harwich and later condemned as a prize because the coal she was carrying came from a mine in the part of Belgium occupied by Germany. *6.12.1917:* Owners became The Shipping Controller, London (Mann, Macneal and Steeves, Glasgow, managers) and renamed POLSTELL. *1920:* Managers became Joseph W. Fisher and Co., Liverpool. *6.1921:* Sold to Louis Liano en Cia., Santander, Spain and renamed ALFREDO. *1923:* Owners became Luis Liano Sociedad en Comandita, Santander. *29.12.1924:* Foundered off the coast of Brittany whilst on a voyage from Ayr to Bayonne with a cargo of coal.

THOMAS GRIEVE
Birkenhead

With just three ships – one of which survived only 14 days – this business needs some justification for inclusion in this book. The author pleads that its ancient ships are themselves of interest, and especially when one of them was thought worthy of renaming at forty years of age. The company's pretensions to offering a regular cargo service also makes it worthy of inclusion, and it is the only coaster company known to have operated from offices in Birkenhead.

Nevertheless, details of the concern are scanty. Thomas Grieve junior was a corn merchant, and sharing offices in Hamilton Square, Birkenhead were Duncan MacNicoll and Henry Henes. In May 1921 Grieve became manager of the 42-year old GALGORM CASTLE, which five months later was transferred to the ownership of her very own company, the Galgorm Castle Steamship Co. Ltd. The onerous task of managing this ship was now spread between Grieve, MacNicoll and Henes.

In September 1921, a concern calling itself the General Shipping and Forwarding Company requested the Mersey Docks and Harbour Board to allocate it quay space for its steam services to Barrow-in-Furness, Workington and Silloth. This company was essentially Grieve, MacNicoll and Henes, and was granted 200 feet of space at the south west side of Clarence Half Tide Dock at which to berth GALGORM CASTLE. One can speculate that, with interests in the grain trade, the partners were mainly concerned with moving imported corn or refined flour from Merseyside to North Lancashire and Cumberland ports, but hoped to eke out their living with what general cargo was offering.

In August 1922 the fleet was expanded. OWAIN TUDUR was only slightly younger than GALGORM CASTLE, but was considered to merit the expense of registering a new name, PEGGY GRIEVE. In that December the partners bought their third ship, MAY, which had once been in the fleet of the Northwich Carrying Co. Ltd. Just two weeks later, however, she was lost in the English Channel.

Services to Barrow-in-Furness, Workington and Silloth did not prosper. The Silloth service had been withdrawn by October 1925, and in February 1926 the creditors of the General Shipping and Forwarding Company were pressing the Mersey Docks and Harbour Board to withdraw its facilities. This they did and the shed – and presumably the service – was taken over by J.S. Monks and Co. Ltd.; quite possibly they had squeezed the little company out of the trade to the north west which Monks considered its own.

There is no record of the old GALGORM CASTLE trading after 1924, and in 1926 she was sold to breakers. PEGGY GRIEVE found another buyer hopeful of trading her, although her iron hull was not to escape the breakers for long. The three partners had spent the bare minimum on ships, yet could not make a coastal shipping service from Liverpool to the far north west of England pay. Even in the twenties, the writing was on the wall for purely coastal shipping.

Peggy Grieve.
National Maritime Museum P12321

Fleet list

1. GALGORM CASTLE 1921-1926 Iron

O.N. 81953 181g 74n 111.0 x 19.4 x 9.0 feet
C. 2-cyl. by John Rowan and Sons Ltd., Glasgow; 9 knots.

6.1879: Launched by Harland and Wolff, Belfast (Yard No. 128) for Alexander McMullin, Ballymena, County

Antrim as GALGORM CASTLE. *21.8.1879:* Completed. *1882:* Owner became Matthew Gault, Ballymena, County Antrim. *1883:* Sold to H. Thompson. *1883:* Sold to Harper Campbell, Sligo. *1888:* Sold to Charles Marshall, Drummore, County Wigtown. *8.12.1891:* Wrecked seven miles from Bangor in the entrance to the Menai Straits whilst on a voyage from Waterford to Whitehaven in ballast. Later salved and repaired. *18.11.1892:* Re-registered in the ownership of William Beesley (James Mawson and Son, managers), Barrow-in-Furness. *10.3.1898:* Sold to James Mawson, Barrow-in-Furness. *11.3.1898:* Sold to John Muir Paton and Peter Donald Hendry, Glasgow. *27.7.1906:* Sold to Walter G. Tilton, Bristol. *11.8.1906:* Owners became Tilton's Trading Steamers Ltd. (W.G. Tilton, manager), Bristol. *31.5.1917:* Sold to John Johnston, Glasgow. *13.5.1921:* Sold to Joseph Long (Thomas Grieve junior, manager), Birkenhead. *17.10.1921:* Acquired by the Galgorm Castle Steamship Co. Ltd. (Thomas Grieve junior, manager), Birkenhead. *1926:* Broken up during the second quarter. *28.5.1926:* Register closed.

Galgorm Castle *John Clarkson*

2. PEGGY GRIEVE 1922-1926 Iron

O.N. 86271 238g 89n 125.9 x 20.1 x 10.2 feet
C. 2-cyl. by Richard Nevill, Llanelli.

10.1882: Launched by Samuel Brothers, Llanelli (Yard No. 25) for the Owain Tudur Steamship Co. Ltd. (Parry, Jones and Co., managers), Liverpool as OWAIN TUDUR. *8.1.1883:* Completed. *18.12.1888:* Sold to William Rowland, Runcorn. *26.9.1906:* Manager became Alfred Rowland, Liverpool. *27.4.1908:* Sold to John R. Rix, Hull. *20.5.1908:* Owners became Humber Steam Coasters Ltd. (Robert Rix and Sons, managers), Hull. *15.7.1916:* Sold to Harry Parker, Grimsby. *25.6.1919:* Owners became Harry Parker (Grimsby) Ltd., Grimsby. *24.8.1922:* Acquired by Thomas Grieve junior, Birkenhead. *8.9.1922:* Owners became the Grieve Steamship Co. Ltd. (Thomas Grieve junior, manager), Birkenhead. *18.9.1922:* Renamed PEGGY GRIEVE. *13.12.1923:* Manager became Duncan MacNicoll, Birkenhead. *26.5.1926:* Sold to Bror. Gosta Hulthen, London. *12.9.1929:* Sold at Wivenhoe to T.W. Ward Ltd. and broken up at Grays, Essex. *28.9.1929:* Register closed.

3. MAY 1922

O.N.118056 263g 56n 115.0 x 22.2 x 10.2 feet
C. 2-cyl. by W.J. Yarwood, Northwich; 8½ knots.

1.1902: Launched by W.J. Yarwood, Northwich (Yard No. 25) for the Northwich Carrying Company Ltd., Northwich as MAY. *3.11.1903:* Completed. *19.1.1920:* Sold to James Kells, Sunderland. *12.4.1922:* Sold to John B. Forster, Sunderland. *5.12.1922:* Acquired by Thomas Grieve junior, Duncan MacNicoll and Henry C. Henes trading as the General Shipping and Forwarding Co., Birkenhead. *19.12.1922:* Foundered in the English Channel whilst on a voyage from Hourdel to Weston Point with a cargo of boulder flints. *3.1.1923:* Register closed.

RICHARD HUGHES AND CO.
RICHARD HUGHES AND CO. (LIVERPOOL) LTD.
HUGHES HOLDEN SHIPPING LTD.
Liverpool

by Roy Griffin and Roy Fenton

Richard Hughes was the largest coastal shipowner that Liverpool, or indeed Wales, produced: not for nothing was his fleet sometimes called the 'Welsh Navy'. His was the only company described here which established for itself a truly national reputation. Indeed, his ships outgrew the local trades, and many could be found adequate employment only by carrying East Coast coal. The life of Richard Hughes' company spanned the period from the earliest bulk-carrying steamers on the West Coast to the ascendancy of the motorship. Tragically, however, his luck or his judgement deserted him in later life – when many men would have retired – and the fleet he built up was lost to him.

Richard Hughes' interest in the sea was a purely commercial one, and had his circumstances been different he might equally well have made his way in the world as an innkeeper or even a grocer. He was born at Gronant, Flintshire in 1858 to Jane and Joseph Hughes, who kept the Gronant Inn. Jane Hughes, although illiterate, had a good head for business and encouraged her husband to diversify into shopkeeping, general carrying, and hiring out machinery to local farmers. Richard inherited his mother's business instincts, and had the unusual advantage for the time of being educated until he was fourteen. As his parents had eight other children to feed, clothe and school, this suggests that their businesses were doing well. Richard's sister Dorothy had married a local man who then moved to Liverpool to work as a clerk in the shipping office of R. and D. Jones. Richard Hughes obtained a position in the same office when he left school: no doubt his brother-in-law had recommended him as a smart lad.

Richard Hughes *H.D. Wallace-Jones collection*

Hughes was certainly smart enough to see that the way to financial advancement was not to work for others. In 1884 he set up in business for himself with some financial help from his parents and fifty pounds borrowed from friends and associates. From offices in Water Street, Liverpool Hughes went ahead and ordered an iron steamer from H. McIntyre and Co. of Paisley. On the day in January 1885 when this ship was launched her name, PRIMROSE, was adopted as the telegraphic code for Richard Hughes and Co. Shortly afterwards, in March 1885, the first of Hughes' single-ship companies, the Primrose Steamship Co. Ltd., was set up to take over the PRIMROSE. Its £4,750 capital was divided into £50 shares of which Hughes initially took just three, later expanding his holding to thirty.

The Primrose Steamship Co. Ltd. was clearly a success, as other single-ship companies followed with increasing frequency. The table below shows the capital, founding and winding-up dates of Richard Hughes' six companies.

Title	Capital	Founded	Dissolved
Primrose Steamship Co. Ltd.	£4,750	14.3.1885	29.1.1907
Wild Rose Steamship Co. Ltd.	£5,000	18.6.1888	13.2.1906
Moss Rose Steamship Co. Ltd.	£7,500	16.6.1890	9.8.1915
White Rose Steamship Co. Ltd.	£4,500	21.1.1891	10.1.1911
Red Rose Steamship Co. Ltd.	£8,500	25.6.1891	9.8.1915
Brier Rose Steamship Co. Ltd.	£9,000	8.7.1892	12.6.1918

As manager of each company, Richard Hughes received a fee of £75 per year, took 7½% of the net earnings (less scrupulous promoters based their remuneration on gross earnings, ensuring they made money whether the ships were making a profit or not) and was entitled to all commissions on brokerage and insurance. The capital of all except the Primrose Steamship Co. Ltd. was divided into £25 shares. There are striking similarities in the pattern of distribution of shareholdings in the six companies, which probably reflect the way the shares were marketed, and probably the respect which Hughes quickly built up. Each company had fifty or so investors, mainly from Liverpool, North Wales and the north of Ireland, although Glasgow and the south of England were well represented. A number of names recur in the list of shareholders of each company: the Belfast shipowner James M. Barkley, the Rea family (described as 'colliery proprietors', but to become better known as collier and tug owners) and the Hutson family of the Kelvinhaugh Engine Works in Glasgow, who pursued a policy of actively buying up shares in Hughes' companies until, as related later, they shared control with the founder. Richard Abel, ship and flat owner of Runcorn, was an initial subscriber to the Primrose Steamship Co. Ltd., but did not repeat his investment. Hughes' family were small but faithful investors, including farmers John and Thomas Hughes, grocer Joseph, joiner Samuel – all of Gronant – and Richard's wife, Mary Jane.

Hughes' initial holding in the companies was modest, representing only five to ten per cent of the capital, but tended to increase over the years (with the exception of the

Primrose, Hughes' first steamer, wrecked in Mount's Bay. *H.D. Wallace-Jones collection*

Hutson period), as he became more prosperous and had the chance to acquire any shares which became available.

The significance of the winding up dates quoted above varies considerably. The Primrose Steamship Co. Ltd. was dissolved soon after the PRIMROSE herself was lost, but the White Rose Steamship Co. Ltd. was allowed to linger on for ten years after the WHITE ROSE had been wrecked, presumably because shareholders had been well satisfied by payments made from her insurance money. For other companies, liquidation followed the sale or the acquisition of the ship by Richard Hughes in person. In the case of the Brier Rose Steamship Co. Ltd., for instance, Hughes made an offer of £12,000 for the BRIER ROSE in June 1918. Although this was thirty per cent higher than her building cost a quarter of a century earlier, war had inflated prices considerably, and she was worth even more. But Hughes' holding over half of the shares made sure the company accepted his offer.

To return to 1892, Richard Hughes was by now sufficiently well established to begin owning ships under his own name, financing them with the help of mortgages from associates such as Guybon Hutson. Apart from the PINK ROSE, bought new, such acquisitions were considerably older than the rest of the fleet: in 1894 he bought the 22-year-old FOYLE and the 29-year-old AVON, the latter being registered under a single-ship company. The FOYLE was to be the fleet's first casualty when abandoned off Bardsey in August 1897. Hughes had an eye for a bargain: in 1897 he bought the EMERALD, which had been wrecked off Burntisland under a previous owner. Several other ships were acquired under similar circumstances, including the LILY in 1899. At this time new and old ships were joining the fleet almost simultaneously. In 1898 came the new PANSY and the 20-year-old NORTHCOTE which, larger than anything bought so far, was intended for trading further afield. Unfortunately, after being renamed VIOLET, she was wrecked in the Baltic in 1901.

Seen here at Cardiff, **Brier Rose** (1) was one the longest-lived of the Rose Boats.

Welsh Industrial and Maritime Museum 519/H793

Mersey at Fowey. The tiny steamer alongside is the **Edith** (34/1895) of Bristol supplying bunker coal. Note the white dust from loading the china clay. *W.S.P.L.*

The trade in which Richard Hughes and Co. prospered was carrying china clay from Fowey, Par and Charlestown to ports in the North West, including Preston, Fleetwood, Ellesmere Port and - most importantly - Runcorn. At the two Mersey ports the clay was unloaded into narrow boats for delivery to the Potteries. One of the attractions of this trade was that coal from Garston made a useful return cargo, although in 1893 Hughes was advertising a regular service for general cargo from the Mersey for Devon and Cornwall, taking his ships into Penzance and Plymouth. The china clay trade became so important to the company that over the years offices were opened at Par (telegraph code 'RAP') and Fowey (more prosaically coded 'HUGHES'), as well as Runcorn (code 'CLAYROSE') and Garston. The company also owned a number of rail wagons to transport clay from the mines to the Cornish ports, as well as a wagon repair works at Par. Hughes never devoted his fleet entirely to the china clay trade, however, and his larger ships in particular traded more widely. For instance, the large LILY worked out of Blyth, Hull and Swansea with coal, and even managed to visit Aberystwyth, presumably for ore. Even the regular ships in the china clay trade would carry coal on the East Coast, frequently to Shoreham.

By the turn of the century, the fleet consisted of twelve ships, but with a particularly deep depression affecting trade a whole decade was to go by without further acquisitions. By then numbers had been reduced to seven by sales and losses, including that of the pioneer PRIMROSE which was wrecked in Mounts Bay in August 1906.

There is evidence that, during the first decade of the twentieth century, Richard Hughes may have wished to leave shipowning, or at least reduce his financial exposure by taking on a partner. Over the period from December 1904 to February 1906, four of his ships were sold outright to Alexander Hutson, who moved from Kelvinside, Glasgow to share Richard Hughes' office in James Street, Liverpool. In recognition of this partnership, *Lloyds Register* began referring to the company as Hughes and Hutson. At this time, Richard Hughes also sold many of the shares in his single-ship companies, the Hutson family's holdings increasing concurrently. The Hutsons had been closely associated with Hughes for many years. Until his death in December 1902, the engineer Guybon Hutson had been the mortgagee for several of Hughes' ships and a shareholder in his companies since at least 1891; the EMERALD had been purchased from Hutson and Son who had presumably repaired her; and Hughes' earliest ships had been engined by Hutson and Corbett - the earlier title of this engineering business based at Kelvinhaugh in Glasgow. But the partnership was short-lived, and in July 1909 the four ships sold to Hutson were reacquired by Hughes.

Although, as events in 1920 will show, Hughes was quite open to offers for his ships, he continued to run his fleet himself, so perhaps the Hutson partnership had convinced him he was better off managing ships himself. Indeed, once the trade depression was over, Hughes started expanding his fleet again, a process that was to continue virtually unchecked for twenty years. Again, new and old ships were to join the fleet simultaneously; a brand new PRIMROSE in 1910 and the 18-year-old MERSEY in 1910, the latter destined not to receive its 'Rose' name for another twenty years. In 1911 came his shortest-lived vessel, the second WHITE ROSE, which disappeared eight months later. The next new buildings represented something of a departure, for three out of the next five ships came from a yard at Hardinxveld in Holland. Since the 1890s Dutch yards had built a few small coasters for British owners, but this was one of the first times an established company had placed a substantial order in Holland - a taste of things to come.

As part of his expansion, Hughes had begun services from South Wales to French ports, almost invariably carrying coal outward but often loading general cargo homewards. Offices were opened at Cardiff (telegraph code 'ROSES') and at Newport for this trade.

The outbreak of the Great War did not stem the flow of new ships for the fleet, but did bring a departure from the purely 'flower' nomenclature with names honouring Allied generals – FRENCH ROSE and JOFFRE ROSE; a series that was eventually to include a couple of admirals. Mined in November 1917, FRENCH ROSE was the company's only confirmed loss due to enemy action, although the RED ROSE disappeared in May 1918 and the PINK ROSE was wrecked off the east of Scotland carrying coal northwards for the Grand Fleet.

Hughes owned a total of 14 ships during the war, and almost all were at some time taken over for Government service. One of the few exceptions was the little DUNMORE, acquired from her repairers after severe damage. Indeed, had it not been for the war she would probably have been scrapped: certainly the Admiralty thought she was worth little and had held her from November 1914 to April 1915 as a possible blockship. The most frequent use made of the 'Rose Boats' by the Government was to carry the enormous variety and quantity of stores required by the British Expeditionary Force in France. The major ports used were Dover, Littlehampton and Newhaven but stores were also loaded on the Thames. Most of the cargoes of stores are not detailed in official lists, but occasional mentions of road-making materials in the MOSS ROSE and timber in PANSY and RED ROSE are reminders of the enormous and appallingly wasteful construction work that went into sustaining trench warfare for over four years. Employment on Government service was rarely continuous: MERSEY probably held the record, being hired from September 1914 until the end of 1917. Even after the Armistice the ships were still required, often to bring back materials they had earlier taken to France. For instance, PANSY remained on hire until September 1919. Just before the Armistice WHITE ROSE brought back an ominous-sounding cargo: rags from Le Havre to Goole. Could these once have been military uniforms?

The outbreak of peace late in 1918 saw most shipowners expecting a continuing period of prosperity aided by continuing Government use of their ships, even though it must have become apparent that the flow of new ships coming from British and Dutch yards would soon exceed demand. Hughes seems to have hedged his bets in an extraordinary way. He first ordered three very large coasters from Fullertons but, three months before the first of these was delivered, he actually sold his entire existing fleet. In all ten ships passed on 11th March 1920 to Robert Leeson of the Liverpool-based John Edwards and Co. and Owen Donnelly, a Dublin coal merchant.

Just two months after their expensive acquisitions, the freight rate bubble burst, and

Launch of **Jellicoe Rose** at Paisley. *H.D. Wallace-Jones collection*

Donnelly and Leeson found themselves trading in a spectacularly depressed market. To add to their troubles partition of Ireland and the ensuing civil war left the banking community – many of whom were hostile to the Irish Free State – with no stomach for propping up an ailing shipping company. The National Bank in London foreclosed on the ships' mortgages and Donnelly was declared bankrupt. Hughes bought the nine survivors back from the bank in September 1921 – the WHITE ROSE (never a fortunate name in the fleet) having been lost just nine days after her sale.

It would seem most likely that Hughes sold on a rising market because he believed strongly that bigger ships and larger cargoes would be the norm in the post-war world, and took the opportunity to dispose of his existing craft at a good price. Hughes was without ships for just three months, and in June 1920 the first of the big new coasters from Paisley, the JELLICOE ROSE, arrived to be followed at three-monthly intervals by the BEATTY ROSE and HAIG ROSE. One would have thought that, with freight rates depressed after 1921, the re-absorption of the nine Donnelly and Leeson ships into the

Foch Rose shares a lock with Zillah's **Amy Summerfield,** and emphasises how much larger were the big Hughes boats compared with the average Irish Sea coaster.
John Clarkson

A sequence of snapshots taken at the launch of **Louie Rose** at Fullerton's yard. *H.D. Wallace-Jones collection*

fleet would have given Richard Hughes enough to think about, but no, he immediately embarked on an expansion scheme, taking delivery of three new ships (including FOCH ROSE) and one secondhand in 1922, buying the 30-year-old HAYLE in 1923, two more large new coasters in 1924 and yet another in 1925. With 20 ships, the fleet was now larger than it had ever been, and in the LOUIE ROSE and FULLERTON ROSE it had its biggest ships ever.

The latter was named as a tribute to her Paisley builder: a nice touch as Fullerton's yard had now completed a total of 14 ships for the fleet. But sadly the FULLERTON ROSE was to be the last, for this old and well-respected steam coaster building yard delivered its final ship in 1927.

The expanded Hughes fleet needed new trades, and the 'Rose Boats' were seen regularly in harbours where they had rarely ventured before, such as Shoreham, Poole and Torquay where they brought East Coast coal for the local gas works or coal merchants. BRIER ROSE visited Penmaenmawr and the Llŷn for stone, whilst the big LOUIE ROSE had a regular contract to carry steel between Ghent, the Bristol Channel and Birkenhead. LOUIE ROSE was named in memory of Hughes wife, who had died in 1923.

Christened Mary Jane Lewis, Hughes always called her Louie.

Like other shipping companies, Hughes was hit by the 1926 coal strike, and the FULLERTON ROSE was laid up on the Tyne from April to August 1926, the BRIER ROSE languishing at Runcorn from May to November. At the height of the strike some Hughes ships brought coal from Ostend to bunker other members of the fleet which were anchored fuel-less off Fowey.

Surviving the slump called for strict economies and the Hughes' ships gained – or perhaps just strengthened – their reputation for frugality during this period. Those who served in the ships frequently speak of them being 'run on a shoe-string'. About this time the old custom of letting a coaster's crew buy and cook their own food ended in the larger ships and a full time cook was employed. Hughes, however, deducted the cost of the food from the crews' wages, which earned him the title 'Hungry Dick'.

Richard Hughes, smoking, with John Fullerton (above) and (below left) during trials on the Clyde of one of the Fullerton-built steamers. *H.D. Wallace-Jones collection*

The year 1927 saw some ships depart: the DUNMORE sold after a long lay-up; and the BEATTY ROSE and MOSS ROSE lost whilst on the company's customary services, Mersey to Cornwall and South Wales to France, respectively. These losses were soon made up by the acquisition of three relatively modern steamers, a number of which were coming on to the market at knock-down prices as companies such as Cornish Traders Ltd. – owners of CORNISH MERCHANT and CORNISH TRADER – who had optimistically bought ships in the heady years soon after the war gave up the struggle and cut their losses.

In the late 1920s Richard Hughes' excellent commercial judgement deserted him. The sudden death of his wife from a heart attack in 1923 affected him deeply, and he was never quite the same again. It should also be borne in mind that he was now an old man, well past today's retiring age. With a modest upturn in trade in the late 1920s he perhaps expected the 1930s to bring renewed prosperity to coastal shipping, and embarked on an ambitious but ultimately ruinous new building programme. Between December 1929 and July 1931 no fewer than eleven new ships were delivered from two yards – the old

Dennis Wallace-Jones (left) launches **Dennis Rose** at the Meadowside yard of D. & W. Henderson and Co. Ltd. whilst Sir Frederick Henderson looks on (above left). The Hendersons were major creditors of Richard Hughes, and were partly instrumental in his bankruptcy. *H.D. Wallace-Jones collection*

friends at Hardinxveld plus a Clyde yard not normally associated with coaster-building but driven to it by the recession, D. and W. Henderson and Co. Ltd.

The new ships brought fresh names into the fleet, including names of family members such as WALLACE ROSE and DUDLEY ROSE and place names including GRONANT ROSE, PRESTATYN ROSE, ANGLESEA ROSE and AMLWCH ROSE. Even the old MERSEY was finally renamed MERSEY ROSE, only to be lost soon afterwards. The Anglesey place names were particularly appropriate as many Hughes crews were recruited from the towns and villages on the island, from whence also came the Marine Superintendent Captain Griffith. Crew members also came from the Llŷn, and the ships would often pass within sight of their homes. Richard Roberts, who was an engineer on the PANSY, came from Uwchmynydd – on the tip of the peninsula – and would write from Haverfordwest to tell his family when he would be passing so that they could climb nearby Pen-y-Foel and wave a home-made flag at the PANSY. Such was the preponderance of Anglesey and Llŷn men in the crews that Dr. David Jenkins of the Welsh Industrial and Maritime Museum recalls that his great-uncle Captain Samuel Jenkins of Aberporth near Cardigan claimed that, whilst in command of the GUELDER ROSE and WALLACE ROSE, he was the only non-North Walian master in the fleet.

No boom in the 1930s came and Hughes' ambitious expansion programme overtaxed even his considerable financial resources, such that the Official Receiver was called in by two of his principal creditors, Martin's Bank and Hendersons the shipbuilders. Hughes was now 76 and in such poor health that he had to leave his home at Bryn Coch Hall, Mold for his daughter's holiday home at Abersoch on the Llŷn. It was here that he died on 23rd April 1936. He left just over £3,300 – not a great fortune after almost fifty years in control of one of Britain's foremost coaster companies.

What sort of a man had Richard Hughes been? There is no denying that he ran a successful company, in a business where sentiment meant next to nothing, hard economics almost all. The company he built up almost singlehanded was certainly well-found: it survived the storms of the twenties and only foundered when its ageing owner over-reached himself. To survive in shipping as long as he did one had to be tough when times were hard. It is said, for instance, that no nightwatchmen were employed on Hughes' ships when in port, the crews being expected to do the job themselves. And, as was common in the coasting trade, captains were encouraged to obtain pilotage certificates for ports to which they frequently traded to save the company the cost of a pilot. One odd aspect of Richard Hughes' character was the rigid enforcement of a rule forbidding women on board his ships. The DUNMORE was laid up at Runcorn for two years in the twenties with an Amlwch man left in charge. When his wife made the long journey from Anglesey to visit him, she was not allowed on board. But as if to balance this hardness, Hughes showed considerable loyalty and even generosity to those who served him well, and both Hughes and his successor kept their crews year in, year out. An outstanding example was Richard Vaughan who joined the FOCH ROSE as a seaman when she was new in 1922. He was still with her as bosun when she was sold to the breakers in 1956. When times were good, crews were often paid more than the basic wage rate. This crude profit sharing, with wages reflecting the company's fortunes, made Hughes and others who practised it unpopular with seamen's unions, so perhaps the sobriquet 'Hungry Dick' was somewhat unfairly applied to him.

Outside shipping, his philanthropic work was considerable. During the First World War he presented ambulances to the French and British Red Cross, supplied boots for the entire child population of a French village in the war zone and gave two wards to the Liverpool Merchant's Mobile Hospital. It was at this hospital at Etaples, incidentally, that his daughter Dorothy met her future husband, Dr. Henry Wallace-Jones. In 1924, remembering his own childhood when there were no leisure facilities for young men, Hughes presented his native village of Gronant with a splendidly equipped village hall and endowed it with sufficient railway shares to meet its future running costs. He was also a devoted husband, father and grandfather, and this is reflected in his use of his wife's, daughter's, son-in-law's and grandsons' names for ships in the fleet.

Although probably considered to be a little eccentric at times, Hughes made decisions rapidly both in and out of business. For example, on one occasion, having heard that the old Flint County Jail – which was situated opposite his home in Mold – might be re-opened as a prison, he promptly bought the entire building. Its only use for years afterwards was as a playground for his grandchildren.

After Hughes' enforced retirement, his ships were not sold off piecemeal, perhaps because the creditors would have faced a very considerable loss this way. Instead the receiver found someone willing and able to take on the whole fleet, a Cardiff shipbroker who handled Hughes' business in that port, Thomas J. Tierney. Tierney became chairman and managing director, but the Hughes name was valued highly enough to be retained, the new company registered on 10th April 1934 being entitled Richard Hughes and Co. (Liverpool) Ltd. Nor was the Hughes' family's interest completely extinguished, as Richard Hughes' son-in-law Henry Wallace-Jones became a director. Dr. Wallace-Jones was a practising heart specialist: the rough and tumble of shipowning must have made an interesting contrast to cardiology.

Tierney continued the frugal management style which Hughes had practised, but there were to be no grandiose plans for expansion. In fact, after the arrival of the MOELFRE ROSE in 1931, no new ships joined the fleet for over twenty years. Instead, ships were disposed of as circumstances permitted, the two big Fullerton sisters leaving the fleet in 1936 and 1937, the LOUIE ROSE to begin what was for a coal carrier a rather exotic second career as a wine tanker in the Mediterranean. The recently built PINK ROSE reduced the fleet further by sinking after a collision in March 1936, whilst the HAYLE of 1893 was sold to shipbreakers in 1937 after spending her last years as a coal hulk in Cornwall. Remarkably, she was the first Hughes ship ever to be broken up.

Twenty-five ships remained on the company's books on the outbreak of the Second World War, but the fleet was not to escape as lightly in this conflict as it did in the First World War. Apart from marine losses, which were heavy enough, and a number of disappearances, the overwhelming cause of loss was air attack. Hughes ships were often larger than the average coaster, and must have presented tempting targets to the Luftwaffe on its offensive patrols of British waters.

February 1940 saw the stranding of the JELLICOE ROSE in the Wear. In peacetime the damage she sustained would probably have meant a voyage to the breakers, but it was wartime and she was of great value, so she was duly repaired. November saw the tragic disappearance of her sister HAIG ROSE and in December the AMLWCH ROSE also went missing. German propaganda made the surprising claim that she had been sunk by a U-boat in November 1944. During 1940 the company managed its only ship, the captured Deutsche Levante Linie steamer MOREA, which soon passed to South Wales managers and sank later that year, just escaping being expended as a blockship.

The crew of the DORRIEN ROSE were amongst the many heroes of the Dunkirk evacuation, making two trips and rescuing sixteen hundred men. Of these, six hundred came from the stricken passenger ship QUEEN OF THE CHANNEL (1,162/1935), rescued – it is said – without even one man getting his feet wet, in spite of continual bombing. Distinguished Service Crosses were awarded to the master, mate and chief engineer of the DORRIEN ROSE, whilst her bosun and gunner also received medals. Although in less hazardous circumstances, the WALLACE ROSE won fame by repatriating allied airmen interned by neutral Eire. Her master also won the D.S.C. and a bar during numerous encounters with the Luftwaffe.

In terms of losses, 1941 had far worse in store than 1940. In January the PRIMROSE capsized and sank off Ireland. In March the BRIER ROSE disappeared in the Irish Sea; she had been built for Richard Hughes almost half a century before, and had the ignominious experience of being taken over by the Admiralty in July 1940 as a possible blockship.

Then began a grim catalogue of Luftwaffe attacks and sinkings. On 2nd April the WILD ROSE had to run ashore after she had been attacked off the Tuskar Rock. Just seven days later the DUDLEY ROSE was bombed and sunk in the English Channel and in another seven days the ANGLESEA ROSE suffered the same fate off St. Ives. Early in May the PINK ROSE caught fire and sank following a collision.

Before dawn on the 16th May, the JOFFRE ROSE was bombed and then repeatedly strafed by a Focke Wolf Fw200 *Condor* off St. Anne's Head in the Irish Sea. A near miss astern disabled the engines, started a leak and injured two engineers. Soon after daylight the OBSIDIAN (811/1922) belonging to William Robertson of Glasgow came alongside, took off the injured and began towing the JOFFRE ROSE toward Milford Haven. She was eventually beached at Dale, just inside the Haven. By an uncomfortable coincidence, her master Captain Alcorn was attacked in exactly the same place whilst in command of the BLUSH ROSE in February 1942. Again a near miss caused leaks and

Dennis Rose in wartime. *National Maritime Museum P21973*

disabled her engines, but this time it was the WILD ROSE – repaired after her misadventures in 1941 – that assisted her into Milford Haven so that she could be beached at Dale, a spot becoming all too familiar to Captain Alcorn.

To return to the disasters of 1941, in July the FOWEY ROSE was attacked and sunk off the Pembroke coast, and in September the GUELDER ROSE suffered damage in the North Sea.

These casualties plus the sale of two ships reduced the fleet to fifteen, but mercifully there were to be no more war losses. The coming of peace, however, did little to abate the danger from marine hazards. In August 1945 the BLUSH ROSE went down after colliding with Alfred Holt's steamer GLAUCUS off Holyhead and in November the STURDEE ROSE capsized and sank off Trevose Head. It seems remarkable that in an age of radio and sophisticated air-sea rescue techniques her eight survivors could spend over a week adrift just off the English coast. This chapter of accidents ends with the JELLICOE ROSE in further trouble, coming off worst in an encounter with a Liberty steamer in the English Channel. Once again she lived to sail another day.

The war was not entirely unkind to Thomas Tierney, however, as by 1944 he had paid off the company's creditors and had bought out the Wallace-Jones' interest so that he now owned all eleven thousand shares. His long-term view of the coastal shipping was a gloomy one but – as it turned out – realistic, and he took every opportunity to sell his ships. In 1947 for instance the DENNIS ROSE, DOROTHY ROSE and MAURICE ROSE were sold to companies in the Coast Lines group for a total of £180,000 – a very satisfactory price for tramp steamers almost twenty years old. Soon after the war he moved the company's head office to Fenchurch Street, London, although an office was maintained in Castle Street, Liverpool. Tierney's son, John, joined the company but was firmly discouraged from taking over on his father's retirement. Instead the concern was sold in 1952 to a Swansea man, Philip E. Holden.

A new company was now formed, Hughes Holden Shipping Ltd., and operations moved again, this time to Swansea. To mark this new beginning came the delivery of the first new ship for over twenty years, the BRIER ROSE – the fleet's first motorship. It is said that Holden was not particularly pleased with his purchase of six ageing and worn-out steamers. Certainly he did not lose much time in disposing of them, PRESTATYN ROSE going in 1953, even the new BRIER ROSE being sold in 1954, the year in which the WALLACE ROSE was terminally damaged in a collision on the Thames. Also in 1954 came the last ship to join the fleet, the RAMBLER ROSE – virtually a repeat of the BRIER ROSE. Strangely, Hughes had never used this name, perhaps because it was an obvious one for a tramp. Between 1956 and 1958 the remaining steamers were sold, leaving the solitary motorship to ramble on until 1961. Her departure to new owners marked the end of the fleet and broke the last link with a Liverpool-Welsh entrepreneur who built up, if not the biggest, then almost certainly one of the best known British coaster fleets.

Rambler Rose: last of the Rose Boats. *Roy Griffin collection*

Fleet list

1. PRIMROSE (1) 1885-1906 Iron

O.N. 91184 272g 79n 135.0 x 20.1 x 9.8 feet
C. 2-cyl. by Hutson and Corbett, Glasgow.

1.1885: Launched by H. McIntyre and Co., Paisley (Yard No. 117) for Richard Hughes and Co., Liverpool as PRIMROSE. *28.2.1885:* Completed. *19.3.1885:* Owners became the Primrose Steamship Co. Ltd. (Richard Hughes and Co., managers), Liverpool. *23.8.1906:* Wrecked in fog on Low Lee Rocks in Mounts Bay near Newlyn whilst on a voyage from Garston to Newlyn with a cargo of coal. *21.9.1906:* Register closed.

The end of **Primrose** *W.S.P.L.*

2. WILD ROSE (1) 1888-1919 Iron

O.N. 93781 252g 93n 135.0 x 20.1 x 9.8 feet
C. 2-cyl. by Hutson and Corbett, Glasgow.

1.5.1888: Launched by John Fullerton and Co., Paisley (Yard No. 82) for Richard Hughes and Co., Liverpool as WILD ROSE. *11.6.1888:* Completed. *6.7.1888:* Owners became the Wild Rose Steamship Co. Ltd. (Richard Hughes and Co., managers), Liverpool. *12.2.1906:* Owner became Alexander Hutson, Liverpool. *21.7.1909:* Owners became Richard Hughes and Co., Liverpool. *19.4.1919:* Sank after a collision with the steamer AFON LLIEDI (1,015/04) in the Bristol Channel eighteen miles north by east of Godrevy Light, Cornwall whilst on a voyage from Garston to Hayle with a cargo of coal. Four of her crew of nine were lost; the remainder were picked up by the AFON LLIEDI and landed at Llanelli. *2.12.1919:* Register closed.

3. MOSS ROSE (1) 1890-1920/1921-1927

O.N. 97787 371g 171n 150.0 x 23.1 x 9.7 feet
C. 2-cyl. by Hutson and Corbett, Glasgow; 11 knots.

19.4.1890: Launched by the Grangemouth Dockyard Co., Grangemouth (Yard No. 129) for Richard Hughes and Co., Liverpool as MOSS ROSE. *3.6.1890:* Completed. *25.6.1890:* Owners became the Moss Rose Steamship Co. Ltd. (Richard Hughes and Co., managers), Liverpool. *8.1.1912:* Owners became Richard Hughes and Co., Liverpool. *11.3.1920:* Sold to Owen H. Donnelly, Dublin and Robert Leeson, Liverpool. *28.7.1921:* Re-acquired by Richard Hughes and Co., Liverpool. *28.10.1927:* Dragged anchors and wrecked at Peniel Point in Holyhead Bay whilst on a voyage from Runcorn to Fowey in ballast. *20.12.1927:* Register closed.

Moss Rose (1) *E.N. Taylor*

4. MATLOCK/WHITE ROSE (1) 1890-1901 Iron

O.N. 89711 336g 202n 150.8 x 22.1 x 10.3 feet
C. 2-cyl. by James S. Hume and Co., Glasgow.

9.6.1884: Launched by W. Harkess and Son, Middlesbrough (Yard No. 119) for Edward W. Harkess (J.M. Lennard and Sons, managers), Middlesbrough as MATLOCK. *7.7.1884:* Completed. *4.1889:* Sold to Meyer and Co., Amsterdam, Holland and renamed VOORWAARTS. *1890:* Owners became Stoomvaart Maatschappij Vooruit (Meyer and Co., managers), Amsterdam, Holland. *5.12.1890:* Acquired by Richard Hughes and Co., Liverpool and renamed MATLOCK. *17.1.1891:* Owners became the White Rose Steamship Co. Ltd. (Richard Hughes and Co., managers), Liverpool and later renamed WHITE ROSE. *5.2.1901:* Wrecked on Udder Rock, three miles east of Fowey Harbour, whilst on a voyage from Plymouth to Fowey in ballast. The crew was rescued.

White Rose (1) wrecked off Fowey in February 1901. The vessel assisting her appears to be **Red Rose**.
H.D. Wallace-Jones collection

Red Rose *John Clarkson*

5. RED ROSE 1891-1918 Steel and iron

O.N. 97854 423g 167n 160.3 x 23.1 x 10.0 feet
C. 2-cyl. by Hutson and Corbett, Glasgow; 10 knots.

23.4.1891: Launched by John Fullerton and Co., Paisley (Yard No. 94) for Richard Hughes and Co., Liverpool as RED ROSE. *27.4.1891:* Completed. *19.1.1895:* Owners became the Red Rose Steamship Co. Ltd. (Richard Hughes and Co., managers), Liverpool. *8.1.1912:* Owners became Richard Hughes and Co., Liverpool. *21.5.1918:* Left Littlehampton for Havre with a cargo of Government stores and disappeared. *3.9.1918:* Register closed.

Pink Rose (1) at Fowey in 1910. *H.D. Wallace-Jones collection*

BRIER ROSE
LIVERPOOL

The Palm Line cargo ship Lagos Palm, 5,120grt, which was built by the Wear Division of the Shipbuilding Corporation, Sunderland. The ship was laid down as the Empire Ronaldsay and she was completed as the Lagosian of the United Africa Co., London, in July, 1947. The ship was transferred to the company's Palm Line and renamed in 1949, being renamed Oguta Palm in 1961, so the name could be used for a new cargo ship. In 1964, the ship was sold to Greek own-

6. PINK ROSE (1) 1892-1917 Steel and iron

O.N. 99362 334g 117n 140.0 x 22.1 x 10.2 feet
C. 2-cyl. by Hutson and Corbett, Glasgow; 10 knots.

17.12.1891: Launched by John Shearer and Son, Glasgow (Yard No. 6) for Richard Hughes and Co., Liverpool as PINK ROSE. *19.1.1892:* Completed. *23.12.1904:* Owners became Alexander Hutson, Liverpool. *21.7.1909:* Owners became Richard Hughes and Co., Liverpool. *23.12.1917:* Wrecked four miles east of Lossiemouth whilst on a voyage from the Tyne to Cromarty with a cargo of coal. *14.1.1918:* Register closed.

Brier Rose (1) heads up the Manchester Ship Canal from Eastham. *W.S.P.L. Cochrane collection*

7. BRIER ROSE (1) 1892-1920/1921-1941 Steel and iron

O.N. 99394 497g 180n 165.0 x 25.1 x 10.3 feet
C. 2-cyl. by Hutson and Corbett, Glasgow; 11 knots.

19.3.1892: Launched by John Shearer and Son, Glasgow (Yard No. 7) for Richard Hughes and Co., Liverpool as BRIER ROSE. *8.4.1892:* Completed. *9.7.1892:* Owners became the Brier Rose Steamship Co. Ltd. (Richard Hughes and Co., managers), Liverpool. *18.6.1918:* Owners became Richard Hughes and Co., Liverpool. *11.3.1920:* Sold to Owen H. Donelly, Dublin and Robert Leeson, Liverpool. *28.7.1921:* Re-acquired by Richard Hughes and Co., Liverpool. *20.4.1934:* Owners became Richard Hughes and Co. (Liverpool) Ltd. (Thomas J. Tierney, manager), Liverpool. *25.3.1941:* Left Belfast for Cardiff with a cargo of steel billets and disappeared. *12.6.1941:* Register closed.

8. AVON 1894-1909 Iron

O.N. 45549 572g 277n 192.3 x 28.0 x 14.9 feet
C. 2-cyl. by Barclay, Curle and Co., Glasgow.

6.10.1865: Launched by Barclay, Curle and Co., Glasgow (Yard No. 139) for the Carron Company, Falkirk as AVON. *21.11.1865:* Completed. *5.1888:* Sold to the Avon Steamship Co. Ltd. (Thomas Jack junior, manager), Larne Harbour. *13.10.1891:* Sold to Henry Williams, Liverpool. *30.4.1894:* Acquired by Richard Hughes and Co., Liverpool. *16.5.1894:* Owners became the Avon Steamship Co. Ltd. (Richard Hughes and Co., managers), Liverpool. *27.4.1897:* Owners became Richard Hughes and Co., Liverpool. *4.2.1905:* Owner became Alexander Hutson, Liverpool. *21.7.1909:* Owner became Richard Hughes and Co., Liverpool. *19.9.1909:* Sunk in a collision with the steamer PACUARE (3,891/1905) in the Crosby Channel, River Mersey whilst on a voyage from Fowey to Liverpool with a cargo of china clay. *14.10.1910:* Register closed.

9. FOYLE 1894-1897 Iron

O.N. 63020 316g 168n 160.0 x 21.1 x 12.1 feet
C. 2-cyl. by Marshall, Osborne and Co., South Shields.

10.1872: Launched by Cole Brothers, Willington Quay-on-Tyne (Yard No. 17) for Michael McChrystal, Londonderry as FOYLE. *4.1.1873:* Completed. *1876:* Sold to James John Joyce, Londonderry. *1877:* Sold to Michael Murphy junior, Dublin. *11.1889:* Sold to Frederick P.W. Campbell and Co., Liverpool. *12.9.1894:* Acquired by Richard Hughes and Co., Liverpool. *19.8.1897:* Abandoned in a sinking condition about twenty miles south west of Bardsey whilst on a voyage from Garston to Fowey with a cargo of coal. The crew landed at Aberdaron in the ship's boat. *10.9.1897:* Register closed.

10. DAISY 1897-1903 Iron

O.N. 62649 933g 568n 217.8 x 29.5 x 16.5 feet
C. 2-cyl. by George Clark, Sunderland; 9 knots.
10.1893: Engines rebuilt by George T. Grey, South Shields.

10.4.1872: Launched by Short Brothers, Sunderland (Yard No. 49) for Edward J. Weatherley, Sunderland as EMERALD. *5.6.1872:* Completed. *1892:* Manager became Robert Weatherley. *19.5.1893:* Sold to James Donald and William G. Taylor, Glasgow. *10.1893:* Engine rebuilt. *19.11.1896:* Stranded off Lammerlaws, Burntisland whilst on a voyage from Bo'ness to Barcelona with a cargo of coal. Later salved. *3.12.1896:* Register closed. *1897:* Sold to Hutson and Son, Glasgow and repaired. *18.6.1897:* Re-registered in the ownership of Richard Hughes and Co., Liverpool. *7.7.1897:* Renamed DAISY. *26.2.1903:* Wrecked in Whitesand Bay whilst on a voyage from Dieppe to Penarth in ballast. *6.3.1903:* Register closed.

Pansy at Preston. *W.S.P.L. Cochrane collection*

11. PANSY/PINK ROSE (3) 1898-1920/1921-1941

O.N. 109433 555g 238n 175.0 x 26.3 x 11.6 feet
T. 3-cyl. by Muir and Houston Ltd., Glasgow; 9 knots.

7.6.1898: Completed by Grangemouth Dockyard Co., Grangemouth (Yard No. 191) for Richard Hughes and Co., Liverpool as PANSY. *23.12.1904:* Owner became Alexander Hutson, Liverpool. *21.7.1909:* Owners became Richard Hughes and Co., Liverpool. *11.3.1920:* Sold to Owen H. Donnelly, Dublin and Robert Leeson, Liverpool. *28.7.1921:* Re-acquired by Richard Hughes and Co., Liverpool. *20.4.1934:* Owners became Richard Hughes and Co. (Liverpool) Ltd. (Thomas J. Tierney, manager), Liverpool. *31.3.1937:* Renamed PINK ROSE. *4.5.1941:* Caught fire after being in collision with the Greek steamer GEORGIOS P (4,052/1903) ten miles south of the South Bishop Light whilst on a voyage from Swansea to Dublin with a cargo of coal. Taken in tow but later sank. *3.7.1941:* Register closed.

Pink Rose (3) was formerly **Pansy** but carried her new name for just four years. *W.S.P.L. collection*

12. NORTHCOTE/VIOLET 1898-1901 Iron

O.N. 69571 946g 473n 216.5 x 30.0 x 16.6 feet
C. 2-cyl. by George Clark, Sunderland.

16.4.1878: Launched by Thomas Turnbull and Son, Whitby (Yard No. 57) for John Holman and Sons, London as NORTHCOTE. *13.5.1878:* Completed. *8.1889:* Sold to Henry Lamont and Co., Glasgow. *13.10.1898:* Acquired by Richard Hughes and Co., Liverpool. *1900:* Renamed VIOLET. *23.10.1901:* Wrecked at Bremoe, Sundsvall, Gulf of Bothnia, Sweden whilst on a voyage from Liverpool to Gefle and Sundsvall with general cargo, iron and woodpulp.

13. LILY 1899-1903 Iron

O.N. 94364 1,214g 747n 242.0 x 33.0 x 16.5 feet
T. 3-cyl. by North Eastern Marine Engineering Co. Ltd., Wallsend-on-Tyne; 9½ knots.

13.1.1888: Launched by the Blyth Shipbuilding Co. Ltd., Blyth (Yard No. 55) for W. Lamplough and Co., London as GODMUNDING. *14.2.1888:* Completed for Thomas B. Williams (W. Lamplough and Co., managers), London. *3.1890:* Sold to John Cory and Sons, Cardiff. *29.8.1896:* Owners became the Godmunding Steamship Co. Ltd. (John Cory and Sons, managers), Cardiff. *1896:* Managers became John Cory and Sons Ltd. *14.5.1898:* Beached at Kilchattan Bay, virtually submerged, following a collision with the paddle steamer VICEROY (236/1875) about three miles north of the Cumbrae Light whilst on a voyage from Cadiz to Glasgow with a cargo of iron ore and empty wine casks. Her crew of 18 was rescued. *23.8.1898:* Register closed. *4.9.1899:* Re-registered in the ownership of Richard Hughes and Co., Liverpool as LILY. *4.1903:* Sold to Dampskibs Aktieselskab Oteren (Thv. B. Heisten, manager), Christiansand, Norway and renamed OTEREN. *1915:* Sold to Aktieselskab Grenmar (H. Haraldsen, manager), Skien, Norway and renamed GRENMAR. *1916:* Sold to Det Strangerske Rederi Aktieselskab (Stranger and Co., managers), Christiania, Norway and renamed HOVDE. *15.10.1917:* Torpedoed and sunk by the German submarine UC 48 in the English Channel eleven miles north west of the Ile de Batz whilst on a voyage from Nantes to Skien with a cargo of cyanide.

Primrose (2) *W.S.P.L. Cochrane collection*

Mersey *W.S.P.L.*

BLUSH ROSE

The Dorelian as a Harrison lin

14. PRIMROSE (2) 1910-1920/1921-1941

O.N. 128044 611g 256n 175.0 x 28.1 x 10.5 feet
T. 3-cyl. by Ross and Duncan, Govan; 10 knots.

31.3.1910: Launched by John Fullerton and Co., Paisley (Yard No. 215) for Richard Hughes and Co., Liverpool as PRIMROSE. *26.4.1910:* Completed. *11.3.1920:* Sold to Owen H. Donnelly, Dublin and Robert Leeson, Liverpool. *28.7.1921:* Re-acquired by Richard Hughes and Co., Liverpool. *20.4.1934:* Owners became Richard Hughes and Co. (Liverpool) Ltd. (Thomas J. Tierney, manager), Liverpool. *30.1.1941:* Capsized and sank when her cargo of maize shifted when she was four miles south east of the Daunt Light Vessel whilst on a voyage from Dublin to Cork. *12.2.1941:* Register closed.

15. MERSEY/MERSEY ROSE 1910-1920/1921-1930

O.N. 99363 536g 226n 173.0 x 25.2 x 11.9 feet
T. 3-cyl. by Harvey and Co. Ltd., Hayle; 10½ knots.

30.11.1891: Launched by Harvey and Co. Ltd., Hayle (Yard No. 153) for Rogers and Bright, Liverpool as MERSEY. *19.1.1892:* Completed. *23.11.1898:* Owners became the Liverpool Steamship Mersey Ltd. (Rogers and Bright, managers), Liverpool. *23.9.1910:* Acquired by Richard Hughes and Co., Liverpool. *11.3.1920:* Sold to Owen H. Donnelly, Dublin and Robert Leeson, Liverpool. *28.7.1921:* Re-acquired by Richard Hughes and Co., Liverpool. *18.7.1930:* Renamed MERSEY ROSE. *12.10.1930:* Sunk in collision with the steamer GLENEDEN (4,761/1909) in the English Channel in position 50.00 N by 02.04 W whilst on a voyage from Goole to Brest with a cargo of coal. Her crew were picked up by the GLENEDEN. *8.5.1931:* Register closed.

16. WHITE ROSE (2) 1911

O.N. 131332 610g 256n 175.0 x 28.1 x 10.5 feet
T. 3-cyl. by Ross and Duncan, Govan; 10 knots.

16.3.1911: Launched by John Fullerton and Co., Paisley (Yard No. 218) for Richard Hughes and Co., Liverpool as WHITE ROSE. *6.4.1911:* Completed. *11.12.1911:* Left La Pallice for Liverpool with a cargo of wheat and disappeared. *17.1.1912:* Posted missing. *26.1.1912:* Register closed.

17. BLUSH ROSE 1913-1920/1921-1945

O.N. 135482 645g 281n 178.4 x 28.1 x 11.1 feet
T. 3-cyl. by Earle's Shipbuilding and Engineering Co.Ltd., Hull; 10¾ knots.

15.7.1913: Completed by N.V. Scheepsbouwwerf 'de Merwede' v/h van Vliet en Co, Hardinxveld, Holland (Yard No. 104) for Richard Hughes and Co., Liverpool as BLUSH ROSE. *11.3.1920:* Sold to Owen H. Donnelly, Dublin and Robert Leeson, Liverpool. *28.7.1921:* Re-acquired by Richard Hughes and Co., Liverpool. *20.4.1934:* Owners became Richard Hughes and Co. (Liverpool) Ltd. (Thomas J. Tierney, manager), Liverpool. *6.2.1942:* Beached in Dale Roads, Milford Haven following an air attack three miles south of St. Ann's Head whilst on a voyage from Dublin to Swansea in ballast. Towed to Milford Haven and later repaired and returned to service. *2.8.1945:* Sunk in collision with the steamer GLAUCUS (7,586/1921) twenty miles off Holyhead in position 53.26.30 N by 05.05 W whilst on a voyage from Dublin to Preston in ballast. *9.8.1945:* Register closed.

Blush Rose *A. Duncan*

18. GUELDER ROSE 1913-1920/1921-1941

O.N. 135512 700g 302n 180.0 x 28.1 x 12.2 feet
T. 3-cyl. by Earle's Shipbuilding and Engineering Co. Ltd., Hull.

31.11.1913: Completed by N.V. Scheepsbouwwerf 'de Merwede' v/h van Vliet en Co., Hardinxveld, Holland (Yard No. 117) for Richard Hughes and Co., Liverpool as GUELDER ROSE. *11.3.1920:* Sold to Owen H. Donnelly and Robert Leeson, Liverpool. *28.7.1921:* Re-acquired by Richard Hughes and Co., Liverpool. *20.4.1934:* Owners became Richard Hughes and Co. (Liverpool) Ltd. (Thomas J. Tierney, manager), Liverpool. *25.2.1941:* Sold to Williamstown Shipping Co. Ltd. (Comben Longstaffe and Co. Ltd., managers), London. *8.5.1942:* Sold to N.W. Spratt Ltd. (N.W. Spratt, manager), Liverpool. *9.3.1943:* Sold to Fredericke R. Browne, London. *12.5.1947:* Renamed RIVERSIDER. *9.11.1951:* Sold to Connell and Grace Ltd., Newcastle-upon-Tyne. *4.12.1951:* Renamed AKENSIDE. *28.9.1954:* Handed over to G. and W. Brunton, Grangemouth for breaking up. *25.6.1956:* Register closed.

Guelder Rose *W.S.P.L. Cochrane collection*

19. WHITE ROSE (3) 1913-1920

O.N. 135517 632g 269n 174.7 x 28.1 x 10.4 feet
T. 3-cyl. by Ross and Duncan, Govan; 10 knots.

14.10.1913: Launched by John Fullerton and Co., Paisley (Yard No. 227) for Richard Hughes and Co., Liverpool as WHITE ROSE. *14.11.1913:* Completed. *11.3.1920:* Sold to Owen H. Donnelly, Dublin and Robert Leeson, Liverpool. *20.3.1920:* Sank after being run down by the steamer FANTEE (5,663/1920) in fog off Trevose Head whilst on a voyage from Boulogne to Llanelli with general cargo. *10.8.1920:* Register closed.

20. FRENCH ROSE 1915-1917

O.N. 137455 465g 223n 153.0 x 25.1 x 10.9 feet
T. 3-cyl. by William Beardmore and Co. Ltd., Coatbridge, Glasgow; 9 knots.

28.5.1915: Completed by N.V. Scheepsbouwwerf 'de Merwede' v/h van Vliet en Co., Hardinxveld, Holland (Yard No. 118) for Richard Hughes and Co., Liverpool as FRENCH ROSE. *24.11.1917:* Mined and sunk six miles south south west of the Shipwash Light Vessel whilst on a voyage from Tréport to Goole in ballast. *12.12.1917:* Register closed.

21. JOFFRE ROSE 1915-1920/1921-1947

O.N. 137458 715g 344n 180.3 x 28.2 x 12.4 feet
T. 3-cyl. by MacColl and Pollock Ltd., South Shields; $9\frac{3}{4}$ knots.

15.6.1915: Completed by Charles Rennoldson and Co., South Shields (Yard No. 169) for Richard Hughes and Co., Liverpool as JOFFRE ROSE. *11.3.1920:* Sold to Owen H. Donnelly, Dublin and Robert Leeson, Liverpool. *28.7.1921:* Re-acquired by Richard Hughes and Co., Liverpool. *20.4.1934:* Owners became Richard Hughes and Co. (Liverpool) Ltd. (Thomas J. Tierney, manager), Liverpool. *16.5.1941:* Beached in Dale Roads, Milford Haven following an air attack off St. David's Head whilst on a voyage from Dublin to Newport in ballast. Later refloated, repaired and returned to service. *14.10.1947:* Sold to the Holderness Steamship Co. Ltd., Hull and renamed HOLDERNENE. *1952:* Sold to Tyson, Edgar Shipping Ltd., London and renamed THEMSLEIGH. *28.10.1955:* Arrived at Dunston-on-Tyne for demolition by Clayton and Davie Ltd.

Joffre Rose *W.S.P.L. Cochrane collection*

22. DUNMORE 1916-1920/1921-1927

O.N. 113926 237g 90n 120.3 x 22.1 x 8.8 feet
C. 2-cyl. by Bow, McLachlan and Co. Ltd., Paisley; 10 knots.

12.12.1900: Launched by J. McArthur and Co., Paisley (Yard No. 138) for John G. Frew, Glasgow as DUNMORE. *27.12.1900:* Completed. *5.2.1901:* Owners became the Home Trade Steam Carrying Co. Ltd. (John G. Frew and Co., managers), Glasgow. *22.2.1914:* Stranded in Ballygally Bay, County Antrim whilst on a voyage from Coleraine to Glasgow in ballast. *4.1914:* Refloated and taken to Belfast. *24.4.1914:* Register closed. Later repaired. *27.11.1915:* Re-registered in the ownership of the Goole Shipbuilding and Repairing Co. Ltd., Goole. *7.7.1916:* Acquired by Richard Hughes and Co., Liverpool. *11.3.1920:* Sold to Owen H. Donnelly, Dublin and Robert Leeson, Liverpool. *28.7.1921:* Re-acquired by Richard Hughes and Co., Liverpool. *21.11.1927:* Sold to Henry Burden Junior and Co. Ltd., Poole. *10.9.1931:* Sold to Jack Brothers, Glasgow and later renamed BURNSIDE. *13.3.1933:* Caught fire and burnt out at Loch Maddy, North Uist whilst on a voyage from Glasgow to Loch Maddy with general cargo which included petrol, paraffin, coal, wood and lime. It is thought that she took the ground and sprang a leak, and that the water ignited the lime in her cargo. *14.3.1933:* Sank. *15.4.1933:* Register closed.

Jellicoe Rose *W.S.P.L.*

23. JELLICOE ROSE 1920-1956

O.N. 143642 1,118g 609n 220.2 x 34.2 x 13.1 feet
T. 3-cyl. by Aitchison, Blair Ltd., Glasgow.

20.4.1920: Launched by John Fullerton and Co., Paisley (Yard No. 265) for Richard Hughes and Co., Liverpool as JELLICOE ROSE. *6.1920:* Completed. *20.4.1934:* Owners became Richard Hughes and Co. (Liverpool) Ltd. (Thomas J. Tierney, manager), Liverpool. *2.2.1940:* Stranded on the north side of Roker Pier, Sunderland whilst on a voyage from Portsmouth to Sunderland in ballast. *19.2.1940:* Refloated and beached. *23.2.1940:* Refloated once again and taken to Sunderland. Although declared a constructive total loss she was repaired and returned to service. *2.7.1946:* Damaged in collision in fog with the United States steamer WILLIAM BREWSTER (7,176/1942) thirty miles east by north of Start Point in position 50.20 N by 02.50 E whilst on a voyage from Newport to Southampton with a cargo of coal. Put into Portland for repairs. *8.5.1952:* Owners became Hughes Holden Shipping Ltd., Swansea. *10.1956:* Sold to Recumar S.A., Panama (Ramon de los Rios Ruiz, Tangier) and renamed CONCHITA. *11.1962:* Laid up at Ceuta, Spain and later sold at auction. *20.4.1964:* Arrived at Cadiz for breaking up.

Haig Rose *A. Duncan*

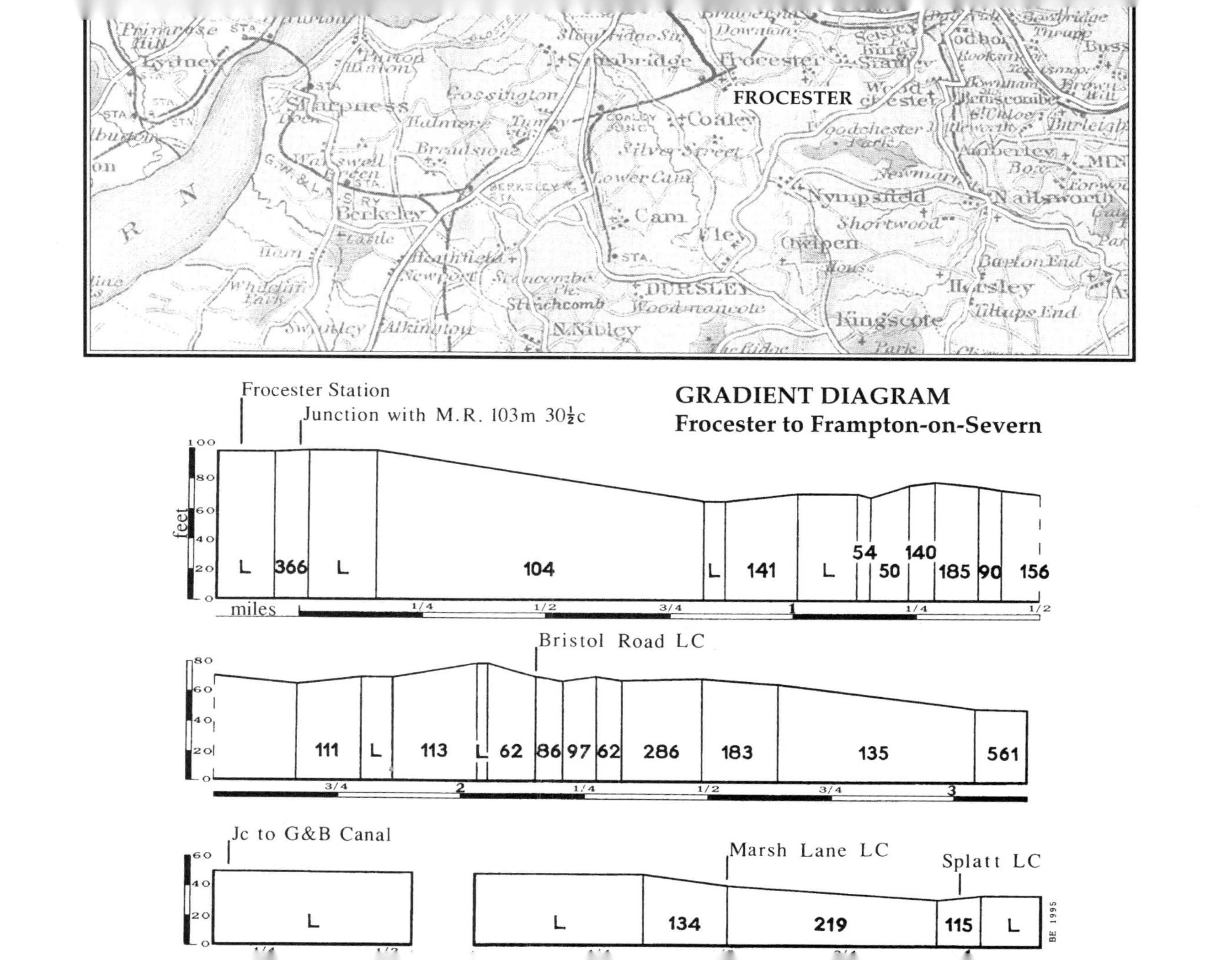
FROCESTER
Frocester
Coaley
Cam
Dursley
Berkeley
Sharpness
Lydney
Nympsfield
Kingscote
Nailsworth
Horsley
GRADIENT DIAGRAM
Frocester to Frampton-on-Severn
Frocester Station
Junction with M.R. 103m 30½c
feet
miles
L
366
L
104
L
141
L
54
50
140
185
90
156
Bristol Road LC
111
L
113
L
62
86
97
62
286
183
135
561
Jc to G&B Canal
L
L
134
Marsh Lane LC
219
Splatt LC
115
L
BE 1995

Often, the longest delay on a barge's voyage from the Humber to or through Goole was the wait in the Ouse to enter the docks. Shipping took precedence and here, in the 1950s, the tanker barge *Middledale H* and dry cargo barge *Hunts Roger* are amongst craft waiting as Hughes Holden Shipping's collier *s.s. Foch Rose* passes. *MT*

24. BEATTY ROSE 1920-1927

O.N. 143668 1,119g 609n 220.2 x 34.2 x 13.1 feet
T. 3-cyl. by William Beardmore and Co. Ltd., Coatbridge, Glasgow; $10^{1}/_{2}$ knots.

2.9.1920: Completed by John Fullerton and Co., Paisley (Yard No. 266) for Richard Hughes and Co., Liverpool as BEATTY ROSE. *1.4.1927:* Foundered in the English Channel seventeen miles north west of the Casquets whilst on a voyage from Swansea to Rouen with a cargo of coal. *25.5.1927:* Register closed.

25. HAIG ROSE 1920-1940

O.N. 143705 1,117g 608n 220.2 x 34.2 x 13.1 feet
T. 3-cyl. by William Beardmore and Co. Ltd., Coatbridge, Glasgow; $10^{1}/_{2}$ knots.

27.10.1920: Launched by John Fullerton and Co., Paisley (Yard No. 267) for Richard Hughes and Co., Liverpool as HAIG ROSE. *28.12.1920:* Completed. *20.4.1934:* Owners became Richard Hughes and Co. (Liverpool) Ltd. (Thomas J. Tierney, manager), Liverpool. *5.11.1940:* Left Barry for Plymouth with a cargo of coal and disappeared. *11.12.1940:* Posted missing. *12.2.1940:* Register closed.

Wild Rose (2) *John Clarkson*

26. WILD ROSE (2) 1922-1951

O.N. 145179 873g 431n 190.0 x 30.1 x 12.5 feet
T. 3-cyl. by the Lytham Shipbuilding and Engineering Co. Ltd., Lytham.

2.1921: Launched by the Hansen Shipbuilding and Ship Repairing Co. Ltd., Bideford (Yard No. 2) for the Hansen Shipping Co. Ltd. (Hansen Brothers Ltd., managers), Cardiff as MONKSTONE. *4.1921:* Completed. *1922:* Acquired by Richard Hughes and Co., Liverpool and renamed WILD ROSE. *20.4.1934:* Owners became Richard Hughes and Co. (Liverpool) Ltd. (Thomas J. Tierney, manager), Liverpool. *2.4.1941:* Beached near Rosslare Harbour following an air attack twelve miles south east of the Tuskar Rock whilst on a voyage from Dublin to Cardiff. Refloated, towed to Dublin and later repaired and returned to sevice. *1951:* Sold to George W. Grace and Co. Ltd., London and renamed SUSSEX ELM. *1953:* Sold to the Holderness Steamship Co. Ltd., Hull and renamed HOLDERNENE. *19.2.1958:* Arrived at Dublin for breaking up by the Hammond Lane Foundry Ltd.

27. FOCH ROSE 1922-1956

O.N. 145960 1,135g 616n 220.2 x 34.2 x 13.2 feet
T. 3-cyl. by Ross and Duncan, Govan.

30.5.1922: Launched by John Fullerton and Co., Paisley (Yard No. 271) for Richard Hughes and Co., Liverpool as FOCH ROSE. *7.1922:* Completed. *20.4.1934:* Owner became Richard Hughes and Co. (Liverpool) Ltd. (Thomas J. Tierney, manager), Liverpool. *8.5.1952:* Owner became Hughes Holden Shipping Ltd., Swansea. *12.1956:* Arrived at Blyth for breaking up by Hughes Bolckow Shipbreaking Co. Ltd.

Foch Rose *Fotoflite incorporating Skyfotos*

28. STURDEE ROSE 1922-1945

O.N. 145983 873g 443n 190.0 x 30.1 x 12.5 feet
T. 3-cyl. by the Lytham Shipbuilding and Engineering Co. Ltd., Lytham; $9\frac{3}{4}$ knots.

21.10.1922: Completed by the Hansen Shipbuilding and Repairing Co. Ltd., Bideford (Yard No. 4) for Richard Hughes and Co., Liverpool as STURDEE ROSE. *20.4.1934:* Owners became Richard Hughes and Co. (Liverpool) Ltd. (Thomas J. Tierney, manager), Liverpool. *16.11.1945:* Capsized and sank off Trevose Head whilst on a voyage from Garston to Plymouth with a cargo of coal. Eight of her crew of twelve were lost; the survivors being picked up eight days later by the steamer TECUMSEH PARK (7,163/1943). *18.12.1945:* Register closed.

29. DORRIEN ROSE 1922-1951

O.N. 145985 1,034g 557n 210.4 x 33.2 x 12.9 feet
T. 3-cyl. by Ross and Duncan, Govan.

21.9.1922: Launched by John Fullerton and Co., Paisley (Yard No. 270) for Richard Hughes and Co., Liverpool as DORRIEN ROSE. *11.1922:* Completed. *20.4.1934:* Owners became Richard Hughes and Co. (Liverpool) Ltd. (Thomas J. Tierney, manager), Liverpool. *7.1951:* Sold to the Fairwood Shipping and Trading Co. Ltd., Swansea and renamed FAIRWOOD ELM. *1956:* Sold to the Glynwood Navigation Co. Ltd., Hull and renamed CUPHOLDER. *1958:* Sold to the Holderness Steamship Co. Ltd., Hull and renamed HOLDERNORE. *14.3.1959:* Arrived at Dublin for breaking up by Hammond Lane Foundry Ltd.

Sturdee Rose *John Clarkson*

Dorrien Rose *S.C. Heal*

Hayle owed her longevity to spending her last years as a coal hulk in Cornwall.
E. N. Taylor

30. HAYLE 1923-1937

O.N. 96562 423g 186n 149.0 x 24.1 x 10.1 feet
1901: 475g 207n 183.2 x 24.1 x 10.1 feet
T. 3-cyl. by Harvey and Co. Ltd., Hayle; 10 knots.

20.3.1893: Launched by Harvey and Co. Ltd., Hayle (Yard No. 156) for Harvey and Co. Ltd., Hayle as HAYLE. *1.8.1893:* Completed. *1901:* Lengthened. *20.1.1923:* Acquired by Richard Hughes and Co., Liverpool. *20.4.1934:* Owners became Richard Hughes and Co. (Liverpool) Ltd. (Thomas J. Tierney, manager), Liverpool. Later used as a coal hulk. *28.4.1937:* Sold to T.W. Ward Ltd. for breaking up at Briton Ferry. *24.9.1937:* Register closed.

Hayle: note the unusual cast nameplate. *John Clarkson*

31. LOUIE ROSE 1924-1936

O.N. 147265 1,596g 955n 250.5 x 37.1 x 16.4 feet
T. 3-cyl. by Ross and Duncan, Govan; $10\frac{1}{2}$ knots.

23.4.1924: Launched by John Fullerton and Co., Paisley (Yard No. 274) for Richard Hughes and Co., Liverpool as LOUIE ROSE. *7.1924:* Completed. *20.4.1934:* Owners became Richard Hughes and Co. (Liverpool) Ltd. (Thomas J. Tierney, manager), Liverpool. *3.1936:* Sold to Guido Montefiore and Victor d'Anchald (Guido Montefiore, manager), Tunis, Tunisia, renamed SAINTE BERNADETTE and converted to a wine tanker. *1941:* Owners became the Société Tunisienne d'Armement et d'Affrètements, Tunis. *1955:* Manager became Panagiotis G. Cottaropoulos, Marseilles, France. *1955:* Sold to Luigi Amico fu Michele, Genoa, Italy. *1.4.1960:* Demolition commenced by Bitici Metalli at Genoa.

Louie Rose *A. Duncan*

32. GRONANT ROSE 1924-1929

O.N. 147286 1,110g 639n 220.5 x 34.2 x 13.2 feet
T. 3-cyl. by Bow, McLachlan and Co. Ltd., Paisley; 10 knots.

16.9.1924: Launched by John Fullerton and Co., Paisley (Yard No. 272) for Richard Hughes and Co., Liverpool as GRONANT ROSE. *16.10.1924:* Completed. *27.9.1929:* Foundered off Pierres Vertes, south of Ushant whilst on a voyage from Cardiff to Brest with a cargo of coal. *30.10.1929:* Register closed.

Gronant Rose *John Clarkson*

33. FULLERTON ROSE 1925-1936

O.N. 147308 1,594g 943n 250.3 x 37.1 x 16.4 feet
T. 3-cyl. by Ross and Duncan, Govan.

24.2.1925: Launched by John Fullerton and Co., Paisley (Yard No. 275) for Richard Hughes and Co., Liverpool as FULLERTON ROSE. *22.4.1925:* Completed. *20.4.1934:* Owner became Richard Hughes and Co. (Liverpool) Ltd. (Thomas J. Tierney, manager), Liverpool. *21.12.1936:* Sold to the Bramhall Steamship Co. Ltd. (Angel, Dalling and Co. Ltd., managers), Cardiff. *29.1.1937:* Renamed BRAMDEN. *18.12.1937:* Owners became Angel, Son and Co. Ltd., Cardiff. *16.9.1939:* Sunk by a British-laid mine south east of Harwich in position 51.22 N by 02.31 E whilst on a voyage from Dunkirk to Blyth in ballast. Three of her crew were lost. *13.12.1939:* Register closed.

Fullerton Rose *University of Glasgow DC101/1166*

Cornish Rose was built for a short-lived company based in Falmouth along with **Fowey Rose**. *E.N. Taylor*

34. CORNISH ROSE 1928-1942

O.N. 137210 471g 189n 141.9 x 25.1 x 11.6 feet.
C. 2-cyl. by MacColl and Pollock Ltd., Sunderland; 9 knots.

17.7.1920: Launched by I.J. Abdela and Mitchell Ltd., Queensferry (Yard No. 454) for Cornish Traders Ltd. (Arthur W. Chard, manager), Falmouth as CORNISH TRADER. *15.11.1920:* Completed. *16.11.1928:* Renamed CORNISH ROSE. *20.11.1928:* Acquired by Richard Hughes and Co., Liverpool. *20.4.1934:* Owners became Richard Hughes and Co. (Liverpool) Ltd. (Thomas J. Tierney, manager), Liverpool. *23.11.1942:* Sold to Ohlson and Co. Ltd. (Sir Eric Ohlson, manager), Hull. *11.9.1946:* Sold to J.P. Katsoulakos (E. Katsoulakos, manager), Piraeus, Greece and renamed TAKIS K. *17.11.1950:* Foundered off the Cyclades Islands in position 36.49 N by 25.07 E whilst on a voyage from Heraklion to Piraeus with a cargo of gypsum.

Fowey Rose at the port whose name she carried.
Roy Griffin collection

35. FOWEY ROSE 1928-1941

O.N. 146387 470g 183n 142.1 x 25.0 x 11.6 feet
C. 2-cyl. by I.J. Abdela and Mitchell Ltd., Brimscombe, Gloucestershire; 9 knots.

13.9.1923: Launched by I.J. Abdela and Mitchell Ltd., Queensferry (Yard No. 463) for Cornish Traders Ltd. (Arthur W. Chard, manager), Falmouth as CORNISH MERCHANT. *23.11.1923:* Completed. *19.11.1928:* Renamed FOWEY ROSE. *20.11.1928:* Acquired by Richard Hughes and Co., Liverpool. *20.4.1934:* Owners became Richard Hughes and Co. (Liverpool) Ltd. (Thomas J. Tierney, manager), Liverpool. *5.7.1941:* Sunk by air attack off the North Bishop, north west of St. David's Head, in position 51.51 N by 05.28 W whilst on a voyage from Penmaenmawr to Swansea with a cargo of stone. Eight of her crew of eleven were lost. *9.7.1941:* Register closed.

Fowey Rose *W.S.P.L.*

Welsh Rose *John Clarkson*

36. WELSH ROSE 1929-1946

O.N. 144860 581g 252n 175.2 x 27.0 x 10.8 feet
T. 3-cyl. by William Beardmore and Co. Ltd., Coatbridge, Glasgow.

23.9.1922: Launched by the Goole Shipbuilding and Repairing Co. Ltd., Goole (Yard No. 241) for Thomas Rose, Sunderland as BROOKSIDE. *10.1922:* Completed. *1929:* Acquired by Richard Hughes and Co., Liverpool and renamed WELSH ROSE. *20.4.1934:* Owners became Richard Hughes and Co. (Liverpool) Ltd. (Thomas J. Tierney, manager), Liverpool. *1946:* Sold to George W. Grace and Co. Ltd., London and renamed SUSSEX BIRCH. *7.1953:* Sold to the Holderness Steamship Co. Ltd., Hull and renamed HOLDERNILE. *15.11.1955:* Arrived at Gateshead for breaking up by C.W. Dorkin and Co.

Dorothy Rose still with her wartime rafts. *Welsh Industrial and Maritime Museum 2605/2639*

37. DOROTHY ROSE 1929-1946

O.N. 161129 1,600g 946n 250.0 x 37.2 x 16.4 feet
T. 3-cyl. by McKie and Baxter Ltd., Govan; 10¾ knots.

31.10.1929: Launched by D. and W. Henderson Ltd., Meadowside, Glasgow (Yard No. 880A) for Richard Hughes and Co., Liverpool as DOROTHY ROSE. *11.1929:* Completed. *20.4.1934:* Owners became Richard Hughes and Co. (Liverpool) Ltd. (Thomas J. Tierney, manager), Liverpool. *1946:* Sold to the Tyne-Tees Steam Shipping Co. Ltd., Newcastle-upon-Tyne and renamed BELGIAN COAST. *24.10.1957:* Breaking up began by L. Engelen, Boom, Belgium.

Dorothy Rose *H.D. Wallace-Jones collection*

38. DUDLEY ROSE 1929-1941

O.N. 161136 1,600g 946n 250.0 x 37.2 x 16.4 feet
T. 3-cyl. by McKie and Baxter Ltd., Govan; 10¾ knots.

4.12.1929: Launched by D. and W. Henderson and Co. Ltd., Meadowside, Glasgow (Yard No. 881M) for Richard Hughes and Co., Liverpool as DUDLEY ROSE. *19.12.1929:* Completed. *20.4.1934:* Owners became Richard Hughes and Co. (Liverpool) Ltd. (Thomas J. Tierney, manager), Liverpool. *9.4.1941:* Sunk by air attack four miles and 150° from Berry Head whilst on a voyage from Plymouth and Dartmouth to Portsmouth with a cargo of coal. Her crew of sixteen was saved. *16.6.1941:* Register closed.

Dudley Rose *Marius Bar*

Pink Rose (2) *John Clarkson*

39. PINK ROSE (2) 1930-1936

O.N. 161148 739g 343n 180.8 x 28.1 x 12.6 feet
T. 3-cyl. by Earle's Shipbuilding and Engineering Co.Ltd., Hull; $10^{1}/_{2}$ knots.

23.1.1930: Launched by N.V. Scheepsbouwwerf 'de Merwede' v/h van Vliet en Co., Hardinxveld, Holland (Yard No. 207) for Richard Hughes and Co., Liverpool as PINK ROSE. *19.3.1930:* Completed. *20.4.1934:* Owners became Richard Hughes and Co. (Liverpool) Ltd. (Thomas J. Tierney, manager), Liverpool. *10.3.1936:* Sank following a collision with the steamer GEORGE FRUSHER (662/1901) about eleven miles south of the Tyne whilst on a voyage from the Tyne to Shoreham with a cargo of coal. *28.4.1936:* Register closed.

40. PRESTATYN ROSE 1930-1953

O.N. 161155 1,151g 670n 220.0 x 34.1 x 14.2 feet
T. 3-cyl. by D. and W. Henderson and Co. Ltd., Meadowside, Glasgow.

28.4.1930: Launched by D. and W. Henderson and Co. Ltd., Meadowside, Glasgow (Yard No. 900M) for Richard Hughes and Co., Liverpool as PRESTATYN ROSE. *5.1930:* Completed. *20.4.1934:* Owners became Richard Hughes and Co. (Liverpool) Ltd. (Thomas J. Tierney, manager), Liverpool. *19.9.1941:* Arrived at Harwich in tow following an air attack in position 51.52.25 N by 01.35.45 E whilst on passage to the Tyne in ballast. *25.9.1941:* Beached. Later repaired and returned to service. *8.5.1952:* Owners became Hughes Holden Shipping Ltd., Swansea. *1953:* Sold to Onesimus Dorey, Guernsey and renamed LANCRESSE. *2.3.1962:* Arrived at Bruges for breaking up by Van Heyghen Frères.

Prestatyn Rose *Fotoflite incorporating Skyfotos*

41. MOSS ROSE (2) 1930-1957

O.N. 161157 739g 343n 180.0 x 28.1 x 12.6 feet
T. 3-cyl. by Earle's Shipbuilding and Engineering Co.Ltd., Hull.
About 1960: Oil engine 2S.C.S.A. 6-cyl. made in 1931 by Franco Tosi S.p.A., Taranto, Italy.

5.4.1930: Launched by N.V. Scheepsbouwwerf 'de Merwede' v/h van Vliet en Co., Hardinxveld, Holland (Yard No. 208) for Richard Hughes and Co., Liverpool as MOSS ROSE. *5.1930:* Completed. *20.4.1934:* Owners became Richard Hughes and Co. (Liverpool) Ltd. (Thomas J. Tierney, manager), Liverpool. *8.5.1952:* Owners became Hughes Holden Shipping Ltd., Swansea. *1957:* Sold to Kontos Brothers, Piraeus, Greece and renamed VIRGINIA K. *About 1960:* Re-engined. *1962:* Sold to Stavros Daifas and Co., Piraeus and renamed SOFIA III. *1964:* Sold to Dionysios N. Theodossis, Piraeus and renamed DIONYSIOS TH. *1968:* Sold to K.E. Papamarkakis and others, Piraeus and renamed OLKAS. *1971:* Sold to M. Koutrouba and S. Giannis, Piraeus and renamed SOTIRIA. *3.1973:* Spiliopolis Brothers began demolition at Perama.

Moss Rose (2) *Welsh Industrial and Maritime Museum 359/657*

Anglesea Rose *E.N. Taylor*

42. ANGLESEA ROSE 1930-1941

O.N. 161159 1,151g 670n 220.0 x 34.1 x 14.2 feet
T. 3-cyl. by D. and W. Henderson and Co. Ltd., Meadowside, Glasgow; $10\frac{3}{4}$ knots.

12.5.1930: Launched by D. and W. Henderson and Co. Ltd., Meadowside, Glasgow (Yard No. 901) for Richard Hughes and Co., Liverpool as ANGLESEA ROSE. *30.5.1930:* Completed. *20.4.1934:* Owners became Richard Hughes and Co. (Liverpool) Ltd. (Thomas J. Tierney, manager), Liverpool. *16.4.1941:* Sunk by air attack north of St. Ives in position 50.25 N by 05.35 W whilst on a voyage from Barry to Plymouth with a cargo of coal. Her crew of 13 was saved. *9.6.1941:* Register closed.

43. MAURICE ROSE 1930-1947

O.N. 162326 1,600g 946n 250.0 x 37.2 x 16.4 feet
T. 3-cyl. by D. and W. Henderson and Co. Ltd., Meadowside, Glasgow.

25.9.1930: Launched by D. and W. Henderson and Co. Ltd., Meadowside, Glasgow (Yard No. 906M) for Richard Hughes and Co., Liverpool as MAURICE ROSE. *10.1930:* Completed. *20.4.1934:* Owners became Richard Hughes and Co. (Liverpool) Ltd. (Thomas J. Tierney, manager), Liverpool. *1947:* Sold to the Tyne-Tees Steam Shipping Co. Ltd., Newcastle-upon-Tyne. *1947:* Owners became A. Coker and Co. Ltd., Liverpool and renamed BALTIC KING. *1947:* Owners became Queenship Navigation Co. Ltd., London and renamed RICHMOND QUEEN. *4.10.1957:* Arrived at Dunston-on-Tyne for breaking up by Clayton and Davie Ltd.

Maurice Rose *John Clarkson*

Dennis Rose *Frank Barr*

44. DENNIS ROSE 1930-1947

O.N. 162328 1,600g 946n 250.0 x 37.2 x 16.4 feet
T. 3-cyl. by D. and W. Henderson and Co. Ltd., Meadowside, Glasgow; 10 3/4 knots.

14.10.1930: Launched by D. and W. Henderson and Co. Ltd., Meadowside, Glasgow (Yard No. 907M) for Richard Hughes and Co. Ltd., Liverpool as DENNIS ROSE. *6.11.1930:* Completed. *20.4.1934:* Owners became Richard Hughes and Co. (Liverpool) Ltd. (Thomas J. Tierney, manager), Liverpool. *12.2.1947:* Sold to the Tyne-Tees Steam Shipping Co. Ltd., Newcastle-upon-Tyne. *23.4.1947:* Renamed VIRGINIAN COAST. *10.1953:* Sold to Aniceto Urain and Lucio Zatica, Bilbao, Spain, registered in Costa Rica and renamed JULIAN PRESA. *3.1.1958:* Arrived at Briton Ferry to be broken up by T.W. Ward Ltd.

Wallace Rose at Fowey. For a period in the 1930s Hughes' ships had their names painted on their hulls, probably reflecting their use in the East Coast coal trade where the practice was quite common. *A. Duncan*

45. WALLACE ROSE 1931-1954

O.N. 162336 632g 277n 175.3 x 27.1 x 11.1 feet
T. 3-cyl. by D. and W. Henderson and Co. Ltd., Meadowside, Glasgow.

1.1931: Completed by N.V. Scheepsbouwwerf 'de Merwede' v/h van Vliet en Co., Hardinxveld, Holland (Yard No. 213) for Richard Hughes and Co., Liverpool as WALLACE ROSE. *20.4.1934:* Owners became Richard Hughes and Co. (Liverpool) Ltd. (Thomas J. Tierney, manager), Liverpool. *8.5.1952:* Owners became Hughes Holden Shipping Ltd., Swansea. *26.1.1954:* Sunk off Erith in the River Thames after colliding with the Swedish motor vessel YVONNE (4,171/1945) whilst on a voyage from Caen to London with a cargo of slag. Later raised and beached, but declared a constructive total loss. *14.4.1954:* Arrived at Grays, Essex for breaking up by T.W. Ward Ltd. *17.6.1954:* Register closed.

Wallace Rose beached in the Thames after a collision in January 1954. *A. Duncan*

Amlwch Rose *H.A. Breton*

46. AMLWCH ROSE 1931-1940

O.N. 162345 632g 277n 175.3 x 27.1 x 11.1 feet
T. 3-cyl. by D. and W. Henderson and Co. Ltd., Meadowside, Glasgow; 9½ knots.

31.12.1930: Launched by Scheepsbouwwerf 'de Merwede' v/h van Vliet en Co., Hardinxveld, Holland (Yard No. 215) for Richard Hughes and Co., Liverpool as AMLWCH ROSE. *14.5.1931:* Completed. *20.4.1934:* Owners became Richard Hughes and Co. (Liverpool) Ltd. (Thomas J. Tierney, manager), Liverpool. *5.12.1940:* Left Partington for Dublin with a cargo of coal and disappeared. Bodies of her crew were later washed ashore at Prestatyn and Rhyl. *8.1.1941:* Posted missing. *12.2.1941:* Register closed.

Moelfre Rose *W.S.P.L.*

47. MOELFRE ROSE 1931-1958

O.N. 162402 631g 277n 175.4 x 27.1 x 11.1 feet
T. 3-cyl. by D. and W. Henderson and Co. Ltd., Meadowside, Glasgow

19.2.1931: Launched by Scheepsbouwwerf 'de Merwede' v/h van Vliet en Co., Hardinxveld, Holland (Yard No. 216) for Richard Hughes and Co., Liverpool as MOELFRE ROSE. *7.1931:* Completed. *20.4.1934:* Owners became Richard Hughes and Co. (Liverpool) Ltd. (Thomas J. Tierney, manager), Liverpool. *8.5.1952:* Owners became Hughes Holden Shipping Ltd., Swansea. *31.12.1958:* Arrived at Briton Ferry to be broken up by Steel Supplies (Western) Ltd. at Neath Abbey Wharf.

48. BRIER ROSE (2) 1952-1954

O.N. 168593 626g 318n 176.6 x 30.2 x 10.9 feet
Oil engine 4S.C.S.A. 6-cyl. by Mirrlees, Bickerton and Day Ltd., Stockport; 10 knots.

4.11.1952: Launched by John Lewis and Sons Ltd., Aberdeen (Yard No. 226) for Hughes Holden Shipping Ltd., Swansea as BRIER ROSE. *12.1952:* Completed. *1954:* Sold to Grand Union (Shipping) Ltd., London and renamed MARSWORTH. *1965:* Owners became the General Steam Navigation Co. Ltd., London. *1969:* Sold to Losinjska Plovidba, Rijeka, Yugoslavia and renamed KIMEN. *1969:* Owners became Brodogradiliste 'Cres', Cres, Yugoslavia. *1977:* Owners became Brodogradiliste 'Cres' Zanatsko Proizvadno i Usluzino Poduzece, Cres, Yugoslavia. *1991:* Owners became the Flanonia Shipping Co. Ltd. (Brodogradiliste 'Cres' Zanatsko, Proizvadno i Usluzino Poduzece, Cres, Croatia, managers) and placed under the flag of St. Vincent and the Grenadines. Still in existence (April 1997).

Brier Rose off the West Pier, Swansea: note the houseflag. *National Maritime Museum P51881*

49. RAMBLER ROSE 1954-1961

O.N. 168594 1,423g 248n 248.2 x 36.8 x 15.2 feet
Oil engine 2S.C.S.A. 3-cyl. by John Lewis and Sons Ltd., Aberdeen.

22.1.1954: Launched by John Lewis and Sons Ltd., Aberdeen (Yard No. 240) for Hughes Holden Shipping Ltd., Swansea as RAMBLER ROSE. *7.1954:* Completed. *10.1961:* Sold to Onesimus Dorey and Sons Ltd., Guernsey and renamed BELVEDERE. *4.1965:* Sold to the Britain Steamship Co. Ltd. (Watts, Watts and Co. Ltd., managers), London and renamed PUTNEY. *5.1965:* Managers became Comben Longstaffe and Co. Ltd., London and renamed BALMORAL QUEEN. *7.1968:* Sold to the Eskgarth Shipping Co. Ltd. (Comben Longstaffe and Co. Ltd., managers), London. *6.1969:* Sold to Elias S. Condos, Leandros Gouliotis, Dionissios Vassilatos and Nicolaos Hadjigeorgiou, Piraeus, Greece and renamed SOLON. *1971:* Sold to Dimsa Compania Maritima S.A. (George Seletopoulos), (International Chartering and Shipping Co. Ltd., managers), Piraeus, Greece and renamed MALENA. *1972:* Sold to Fortuna Shipping Co. Ltd., Limassol and later Famagusta, Cyprus (George Seletopoulos), (International Chartering and Shipping Co. Ltd., Piraeus, Greece, managers). *1975:* Managers became Andreas Katikas and P. Alogoskoufis Ltd., Piraeus. *1979:* Sold to Aristos Kaisis, Limassol, Cyprus and renamed KAISIS 1. *5.1982:* Broken up, reportedly at Limassol by Konitsa Navigation Co. Ltd.

Managed for the Ministry of Shipping

MOREA 1940

O.N. 167523 1,921g 1090n 289.0 x 41.7 x 17.5 feet
T. 3-cyl. by A.G. 'Neptun', Rostock, Germany; 10 knots.

6.10.1922: Launched by Schiffswerke und Dockbauwerft Flender A.G., Lubeck, Germany (Yard No. 62) for the Hamburg America Packetfahrt A.G. (Deutsche Levante-Linie, managers), Hamburg, Germany as MOREA. *20.12.1922:* Completed. *1.8.1935:* Owners became Deutsche Levante-Linie G.m.b.H. (Deutsche Levante-Linie A.G., managers), Hamburg. *12.2.1940:* Captured west of Iceland by the British destroyer H.M.S. HARDY. *23.5.1940:* Registered in the ownership of the Ministry of Shipping, London (Richard Hughes and Co. (Liverpool) Ltd., Liverpool, managers). Later that year owners became the Ministry of War Transport (Richard W. Jones and Co., Newport, managers) and renamed EMPIRE SEAMAN. *4.12.1940:* Register closed after she had foundered whilst on a voyage to Scapa Flow where she was to be used as a blockship.

Nomenclature

From the outset, Richard Hughes gave his ships rather pretty flower names. Names ending ROSE were soon adopted and became standard after 1911, although the early simplicity gave way to increasing sophistication, involving names of Allied military and naval commanders, family and place names. The only two ships built after Hughes relinquished power reverted to real ROSE names. The following list concentrates on the less well-known roses, and on the personal and place names.

AMLWCH ROSE — Amlwch is a small Anglesey seaport.

ANGLESEA ROSE — Hughes manned his ships largely from Anglesey or Ynys Môn as it should now be called. Note the archaic spelling.

BEATTY ROSE — Admiral of the Fleet Sir David Beatty (1871-1936) cultivated the image of the dashing buccaneer, which chimed in well with his command of the battlecruiser squadrons of the Grand Fleet. However, although he successfully fulfilled his role at Jutland by luring the German Home Fleet under the guns of the battleships of the Grand Fleet, the war revealed him to have limited imagination and a pedestrian approach to problems.

BLUSH ROSE — A general term to describe a rose which is a very delicate pink.

BRIER ROSE — Brier is a variant spelling of briar; the widespread local name for the dog rose, or wild rose. It could also refer to three other native British rose species, the Sweet Briar, the Lesser Sweet Briar or the Narrow-leaved Sweet Briar.

DENNIS ROSE — The ship was launched by Richard Hughes' grandson, Dennis Wallace-Jones.

DORRIEN ROSE — General Sir Horace Smith-Dorrien (1858-1930) was a veteran of the Zulu Wars and distinguished himself as a commander at some hard-fought rearguard actions which helped to stop the German offensive in 1914. But he quarrelled with Sir John French and was transferred to the campaign in German East Africa, until invalided home.

DOROTHY ROSE — Dorothy was Richard and Mary Hughes' daughter, named after Richard's sister.

DUDLEY ROSE — Dudley Wallace-Jones is a grandson of Richard Hughes.

FOCH ROSE — Marshal Ferdinand Foch (1851-1929) was an exuberant, optimistic military thinker and writer who was a proponent of the almost mystical *attaque à la outrance* school of military warfare. He had sufficient flexibility of mind, however, to allow his experience as an army commander during the opening stages of the war to modify his views so that his period as Commander-in-Chief of Allied Forces (1917-1919) was less frightful and more successful than it otherwise might have been.

FOWEY ROSE	Hughes' ships were frequent visitors to this china clay port, where the company had an office.
FRENCH ROSE	Sir John French, the First Earl Ypres (1852-1925), started in the Royal Navy before joining the cavalry and, after conspicuous service in the South African War, was Commander-in-Chief of the British Expeditionary Force in August 1914. He had an excitable personality of great courage and determination, but a mind of limited intelligence and with little strategic insight.
FULLERTON ROSE	John Fullerton and Co. of Paisley were one of the finest builders of steam coasters, providing no fewer than fourteen for Hughes' fleet.
GRONANT ROSE	Richard Hughes' birthplace, a village in Flintshire.
GUELDER ROSE	Not a rose at all, but the common name for our native *Viburnus opulus,* a shrub with maple-shaped leaves and bright red berries. The name comes from the Dutch, Geleersche roos - meaning the tree with rose-like blooms from the Dutch province of Guelders, the modern Gelderland.
HAIG ROSE	Sir Douglas Haig, First Earl Bermersyde (1861-1928), was a cavalry officer of courage and a shrewd political soldier with brains and a cool head. As Commander-in-Chief of British Forces 1915 to 1919, however, his belief in himself as 'the man of the hour' made him unself-critical, whilst highly critical of everyone else, and probably cost many men their lives.
JELLICOE ROSE	Admiral of the Fleet Sir John Rushworth Jellicoe (1859-1935) was a competent if self-effacing sailor, known in the Navy as 'Silent Jack', who lacked that final inspirational flair. He commanded the Grand Fleet at the Battle of Jutland where he handled his forces skillfully and was unlucky not to have achieved a more conspicuous victory.
JOFFRE ROSE	Marshal Joseph Joffre (1852-1931) was a skilful engineer-cum-soldier with a strong, phlegmatic personality and a mind that combined commonsense with flexibility. He required all these characteristics when improvising the response that led to the victory on the Marne in September 1914, which finally thwarted the Von Schlieffen Plan that aimed to give Germany victory over France in the first 40 days of the war.
LOUIE ROSE	Richard Hughes' wife was born Mary Jane Lewis, and his pet name for her was Louie.
MAURICE ROSE	Maurice Wallace-Jones is another of Hughes' grandsons.
MOELFRE ROSE	A village on the east coast of Anglesey.
MOSS ROSE	A moss rose is so named because of a curious mossy growth on the flower stalks and sepals. These fragrant roses, highly prized in Victorian times, originated as a sport from the cabbage rose in the sixteenth century.
PRESTATYN ROSE	A seaside town and latterly a holiday resort in North Wales, the nearest town to Hughes' birthplace of Gronant.
RAMBLER ROSE	Mostly hybrids, rambler roses display vigorous lax growth and bear small flowers in clusters.
STURDEE ROSE	Vice Admiral Sir Doveton Sturdee avenged the defeat of Sir Christopher Cradock of Coronel when he defeated Admiral Graff von Spee at the Battle of the Falkland Islands, December 1914. Drake-like, he insisted he had time to eat his breakfast before leaving Port Stanley harbour to do battle, and events proved him right.
WALLACE ROSE	Richard Hughes' daughter married Dr Wallace-Jones, who was later to become a director of the company.

HUME, SMITH AND CO.
Liverpool

James Hume and Harry Smith are important but little known figures in the history of coastal shipowning in Liverpool. They were promoters and managers of one of the first Liverpool fleets of bulk carrying steam coasters, acquiring their first steamers at the same time as the Macks. As so often with pioneers, however, their career in shipping was short.

Hume and Smith's rise to prominence was meteoric: the companies they promoted took delivery of eight new steamers in less than twelve months. No less than five of these were delivered in the latter half of 1882 alone, with two arriving on one day in October. This build-up of the fleet coincided with a boom in shipping in the early 1880s, a boom which encouraged the adoption of steam in the West Coast bulk trades. Before 1882 few bulk carrying steamers were owned in Irish Sea ports, although they were now numerous in the East Coast coal trade.

The choice of builders was wide, and although Murdoch and Murray of Port Glasgow built three, one particularly obscure yard also featured: H. Tipping and Co. of Portsmouth. Yards seem to have been given a fairly free hand, and although most of the steamers were in the range 140 to 155 feet in length, there was considerable variation in size and in material. Two of the ships were clearly not coasters: the ocean-going tramp SCAW FELL (2,192/1882) and the middle-sized RYDAL FELL which was probably intended for the Spanish ore trade. The BOW FELL was to be lost within two weeks of completion, disappearing with all twelve hands in the Irish Sea. The HART FELL – delivered some time after the other ships – may have been a replacement.

Ownership of all but one ship was vested in single-ship companies. The exception was the GRANGE FELL, in which Hume and Smith initially took 64 shares, selling them off to others including Robert and John Evans, her Liverpool builders, who took them in lieu of payment. The other ships were ordered by Hume and Smith, who raised the capital necessary to pay the builders by floating limited liability companies. The capital required - typically £8,400 for one of the coasters – was simply divided into £100 shares. This was a substantial sum in 1882, and Hume and Smith had to cast their net wide to sell the shares. Shareholding was well scattered, although a number of individuals other than Hume and Smith had small holdings in most of the companies. There is no pattern in the share ownership which might suggest which trades the ships were intended for, and subscribers included professional men and small businessmen from Merseyside, Cumberland, Scotland, London and the south of England. Perhaps the most notable investor was shipowner Thomas Ismay of White Star fame.

The principals were based in Liverpool, with offices in Oriel Chambers, Water Street. However, Hume, Smith and Co. also had an office in Workington and the business had a decidedly Cumbrian feel to it. The telegraphic address was HEMATITE, Liverpool, suggesting a link with the West Cumberland iron ore trade. The one common factor about the ships was their names, taken from hills and mountains of the Lake District, and several were mortgaged to banks in Whitehaven. All this suggests that the ships were ordered partly to trade with coal and ore to Cumberland iron and steel works and carry away their products.

Hume, Smith's tenure as managers was short. In April and May 1886 their management was terminated, and in their place George Nelson and Sons became managers of three of the coasters with the two larger ships going to Goodyear and to Gracie, Beazley. The split involved legal proceedings, and it may be that the small shareholders in the companies formed an alliance to oust founders Hume and Smith. The companies' articles of association allowed them to be removed as managers on a simple majority vote. The shipping boom of the early 1880s was short-lived and as it ended steamships with their high capital costs became uneconomic in the bulk trades compared to sail. The blame for the lack of profits would be laid at the feet of Hume and Smith, who had no doubt made extravagant promises in their prospectuses in order to attract the large amounts of capital needed for their steamship-owning ventures.

The GRANGE FELL and SHAP FELL were sold in 1886, but the remaining five ships carried on under the same owning companies and their new managers. The fortunes of the three coasters did not improve, however; and in 1894 the CONISTON FELL, HART FELL and WANS FELL were sold by their mortgagees, who had repossessed them, and the owning companies were wound up. The larger vessels fared slightly better, the SCAW FELL being sold in 1895 and the RYDAL FELL lasting until 1899.

Hume, Smith and the shareholders of these companies paid the price for being pioneers. Other Liverpool owners, including the Mack family and Richard Hughes, were to benefit from the use of steam in the Irish Sea bulk trades which Hume, Smith and Co. and their investors helped to develop.

Fleet list

1. GRANGE FELL 1881-1886 Iron

O.N.84101 245g 143n 120.5 x 22.0 x 10.1 feet
C.2-cyl. by David Rollo and Sons, Liverpool.

2.4.1881: Launched by R. and J. Evans, Liverpool (Yard No. 99) for Hume, Smith and Co., Liverpool as GRANGE FELL. *9.5.1881:* Completed. *1886:* Sold to the Steamship Grange Fell Co. Ltd. (J. J. Mack and Sons, managers), Liverpool. *7.12.1886:* Left Fowey for Liverpool with a cargo of china clay and disappeared. *7.2.1887:* Register closed.

2. RYDAL FELL 1882-1886 Iron

O.N. 84190 601g 384n 180.2 x 26.2 x 14.2 feet
C. 2-cyl. by Dunsmuir and Jackson, Govan.

17.12.1881: Launched by Murdoch and Murray, Port Glasgow (Yard No. 59) for the Rydal Fell Steam Ship Co. Ltd. (Hume, Smith and Co., managers), Liverpool as RYDAL FELL. *1.2.1882:* Completed. *4.5.1886:* Manager became James H. Goodyear, Liverpool. *7.1899:* Sold to Arcangelo Fragalà e Fratelli, Riposto, Sicily, Italy and renamed RIPOSTO. *1909:* Sold to Societa Anonima di Navigazione La Sicania, Trapani, Sicily, Italy and renamed MARSALA. *1914:* Sold to V. Capriola, Torre del Greco, Italy. *1916:* Sold to Societa di Navigazione a Vapore per Trasporti Costieri Liguria Occidentale, Porto Maurizio, Italy and renamed MAURIZIO P. *26.8.1917:* Torpedoed and sunk by the German submarine UC 20 near Marsa Sirocco Bay in position 36.56 N by 00.15 E.

3. WANS FELL 1882-1886 Iron

O.N. 86197 308g 99n 145.0 x 22.0 x 10.1 feet
C. 2-cyl. by Kincaid and Co., Greenock.

30.5.1882: Launched by H.M. McIntyre and Co., Paisley (Yard No. 88) for the Wans Fell Steam Ship Co. Ltd. (Hume, Smith and Co., managers), Liverpool as WANS FELL. *15.7.1882:* Completed. *3.4.1886:* Managers became George Nelson and Sons, Whitehaven and later Liverpool. *20.3.1894:* Sold to Spillers and Bakers Ltd., Cardiff. *4.1906:* Sold to Matthew Taylor, Methil. *2.10.1929:* Beached after a collision with the steam drifter GIRL PAT (97/1920) off Hartlepool. Abandoned as a constructive total loss and sold for scrap.

Wans Fell as pictured by a sale and purchase broker. *C. V. Waine*

4. CONISTON FELL 1882-1886

O.N. 86265 337g 130n 144.6 x 22.0 x 10.0 feet
C. 2-cyl. by David Rollo and Sons, Liverpool.

7.1882: Launched by H. Tipping and Co., Portsmouth for the Coniston Fell Steamship Co. Ltd. (Hume, Smith and Co., managers), Liverpool as CONISTON FELL. *12.12.1882:* Completed. *13.3.1886:* Managers became George Nelson and Sons, Whitehaven and later Liverpool. *28.3.1894:* Manager became William L. Jackson, Liverpool. *2.10.1894:* Sold to David W. Bain and Co., Portreath. *1895:* Owners became Bain, Son and Co., Portreath. *29.11.1899:* Sank off New Brighton pier in the River Mersey following a collision with the steamer SULLY (1,326/1874) whilst on a voyage from London to Birkenhead with a cargo of cement. *14.12.1899:* Register closed.

5. SHAP FELL 1882-1886 Iron

O.N. 86248 351g 220n 155.7 x 10.9 x 14.3 feet
C. 2-cyl. by Dunsmuir and Jackson, Govan.

9.1882: Launched by the Campbeltown Shipbuilding Co., Campbeltown (Yard No. 19) for the Shap Fell Steam Ship Co. Ltd. (Hume, Smith and Co., managers), Liverpool as SHAP FELL. *24.10.1882:* Completed. *1886:* Sold to the Hayburn Steamship Co. Ltd., Liverpool (George Nelson and Sons, Whitehaven and later Liverpool, managers) and renamed HAYBURN. *17.7.1889:* Stranded six miles north of Portpatrick with a cargo of pig iron. Some of the cargo was recovered but salvage of the ship was impossible.

6. BOW FELL 1882 Iron

O.N. 86247 294g 163n 144.8 x 22.1 x 10.1 feet
C. 2-cyl. by Dunsmuir and Jackson, Govan.

16.9.1882: Launched by Murdoch and Murray, Port Glasgow (Yard No. 66) for the Bow Fell Steam Ship Co. Ltd. (Hume, Smith and Co., managers), Liverpool as BOW FELL. *24.10.1882:* Completed. *3.11.1882:* Left Troon for Belfast with a cargo of coal and disappeared with her crew of 12. *24.11.1882:* Register closed.

7. HART FELL 1883-1886

O.N. 87856 319g 136n 139.3 x 21.6 x 10.0 feet
C. 2-cyl. by Dunsmuir and Jackson, Govan.

21.6.1883: Launched by Murdoch and Murray, Port Glasgow (Yard No. 65) for the Hart Fell Steam Ship Co. Ltd. (Hume, Smith and Co., managers), Liverpool as HART FELL. *14.7.1883:* Completed. *15.5.1886:* Managers became George Nelson and Sons, Whitehaven and later Liverpool. *30.3.1894:* Manager became William L. Jackson, Liverpool. *6.11.1894:* Sold to John Gardner, Glasgow. *4.1.1895:* Sold to William C. Young and Donald Macleod (C.F. Morrison and Sons, managers), Elgin. *16.5.1898:* Owners became the North Eastern Shipping Co. Ltd. (George Elsmie and Sons, managers), Aberdeen. *1.3.1902:* Wrecked at Scaurs of Cruden, Port Errol, south of Peterhead whilst on a voyage from Sunderland to Buckie with a cargo of coal. *7.3.1902:* Register closed.

Nomenclature

Hume, Smith steamers took their names from fells in Cumberland and Lancashire. Modern usage has changed some of these names but most are still identifiable.

BOW FELL — Now commonly spelt Bowfell, a mountain just under 3,000 feet, standing between Great Langdale and Eskdale.

CONISTON FELL — Coniston fells rise between the Coniston and Duddon valleys mainly in what was Lancashire but is now Cumbria. The highest of these, to which the name probably refers, is The Old Man of Coniston,

GRANGE FELL — A relatively low but extremely beautiful wooded hill above Grange in Borrowdale.

HART FELL — Not found on modern maps, but may refer to Harter Fell, above Kentmere; or to Hart Crag, between Rydale and Patterdale.

RYDAL FELL — The name given to part of the long ridge to the west of Rydale, above the village and lake of Rydal.

SHAP FELL — To the east of the Lake District; the valleys below Shap Fell are the route taken by railway and road between England and Scotland.

WANS FELL — A ridge between Ambleside and Troutbeck.

DAVID JONES AND CO.
R. AND D. JONES LTD.
Liverpool

Lloyds Register for 1880 lists 123 shipowners named Jones. Fortunately, only two qualify as Liverpool owners for consideration here: Richard and David Jones of 28 Brunswick Street and David Jones of Queen's Pier Head. The owners were almost certainly related: the solitary David Jones may well have been father of the partners Richard and David. R. and D. Jones' first ship was bought from David Jones, and the partners employed several names first used by David Jones.

R. and D. Jones are one of several Welsh shipping companies which meander through the history of Liverpool coastal shipping: never owning a large fleet, but surprising the historian by their capacity to take odd turns. They disappear from time to time as freight rates become unattractive, only to spring forth again when the economic climate improves.

Firstly, David Jones and Co. will be considered. This fleet consisted mainly of wooden and iron sailing ships employed in the South American nitrate trade. Along with these and a small schooner was the iron steamer ALCAZAR (471/1873) which was large enough to trade to Spain, the Mediterranean or the Baltic. The biggest and best of Jones' nitrate sailers was the SNOWDON (1,122/1877), an iron barque built for him by Russell of Port Glasgow. It was SNOWDON that became R. and D. Jones' first ship in 1879.

R. and D. Jones described themselves as shipowners, shipbrokers and commission agents. They had strong connections with Flintshire, being the Liverpool agents for the Mostyn Coal and Iron Company, and the associated Liverpool and Mostyn Line. The latter maintained a passenger service between the ports in its title with the iron paddle steamer SWIFTSURE (115/1861). She was regarded as neither swift nor particularly sure, and the timings of her two or three sailings each week depended more on tide tables than a timetable. The importance of the Flintshire business to R. and D. Jones can be gauged from their use of the telegraphic address MOSTYN. There was one more connection with the region that was to be historically important: Richard Hughes of Gronant gained his first experience of the shipping business in R. and D. Jones' office. These Flintshire connections, and use of local names such as CLWYD and ELWY, suggest that the Joneses were themselves Flintshire men.

The company began owning coasters in 1880, when partner David Jones junior bought the BEE on the bankruptcy of her Flintshire owner. Described as a steam lighter, she was obviously considered capable of setting out across the Irish Sea, but the disaster which befell her in Carlingford Lough during 1888 suggests she was underpowered for coasting. Even steamships were not immune from the hazards of wind and weather which every year took such a toll of sailing ships. ARGOS, acquired in 1883, spent much of her relatively short career with the Joneses in the Irish Sea coal trade, out of Garston or the Scottish coal ports. Arriving at Irvine in a gale in December 1886, she ran aground and was holed. The Liverpool and Glasgow Salvage Association refloated her just before Christmas, but it is possible that R. and D. Jones were not prepared to pay the salvage claim, as ARGOS was registered in the ownership of the Association's secretary, Rundell, and sold by him for breaking up at Ardrossan.

From 1880 to 1883, the fleet managed by R. and D. Jones expanded considerably, and ranged from steamers even tinier than the BEE to the relatively large NANT GWYNANT, which was capable of trading well outside home trade limits. To finance this expansion the brothers floated six single-ship companies, each with a capital reflecting the purchase price of the ship involved: for example, £2,000 for the Bee Steamship Co. Ltd., £4,000 for the Argos Steamship Co. Ltd. and £27,500 for the Nant Gwynant Steamship Co. Ltd. David Jones subscribed to all of the companies, whilst other investors included a remarkably consistent range of merchants and small businessmen from North Wales and Liverpool: timber merchants from the Conwy valley, men from Anglesey in the tobacco business, a Liverpool flour merchant and an insurance broker. A few other Joneses appear, but David Jones was by now in sole charge of the erstwhile partnership R. and D. Jones.

In 1882 R. and D. Jones were given an appropriated berth in Trafalgar Dock, Liverpool. This was for the SWIFTSURE running to Mostyn, a service to Greenfield in Flintshire carried on by sailing ship, and for steamers running to Lancashire, Cumberland and Welsh ports. The SWIFTSURE's service ended in 1893.

By 1886, the fleet included six cargo steamers. But in this year the business of R. and D. Jones changed direction, probably in response to falling cargo rates, and passenger carrying paddle steamers began to be bought. Over the next three years, the company acquired the ageing ex-railway steamers ALEXANDRA (337/1863) and MARSEILLES (432/1864) formerly with the London, Brighton and South Coast Railway, and the QUEEN OF THANET (158/1864) which had served several Scottish railways as the CARHAM. These were put on a service between Liverpool, Llandudno, Beaumaris, Bangor and Menai Bridge. The old paddlers faced competition from newer, faster and larger vessels, and the venture came to an end in 1892. As if the paddlers were sucking capital from the other side of the business, the cargo carrying fleet was run down at this time, with the companies being wound up as their ships were sold. This period also saw the retirement of the solitary David Jones, who sold his last ship in 1889.

The company adopted limited liability status in 1896, becoming R. and D. Jones Ltd. A Thomas Jones, possibly David's son, was now involved in the business. Henceforth, the brokerage and agency business was pursued at the expense of shipowning, and the sailing vessel SNOWDON was sold in 1903 and the steamer NANT FRANCON in 1905. Short-term ownership during 1906 of two aged paddlers – the former Mersey ferry PRIMROSE (292/1879) and the ALERT (172/1865) – indicates that the company may also have been sale and purchase brokers.

As and when conditions seemed propitious, R. and D. Jones Ltd still bought coasters. In 1904 the MAYFLOWER was acquired and quickly transferred to a single-ship company set up to own her. The Mayflower Steamship Co. Ltd. had a paid-up capital of £3,750 which was subscribed mainly by R. and D. Jones Ltd. Two further coasters of similar size were built for the managers: CLWYD in 1909 and the ELWY in 1914, both to be owned by the Clwyd Steamship Co. Ltd. Both names had been used by forerunner David Jones for his sailing ships. Sale of the ELWY in 1917 left the Jones company, for the first time, with no ships.

Elwy *W.S.P.L. Cochrane collection*

By 1922 the company's affairs were largely in the hands of David Richard Jones, born in 1891 to David and Annie Jones – his father having been the dominant partner in R. and D. Jones. The numerous outside appointments David R. Jones held confirm that the company his father had helped form had become respected and influential. A committee member of the Liverpool Shipowners' Association, he represented this body on the River Dee Pilotage – appropriate in view of his company's links with Flintshire although by now these were probably confined to looking after ships visiting the Point of Ayr Colliery and probably Mostyn. David R. Jones became Chairman of the Liverpool Shipowners' Association in 1932, holding the post until 1936 after which he remained a director until 1949. As a leading light in a shipowners' association, it was inappropriate that his company had no ships. So in 1922 it entered the coaster ACME (227/1903) in the Association's register, even though she actually belonged to a Peter Marmion of Liverpool who probably time-chartered her to Jones (see the Henry Seddon fleet list for her details). In 1924 the situation was remedied when the dormant Clwyd Steamship Co. Ltd. took delivery of a new coaster, the GLYNCONWY. She was an unusual choice, as she was too big for the Dublin coal trade, and almost certainly unsuitable for the Point of Ayr trade which required little coasters such as ELWY and CLWYD.

Glynconwy spent the years 1939 to 1958 as **Rockleaze** of Osborn and Wallis, Bristol. *Author's collection*

Following the sale of GLYNCONWY in 1929, R. and D. Jones Ltd. owned no further ships. However, in yet another twist of their story, they became actively involved in looking after coasters again during the Second World War. A considerable number of Dutch coasters had either escaped from Holland during the German invasion in 1940, or were out of Dutch waters and simply stayed away. Most came under British control, and the Ministry of War Transport required companies with experience of dealing with coasters to take on day-to-day activities such as issuing stores, paying wages and organising repairs. R. and D. Jones Ltd. became involved in this, acting as what the Ministry described as managers for a group of Dutch coasters which included ATLAS (334/1938), CASTOR (199/1931) and MAJORI (196/1935). *Lloyd's Register* did not regard the company as managers, and reflecting the company's lack of investment or entrepreneurial risk, these Dutchmen have not been included in the fleet list.

Now wholly concerned with shipbroking and agency work, in the early 1950s R. and D. Jones became a subsidiary of Rea Ltd., the stevedoring arm of the Liverpool towage and bunkering firm, itself part of the Cory and later Ocean Groups. Jones' activities were gradually absorbed by Rea Ltd., but one of its last functions was to act as agents for ore carriers unloaded by Reas in Bidston Dock. The ore was destined for the steelworks of John Summers and Sons Ltd. at Shotton in Flintshire. So, after almost a century, the company ended life as it had begun with strong Flintshire connections.

Fleet lists

David Jones and Co.

1. ALCAZAR 1874-1876 Iron

O.N. 68417 471g 296n 175.0 x 24.8 x 14.9 feet
C. 2-cyl. by John Readhead and Co., South Shields.

21.4.1873: Launched by John Readhead and Co., South Shields (Yard No. 93) for Otway Robinson, London as ALCAZAR. *24.4.1874:* Acquired by David Jones, Liverpool. *24.4.1876:* Sold to Robert Lewis, Holywell. *30.7.1879:* Sank following a collision with the steamer FLAMINGO (1,209/1874) fourteen miles north by half west of Ushant whilst on a voyage from Cardiff to Sables d'Olonne, France with a cargo of coal and one passenger. The passenger and the crew of thirteen were rescued. *16.8.1879:* Register closed.

R. and D. Jones
R. and D. Jones Ltd.

1. BEE 1880-1888 Iron

O.N. 63288 160g 96n 126.0 x 18.0 x 8.0 feet
C. 2-cyl. by MacNab and Co., Greenock.

10.8.1870: Completed by Henry Murray and Co., Port Glasgow for Thomas B. Horsfall and George H. Horsfall, Liverpool as BEE. *11.12.1874:* Owner became George H. Horsfall, Liverpool. *25.6.1875:* Sold to William P. Evans, Greenfield, Denbigh. *4.8.1880:* Acquired by David Jones, Liverpool. *19.12.1883:* Owners became the Bee Steamship Co. Ltd. (R. and D. Jones, managers), Liverpool. *19.10.1888:* Wrecked on Hellyhunter Rocks, Carlingford whilst on a voyage from Runcorn to Newry with a cargo of salt. *29.11.1888:* Register closed.

2. NANT FRANCON 1881-1905 Iron

O.N. 84177 670g 429n 189.8 x 26.7 x 15.0 feet
C. 2-cyl. by John Readhead and Co., South Shields.

11.1881: Launched by John Readhead and Co., South Shields (Yard No. 175) for R. and D. Jones, Liverpool as NANT FRANCON. *6.12.1881:* Completed. *5.6.1882:* Owners became the Nant Francon Steamship Co. Ltd. (R. and D. Jones, managers), Liverpool. *13.11.1896:* Managers became R. and D. Jones Ltd. *27.6.1905:* Sold to Robert Jobson, West Hartlepool. *10.1905:* Sold to the Compañia Argentina de Pesca, Buenos Aires, Argentina and renamed DON PEDRO. *1907:* Renamed CACHALOTE. *1912:* Sold to Hermann Ost, Buenos Aires, Argentina. *1915:* Sold to Compañia Porteña de Navegacion a Vapor (W.R. Grace and Co., managers), Valparaiso, Chile and renamed PORTEÑO. *1916:* Sold to Compañia Carbonifera y de Fundicion Schwager, Valparaiso, Chile. *1923:* Sold to Beeche y Compañia Ltda., Valparaiso, Chile and renamed MERCEDES. *23.9.1925:* Wreckage found on beach at Tubul, Gulf of Aranco. She had been on a voyage from Coronel to Valparaiso with a cargo of coal.

Nant Francon *W.S.P.L. collection*

3. NANT GWYNANT 1883-1895 Iron

O.N. 87851 1,702g 1105n 256.5 x 34.5 x 19.6 feet
C. 2-cyl. by John Readhead and Co., South Shields.

14.6.1883: Launched by John Readhead and Co., South Shields (Yard No. 194) for the Nant Gwynant Steamship Co. Ltd. (R. and D. Jones, managers), Liverpool as NANT GWYNANT. *5.7.1883:* Completed. *7.9.1895:* Sold to the Ulster Steamship Co. Ltd. (G. Heyn and Sons, managers), Belfast and later renamed GLEN HEAD. *8.12.1934:* Wrecked near Nekso, Bornholm Island whilst on a voyage from Riga and Liepaja to Cork and Londonderry with general cargo and wood.

4. ARGOS 1883-1887 Iron

O.N. 60839 241g 178n 165.2 x 20.1 x 9.7 feet
Inverted 2-cyl. by R. and W. Hawthorn, Hebburn-on-Tyne.

8.6.1868: Launched by A. Leslie and Co., Hebburn-on-Tyne (Yard No. 98) for Jules Gaudet, London as ARGOS. *9.7.1868:* Completed. *1873:* Owners became the Gaudet Frères London and Paris Steamship Co. Ltd., London. *1876:* Sold to Edward J. Hough and Co., London. *6.1883:* Acquired by R. and D. Jones, Liverpool. *15.12.1883:* Owners became the Argos Steamship Co. Ltd. (R. and D. Jones, managers), Liverpool. *6.12.1886:* Stranded at North Perch, Irvine Bar whilst on a voyage from Belfast to Irvine in ballast. *23.12.1886:* Refloated and taken to Ardrossan. *17.2.1887:* Sold to Nicholas Rundell, Liverpool. *1887:* Sold to the Ardrossan Shipbuilding Co., Ardrossan for breaking up.

5. CRAIGNAIR 1883-1913 Iron

O.N. 58805 105g 59n 87.8 x 18.5 x 7.2 feet.
C. 2-cyl. by R.H. Pearson and Co., Glasgow.

27.8.1881: Launched by Dobson and Charles, Grangemouth (Yard No. 68) for Thomas Biggar and Sons, Dalbeattie, Dumfries-shire as CRAIGNAIR. *10.1882:* Sold to William G. Richardson, Liverpool. *8.1883:* Acquired by R. and D. Jones, Liverpool. *15.12.1883:* Owners became the Craignair Steamship Co. Ltd. (R. and D. Jones, managers), Liverpool. *13.11.1896:* Owners became R. and D. Jones Ltd. *3.4.1913:* Sold to James and William Roberts, Probus, Cornwall. *9.12.1913:* Sold to the Anglo-Ottoman Steamship Co. Ltd. (Demetrius Lambiri, manager), Newcastle-upon-Tyne. *9.10.1914:* Sold to the Levant Transport Co. Ltd. (Henry Tyrer and Co., managers), Liverpool. *9.3.1915:* Sold to Thomas W. Ward Ltd., Sheffield. *7.8.1918:* Wrecked near Glasserton Shore, Luce Bay whilst on a voyage from Whithorn to Morecambe with a cargo of scrap. Later declared a constructive total loss. *3.10.1918:* Register closed.

6. ANT 1883-1906 Iron

O.N. 65934 188g 107n 110.3 x 20.5 x 10.3 feet
Inverted 2-cyl. simple by Kincaid, Donald and Co., Greenock.
1878: Engines compounded by S. Baker, Liverpool.

4.1872: Launched by J. Reid and Co., Port Glasgow (Yard No. 4a) for Thomas B. Horsfall and George H. Horsfall, Liverpool as ANT. *8.5.1872:* Completed. *18.12.1874:* Owner became George H. Horsfall, Liverpool. *12.2.1883:* Acquired by David Jones, Liverpool. *1878:* Engines compounded. *13.2.1884:* Owners became the Ant Steamship Co. Ltd. (R. and D. Jones, managers), Liverpool. *13.11.1896:* Managers became R. and D. Jones Ltd. *31.11.1906:* Sold to Thomas Perry, Liverpool. *12.6.1912:* Sold to Joseph Forster, Liverpool. *14.8.1912:* Sold to the Ant Steam Flat Co. Ltd. (T.J. May and Co., managers), Liverpool. By 1935 in use as a dumb barge, although her engines were still in place. *6.1.1937:* Register closed after she had been broken up.

7. MAYFLOWER 1904-1912

O.N. 110519 258g 93n 128.9 x 22.0 x 6.6 feet
C. 2-cyl. by Muir and Houston, Glasgow; 10 knots.

26.4.1900: Launched by the Larne Shipbuilding Co., Larne (Yard No. 12) for the Mayflower Steamship Co. Ltd. (Hugh Foster, manager), Belfast as MAYFLOWER. *31.5.1900:* Completed. *18.3.1902:* Sold to the Coast Transit Co. Ltd. (James Boyle, manager), Falkirk. *10.6.1902:* Sold to the Cardigan Commercial Steam Packet Co. Ltd. (David I. Evans, manager), Cardigan. *17.3.1904:* Acquired by R. and D. Jones Ltd., Liverpool. *3.5.1904:* Owners became the Mayflower Steamship Co. Ltd. (R. and D. Jones Ltd., managers), Liverpool. *7.9.1912:* Sold to Frederick W. Horlock, Mistley. *20.4.1915:* Sold to the Cotton Powder Co. Ltd. (William J. Douglas, manager), London. *10.5.1920:* Sold to Bickford, Smith and Co. Ltd., London. *1.6.1922:* Sold to Coast Lines Ltd., Liverpool. *29.6.1922:* Renamed IRISH COAST. *12.9.1938:* Sold to Charles S. Kendall, Southsea. *10.5.1940:* Sold to the Vectis Transport Co. Ltd. (E.W. Gilbert, manager), Portsmouth. *16.3.1942:* Sold to the British Iron and Steel Corporation (Salvage) Ltd. (Arthur H. Turner, manager), Glasgow. *31.3.1949:* Renamed ARCLIFF. *6.7.1949:* Sold to the Ministry of Transport, London. *14.2.1951:* Register closed after being broken up by Arnott, Young and Co. Ltd., Troon.

8. CLWYD 1909-1916

O.N. 127956 289g 124n 125.2 x 22.7 x 9.5 feet
C. 2-cyl. by J.P. Rennoldson and Sons, South Shields; 9½ knots.

25.11.1908: Launched by J.P. Rennoldson and Sons, South Shields (Yard No. 256) for the Clwyd Steamship Co. Ltd. (R. and D. Jones Ltd., managers), Liverpool as CLYWD. *14.1.1909:* Completed. *19.1.1916:* Sold to the Point of Ayr Collieries Ltd. (George W. Dishart and Alfred Stabback, managers), Liverpool. *19.12.1917:* Sunk in collision with the steamer PARAGON (408/1889) twelve miles north of the Skerries, Anglesey whilst on a voyage from Dublin to Point of Ayr in ballast. *29.12.1917:* Register closed.

9. ELWY 1914-1917

O.N. 137400 293g 135n 128.0 x 23.0 x 9.8 feet
C. 2-cyl. by the Shields Engineering and Dry Dock Co. Ltd., North Shields; 8½ knots.

23.9.1914: Completed by Charles Rennoldson and Co., South Shields (Yard No. 166) for the Clwyd Steamship Co. Ltd. (R. and D. Jones Ltd., managers), Liverpool as ELWY. *27.8.1917:* Sold to Abraham Lazarus, London. *28.12.1918:* Sold to the Elwy Steamship Co. Ltd. (Claude Langdon Ltd., manager), Liverpool. *21.1.1920:* Sold to William R. Warden, Samuel Stewart and Charles S. Orr (James Waterson and Son, managers), Belfast. *19.9.1922:* Owners became Charles S. Orr and William Stewart (James Waterson and Son, managers), Belfast. *14.2.1931:* Sold to Spillers Ltd., Liverpool. *3.3.1931:* Renamed WHEATFEED. *27.7.1933:* Sold to the Point of Ayr Collieries Ltd. (George W. Dishart and Alfred Stabback, managers), Liverpool. *9.11.1933:* Renamed TANLAN. *6.1.1950:* Owners became the National Coal Board (North Western Division), Liverpool. *25.5.1958:* Arrived at Cork for breaking up by Haulbowline Industries Ltd. *10.9.1958:* Register closed.

10. GLYNCONWY 1924-1929

O.N. 147248 486g 196n 156.2 x 25.6 x 9.8 feet
T. 3-cyl. by William Beardmore and Co. Ltd., Coatbridge, Glasgow; 9 knots.

23.2.1924: Launched by the Goole Shipbuilding and Repairing Co. Ltd., Goole (Yard No. 253) for the Clwyd Steamship Co. Ltd. (R. and D. Jones, Ltd., managers), Liverpool as GLYNCONWY. *4.1924:* Completed. *1929:* Sold to R. and W. Paul Ltd., Ipswich and renamed GOLDCREST. *9.1934:* Sold to the Ald Shipping Co. Ltd., Bristol. *29.10.1934:* Renamed MONKTON COMBE. *6.12.1938:* Sold to Osborn and Wallis Ltd., Bristol. *19.1.1939:* Renamed ROCKLEAZE. *21.5.1958:* Arrived at Llanelli for breaking up by the Rees Shipbreaking Co. Ltd. *8.12.1958:* Register closed.

Glynconwy *National Maritime Museum P10523*

Nomenclature

The five ships delivered new into R. and D. Jones' ownership all took names of rivers or valleys in North Wales.

CLWYD	One of the major rivers of North Wales which drains the hills of Flintshire and east Denbighshire and flows into the Irish Sea at Rhyl. It has given its name to the surrounding hills and, more recently, to an administrative county.
ELWY	A tributary of the Clwyd, rising on the moors of Denbighshire and flowing eastwards to join it near Rhuddlan, some four miles from the sea.
GLYNCONWY	The valley of the Conwy, another major river of North Wales, which rises in the upland area of Migneint above Ffestiniog and flows northwards to the sea.
NANT FRANCON	The valley of the Afon Ogwen, running north east from Llyn Ogwen to Bethesda.
NANT GWYNANT	Arguably the most beautiful valley of North Wales, south east of Snowdon.

LOWDEN, CONNELL AND CO.
Liverpool

The coaster-owning activities of Lowden, Connell and Co. represent the rather ignominious end of a once proud and successful deep sea sailing ship operation. They also serve to demonstrate, once again, the difficulties of making a living in the coastal trade between the wars. Their interest lies also in their brief ownership of a novel and innovative – albeit not completely successful – Mersey-built coaster.

Captain William Lowden served with Whitehaven and Liverpool shipowners Thos. and Jno. Brocklebank Ltd., working his way up from apprentice to master. In 1864 he left this company to command with some success the Workington-built teak barque HUASQUINA (428/1864) which was managed by his brother, Samuel Lowden. On the death of Samuel in 1872, William Lowden left the sea and took over the management of the small fleet which had been built up. In 1874 John Edgar, a native of Dumfries-shire, became a partner, the company becoming Lowden, Edgar and Co. The company concentrated on small, handy-sized sailing vessels, built mainly in Cumberland and running to the West Coast of South and North America. The partnership with Edgar was dissolved in 1890, William Lowden then taking his nephew Robert Lowden Connell into partnership. W. Lowden and Co. took the bulk of the fleet, adding a number of other ships as British owners slowly quit sail. Lowden's biggest venture was the steel four-masted barque MASHONA (2,499/1891) built of steel at Londonderry. Captain William Lowden retired about 1904 and died in 1914 at the age of 85.

With William Lowden retired, Robert Lowden Connell accelerated the process of replacing sail with steam, which had begun when the ATHENA (3,427/1899) had been delivered by Short Brothers of Sunderland. The last sailing ship, MASHONA, was sold to Norwegian owners in 1906. The British and Chilian Steamship Co. Ltd. was formed to finance the steamers, its title reflecting Lowden's continuing interest in the South American trade. For instance, the ATHENA was to be wrecked in March 1902 whilst carrying a cargo of saltpetre from Iquique in Chile to Las Palmas. Under British and Chilian and other titles, Lowden owned a total of eight ocean-going steamers, although sales and losses ensured there were never more than three owned at one time. Last to go was the WABANA (4,804/1911) which was sold in 1921.

A further South American interest was the management between 1912 and 1922 of the Falkland Islands Transport Co. Ltd., whose steamer FALKLAND (452/1906) sailed between the River Plate and the Falkland Islands. She had once been familiar on the British West Coast as Spillers' WHEATSHEAF.

A venture which was to take an interesting turn began in 1905 with the formation of the Manx Isles Steamship Co. Ltd. to take delivery of the MANX ISLES (2,642/1905). Initially, the company was set up in the Isle of Man - there being nothing new about the current practice of operating under the Manx flag. Most of the shares of the Manx Isles company were held by the British and Chilian Steamship Co. Ltd. In 1915 MANX ISLES was converted to a molasses tanker and from 1917 ran on charter to the British Molasses Co. Ltd. This company originated in Liverpool and was the major British player in the molasses trade. Their satisfaction with the MANX ISLES' performance was evident from their purchase of the ship in July 1921, to become the first of what was to be a major fleet of tankers. Subsequent acquisitions were given names beginning ATHEL-, and one of these was also managed briefly by Lowden, Connell: the ATHELMERE (5,656/1914) a former Norwegian oil tanker. When British Molasses became United Molasses Co. Ltd. in 1926 Lowden, Connell's management of MANX ISLES ceased, but not their connection with the company as Sir Robert Connell became a director of the United Molasses. Indeed, investment in the molasses business may have absorbed some of the profits which Lowden, Connell had made from shipping during the First World War.

Sale of the MANX ISLES in 1921 raised £15,000 - only slightly less than she had cost 16 years earlier - and some of these proceeds were spent buying the coaster FULLAGAR, which was renamed CARIA. Few coasters in this book can make so many claims to fame as FULLAGAR. She was one of very few coasters built by Cammell, Laird and Co. Ltd.

Fullagar, seen here on trials in the Mersey in July 1920, was renamed **Caria** after purchase by the Manx Isles Steamship Co. Ltd. *Williamson Art Gallery, Birkenhead*

and the only coaster (as opposed to river craft) owned by Thos. and Jno. Brocklebank Ltd. But what set her apart was the innovative use of electric welding on her hull, and the fitting of a novel oil engine, built by Cammell, Laird to the design of a Mr. Fullagar. Both builders and owners were probably only interested in her as a test bed for this new technology. Brocklebanks were clearly serious about trying motorships, and fitted a similar Fullagar engine into their ocean-going MALIA (3,872/1921) and tried a different installation in their LYCIA (2,338/1924). None were successful, and it was almost 40 years before the company returned to diesels. The welded hull seems to have been a success, offering considerable improvements in strength over a rivetted hull. In passing, it is interesting to note how contemporary technical journals suggested that an unusually high degree of skill was needed for electric welding which would not be readily available in shipyards: just over twenty years later unskilled men and women who had never seen a ship before would be welding together Liberty ships in U.S. yards. The Cammell Laird-Fullagar engine was a very different matter, however. It was an opposed piston design, so that upper and lower pistons were driven apart during a firing stroke. This gave advantages in terms of simplified cylinder cover design. However, despite extensive testing before fitting, the engine proved totally unsuccessful, both in FULLAGAR and in MALIA. Just 15 months after completion, the Manx Isles company paid £6,000 for FULLAGAR, which can only have been a fraction of her cost, and immediately installed another oil engine, this time made by Beardmores, and renamed her CARIA.

In 1921, Lowden, Connell - a title adopted only in 1916 – were clearly making an attempt to break into the coasting trade. On his own account, Alfred Connell – Robert's son – had recently bought the small and aged coaster GLENMAY, selling her almost immediately to a Whitehaven company but later taking back her management. CARIA represented an opportunity to obtain an almost new coaster at a knock-down price: rather like buying a demonstrator from the local car dealer. CARIA traded out of the Mersey, running mainly between Garston and Waterford with coal. Despite her modest purchase price, her owners did not make money out of her, and the accounts of the Manx Isles Steamship Co. Ltd. show a loss for several years. CARIA's lack of profit must have been at least partly due to the engine trouble which beset most early motor coasters, although this was often compounded by the owner's decision to employ engineers whose knowledge of the internal combustion engine was sketchy. A few entries from the

Casualty Returns indicate typical problems. On 24th February 1923 she had engine damage which forced her to put back into Waterford. CARIA again reported engine trouble on arriving at Waterford on 9th September 1923 after a stormy passage from Liverpool, and was in port earning no money for almost two weeks.

It is not known what part engine failure played in the incident which led to the CARIA's sale. On 21st June 1924 she grounded at Hale Head in the Upper Mersey and although refloated with the tide had sustained sufficient damage to need immediate dry docking. It is not clear whether she was heading up the Mersey for Runcorn or Widnes, or had been carried up the river with the tide following an engine failure when bound for her usual destination of Garston. The Manx Isles company had clearly had enough of her, and in July 1924 sold her hulk for a mere £1,125, later recovering over £4,000 from their underwriters. The company did not trade again, and was liquidated in 1928 giving its investors a handsome return.

Of Lowden, Connell's involvement with coasters, there is little more to report. When they took over the management of the Solway Shipping Co. Ltd. in 1923, both GLENMAY and SODIUM came under their control. GLENMAY continued to run, as she had done most of her life, to the Isle of Man and SODIUM, which was later renamed PENTON, probably did so too. Management ceased in 1926 and 1927, respectively, when the ships were sold. The small coasters PEMBREY and ROMA were also owned by Lowden, Connell and Co. for brief periods in 1923 and 1924.

The company's interests in South American shipping were resurrected in 1932. Lowden, Connell and Co. Ltd., as it had now become, acted as managers for a group of three ships which had been returned to their Clydeside builders by the Compania Sud-Americana de Vapores, who were having financial difficulties. Lowden, Connell had acted as agents for this Chilian company and were owed a considerable sum. Of the three ships, ACONCAGUA (7,289/1922), TENO (7,289/1922) and TOLTEN (5,348/1930), only TOLTEN was managed for any length of time, passing to other owners in 1938. Since then the company has not been listed as owners or managers.

For Lowden, Connell coaster-owning had been a brief and unsatisfactory postscript to what was a long and otherwise successful career in the shipping business.

Roma *John Clarkson*

Fleet list

1. GLENMAY 1921-1926

O.N.102899 154g 63n 101.6 x 17.5 x 9.3 feet
C. 2-cyl. by Kincaid and Co. Ltd., Greenock.

8.1894: Completed by T.B. Seath and Co., Glasgow (Yard No. 292) for Thomas B. Briggs, Sunderland as READY. *29.3.1895:* Sold to Charles H. Pile, London. *1.8.1895:* Sold to Perroud et Compagnie, Nantes, France and renamed MARCHE DROIT. *1898:* Sold to Y. Lefiblec et Compagnie, Lannion, France. *2.1.1902:* Sold to Edwin Qualtrough, Peel, Isle of Man and renamed READY. *18.1.1902:* Renamed GLENMAY. *5.2.1902:* Sold to Steamship Glenmay Ltd. (Henry Quayle, manager), Peel, Isle of Man. *10.12.1902:* Manager became Edwin Qualtrough. *4.2.1914:* Sold to William Darlington, Garston. *8.8.1921:* Acquired by Alfred H. Connell, Liverpool. *20.9.1921:* Sold to the Solway Shipping Co. Ltd. (James B. Care, manager), Whitehaven. *1.11.1923:* Manager became Alfred H. Connell. *16.6.1926:* Sold to Edwin I. Murphy, Waterford. *20.2.1928:* Sold to the Ramsey Steamship Co. Ltd., Ramsey. *17.10.1928:* Renamed BEN MAY. *9.8.1937:* Sold to Samuel Gray, Belfast. *14.9.1938:* Sold to William Trohear, Dundrum. *14.11.1938:* Sprang a leak in the North Channel and foundered in East Tarbert Bay, off the Mull of Galloway, whilst on a voyage from Workington to Dundrum with a cargo of coal. Her crew of four got away in the ship's boat.

Glenmay spent the last ten years of her life with Ramsey Steamship Co. Ltd. as **Ben May** *W.S.P.L.*

2. CARIA 1921-1924

O.N. 143649 398g 185n 150.0 x 23.7 x 10.1 feet
Oil engine 4-cyl. 2S.C.S.A. by Cammell, Laird and Co. Ltd., Birkenhead, 9½ knots.
11.1921: Oil engine 4-cyl. 2S.C.S.A. by William Beardmore and Co. Ltd., Coatbridge, Glasgow; 9½ knots.

5.2.1920: Launched by Cammell, Laird and Co. Ltd., Birkenhead (Yard No. 882) for Thos. and Jno. Brocklebank Ltd., Liverpool as FULLAGAR. *2.7.1920:* Completed. *18.10.1921:* Acquired by the Manx Isles Steamship Co. Ltd. (Lowden, Connell and Co., managers), Liverpool, and re-engined. *9.11.1921:* Renamed CARIA. *30.7.1924:* Sold to John Fletcher, Kinghorn, Fife. *27.11.1924:* Sold to James A. White, London. *1.1.1925:* Sold to the British Columbia Cement Co. Ltd., Victoria, British Columbia. *29.8.1925:* Renamed SHEAN; it had been intended to name her GULL. *9.1935:* Sold to O.L. Rodriguez, Ensenada, Mexico and renamed CEDROS. *31.8.1937:* Sank following a collision with the Mexican motor vessel HIDALGO (1,060/1900) thirty miles south of Ensenada whilst on a voyage from Ensenada to Manzanillo with a cargo of fish and flour.

3. SODIUM/PENTON 1921-1927

O.N. 92861 147g 71n 100.0 x 20.1 x 8.1 feet
C. 2-cyl. by the Wallsend Slipway and Engineering Co., Wallsend-on-Tyne.

27.4.1887: Launched by Wood, Skinner and Co., Bill Quay-on-Tyne (Yard No. 5) for Wilton Allhusen, Newcastle-upon-Tyne as SODIUM. *23.5.1887:* Completed. *13.3.1891:* Owners became the United Alkali Co. Ltd. (Eustace Carey, manager), Liverpool. *2.3.1906:* Sold to Thomas Thompson and Son, Newcastle-upon-Tyne. *18.10.1906:* Owners became 'T' Steam Coasters Ltd. (Robinson, Brown and Co., managers), Newcastle-upon-Tyne. *7.5.1917:* Sold to John Harrison Ltd., London. *24.12.1917:* Sold to William Darlington, Garston. *8.8.1921:* Acquired by Lowden, Connell and Co., Liverpool. *20.9.1921:* Owners became the Solway Shipping Co. Ltd. (T. Wilson and Co., managers), Whitehaven. *1.11.1923:* Managers became Lowden, Connell and Co., Liverpool. *6.3.1923:* Renamed PENTON. *16.6.1927:* Sold to James D. Ormiston, Leith. *22.7.1927:* Sold to Alexander Hannah, Leith. *4.9.1930:* Sold to the Sandwich Hoy Company (Ernest A. Fagg, manager), Sandwich. *18.1.1937:* Stranded one mile south of Gorleston Coast Guard Station whilst on a voyage from Great Yarmouth to London in ballast. Her crew was rescued. *10.1937:* Refloated and sold for breaking up. *13.11.1937:* Whilst in tow of QUEENS CROSS (286/1921) for Whitby the tow parted off Skinningrove during heavy weather and she went aground at Kettleness, four miles north of Whitby, and became a total loss. *22.1.1941:* Register closed.

Penton aground at Gorleston in 1937. Although refloated, she cheated the breakers, and whilst on tow broke free and was wrecked near Whitby.

Author's collection

4. PEMBREY 1923

O.N. 130059 549g 242n 165.8 x 25.4 x 10.7 feet
T. 3-cyl. by N.V. Industriele Maatschappij 'Hera', Ymuiden, Holland; 9½ knots.

6.6.1920: Launched by Firma D. Boot, Alphen a/d Rijn, Holland probably for the builder's own account. *2.8.1920:* Sold to the Pembrey Steamship Co. Ltd. (Francis J. Evans, manager), Burry Port. *21.9.1920:* Completed as PEMBREY. *31.1.1923:* Owners became the Burryside Steamship Co. Ltd. (Francis J. Evans, manager), Burry Port. *16.6.1923:* Acquired by Alfred H. Connell, Liverpool. *21.7.1923:* Sold to the Island Steamship Co. Ltd. (John B. Kee, manager), Ramsey. *8.1928:* Sold to the Société Belge d'Armament Maritime S.A., Antwerp, Belgium and renamed IDA. *22.9.1930:* Wrecked in fog one cable west of Prawle Point whilst on a voyage from Cardiff to Portsmouth with a cargo of coal. The crew of 12 were rescued by breeches buoy. *9.10.1930:* Wreck broke in two and by November 1930 was virtually broken up.

5. ROMA 1924

O.N. 116007 158g 49n 95.0 x 18.9 x 8.5 feet
1913: 181g 67n 106.0 x 18.9 x 8.5 feet
C. 2-cyl. by Muir and Houston Ltd., Glasgow.

1903: Completed by the Larne Shipbuilding Co., Larne (Yard No. 25) for W.J.R. Harbinson and C.L. Mackean, Belfast as ROMA. *1913:* Lengthened. *1917:* Sold to Henry Renny (Earl J. Leslie, manager), Forfar. *1920:* Sold to the Sea Navigation Co. Ltd. (W.J. Stewart and Douglas Cable, managers), London. *1924:* Acquired by Lowden, Connell and Co., Liverpool. *1924:* Sold to the Straits Steamship Co. Ltd., Liverpool. *1938:* Sold to Alfred J. Smith, Bristol. *1949:* Sold to Bristowe Shippers Ltd. (Arthur Smith, manager), Bristol. *1958:* Sold to Renwick, Wilton and Dobson Ltd., Torquay. *10.4.1959:* Arrived at Newport, Monmouthshire to be broken up by John Cashmore Ltd.

JOHN J. MACK AND SONS
Liverpool

The Mack family were involved in an impressive cross section of Liverpool's coastal, river and dock trades. They had substantial interests in major towing, lighterage and grain elevator companies; in a cargo liner service from the Mersey to Belfast; and in Liverpool's best known owners of excursion steamers. The company's funnel colours were a feature of trading craft on the Mersey for 90 years, and indeed can still be seen on several preserved vessels. Strong supporters of the Methodist Church, the temperance movement and liberalism, Mack family members also found time to become involved with local government in Bootle. But of particular relevance to this book is their pioneering use of steam in the coastal bulk trades.

The founder of the family's shipping businesses, John Jermyn Mack, ran away to sea in the first half of the nineteenth century and served in Guion and Inman Line steamers. But after he had gained his master's ticket he sensibly decided on a job connected with shipping on land, and went into partnership in the stevedoring business as Durant and Mack. He married his partner's sister Amelia, and Durant has been used as a middle name over several generations of Macks. Mersey flats and lighters were used in the stevedoring business, and by 1880 John's son William Durant Mack is listed as the owner of at least seven Mersey sailing flats. The family is said to have begun carrying coal, bulk grain and flour from Liverpool to Belfast as early as 1877, but no record can be found of their owning sea-going ships until the arrival of the steamers ADA and HERBERT in 1881. Although steamers had been carrying bulk cargoes of coal on the East Coast since the 1840s, steam on the Irish Sea was still largely confined to carrying passengers and high value, often perishable, goods which could bear the extra cost of steamers over sailing vessels. Macks were the first Liverpool steamship owners to successfully venture into home trade tramping, following Glasgow owners such as William Robertson and James Hay who had begun to grasp the possibilities which steam offered in the late 1870s. Macks' fleet was built up on the same wave of optimism which saw Hume, Smith and Co. invest heavily in steam, but Macks proved much more durable. Like their Liverpool competitors, rapid expansion was financed largely by floating single-ship companies.

Within a few days during September 1881, the Macks acquired an almost new steamer, which they renamed ADA, and took delivery of the slightly larger HERBERT from a Liverpool shipbuilder. Part of HERBERT's machinery may well have been to sea before the hull, as the machinery was built in Caernarfon by De Winton and Co., who made a practice of launching boilers into the water and having them towed to Liverpool to be fitted into a ship.

The Clyde-built FLORENCE joined the fleet just over a year later; the swiftness of this addition and her larger size providing evidence of Macks' confidence in the future of steam. Three more steamers were added over the next 18 months; the Barrow-built, engines-amidships sisters ANNIE and DOLLIE showing a further increase in size.

Although William D. Mack appears as the registered owner and later manager of the HERBERT, the title J. J. Mack and Sons was adopted about the same time. Those involved were James Jermyn, John Sutton and Isaac A. Mack, to whom were later added Harold B. (son of James), Charles Garrett Mack and Lovell D.(sons of Isaac).

Following the addition of GRANGE FELL in 1886 there was a temporary lull in the fleet's expansion. This may have reflected the disappearance of the GRANGE FELL – the first of many losses – but probably resulted from the family investing its energy and capital in other areas as the boom in the early 1880s turned to recession. Macks along with John Jermyn's partner Durant were subscribers to the Alexandra Towing Co. Ltd. which was formed in 1887 and eventually became Liverpool's and later the U.K.'s most important towage company. Macks also had an interest in the Liverpool and North Wales Steamship Co. Ltd. formed in 1891 to operate excursion steamers to Llandudno. In response to a recession in the 1890s the family persuaded a number of flat owners to amalgamate. The result was the formation in September 1896 of the Liverpool Lighterage Co. Ltd. which had the largest fleet of flats and barges in the port, totalling about 150 by 1914. From 1912 this company also had its own yard at Northwich, where twelve men were capable of carrying out major repairs to barges, and owned a number of lighterage tugs which wore the same funnel colours as Mack's steam coasters. One of these, KERNE (63/1913), has been preserved.

The Mack family's other major ventures had a much higher profile, the Belfast and Mersey Steamship Co. Ltd. and its successor the Belfast, Mersey and Manchester Steamship Co. Ltd. As short-sea liner companies, their story is beyond the scope of this work, but needs to be mentioned as Mack's other ships occasionally ran in their services or were transferred; for instance, LANCASHIRE was running general cargo from Belfast to Liverpool when sunk in 1902, and FLESWICK was transferred in 1929. Run initially in conjunction with Samuel Lawther and Sons of Belfast, the companies provided a general cargo service between Liverpool and later Manchester and Belfast in direct and often litigious opposition to the Belfast Steamship Co. Ltd. By keeping one step ahead of the latter company, the Belfast, Mersey and Manchester remained a thorn in its side even when both became part of the Coast Lines group. The ageing CALEDONIAN was bought by Macks in 1894 to supplement Belfast and Mersey's own ships.

Involvement with the Belfast and Mersey Steamship Co. Ltd. did not inhibit the expansion of Macks' own steamer fleet. TOPAZ was bought from William Robertson of Glasgow in 1891, but like her immediate predecessor GRANGE FELL was to be lost within a year, the year which had begun with the wreck of the pioneering ADA. Undeterred, Macks went to Fullertons of Paisley for a series of coasters named after English counties. The smallest of these, CUMBERLAND and YORKSHIRE, were clearly ordered with the Dublin coal trade in mind, being built to the maximum length to enter Ringsend Basin, but being unusually broad in the beam to increase their carrying capacity.

Of Macks' earlier ships, most photographs are of the ships in later life under the ownership of companies controlled by John Kelly Ltd. This is **Lancashire** which was nominally owned by Wm. Barkley and Sons Ltd. although sporting a Kelly funnel. *W.S.P.L. Cochrane collection*

Yorkshire on trials.

University of Glasgow DC101/1648

Casualties in Macks' Irish Sea trades were heavy. In addition to the three already listed, HERBERT foundered in 1885, FLORENCE had been lost near the Isle of Man in 1889 whilst carrying Lancashire coal to Belfast, JOHN BURBERRY was wrecked in 1899, LANCASHIRE sank after a collision in the foggy Mersey in 1902, DOLLIE went missing in 1905, FLESWICK sank in collision off Cork in 1908, YORKSHIRE was damaged in collision off Anglesey in 1916 and – last of the tramping fleet – CHESHIRE disappeared in 1922. The voyages on which the vessels were lost suggest that carrying coal from the Mersey to Belfast, Dublin, Cork and other ports around the Irish Sea was the principal business of Macks' coastal tramps. But they could also be found bringing bog ore from the west of Ireland to Scottish ironworks, serving the West Cumberland ironworks, carrying rails for Irish railways, and would occasionally stray outside the Irish Sea to load china clay or take coal to continental Europe. They also helped out frequently on the liner services between Manchester, Liverpool and Belfast. Only a few of Macks' fleet survived to be sold, all but one going to other Irish Sea operators, most notably companies associated with John Kelly who took four, including the salved LANCASHIRE.

FLESWICK was the last steamer acquired by J. J. Mack and Sons. Evidence of a misadventure off Cork indicates she also hauled coal, and she spent time running between South Wales and Hayle in Cornwall. But her main employment was to be as a running mate to the MANCHESTER (506/1891) of the Belfast and Mersey Steamship Co. Ltd. in the general cargo trade, and after being hauled out of Cork Harbour and repaired she was to continue in this for many years.

The late 1920s saw the Mack family, invigorated by new blood in the shape of Harold and Charles Mack, take a renewed interest in the Belfast trade. As if in preparation, the family firm was incorporated as J.J. Mack and Sons Ltd. in December 1928, and within weeks the Belfast, Mersey and Manchester Steamship Co. Ltd. was registered. Mack's last steamer – FLESWICK – was to be formally transferred to the Belfast, Mersey and Manchester company in 1929.

Fleswick in the buff funnel with black top of the Belfast, Mersey and Manchester Steamship Co. Ltd. She was formally transferred to the ownership of this company in 1929. *W.S.P.L. Cochrane collection*

There is one further chapter in the Macks' career as coastal shipowners. Around 1924, an Alfred Capper of Wavertree, Liverpool had formed the Straits Steamship Co. Ltd. The name was all it had in common with the rather grand Singapore company; the title referring to the Menai Straits, and its sole ship being the tiny and ageing steam coaster ROMA. She was a frequent visitor to Caernarfon with supplies for local grocers, being one of the last vessels in a time-honoured trade. The ROMA was sold in 1938, but the Straits company and its goodwill passed to Macks. Another tiny and ancient steamer, once owned by Henry Seddon, was bought and renamed PENRHOS; her name honouring Penrhos College in North Wales, of which Isaac Mack was a director. To supplement her the little motor vessel CRISTO was bought, but was registered in the ownership of Liverpool Lighterage Ltd. PENRHOS was soon to become a mine victim and it was not until 1954 that a further coaster, the PENRHYN, was registered in the ownership of the Straits Steamship Co. Ltd., although the lighterage tug KERNE was transferred to the company's ownership. Another Northwich-built vessel, the PENRHYN was employed alongside CRISTO in taking Bibby's cattle feed from Waterloo Dock, Liverpool to Caernarfon and returning to the Mersey and Manchester Ship Canal ports with stone from quarries at Dinmor, Trevor, Penmaenmawr and Llanddulas. For a time the company had its registered office in Caernarfon. Although the houseflag used by Capper with a red letter S on white was retained, PENRHYN carried Macks' by now time-honoured black funnel with a white-edged blue band. Her transfer to the Liverpool Lighterage Co. Ltd. in 1965 was little more than a formality and she was sold for scrap soon after: the CRISTO – now converted to a motorship – having already been sold. In 1965 the company also gave up its stevedoring and warehousing activities, which had been restarted in 1955 under the title Straits Stevedoring Co. Ltd. This company acted for Spain's Trafrume Line in Toxteth Dock, Liverpool.

In 1971, most of the lighterage business of Liverpool Lighterage Co. Ltd. passed to Bulk Cargo Handling Services Ltd., a subsidiary of Alexandra Towing Co. Ltd., although Liverpool Lighterage remains in business, latterly as a property company run by Paul Mack (great grandson of the founder), owning premises behind the old barge yard at Northwich which was itself given up in 1972. It will be recalled that Alexandra was itself an interest of the Macks.

Throughout the twentieth century, coasters have kept turning up in the ownership of companies which have been involved in Mersey river and dock trades, presenting an enigma as to whether or not they should be included in this book. Macks provided the last of these, purchasing for their lighterage trade one ship which had been a coaster and buying five new hulls at least one of which subsequently became a coaster. The resurgence in lighterage followed the opening of the Royal Seaforth Dock in 1972 and its large grain silo, which received most of the North West's grain imports, a proportion of which had previously gone direct to mills at Manchester via the Ship Canal. Bulk Cargo Handling Services moved much of this grain, buying in 1972 a Dutch coaster which it renamed SEAFORTH TRADER (480/1952). Further motor barges were ordered, based on a coaster hull designed by the Yorkshire Dry Dock Co. Ltd. of Hull: the SEACOMBE TRADER (480/1974), SEALAND TRADER (498/1974), SEABOURNE TRADER (499/1975) and IRWELL TRADER (492/1977). A near-sister, MERSEY TRADER (496/1977), was built locally by McTay Marine Ltd. at Bromborough. All were owned in the name of Alexandra Towing Co. Ltd. although carrying the colours of Bulk Cargo Handling Services Ltd. Alas, the trade proved vulnerable to road competition and between 1987 and 1989 these motor barges were sold, to become bunkering craft and, in at least one case, a coaster: the SEABOURNE TRADER has run in the stone trade as YEOMAN ROSE.

The final severance between the Mack family and Liverpool's coastal and river trade, in which it had been actively and successfully involved for over a century, was not to be long delayed, and came when the highly successful Alexandra Towing Co. Ltd. was sold to Australia's Howard Smith group.

Fleet lists

J.J. Mack and Sons

1. ADA 1881-1891 Iron

O.N. 62776 165g 90n 108.7 x 19.6 x 8.9 feet
C.2-cyl. by Ross and Duncan, Govan.

9.4.1880: Launched by the Campbeltown Shipbuilding Co., Campbeltown (Yard No. 7) for Samuel Connor, Felix O'Hagan, Abraham R. Walker and Allan Macdonell, trading as the Newry Salt Works Co., Newry as ALLAN MACDONELL. *17.5.1880:* Completed. *8.1881:* Acquired by William D. Mack, Liverpool. *11.8.1881:* Renamed ADA. *16.9.1881:* Owners became the Steamship Ada Co. Ltd. (John J. Mack and Sons, managers), Liverpool. *1.1.1891:* Wrecked off the Garvan Islands, near Malin Head, whilst on a voyage from Ballina to Glasgow with a cargo of bog ore. *16.1.1891:* Register closed.

2. HERBERT 1881-1885 Iron

O.N. 84149 165g 98n 115.4 x 19.2 x 9.3 feet
C.2-cyl. by De Winton and Co., Caernarfon.

15.8.1881: Launched by R. and J. Evans and Co., Liverpool (Yard No. 105) for William D. Mack, Liverpool as HERBERT. *26.9.1881:* Completed. *1.12.1881:* Owners became the Steamship Herbert Co. Ltd (William D. Mack, manager), Liverpool. *1882:* Managers became John J. Mack and Sons. *19.11.1885:* Foundered off the Skerries whilst on a voyage from Holyhead to Harrington with a cargo of clay.

3. FLORENCE 1882-1889 Iron

O.N. 86244 281g 135n 149.8 x 22.2 x 10.7 feet
C. 2-cyl. by William King and Co., Glasgow.

14.9.1882: Launched by T. B. Seath and Co., Rutherglen (Yard No. 214) for the Steamship Florence Co. Ltd. (John J. Mack and Sons, managers), Liverpool as FLORENCE. *18.10.1882:* Completed. *20.9.1889:* Foundered off the Calf of Man whilst on a voyage from Garston to Belfast with a cargo of coal. All the crew except one was lost. *10.10.1889:* Register closed.

4. JOHN BURBERRY 1883-1899 Iron

O.N. 84660 301g 109n 145.0 x 22.1 x 9.3 feet
C.2-cyl. by J. and T. Young, Ayr.

6.8.1881: Launched by the Campbeltown Shipbuilding Co., Campbeltown (Yard No. 15) for Dowson and Harley, Cardiff as JOHN BURBERRY. *1881:* Owner became John W. Dowson, Cardiff. *3.1883:* Acquired by William D. Mack, Liverpool. *5.6.1883:* Owners became the Steamship John Burberry Co. Ltd. (John J. Mack and Sons, managers), Liverpool. *21.9.1899:* Wrecked at Lowca Point between Harrington and Whitehaven, whilst on a voyage from Garston to Harrington with a cargo of coal. *16.11.1899:* Register closed.

5. ANNIE 1883-1900 Iron

O.N. 87863 411g 237n 160.0 x 23.2 x 11.0 feet
C.2-cyl. by the Barrow Shipbuilding Co. Ltd., Barrow-in-Furness.

23.6.1883: Launched by the Barrow Shipbuilding Co. Ltd., Barrow-in-Furness (Yard No. 108) for the Steamship Annie Co. Ltd. (John J. Mack and Sons, managers), Liverpool as ANNIE. *16.8.1883:* Completed. *21.4.1900:* Sold to Rederi Aktiebolag Olof (Edvard Persson, manager), Limhamn, Sweden. *11.1902:* Manager became Gottfrid Sjøberg, Malmo. *3.1904:* Owners became Rederi Aktiebolag Annie (Gottfrid Sjøberg, manager), Malmo, Sweden. *3.2.1910:* Sank in the Lower Elbe after a collision with the German sailing ship SUSANNA (1,975/1892) whilst on a voyage from Hamburg to Falkenberg with a cargo of grain. Later refloated. *9.1910:* Broken up at Hamburg.

6. DOLLIE 1884-1905 Iron

O.N. 87952 403g 201n 160.0 x 23.2 x 11.0 feet
C.2-cyl. by the Barrow Shipbuilding Co. Ltd., Barrow-in-Furness.

1.3.1884: Launched by the Barrow Shipbuilding Co. Ltd., Barrow-in-Furness (Yard No. 120) for the Steamship Dollie Co. Ltd. (John J. Mack and Sons, managers), Liverpool as DOLLIE. *17.4.1884:* Completed. *14.3.1905:* Left Garston for Dublin with a cargo of coal and disappeared. *14.4.1905:* Register closed.

7. GRANGE FELL 1886 Iron

O.N. 84101 245g 143n 120.5 x 22.0 x 10.1 feet
C.2-cyl. by David Rollo and Sons, Liverpool.

2.4.1881: Launched by R. and J. Evans, Liverpool (Yard No. 99) for Hume, Smith and Co., Liverpool as GRANGE FELL. *9.5.1881:* Completed. *26.2.1886:* Acquired by the Steamship Grange Fell Co. Ltd. (John J. Mack and Sons, managers), Liverpool. *7.12.1886:* Left Fowey for Liverpool with a cargo of china clay and disappeared. *7.2.1887:* Register closed.

8. TOPAZ 1891 Iron

O.N. 87723 353g 168n 160.1 x 23.2 x 11.1 feet
C. 2-cyl. by William King and Co., Glasgow.

6.11.1883: Launched by T. B. Seath and Co., Rutherglen (Yard No. 237) for William Robertson, Glasgow as TOPAZ. *4.12.1883:* Completed. *4.4.1891:* Acquired by John J. Mack and Sons, Liverpool. *28.12.1891:* Struck Dunany Point and foundered off Dundalk Bay whilst on a voyage from Workington to Dundalk with a cargo of rails. *12.1.1893:* Register closed.

9. LANCASHIRE 1892-1916 Iron

O.N. 102053 413g 172n 160.2 x 23.1 x 11.5 feet
C.2-cyl. by Ross and Duncan, Govan.

15.11.1892: Completed by John Fullerton and Co., Paisley (Yard No. 109) for John J. Mack, Liverpool. *2.12.1892:* Owners became the Steamship Lancashire Co. Ltd. (John J. Mack and Sons, managers), Liverpool as LANCASHIRE. *8.2.1902:* Sank in collision during fog with the Norwegian steamer ASLAK (872/1882) in the Crosby Channel, River Mersey whilst on a voyage from Belfast to Liverpool with general cargo. *13.2.1902:* Register closed. Later raised and repaired. *2.6.1902:* Re-registered. *12.2.1916:* Sold to Mann, Macneal and Co. Ltd., Glasgow. *11.3.1926:* Sold to William M. Barkley and Sons Ltd. (William Clint, manager), Belfast. *15.11.1934:* Sold to Alfred H. Smith, Shenfield, *Essex. 12.1.1934:* Sold to T. G. Irving Ltd., Sunderland. *13.1.1936:* Sold to John Carter (Poole) Ltd., Poole. *10.11.1936:* Register closed after being broken up by Thomas Young and Co., Sunderland.

10. CUMBERLAND 1893-1916 Steel and iron

O.N. 102092 396g 159n 142.2 x 25.2 x 11.5 feet
C.2-cyl. by Ross and Duncan, Govan; 9½ knots.

18.4.1893: Launched by John Fullerton and Co., Paisley (Yard No. 113) for the Steamship Cumberland Co. Ltd. (John J. Mack and Sons, managers), Liverpool as CUMBERLAND. *8.5.1893:* Completed. *2.5.1916: S*old to John Kelly Ltd. (Samuel Kelly, manager), Belfast. *25.2.1919:* Renamed DINGLE. *28.7.1920:* Sold to Cullen, Allen and Co. Ltd. (Wilson and Reid, managers), Belfast. *30.11.1921:* Wrecked on Rue Point, Rathlin Island whilst on a voyage from Belfast to Portrush in ballast.

11. YORKSHIRE 1893-1916 Steel and iron

O.N. 102116 394g 156n 142.2 x 25.2 x 11.5 feet
C. 2-cyl. by Ross and Duncan, Govan; 9½ knots.

16.10.1893: Launched by John Fullerton and Co., Paisley (Yard No. 114) for John S. Mack, Liverpool. *6.11.1893:* Completed. *15.12.1894:* Owners became the Steamship Yorkshire Co. Ltd. (John J. Mack and Sons, managers), Liverpool as YORKSHIRE. *11.8.1916:* In collision with the steamer SKERNAHAN (530/1902), which sank, seven miles south west of the Stack, Holyhead whilst on a voyage from Garston to Waterford with a cargo of coal. *19.9.1916:* Sold to William Barkley and Sons Ltd. (Samuel Kelly, manager), Belfast. *11.3.1919:* Renamed STRAMORE. *20.6.1920:* Sold to Samuel Gray, Belfast. *8.2.1922:* Struck submerged wreck and sank ten miles west of Inishowen Head whilst on a voyage from Belfast to Sligo with a cargo of maize. *6.3.1922:* Register closed.

12. CALEDONIAN 1894-1902 Iron

O.N. 67497 553g 331n 201.0 x 26.1 x 12.9 feet
C. 2-cyl. by John Elder and Co., Govan.

30.4.1874: Launched by John Elder and Co., Govan (Yard No. 170) for Robert Henderson Senior, Belfast as CALEDONIAN. *1876:* Owner became Robert Henderson junior, Belfast and later that year the Ardrossan Shipping Co., Ardrossan (Robert Henderson and Sons, Belfast, managers). *7.1891:* Sold to William Sloan and Co., Glasgow. *7.1894:* Acquired by John J. Mack and Sons, Liverpool. *1.2.1902:* Sold to William B. Baring (William W. Craig, manager), Liverpool. *4.1902:* Sold to Salgado and Co., Rio de Janeiro, Brazil and renamed GUASCA. *5.12.1907:* Sunk in collision with a vessel reported to be the Brazilian steamer SAN LOURENCO off Paranagua whilst on a voyage from Paranagua to Santos. Thirty of those on board were drowned.

13. DEVONSHIRE 1894-1918

O.N. 102183 500g 176n 175.0 x 26.6 x 10.3 feet
C. 2-cyl. by Ross and Duncan, Govan; 10 knots.

31.10.1894: Launched by John Fullerton and Co., Paisley (Yard No. 120) for the Steamship Devonshire Co. Ltd. (John J. Mack and Sons, managers), Liverpool as DEVONSHIRE. *6.12.1894:* Completed. *28.2.1918:* Sold to John Kelly Ltd. (Samuel Kelly, manager), Belfast. *25.2.1919:* Renamed BLACKSOD. *26.11.1923:* Manager became William Clint. *15.4.1949:* Sold to W. N. Lindsay Ltd., Leith. *1.1954:* Broken up by Shipbreaking Industries Ltd., Charlestown, Fife. *10.3.1954:* Register closed.

Mack's **Devonshire** ran as **Blacksod** from 1919 to 1954. *W.S.P.L. Cochrane collection*

14. CHESHIRE 1904-1922

O.N. 118144 633g 237n 178.0 x 29.1 x 10.7 feet
C. 2-cyl. by Ross and Duncan, Govan; 10$^1/_2$ knots.

27.9.1904: Launched by John Fullerton and Co., Paisley (Yard No. 178) for the Steamship Cheshire Co. Ltd. (John J. Mack and Sons, managers), Liverpool as CHESHIRE. *3.11.1904:* Completed. *6.3.1922:* Left Port Talbot for Fécamp with a cargo of coal and disappeared. *7.3.1922:* Last seen passing the Lizard. *19.5.1922:* Register closed.

15. FLESWICK 1907-1929

O.N. 102470 647g 195n 179.3 x 28.0 x 11.2 feet
C. 2-cyl. by McKie and Baxter, Glasgow.

16.12.1899: Launched by the Ailsa Shipbuilding Co., Troon (Yard No. 85) for Robert Simpson, Whitehaven as FLESWICK. *17.3.1900:* Completed. *18.3.1907:* Acquired by the Steamship Fleswick Co. Ltd. (John J. Mack and Sons, managers), Liverpool. *17.10.1908:* Sank following a collision with the steamer KILLARNEY (1,232/1891) in Monkstown Bay, Cork Harbour whilst on a voyage from Garston to Cork with a cargo of coal. One fireman was lost. *18.3.1909:* Raised and later repaired. *30.6.1909:* Re-registered. *31.1.1929:* Owners became the Belfast, Mersey and Manchester Steamship Co. Ltd. (John J. Mack and Sons, managers), Liverpool. *15.10.1936:* Sold to Monroe Brothers Ltd., Liverpool. *3.12.1936:* Owners became the Kyle Shipping Co. Ltd. (Monroe Brothers, managers), Liverpool. *8.10.1941:* Sold to the Culliford Shipping Co. Ltd. (Culliford and Clark Ltd., managers), London. *23.1.1945:* Sold to Charles Strubin and Co. Ltd., London. *7.1946:* Sold to the Bienvenido Steamship Co. (J. Livanos and Sons, managers), Panama and renamed LEANDROS. *12.2.1949:* Foundered north of Corsica whilst on a voyage from Marseilles to Heraklion with a cargo which included carbon disulphide.

Straits Steamship Co. Ltd.

1. ROMA 1924-1938

O.N. 116007 158g 49n 95.0 x 18.9 x 8.5 feet
1913: 181g 67n 106.0 x 18.9 x 8.5 feet
C. 2-cyl. by Muir and Houston Ltd., Glasgow.

1903: Completed by the Larne Shipbuilding Co., Larne (Yard No. 25) for W.J.R. Harbinson and C.L. Mackean, Belfast as ROMA. *1913:* Lengthened. *1917:* Sold to Henry Renny (Earl J. Leslie, manager), Forfar. *1920:* Sold to the Sea Navigation Co. Ltd. (W.J. Stewart and Douglas Cable, managers), London. *1924:* Sold to Lowden, Connell and Co., Liverpool. *1924:* Acquired by the Straits Steamship Co. Ltd. (Alfred Capper, manager), Liverpool. *1938:* Sold to Alfred J. Smith, Bristol. *1949:* Sold to Bristowe Shippers Ltd. (Arthur Smith, manager), Bristol. *1958:* Sold to Renwick, Wilton and Dobson Ltd., Torquay. *10.4.1959:* Arrived at Newport, Monmouthshire to be broken up by John Cashmore Ltd.

Roma *John Clarkson*

2. PENRHOS 1939-1942

O.N. 118125 187g 87n 101.0 x 21.8 x 10.6 feet
C. 2-cyl. by W.J. Yarwood, Northwich; 8 knots.

25.3.1904: Launched by W.J. Yarwood, Northwich (Yard No. 31) for Henry Seddon, Middlewich as STANLEY. *13.9.1904:* Completed. *31.10.1904:* Owners became the Stanley Steamship Co. Ltd. (Henry Seddon, manager), Liverpool. *3.6.1927:* Sold to William B. Kyffin, Birkenhead. *24.8.1927:* Sold to Alfred B. Wade, Cardiff. *20.10.1927:* Sold to Steam Coasters Ltd. (William A. Andrew, manager), Cardiff. *4.12.1939:* Acquired by the Straits Steamship Co. Ltd. (Lovell D. Mack, manager), Liverpool. *16.1.1940:* Renamed PENRHOS. *1.1.1942:* Mined and sunk one mile and approximately 243° from the North Constable Buoy, Liverpool Bay whilst on a voyage from Penmaenmawr to Liverpool with a cargo of stone chippings. Her crew of four was lost. *16.2.1942:* Register closed.

3. PENRHYN 1954-1965

O.N. 113442 211g 72n 100.5 x 21.6 x 9.7 feet
C. 2-cyl. by W.J. Yarwood, Northwich.
3.1932: Oil engine 3-cyl. 4S.C.S.A. made by N.V. Machinefabriek Bolnes, Bolnes, Holland in 1930 .
7.1946: Engine removed.
1948: Oil engine 4-cyl. 2S.C.S.A. made by J.G. Kincaid and Co. Ltd., Greenock in 1940.

18.11.1901: Completed by W.J. Yarwood, Northwich (Yard No. 10) for the Northwich Carrying Co. Ltd., Northwich as ALEXANDRA. *9.10.1923:* Sold to Joseph Bowles, Cardiff. *3.1932:* Fitted with an oil engine. *1935:* Owners became F. Bowles and Sons (Joseph Bowles, manager), Cardiff. *25.8.1944:* Sold to Hubert F. Ashmead, Bristol. *11.7.1946:* Re-registered as a sailing vessel after engines had been removed. *1948:* Sold to I.P. Langford (Shipping) Ltd. (Victor W. Rowles and Co., managers), Gloucester, renamed DIANA MARY and fitted with an oil engine. *1954:* Acquired by the Straits Steamship Co. Ltd., Caernarfon (Lovell D. Mack, Liverpool, manager) and renamed PENRHYN. *1965:* Owners became the Liverpool Lighterage Co. Ltd., Liverpool. *17.8.1965:* Arrived at Troon to be broken up by W.H. Arnott, Young and Co. Ltd.

Penrhyn was a regular trader to the Manchester Ship Canal. *K. Cunnington*

Liverpool Lighterage Co. Ltd.

CRISTO 1940-1963

O.N. 135929 140g 70n 89.0 x 19.1 x 9.1 feet
Oil engine 2S.C.S.A. by J. och C.G. Bolinders Mekaniska Verksted A/B, Stockholm, Sweden.
1958: Oil engine 4-cyl. 4S.C.S.A. made by R.A. Lister and Co. Ltd., Dursley.

4.1916: Completed by the Rennie Forrestt Shipbuilding Co. Ltd., Wivenhoe (Yard No. 1268) for Wilfred Christophersen, Ipswich as CRISTO. *1918:* Sold to Harry O. Blackwood (Matthew Butcher, manager), Great Yarmouth. *1919:* Owners became the Blackwood Shipping Co. Ltd. (Richards, Longstaffe and Co. Ltd., managers), London. *1920:* Sold to Van Oppen and Co. Ltd. (Anglian Steamship Co. Ltd., managers), London. *1922:* Sold to the Darwen and Mostyn Iron Co. Ltd., Mostyn. *1933:* Sold to Cristo Ltd., Bristol. *1940:* Acquired by the Liverpool Lighterage Co. Ltd., Liverpool. *1958:* Fitted with a new oil engine. *1963:* Sold to the Light Shipping Co. Ltd. (Ross and Marshall Ltd., managers), Glasgow. *1964:* Renamed LIMELIGHT. *10.10.1966:* Wrecked near Port Ellen, Islay whilst on a voyage from Irvine to Port Ellen with a cargo of cement and bricks.

MANCHESTER, LIVERPOOL AND NORTH WALES STEAMSHIP CO. LTD.
Liverpool

The opening of the Manchester Ship Canal in 1894 began a flurry of commercial activity in Manchester as shipping and associated companies were formed to exploit the great new waterway. The name Manchester now appeared almost for the first time in the titles of shipping companies, such as the specific if long-winded Manchester, Liverpool and North Wales Steamship Co. Ltd. This company is of particular interest in being formed not by a shipbroker, ship's master or merchant, but by a retired admiral.

Rear Admiral John Parry Jones-Parry (1829-1920) retired from the Royal Navy in 1873, after a career in which he saw service throughout the Crimean War as gunnery officer in H.M.S. TERRIBLE. He is also credited with the invention of the non-recoil gun carriage. John Parry Jones-Parry was a son of the Llŷn peninsula; the Jones-Parry family lived at Madryn Castle. The Rear Admiral's father, another John, was a younger son of the family, and in 1822 became rector at the nearby village of Edern, the living being in the gift of the family. Our hero's uncle, Sir Love Parry Jones-Parry (1781-1853), enjoys an almost legendary status. He had soldiered in the Peninsula War, was Member of Parliament for Caernarfon and seems to have exercised almost feudal rights over his estates. He is perhaps best known for the survey work he undertook for the Welsh settlement in Patagonia which became known as the Chubut Colony. His impressions of the bare and arid land along the Chubut river were unfavourable, but the settlers nevertheless went ahead and colonised the region, being most impressed by the unsurprising lack of any other European settlers. In honour of Jones-Parry, the colony's port took its name from his family seat and became Puerto Madryn.

By the 1890s Rear Admiral John Parry Jones-Parry was settled at Thelwall Hall, Warrington. Here he became a local magistrate, his initials now being J.P. J-P. J.P. He was referred to as Terrible John, although it is not known if this was a reflection of his naval posting or his sentencing policy.

John Parry Jones-Parry's connections with merchant rather than naval shipping were rather distant ones. His first wife was the daughter of Caernarfon ironmaster Jeffrey de Winton, who built a number of engines, boilers and hulls. The Jones-Parry family had cherished an ambition that the nearby Porthdinllaen should take over from Holyhead as the major packet port for Ireland. Jones-Parry inherited a shareholding in the Oakley Slate Quarry, and this and a patriarchal interest in developing his native Llŷn may have convinced him that the local stone industry would benefit from the use of steamships. The first vessel he is known to have owned was the small steamer FLAGSTAFF, which regularly loaded at Yr Eifl Quarry, a few miles north of Edern.

In May 1895 Jones-Parry was instrumental in forming the Manchester, Liverpool and North Wales Steamship Co. Ltd. Of the 500 £5 paid-up shares in the company, Jones-Parry had 494, with just one owned by each of the other six subscribers which company law required. Jones-Parry was already in possession of the W.S. CAINE and transferred her to the company. Despite the pre-eminence of Manchester in its title, the company had its head office in Liverpool, at South John Street. The fleet was built up cautiously by purchasing small, secondhand steamers at intervals and financing them with mortgages. The steamers' main employment was carrying stone from quarries on the North Wales coast to the Mersey ports and to Manchester, Fleetwood, Lancaster and Preston. The W.S. CAINE. for instance, regularly loaded at Yr Eifl for Runcorn.

This was not to be Jones-Parry's sole interest in steamship companies, as in 1896 he became Chairman of the troubled Liverpool, Caernarfon and Menai Straits Steamship Co. Ltd. He retained a substantial shareholding in its successor, the Liverpool and Menai Straits Steamship Co. Ltd. of 1901.

Towards the end of 1903, Jones-Parry began to restructure the company in preparation for his retirement: he was now almost 75. This involved bringing new capital and new managers into the company, and this was achieved by increasing the company's capital from £5,000 to £20,000 and finding new shareholders. Jones-Parry was still the largest single shareholder, but next to him was salt proprietor Henry Seddon. Most of the other new investors were business associates of Seddon: most notably Richard R.

Clark and his shipbroking partner George Grounds, but also salt merchants and salt brokers, a fish curer from Lerwick, and small businessmen including shipbuilders and engineers from Northwich. In April 1904 Jones-Parry stood down as manager in favour of Robert R, Clark. As described in an earlier chapter, Clark was already a successful shipbroker and sailing ship owner, specialising in the North Wales stone trade. He moved into the offices of the Manchester, Liverpool and North Wales Steamship Co. Ltd. which were now in Albert Buildings, Liverpool. Jones-Parry remained a director until 1908, when he passed the job on to his son William.

The increase in capital helped the company acquire its first new ships. Named in honour of the company's founder, ADMIRAL was one of the last steamers built at Maryport. And even though W.J. Yarwood had not invested in the company, his Northwich yard received an order for the smaller CONSTANCE.

Richard Clark seems not to have distinguished between the various ships he operated: those he owned himself, or those managed for Henry Seddon or the Manchester, Liverpool and North Wales Steamship Co. Ltd. A letter written by Clark in May 1906 simply reports that his 'boats' had loaded almost 150,000 tons of Welsh stone in the previous year. They also carried coal, iron, timber, corn and general cargo to Ireland and elsewhere; the larger vessels running to the Bristol Channel and as far as the Thames.

In 1911, Clark floated his own company, the Overton Steamship Co. Ltd., and new ships were acquired for this company whilst the fleet of the Manchester, Liverpool and North Wales Steamship Co. Ltd. was allowed to decline slowly. All may not have been well with the company financially: the tiny CAREW was repossessed by her mortgagee and sold, and the W.S. CAINE also left the fleet. The SOLWAY PRINCE was left a constructive total loss after a collision in the Manchester Ship Canal in 1913, two ships were sunk by U-boats during the First World War whilst the CONSTANCE was sold in 1919, just before her loss. Only the ADMIRAL now remained.

In 1920, over £18,000 of the profits from ship sales was capitalised by creating new shares which were divided up amongst the existing shareholders – a device which may

Admiral had a grey hull when new, as did some of the company's other vessels. She is seen at Neath about 1909 with the tug **Gipsy** alongside. Judging by the ladies in the stern of the **Gipsy,** it rather than the **Admiral** was the photographer's prime objective. *Welsh Industrial and Maritime Museum*

A splendid view of **Constance** with her funnel emblazoned with crossed battleaxes and smoking strongly.

John Clarkson

Launch of **Edern**. *Courtesy Mrs Christine Evans*

have reduced the company's tax liability. As events would show, this was a mistake. At the same time there was another massive increase in nominal capital of £95,000. Only a fraction of this was paid-up, but the aim was to increase the size and efficiency of the fleet, and one of four sisters which Clark had ordered from Cochranes of Selby was delivered to the Manchester, Liverpool and North Wales Steamship Co. Ltd. as EDERN, her name recalling its founder's connections with the Llŷn. Neither were the old company's colours forgotten, as the EDERN had the crossed battleaxes painted bravely on her funnel. With ADMIRAL, however, she was run as just another member of Clark's fleet.

Jones-Parry died in 1920 at his home – also called Edern – at Boscombe, Hampshire. Much of his now substantial holding in the Manchester, Liverpool and North Wales Steamship Co. Ltd. passed to his son William and his wife. Other family members had held small holdings in the company, including son Geoffrey Jones-Parry, an army captain who was killed in action in August 1915, and Thomas who became a poultry farmer in Lancashire. Seddon and Clark remained the most important shareholders outside the family.

The ADMIRAL was sold in 1930, and in August 1932 the EDERN was transferred to the ownership of the Overton Steamship Co. Ltd. Why was this done? The EDERN is known to have cost about £29,000 when new, but this had been during the post-war boom when ship prices were grossly inflated: her sisterships were changing hands for less than half this price within a few years, and values had not increased over the next decade. As a result, not only were companies like the Manchester, Liverpool and North Wales Steamship Co. Ltd. not making profits during the depressed trading conditions, but their capital did not reflect the value of their assets which comprised their now much-depreciated steamers. Keeping the companies going was just not worth the administrative effort. Transfer of the EDERN was something of a tidying-up operation, allowing the owning company to be liquidated, and a general meeting agreed to this in October 1932. The return to the shareholders was, however, minute. There was an outstanding mortgage on EDERN of just over £2,600. It is not known if ADMIRAL had been mortgaged, but the net result of the sale of the two ships was that just £171 was available for distribution amongst owners of 21,000 shares. The largest shareholder, William Jones-Parry, walked away with £53.

The financial fortunes of the Manchester, Liverpool and North Wales Steamship Co. Ltd. help to illustrate just why investment in coastal shipping became unpopular after 1920. The company had been soundly based and was run with discretion. Undoubtedly dividends had been good for the latter part of the war and for a year or two thereafter, but the final pay-out represented just 7% of an initial total investment of almost £2,500 - a figure which had been substantial increased over the years.

Fleet lists

John P. Jones-Parry

1. FLAGSTAFF 1893-1895 Iron

O.N. 97233 113g 48n 75.0 x 19.7 x 8.1 feet
C. 2-cyl. by G.K. Stothert and Co., Bristol.

7.2.1890: Completed by G.K. Stothert and Co., Bristol for William E. Davies, London as FLAGSTAFF. *11.12.1893:* Acquired by John P. Jones-Parry, Liverpool. *7.3.1895:* Sold to David C. Pritchard, Caernarfon. *1900:* Sold to Spillers and Bakers Ltd., Cardiff. *1903:* Sold to Patrick Hallinan, Middleton, County Cork. *1932:* Sold to the Middleton Milling (Parent) Co. Ltd., Middleton. *1938:* Broken up. *9.1938:* Register closed.

Manchester, Liverpool and North Wales Steamship Co. Ltd.

1. W.S. CAINE 1895-1911 Iron

O.N. 87232 183g 79n 122.4 x 21.1 x 7.9 feet
C. 2-cyl. by De Winton and Co., Caernarfon.

4.1883: Launched by William Thomas and Sons, Amlwch (Yard No. 15) for William Thomas and Co., Amlwch as W.S. CAINE. *2.5.1883:* Completed. *12.3.1886:* Owners became the Steamship W.S. Caine Co. Ltd. (William Thomas and Co., managers), Liverpool. *9.3.1895:* Acquired by John P. Jones-Parry, Liverpool. *18.6.1895:* Owners became the Manchester, Liverpool and North Wales Steamship Co. Ltd., (John P. Jones-Parry, manager), Liverpool. *28.3.1904:* Manager became Robert R. Clark. *28.3.1911:* Sold to William Rouse and Sons, Neyland, Pembrokeshire. *27.12.1918:* Sold to John W. Robertson, Lerwick. *20.2.1920:* Sold to John Johnston, Glasgow. *11.4.1922:* Sold to William Cubbin Ltd., Liverpool for demolition. *5.1922:* Broken up at Birkenhead. *17.6.1922:* Register closed.

2. ADELAIDE 1897-1899 Iron

O.N. 76722 70g 27n 65.4 x 17.7 x 7.5 feet
2-cyl. by Manderson, Hutson and Corbett, Glasgow.
2.1904: C. 2-cyl. by Plenty and Sons, Newbury; 7 knots.

25.11.1876: Completed by John Hay, Kirkintilloch for James and John Hay, Glasgow as ADELAIDE. *27.9.1895:* Sold to William Walker junior, Maryport. *10.3.1897:* Acquired by the Manchester, Liverpool and North Wales Steamship Co. Ltd. (John P. Jones-Parry, manager), Liverpool. *1.9.1899:* Sold to Henry Ensor, Queenstown, Cork. *2.1904:* Fitted with new engine. *30.9.1935:* Register closed, having been broken up at Milford Haven by Thomas W. Ward Ltd.

3. TRAFFORD 1899-1915

O.N. 105675 231g 47n 128.0 x 20.1 x 9.4 feet
C. 2-cyl. by Muir and Houston Ltd., Glasgow; 10 knots.

20.8.1896: Launched by Mackie and Thomson, Govan (Yard No. 113) for the Trafford Steamship Co. Ltd., Manchester (John K. Morris, Seacombe, manager) as TRAFFORD. *15.9.1896:* Completed. *4.5.1898:* Manager became Charles Baybut, Manchester. *26.11.1898:* Managers became Fletcher, Woodhill and Co., Manchester. *9.10.1899:* Acquired by the Manchester, Liverpool and North Wales Steamship Co. Ltd. (John P. Jones-Parry, manager), Liverpool. *28.3.1904:* Manager became Richard R. Clark. *16.6.1915:* Sunk by gunfire from the German submarine U 22 thirty miles west north west of the Smalls whilst on a voyage from Newport to Lydney in ballast. *25.6.1915:* Register closed.

4. CAREW 1900-1911

O.N. 102161 133g 64n 95.0 x 20.0 x 7.2 feet
T. 3-cyl. by the North Eastern Marine Engineering Co. Ltd., Newcastle-upon-Tyne; 8½ knots.

5.7.1894: Launched by McAndrew, Cowan and Potts, South Hylton, Sunderland for John Bacon Ltd., Liverpool as CAREW. *31.7.1894:* Completed. *9.5.1900:* Acquired by John P. Jones- Parry, Liverpool. *21.5.1900:* Owners became the Manchester, Liverpool and North Wales Steamship Co. Ltd. (John P. Jones-Parry, manager), Liverpool. *28.3.1904:* Manager became Robert R. Clark. *25.7.1911:* Sold to Irish Industrial Minerals Ltd. (Laurence W. Carder, manager), Westport, County Mayo. *9.1912:* Sold to Trasporti Marittimi Costieri (Carlo Givone, manager), Genoa, Italy and renamed CARLO GIVONE. *1913:* Sold to F. Paoletti, Genoa and renamed TERZO. *1916:* Sold to S. Pellegrino, Bengasi, Tripoli and placed under the Italian flag. *1919:* Sold to Francesco Fabiano, Port Said, Egypt. *1922:* Sold to F.E. Montu (Costi Xydia and Son, managers), Alexandria, Egypt. *1924:* Sold to Apostolis Vrahamis, Constantinople, Turkey and renamed ELIF. *10.9.1927:* Foundered near Zonguldak whilst on a voyage from Zonguldak to Constantinople with a cargo of coal.

5. EXCHANGE 1901-1917 Iron

O.N. 87965 295g 93n 135.0 x 22.3 x 9.9 feet
C. 2-cyl. by De Winton and Co., Caernarfon.

2.1884: Launched by William Thomas and Sons, Amlwch (Yard No. 16) for William Thomas junior, Amlwch as EXCHANGE. *9.5.1884:* Completed. *15.5.1884:* Owners became the Steamship Exchange Co. Ltd. (William Thomas and Co., managers), Liverpool. *10.12.1901:* Acquired by the Manchester, Liverpool and North Wales Steamship Co. Ltd. (John P. Jones-Parry, manager), Liverpool. *28.3.1904:* Manager became Robert R. Clark. *23.3.1917:* Sunk by gunfire from the German submarine UB 39 thirty miles north west of Cayeux whilst on a voyage from St. Valery-sur-Somme to Newhaven in ballast. *20.4.1917:* Register closed.

Exchange *E.N. Taylor*

6. SOLWAY PRINCE 1902-1913 Iron

O.N. 94034 349g 99n 145.3 x 23.2 x 9.0 feet
C. 2-cyl. by the Penarth Shipbuilding and Ship Repairing Co. Ltd., Penarth Dock.

25.8.1890: Completed by the Penarth Shipbuilding and Ship Repairing Co. Ltd., Penarth Dock (Yard No. 11) for the Solway Steamship Co. Ltd., Whitehaven as SOLWAY PRINCE. *19.3.1895:* Managers became Burnyeat, Dalzell and Co. *12.1.1899:* Sold to William Postlethwaite, Millom. *29.11.1902:* Acquired by the Manchester, Liverpool and North Wales Steamship Co. Ltd. (John P. Jones-Parry, manager), Liverpool. *29.3.1904:* Manager became Robert R. Clark. *22.3.1913:* Sank in collision with the steamer ROSSMORE (627/1907) in the Manchester Ship Canal whilst on a voyage from Partington to Malpas with a cargo of coal. *22.3.1913:* Register closed. Although declared a constructive total loss, she was refloated, taken to Manchester and repaired. *16.2.1914:* Re-registered in the ownership of Frederick W. Horlock, Harwich. *13.10.1915:* Sold to Care and Young Shipping Co. Ltd., Cardiff. *20.2.1917:* Sold to Thomas Stone and Joseph Rolfe, Llanelli. *24.5.1917:* Owners became Channel Transport Ltd. (Thomas Stone and Joseph Rolfe, managers), Llanelli. *27.6.1917:* Sunk by explosives after being captured by the German submarine UB 40 eight miles north of Alderney whilst on a voyage from Poole to Jersey in ballast. *11.7.1917:* Register closed.

7. ADMIRAL 1906-1930

O.N. 120914 263g 170n 121.2 x 22.1 x 9.5 feet
C. 2-cyl. by James Ritchie, Partick, Glasgow; 9 3/4 knots.

29.11.1905: Launched by William Walker, Maryport (Yard No. 90) for the Manchester, Liverpool and North Wales Steamship Co. Ltd. (Robert R. Clark, manager), Liverpool as ADMIRAL. *19.1.1906:* Completed. *19.11.1930:* Sold to the Eastbrook Trading Co. (Robert Monroe, manager), Liverpool. *20.1.1931:* Owners became Monroe Brothers Ltd., Liverpool. *15.3.1935:* Sold to Andrew McKay, Islandmagee, County Antrim. *20.4.1935:* Sold to Isaac Stewart trading as the Admiral Shipping Co., Belfast. *1940:* Owners became Isaac Stewart (Stewart and Partners, managers), Belfast and renamed FIRST. *1957:* Sold to Mrs. J.M. McLennan, Dundee. *1958:* Renamed MIDDLEBANK. *1962:* Sold to Smith, Hood and Co. Ltd., Dundee. *1962:* Sold to the Tay Sand Co. Ltd., Dundee. *5.1964:* Sold to Malcolm Brechin for demolition at Granton.

8. CONSTANCE 1907-1919

O.N. 124053 209g 76n 112.0 x 22.0 x 8.9 feet
C. 2-cyl. by W.J. Yarwood and Sons, Northwich; 9 knots.

1.12.1906: Launched by W.J. Yarwood and Sons, Northwich (Yard No. 75) for the Manchester, Liverpool and North Wales Steamship Co. Ltd. (Robert R. Clark, manager), Liverpool as CONSTANCE. *2.4.1907:* Completed. *15.11.1919:* Sold to William Clint, Belfast. *18.12.1919:* Left Garston for Belfast with a cargo of coal and disappeared. She is believed to have foundered near the Mersey Bar. *13.1.1920:* Register closed.

Edern in original condition with the crossed battleaxes on her funnel. She later lost them in favour of a plain buff funnel. *E.N. Taylor*

9. EDERN 1921-1932

O.N. 143710 466g 192n 152.0 x 25.2 x 10.8 feet
T. 3-cyl. by C.D. Holmes and Co. Ltd., Hull; 9½ knots.

15.9.1920: Launched by Cochrane and Sons, Selby (Yard No. 748) for the Manchester, Liverpool and North Wales Steamship Co. Ltd. (Robert R. Clark, manager), Liverpool as EDERN. *26.1.1921:* Completed. *29.8.1932:* Owners became the Overton Steamship Co. Ltd. (Robert R. Clark, managers), Liverpool. *16.6.1942:* Sold to the Williamstown Shipping Co. Ltd. (Comben Longstaff and Co., managers), London. *31.3.1944:* Sold to Challis, Stern and Co. Ltd. (Warren Shipping Co. Ltd., managers), London. *3.7.1946:* Renamed WARREN CHASE. *5.5.1952:* Owners became the Warren Shipping Co. Ltd., London. *15.6.1954:* Arrived at Gateshead to be broken up by J.J. King and Co. *20.10.1954:* Register closed.

Nomenclature

ADMIRAL	Named in honour of Rear-Admiral J.P. Jones-Parry J.P., the company's founder.
CONSTANCE	Named after Jones-Parry's second wife, Marion Constance.
EDERN	Jones-Parry was born in this village on the Llŷn.

MERSEY PORTS STEVEDORING CO. LTD.
Liverpool

Mersey Ports Stevedoring Co. Ltd. was unusual for a company in the coastal trade in being founded by a deep-sea master mariner, albeit one who had specialised in port services. As such, it provides a unique example in this book of a company moving from these services into coastal shipowning. What is known about the company is largely that recorded by Captain Owen Spargo, who worked for it as seaman at the beginning of its existence and as master towards the end.

Behind the company was Captain Robert McClure, who had been master in deep sea sail and finished as captain with Ritson's of Sunderland who owned big cargo vessels with names ending BRANCH and a forest of derricks. With a William McKnight, McClure ran a stevedoring business. This probably had its origins in the Mersey Derricking and Coaling Co. Ltd. which, in 1921, bought a small wooden steamer that had spent part of its life as a sailing lugger, the CONCORD (65/1917). Her manager was initially a Richard Bennett, but in 1924 Robert McClure took over. As the CONCORD was transferred to the ownership of the Mersey Ports Stevedoring Co. Ltd. in 1926, it is reasonable to assume McClure had an interest in both concerns. Shortly before acquiring CONCORD, the Mersey Ports company had purchased another wooden steamer, this time built in Canada, the SALVATOR (92/1917). Both were converted to derrick barges for use in and between the ports on the Mersey.

The Mersey Ports Stevedoring Co. Ltd. began buying coasters in 1931 with the DENESIDE, continuing with the SHELLIE which was renamed DELLSIDE in a short-lived enthusiasm for a naming scheme. Each was sold after four years, but considerably larger coasters were then bought: ARDGARROCH, ESKWOOD and KILREA were in the 190-200 feet range. Both derrick barges were broken up in 1936, after which the company concentrated on coasters.

The DENESIDE had a fairly regular run to Kilrush in the mouth of the River Shannon, usually with bulk maize and sometimes with coal, plus a small amount of general cargo in the hold. Return cargoes were sometimes available from the quarry at Liscannor which produced flagstones, or granite chippings from Crookhaven. The DENESIDE also used to load in the china clay ports for Runcorn or Glasson Dock.

The company's ships were often bought and sold quite rapidly, and Captain Spargo suggests that the owners acquired coasters almost as the fancy took them. They were probably looking out for a good purchase or sale, with an eye on the chance of a quick profit. The company suffered no major disasters, and with the exception of its early wooden steamers, all its ships were sold on to other owners, several of whom were in

Kilrea *John Clarkson*

Perdita in Gilchrist's colours.

W.S.P.L.

the coastal liner trades. Some ships had come out of this trade, including the post-war acquisition PERDITA which had been built for the South Wales to Liverpool service of Gilchrists, whilst the CELIA MARY – although built as a collier – had been the PERSIAN COAST of the Tyne-Tees Steamship Co. Ltd. PERDITA was remembered as a particularly fast steamer, making all of the 11 knots with which she was officially credited. Having kept her in good condition, the company sold her to Italian owners in the spring of 1951.

The last ship of Mersey Ports Stevedoring Co. Ltd., CELIA MARY, was sold in 1955, Hull owners squeezing a few more months' work from her. This year saw the post-war

Enid Mary

J.K. Byass

boom in coastal freight rates end, and began a wholesale scrapping of steam coasters which meant only a few survived into the 1960s. With good judgement, the company had picked the right time to quit shipowning.

Robert McClure is recalled as a very fair man and a good employer. He did not resort to half-pay for his men when a ship could not work, as happened to the DENESIDE after she had suffered a fire, but kept the officers on full pay. Also unusual in the coasting trade, he paid skippers their full pilotage. Coastal ship masters often held pilotage certificates for several ports, which exempted their ship from pilotage dues. Usually, it was the owner who pocketed the saving; indeed, when times were hard some owners would only employ skippers with pilotage certificates. But deep sea men did not always understand the coasting trade: Captain Spargo recalls that McClure never really appreciated why coasters spent so much of their time windbound.

The fleet of the Mersey Ports Stevedoring Co. Ltd. was short-lived but was a significant part of the Liverpool coaster business of the time. Captain McClure showed that, to make a good living from coasters, you did not have to be brought up in them, nor to adopt an intolerant and penny-pinching attitude to those who earned you your money.

Fleet list

1. DENESIDE 1931-1935

O.N. 132051 329g 130n 133.9 x 23.1 x 9.3 feet
C. 2-cyl. by George T. Grey, South Shields.

8.8.1910: Launched by J.T. Eltringham and Co., South Shields (Yard No. 279) for the Wear Steam Shipping Co. Ltd. (Thomas Rose, manager), Sunderland as DENESIDE. *8.1910:* Completed. *1917:* Owners became the Wear Steam Shipping Co. (1917) Ltd. (Thomas Rose, manager), Sunderland. *1921:* Sold to William K. Griffin and Norman S. Race, Cardiff. *1922:* Owners became the Deneside Steamship Co. Ltd. (Griffin and Race, managers), Cardiff. *1931:* Acquired by the Mersey Ports Stevedoring Co. Ltd., Liverpool. *1935:* Sold to the Larne Steamship Co. Ltd., Belfast. *1953:* Sold to H.T. Browne and resold to the Tay Sand Co. Ltd. (J. Neilson, manager), Dundee. *18.5.1961:* Arrived in the Nieuw Waterweg in tow of BLANKENBURG (124/1938) for breaking up by Ijssel N.V. Heuvelman. *3.7.1961:* Work began at Krimpen a/d Ijssel, Holland.

Deneside *John Clarkson*

2. SHELLIE/DELLSIDE 1932-1935

O.N. 107004 339g 130n 145.0 x 24.1 x 10.4 feet
C. 2-cyl. by Ross and Duncan, Govan; 10 knots.

30.10.1905: Launched by the Dublin Dockyard Co., Dublin (Yard No. 52) for Samuel Lockington and Co. Ltd., Dundalk as SHELLIE. *25.11.1905:* Completed. *15.5.1917:* Sold to Cunningham, Shaw and Co. Ltd. (Vernon S. Lovell, manager), London. *20.7.1917:* Sold to John Harrison Ltd., London. *13.7.1922:* Sold to the Loughrigg Shipping Co. Ltd. (James A. Johnstone, manager), Fleetwood. *29.9.1927:* Sold to William R. Davies and Co., Liverpool. *1928:* Owners became William R. Davies and Co. Ltd., Liverpool. *2.12.1932:* Acquired by the Mersey Ports Stevedoring Co. Ltd., Liverpool. *3.2.1933:* Renamed DELLSIDE. *6.12.1935:* Sold to John Campbell, Irvine. *4.1.1936:* Sold to the Plymouth, Channel Islands and Brittany Steamship Co. Ltd. (John W.H. Stokes, manager), Plymouth. *5.2.1936:* Renamed NEW VERDUN. *13.12.1938:* Sold to Richard C.L Pike, London. *17.1.1938:* Renamed EFFORD. *29.3.1938:* Sold to the Don David Sand and Gravel Co. Ltd. (Albert H. Russell, manager), Hove, Sussex. *15.5.1940:* Sold to the Efford Shipping Co. Ltd., London. *16.5.1940:* Owners became Springfal Shipping Co. Ltd. (Francis P. Longton, manager), London. *22.5.1940:* Sank following a collision with the French steamer TLEMCEN (4,425/1912) about one mile south of Dover whilst on a voyage from the Tyne to Fowey with a cargo of coal. *17.6.1940:* Register closed.

Shellie in a former owner's colours. *John Clarkson*

3. ARDGARROCH 1936-1937

O.N. 142743 968g 501n 200.2 x 31.2 x 13.2 feet
T. 3-cyl. by Aitchison, Blair Ltd., Clydebank; 10 knots.

13.12.1918: Completed by the Ardrossan Dry Dock and Shipbuilding Co. Ltd., Ardrossan (Yard No. 271) for Mead, Son and Hussey, London as PORTLAND HOUSE. *15.4.1920:* Sold to P. McCallum and Sons Ltd. (Lang and Fulton Ltd., managers), Greenock. *12.5.1920:* Renamed ARDGARROCH. *18.8.1936:* Acquired by the Mersey Ports Stevedoring Co. Ltd., Liverpool. *2.9.1937:* Sold to the Bristol Steam Navigation Co. Ltd., Bristol. *5.11.1937:* Renamed CAPITO. *7.1950:* Sold to the Société Navale Caennaise (G. Lamy et Compagnie, managers), Caen, France and renamed NEREE. *29.11.1952:* Arrived on the Thames to be broken up by T.W. Ward Ltd. *2.12.1952:* Work began at Grays, Essex.

4. ESKWOOD 1937-1944

O.N. 128813 803g 378n 201.8 x 30.0 x 11.6 feet
T. 3-cyl. by Blair and Co. Ltd., Stockton-on-Tees.

25.7.1911: Launched by W. Harkess and Son Ltd., Middlesbrough (Yard No. 189) for the Meteor Steamship Co.

Ardgarroch *W.S.P.L.*

Eskwood in Stone and Rolfe's colours. *E.N. Taylor*

Ltd. (R.A. Constantine and T.H. Donking, managers), Middlesbrough as ESKWOOD. *30.8.1911:* Completed. *1918:* Sold to E. Johnson and Co. Ltd., Goole. *1926:* Sold to S. and R. Steamships Ltd. (Stone and Rolfe Ltd., managers), Llanelli. *1937:* Acquired by the Mersey Ports Stevedoring Co. Ltd., Liverpool. *1944:* Sold to Grand Union (Shipping) Ltd., London. *1946:* Renamed KILWORTH. *1950:* Sold to the Fenchurch Shipping Co. Ltd. (George A. Tom and Co. Ltd., managers), London. *1951:* Renamed FENCHURCH. *1951:* Sold to the Holderness Steamship Co. Ltd., Hull and renamed HOLDERNOLL. *20.1.1956:* Arrived at Gateshead to be broken up by J.J. King and Co. Ltd.

5. KILREA 1937-1941

O.N. 135158 767g 370n 190.4 x 30.0 x 11.7 feet
T. 3-cyl. by George T. Grey, South Shields; 9¾ knots.

11.11.1912: Completed by the Dundee Shipbuilding Co. Ltd., Dundee (Yard No. 346) for M.A. Ray and Sons, London as WANSTEAD. *27.12.1918:* Sold to Coombes, Marshall and Co. Ltd., Middlesbrough. *11.6.1920:* Renamed TEESBURN. *28.6.1926:* Owners became Coombes (Middlesbrough) Ltd., Middlesbrough. *7.11.1928:* Sold to R. and D.A. Duncan Ltd. (William Clint, manager), Belfast. *15.12.1928:* Renamed KILREA. *24.6.1937:* Acquired by the Mersey Ports Stevedoring Co. Ltd., Liverpool. *14.5.1941:* Sold to Western Isles Steamer Services Ltd. (John Campbell, manager), Irvine. *31.8.1943:* Sold to Frederick G. Browne, London. *15.2.1944:* Sank following a collision with the tug LYNCH (211/1924) north of Flamborough Head whilst on a voyage from Aberdeen to Ridham Dock, Kent with a cargo of woodpulp. Her crew was saved. *18.4.1944:* Register closed.

6. PERDITA 1945-1951

O.N. 131309 543g 211n 175.0 x 26.1 x 10.7 feet
T. 3-cyl. by McColl and Pollock, Sunderland; 11 knots.

15.11.1890: Launched by Mackay Brothers, Alloa (Yard No. 14) for the South Wales and Liverpool Steamship Co. Ltd. (Robert Gilchrist and Co., managers), Liverpool as PERDITA. *12.1890:* Completed. *16.4.1943:* Owners became Coast Lines Ltd., Liverpool. *15.1.1945:* Acquired by the Mersey Ports Stevedoring Co. Ltd., Liverpool. *5.1951:* Sold to Giovanni Fornara, Genoa, Italy. *1952:* Renamed SEDULA. *1953:* Renamed SUSANNA. *12.2.1953:* Stranded on Abu Faramish Reef about thirty miles north of Jeddah whilst on a voyage from Naples to Jeddah. Later sank.

7. ENID MARY 1946-1953

O.N. 143539 582g 291n 174.5 x 28.6 x 10.9 feet
T. 3-cyl. by Aitchison, Blair Ltd., Clydebank.

24.2.1921: Launched by Taw Shipyards Ltd., Barnstaple (Yard No. 18) for William A. Philips, Cardiff as ENID MARY. *5.1921:* Completed. *1933:* Sold to William G. James (William G. James and Sons, managers), Cardigan. *1935:* Owners became British Isles Coasters Ltd., Cardigan. *1946:* Acquired by the Mersey Ports Stevedoring Co. Ltd., Liverpool. *1953:* Sold to the Laverock Shipping Co. Ltd., Leith. *1955:* Owners became the Enid Shipping Co. Ltd. (W.B.W. Lyle, manager), Leith. *1956:* Sold to John S. Monks and Co. Ltd., Liverpool and renamed RIVERVILLE. *14.6.1960:* Arrived at Preston for breaking up by T.W. Ward Ltd.

8. CELIA MARY 1951-1955

O.N. 143040 744g 323n 190.9 x 29.2 x 13.8 feet
T. 3-cyl. by Forth Shipbuilding and Engineering Co. Ltd., Alloa.

2.1919: Completed by Forth Shipbuilding and Engineering Co. Ltd., Alloa (Yard No. 29) for J. Leete and Sons, London as CATHERINE ANNIE. *1922:* Sold to J. Hay and Sons Ltd., Glasgow and renamed THE PRESIDENT. *1933:* Sold to the Tyne-Tees Steamship Co. Ltd., Newcastle-upon-Tyne and renamed GATESHEAD. *1946:* Renamed PERSIAN COAST. *1951:* Acquired by the Mersey Ports Stevedoring Co. Ltd., Liverpool and renamed CELIA MARY. *1955:* Sold to the Glynwood Navigation Co. Ltd., Hull and renamed CUPHOLDER. *26.4.1956:* Arrived at Hendrik ido Ambacht, Holland for breaking up by N.V. Holland.

Celia Mary *Fotoflite incorporating Skyfotos*

JOHN K. MORRIS
Liverpool

John Kemp Morris was an entrepreneur who would try almost any aspect of the coastal shipping business. He was a shipbroker, managed ships – albeit briefly – for Manchester businesses, engaged in a minor arm of the liner trade, and was one of the final Liverpool owners in coastal sail: indeed, he was probably the last to buy sailing ships. None of these ventures, however, made him rich.

Morris undoubtedly came from the West Country: he established enduring trading links with Devon, and named his Liverpool home Clovelly. His first shipping venture which has been traced was management of two steamers ordered by Manchester interests soon after that city became a port. TRAFFORD and LATCHFORD were delivered in 1896 and 1897: the former to the Trafford Steamship Co. Ltd. under Morris management, the latter to the joint ownership of Morris and a Salford businessman. In early 1898 Morris, who remained based at Seacombe on Merseyside, lost or relinquished the management of these ships to Manchester men. Morris took shares in both the Trafford and the Latchford Steamship companies, which were owned by a variety of small and large businessmen in Manchester, but sold his holdings soon after ceasing to be manager.

Morris's energies then turned to establishing a regular steamer service between the Mersey and ports in the West Country. This concentrated on ports which were not served by the major coastal liner companies who preferred to make their calls at Falmouth and Plymouth. However, Morris's service would be in competition with Richard Hughes, who offered a general cargo service to the West Country in the 1890s.

Morris formed first the Liverpool and North Devon Steamship Co. Ltd. and then the Liverpool and Cornwall Steamship Co. Ltd. He was the major shareholder in both companies, other subscribers including Liverpool businessmen and merchants from Barnstaple and Exeter for the Liverpool and North Devon company. Cornishmen showed little interest in the Liverpool and Cornwall company, and by 1906 the only investor outside Liverpool was a man from Bude. Morris took the bold step of ordering new ships for both companies' services, first to be delivered being the FREMINGTON for the

Latchford on trials *University of Glasgow DC101/0363*

Taunton as **Porthleven** in William J. Ireland's colours. *W.S.P.L. Cochrane collection*

Liverpool and North Devon company in 1899. She traded regularly from the Mersey; in January 1900 clearing the river for Fremington itself and for Padstow; the latter suggesting that the North Devon in the title was not to be taken literally. Equally, the Liverpool and Cornwall company was not to confine itself to Cornish ports.

The first ship bought for the Liverpool and Cornwall Steamship Co. Ltd. was the antique ROBERT BURNS, which after a period in liner service was now tramping round the Irish Sea. ROBERT BURNS was not entirely a stop gap, and remained under the company's ownership well after its two newbuildings had been delivered, TORRINGTON and the Garston-built TAUNTON. The company's accounts quote the cost of the steamers: £6,913 for the TORRINGTON from Selby and £6,374 for the TAUNTON from Garston. The lower cost of the slightly larger TAUNTON suggests that Merseyside builders could compete well on price with shipyards elsewhere.

Neither of Morris's companies prospered. The Liverpool and North Devon company sold the FREMINGTON in February 1902 and then proceeded to wind itself up. In an application for a dedicated berth at Liverpool, Morris claimed in 1903 that the two companies had amalgamated, presumably meaning that their services had been amalgamated, as the Liverpool and Cornwall company was now running to Fremington in Devon. After several unsuccessful applications, in 1900 Morris was granted the use of facilities without railway access in Clarence Half Tide Dock: the Mersey Docks and Harbour Board demonstrating its disdain for the coastal trade.

The Liverpool and Cornwall company was never financially healthy. The first decade of the century was not a profitable period for shipping, and it is unlikely that there was a lot of money to be made offering a service to the West Country. The company's planned £10,000 capital was nowhere near subscribed, and in 1904 it took out debentures with several of its shareholders to raise £7,500, using its three steamers as security. Accounts for the years from 1907 show only one year in which a profit was made, and this was of

£4-10s-10d. Debts mounted, and the only recourse was to sell off the ships, ROBERT BURNS going to breakers in 1906 and the TORRINGTON being sold in 1911 to help pay off the debenture holders. Even this did not save the company, and in August 1914 the Liverpool and Cornwall company was placed in receivership. Its surviving steamer, TAUNTON, was sold in March 1915.

Morris continued as a shipbroker, but despite his recent unhappy experiences, he could not resist the lure of shipowning. In 1916 with the war creating profitable work for any type of ship – especially those which would not be taken over for Government service – he bought the wooden barquentines HUNTLEYS (186/1865), MAGGIE A (211/1877) and SELA 198/1859) and the three masted schooner ZEBRINA (187/1873) from the Whitstable Shipping Co. Ltd. All could tell stories of the East Coast trade under sail: the MAGGIE A and SELA had been part of the massive shipbuilding effort of Prince Edward Island in the mid-nineteenth century, and the ZEBRINA had been designed to carry cement to South America, spending seven years in the River Plate as a lighter. Exciting times continued under Morris's ownership: on 25th March 1917 the Sunderland-built HUNTLEYS was stopped and sunk by a German submarine in the English Channel whilst carrying pitch from Bristol to Dieppe, her crew being allowed to escape. Perhaps this incident, or the ever-increasing prices being offered even for nautical antiques, persuaded Morris to sell off his remaining ships. ZEBRINA was to have one more big adventure. In 1918 she left Falmouth for France but was found off the French coast several days later with sails set and gear intact, but with no-one on board.

Morris continued as a shipbroker after the war. In 1924 he was applying for a berth in Trafalgar Dock, Liverpool for ships trading to his old haunt of Fremington, as well as Bridgwater and the Channel Islands. In association with John S. Sellers, he took a berth at Liverpool in early summer each year for ships in the potato trade from Jersey. The prosperity of this operation is in doubt: on two occasions the Mersey Docks and Harbour Board had to resort to or threaten legal action to recover its dues. The last use of this facility was in 1935, and thereafter Morris drops out of local directories, either because he retired and moved away from Liverpool or because he died. His ventures in shipowning were bold and imaginative if never very profitable, and he added a touch of colour to the Liverpool coastal shipping business.

Fleet list

1. TRAFFORD 1896-1898

O.N. 105675 231g 47n 128.0 x 20.1 x 9.4 feet
C. 2-cyl. by Muir and Houston Ltd., Glasgow; 10 knots.

20.8.1896: Launched by Mackie and Thomson, Govan (Yard No. 113) for the Trafford Steamship Co. Ltd., Manchester (John K. Morris, Seacombe, manager) as TRAFFORD. *15.9.1896:* Completed. *4.5.1898:* Manager became Charles Baybut, Manchester. *26.11.1898:* Managers became Fletcher, Woodhill and Co., Manchester. *9.10.1899:* Sold to the Manchester, Liverpool and North Wales Steamship Co. Ltd. (John P. Jones-Parry, manager), Liverpool. *29.3.1904:* Manager became Richard R. Clark. *16.6.1915:* Sunk by gunfire from the German submarine U 22 thirty miles west north west of the Smalls whilst on a voyage from Newport, Monmouthshire to Lydney in ballast. *25.6.1915:* Register closed.

2. LATCHFORD 1897-1898

O.N. 105677 458g 125n 160.0 x 24.1 x 9.3 feet
C. 2-cyl. by Shanks, Morrice and Co., Pollokshields, Glasgow; 10 knots.

3.5.1897: Launched by S. McKnight and Co. Ltd., Ayr (Yard No. 51) for John K. Morris, Seacombe and John Roberts, Salford as LATCHFORD. *19.6.1897:* Completed. *20.4.1898:* Sold to the Latchford Steamship Co. Ltd. (Charles Baybut, manager), Manchester. *26.11.1898:* Managers became Fletcher, Woodhill and Co., Manchester. *24.8.1899:* Sold to Mann, Macneal and Co., Glasgow. *6.2.1912:* Owners became the Ford Shipping Co. Ltd. (Mann, Macneal and Co., managers), Glasgow. *4.6.1915:* Sold to John Harrison Ltd., London. *7.6.1915:* Renamed FORDHAM. *31.12.1917:* Sold to the London Transport Co. Ltd. (Brown, Jenkinson and Co., managers), London. *12.4.1920:* Manager became Ernest J. Heinz. *20.12.1926:* Sold to Oxford House Ltd. (Peter Bossalini, manager), London. *1.1929:* Sold to the Lola Steamship Co., Antwerp, Belgium and renamed LOLA. *20.10.1929:* Foundered off Selsey Bill whilst on a voyage from Porthoustock to London with a cargo of macadam.

3. FREMINGTON 1899-1902

O.N. 110541 344g 87n 136.0 x 23.2 x 8.8 feet
C. 2-cyl. by Hedley and Boyd, North Shields.

14.12.1898: Launched by R. Thompson and Sons, Sunderland (Yard No. 207) for the Liverpool and North Devon Steamship Co. Ltd. (John K. Morris, manager), Liverpool as FREMINGTON. *15.2.1899:* Completed. *20.2.1902:* Sold to J. Japp, Liverpool. *4.1902:* Sold to Compagnie Marseillaise de Navigation à Vapeur (Fraissinet et Compagnie, managers), Marseilles, France and renamed FARAMAN. *1909:* Sold to Société Anonyme des Transports Cotiers, Marseilles. *1912:* Sold to Joseph Lasry, Oran, Algeria. *1913:* Sold to M. Mazella and Compagnie, Oran, Algeria. *1929:* Sold to Union d'Entreprises Marocaines, Casablanca, Morocco. *1930:* Renamed CAID AZIZ. *1933:* Sold to J. Trujillo Zafra e Hijos, Ceuta, Morocco and renamed JOSE TRUJILLO under the Spanish flag. *1941:* Sold to Compañia Comercial Maritima de Transportes, Madrid, Spain and renamed CRESPI. *7.1943:* Owners became Mittelmeer Reederei G.m.b.H., Berlin, Germany. *23.7.1943:* Damaged by aircraft rocket attack between Nikaria and Mykonos. *25.7.1943:* Sank after arriving at Piraeus. *31.7.1943:* Refloated and later repaired. *9.1944:* Renamed CELSIUS. *9.10.1944:* Scuttled at Piraeus during evacuation of German forces.

4. ROBERT BURNS 1901-1906 Iron

O.N. 25063 130g 54n 106.0 x 18.5 x 8.2 feet
Inverted 2-cyl. by A. and J. Inglis, Glasgow.

1857: Completed by T.B. Seath and Co., Rutherglen for the Dundrum and Newcastle Steam Packet Co. Ltd., Dundrum as ROBERT BURNS. *1866:* Sold to John Forsyth, Downpatrick, County Down. *1884:* Sold to A.R. Walker, Newry. *1886:* Sold to Felix O'Hagan, Newry. *22.2.1898:* Manager became Patrick McDonald, Newry. *28.9.1900:* Sold to Thomas K. Hayes, Liverpool. *18.2.1901:* Acquired by the Liverpool and Cornwall Steamship Co. Ltd. (John K. Morris, manager), Liverpool. *1.1906:* Broken up. *17.2.1906:* Register closed.

5. TORRINGTON 1901-1911

O.N. 113475 286g 95n 130.0 x 22.1 x 9.3 feet
C. 2-cyl. by Crabtree and Co. Ltd., Great Yarmouth; 10 knots.

20.4.1901: Launched by the Selby Shipbuilding and Engineering Co. Ltd., Selby (Yard No. 48) for the Liverpool and Cornwall Steamship Co. Ltd. (John K. Morris, manager), Liverpool as TORRINGTON. *6.7.1901:* Completed. *14.12.1911:* Sold to H. and C. Grayson, Liverpool. *29.12.1911:* Sold to Mann, Macneal and Co., Glasgow. *29.1.1912:* Renamed WATFORD. *26.4.1913:* Sold to Cuthbert Pyke, Preston. *9.9.1915:* Sold to Henry Tyrer and Co., Liverpool. *31.1.1916:* Sold to Albert Chester, Middlesbrough. *18.11.1916:* Wrecked on Little Sunk Sand whilst on a voyage from the Tyne to Dunkirk with a cargo of coal. *10.5.1917:* Register closed.

6. TAUNTON 1903-1915

O.N. 118061 342g 143n 136.3 x 23.9 x 9.9 feet
C. 2-cyl. by McKie and Baxter, Glasgow.

21.10.1903: Launched by the Garston Graving Dock and Shipbuilding Co. Ltd., Garston (Yard No. 26) for the Liverpool and Cornwall Steamship Co. Ltd. (John K. Morris, manager), Liverpool as TAUNTON. *14.11.1903:* Completed. *6.3.1915:* Sold to Robert Whitfield (Rose Brothers, managers), Sunderland. *23.12.1915:* Sold to the Leith Coasters Shipping Co. (A.F. Henry and MacGregor Ltd., managers), Leith. *15.6.1916:* Renamed ST. ABBS HEAD. *3.7.1917:* Sold to John Harrison Ltd., London. *24.11.1921:* Sold to the Deansgate Steamship Co. Ltd. (R.P. Care and Co. Ltd., managers), Cardiff. *28.3.1923:* Renamed PORTHLEVEN. *14.12.1926:* Owners became the Richard England Steamship Co. Ltd., Cardiff. *13.11.1929:* Sold to John M. Piggins, Montrose. *6.2.1936:* Sold to William J. Ireland, Liverpool. *4.11.1937:* Owners became the Ribble Shipping Co. Ltd. (William J. Ireland, manager), Liverpool. *9.1939:* Broken up by the Rees Shipbreaking Co. Ltd., Llanelli. *13.5.1940:* Register closed.

Nomenclature

Morris's ships had names taken from places in Manchester, Devon or both.

FREMINGTON	A village west of Barnstaple in Devon.
LATCHFORD	A district of Warrington, best known for the locks on the Manchester Ship Canal.
TAUNTON	Not just the county town of Devon, but also part of Ashton-under-Lyne.
TORRINGTON	A town overlooking the River Torridge in Devon.
TRAFFORD	To the north west of Manchester, Trafford is known for its cricket and football grounds and Trafford Park, the original industrial estate.

MOUNTWOOD SHIPPING CO. LTD.
Liverpool

This was the last of the companies featured in this book to be established, and the only one to own nothing but motor vessels. It was also notable for the way it moved from coaster owning to a novel trade.

The founder, Joseph Wilson, was brought up in a shipping family and from boyhood cherished an ambition to own ships. He had an excellent grounding in the shipping business with two Liverpool shipowners, Chas. G. Dunn and Co. and James Chambers and Co. On demobilisation from the Army after the Second World War he began searching for a motor coaster to purchase. However, inspection revealed that most were suffering from neglected maintenance during the war and from unavailability of engine spares. Joseph Wilson took a typically creative approach to this problem, first buying a Lister marine diesel and then looking for a sound hull to put it in. In a Bideford dry dock he came across the PLYMPTON, with a strongly-built hull but a German engine which it had proved difficult to maintain. Her problems were solved by fitting the Lister engine, and renamed TORWOOD she proved a strong and exceptionally good sea boat for her size. TORWOOD soon gained an excellent reputation amongst coastal shippers, much of which her owner generously attributed to her masters, Barney Thomas and later his brother Vivian Thomas. The name of the owning company came from Joseph Wilson's home address in Mountwood Road, Birkenhead.

Torwood. *John Clarkson*

Mountwood's motorships were run largely in Irish Sea trades. Those that knew the company remember that they did not often go 'round the corner' beyond Land's End, but they did occasionally load china clay at Fowey, Par, Charlestown and Teignmouth for Runcorn and Preston. Other cargoes included carbide from Port Talbot to Fleetwood or Irvine for I.C.I. One of the coasters spent almost two years on charter to Burns and Laird Line for a service from Greenock to Coleraine, Londonderry and Belfast. Such regular employment was popular with the management but not with the crews, as the schedule did not give them a weekend in port, and Viv Thomas recalls that a total of 30 men came and went over a period of 22 months.

In 1951 a slightly younger and larger Dutch coaster was bought and renamed BENWOOD, remaining with the company until 1959. In 1960 the modern FRIENDSHIP was bought, another Dutch-built motorship. In July 1960 she began a container service between Preston and Greenore which saw the Irish port reopen for business. Running for Greenore Ferry Services – which later went on to own its own ships – FRIENDSHIP had an unusual chocolate-brown hull. Although replaced on this service in early 1962, FRIENDSHIP continued to be a frequent visitor to Preston, running at various times to Dublin for British and Irish Steam Packet Co. Ltd., to Londonderry for Anglo-Irish Transport, to Larne for Northern Irish Trailer Services and to Dublin and Drogheda for Atlantic Steam Navigation. Although sold in 1962, FRIENDSHIP was taken back on bareboat charter until 1967.

A remark by car manufacturer Mr. Brian Rootes on the U.K.'s future transport requirements should it join the European Economic Community gave Joseph Wilson the idea for Mountwood's big innovation, the specialised roll-on, roll-off vehicle carrier. The company engaged a naval architect to develop the design and took an active interest, but it was clear that the cost of the project would exceed Mountwood's resources. At this point Elder, Dempster were approached and after carefully appraising the project agreed to finance it and place the management of the ships with Mountwood.

The first vessel, the side-loading CARWAY, was delivered in 1967, and by 1970 the fleet under Mountwood management comprised:

CARWAY	1967/866g,	built U.K.
CLEARWAY	1967/1207g,	built Germany, acquired 1969
SPEEDWAY	1970/1160g,	built U.K.
SKYWAY	1968/1175g,	built Norway, acquired 1970

CLEARWAY and SPEEDWAY swapped names in 1970.

CARWAY initially ran from Felixstowe to Copenhagen and Gothenburg, largely exporting British-built cars. She was chartered to Seaway Car Transporters, an Elder, Dempster subsidiary. In 1971 CLEARWAY (ex-SPEEDWAY) was transferred from the Baltic services to Elder, Dempster's West African trade where congestion at traditional berths in Nigeria made a side-loader attractive. It was a pioneering venture, which anticipated the way almost all vehicles are now shipped, but the relative smallness of the vessels and the turmoil through which British shipping and the British motor industry were passing at the time told against it.

Joseph Wilson who is now in retirement in Wiltshire is remembered as an owner who was remarkably considerate to those who served him. A lamp-trimmer who had recently joined the TORWOOD was completely non-plussed when Joseph came on board and wished him happiness in his new berth. Viv Thomas recalls that a surly Dublin agent had asked him "where had he been?" when arriving a little late after an exceptionally hard blow in the Irish Sea. On being told of this, Joseph Wilson immediately wrote to Dublin reminding the agent that he was just that, and that Wilson had implicit faith in his masters. Joseph Wilson showed that a shipowner could achieve success whilst being considerate to those who worked and at times took risks for him.

Fleet list

1. TORWOOD 1948-1959

O.N. 162495 264g 130n 117.0 x 23.2 x 9.0 feet
Oil engine 4-cyl. 4S.C.S.A. by Motorenfabrik "Deutz" A.G., Koln-Deutz, Germany.
6.1948: Oil engine 4S.C.S.A. 5-cyl. by R.A. Lister (Marine Sales) Ltd., Dursley.
1965: Oil engine 4S.C.S.A. 6-cyl. by the Caterpillar Tractor Co., Peoria, Illinois, U.S.A.

10.1930: Completed by J. Koster Hzn. Scheepsbouwwerft "Gideon", Groningen, Holland (Yard No. 128) for Thomas J. Metcalf, London as ELLEN M. *1936:* Acquired by Robert Rix and Sons, Hull and renamed NORRIX. *1945:* Sold to Martin's Coastal Steamships Ltd. (Charles E.C. Martin, manager), London. *1946:* Renamed DARTMEET. *1947:* Sold to the Plym Shipping Co. Ltd., Plymouth and renamed PLYMPTON. *1948:* Acquired by the Mountwood Shipping Co. Ltd., Liverpool, fitted with a new engine and renamed TORWOOD. *1959:* Sold to William G. Dennison, Kirkwall and renamed ELWICK BAY. *1960:* Owners became the Elwick Bay Shipping Co. Ltd., Kirkwall. *1965:* Fitted with new engine. *5.1981:* Broken up by David Stewart (Metals) Ltd., Aberdeen.

2. BENWOOD 1951-1955

O.N. 167408 341g 152n 133.3 x 23.1 x 9.5 feet
Oil engine 6-cyl. 4S.C.S.A. by Motoren Werke Mannheim A.G., vorm Benz and Co., Mannheim, Germany; 9¾ knots.
5.1960: Oil engine 4-cyl. 2S.C.S.A. by Skandiaverken A/B, Lysekil, Sweden.

28.4.1936: Launched by N.V. Noord-Nederlandsche Scheepswerven, Groningen, Holland (Yard No. 152) for M. Oosterhuis (N.V. Wijnne and Barends, managers), Delfzijl, Holland as DR. COLIJN. *1.7.1936:* Completed. *15.3.1940:* Taken over by the Ministry of Shipping (Otto Andersen, manager), London and renamed EMPIRE CROCUS. *3.6.1940:* Managers became T.H. Donking and Sons Ltd., Middlesbrough. *8.1941:* Owners became the Ministry of War Transport, London. *18.10.1946:* Sold to G. and S. Shipping Co. Ltd. (Robert A. Grayson, manager), Middlesbrough. *21.10.1947:* Renamed STAINTON. *6.7.1948:* Sold to Erimus Shipping Co. Ltd. (H.P. Marshall and Co. Ltd., managers), Middlesbrough. *11.7.1951:* Acquired by the Mountwood Shipping Co. Ltd., Liverpool. *7.8.1951:* Renamed BENWOOD. *4.1955:* Sold to Rederi A/B Henrik Selên, Borga, Finland and renamed MONICA. *1957:* Sold to N.O. Olausson Partrederi, Skarhamn, Sweden and renamed MONA. *5.1960:* Fitted with a new engine. *1962:* Sold to L. Skovgaard, Rønne, Denmark. *11.1963:* Sold to I/S m.s. Scantic (L.J. Hansen, manager), Rønne and renamed SCANTIC. *7.12.1964:* Foundered after springing a leak in heavy weather in St. George's Channel in position 51.10 N by 07.15 W whilst on a voyage from Preston to Goole with a cargo of lime. The crew of eight was rescued by the motor vessel ARTHUR ALBRIGHT (6,646/1960).

Friendship ran for several different container services across the Irish Sea. At the time she had a chocolate coloured hull and green boot topping. *A. Duncan*

3. FRIENDSHIP 1959-1962

O.N. 301328 560g 273n 200.3 x 30.8 x 11.8 feet
Oil engine 6-cyl. 4S.C.S.A. by N.V. Werkspoor, Amsterdam, Holland; 10½ knots.

22.6.1957: Launched by Scheepswerven Gebroeder van Diepen N.V., Waterhuizen, Holland (Yard No. 944) for N.V. Rederij Friendship (H. van der Broek and others) (W.H. James en Co.'s Scheepvaart en Handel Maatschappij N.V., managers), Rotterdam, Holland as FRIENDSHIP. *14.9.1957:* Completed. *12.1959:* Acquired by Mountwood Shipping Co. Ltd., Liverpool. *3.1962:* Sold to Thomas Stone (Shipping) Ltd., Swansea. *8.1968:* Sold to Fostersons Co. Ltd. (Foster Trade Co. Ltd.), Cayman Brac, Cayman Islands. *9.1981:* Sold to Maritime Mar Associates S.A., Panama and renamed STEDMAN SMITH. *20.1.1982:* In difficulties in position 12.25 N by 82.25 W during a storm whilst on a voyage from Puerto Limon to Houston with a cargo of wood pulp. The crew was taken off the next day. *22.1.1982:* Stranded on the coast of Nicaragua, and later broke in two and became a total loss.

EDWARD NICHOLSON LTD.
Garston

Edward Nicholson Ltd. is one of only two companies described in this book which are still in existence. The company was founded in 1879 yet, in a history lasting almost a century and a quarter, they were shipowners for just sixteen years. This and their longevity may not be unconnected: shipowning could yield big profits in good years but could also lead to heavy losses in bad ones, and agency aspects of the shipping business gave better prospects for steady employment.

The Nicholson business originated with a Marshall Stevens, who ran a service between the Mersey and the Channel Islands, which frequently loaded at Garston. Here, Marshall Stevens had an office managed by an Edward Nicholson. When the Manchester Ship Canal opened in 1894, Stevens was offered a managerial position with the canal company, and sold the Garston office to Nicholson. His tenure was short, however, as he soon died, and his widow decided that her vocation was to be a missionary in India. The business was bought by William Harris, great grandfather of the present owners and whose ambition and energy more than compensated for his lack of capital. Harris arranged with Mrs. Nicholson to provide her with a pension to carry out her missionary business in exchange for the company, which retains Nicholson's name to this day. Harris's son-in-law, Eric Cowan, joined the company after the First World War, and made good use of his shore experience with liner owners T. and J. Harrison to successfully develop the ships' agency side of the business.

In 1929 Nicholsons took a half share in the Dhoon Glen Quarry near Laxey on the Isle of Man, which shipped stone to Liverpool. Soon afterwards, William Harris – who knew next to nothing about ships – bought a steamer to carry the stone at an auction. This was the GERTIE, whose survival for over a third of a century was remarkable for a wooden steam barge. Her luck ran out soon after her purchase, however, and she was lost in Liverpool Bay in July 1930.

Within days of the loss of the GERTIE, the OAK VILLA was bought to carry on the business, which now included shipping coal from Garston to the Isle of Man, so giving a shipowner's dream of a cargo both ways. OAK VILLA traded from Liverpool, Preston and Runcorn to Douglas and Castletown on the Isle of Man, as well as the quarry jetties of North Wales. Serving the latter she was eventually to come to grief, like her predecessor. Nicholson's interest in the Isle of Man quarry was reflected in their giving the next purchase the name DHOON GLEN – renaming being a condition of her purchase as her former name MILLOCRAT was a brand name of Ranks the millers. Even at just 130 feet long, she was to be the largest ship owned, reflecting the need for smaller ships to trade to Manx and other small ports around the Irish Sea.

Nicholsons were also becoming involved in managing small ships for other owners, and the MARJORIE owned by Antonio M. Ralli was placed under their management in 1931. Ralli owned two small coasters, also having the MIA which was one of a quartet of single-hatch coasters built for Irish Sea work at Ellesmere Port. MARJORIE and MIA ran to small ports around the Irish Sea, and MIA became associated with short-distance trades from Liverpool to the River Conwy and Caernarfon. MIA was sold in 1932 and there is no evidence that she came under Nicholson's management, but for completeness she is included in the fleet lists below. Ralli described himself as a barge owner and previous to that as a team owner: before the days when businessmen bought football teams the latter signified that he owned heavy horses, and could be regarded as a haulage contractor. His shipowning was not completely successful, however, and MARJORIE was bought outright by Nicholsons early in 1933. She was to be lost whilst trading to Annagassan, a village south of Dundalk.

Nicholson's loss of the OAK VILLA in 1937 was followed by the almost immediate purchase of another small steamer, the COOMBE DINGLE, which had already traded on the Irish Sea although for some years she had been owned by liner companies operating to the Channel Islands. The COOMBE DINGLE was to trade to the Isle of Man, but as with Nicholson's other ships not exclusively so, and she also visited Coleraine. A notable

Oak Villa in William J. Ireland's colours before being bought by Edward Nicholson Ltd.
John Clarkson

Coombe Dingle in a former owner's colours.
John Clarkson

Mia was one of four coasters built at Ellesmere Port.
John Clarkson

entry on her certificate in 1940 indicates a change of master at Warrington, and this suggests she navigated the Upper Mersey to call at Bank Quay. She must have been one of the last sea-going ships to do so.

The company's interest in the coal trade to the Isle of Man continued after the sale of the Dhoon Glen Quarry, which was unable to compete with quarries in North Wales. Suitable small steamers were not always easy to find, however, and the SPEKE – which had been built for owners in Port St. Mary as GLENMONA – was acquired from Belgium. The cause of her loss in the Irish Sea in wartime was the subject of lengthy litigation and debate, although the mystery seems to have been solved recently by an amateur diver.

On the evening of 27th September 1943, SPEKE left Liverpool for the short voyage to Preston with 144 tons of woodpulp in her hold and on deck. With Preston's Baltic trade severed by the war, this cargo came from Canada and was transhipped to SPEKE in the Alexandra Dock. Somewhere between the Bar Light Vessel and the Ribble the SPEKE disappeared. The bodies of the crew of seven and her two D.E.M.S. gunners were washed ashore, but no wreckage other than her boats was found. This suggested that she had not been mined: in fact she was in a swept channel, and no aircraft had been sighted which might have dropped mines or bombed the ship. Speculation was prompted as to whether the SPEKE had capsized through poor stowage of her cargo. It was unlikely that a poor seaman's family could have pursued such a case through the law courts, but the widow of one of the D.E.M.S. gunners brought such an action against the stevedores who had loaded the SPEKE. Evidence was heard that her hold had not been filled completely, and that the deck cargo may not have been properly secured. Perhaps more importantly, the guns fitted to the SPEKE and the protection added around her wheelhouse may well have affected her stability. The judge hearing the case decided that negligence had not been proven.

A wreck has since been located and identified with some certainty as the SPEKE. Its position is consistent with her capsizing as she altered course to the north east around the end of Jordan's Spit in Liverpool Bay. Waves are particularly steep at this point, and may well have caused her cargo to shift so that she capsized before the crew could have taken to the boats or fired distress rockets.

Nicholson's remaining steamers, JESMOND and SEA NYMPH, were sold in 1945 and 1946 respectively. The company clearly hoped to continue in shipowning, and asked Cammell Laird to quote for building a motor coaster. But with shipyards having all the work they wanted, the price proved much too high. Instead, Edward Nicholson Ltd. took a number of Dutch coasters on time charter, and actually managed some for their captain-owners until the gradual move to company ownership meant there was little need for this activity. There remains a close involvement with shipping, and in late 1996 the company was operating three coasters on behalf of their time charterers.

Nicholsons were also to continue in business at Garston, Liverpool, Preston and Runcorn (to where the head office was moved in 1996) as agents, and have opened offices further afield, including one at Immingham. They have also became haulage contractors, reflecting the growth in the importance of the through-rate concept in freight transport. A nice touch has been the painting of the company's houseflag on their lorries, which are grey as were many members of the coaster fleet, which was inevitably dubbed 'the Garston Navy'. These are signs that Nicholsons consider their shipping and shipowning activities to have been important parts of their business, notwithstanding the short-lived nature of the latter.

Fleet list

1. GERTIE 1930 Wood

O.N. 102054 114g 55n 76.7 x 20.5 x 8.6 feet
C. 2-cyl. by Cleghorn and Wilkinson, Northwich; 8 knots.

15.11.1892: Completed by John Woodcock, Northwich for Isaac Bradburn, Liverpool as GERTIE. *6.12.1900:* Owners became the Executors of Isaac Bradburn, Liverpool. *1930:* Acquired by Edward Nicholson Ltd., Garston. *9.7.1930:* Foundered in Liverpool Bay whilst on a voyage from Trevor to Liverpool with a cargo of crushed granite. *30.8.1930:* Register closed.

2. OAK VILLA 1930-1937

O.N. 115700 200g 37n 105.0 x 20.2 x 9.2 feet
1916: 222g 84n 118.9 x 20.2 x 9.1 feet
C. 2-cyl. by Fisher and Co., Paisley; 9 knots.

8.7.1902: Launched by Scott and Sons, Bowling (Yard No. 155) for the Glasgow Steam Coaster Co. Ltd. (Paton and Hendry, managers), Glasgow as NORWOOD. *1.8.1902:* Completed. *11.9.1916:* Re-registered after having been lengthened by the Ailsa Shipbuilding Co. Ltd., Ayr. *3.3.1919:* Sold to James F. Brice, Bangor, County Down. *7.3.1919:* Sold to William D.H. Arthur, Newcastle-upon-Tyne. *17.6.1919:* Sold to Villa Steam Coasters Ltd. (William A. Green, manager), Cardiff. *31.5.1920:* Renamed OAK VILLA. *13.2.1923:* Sold to William J. Ireland, Liverpool. *17.7.1930:* Acquired by Edward Nicholson Ltd., Garston. *15.10.1937:* Stranded at Port Rivals, Caernarfonshire whilst leaving for Liverpool with a cargo of roadstone. *21.10.1937:* Refloated but subsequently broken up. *25.3.1938:* Register closed.

Dhoon Glen at Liverpool. *Courtesy of Robert Cowan*

3. DHOON GLEN 1931-1937

O.N. 145447 325g 123n 130.2 x 22.6 x 9.6 feet
C. 2-cyl. by Cran and Somerville Ltd., Leith; 9 knots.

27.1.1921: Launched by Cran and Somerville Ltd., Leith (Yard No. 124) for Cheviot Coasters Ltd. (G.T. Gillie and Co., managers), Newcastle-upon-Tyne as BRUNTON. *20.5.1921:* Completed. *12.10.1922:* Sold to the B.I. Transport Co. Ltd. (William H. Buckley, manager), London. *20.11.1922:* Renamed MILLOCRAT. *13.2.1931:* Acquired by Edward Nicholson Ltd., Garston. *4.8.1931:* Renamed DHOON GLEN. *19.1.1937:* Sold to John Urquhart, Glasgow. *29.1.1937:* Renamed RUMORE. *1.3.1937:* Owners became the Point Steamship Co. Ltd. (C. McPhail, Urquhart and Co., managers), Glasgow. *27.1.1938:* Left Waterford for Barry in ballast and disappeared. *2.4.1938:* Register closed.

4. MARJORIE 1933-1938

O.N. 118732 179g 72n 100.3 x 21.0 x 8.7 feet
C. 2-cyl. by Menzies and Co., Leith; 8½ knots.

14.5.1903: Launched by the Dundee Shipbuilders Co. Ltd., Dundee (Yard No. 141) for D. and J. Nicol, Dundee as MARJORIE. *24.6.1903:* Completed. *9.10.1907:* Sold to Frederick Fish and Randal Hopley, trading as the Hudson Steamship Co. Ltd., Goole. *25.11.1912:* Sold to Joseph Crosfield and Sons Ltd., Warrington. *17.10.1922:* Sold to Antonio M. Ralli and Son (Michael H. Ralli, manager), Liverpool. *23.7.1931:* Owners became A.M. Ralli and Son Ltd. (Edward Nicholson Ltd., managers), Garston. *12.1.1933:* Acquired by Edward Nicholson Ltd., Garston. *15.10.1938:* Foundered 16 miles south east of St. John's Point, County Down whilst on a voyage from Birkenhead to Annagassan with a cargo of salt. *21.11.1938:* Register closed.

5. COOMBE DINGLE 1937-1941

O.N. 129758 261g 97n 120.5 x 21.6 x 9.0 feet
C. 2-cyl. by Hepple and Co. Ltd., South Shield; 9 knots.

23.7.1910: Launched by Hepple and Co. Ltd., South Shields (Yard No. 607) for Glen Coasters Ltd. (Matthew Worth, manager), Newcastle-upon-Tyne as GLENSIDE. *6.9.1910:* Completed. *16.11.1912:* Sold to Joseph Monks and Co. Ltd., Liverpool. *29.4.1919:* Sold to Albert Chester and Ernest Harrison, Middlesbrough. *17.11.1919:* Owners became the Glenside Steamship Co. Ltd. (Albert Chester, manager), Middlesbrough. *9.1.1920:* Sold to the Bristol City Line Steamers Ltd., Bristol. *6.2.1920:* Renamed COOMBE DINGLE. *17.6.1937:* Sold to the Plymouth, Channel Islands and Brittany Steamship Co. Ltd., Plymouth. *27.10.1937:* Acquired by Edward Nicholson Ltd., Garston. *2.4.1941:* Stranded at Carnalea, Bangor whilst on a voyage from Garston to the Isle of Man in ballast and became a total loss. *17.5.1941:* Register closed.

6. SPEKE 1938-1943

O.N. 91460 217g 92n 112.3 x 21.6 x 8.9 feet
C. 2-cyl. by Charles D. Holmes and Co. Ltd., Hull; 9 knots.

19.5.1913: Launched by Cochrane and Sons Ltd., Selby (Yard No. 564) for the Port St. Mary Steamship Co. Ltd. (Edwin Qualtrough, manager), Port St. Mary, Isle of Man as GLENMONA. *7.1913:* Completed. *1916:* Sold to John Pattinson and Son Ltd., Whitehaven. *1930:* Sold to Eugène Rau, Ostend, Belgium and renamed RAYMOND. *17.11.1938:* Acquired by Edward Nicholson Ltd., Garston. *10.1.1939:* Renamed SPEKE. *27.9.1943:* Left Liverpool for Preston with a cargo of woodpulp and disappeared. Presumed to have foundered during heavy weather in Liverpool Bay. *21.10.1943:* Register closed.

Speke with a deck cargo of timber. *Courtesy of Robert Cowan*

7. JESMOND 1939-1945

O.N. 122823 192g 89n 112.7 x 20.2 x 8.9 feet
C. 2-cyl. by the Shields Engineering and Dry Dock Co. Ltd., North Shields; $8\frac{1}{2}$ knots.

5.6.1905: Launched by Smith's Dock Co. Ltd., North Shields (Yard No. 772) for Robert Mason, Newcastle-upon-Tyne as JESMOND. *1913:* Sold to L.S. Carr and Co., Newcastle-upon-Tyne. *7.1905:* Completed. *10.12.1917:* Sold to Cunningham, Shaw and Co. Ltd. (Vernon S. Lovell, manager), London. *21.2.1919:* Managers became

Cunningham, Shaw and Co. Ltd. *5.9.1919:* Sold to the Coastcon Steamship Co. Ltd. (William T.F. Williams, manager), Cardiff. *7.2.1920:* Sold to the Kelston Shipping Co. Ltd. (Samuel L. Carr and Frank Clark, managers), Cardiff. *11.5.1921:* Sold to Isaac Milne, Nairn. *20.8.1939:* Acquired by Edward Nicholson Ltd., Garston. *1.12.1945:* Sold to the Tay Sand Co. Ltd. (John Nielson, manager), Perth. *11.6.1953:* Demolition commenced by G. and W. Brunton Ltd., Grangemouth.

8. SEA NYMPH 1942-1946

O.N. 117991 246g 96n 119.9 x 22.1 x 8.9 feet
C. 2-cyl. by Colin Houston and Co., Glasgow; 10 knots.
10.1947: Oil engine 2-cyl. 2S.C.S.A. by A/S Volund, Copenhagen, Denmark.

7.12.1905: Launched by George Brown and Co., Greenock (Yard No. 30) for the East Coast Steamship Co. Ltd., Kings Lynn as SEA NYMPH. *3.1.1906:* Completed. *9.1.1942:* Acquired by Edward Nicholson Ltd., Garston. *4.2.1946:* Sold to Lynd Carriers Ltd., Hull. *30.12.1946:* Sold to Rederiet "Nordhavet" A/S (C.W. Folting, manager), Copenhagen, Denmark. *10.2.1947:* Renamed DUNJA. *10.1947:* Fitted with new engine. *16.2.1962:* Wrecked on the Grosser Knecht Sand, near Cuxhaven in heavy weather whilst on a voyage from Rotterdam to Rudkoping with a cargo of fertilisers. She was partly broken up in situ, and her remains left as an artificial fish reef. *14.6.1962:* Register closed.

Sea Nymph in the Avon. Note the falls for the liferaft, in this view dated 25th July 1945. *E.N. Taylor*

Antonio M. Ralli and Son

Vessels managed by Edward Nicholson Ltd. 1932-1933

1. MARJORIE 1922-1933 (see 4 above)

2. MIA 1923-1932

O.N. 147211 266g 99n 120.0 x 22.1 x 9.1 feet
C. 2-cyl. by Manchester Dry Docks Co. Ltd., Manchester; 9 knots.

19.5.1920: Launched by the Manchester Dry Docks Co. Ltd., Ellesmere Port (Yard No. 72) as LOSSIE. She had been laid down for The Shipping Controller as WAR LOSSIE, but was cancelled in November 1918. *5.1923:* Completed for A. M. Ralli and Son, Liverpool as MIA. *1930:* Owners became the Mia Steamship Co. Ltd. (Antonio M. Ralli and Son, managers), Liverpool. *1932:* Sold to William F. Cook, Aberdeen. *1937:* Sold to the Wilson Steamship Co. Ltd. (T.W. Dixon, manager), Whitehaven and renamed BEACONIA. *1954:* Sold to the Ramsey Steamship Co. Ltd., Ramsey and renamed BEN VARREY. *24.3.1957:* Arrived at Dublin for breaking up by the Hammond Lane Foundry Ltd.

NORTHWICH CARRYING CO. LTD.
Northwich and Liverpool

The Northwich Carrying Co. Ltd. is an example, virtually unique on the Mersey, of a company dedicated to inland waterway transport graduating to the coasting trade. To do this it had to make considerable changes in its organisation, not least because its later coasters were too large to reach its home port.

The company was incorporated in January 1883 in order to provide a carrying service between Northwich and Liverpool. Subscribers to the limited company included a variety of small businessmen and shopkeepers from Northwich who would benefit from this service: a rope maker, a builder, a farmer, a draper, a grocer and a flat owner to provide some knowledge of river craft. Slate merchant Thomas Moore was amongst the largest shareholders, and probably the moving spirit behind the company as he became managing director. Moore, his wife Mary and his son, also Thomas, were to be intimately associated with the company for fifty years. Indeed, the Moores were one of the few constant factors in the company's fortunes. Shareholders came and went, the capital was increased, reduced and increased again, the registered office moved from Northwich to Liverpool (an office had been maintained there since 1895), but a Thomas Moore was always amongst the directors.

To provide its service the company built up a fleet of sailing flats which had a mixture of personal and country names, so that JANE might rub shoulders with JAPAN, INDIA with SAM. It also bought three small steamers: ALICE CAPPER (96/1875), HERBERT (105/1878) and VICTORIA (142/1898).

The first recognisable coaster in the fleet was the ALEXANDRA of 1901. By then Northwich shipbuilder W.J. Yarwood was a shareholder in the company, and could expect and indeed obtained most orders for new vessels and repair work from the Northwich Carrying Co. Ltd. In fact, Yarwood's repair book indicates that the carrying company made a substantial contribution to the yard's work. ALEXANDRA, for instance, came to the yard once a year for her first ten years, and then even more often as she advanced into middle age. Indeed, the regularity which she turns up suggests that she was trading from Northwich. In contrast, the Yarwood-built MAY is recorded just twice and the same yard's ALISON never, suggesting they were not that often in Northwich. MAY is known to have traded to Fleetwood.

The SALTOM acquired second hand in 1906 was, at 137 feet, the first company vessel which would have found visiting Northwich tricky. And for the slightly larger HARTFORD of 1912, the company had to go to an outside builder, and the major connection with Cheshire was her name.

Both MAY and ALISON were called up for Government service during November 1915. MAY was retained until July 1917, in a service category which was described rather vaguely as "steam launches, water boats etc." ALISON was described more succinctly as running with "cross channel stores", and it was doing this that she was caught and captured by a German submarine in November 1916: the company's only loss.

As with so many British businesses, things were never to be the same again after the Great War. Canal and river transport were particularly affected, as increased wages and shorter working hours reduced their competitiveness. As well as business lost to railways the carriers faced a new and very flexible form of competition from motor lorries. But there was another factor in the equation for a company like Northwich Carrying which was in shipping: very high profits made out of the war. In May 1920 the company was getting round excess profits tax by capitalising £20,000 of its undivided profits (further profits had, presumably, been already divided up) and distributing the new shares as a tax-free bonus to its existing shareholders, who were largely members of the Moore family, plus shipbuilder William Yarwood.

With its old river carrying business in decline but with money in the bank and prospects in shipping looking (at the time) rosy, the company took a new direction. This was helped by having much of the shareholding within the Moore family. Thomas Moore the founder had died, leaving his widow as the major shareholder, with son

Alexandra *John Clarkson*

Thomas taking his place and daughters and daughter-in-law having substantial holdings. The Moores had steadily increased their hold on the company and had sufficient funds to provide mortgages for at least some of the company's craft.

The 1920s saw the river craft sold off, and one large and two medium-sized coasters built for the company on the East Coast. The new coasters traded widely. PICKMERE is recorded as making voyages from Goole to Barnstaple – presumably with coal – in January 1929 and from Lerwick to Lowestoft with herring barrels, some of which were carried as deck cargo and were lost off the Humber in October 1930.

The largest coaster, PICKMERE, would not have been able to reach Northwich; the slightly smaller REDESMERE and HATCHMERE could do so only with difficulty. The ending of any practical links with Northwich was acknowledged in 1923, when the registered office of the company was moved to the business district of Liverpool. A more significant change, however, was the recruitment to the board during the late 1920s of a coastal shipping professional, Joseph E. Fisher. As related in an earlier chapter he had already built up a modest fleet of coastal steamers of his own.

As will be apparent from the number of businesses in this book which disappeared or had crises between the wars, coastal shipping was now in a very depressed state, and companies like Northwich Carrying would have done poorly out of their considerable investment in new coasters. This is reflected in the run down of the fleet: beginning with the pre-war steamers, virtually one a year was sold until only the PICKMERE was left in 1926. Perhaps it was the sorry state of the business that led to Joseph Fisher being appointed. It is quite likely he advised the company to do as he was busy doing and quit shipowning. The PICKMERE was sold in 1931, and proceedings for winding up begun in April 1932. The company was by no means broke, with several thousand pounds in the bank, but one amusing item appears in the winding up resolution: the sale of the name Northwich Carrying Co. Ltd. for five pounds.

The title had been a very appropriate one at the company's inception. But although they took the name of Northwich to a wide variety of ports, its coasters had in truth little to do with the Cheshire port and its own modest trade in salt and chemicals.

Fleet list

1. ALEXANDRA 1901-1923

O.N. 113442 211g 72n 100.5 x 21.6 x 9.7 feet
C. 2-cyl. by W.J. Yarwood, Northwich; 8 knots.
3.1932: Oil engine 3-cyl. 4S.C.S.A. made by N.V. Machinefabriek Bolnes, Bolnes, Holland in 1930 .
1946: Engine removed.
1948: Oil engine 4-cyl. 2S.C.S.A. made by J.G. Kincaid and Co. Ltd., Greenock in 1940.

18.11.1901: Completed by W.J. Yarwood, Northwich (Yard No. 10) for the Northwich Carrying Co. Ltd., Northwich as ALEXANDRA. *9.10.1923:* Sold to Joseph Bowles, Cardiff. *3.1932:* Fitted with an oil engine. *1935:* Owners became F. Bowles and Sons (Joseph Bowles, manager), Cardiff. *25.8.1944:* Sold to Hubert F. Ashmead, Bristol. *11.7.1946:* Re-registered as a sailing vessel after her engine had been removed. *1948:* Sold to I.P. Langford (Shipping) Ltd. (Victor W. Rowles and Co., managers), Gloucester, renamed DIANA MARY and fitted with an oil engine. *1954:* Sold to the Straits Steamship Co. Ltd., Caernarfon (Lovell D. Mack, Liverpool, manager), and renamed PENRHYN. *1965:* Owners became the Liverpool Lighterage Co. Ltd., Liverpool. *17.8.1965:* Arrived at Troon to be broken up by W.H. Arnott, Young and Co. Ltd.

2. MAY 1903-1920

O.N.118056 263g 56n 115.0 x 22.2 x 10.2 feet
C. 2-cyl. by W.J. Yarwood, Northwich; 8½ knots.

1.1902: Launched by W.J. Yarwood, Northwich (Yard No. 25) for the Northwich Carrying Co. Ltd., Northwich as MAY. *3.11.1903:* Completed. *19.1.1920:* Sold to James Kells, Sunderland. *12.4.1922:* Sold to John B. Forster, Sunderland. *5.12.1922:* Sold to Duncan MacNicoll, Henry C. Henes and Thomas Grieve junior trading as the General Shipping and Forwarding Co., Birkenhead. *19.12.1922:* Foundered in the English Channel whilst on a voyage from Hourdel to Weston Point with a cargo of boulder flints. *3.1.1923:* Register closed.

May alongside W.J. Yarwood's shipyard in Northwich where she was built. *David Donnan collection*

3. SALTOM 1906-1923

O.N. 113131 293g 72n 137.2 x 22.6 x 9.7 feet
C. 2-cyl. by Muir and Houston Ltd., Glasgow; 9 knots.

10.11.1900: Launched by the Ailsa Shipbuilding Co., Troon (Yard No. 92) for Robert Simpson, Whitehaven as SALTOM. *12.1900:* Completed. *6.1906:* Acquired by the Northwich Carrying Co. Ltd., Northwich. *16.11.1923:* Sold to Frederick E. Peters, Bristol. *9.4.1924:* Owners became the Bristol Sand and Gravel Co. Ltd. (Frederick E. Peters, manager), Bristol. *7.1.1957:* Sprang a leak and foundered in shallow water at her moorings at Cumberland Wharf, Bristol with a cargo of sand. Later raised but beyond economical repair. *18.2.1957:* Arrived at Newport, Monmouthshire for breaking up by John Cashmore Ltd.

Saltom as a suction dredger underway on the River Avon in December 1937.
National Maritime Museum P30091

4. ALISON 1908-1916

O.N. 127946 286g 98n 120.5 x 22.6 x 9.4 feet
C. 2-cyl. by W.J. Yarwood and Sons, Northwich; 8 knots.

30.7.1908: Launched by W.J. Yarwood and Sons, Northwich (Yard No. 106) for the Northwich Carrying Co. Ltd., Northwich as ALISON. *28.11.1908:* Completed. *28.11.1916:* Captured by the German submarine UB 39 and sunk by bombs eight miles east south east of the Owers Light Vessel whilst on a voyage from Havre to Littlehampton with Government cargo. *4.12.1916:* Register closed.

Alison alongside her builder's yard. *Courtesy Clive Guthrie*

Hartford in the colours of the Cement Marketing Co. Ltd.
A. Duncan

5. **HARTFORD 1912-1925**

O.N. 131426 407g 156n 144.0 x 24.4 x 10.5 feet
C. 2-cyl. by J.P. Rennoldson and Sons, South Shields; 9 knots.

15.2.1912: Launched by J.P. Rennoldson and Sons, South Shields (Yard No. 275) for the Northwich Carrying Co. Ltd., Northwich as HARTFORD. *13.3.1912:* Completed. *21.10.1925:* Sold to William A. Wilson, Southampton. *26.7.1927:* Sold to the Cement Marketing Co. Ltd., London. *25.8.1936:* Sold to Frederick T. Everard and Sons Ltd., London. *22.10.1937:* Sold to F. Bowles and Sons (Joseph Bowles, manager), Cardiff. *2.1939:* Converted to a sand pump dredger. *14.7.1948:* Owners became F. Bowles and Sons Ltd. *3.8.1948:* Manager became David M. Bowles. *24.6.1950:* Sold to Archibald J. Lane, Ashurst, Hampshire. *9.1950:* Sold to the Seaborne Aggregate Co. Ltd., Southampton and renamed SEABORNE ALPHA. *3.1966:* The Metcalfe Marine Salvage Co. Ltd. began demolition at Southampton.

Pickmere *E.N. Taylor*

6. PICKMERE 1920-1931

O.N. 143692 466g 192n 152.0 x 25.2 x 10.8 feet
T. 3-cyl. by C.D. Holmes and Co. Ltd., Hull.

20.7.1920: Launched by Cochrane and Sons, Selby (Yard No. 746) for the Northwich Carrying Co. Ltd., Northwich as PICKMERE. *11.1920:* Completed. *1931:* Sold to John S. Monks and Co. Ltd., Liverpool and renamed SPRAYVILLE. *20.6.1958:* Arrived at Barrow for breaking up by T.W. Ward Ltd.

7. REDESMERE 1921-1926

O.N. 145870 345g 133n 135.0 x 23.1 x 9.0 feet
T. 3-cyl. by Charles D. Holmes and Co. Ltd., Hull; $9\frac{1}{2}$ knots.

23.3.1921: Launched by Cook, Welton and Gemmell Ltd., Beverley (Yard No. 441) for the Northwich Carrying Co. Ltd., Northwich as REDESMERE. *9.1921:* Completed. *1926:* Sold to the Ald Shipping Co. Ltd. (Alfred L. Duggan, manager), Bristol and renamed BROCKLEY COMBE. *1937:* Sold to George Couper and Co. Ltd., Helmsdale and renamed LOTHDALE. *1942:* Manager became Duncan and Jamieson Ltd., Aberdeen. *1944:* Managers became Bloomfields Ltd. (Coastal Shipping Department), Aberdeen. *1946:* Owners became C.B. Simpson, Helmsdale. *1953:* Sold to Bremner and Co. (John R. Bremner, manager), Kirkwall. *22.6.1953:* Renamed ORKNEY DAWN. *6.8.1955:* Sold to Captain William Bennett (John B. Moffat, manager), Whitehaven. *3.7.1957:* Arrived at Troon to be broken up by the West of Scotland Shipbreaking Co. Ltd.

Redesmere became the Bristol-owned **Brockley Combe.** *W.S.P.L.*

8. HATCHMERE 1921-1926

O.N. 145880 345g 133n 135.0 x 23.1 x 9.0 feet
T. 3-cyl. by C.D. Holmes and Co. Ltd., Hull; $9\frac{1}{2}$ knots.

23.3.1921: Launched by Cook, Welton and Gemmell Ltd., Beverley (Yard No. 442) for the Northwich Carrying Co. Ltd., Northwich as HATCHMERE. *4.10.1921:* Completed. *15.6.1926:* Sold to the Cement Marketing Co. Ltd., London. *21.12.1927:* Struck a rock and foundered near White Head, Belfast Lough whilst on a voyage from Ardrossan to Magheramorne with a cargo of coal. *16.2.1928:* Register closed.

Nomenclature

The company originally used Christian names, possibly including those of members of the Royal family: Alexandra and May. Later coasters were given local names, those of lakes in north Cheshire being favoured.

HARTFORD Village south west of, and now joined with, Northwich
HATCHMERE Hatch Mere is a lake and Hatchmere a hamlet on the edge of Delamere Forest.
PICKMERE Pickmere is a village on Pick Mere, about three miles north east of Northwich.
REDESMERE Redes Mere is a lake about five miles west of Macclesfield.

ROBERT OWEN AND CO.
Liverpool

Liverpool is popularly supposed to be an Irish city, a way station between the Emerald Isle and the New World, populated by emigrants who did not go the full distance. It could equally well be regarded as a Welsh city, attracting more of the inhabitants of Mid and North Wales than did Cardiff. Despite the importance of Ireland to Liverpool's local trades, few Irishmen figured amongst local shipowners. The Welsh, however, had a significant share in small and not-so-small shipping businesses, as is apparent from the Edwards, Hughes, Jones, Owens, Roberts and Thomases in this book.

Robert Owen was not a large coastal shipowner by the standards of Richard Hughes – indeed, no-one was. But his modest ownership of coasters belies his significance in the Liverpool-Welsh shipping community. There were few companies serving the minor Welsh ports from Liverpool which achieved any degree of success without his involvement. The stories of these companies were told in detail in *Cambrian Coasters,* and a short review of Owen's involvement must suffice here.

He is first encountered in 1888 taking shares in the Aberystwyth and Aberdovey Steam Packet Co. Ltd., a stake necessary to secure him the job as Liverpool agent, which in effect meant he managed the ship. He graduated to shipowning in 1890 with a few shares in the TELEPHONE, other shareholders including master mariner Owen Griffiths and others who had positions in the wholesale grocery company David Jones and Co., with which Owen was to remain associated.

David Jones had been born in 1822 in the farming community of Llanderfel, between Corwen and Bala. Having built up a grocery business in his home village, Jones moved to Liverpool in 1862 to do the same, leaving his partner R.D. Roberts to manage the original shop. The Liverpool business, David Jones and Co. Provision Merchants, prospered and became heavily involved in operating shipping services to many small Welsh ports, a large proportion of whose cargoes comprised groceries. Robert Owen's precise relationship to the grocery company has not been established, but it is most likely that as a member of the Liverpool-Welsh community he was a trusted business associate, and valued because of his knowledge of ships and shipbroking.

In 1892 David Jones and Co. helped set up the Aberdovey and Barmouth Steamship Co. Ltd. to which Owen's TELEPHONE was sold. Over the next few years, TELEPHONE moved into and out of Owen's management, and that of John D. Penney who held various jobs including office manager during a long career with David Jones and Co. Other companies which the grocers were instrumental in forming were the Carnarvon and Liverpool Steamship Co. Ltd., the Liverpool and Cardigan Bay Steamship Co. Ltd. and the Liverpool and Menai Straits Steamship Co. Ltd. In all of these, Owen had a shareholding and was at some point involved as secretary, agent or manager. These responsibilities he took seriously: in 1895 when the Carnarvon and Liverpool company's IBIS (171/1881) came to grief uninsured, Owen took some of the financial loss on himself.

By 1903 Owen could boast of an impressive list of Welsh ports connected by "Regular steam services from Liverpool": Aberaeron, Barmouth, Bangor, Beaumaris, Caernarfon, Cardigan, Fishguard, Newquay, Porthmadog, Pwllheli, Porth Dinllaen, Port Dinorwic and Pwllfanog (for Anglesey). Part of his early shipowning involved ships which supplemented these services: note how both TELEPHONE and MARGARET passed to companies with which he was involved.

An oddity was the elderly barque CARPASIAN (299/1875) which Owen bought from a namesake in Porthmadog in 1908. She was wrecked on the coast of Jamaica on 13th November 1909 having just left Oracabessa with timber for Le Havre.

Robert Owen died in 1913, but his company's reputation was such that its name continued unchanged for twenty years. At the helm now was Griffith Davies, who was to expand the shipowning activities of Robert Owen and Co. In 1915 he joined forces with others to buy a small steamer which was registered in the name of the Esperanto Steamship Co. Ltd. One of his fellow shareholders was grocer William Owen Roberts, son of the R.D. Roberts who had been David Jones' partner. William Roberts had a

Christiana
E.N. Taylor

shipowning career of his own, and in the late 1920s managed the Waldos Shipping Co. Ltd. and its steamer ARKLESIDE (1,567/1924).

The First World War all but wiped out the regular services to Wales which had been provided by small steamers under Owen's management. But as if to compensate, the company acquired other ships, which it eventually registered in the ownership of the Moorcroft Shipping Co. Ltd. One of these was the CHRISTIANA, which had previously been managed by Owen and was taken over when the Liverpool and Menai Straits Steamship Co. Ltd. was wound up. With the ending of regular services to Wales, the steamers had to make a living in the tramp trades, and CHRISTIANA is remembered as running coal from Garston to small Irish ports, with a crew drawn mainly from Caernarfon. Such a living became harder to make as economic conditions grew harsher, and in 1930 its three ships were sold and the Moorcroft company wound up. Robert Owen and Co, shipowners and shipbrokers, disappear from Liverpool directories in 1932.

The list of ships below is short, and indeed only two of the six were owned during Robert Owen's lifetime. Owen's significance, however, is as a manager of ships for companies which were small but important to the communities they served (not all of these ships are listed here), and for being a steady pair of hands which successfully guided such companies through the sometimes murky waters of shipping business.

Fleet list

1. TELEPHONE 1890-1892 Iron

O.N. 68289 165g 63n 110.6 x 18.2 x 8.8 feet
C. 2-cyl. by Muir and Houston, Glasgow.

20.2.1878: Launched by H. McIntyre and Co., Paisley (Yard No. 17) for David J. McGowan and Henry Lane, Londonderry as TELEPHONE. *18.3.1878:* Completed. *10.1880:* Sold to the Dublin, Belfast and Londonderry Steam Ship Co. Ltd., Londonderry. *3.1882:* Sold to Donald MacDonald, Larne. *15.11.1883:* Sold to Peter Barr, Stranraer. *24.8.1889:* Sold to William Newall and Edward W. Turner, Garston. *10.10.1890:* Acquired by Robert Owen, Liverpool and Owen Griffith, Portmadog. *2.6.1892:* Sold to the Aberdovey and Barmouth Steamship Co. Ltd. (John D. Penney, manager), Liverpool. *22.8.1900:* Sold to William T. Roberts, Liverpool. *2.11.1900:* Sold to the Liverpool and Cardigan Bay Steamship Co. Ltd. (Robert Owen and Co., managers), Liverpool. *3.4.1905:* Owners became the Liverpool and Menai Straits Steamship Co. Ltd. (John D. Penney, manager), Liverpool. *9.3.1915:* Sold to Thomas M. Collier, Bray, Wexford. *1.11.1916:* Renamed BRAEBEG. *6.1.1917:* Sold to William O. Roberts, Henry M. Grayson, Griffith Davies and John S. Jones, Liverpool. *30.4.1917:* Sold to John J. Murphy, Waterford. *11.12.1922:* Sold to Samuel Gray (Thomas J. Wilson, manager), Belfast. *17.5.1923:* Sold to Harry J. Wright, Llanbedr, Merionethshire. *16.9.1924:* Sold to the Fox Shipping Co. Ltd. (Walter R.S. Smith, manager), Norwich. *20.12.1927:* Demolition began at Grays, Essex by T.W. Ward Ltd. *12.6.1928:* Register closed.

2. MARGARET 1895-1902 Iron

O.N. 96039 33g 27n 66.5 x 13.5 x 4.5 feet
Single cylinder steam engine by Turnbull, Grant and Jack, Glasgow.

Completed by D.M. Cumming, Blackhill, Glasgow. *14.1.1889:* Registered in the ownership of David MacBrayne, Glasgow as MARGARET. *10.6.1892:* Sold to Owen Edwards, Newton-le-Willows. *1.7.1892:* Sold to William H. Arnott, Newton-le-Willows. *6.4.1895:* Acquired by Robert Owen, Liverpool. *28.4.1902:* Owners became the Liverpool and Cardigan Bay Steamship Co. Ltd. (Robert Owen, manager), Liverpool. *19.4.1905:* Owners became the Liverpool and Menai Straits Steamship Co. Ltd. (Griffith Davies, manager), Liverpool. *20.3.1914:* Sold to Howard A.E. Thomas, Cardigan. *13.7.1920:* Sold to John J. David, Cardiff. *5.5.1921:* Sold to Philip O. Walters, Cardiff. *7.12.1923:* Register closed after vessel had been wrecked.

3. ESPERANTO 1915-1919

O.N. 125752 217g 81n 115.2 x 22.1 x 8.1 feet
C. 2-cyl. by Crabtree and Co. Ltd., Great Yarmouth; 8½ knots.

12.10.1908: Launched by Cochrane and Sons, Selby (Yard No. 444) for Beckwith and Co., Colchester as ESPERANTO. *2.1.1909:* Completed. *5.3.1915:* Acquired by Griffith Davies, William O. Roberts and Thomas L. Roberts, Liverpool. *5.4.1915:* Owners became the Esperanto Steamship Co. Ltd. (Robert Owen and Co., managers), Liverpool. *2.10.1919:* Sold to William J. Kelly, Belfast. *29.12.1923:* Sold to James Downey and Patrick Neville, Dublin. *4.3.1925:* Sold to Frederick W. Taylor, Sunderland. *9.4.1925:* Renamed ELEMORE. *9.3.1927:* Sold to T. Small and Co. (Great Yarmouth) Ltd., Great Yarmouth. *14.4.1927:* Renamed NORWICH TRADER. *17.12.1931:* Sold to the Great Yarmouth Shipping Co. Ltd., Great Yarmouth. *7.1.1942:* Mined and sunk in position 51.55.07 N by 01.32.05 E whilst on a voyage from London to Yarmouth with general cargo. Her crew of six and one D.E.M.S. gunner were lost. *1943:* Wreck dispersed.

Esperanto *E.N. Taylor*

4. CHRISTIANA 1920-1930

O.N. 106791 295g 67n 130.0 x 23.0 x 9.2 feet
C. 2-cyl. by Hall-Brown, Buttery and Co., Glasgow; 9 knots.

18.6.1896: Completed by John Fullerton and Co., Paisley (Yard No. 131) for William O. Roberts, Liverpool as CHRISTIANA. *3.6.1901:* Owners became the Liverpool and Menai Straits Steamship Co. Ltd. (John D. Penney, manager), Liverpool. *1906:* Manager became Robert Owen. *1913:* Manager became Griffith Davies. *1913:* Manager became Robert Owen and Co. *1.7.1920:* Owners became Robert Owen and Co., Liverpool. *4.4.1922:* Owners became the Moorcroft Shipping Co. Ltd. (Robert Owen and Co., managers), Liverpool. *30.9.1930:* Sold to James D. Ormiston, Leith. *6.4.1935:* Register closed after vessel had been broken up.

5. LOCHABER 1922-1930

O.N. 113976 263g 99n 125.0 x 22.6 x 9.7 feet
C. 2-cyl. by Muir and Houston Ltd., Glasgow.

13.7.1901: Launched by Scott and Sons, Bowling (Yard No. 148) for John G. Stewart, Glasgow as LOCHABER. *29.8.1901:* Completed. *21.10.1915:* Sold to James Leslie, Anstruther. *6.6.1916:* Sold to William J. Duncan and William A. Leith, Aberdeen. *15.6.1916:* Sold to John Kelly Ltd. (Samuel Kelly, manager), Belfast. *1.8.1916:* Owners became the Brigadier Steamship Co. Ltd. (Samuel Kelly, manager), Belfast. *4.6.1917:* Sold to Abraham Lazarus, London. *28.12.1917:* Sold to the Langdon Steamship Co. Ltd. (Claude Langdon, manager), London. *28.7.1919:* Sold to Atkins Brothers Ltd., Cardiff. *6.10.1919:* Owners became the Kirk Shipping Co. Ltd. (Atkins Brothers, managers), Cardiff. *27.10.1922:* Acquired by the Moorcroft Shipping Co. Ltd. (Robert Owen and Co., managers), Liverpool. *14.8.1930:* Sold to the Whiteabbey Shipping Co. Ltd., Belfast. *13.10.1930:* Renamed WHITEABBEY. *29.10.1934:* Wrecked off Ballyshannon, County Donegal whilst on a voyage from Whitehaven to Ballyshannon with a cargo of coal. *31.1.1935:* Register closed.

Lochaber *E.N. Taylor*

6. EDDIE 1922-1930

O.N. 118447 219g 86n 115.0 x 20.1 x 9.0 feet
C. 2-cyl. by the North Eastern Marine Engineering Co. Ltd., Wallsend-on-Tyne; $8^{1}/_{2}$ knots.
1933: Oil engine 6-cyl. 4S.C.S.A. by W.H. Allen, Sons and Co. Ltd., Bedford; 7 knots.

12.5.1904: Launched by Wood, Skinner and Co. Ltd., Bill Quay-on-Tyne (Yard No. 120) for Stephenson Clarke and Co., London as EDDIE. *8.6.1904:* Completed. *18.5.1909:* Sold to John S. Cole, Newcastle-upon-Tyne. *14.3.1922:* Acquired by John Owens and James Owens (Robert Owen and Co., managers), Liverpool. *4.4.1922:* Owners became the Moorcroft Shipping Co. Ltd. (Robert Owen and Co., managers), Liverpool. *20.11.1930:* Sold to the Colonial Lands Improvement Co. Ltd., St. Lawrence, Jersey. *29.5.1933:* Sold to the Union Drydock and Engineering Co. Ltd., Hull and fitted with an oil engine. *7.5.1934:* Re-registered as a motor ship. *12.10.1934:* Stranded and sank off Goole whilst on passage to Selby with a cargo of sugar beet. *13.6.1935:* Register closed.

POLLEXFEN AND CO. LTD.
Liverpool

The Pollexfens are notable as one of Liverpool's very few Irish shipowners, although their loyalty to their home town meant that their operations out of Liverpool were rather sporadic.

The Pollexfen family were from Sligo on the West Coast of Ireland, and are probably best known for producing one of Ireland's most celebrated poets, W.B. Yeats. The family's interests included grain importing and milling, and in connection with this they had a fleet of sailing ships working to the Black Sea grain ports, and later a number of coastal schooners. Their connection with Liverpool and steam began in October 1856, when the company of Pollexfen and Middleton chartered a steamer for a service between Sligo and Liverpool. Chartering was an interim measure until their own steamer, the first SLIGO (282/1857), was delivered, allowing a call at Glasgow to be added to their service. Later, calls were made at Dublin, Belfast and Portrush. The title Sligo Steam Navigation Co. was adopted by 1867.

The connection between Sligo and Liverpool generated a considerable traffic in Pollexfens between the two ports. The earliest one of these to appear in *Lloyds Register's* list of shipowners is Charles W. Pollexfen who ran a number of ocean-going steamers and one or two very small ones, probably confined to the Mersey, from an office in Brunswick Street, Liverpool. The family's first steam coaster was the BALLINA, owned by Charles and George Pollexfen, uncles of W.B. Yeats. BALLINA was run from a nearby office and occasionally used on the service from Ballina to Liverpool. Her loss in 1882 did not deter members of the family from further coastal shipowning, and a motley

Although owned in Liverpool, **Polglen** and her running mates spent most of their time in the East Coast coal trade. **Polglen** is seen here discharging at Portsmouth. *David Eeles*

Polgarth in Southampton Water in August 1937. *National Maritime Museum P29913*

collection of wood and iron steamers, auxiliaries and sailing ships was built up, but these were owned in Sligo and do not qualify for the fleet list in this book. A further member of the family to open a Liverpool office was Francis H. Pollexfen, who took delivery of the Sunderland-built HURSTDALE (2,752/1902).

But this spurt of activity had run its course by the 1910, and the Pollexfens then concentrated on their grain business, Sligo Steam Navigation Co. Ltd. and a spot of shipbroking in Liverpool. The Sligo company was acquired by the Coast Lines group in 1919, but retained its services until August 1936 when it was merged with Burns and Laird Lines Ltd., who had been operating services between Sligo and Glasgow. Well after they had sold out to Coast Lines, however, the Pollexfens returned to shipowning with a small fleet of coasters run from Liverpool. POLGLEN and POLGRANGE were bought and duly renamed in 1929 and 1930, and placed under the ownership of the Brunswick Steamship Co. Ltd., which took its name from the street in which the company had its offices. Later, in 1937, the POLGARTH was added and registered under its own single-ship company. These ships were suspiciously large for Irish Sea trades, and evidence suggests they were used mainly to carry East Coast coal: certainly, two were to become war losses in this trade. The style of the management company was Pollexfen and Co. Ltd., but it is hard to discern which Pollexfen, if any, was running the operation. The ship's husband – he who took the blame if a vessel caused trouble – was yet another Welshman, John Lewis Jones. It is hard to escape the conclusion that Pollexfens provided the finance and names for these three coasters but were then content to let others run them.

The POLGLEN was sold for £18,000 in June 1940, and next month POLGRANGE succumbed to the dangers of Channel convoys when bombed and sunk off Dover. When the POLGARTH was mined in 1942 Pollexfen's venture into shipowning was over, although the CHORZOW continued to be managed for the Ministry of War Transport until 1944. It is worth noting that all three owned ships were to be victims of the Second World War: the POLGLEN being sunk by a rogue mine three years after the war in Europe had ended.

A few years later, the Polgarth Steamship Co. Ltd. resurfaced. From 1946 to 1949 it was the registered owner of the GLENBRIDE, which will be found in the fleet of Summerfield Steamship Co. Ltd. as JESSIE SUMMERFIELD. However, by then it was based in London which suggests that the company name had been sold by the Pollexfens.

Fleet lists

George T. Pollexfen

1. BALLINA 1878-1882 Iron

O.N. 78780 341g 210n 170.5 x 23.2 x 11.4 feet
C. 2-cyl. by the Barrow Shipbuilding Co. Ltd., Barrow-in-Furness.

21.5.1878: Completed by the Barrow Shipbuilding Co. Ltd., Barrow-in-Furness for George T. Pollexfen and Charles W. Pollexfen, Liverpool as BALLINA. *5.1.1882:* Left Liverpool for Ballina with general cargo and disappeared with her crew of fifteen. Her bell was later discovered off the Isle of Man. *2.2.1882:* Register closed.

Pollexfen and Co. Ltd.

1. POLGLEN 1929-1940

O.N. 133262 795 368n 186.3 x 29.4 x 12.4 feet
T. 3-cyl. by Ross and Duncan, Govan.

18.1.1915: Launched by R. Williamson and Son, Workington (Yard No. 220) for R. Williamson and Son, Workington as ARLEIA. *2.3.1915:* Completed. *14.5.1923:* Owners became the Northwest Shipping Co. Ltd., Workington. *3.1.1929:* Acquired by the Brunswick Steamship Co. Ltd. (Pollexfen and Co. Ltd., managers), Liverpool. *12.2.1929:* Renamed POLGLEN. *7.6.1940:* Sold to Charles Strubin and Co. Ltd., London. *15.5.1948:* Mined and sunk fourteen miles east north east of Borkum whilst on a voyage from Hamburg to London with a cargo of pitprops. *5.7.1948:* Register closed.

Polglen *David Eeles*

2. POLGRANGE 1930-1940

O.N. 144784 804g 378n 186.5 x 29.4 x 12.4 feet
T. 3-cyl. by McKie and Baxter, Glasgow; 9 knots.

14.9.1920: Launched by R. Williamson and Son, Workington (Yard No. 237) for Adam Brothers Ltd., Aberdeen as ARDSHEAN. *22.10.1920:* Completed. *19.9.1921:* Sold to the Constantine and Donking Steamship Co. Ltd. (R.A. Constantine and T.H. Donking, managers), Middlesbrough. *15.5.1923:* Owners became the Joseph Constantine Steamship Line Ltd. *24.1.1924:* Renamed EDENWOOD. *11.6.1930:* Acquired by the Brunswick Steamship Co. Ltd. (Pollexfen and Co. Ltd., managers), Liverpool. *3.7.1930:* Renamed POLGRANGE. *25.7.1940:* Bombed and sunk off Dover whilst on a voyage from Blyth to Cowes with a cargo of coal. Two of her crew of fourteen were lost. *24.9.1940:* Register closed.

Polgrange at Portsmouth *David Eeles*

3. **POLGARTH 1937-1942**

O.N. 144055 794g 375n 185.1 x 31.0 x 11.7 feet
T. 3-cyl. by Earle's Shipbuilding and Engineering Co. Ltd., Hull; 9½ knots.

20.5.1920: Launched by Cochrane and Sons Ltd., Selby (Yard No. 697) for Humber Steam Coasters Ltd. (J.R. Rix, managers), Hull as MAYRIX. *9.9.1920:* Completed. *15.1.1934:* Sold to H. Harrison (Shipping) Ltd., London. *24.1.1934:* Renamed KEMPTON. *4.1.1937:* Acquired by the Polgarth Steamship Co. Ltd. (Pollexfen and Co. Ltd., managers), Liverpool. *22.1.1937:* Renamed POLGARTH. *1.3.1942:* Mined and sunk two miles south south west of Aldeburgh Light Float in position 52.09 N by 01.42.33 E whilst on a voyage from Blyth to Southampton with a cargo of 856 tons of coal. The crew of sixteen was saved. *9.4.1942:* Register closed.

Managed for the Ministry of War Transport

CHORZOW 1941-1944

845g 489n 212.9 x 31.4 x 13.2 feet
T. 3-cyl. by Machinefabriek Delftshaven, Rotterdam, Holland.

20.4.1921: Launched by N.V. Werf 'Zeeland', Hansweert, Holland (Yard No. 61) for A/S D/S Vesterhavet (J. Lauritzen, manager), Copenhagen, Denmark as HELGA. *11.7.1921:* Completed. *1927:* Owner became J. Lauritzen, Copenhagen. *1930:* Sold to Pantswowe Przedsiebiorstwo 'Zegluga Polska', Gdynia, Poland and renamed CHORZOW. *1933:* Owners became Zegluga Polska S.A., Gdynia. *1939:* Owners became the Polish Steamship Agency Ltd., London. *14.7.1941:* Chartered by the Ministry of War Transport, London (Pollexfen and Co. Ltd., Liverpool, managers). *1944:* Managers became Monroe Brothers Ltd., Liverpool. *17.12.1944:* Stranded off Shoreham whilst on a voyage from Newport to Shoreham with a cargo of coal. *16.1.1945:* Refloated and taken to Shoreham. *2.1945:* Declared a constructive total loss. *1945:* Sold to W. Bartosiak, London, although still registered in Gdynia. *1947:* Sold to Compañia de Navegacion Interoceanica, Panama and renamed STELLA MARIS. *8.12.1953:* Wrecked south of Cidreira Lighthouse, 150 miles north of Rio Grande, Brazil whilst on a voyage from Itajahy to Montevideo with a cargo of railway sleepers.

RAYNES, KNEESHAW AND LUPTON
Liverpool

Quarrying of low-value stone on a large scale has been economic only where it can be carried away by sea. Hence, apart from slate, stone extraction in North Wales has been concentrated round the coast. The scars at Llanddulas, the Great Orme, Penmaenmawr and along the Llŷn testify to the scale of this quarrying, yet few of the operators owned their own ships, preferring to let others worry about the hazards of berthing at exposed jetties on rock-bound coasts. Of the two exceptions, Brundrits have already been dealt with. This chapter looks at the individual and collective steamer-owning activities of a loose group of quarry owners drawn from the Raynes, Kneeshaw and Lupton families. At various times, these Liverpool-based gentlemen owned many of the major limestone and granite quarries in North Wales and along with the slate barons can be considered amongst North Wales' major businessmen. Of particular importance to this book, they were also instrumental in introducing steam ships to the local bulk trades.

By 1840 James Trevelyan Raynes, who was born in Yorkshire, and William Lupton senior from Tyneside were quarrying limestone at Llysfaen near Llanddulas. In that year they took over a granite quarry at Penmaenmawr in partnership with Richard Kneeshaw.

Granite has been won from Penmaenmawr since the stone age: a neolithic axe factory has been identified above the present town. But the real stimulus to quarrying came in the 1820s with the arrival in the district of Thomas Telford to build his London to Holyhead road, which needed broken granite for its macadam surface. The Brundrits also contributed to the growth of quarrying when they discovered that Penmaenmawr yielded a rock suitable for making setts to pave streets. In 1834 the railway contractor Thomas Brassey began working the Graiglwyd Quarry to the east of the town, but wishing to follow other interests he sold this to Raynes, Kneeshaw and Lupton in 1840. The new owners transferred quarrymen from their Llysfaen workings, brought in quarrymen from Kirkcudbrightshire who were experienced in sett making, and began shipping stone to Liverpool from Graiglwyd Quarry's pier.

Raynes and Lupton are known to have owned ships since at least 1858 when they took delivery of the sloop JAMES (67/1858) and schooner HENRY (78/1858). The composite LLYSFAEN delivered in 1867 was one of the first steamers to enter the bulk trades on the Irish Sea, and was followed in 1874 by the secondhand PERI. As discussed in the introduction, this early adoption of steam was a result of the partners owning both the quarry and the steamer so that they could ensure the latter was loaded immediately she arrived, thus exploiting the steam ship's advantage of being able to make many more voyages than a sailing vessel.

The build up of the partners' fleet coincided with major developments in their limestone business, with the new Llanddulas Quarry opening and the acquisition of a nearby quarry from Brundrit and Whiteway, which became known as Raynes Quarry. The latter transaction also brought several more sailing ships to the partners' fleet.

The growth of the Raynes, Lupton and Kneeshaw steamer fleet owed much to their granite quarrying interests, and particularly to their move from Penmaenmawr to the Llŷn. This followed the expiry of the lease on the Graiglwyd Quarry and the failure to agree terms for its extension. The quarrying equipment including tramways was stripped out and moved, together with many quarrymen, to an existing site at Porth-y-Nant near Trevor. Here was granite quite as good as at Graiglwyd and already being used to pave Liverpool's streets. But conditions for ships loading at the quarry were even worse than at Penmaenmawr, with a spindly jetty having even less protection from westerly winds. A contemporary account speaks of "vessels forced to lie off Porth Dinllaen a week or more before venturing the four miles to snatch a cargo."

Given such conditions, steamers offered a safer and more certain way of carrying away the granite than did sailing ships. In 1877 a start was made in building up a fleet of steam coasters to serve the quarry, with the delivery of the TOLFAEN. The Llŷn fleet was never large: over twenty years just six steamers were built, and sales and accidents meant that there were never more than three ships owned at one time. Given the treacherous coast of the Llŷn, it is a tribute to the crews that there was only one serious loss. In 1904 the GWYNFAEN was wrecked in Porth Dinllaen Bay, having just snatched a cargo and two passengers for Birkenhead. ITHFAEN had a particularly short career with the company, and her sale to a Troon shipbuilder to be fitted with a new engine suggests that her original machinery was defective or had been damaged in some way.

The 1870s saw the separation of the interests of Kneeshaw and Lupton, who concentrated on Porth-y-Nant granite, from those of the Raynes, who devoted themselves to quarrying limestone at Llysfaen. The limestone workings would have been served by the steamers LLYSFAEN and PERI, and by a host of small schooners and smacks. Evidence for this comes largely from the details of the great number of casualties which occurred amongst the traders to Llysfaen. Brundrit's smack PARKER (58/1866) was wrecked in the Mersey in March 1886, the HENRY burned on a voyage to Fleetwood in October 1897, Raynes' flat FAIR TRADE (76/1888) in trouble on the East Hoyle Bank whilst on passage to Widnes in October 1904 and his flat RECIPROCITY (75/1890) driven ashore in Colwyn Bay whilst waiting to come alongside the quarry jetty, and the JAMES lost in collision in January 1911. Nor was steam immune: the LLYSFAEN herself was driven from the jetty and wrecked in August 1900.

In December 1886 James T. Raynes died at his home in Rock Ferry, near Birkenhead. He was succeeded by his sons James W. and George T. Raynes, both already shipowners in their own right. Although the Raynes had been early users of steam, they remained loyal to sail, even taking the engines out of the PERI in 1884 and trading her as a pure schooner. Many of their sailing ships were small and they can usually only be identified when they came to grief. From 1881, however, a notable series of schooners named after Earls was built for the Raynes family at Connah's Quay by Ferguson and Baird. Indeed, the fourth of these, the EARL OF BEACONSFIELD (169/1903), was one of the last wooden trading schooners built on the Dee.

In 1899 James W. Raynes bought the last steamer to be acquired by any of the erstwhile partners, the ELEANOR, which was later to inaugurate a unique service. Her origins are somewhat unusual, as she was built in 1897 at Inverkeithing for the fruit trade of her French owners. They may have defaulted on payment, as March 1899 found ELEANOR being auctioned by court order in Leith. The advertisement of her impending sale makes no mention of her being other than a conventional cargo steamer, and Raynes at first used her as such. Her main employment was carrying limestone from Llysfaen to the Clyde where it was used in steel making. In August 1904, however, ELEANOR began regular sailings from Deganwy on the River Conwy to Glasgow offering facilities for both passengers and cargo. She left Deganwy on Saturdays, returning from Glasgow on Wednesday; the passage taking about 20 hours. Quite what facilities the passengers enjoyed on what was basically a cargo ship is not clear; perhaps in the best traditions of the North Wales coast steamships they could brave it on deck or huddle in the saloon for a small extra payment. The initiative for the service came from ELEANOR's master, Captain T. Roberts of Colwyn Bay. The initial aim was to build up the cargo service; the shipment of Welsh slate to Scotland being stressed in the newspaper announcement of the new service.

The trade in slate probably reflected Raynes' management of the Prince of Wales Slate Quarry at Garn Dolbenmaen near Porthmadog. Deganwy was not the nearest port, but it is possible that the influence of other slate quarry owners made Porthmadog unattractive. The London and North Western Railway's Conwy Valley line provided a rail connection between the quarry and the Deganwy wharf.

When sold in 1913 the ELEANOR was the last ship which can be traced in Raynes' ownership; those sailing vessels which survived the hazards of the North Wales coast being disposed of around 1906. It is quite likely that under her subsequent ownership by Zillah ELEANOR returned frequently to the quarries and jetties of North Wales, although coasters owned by William Robertson of Glasgow took over much of the local limestone trade.

In the early 1920s the limestone workings around Llanddulas were sold. Raynes Quarry went to the United Alkali Co. Ltd. (g.v), whose Fleetwood works was already taking much of the quarry's output. In 1926 this company became a founder member of Imperial Chemical Industries Ltd., who continued extracting limestone. Since 1972, the quarry has been operated by Northwest Aggregates Ltd., a subsidiary of Ready Mixed Concrete Ltd. Stone is still extracted, and now mainly shipped to the south coast of England, but for some years the quarry's output went exclusively to Bramley Moore Dock, Liverpool in the appropriately named motorship RAYNESTONE and later the one-time sand carrier SAND SKUA which are listed in the chapter on William Cooper.

In 1922 Llanddulas Quarry passed to the Glasgow shipowner William Robertson who operated it under a subsidiary company entitled Kneeshaw, Lupton and Co. Ltd., using his own steamers to ship out the limestone. William Robertson Shipowners Ltd. were taken over by Powell Duffryn in 1971, and in 1984 this group merged their quarry interests with those of the Amey Roadstone Corporation to form A.R.C.P.D., which operates the quarry today. By an odd quirk of fate, the jetty is now also used to export granite from the former Kneeshaw, Lupton-owned Graiglwyd Quarry. The third ex-Kneeshaw, Lupton quarry near Llanddulas was closed in 1962 when its working face came too close to the North Wales coast railway, which is tunnelled hereabouts. The quarry floor now carries the North Wales Expressway.

Further west, Kneeshaw, Lupton and Co. also sold out at Porth-y-Nant in 1922. Their last ship, CALCHFAEN, was sold in 1916 but was to have a long and adventurous further career. She was acquired by an Estonian in 1937, but in 1940 found herself back under British registry when her owner's homeland was overrun by Germany. Having no desire to hand over his little vessel to Russian ownership after the war, Albert Toop elected to continue trading in British waters under the Red Ensign, until the 65-year-old ANNA TOOP sank off Arklow in 1958.

With nine individuals drawn from three families, this story has been a complicated one, notwithstanding the small number of ships involved. But the Raynes, Kneeshaws and Luptons are significant in having demonstrated that steam coasters were viable in the Irish Sea bulk trades, at least when given favourable loading arrangements. Shipowners such as William Savage went on to exploit this situation so that stone became a important trade for Merseyside's coastal shipowners.

Calchfaen survived longer than any other Kneeshaw, Lupton vessel, and finally became **Anna Toop** after the Second World War. Remarkably, she retained her open bridge, and apart from the odd cluster of lights atop what is left of her mizzen mast, must have been in remarkably original condition. *John Clarkson*

A note on ownership

The details of ownership of the steamers in this fleet give useful clues as to which of the Raynes, Kneeshaw and Lupton interests were active at any one time. Evidently James T. Raynes was originally the major player, but by the 1870s the Kneeshaws and Luptons held most of the shares in the steamers. This may have reflected the retirement of Raynes senior, who from 1877 until his death was an alderman of Birkenhead. His sons did not involve themselves with the Kneeshaws and Luptons, but owned ships in their own right.

The 64 shares in the LLYSFAEN were originally held as follows:

James Trevelyan Raynes	22	Henry Kneeshaw	8
Richard Kneeshaw	18	Banister Lupton	16

Notwithstanding the ownership of 26 shares by Kneeshaws, the contemporary *Mercantile Navy List* gives LLYSFAEN's owners as Raynes, Lupton and Co. This is but one example of the need for registers to summarise the often complex ownership of ships owned under the sixty-fourth share system, a summary which did not always reflect the actual distribution of shares. The later ships with names ending -FAEN were regarded by *Lloyd's Register* as being owned or managed by Kneeshaw, Lupton and Co. of Liverpool, but again the actual share ownership varied from ship to ship and from time to time as packets of shares were transferred between members of the families.

The SYLFAEN of 1883 was unique in coming under the ownership of a single-ship company, the Sylfaen Steamship Co. Ltd. This was registered in 1884 and almost all of its 64 shares were owned by members of the Lupton family, only one being taken up by Henry Kneeshaw who was by then living in retirement at Penmaenmawr.

For the purposes of the list which follows, all the steamers mentioned are regarded as being part of one fleet and are listed in chronological order of acquisition. The ownership given for each is that reported in *Lloyd's Register* or the *Mercantile Navy List.*

The following members of the three familes are known to have had shareholdings in steamers: James Trevelyan Raynes, James William Raynes, George T. Raynes, William Lupton, Henry Lupton, Banister Lupton senior, Banister Lupton junior, Richard Kneeshaw and Henry Kneeshaw.

Fleet list

1. LLYSFAEN 1867-1900 Iron and wood

O.N. 55098 76g 52n 73.8 x 19.6 x 7.9 feet
Single cylinder engine.

8.7.1867: Completed at Lancaster for Raynes, Lupton and Co., Liverpool as LLYSFAEN. *2.4.1873:* Owner became Henry Lupton, Liverpool. *3.8.1900:* Drove from Llanddulas Jetty and ran ashore near Abergele after arriving from Widnes, light. *27.8.1900:* Register closed.

2. PERI 1874-1888 Wood

O.N. 67362 104g 65n 89.8 x 20.3 x 9.1 feet
Inverted two cylinder simple engine by Bowden Brothers, Newcastle-upon-Tyne.

7.1872: Launched by the Union Cooperative Shipbuilding Society, Blyth (Yard No. 5) for Robert Fell junior, Newcastle-upon-Tyne as PERI. *16.9.1872:* Completed. *3.1873:* Sold to John Whitney, Livingstone. *7.1874:* Acquired by James T. Raynes, Liverpool. *8.2.1883:* Reregistered as a schooner after her engines had been removed; manager George T. Raynes, Liverpool. *26.10.1888:* Sold to Michael Moloney, Dungarvan, County Waterford. *2.11.1907:* Wrecked at Sea View, Helwick Head. Two members of her crew of four were lost.

3. TOLFAEN 1878-1891 Iron

O.N. 78753 187g 117n 131.2 x 18.1 x 10.8 feet
C. 2-cyl. by William Allsup and Sons, Preston.

11.1877: Launched by William Allsup and Sons, Preston (Yard No. 52) for Henry Kneeshaw, Liverpool as TOLFAEN. *6.2.1878:* Completed. *1886:* Owners became Kneeshaw, Lupton and Co., Liverpool. *30.5.1891:* Sold to Stubbs Brothers Ltd., Winsford. *1.1893:* Sold to Hinard and Langevin, Bordeaux, France and renamed PONTAILLAC. *1895:* Owner became J.R. Hinard and Co., Bordeaux. *3.4.1897:* Sailed from Socoa, where she had taken refuge, for Bordeaux with a cargo of 270 casks of wine and disappeared. Wreckage was later found between Lacanau and Carcaus.

4. SYLFAEN 1883-1900 Iron

O.N. 87908 350g 169n 160.0 x 23.1 x 10.9 feet
C.2-cyl. by William King and Co., Glasgow.

3.10.1883: Launched by John Fullerton and Co., Paisley (Yard No. 59) for the Sylfaen Steamship Co. Ltd. (Kneeshaw, Lupton and Co., managers), Liverpool as SYLFAEN. *17.11.1883:* Completed. *8.8.1900:* Sold to George Couper, Helmsdale. *2.3.1905:* Sold to Mann, Macneal and Co., Glasgow. *14.3.1905:* Renamed EARLFORD. *10.1.1912:* Owners became the Ford Shipping Co. Ltd. (Mann, Macneal and Co., managers), Glasgow. *31.12.1914:* Sold to the Channel Shipping (Cardiff) Co. Ltd. (John G. Legros, manager), Cardiff. *18.2.1915:* Renamed JERSEYMAN. *1915:* Managers became Emlyn-Jones and Williams, Cardiff. *24.11.1916:* Abandoned after striking a mine thirty miles north west of Dieppe whilst on a voyage from Swansea to Tréport with a cargo of coal. *12.12.1916:* Register closed.

A fine photograph of **Earlford,** ex-**Sylfaen,** at Bristol. *E.N. Taylor*

5. GWYNFAEN 1887-1904 Iron

O.N. 93731 255g 99n 139.9 x 20.3 x 9.9 feet
C. 2-cyl. by John Jones and Co., Liverpool.

5.1887: Launched by John Jones and Co., Liverpool (Yard No. 52) for Kneeshaw, Lupton and Co., Liverpool as GWYNFAEN. *10.10.1904:* Stranded on Whistle Rock, Porth Dinllaen Bay, Caernarfonshire whilst on a voyage from Port Nant, Caernarfonshire to Birkenhead with a cargo of roadstone. Her crew of eight and two passengers got ashore, after which the ship slipped off and sank in deep water.

6. ITHFAEN 1892-1893

O.N. 99449 427g 160n 160.0 x 23.1 x 10.5 feet
C. 2-cyl. by Ross and Duncan, Govan.
1893: C. 2-cyl. by Muir and Houston, Glasgow; 10 knots.

21.10.1892: Launched by Scott and Co., Bowling (Yard No. 94) for Kneeshaw, Lupton and Co., Liverpool as ITHFAEN. *4.11.1892:* Completed. *4.5.1893:* Sold to Alexander McCredie, Troon and fitted with a new engine. *18.10.1893:* Renamed MAGGIE BAIN. *20.10.1893:* Sold to Walter B. Niven, Renfrew. *3.11.1899:* Sold to Mann, Macneal and Co., Glasgow. *2.1.1900:* Renamed ASHFORD. *10.1.1912:* Owners became the Ford Shipping Co. Ltd. (Mann, Macneal and Co., managers), Glasgow. *16.8.1915:* Sold to Charles Harris, Bray, County Wicklow. *12.11.1915:* Owners became the Bray Steamship Co. Ltd. (Charles Harris, manager), Bray. *21.9.1916:* Renamed BRAEFIELD. *30.3.1917:* Sailed from Cork for Cardiff in ballast and disappeared. She is believed to have been torpedoed by the German submarine U 57 in the Bristol Channel on 31.3.1917. *6.12.1917:* Register closed.

7. CALCHFAEN 1893-1916

O.N. 102112 421g 145n 160.0 x 24.6 x 10.8 feet
C. 2-cyl. by Ross and Duncan, Govan; 10 knots.

19.8.1893: Launched by the Ailsa Shipbuilding Co., Troon (Yard No. 41) for Kneeshaw, Lupton and Co., Liverpool as CALCHFAEN. *7.10.1893:* Completed. *1.6.1916:* Sold to the Antrim Iron Ore Co. Ltd., Belfast and later renamed GLENSHESK. *1927:* Sold to the Raglan Steamship Co. Ltd. (Francis J. Tyrrell, manager), Cardiff. *1934:* Sold to John Tyrrell Ltd., Cardiff and renamed RIVER AVOCA. *1937:* Sold to Albert Toop, Tallinn, Estonia and renamed ANNA. *15.10.1940:* Taken over by the Ministry of Shipping, later Ministry of War Transport and finally Ministry of Transport, London (John Tyrrell Ltd., Cardiff, manager) and renamed ANNA II. *1950:* Sold to Albert W. Toop and Co. Ltd., Cardiff and renamed ANNA TOOP. *21.1.1958:* Stranded on Arklow Bank whilst on a voyage from Port Talbot to Londonderry with a cargo of steel plates. Later refloated by the tug EMPIRE NETTA (290/1945) but sank near Arklow Bank on 22.1.1958. *6.2.1958:* Registry closed.

8. ELEANOR 1899-1913

O.N. 111214 490g 196n 165.0 x 25.1 x 10.2 feet
C. 2-cyl. by J. Cran and Co., Leith; 10 knots.

7.1.1897: Launched by Cumming and Ellis, Inverkeithing (Yard No. 24) for Compagnie Depeaux, Rouen, France as MARGUERITE DEPEAUX. *7.1897:* Completed. *8.1899:* Acquired by James W. Raynes, Llysfaen and renamed ELEANOR. *19.5.1913:* Sold to the Zillah Shipping and Carrying Co. Ltd. (William A. Savage, manager), Warrington. *27.1.1915:* Sold to the Antrim Iron Ore Co. Ltd., Belfast. *26.2.1915:* Renamed GLENARIFF. *30.12.1915:* Left Newport, Monmouthshire for Belfast with a cargo of coal and disappeared. *25.1.1916:* Register closed. *9.2.1916:* Posted missing.

Eleanor discharging limestone chippings at Queen's Dock, Glasgow. *Courtesy Mrs. M. Rawcliff*

Nomenclature

The quarry at Llysfaen gave its name to the first steamer in the fleet and inspired names for most of the others – quite appropriate as 'faen' means 'stone', although it is usually spelt 'maen'. Interestingly one name, near at hand, was neglected; possibly to avoid confusion with Llysfaen. The village of Llithfaen is the nearest settlement to Porth-y-Nant Quarry. The derivation of the name TOLFAEN is not known.

CALCHFAEN Lime stone
GWYNFAEN White stone
ITHFAEN Granite
LLYSFAEN Stone hall. The village of Llysfaen lies near the quarries at Llanddulas
SYLFAEN Foundation stone

WILLIAM ROWLAND
Runcorn and Liverpool

William Rowland was a classic example of a man of humble origins whom hard work as first a seafarer and then a shipowner was to elevate to a position of considerable wealth and respect.

He was born in February 1841 at Runcorn. During the middle years of the nineteenth century the port was enjoying a boom, and life on Runcorn's flats and schooners must have appealed to a hard working and industrious, if impecunious, young man as offering good prospects of advancement. William Rowland worked on the sailing vessels carrying stone from North Wales to the Mersey, and seems to have progressed speedily, probably becoming a master in his late twenties. At the age of thirty he had accumulated enough capital to take 21 shares in the sailing flat CHARLES (58/1848). Indeed, this quite substantial holding suggests that he may have had earlier shareholdings, although none have been traced. His partners in this venture were John Beckett, another master mariner and his neighbour at Leinster Terrace in Runcorn, and William Beckett described as "a gentleman" presumably because of a lack of any other useful serious occupation. The CHARLES was run in the North Wales trade, and was so engaged when lost in the Dee Estuary some twelve years later.

Runcorn shipowners were in general reluctant to take to steam, but William Rowland and his partners clearly saw this as the way ahead, and in 1881 they had the wooden HANNAH BECKETT built and engined at Northwich. Rowland initially took 16 shares, whilst the Becketts also had 16 each, as did a manager of a local salt works, giving a clue to her intended trade. The first steamer wholly registered in Rowland's name was the

A fine view of **Owain Tudur** in Rix ownership at Bristol. *E.N. Taylor*

Annie *John Clarkson*

wooden LADY KATE, in 1884. About this time Rowland's name appeared as the owner of the ageing Baltic-built barquentine WINDAU (282/1856). In 1886 she was sold to Liverpool owners, and was evidently considered still capable of a trans-Atlantic voyage, although perhaps not by her crew who abandoned her when she went ashore off Queenstown in August 1886.

Despite this flirtation with sail, Rowland was carefully advancing the size and sophistication of the ships he owned, adding the iron coasters HEBE and OWAIN TUDUR and the wooden HAWARDEN CASTLE. The last-named was sold to a diver, John Gibney, in 1892 and went on to have a long life in the salvage business. Rowland's fleet remained relatively stable throughout the nineties; increasing when the IBIS was bought in 1896, but declining again with the loss of the HEBE during a December gale in 1897. Rowland also invested in other people's ships, buying six shares in William Savage's first steamer ZILLAH in 1891. His name was notably absent from the list of investors in son Alfred's shipowning ventures which also began in 1891, suggesting a rift within the family. However, in 1901 and 1902 Alfred began acquiring shares in some of his father's ships, including JESSIE, ANNIE and the second BLANCHE.

As if to show that his sights were on more distant horizons, William Rowland moved his business from his home in Runcorn to an office in Canning Place, Liverpool towards the end of the 1890s. Dramatic expansion followed this move, and from 1898 to 1905 eight steamers were built for the fleet at Ayr, Troon and Dublin. The coasters took the names of his daughters, of whom there were five. Ranging in length from 140 to 150 feet, these – the ships not the daughters – were all single hatch coasters of a type widely used on the Irish Sea. The ships might be new, but finance was obtained in the time-honoured fashion of sixty-fourth shares. These were bought by a large number of family, business associates and other investors mainly on Merseyside and in North Wales: there were some forty shareholders in ANNIE of 1902, for instance.

The growth of the fleet may owe a lot to William Rowland's involvement in the gravel trade. His obituary in a Runcorn newspaper recalled that he had obtained a contract to supply "millions of tons" of gravel, but dates this from the construction of the

On trial: **Jessie** (above) and **Jane Rowland** (below) *University of Glasgow DC101/0322 and DC101/1245*

Manchester Ship Canal. However, when this work got underway in 1887, Rowland's fleet was very modest and it seems likely that the gravel contract was obtained ten years later. The FLORENCE of 1898 was built with a pump in her hold to dewater gravel cargoes, and this proved useful to later owners when loading from a dredger in the Solway. Rowland's coasters brought gravel cargoes from Walney Island and Fleetwood to Liverpool and probably up the Ship Canal itself. The first and second BLANCHEs were lost on such voyages.

William Rowland died on 4th May 1903 at Eversley, the home he had built for himself in Runcorn. Although he had never been a public figure, his funeral attracted considerable attention from the three local papers, and a large number of mourners amongst whom were numbered several local shipowners, including William Kennaugh and members of the Grounds and Savage families. His obituaries recalled William Rowland's probity and rectitude, and maintained that in spite of his great intuition and shrewdness, he was esteemed for his straightforward dealing and transparent honesty of purpose. They also spoke of his hearty and generous nature earning him considerable respect and popularity. As befitted a Methodist, he was not an ostentatious man, according to his obituaries, but his remains were interred in a rather ornate tomb in Runcorn Cemetery.

In his honour, the next ship to be delivered from Troon was named WILLIAM ROWLAND, and the final member of the series became the JANE ROWLAND after his widow. According to William Rowland's will his shareholdings in his ships were to be distributed amongst his wife, daughters and three sons. His executors were his wife, a shipwright named Richard Hough who had been a shareholder in many of his ships, and his son William Ernest Rowland, who worked in his father's office. But clearly all was not well amongst the Rowlands; there was something nasty in the woodshed at Eversley. Alfred, the most successful businessman amongst Rowland's sons, who had been buying shares in many of his father's ships was set to become managing owner, in other words he would control the ships. It seems that not all the family were happy about this, and from August 1906 High Court rulings prevented any transfer of shares in WILLIAM ROWLAND and some other ships until December 1906. Matters were then settled, and in January 1907, almost four years after William Rowland's death, Alfred Rowland became manager of the WILLIAM ROWLAND and JANE ROWLAND. Reflecting Alfred's unsentimental approach to business, the entire fleet was sold off over the next few years, forming the nucleus of a fast-expanding Liverpool fleet, that of James and John Monks. As the next chapter shows, Alfred Rowland's career as a shipowner was more spectacular than that of his father, but was not to end on such a high note.

Fleet list

1. HANNAH BECKETT 1881-1889 Wooden steam flat

O.N. 84139 88g 33n 77.0 x 19.6 x 8.5 feet
C. 2-cyl. by W.E. Bates, Northwich.

5.1881: Launched by Charles Bracegirdle, Northwich for John Beckett, William Bennett, William Rowland and John Aspey, Runcorn as HANNAH BECKETT. *2.9.1881:* Completed. *12.7.1887:* Owner became William Rowland, Runcorn. *12.1.1889:* Sold to William E. Davies, London. *8.11.1898:* Sold to Ernest J. Fawke, Liverpool. *14.5.1900:* Sold to John Marmion, Liverpool. *31.12.1930:* Register closed after being broken up.

2. LADY KATE 1884-1903 Wood

O.N. 74758 136g 78n 99.7 x 21.9 x 9.8 feet
C. 2-cyl. by De Winton and Co., Caernarfon.

1.2.1881: Launched by William Thomas & Co., Millom (Yard No. 3) for John Thomas, Millom as LADY KATE. *29.4.1881:* Completed for the Lady Kate Steamship Co. Ltd. (John Thomas, manager), Millom. *12.1881:* Sold to George Farren and Co., Caernarfon. *12.1884:* Acquired by William Rowland, Runcorn. *28.1.1903:* Sold to John Gibney and Sons, Liverpool. *21.1.1910:* Owners became John Gibney, Sons and Co. Ltd., Liverpool. *9.2.1912:* Sold to the Liverpool Association for the Protection of Commercial Interests as Respects Wrecked and Damaged Property, Liverpool. *24.11.1920:* Sold to the Liverpool Derricking and Stevedoring Co. Ltd. (John W. Jones, manager), Liverpool. *31.8.1922:* Sold to the Wadsworth Lighterage and Coaling Co. Ltd., Liverpool. *23.11.1948:* Register closed after being broken up on Tranmere Beach earlier that year.

3. HEBE 1886-1897 Iron

O.N. 86534 133g 68n 101.5 x 18.1 x 9.2 feet
C. 2-cyl. by McIlwaine and Lewis, Belfast.

30.8.1882: Launched by McIlwaine and Lewis, Belfast (Yard No. 15) for Dunn, Sefton and Walker, Newtownards, County Down as ARDS. *6.10.1882:* Completed. *1.1884:* Sold to Meredith Townsend, Liverpool. *11.1.1884:* Renamed HEBE. *8.3.1884:* Owners became the Hebe Steamship Co. Ltd. (Townsend and Southam, managers), Liverpool. *25.9.1886:* Acquired by William Rowland, Runcorn. *29.12.1897:* Foundered in a gale about five miles east south east of the Morecambe Bay Light Vessel whilst on a voyage from Millom to Ellesmere Port with a cargo of steel rails. Her crew of six was landed at Bispham.

4. HAWARDEN CASTLE 1889-1892 Wood

O.N. 76558 95g 60n 78.6 x 20.8 x 9.0 feet
C. 2-cyl. by W.E. Bates, Northwich.
1897: C. 2-cyl. engine by Plenty and Sons, Newbury.

5.5.1881: Completed by Ferguson and Baird, Connah's Quay for the Connah's Quay Alkali Co. Ltd, Connah's Quay as HAWARDEN CASTLE. *11.1886:* Sold to Coppack, Carter and Co., Connah's Quay. *7.1889:* Acquired by William Rowland, Liverpool. *12.1.1892:* Sold to John Gibney, Liverpool. *6.1892:* Renamed GLEANER. *1.1910:* Owners became John Gibney, Sons and Co. Ltd., Liverpool. *12.1911:* Owner became John Gibney the younger, Liverpool. *7.1917:* Owners became John Gibney Junior Ltd., Wallasey. *8.1931:* Sold to the Liverpool Derricking and Carrying Co. Ltd., Liverpool. *15.1.1940:* Sold to the Norwest Construction Co. Ltd. (James S. Baucher, manager), Liverpool. *24.1.1940:* Sank off Preston Bar.

5. OWAIN TUDUR 1888-1908 Iron

O.N. 86271 227g 91n 125.9 x 20.1 x 10.2 feet
C. 2-cyl. by Richard Nevill, Llanelli.

14.10.1882: Launched by Samuel Brothers, Llanelli (Yard No. 25) for the Owain Tudur Steamship Co. Ltd. (Parry, Jones and Co., managers), Liverpool as OWAIN TUDUR. *8.1.1883:* Completed. *18.12.1888:* Acquired by William Rowland, Runcorn. *26.9.1906:* Manager became Alfred Rowland, Liverpool. *27.4.1908:* Sold to John R. Rix, Hull. *20.5.1908:* Owners became Humber Steam Coasters Ltd. (Robert Rix and Sons, managers), Hull. *15.7.1916:* Sold to Harry Parker, Grimsby. *25.6.1919:* Owners became Harry Parker (Grimsby) Ltd., Grimsby. *24.8.1922:* Sold to Thomas Grieve, Birkenhead. *8.9.1922:* Owners became the Grieve Steamship Co. Ltd. (Thomas Grieve Junior, manager), Birkenhead. *18.9.1922:* Renamed PEGGY GRIEVE. *13.12.1923:* Manager became Duncan MacNicoll, Birkenhead. *26.5.1926:* Sold to Bror. Gosta Hulthen, London. *12.9.1929:* Sold at Wivenhoe to T.W. Ward Ltd. and broken up at Grays, Essex. *28.9.1929:* Register closed.

6. IBIS 1896-1899 Iron

O.N. 82554 171g 64n 110.2 x 20.1 x 9.0 feet
C. 2-cyl. by John Payne, Bristol.
1890: C. 2-cyl. by Muir and Houston, Glasgow.

15.6.1881: Completed by John Payne, Bristol for Henry Burton, Newport as IBIS. *2.1888:* Sold to William E. Davies, London. *4.8.1893:* Sold to the Carnarvon and Liverpool Steam Ship Co. Ltd., Liverpool. *15.11.1895:* Beached after collision with the steamer ALARM (225/1885) in the River Mersey. *12.12.1895:* Register closed. Later refloated and repaired. *15.4.1896:* Re-registered in the ownership of John J. Marks, Liverpool. *6.7.1896:* Acquired by William Rowland, Liverpool. *27.1.1899:* Sold to the Wilson Brothers Bobbin Co. Ltd. (Edward W. Turner, manager), Garston. *4.10.1912:* Sold to the Ribble Shipping Co. Ltd. (John S. Sellers, manager), Liverpool. *16.11.1923:* Wrecked on Taylor's Bank Revetment, Crosby Channel, River Mersey whilst on a voyage from Liverpool to Dublin with general cargo. *1.12.1923:* Register closed.

7. FLORENCE 1898-1909

O.N. 109396 347g 54n 141.7 x 24.1 x 9.8 feet
C. 2-cyl. by Ross and Duncan, Govan; 9 knots.

8.3.1898: Completed by S. McKnight and Co. Ltd., Ayr (Yard No. 52) for William Rowland, Liverpool as FLORENCE. *26.9.1906:* Manager became Alfred Rowland, Liverpool. *6.10.1909:* Sold to James H. Monks (Preston) Ltd., Preston and later Liverpool. *19.2.1924:* Owners became John S. Monks and Co. Ltd., Liverpool. *17.3.1938:* Sold to Mrs. Florence G. Follows (John C. Johnson, manager), Liverpool. *3.10.1938:* Dragged anchor and wrecked on rocks outside Arbroath whilst inward bound from Bo'ness with a cargo of coal. *11.10.1938:* Register closed.

8. BLANCHE (1) 1899-1901

O.N. 110598 363g 64n 145.0 x 24.2 x 10.1 feet
C. 2-cyl. by Ross and Duncan, Govan; 11 knots.

13.6.1899: Launched by S. McKnight and Co. Ltd., Ayr (Yard No. 57) for William Rowland, Liverpool as

BLANCHE. *26.8.1899:* Completed. *13.6.1901:* Foundered ten miles off Southport Pier whilst on a voyage from Walney Island to Liverpool with a cargo of gravel. *16.7.1901:* Register closed.

9. JESSIE 1901-1911

O.N. 113468 364g 84n 146.9 x 24.1 x 10.3 feet
C. 2-cyl. by Ross and Duncan, Govan; 10 knots.

19.3.1901: Launched by S. McKnight and Co. Ltd., Ayr (Yard No. 59) for William Rowland, Liverpool as JESSIE. *8.5.1901:* Completed. *26.9.1906:* Manager became Alfred Rowland, Liverpool. *8.11.1911:* Sold to David M. Walker and Walter Bain, Grangemouth. *16.12.1911:* Sold to the Shield Steam Ship Co. Ltd. (Walker and Bain, managers), Grangemouth. *2.11.1917:* Damaged by gunfire from the German submarine UB 35 two miles off Speeton Cliff, Flamborough Head whilst on a voyage from Calais to Middlesbrough in ballast. Beached but later declared a constructive total loss. *6.12.1917:* Register closed.

10. ANNIE 1902-1911

O.N. 115281 343g 91n 150.0 x 24.4 x 10.4 feet
C. 2-cyl. by Ross and Duncan, Govan; 11 knots.

6.5.1902: Launched by the Ailsa Shipbuilding Co. Ltd., Ayr (Yard No. 66) for William Rowland, Liverpool as ANNIE. *2.6.1902:* Completed. *26.9.1906:* Manager became Alfred Rowland, Liverpool. *2.11.1911:* Sold to James Henry Monks (Preston) Ltd., Preston and later Liverpool. *19.2.1924:* Owners became John S. Monks and Co. Ltd., Liverpool. *21.9.1924:* Wrecked in Church Bay, Holyhead whilst on a voyage from Swansea to Liverpool in ballast. *12.11.1924:* Register closed.

Gertie in Monks' ownership. *John Clarkson*

11. GERTIE 1902-1911

O.N. 115333 370g 84n 150.0 x 24.2 x 10.2 feet
C. 2-cyl. by Ross and Duncan, Govan; 10 knots.

8.11.1902: Completed by the Dublin Dockyard Co., Dublin (Yard No. 37) for William Rowland, Liverpool as GERTIE. *26.9.1906:* Manager became Alfred Rowland, Liverpool. *17.2.1911:* Sold to James Henry Monks (Preston) Ltd., Preston and later Liverpool. *19.2.1924:* Owners became John S. Monks and Co. Ltd., Liverpool. *8.12.1941:* Sunk by a floating British mine off the Tuskar Rock whilst on a voyage from Port Talbot to Waterford with a cargo of coal. Her crew was saved. *23.1.1942:* Register closed.

12. BLANCHE (2) 1903-1904

O.N. 118006 371g 87n 150.0 x 24.4 x 10.4 feet
C. 2-cyl. by Ross and Duncan, Govan; 11 knots.

4.2.1903: Launched by by the Ailsa Shipbuilding Co. Ltd., Ayr (Yard No. 113) for William Rowland, Liverpool as BLANCHE. *11.3.1903:* Completed. *30.11.1904:* Sunk in collision with the steam hopper NUMBER 66 (462/1899) in the Queen's Channel, Liverpool Bay whilst on a voyage from Fleetwood to Liverpool with a cargo of gravel. Seven of her crew of nine were lost. *23.2.1905:* Register closed.

William Rowland between 1911, when sold to Monks, and 1913 when renamed **Susetta.** *E.N. Taylor*

13. WILLIAM ROWLAND 1904-1911

O.N. 118089 363g 75n 150.2 x 24.4 x 10.4 feet
C. 2-cyl. by Ross and Duncan, Govan; 11 knots.

7.3.1904: Launched by the Ailsa Shipbuilding Co. Ltd., Troon (Yard No. 125) for William Rowland, Liverpool as WILLIAM ROWLAND. *2.4.1904:* Completed. *23.1.1907:* Manager became Alfred Rowland, Liverpool. *21.11.1911:* Sold to James Henry Monks (Preston) Ltd., Preston and later Liverpool. *3.4.1913:* Renamed SUSETTA. *19.2.1924:* Owners became John S. Monks and Co. Ltd., Liverpool. *31.12.1934:* Renamed BANKVILLE. *8.5.1957:* Arrived at Dublin for breaking up by Hasmmond Lane Foundry Ltd. *22.8.1957:* Register closed.

14. JANE ROWLAND 1905-1911

O.N. 120885 365g 74n 150.0 x 24.4 x 10.4 feet
C. 2-cyl. by Ross and Duncan, Govan; 11 knots.

12.9.1905: Launched by the Ailsa Shipbuilding Co. Ltd., Ayr (Yard No. 141) for William Rowland, Liverpool as JANE ROWLAND. *4.10.1905:* Completed. *23.1.1907:* Manager became Alfred Rowland, Liverpool. *21.11.1911:* Sold to James Henry Monks (Preston) Ltd., Preston and later Liverpool. *3.4.1913:* Renamed ALETTA. *19.9.1917:* Sunk in collision with the steamer IBEX (951/1891) twenty miles south west by half west of Portland Bill whilst on a voyage from Weymouth to Guernsey with general cargo. *23.10.1917:* Register closed.

ALFRED ROWLAND
Liverpool

Alfred Rowland was the son of William Rowland (q.v.), and truly represented another generation of shipowners. Alfred was not content merely to trade ships, as had his father. A master mariner, William Rowland had built up his fleet in the traditional way, beginning with small, wooden vessels and slowly progressing to new-buildings financed on the sixty-fourth share system. In contrast, Alfred Rowland built new ships from the start, later floating limited companies to finance them. He treated his ships as capital speculations and was quite ready to buy and sell them whenever profitable opportunities arose. Indeed, the size of Alfred Rowland's fleet showed considerable fluctuations, with its minima in phase with the strength of the demand for ships.

It may not be too fanciful to imagine Alfred frustrated by the old-fashioned ways of his father who was still running his business from his home in Runcorn, and taking himself off to Liverpool to show the family how he could make his fortune as a shipbroker and ship owner. The absence of investment by his father or other members of his family in Alfred's fleet, coupled with the tardiness with which Alfred took over his father's ships on the latter's death, suggests a certain coolness in their relationship.

In 1891 Alfred Rowland took delivery of an iron and steel steamer which was considerably larger than anything his father owned, the BLACK ROCK. Over the next five years she was joined by six further ships built at Workington and Troon. Of these, two pairs could be considered sisters: the Williamson-built, iron and steel BLACK ROCK and BELL ROCK; and the Ailsa-built BISHOP ROCK and BEACON ROCK. All were relatively large, two hatch coasters with an open bridge amidships and compound two cylinder or, in one case, triple expansion engines, placed aft. The arrival of the fourth of this group, the BLANCHE ROCK, saw the method of financing change. She was owned by a single-ship company, rather than on the traditional sixty-fourth share system. This financing method was adopted not only for subsequent steamers but was also applied to two of the fleet's existing ships, so that by 1899 Alfred Rowland controlled seven ships, six owned by single-ship companies.

It is interesting to consider why Rowland adopted this method of financing. It was clearly not to make individual shares smaller and hence more attractive to small investors: Rowland's coasters cost in the region of £6,000, and a sixty-fourth share would represent an investment of just under £100, yet Alfred Rowland chose to divide the issued capital of the companies he formed into shares worth £100. Probably the main advantage of Rowland's single-ship companies was that, in case of an accident, the liability was limited to the assets of the company, which rarely exceeded the value of the ship. As manager Alfred Rowland took an annual fee usually of £75 plus 7% of the net earnings of each company's ship, and kept any brokerage fees.

Alfred Rowland relied on a group of investors mostly resident in Liverpool and Cheshire, and several supported almost all his ventures. These included Alexander Bicket, then a stevedore but later a steamship manager in his own right with the Kyle Shipping Co. Ltd., a consulting engineer, and a solicitor. The other shareholders were shipping men such as shipowner Alfred Connell, master mariner John Summerfield, manufacturers and quarry proprietors, men involved in both marine and non-marine trades and professions and their wives, plus one nun. Notably absent from the list of investors were any members of the Rowland family other than Alfred and his wife Mary. Tight control was kept on the number of shareholders: the companies' articles often contained a clause whereby Rowland was allowed sixty days to find a buyer for any share which a subscriber wished to sell.

The ROCKs were substantial coasters suitable for trading anywhere around the British Isles and even further afield, but they were often to be found running coal to Belfast, having loaded predominantly at Garston but also at Ardrossan, Ayr, Troon, Partington and at Lydney on the Severn. They also carried salt from Runcorn to East Coast fishing ports such as Fraserburgh, returning with grain, flour or cattle feed; or lifting a cargo of coal for the Thames, Southampton or Plymouth.

In 1899 Alfred Rowland made a departure from his policy of buying only new ships, acquiring the TILSCO which had been wrecked the previous February. In 1901 he bought a French-built steamer which had also been salvaged and repaired after being a casualty late in 1898. This took the name of the first BASS ROCK, which had been sold in 1900 when only eight years old. In 1902 he purchased another vessel which had been a total loss, the Cardiff steamer RAGLAN, which was as big as any ship he owned, being quite capable of lengthy voyages. In 1906, for instance, she left the Tyne on 15th June for Gibraltar with coal, returning to Liverpool via Lisbon during July. In September she loaded at Penarth for Gandia, returning to Liverpool from where she made a voyage out to Copenhagen, returning to Methil. Reflecting the extra responsibilities involved in such a trading pattern, Rowland received an annual fee of £200 for managing the Steamship Raglan Co. Ltd.

There is something of a mystery surrounding Rowland's involvement with two other ships. His letterheads list, in addition to his known companies, the Steamship Holme Wood Co. Ltd. in 1899 and the Steamship Snipe Co. Ltd. in 1906. The iron steamers HOLME WOOD (229/1883) and SNIPE (306/1884) were real enough, but at no time in their lives did these companies own them and nor did Rowland own or manage them, according to their closed registers. Rowland might have been running them for their owners or charterers, but why invent owning companies for them?

The pace of expansion of Alfred Rowland's small shipping empire slowed in the 1900s, as shipping went through one of its periodic depressions. However, in September 1906 he was appointed manager of the seven surviving ships of his father, who had died three years earlier. His policy was to sell these small coasters as soon as practicable and, once they were gone, to dispose of his own larger ships as ship prices rose when trade recovered after 1910. As the ships went the companies which had owned them were quickly liquidated and the money made available for further investment. When the first ROCK of all, the BLACK ROCK, sank in collision near the Mersey Bar in August 1913, Rowlands fleet was down to just two ships.

Regeneration of the fleet began early in 1914 under a new name, the West Lancashire Steamship Co. Ltd. This company was the most ambitious of Rowland's ventures, with a capital of £50,000. Alfred took the largest single holding of eighty £100 shares and for the rest of the capital relied on his usual business associates, who had probably done well out of the other recently-liquidated companies managed by Rowland. A notable feature of the financing of this fleet was the mortgaging of some ships, including ALLERTON, to a shipping bank in Groningen, Holland. Dutch banks were reckoned to be more sympathetic to the needs of shipowners than their British counterparts, but it was very unusual for a British owner to make use of their services.

Between 1914 and 1918 three pairs of ships were delivered from Fullerton of Paisley, their lengths of 170 to 195 feet making them a size larger than the ROCKs, although still with engines aft. The first pair had been ordered from Fullerton under Alfred Rowland's name in October 1912, and the builders accepted fifteen shares in part payment. A new naming scheme was adopted - suburbs of Liverpool, initially being allocated in alphabetical order.

At no time did the West Lancashire Steamship Co. Ltd. own more than four ships. Two were lost during the war; the AIGBURTH was only three months old when torpedoed. The other West Lancashire ships were sold as Alfred Rowland took advantage of the vastly inflated prices available for good quality steamers, as the products of the Paisley yard undoubtedly were. Sale of the CROXTETH in 1919 left the company entirely without ships although, thanks to the survival of the second BASS ROCK until 1923, Alfred Rowland could still claim to be a shipowner.

The West Lancashire Steamship Co. Ltd. now had no ships and, as was the custom, liquidation quickly followed, distributing considerable profits to investors. Alfred Rowland stood to gain most, and his earnings allowed him to acquire ships entirely in his own right. In June 1922 he took delivery of the Cowes-built ALLERTON, representing a further size increase over the largest Paisley-built ships, and giving him ships of a size with those of Richard Hughes. Four months later another product of Cowes was bought secondhand, an engines amidships, Baltic-type steamer which became the AINTREE.

Beacon Rock

Glasgow University Archives DC101/0058

Aigburth *E.N. Taylor*

Clearly Rowland was now looking at more distant trades, and a pair of similar, newly-built, engines amidships steamers were bought from Norwegian owners during 1923, becoming AUGHTON and AIGBURTH. The contracts for the ALLERTON and AINTREE would have been placed at the inflated prices which ruled during the shipbuilding boom which followed the First World War. After the ships were delivered Rowland would have had expensive assets with which even he would have difficulty in earning a profit. The rejuvenation of his fleet was therefore short-lived, and in 1925 all four ships were sold, the Cowes-built pair incurring a very considerable loss.

In contrast to his father, Alfred Rowland was very much a twentieth century shipowner, treating his coasters largely as assets which could make modest earnings while trading until a boom came along which allowed him to make a more spectacular profit. The art in this was, of course, knowing when to sell and - especially - when to buy, and Rowland's failure to get the latter right in immediate post-war years led to his downfall. Nevertheless, with a total fleet of 27 ships, Alfred Rowland made a notable contribution to Liverpool's coasting fleet.

Alfred Rowland's companies were:

Steamship Blanche Rock Co. Ltd.	1894-1913
Steamship Bishop Rock Co. Ltd.	1895-1913
Steamship Beacon Rock Co. Ltd.	1895-1912
Steamship Brest Rock Co. Ltd.	1896-1912
Steamship Bass Rock Co. Ltd.	1897-1923
Steamship Black Rock Co. Ltd.	1899-1913
Steamship Tilsco Co. Ltd.	1899-1911
Steamship Raglan Co. Ltd.	1902-1910
West Lancashire Steamship Co. Ltd.	1914-1920

Fleet list

1. BLACK ROCK 1891-1913 Iron and steel

O.N. 99324 362g 130n 152.3 x 23.6 x 8.7 feet
C. 2-cyl. by Dunsmuir and Jackson, Glasgow.

6.10.1891: Completed by R. Williamson and Son, Workington (Yard No. 96) for Alfred Rowland, Liverpool as BLACK ROCK. *10.7.1899:* Owners became the Steamship Black Rock Co. Ltd. (Alfred Rowland, manager), Liverpool. *12.8.1913:* Sank after a collision with the steamer BALNIEL II (628/1909) near the Bar Light Vessel, Liverpool Bay whilst on a voyage from Fleetwood to Garston with a cargo of rock salt. Two members of her crew were lost. *29.9.1913:* Register closed. Later that year refloated and sold to William Thomas and Sons, Amlwch who eventually repaired her. *10.5.1918:* Re-registered as ELETH. *19.7.1940:* Sold to the Ministry of War Transport, London (William Thomas and Co. Amlwch, managers) and renamed EMPIRE LETHE. *11.4.1946:* Resold to William Thomas and Sons, Amlwch. *9.8.1946:* Renamed ELETH. *1.2.1951:* Foundered off St. John's Point, County Down about thirty miles south east of Dundalk, whilst on a voyage from Garston to Dundalk with a cargo of coal. Nine of her crew of ten were lost. *24.7.1951:* Register closed.

Black Rock *E.N. Taylor*

2. BASS ROCK (1) 1892-1900

O.N. 99406 493g 198n 164.7 x 26.1 x 11.5 feet
T. 3-cyl. by Dunsmuir and Jackson, Govan; 10 knots.

30.4.1892: Launched by the Ailsa Shipbuilding Co., Troon (Yard No. 33) for Alfred Rowland and Co., Liverpool as BASS ROCK. *24.5.1892:* Completed. *31.12.1897:* Owners became the Steamship Bass Rock Co. Ltd. (Alfred Rowland and Co., manager), Liverpool. *24.9.1900:* Sold to Hallands Ångbåts Aktiebolag (Ludvig Kollberg, manager) Halmstad, Sweden and renamed NISSAN. *1.1.1908:* Manager became R.H. Möller. *1921:* Manager became Hjalmar Blomberg, Halmstad and later Gothenburg. *6.1928:* Owners became Rederi Aktiebolag Halland and Nornan (Hjalmar Blomberg, manager), Gothenburg. *8.1934:* Ownership reverted to Hallands Ångbåts Aktiebolag, Gothenburg. *1935:* Manager became Harry Trapp, Gothenburg. *20.11.1937:* Sold for £1,450 to thc International Shipbuilding and Engineering Co. Ltd., Danzig for breaking up.

3. BELL ROCK 1893-1914 Iron and steel

O.N. 102080 368g 127n 153.2 x 23.6 x 9.0 feet
C. 2-cyl. by Dunsmuir and Jackson, Govan; 10 knots.

6.2.1893: Launched by R. Williamson and Son, Workington (Yard No. 99) for Alfred Rowland, Liverpool and Richard Williamson, Workington as BELL ROCK. *4.3.1893:* Completed. *13.4.1893:* Owners became the Steamship Bell Rock Co. Ltd. (Alfred Rowland, manager), Liverpool. *7.1914:* Sold to Joseph Larran, Peyrehorade, France and renamed NORMAND. *1922:* Sold to Juan Llovet, Valencia, Spain and renamed FRUTERO. *9.6.1938:* Sunk by Nationalist air attack at Benicasim during the Spanish Civil War. Later refloated but apparently not repaired.

4. BLANCHE ROCK 1894-1913

O.N. 102131 471g 172n 162.0 x 25.6 x 11.5 feet
C. 2-cyl. by Muir and Houston, Glasgow; 11 knots.

25.1.1894: Launched by the Ailsa Shipbuilding Co., Troon (Yard No. 43) for Alfred Rowland, Liverpool as BLANCHE ROCK. *26.2.1894:* Completed. *14.6.1894:* Owners became the Steamship Blanche Rock Co. Ltd. (Alfred Rowland and Co., managers), Liverpool. *16.8.1913:* Sold to the Rayford Shipping Co. Ltd. (Mann, Macneal and Co., managers), Glasgow. *27.8.1913:* Renamed RAYFORD. *1915:* Managers became Mann, Macneal and Co. Ltd. *22.10.1917:* Sold to Matthew Taylor, Methil. *29.8.1937:* Sank in collision with the steamer LONDON (1,499/1921) one mile east north east of the Humber Light Vessel whilst on a voyage from Sunderland to Lowestoft with a cargo of coal. *8.9.1937:* Register closed.

Blanche Rock on trials. *Glasgow University Archives DC101/0070*

5. BISHOP ROCK 1895-1913

O.N. 105302 495g 146n 170.0 x 25.9 x 11.7 feet
C. 2-cyl. by Muir and Houston, Glasgow; 10 knots.

13.4.1895: Launched by the Ailsa Shipbuilding Co., Troon (Yard No. 50) for Alfred Rowland, Liverpool as BISHOP ROCK. *15.5.1895:* Completed. *11.6.1895:* Owners became the Steamship Bishop Rock Co. Ltd. (Alfred Rowland and Co., managers), Liverpool. *16.7.1913:* Sold to James Henry Monks (Preston) Ltd., Preston and later Liverpool. *9.9.1913:* Renamed ISABEL MONKS. *24.9.1915:* Sunk in collision with the steamer YDUN (1,266/1899) about ten miles north east of the Tuskar whilst on a voyage from Garston to Waterford with a cargo of coal. Both crews were saved. *2.11.1915:* Register closed.

Bishop Rock on trials. *University of Glasgow DC101/0068*

6. BEACON ROCK 1895-1912

O.N. 105315 495g 146n 170.0 x 25.9 x 11.7 feet
C. 2-cyl. by Muir and Houston, Glasgow; 11 knots.

25.5.1895: Launched by the Ailsa Shipbuilding Co., Troon (Yard No. 51) for Alfred Rowland, Liverpool as BEACON ROCK. *12.6.1895:* Completed. *10.7.1895:* Owners became the Steamship Beacon Rock Co. Ltd. (Alfred Rowland and Co., managers), Liverpool. *3.9.1912:* Sold to the Ford Shipping Co. Ltd. (Mann, Macneal and Co., managers), Glasgow. *24.9.1912:* Renamed NORTHFORD. *1915:* Managers became Mann, Macneal and Co. Ltd. *28.8.1916:* Sold to Northford and Co. Ltd. (Alfred H. Neale, manager), Liverpool. *15.2.1918:* Sold to Donald Macleod, London. *22.6.1918:* Sold to Samuel Kelly (William Clint, manager), Belfast. *27.2.1919:* Renamed ORANMORE. *4.11.1925:* Owner became John Kelly Ltd., Belfast. *15.4.1949:* Sold to W.N. Lindsay, Leith. *7.3.1955:* Arrived at Charlestown, Fife for breaking up by Shipbreaking Industries Ltd. *9.7.1955:* Register closed.

Beacon Rock with non-standard funnel colours. *E.N. Taylor*

Monks' **Claretta** was built for Rowland as **Brest Rock**
E.N. Taylor

7. BREST ROCK 1896-1912

O.N. 106822 533g 200n 167.5 x 26.1 x 11.5 feet
C. 2-cyl. by Ross and Duncan, Govan.

22.10.1896: Launched by R. Williamson and Son, Workington (Yard No. 117) for Alfred Rowland, Liverpool and Richard Williamson, Workington as BREST ROCK. *13.11.1896:* Completed. *25.5.1897:* Owners became the Steamship Brest Rock Co. Ltd. (Alfred Rowland and Co., managers), Liverpool. *26.9.1912:* Sold to James Henry Monks (Preston) Ltd., Preston and later Liverpool. *27.3.1913:* Renamed CLARETTA. *19.2.1924:* Owners became John S. Monks and Co. Ltd., Liverpool. *31.8.1930:* Sunk in collision with the steamer BORDERLAND (1,753/1912) eleven miles north of the Longships whilst on a voyage from Cardiff to Granville with a cargo of coal. *7.10.1920:* Register closed.

8. TILSCO 1899-1911 Iron

O.N. 91488 205g 87n 120.0 x 21.1 x 9.8 feet
C. 2-cyl. by North Eastern Marine Co. Ltd., Wallsend-on-Tyne.
1938: Oil engine 6-cyl. 4S.C.S.A. built by Waggon-und Maschinenbau A.G., Gorlitz, Germany.

4.1885: Launched by Wood, Skinner and Co., Bill Quay-on-Tyne (Yard No. 1) for the International Line Steamship Co. Ltd. (Christopher Marwood, manager), Whitby as TILSCO. *18.5.1885:* Completed. *1888:* Sold to Edward F. Sewell (Christopher Marwood, manager), Whitby. *1888:* Sold to John Stevenson, Whitby. *30.5.1892:* Sold to Charles Smales (W. Rayment, manager), Whitby. *5.6.1897:* Sold to James Reid and Co., Glasgow. *5.2.1898:* Stranded near Bruichladdich whilst on a voyage from Glasgow to Bruichladdich with a cargo of barley. Later refloated. *11.2.1899:* Re-registered in the ownership of the Steamship Tilsco Co. Ltd. (Alfred Rowland and Co., managers), Liverpool. *7.1911:* Sold to M. Mazella and Co., Oran, Algeria and renamed FRANCE. *1928:* Sold to Union d'Enterprise Marocaines, Casablanca, Morocco. *1931:* Sold to Edoard Accinelli, Spezia, Italy and renamed TERESITA. *1933:* Sold to Franco Maresca, Genoa, Italy and renamed DECIO. *1938:* Fitted with oil engine. *1950:* Sold to Stefano Costanzo, Porto San Stefano, Italy and renamed ANGELO COSTANZO. *1954:* Sold to Giovanni Penzo, Venice, Italy. *1957:* Sold to Paolo Gabutti, Cagliari, Italy. *1968:* Sold to Agostino Peloso, Carloforte, Sardinia. *1.10.1971:* Demolition commenced by Cantiere Navale Lotti, La Spezia.

9. BASS ROCK (2) 1901-1923

O.N. 113448 628g 358n 187.6 x 28.0 x 15.4 feet
C. 2-cyl. by Ateliers et Chantiers de la Loire, Nantes, France.

1889: Completed by Ateliers et Chantiers de la Loire, Nantes, France for Compagnie Parissienne de Navigation à Vapeur, Paris, France as BERCY. *1894:* Sold to Mademoiselle Govaerts, St. Valery-sur-Somme, France. *1896:* Sold to A/S Parisien (Chr. Hannevig, manager), Christiania, Norway and renamed PARISIEN. *30.12.1898:* Wrecked at Cape d'Erquy. Later salved and sold to Beliard and Fletcher, Antwerp, Belgium. *4.2.1901:* Registered in the ownership of the Steamship Bass Rock Co. Ltd. (Alfred Rowland and Co., managers), Liverpool as BASS ROCK. *30.10.1923:* Sold to James Kell, Sunderland. *12.1923:* Sold to Viktor Schuppe, Berlin, Germany. *1926 or 1927:* Broken up.

10. RAGLAN 1902-1910 Iron

O.N. 87499 1027g 649n 220.5 x 31.7 x 15.5 feet
C. 2-cyl. by Palmers' Shipbuilding and Iron Co. Ltd., Jarrow.

3.10.1883: Launched by Palmers' Shipbuilding and Iron Co. Ltd., Jarrow (Yard No. 514) for John Cory and Sons, Cardiff as RAGLAN. *9.11.1883:* Completed. *1899:* Owners became John Cory and Sons Ltd., Cardiff. *28.7.1901:* Stranded whilst entering Workington with a cargo of iron ore from Castro and broke her back. Declared a constructive total loss. *19.10.1901:* Register closed. Later salved and repaired. *3.3.1902:* Re-registered in the ownership of the Steamship Raglan Co. Ltd. (Alfred Rowland, manager), Liverpool. *10.1910:* Sold to Stevano Cavassa, Bogliasco, Italy and renamed MONGIBELLO. *1914:* Sold to Luigi Risso, Bogliasco. *1916:* Sold to E. Arditi (Vassallo and Narrizanno, managers), Genoa, Italy. *1921:* Sold to Société Anonyme Les Affreteurs Reunis (Jean Stern, manager), Paris, France and renamed MINERVA. *1926:* Sold to M. Barrel, La Seyne, France and broken up.

Of the two ships named **Bass Rock,** this one looks nothing like the other Ailsa-built ships, and is almost certainly the second of the name, built in France. *E.N. Taylor*

Raglan: the letter on Rowland's funnel is a mystery.  *E.N. Taylor*

Allerton (1) in later life as Henry and MacGregor's **St. Abbs Head.** *W.S.P.L.*

11. OWAIN TUDUR 1906-1908
[see William Rowland no.5]

12. FLORENCE 1906-1909
[see William Rowland no.7]

13. JESSIE 1906-1911
[see William Rowland no.9]

14. ANNIE 1906-1911
[see William Rowland no.10]

15. GERTIE 1906-1911
[see William Rowland no.11]

16. WILLIAM ROWLAND 1906-1911
[see William Rowland no.13]

17. JANE ROWLAND 1906-1911
[see William Rowland no.14]

18. ALLERTON (1) 1914-1916

O.N. 135535 616g 257n 174.8 x 28.1 x 10.4 feet
T. 3-cyl. by Ross and Duncan, Govan; 10 knots.

11.12.1913: Launched by John Fullerton and Co., Paisley (Yard No. 230) for the West Lancashire Steamship Co. Ltd. (Alfred Rowland and Co., managers), Liverpool as ALLERTON. *9.1.1914:* Completed. *20.4.1916:* Sold to J.N. Russell and Sons Ltd., Limerick. *24.7.1916:* Renamed MONALEEN. *12.1.1918:* Sold to the Clyde Shipping Co. Ltd., Glasgow. *7.2.1918:* Renamed FASTNET. *16.5.1923:* Sold to A.F. Henry and Macgregor Ltd., Leith. *9.6.1923:* Renamed ST. ABBS HEAD. *9.12.1953:* Handed over to Shipbreaking Industries Ltd., Rosyth for breaking up. *15.1.1954:* Register closed.

Broadgreen on trials. *Glasgow University Archives DC101/1774*

19. BROADGREEN 1914-1917

O.N. 135551 622g 264n 175.2 x 28.1 x 10.4 feet
T. 3-cyl. by Ross and Duncan, Govan; 10 knots.

16.1.1914: Launched by John Fullerton and Co., Paisley (Yard No. 231) for the West Lancashire Steamship Co. Ltd. (Alfred Rowland and Co., managers), Liverpool as BROADGREEN. *20.2.1914:* Completed. *3.4.1917:* Sold to T.G. Beatley and Son (Thomas E. Brooke, manager), London. *11.1.1918:* Renamed MADAME BROOKE. *22.11.1921:* Sold to Onesimus Dorey, Guernsey. *23.12.1921:* Renamed BROADGREEN. *7.11.1931:* Owners became Onesimus Dorey and Sons Ltd., Guernsey. *16.11.1933:* Sold to Monroe Brothers Ltd. (Monroe Brothers, managers), Liverpool. *16.4.1934:* Renamed KYLEGORM. *1.12.1936:* Owners became the Kyle Shipping Co. Ltd. (Monroe Brothers, managers), Liverpool. *12.10.1937:* Owners became the Walton Steamship Co. Ltd. (F.L. Dawson, manager), Newcastle. *5.1946:* Sold to Compañia Marittima "Laguna" S.A., Panama and renamed SEMIRAMIS. *28.3.1951:* Foundered off Mersa Matrou whilst on a voyage from Alexandria to Benghazi with general cargo.

Childwall on trials. *Glasgow University Archives DC101/1031Y1*

20. CHILDWALL 1914-1915

O.N. 135596 593g 248n 170.0 x 28.1 x 10.3 feet
T. 3-cyl. by Ross and Duncan, Govan; 10 knots.

16.5.1914: Launched by John Fullerton and Co., Paisley (Yard No. 233) for the West Lancashire Steamship Co. Ltd. (Alfred Rowland and Co., managers), Liverpool as CHILDWALL. *7.7.1914:* Completed. *1.4.1915:* Sunk in collision with the steamer TRINCULO (5,203/1908) off Lundy Island, twenty miles north east by east of Hartland Point, whilst on a voyage from Cherbourg to Swansea in ballast. No lives were lost. *21.4.1915:* Register closed.

21. DINGLE 1914-1916

O.N. 137399 593g 248n 170.0 x 28.1 x 10.3 feet
T. 3-cyl. by Ross and Duncan, Govan; 10 knots.

8.7.1914: Launched by John Fullerton and Co., Paisley (Yard No. 234) for the West Lancashire Steamship Co. Ltd. (Alfred Rowland and Co., managers), Liverpool as DINGLE. *11.9.1914:* Completed. *8.2.1916:* Sold to Dale Coasters Ltd. (James Lythgoe, manager), Sunderland. *20.2.1916:* Mined and sunk ten miles south east of the Kentish Knock Light Vessel whilst on a voyage from Sunderland to Caen with a cargo of coal. There was only one survivor who clung to an upturned boat for fifteen hours until rescued by a warship. *14.3.1916:* Register closed.

22. AIGBURTH (1) 1917

O.N. 140537 824g 392n 194.9 x 31.2 x 11.8 feet
T.3-cyl. by Ross and Duncan, Govan; 10 knots.

24.9.1917: Completed by John Fullerton and Co., Paisley for the West Lancashire Steamship Co. Ltd. (Alfred Rowland and Co., managers), Liverpool as AIGBURTH. *5.12.1917:* Torpedoed and sunk by the German submarine UB 75 ten miles south of Whitby whilst on a voyage from the Tyne to Tréport with a cargo of coal. *2.1.1918:* Register closed.

Croxteth spent most of her long life as Kennaugh's **Dalegarth Force,** as seen here. *W.S.P.L. Cochrane collection*

23. CROXTETH 1918-1919

O.N. 140565 825g 393n 195.0 x 31.2 x 11.8 feet
T. 3-cyl. by Ross and Duncan, Govan; 10 knots.

16.3.1918: Completed by John Fullerton and Co., Paisley (Yard No. 244) for the West Lancashire Steamship Co. Ltd. (Alfred Rowland and Co., managers), Liverpool as CROXTETH. *16.10.1919:* Sold to the West Coast Shipping Co. Ltd. (W.S. Kennaugh and Co., managers), Liverpool and later renamed DALEGARTH FORCE. *5.2.1959:* Arrived at Granton for breaking up by Malcolm Brechin.

24. ALLERTON (2) 1922-1925

O.N. 145953 904g 410n 198.3 x 30.7 x 12.2 feet
T. 3-cyl. by J. Samuel White and Co. Ltd., East Cowes; 9 knots.

1922: Launched by J. Samuel White and Co. Ltd., East Cowes (Yard No. 1553) for Albert Chester, Middlesbrough as ACKLAM. *16.6.1922:* Completed for Alfred Rowland, Liverpool as ALLERTON. *31.3.1925:* Sold to John Cook and Son, Aberdeen and later renamed GLEN GAIRN. *27.12.1928:* Sold to the South Georgia Co. Ltd (Christian Salvesen and Co., managers), Leith. *23.4.1942:* Sold to the Brook Shipping Co. Ltd. (Comben Longstaff and Co. Ltd., managers), London. *16.10.1945:* Renamed SURREYBROOK. *23.2.1946:* Owners became the Williamstown Shipping Co. Ltd. (Comben Longstaff and Co. Ltd., managers), London. *1.9.1948:* Sold to A.G. Tsavliris Ltd. (Tsavliris (Shipping) Ltd., managers), London and renamed GEORGE T. *5.1952:* Sold to Nicholas T. Papadotas, Piraeus, Greece and renamed IOANNA MARIA. *1955:* Sold to Dinos E. Mitropoulos, Piraeus. *1955:* Owners became Ntinos Mitropoulos and Co., Piraeus and renamed ALKIS. *8.4.1958:* Foundered off Skyros whilst on a voyage from Stratoni to Lavrion with a cargo of iron ore.

25. AINTREE 1922-1925

O.N. 145981 1173g 606n 221.0 x 34.2 x 14.6 feet
T. 3-cyl. by J. Samuel White and Co. Ltd., East Cowes.

17.9.1920: Launched by J. Samuel White and Co. Ltd., East Cowes (Yard No. 1548) for A/S Atlas (Jacobsen and Co., managers), Langesund, Norway as ATLAS. *11.1920:* Completed. *12.1922:* Acquired by Alfred Rowland and Co., Liverpool and renamed AINTREE. *4.1925:* Sold to Christian Salvesen and Co., Leith and renamed FOLDA. *6.1927:* Owners became the South Georgia Co. Ltd. (Christian Salvesen and Co., managers), Leith. *19.11.1940:* Damaged in an air attack in Barrow Deep. *30.3.1956:* Arrived at Rosyth for breaking up by Shipbreaking Industries Ltd. at Inverkeithing.

Aintree, seen here as Salvesen's **Folda,** was built for Norwegian owners. *A. Duncan*

26. AUGHTON 1922-1925

O.N. 147193 1123g 624n 220.5 x 35.2 x 13.8 feet
T. 3-cyl. by Earle's Shipbuilding and Engineering Co. Ltd., Hull; 10 knots.

11.11.1920: Launched by the Ouse Shipbuilding Co. Ltd., Goole (Yard No. 77) for D/S A/S Borg (Thr. Halvorsen, manager), Bergen, Norway as LYSLAND. *5.1921:* Completed. *12.1922:* Acquired by Alfred Rowland and Co., Liverpool. *26.1.1923:* Renamed AUGHTON. *22.4.1925:* Sold to the Leith, Hull and Hamburg Steam Packet Co. Ltd. (James Currie and Co., managers), Leith. *14.5.1925:* Renamed MINORCA. *25.7.1940:* Owners became the Currie Line Ltd., Leith. *26.2.1941:* Sunk by a German E-boat ten miles north east of Cromer in position 53.04 N by 01.21 E whilst on a voyage from London to Grangemouth with a cargo of cement. Seventeen of her crew of nineteen and two of her three passengers were lost. *10.3.1941:* Register closed.

27. AIGBURTH (2) 1922-1925

O.N. 147196 1126g 589n 220.0 x 35.1 x 13.8 feet
T. 3-cyl. by Earle's Shipbuilding and Engineering Co. Ltd., Hull.

30.9.1920: Launched by the Ouse Shipbuilding Co. Ltd., Goole (Yard No. 76) for D/S A/S Borg (Thv. Halvorsen, manager), Bergen, Norway as FAEDRELAND. *3.1921:* Completed. *1922:* Owners became D/S A/S Kistransport (Thv. Halvorsen, manager), Bergen. *12.1922:* Acquired by Alfred Rowland and Co., Liverpool and renamed AIGBURTH. *4.1925:* Sold to the Leith, Hull and Hamburg Steam Packet Co. Ltd. (James Currie and Co., managers), Leith and renamed MAJORCA. *1940:* Owners became the Currie Line Ltd., Leith. *1949:* Sold to the Virtu Steamship Co. Ltd., Malta. *6.9.1955:* Arrived at Briton Ferry for breaking up by T.W. Ward Ltd.

Nomenclature

BLACK ROCK and BEACON ROCK have proved difficult to locate, but the inspiration for the other names Rowland gave to his ships is readily apparent.

AIGBURTH	A south eastern district of Liverpool, its name means "oak hill" in old Norse.
AINTREE	Best known for its racecourse, Aintree is north east of Liverpool.
ALLERTON	Adjacent to Garston.
AUGHTON	A Lancashire village near Ormskirk.
BASS ROCK	Small island of basalt in the Firth of Forth.
BELL ROCK	Also known as the Inchcape Rock, a rock lighthouse off the mouth of the Tay.
BISHOP ROCK	Rock lighthouse at the western end of the Scillies.
BLANCHE ROCK	Probably named after Rowland's sister.
BREST ROCK	Named after the town and naval base in Brittany.
BROADGREEN	Broad Green is to the east of Liverpool.
CHILDWALL	Also to the east of Liverpool.
CROXTETH	An inland district of Liverpool, which makes the derivation of the name as 'Croc's landing place' difficult to explain.
DINGLE	Best known as the southern terminus of the Liverpool Overhead Railway.

HENRY SEDDON
H. SEDDON AND SONS LTD.
Middlewich

Henry Seddon was a Cheshire salt producer, and it could be assumed that his modest fleet of small coasters was run in conjunction with his business. However, the weight of evidence suggests that his ships were intended more for the North Wales stone and other trades.

Henry Seddon's father Ralph owned the Kinderton Salt Works until sold to the Salt Union Ltd. in 1888. Henry took over a salt works in Middlewich about 1890; somewhat quirkily, its address was Pepper Street. This works as first established in 1756, and Seddon rather misleadingly claimed this as the date for the foundation of his business. He expanded in 1911 by purchasing three nearby works of the Dairy and Domestic Salt Co. Ltd.

Brine pumping in Cheshire was causing very considerable damage to property in certain areas: buildings could literally fall into large holes which were due to the underlying strata collapsing. Middlewich was considered to be outside the area where this subsidence was worst, and hence local works escaped inclusion in the Brine Pumping (Compensation for Subsidence) Bill, giving them a competitive advantage. Seddon's works already had an advantage in not being part of the huge but unprofitable and poorly managed Salt Union, widely regarded as an industrial dinosaur.

What Henry Seddon did have in common with the Salt Union was his firm belief in looking after the transportation of his own salt. His works were adjacent to the Trent and Mersey Canal, and from 1898 Seddon built up a fleet of narrow boats to carry salt and also bring in coal from North Staffordshire. The salt destined for shipment coastwise or abroad was carried the short distance to Anderton, where the canal passed close to – but well above – the River Weaver. The Anderton lift was built here to transfer narrow boats from one waterway to the other, but Seddon used a cruder and cheaper method. His bags of salt were sent down by chutes to the lower level, where they were loaded into his larger steamers for delivery to Liverpool, or perhaps further afield. The Weaver Navigation Trustees employed a six-man gang on this work in the 1920s.

Trading between Anderton and Liverpool, his river craft became something of an institution on the Weaver and Mersey. First was the PRIDE O'TH'WEAVER (178/1898) owned by the Weaver Steamship Co. Ltd. and built by W.J. Yarwood at Northwich. The WEAVER BELLE (156/1900) followed, which habitually towed the barge GOWANBURN (164/1902) and a further dumb barge DANEHURST (168/1904) which was converted to steam in 1914. At Liverpool or Birkenhead Docks these craft would often load the salt directly into ocean-going steamers, Nigeria being a frequent destination.

In 1903, Henry Seddon began taking delivery of craft capable of loading at Anderton but trading coastwise. The wooden ENTERPRISE he owned in person, but for the ACME, STANLEY and TREVOR he established single ship companies and invited business associates to subscribe. For instance, amongst the 27 persons subscribing £4,000 to the Stanley Steamship Co. Ltd. in 1903 were salt brokers, quarry employees, master mariners, stevedores and ships chandlers. Of more significance as subscribers were John P. Jones-Parry, in whose Manchester, Liverpool and North Wales Steamship Co. Ltd. Seddon was about to invest, and Richard R. Clark who was to manage Seddon's coasters from his Liverpool office. The builder of most of Seddon's river and coastal vessels, W.J. Yarwood, also had a substantial shareholding.

All four coasters were of a suitable size for loading at Anderton and taking salt cargoes to Irish Sea ports, and a photograph exists of the ACME loading salt on the Weaver. However, Seddon had just sunk a significant amount of capital into the Manchester, Liverpool and North Wales Steamship Co. Ltd. and was heavily involved with a fleet which, at its peak, totalled ten coasters. This was more than required for the salt trade, and indeed Richard Clark was keeping the coasters under his management, including Seddon's, employed mainly with stone, but also carrying coal, timber, corn, iron and general cargo about the Irish Sea. In a letter to Yarwoods describing the trades

Acme just completed at Pimblott's yard, Northwich. *Courtesy Derek Blackhurst and Clive Guthrie*

of his ships, the one cargo Richard Clark does not mention is salt, although it is known the occasional cargo was carried. The name TREVOR chosen for the final Seddon ship confirms she was intended for the North Wales stone trade, where the Trevor Quarry was a frequent destination. The wooden ENTERPRISE may well have been the exception, and could have been employed as a river craft. However, she has been given the benefit of the doubt and included in the fleet list as a coaster because she did go to sea with stone during her career.

Seddon was acting as provider of capital and, notwithstanding Seddon's name appearing as manager in registration documents, Clark was supplying the expertise for building and running the ships as he saw fit. For instance, as builders Yarwoods were dealing with Clark and not Seddon.

Did Seddon do well out of his shipping venture? Keeping three of the ships running through the First World War he could hardly fail to make a good profit, especially as none were called on for Government service which was usually rewarded at a rate shipowners considered low. ACME and TREVOR would also yield good returns when sold in 1917 and 1919, although STANLEY which was kept until 1927 would not. Seddon's unfortunate experience as investor in the Manchester, Liverpool and North Wales Steamship Co. Ltd. would ensure he had no faith, or money, to put into further shipping ventures. Sale of STANLEY in 1927 ended Seddon's shipowning, but not the carriage of his salt by water. WEAVER BELLE and GOWANBURN survived until 1960, when both narrow boats and Weaver packets were given up.

Henry Seddon and Sons Ltd. – a title adopted in 1907 – continued producing salt until 1952, when the business was sold to the Cerebos Salt Co. Ltd. This company even resumed coastal shipowning, purchasing in 1959 the motor coaster PURBECK (199/1936) which was to be seen loading at Anderton. A photograph and details of PURBECK appear in Graeme Somner's *Dundee, Perth and London.* The company was sold again in 1969, and in 1996 the works remain in production as part of what is now known as RHM Foods Ltd.

Fleet list

1. ACME 1903-1917

O.N. 118041 227g 79n 110.0 x 21.7 x 9.7 feet
C. 2-cyl. by Cleghorn and Wilkinson, Northwich; 8 knots.

31.8.1903: Completed by Isaac Pimblott and Sons, Northwich for the Acme Steamship Co. Ltd. (Henry Seddon, manager), Liverpool as ACME. *18.12.1917:* Sold to the Carlisle Coasting Co. (John W.H. Stokes, manager), Plymouth. *20.7.1920:* Sold to the Coastwise Union Shipping Co. Ltd. (Arthur J. Jolly, manager), Liverpool. *23.3.1921:* Sold to Peter Marmion, Liverpool. *18.12.1925:* Sold to Mrs. Lena Fielding (Arthur Fielding, manager), Liverpool. *28.6.1928:* Capsized and sank off the South Stack, Anglesey when her deck cargo of timber shifted in a storm whilst on a voyage from Dublin to Liverpool. The crew of seven was rescued by the Norwegian steamer RIMFAKSE (1,334/1921). The position of her loss was initially reported to be about sixty miles south east of the Isle of Man. *8.8.1928:* Register closed.

2. ENTERPRISE 1904-1908 Wood

O.N. 118083 160g 89n 93.4 x 21.6 x 10.0 feet
C. 2-cyl. by W.J. Yarwood, Northwich; 8 knots.

4.3.1904: Completed by W.J. Yarwood, Northwich (Yard No. 26) for Henry Seddon, Middlewich as ENTERPRISE. *7.1.1908:* Sold to the Liverpool Association for the Protection of Commercial Interests as Respects Wrecked and Damaged Property, Liverpool. *19.7.1912:* Sold to the Mersey Bunkering Co. Ltd. (John T. Makinson, manager), Liverpool. *29.6.1913:* Foundered at the entrance to the River Ribble whilst on a voyage from Penmaenmawr to Preston with a cargo of granite. *4.10.1913:* Register closed.

Stanley *John Clarkson*

3. STANLEY 1904-1927

O.N. 118125 187g 87n 101.0 x 21.8 x 10.6 feet
C. 2-cyl. by W.J. Yarwood, Northwich.

25.3.1904: Launched by W.J. Yarwood, Northwich (Yard No. 31) for Henry Seddon, Middlewich as STANLEY. *13.9.1904:* Completed. *31.10.1904:* Owners became the Stanley Steamship Co. Ltd. (Henry Seddon, manager), Liverpool. *3.6.1927:* Sold to William B. Kyffin, Birkenhead. *24.8.1927:* Sold to Alfred B. Wade, Cardiff. *20.10.1927:* Sold to Steam Coasters Ltd. (William A. Andrew, manager), Cardiff. *4.12.1939:* Sold to the Straits Steamship Co. Ltd. (Lovell D. Mack, manager), Liverpool. *16.1.1940:* Renamed PENRHOS. *1.1.1942:* Mined and sunk one mile and approximately 243° from the North Constable Buoy, Liverpool Bay whilst on a voyage from Penmaenmawr to Liverpool with a cargo of stone chippings. Her crew of four was lost. *16.2.1942:* Register closed.

Trevor *John Clarkson*

4. TREVOR 1906-1919

O.N.123989 196g 69n 106.0 x 22.0 x 8.9 feet
C. 2-cyl. by W.J. Yarwood and Sons, Northwich.

27.7.1906: Completed by W.J. Yarwood and Sons, Northwich (Yard No. 45) for the Trevor Steamship Co. Ltd. (Henry Seddon, manager), Liverpool as TREVOR. *11.1.1919:* Sold to the Douglas Shipping Co. Ltd. (George E. Kelly, manager), Douglas, Isle of Man. *19.9.1930:* Manager became Leonard M. Callow. *28.4.1932:* Sold to Stephen A. Portus, Garston. *4.5.1932:* Sold to William N. George, Llanelli. *27.2.1933:* Owner became Gaynor George, Llanelli. *21.6.1934:* Sold to Coppack Brothers and Co., Connah's Quay. *30.7.1937:* Register closed after being broken up on Tranmere Beach.

THOMAS J. SHARP AND CO.
Liverpool

Thomas James Sharp made an impressive entry to coaster management, but his timing was bad. His small fleet is of interest partly because two ships were built locally, and their construction and financing involved one of Liverpool's most important shipbuilders and repairers.

In 1902 Sharp acted as a shipping and commission agent from offices in India Buildings in Liverpool, and a branch office in Fowey indicates an interest in the china clay trade. Seeking to further this business by owning his own ships, he floated two companies in 1901 and 1902, the British Monarch Steamship Co. Ltd. and the British Empire Steamship Co. Ltd., each with a nominal capital of £6,500. Appointed as manager, Sharp was the largest subscriber to both companies, other shareholders including a Birkenhead pawnbroker, together with some Liverpool and Garston shipbrokers and Henry Grayson, who was to play a big part in the story. Sharp's ships were ordered from Grayson's new shipyard.

Henry Mulleneux Grayson was the sixth member of his family to enter their ship building and repairing business at Liverpool. For some years Graysons had concentrated on repairing and lengthening ships, partly because the dock authorities had not considered shipbuilding a priority industry, and Grayson's yards had to be given up to further dock expansion. Henry Grayson entered the family firm in 1886, but not until his father retired in 1899 could he realise his ambition of taking the family back into shipbuilding. He acquired a site at Garston, and in 1901 formed the Garston Graving Dock and Shipbuilding Co. Ltd. Its first seagoing vessel was delivered in April 1902, Sharp's BRITISH MONARCH, followed a few months later by the BRITISH EMPIRE. Yard numbers 14 and 21 were allocated to this pair, but no lower yard numbers have been identified, other numbers being allocated to pontoons and the like.

Grayson quickly increased his holdings in Sharp's companies, and his shipyard provided a mortgage of £4,000 on the BRITISH MONARCH. Sharp, with no record of ship management, was having great difficulty attracting enough capital and Grayson, anxious for orders for his new yard, was willing to make up the shortfall. He would come to regret it.

The first decade of the twentieth century was a difficult one for most aspects of British shipping, following a period of prosperity in the 1890s when, for instance, considerable numbers of steam coasters had been built. The British Monarch and British Empire companies did not do well, and consistently lost money. Grayson was owed £6,258 in mortgages and running costs by the British Empire company alone, and his company had at least £4,000 outstanding on the BRITISH EMPIRE. To satisfy his financial interests he took over both ships in April 1909, and little was left for other creditors. There was an attempt to put the British Monarch company into voluntary liquidation a month later, but the meeting attracted too few subscribers: they had lost their money anyway. Both companies were compulsorily wound up in 1911.

The Garston shipyard does not seem to have been the success that Grayson hoped. In 1912 its name became Henry and Charles Grayson Ltd., suggesting that the original company had failed. Work was brisk throughout the war, but the company gave up shipbuilding in 1922. Around 30 of its products can be identified from sources such as *Lloyds Register's Appendix,* although yard numbers reached 119. Henry Grayson did himself well out of the war, becoming Director of Ship Repairs in December 1917, for which he was handsomely rewarded with a knighthood, a K.B.E. and the rank of Lieutenant-Colonel.

Thomas J. Sharp went back to his agency and shipbroking work after the repossession of his companies' coasters. He did briefly return to coaster owning in July 1921, but was no more successful. He bought the 43-year old steamer ETHEL from a Garston man, again forming a limited company to own her and taking out a mortgage. But times were even harder than twenty years earlier, and for the sake of a mortgage which was just £375, the Midland Bank repossessed the ETHEL in December 1924 and sold her.

Fleet list

1. BRITISH MONARCH 1902-1909

O.N. 115271 523g 229n 160.0 x 24.7 x 11.0 feet
C. 2-cyl. by Ross and Duncan, Govan; 10 knots.

9.4.1902: Launched by the Garston Graving Dock and Shipbuilding Co. Ltd., Garston (Yard No. 14) for the British Monarch Steamship Co. Ltd. (Thomas J. Sharp and Co., managers), Liverpool as BRITISH MONARCH. *28.4.1902:* Completed. *7.4.1909:* Sold to Henry and Charles Grayson, Liverpool. *29.6.1909:* Sold to the Ribble Shipping Co. Ltd. (John S. Sellers, manager), Liverpool. *8.7.1909:* Renamed RIBBLEDALE. *1924:* Sold to Park and Henderson Ltd., Newcastle-upon-Tyne. *27.12.1926:* Wrecked at Litacquerol Point, Bouley Bay, Jersey after dragging her anchor whilst on a voyage from London to Jersey in ballast. *27.5.1927:* Register closed.

2. BRITISH EMPIRE 1902-1909

O.N.115335 557g 237n 167.5 x 26.6 x 11.5 feet
C. 2-cyl. by Ross and Duncan, Govan; 10 knots.

2.10.1902: Launched by the Garston Graving Dock and Shipbuilding Co. Ltd., Garston (Yard No. 21) for Henry M. Grayson, Liverpool. *11.1902:* Completed. *20.12.1902:* Acquired by the British Empire Steamship Co. Ltd. (Thomas J. Sharp and Co., managers), Liverpool as BRITISH EMPIRE. *14.7.1909:* Sold to H. and C. Grayson, Liverpool. *24.8.1909:* Sold to the Manchester Coasting and General Shipping Co. Ltd. (Alfred E. Bowen, manager), Manchester. *23.5.1910:* Sank following a collision with the Swedish steamer HALFDAN (1,142/1884) near Stanlow in the Manchester Ship Canal whilst on a voyage from Weston Point to Lerwick with a cargo of salt. *8.6.1910:* Raised and beached near Eastham. *1911:* Sold to the Greenock and Grangemouth Dockyard Co. Ltd. and repaired. *1911:* Sold to William Eadie, Vancouver, Canada. *1916:* Sold to the Solar Steamship Co. Ltd. (T.W. Smyth, manager), London and renamed SOLAR. *21.12.1917:* Struck a submerged object six miles south west of Cape Barfleur whilst on a voyage from Guernsey to Tréport with a cargo of stone. *29.7.1918:* Refloated, but later declared a constructive total loss.

British Monarch on the gridiron at Bristol following a collision in February 1908. *Robin Craig collection*

3. ETHEL 1921-1924

O.N. 67509 178g 91n 120.2 x 19.9 x 8.4 feet
C. 2-cyl. by Pattison and Atkinson, Newcastle-upon-Tyne; 8 knots.

5.1878: Launched by R. Craggs and Sons, Middlesbrough (Yard No. 23) for Richard H. Appleton and Co., Stockton-on-Tees as ETHEL. *8.7.1878:* Completed. *1887:* Owners became the Cleveland Steamship Co. Ltd. (Richard H. Appleton and Co., managers), Stockton-on-Tees. *25.3.1909:* Owners became Cleveland Steam Shipping Co. Ltd., Stockton-on-Tees. *15.11.1912:* Sold to John R. Dickson junior and Co., Glasgow. *23.5.1913:* Owners became the Steamship Cliftondale Co. Ltd. (John R. Dickson junior and Co., managers), Glasgow. *2.5.1916:* Sold to John Joseph Murphy, Waterford. *2.7.1919:* Sold to the Leadenhall Shipping and Forwarding Co. Ltd. (George R. Smith, manager), London. *31.3.1921:* Sold to John Hyland, Garston. *26.7.1921:* Acquired by Thomas J. Sharp, Liverpool. *21.10.1921:* Owners became the Ethel Steamship Co. Ltd. (Thomas J. Sharp and Co., managers), Liverpool. *30.12.1924:* Sold to the Eltham Shipping Co. Ltd. (T.B. Stott and Co. Ltd., manager), Liverpool. *27.3.1925:* Capsized and sank fifteen miles north north west of Strumble Head whilst on a voyage from Newport, Monmouthshire to Dublin with a cargo of coal. *29.5.1925:* Register closed.

THOMAS B. STOTT
Liverpool

The Stott family were amongst Merseyside's best known shipbrokers and, like many in the business, they aspired to shipowning. In Thomas Stott's case, however, dabbling in coasters merely lost him and his associates money.

W.H. Stott began in the business at the age of 17 in 1852, and by 1866 was heading his own company. W.H. Stott and Co. owned a few sailing vessels and from 1886 some modest-sized steamers, such as STARLIGHT (1,513/1886), trading mainly from the Mersey to the Baltic. Thomas Buckley Stott was the founder's second son, and joined the business in 1890 after a period as a consulting engineer. From 1896 to 1912 a number of steamers were registered under his name, again mostly of a size suitable for the Baltic trades. Some were disposed of quickly: successive, newly-built SPARTAN CHIEFs (1,546/1898 and 1,813/1899) were each sold after barely twelve months' service.

Thomas Stott left the family company in 1915 to set up in business on his own account, initially as a shipbroker. But even in the last years of the First World War, when prices of ships were vastly inflated, he felt the lure of shipowning, and briefly operated the tug DISPATCH (280/1870) and the ex-Mersey ferry WIRRAL (391/1890). From 1920 a serious effort was made to build up a fleet; initially the ships bought were intermediate-size vessels like those previously owned by the family, but from 1922 coasters were acquired and registered in the name of the Eltham Shipping Co. Ltd. The little FLORENCE and ETHEL were over 40-years old, and although Stott's subsequent purchases were larger they too were of advanced years. The coasters were of a size suitable for trading round the Irish Sea. ETHEL, for instance, was taking South Wales coal to Ireland when she found the March weather in St. George's Channel too much for her.

Stott's other ventures were less successful. The ancient collier STOTTGATE (620/1875) was bought from Greek owners in February 1923 only to be sold by her mortgagees just over a year later. Even more of a blow must have been the similarly enforced sale of the steamer STOTTPOOL (1,259/1924). Stott's only new-building, she was completed at Sunderland by Swan Hunter and Wigham Richardson Ltd. in May 1924 for the Stottpool Steamship Co. Ltd., financed partly by a mortgage from her builders. Her certificate, which survives in the Public Record Office, is in such pristine condition that it is likely she never traded. The builders, as mortgagees, repossessed her in December 1925 and sold her to Norwegian owners. The third of this group, the STOTTFIELD (618/1890) which had

Ethel *E.N. Taylor*

been T. and J. Harrison's JARNAC, escaped a similar fate probably because the mortgagee was Stott's wife Constance, but Stotts sold the ship to Italian owners in June 1925.

Stott bought or ordered these ships cheaply at a time of favourable prices in the early 1920s in the not-unreasonable expectation that no shipping recession would last more than a few years. But this recession did last, almost until the next war. After 1925, Stott's interest was purely in coasters. BRYNAWEL could be considered as a replacement for the ETHEL, although larger and not quite so old. DINORWIC, bought in 1927 in the name of the Stottdale Steamship Co. Ltd., had for 25 years been a familiar visitor to the Mersey with slate cargoes from Dinorwic Quarries.

In 1929, Thomas Stott and others floated a new owning company, the unappealingly named Camrat Steam Ship Co. Ltd., to which the BRYNAWEL was transferred. Was it just coincidence that the name was a back-spelling of Tarmac, or was the company intended to trade with roadstone? If the latter, there is no clue in its articles of association or subscribers. The company came woefully short of raising its nominal capital of £10,000, and was dissolved after making just one annual return. It seems to have been Thomas Stott's last throw as a shipping entrepreneur, and although the DINORWIC steamed on until 1932 under his management, the BRYNAWEL's management passed to a George Canning in 1930.

Canning also inherited the management of the Eltham Shipping Co. Ltd., and was bold enough to order a new coaster, the BRIGHTSIDE, from a yard on the Dee. Despite her name, the future was not bright for coastal shipping. BRIGHTSIDE was repossessed and sold by her mortgagee within two years of delivery, and in 1933 BRYNAWEL suffered the same fate and was sold for scrap.

With hindsight, Thomas Stott and his associates would have been better sticking to shipbroking: the family firm W.H. Stott and Co. Ltd. had sold their ships in 1924, but continued very successfully as shipbrokers in Liverpool and Manchester.

Fleet list

1. FLORENCE 1922-1923 Iron

O.N. 67575 207g 123n 121.8 x 21.2 x 8.7 feet
C. 2-cyl. by Blair and Co. Ltd., Stockton-on-Tees.

15.2.1881: Launched by R. Craggs and Sons, Middlesbrough (Yard No. 27) for Richard H. Appleton and Co., Stockton-on-Tees as FLORENCE. *17.3.1881:* Completed. *18.3.1903:* Sank following a collision with the steamer BARON SELBORNE (882/1872) half a mile below Broadness Point in Northfleet Reach, River Thames whilst on a voyage from Middlesbrough to London with a cargo of steel rails. Her crew was saved. Later refloated, repaired and returned to service. *11.8.1909:* Owners became the Cleveland Steam Shipping Co. Ltd. (Thomas Nattras, manager), Stockton-on-Tees. *5.6.1914:* Sold to Harry Barnett, London. *10.1.1916:* Sold to Cunningham, Shaw and Co. Ltd., Liverpool (Vernon S. Lovell, London, manager). *15.12.1916:* Sold to Edward W. Broadbent, Leeds (Herbert Smart, London, manager). *20.6.1917:* Owners became the U.K. Steamship Co. Ltd., Leeds (Herbert Smart, London, manager). *6.3.1922:* Acquired by the Eltham Shipping Co. Ltd. (Thomas B. Stott and Co., manager), Liverpool. *30.7.1923:* Sold to Elias T. Elias and Harry Maiden, Liverpool. *2.1.1924:* Foundered off Buncrana whilst on a voyage from Portnalong to Manchester with a cargo of granite. *6.2.1924:* Register closed.

2. STOTTGATE 1923-1924

O.N. 73567 620g 376n 186.3 x 30.0 x 12.0
C. 2-cyl. by John Dickinson, Sunderland; 9 knots.

27.7.1875: Launched by James Laing, Sunderland (Yard No. 370) for H.T. Morton and Co., Sunderland and William Milnes, London as DEVONSHIRE. *30.9.1875:* Completed. *1881:* Owner became William S. Milnes, London. *17.3.1891:* Sold to John G. Lambton (Earl of Durham), Sunderland. *26.8.1896:* Owners became Lambton Collieries Ltd. (Thomas Nicholson, manager), Sunderland. *2.11.1903:* Manager became Edward T. Nisbet. *21.8.1911:* Owners became Lambton and Hetton Collieries Ltd. (Edward T. Nisbet, manager), Sunderland. *1912:* Sold to D.J. Theophilatos, Andros, Greece and renamed ANTONIOS. *1913:* Sold to Antonios Georgandis, N.A. Dallas and M.M. Pithis, Syra, Greece. *1917:* Owner becomes Antonios Georgandis, Syra. *1919:* Sold to D.J. Theophilatos, Andros, Greece. *2.1923:* Acquired by Jura Steamers Trading Co. Ltd. (Thomas B. Stott, manager), Liverpool. *15.2.1923:* Renamed STOTTGATE. *3.1924:* Sold to Prvo Dalmatinsko Trgovacko Drustvo (First Dalmatian Trading Co), Dubrovnik, Yugoslavia and renamed PRVI DALMATINSKI. *1928:* Renamed AURORA. *1928:* Sold to Luigi fu A. Panunzio, Molfetta, Italy and renamed AIDA. *1930:* Sold to Paolo De Gennaro, Molfetta. *1933:* Broken up.

3. ETHEL 1924-1925

O.N. 67509 178g 91n 120.2 x 19.9 x 8.4 feet
C. 2-cyl. by Pattison and Atkinson, Newcastle-upon-Tyne, 8 knots.

5.1878: Launched by R. Craggs and Sons, Middlesbrough (Yard No. 23) for Richard H. Appleton and Co., Stockton-on-Tees as ETHEL. *8.7.1878:* Completed. *1887:* Owners became the Cleveland Steamship Co. Ltd. (Richard H. Appleton and Co., managers), Stockton-on-Tees. *25.3.1909:* Owners became Cleveland Steam Shipping Co. Ltd., Stockton-on-Tees. *15.11.1912:* Sold to John R. Dickson junior and Co., Glasgow. *23.5.1913:* Owners became the Steamship Cliftondale Co. Ltd. (John R. Dickson junior and Co., managers), Glasgow. *2.5.1916:* Sold to John Joseph Murphy, Waterford. *2.7.1919:* Sold to the Leadenhall Shipping and Forwarding Co. Ltd. (George R. Smith, manager), London. *31.3.1921:* Sold to John Hyland, Garston. *26.7.1921:* Sold to Thomas J. Sharp, Liverpool. *21.10.1921:* Owners became the Ethel Steamship Co. Ltd. (Thomas J. Sharp and Co., managers), Liverpool. *30.12.1924:* Acquired by the Eltham Shipping Co. Ltd. (Thomas B. Stott and Co., manager), Liverpool. *27.3.1925:* Capsized and sank fifteen miles north north west of Strumble Head whilst on a voyage from Newport, Monmouthshire to Dublin with a cargo of coal. *29.5.1925:* Register closed.

4. BRYNAWEL 1925-1933

O.N. 99878 410g 163n 142.5 x 25.1 x 11.0 feet
C. 2-cyl. by Bow, McLachlan and Co., Paisley.

18.1.1893: Launched by J. McArthur and Co., Paisley (Yard No. 8) for John M. Paton and Peter D. Hendry, Glasgow as FERGUSLIE. *30.1.1893:* Completed. *25.2.1898:* Owners became the Glasgow Steam Coasters Co. Ltd. (John M. Paton and Peter D. Hendry, managers), Glasgow. *11.9.1908:* Sold to George Webster and Co., Glasgow. *12.10.1911:* Sold to Mann, Macneal and Co., Glasgow. *21.5.1913:* Renamed JEDFORD. *22.2.1915:* Sold to William L. Lewis, Aberaeron. *12.5.1915:* Renamed BRYNAWEL. *14.2.1916:* Sold to the Bryn Steam Navigation Co. Ltd. (Emlyn Jones and Co. Ltd., managers), Cardiff. *12.11.1919:* Sold to the Brynawel Steamship Co. Ltd. (Francis J. Evans, manager), Burryport. *2.3.1923:* Sold to Evan Jones, Llanelli. *14.5.1925:* Sold to Hannevig Brothers, London. *15.5.1925:* Acquired by the Eltham Shipping Co. Ltd. (Thomas B. Stott, manager), Liverpool. *8.1.1930:* Owners became the Camrat Steamship Co. Ltd. (Thomas B. Stott and Co., managers), Liverpool. *26.8.1930:* Manager became George Canning. *11.2.1933:* Sold to shipbreakers.

Brynawel in Hotwell Dock, Bristol on 6th July 1919. *National Maritime Museum P28958*

5. DINORWIC 1927-1932

O.N. 92205 276g 111n 128.0 x 23.0 x 10.4 feet
C. 2-cyl. by William Kemp, Glasgow; 10 knots.

8.12.1891: Launched by S. McKnight and Co., Ayr (Yard No. 33) for George W.D. Assheton-Smith (Walter W. Vivian, manager), Port Dinorwic as DINORWIC. *21.1.1892:* Completed. *22.6.1907:* Owner became Walter W. Vivian (Ernest Neele, manager), Port Dinorwic. *19.9.1919:* Sold to Owen H. Donnelly, Dublin. *19.2.1923:* Sold to Arthur Monks, Liscard, Cheshire. *14.4.1924:* Owner became Mrs. Margaret J. Monks (Humphrey Roberts, manager), Liscard. *21.7.1927:* Acquired by the Stottdale Steamship Co. Ltd. (Thomas B. Stott and Co., managers), Liverpool. *20.12.1932:* Sold to James C. Screech, Appledore. *16.6.1933:* Sold to William V. Lunt, Par. *17.1.1934:* Capsized in heavy weather whilst discharging at Cleavehouses on the River Torridge having arrived from Goole with a cargo of coal. She was later refloated and broken up. *12.2.1934:* Register closed.

Dinorwic *E.N. Taylor*

6. BRIGHTSIDE 1930-1932

O.N. 162324 476g 189n 142.2 x 25.2 x 11.5 feet
C. 2-cyl. by Abdela-Mitchell, Queensferry; 9 knots.

25.8.1930: Completed by Abdela-Mitchell, Queensferry (Yard No. 464) for the Eltham Shipping Co. Ltd. (George Canning, manager), Wallasey as BRIGHTSIDE. *31.3.1932:* Sold to Leslie Knopp (James W. Harvie, manager), London. *29.3.1933:* Sold to the Fortis Steamship Co. Ltd. (T.H. Donking and Sons Ltd., manager), Middlesbrough. *5.2.1946:* Sold to Robert Taylor and Sons Ltd., Dundee (G.T. Gillie and Blair Ltd., managers, Newcastle-upon-Tyne). *24.9.1949:* Wrecked one and a half miles south of Collieston during fog whilst on a voyage from London to Inverness with a cargo of cement. *16.11.1949:* Register closed.

Brightside *E.N. Taylor*

SUMMERFIELD STEAMSHIP CO. LTD.
Liverpool

Of the many shipping companies formed in the heady days of high earnings following the First World War, a number were blatant and cynical speculations, organised by greedy financiers with little interest or experience in shipping. But in the subsequent crash of freight rates and ship prices, almost all these companies succumbed, including those that were soundly financed and had experienced management.

The Summerfield Steamship Co. Ltd. was registered in July 1919 to take over from Samuel Summerfield and George Henshall the contracts for a number of coasters already under construction. Summerfield came from a Warrington family that had, since at least the 1870s, been involved with sailing flats and other vessels. A John Summerfield had shares in the flat ANNE (63/1861) of Runcorn and a William Summerfield shares in the flat HARRIET (66/1840). Captain Samuel Summerfield took over the command of William Savage's first steamer ZILLAH in 1895, and had a close association with the Zillah Shipping and Carrying Co. Ltd. One of this company's largest steamers was named SUMMERFIELD in honour of the family. Whether or not he had the blessing of his former employer in his new venture, Samuel Summerfield was certainly to draw on his experience with the Zillah company.

Captain Samuel Summerfield was the single largest subscriber, and with his wife Hannah held 10,400 of the company's 70,000 £1 shares. George Henshall was a provision merchant in Warrington; other directors included George Summerfield of Garston, probably Samuel's brother and himself a master mariner; a Dublin coal importer; a painter and a consulting engineer. There seemed little difficulty in selling the shares, at least initially. There were some 150 subscribers, mostly from Liverpool and Warrington. They ranged from widows to wire-drawers, plumbers to publicans, and bargemen to bank clerks.

The first ship to be completed was the JESSIE SUMMERFIELD, delivered from Troon in December 1919. She was something of an anachronism, and was almost indistinguishable from ships delivered by the same yard to the Zillah company almost twenty years earlier. It was as if Ailsa had merely dusted off the plans for the second ZILLAH of 1901 and her contemporaries. Two design features were particularly significant. The small hatch ahead of the mainmast was to allow for trimming when heavy stone cargoes were carried, and her length of 143 feet was to fit the locks at Ringsend Basin, Dublin. Stone carrying and exporting coal to Dublin were the two trades in which Zillah specialised, and both would be familiar to Captain Samuel Summerfield. The directorship given to Stephen Kelly, a Dublin coal importer, helps confirm that the young company was aiming at this trade.

Jessie Summerfield *W.S.P.L. collection*

Such was the pressure on shipbuilders at this time that it was over a year before the company's further ships appeared, the MARY SUMMERFIELD and AMY SUMMERFIELD. Although outwardly identical to the JESSIE SUMMERFIELD, they were built at a different yard, Day, Summers and Co. Ltd. at Southampton, but clearly from plans supplied by Ailsa. Comparison of the prices paid for three similar ships shows how shipbuilding costs were increasing:

JESSIE SUMMERFIELD	December 1919	£27,569
MARY SUMMERFIELD	February 1921	£29,926
AMY SUMMERFIELD	March 1921	£32,876

Despite this price inflation, the directors were clearly optimistic about the prospects for shipowning, and less than a year after founding the company increased its capital by £50,000. Subscribers were not so confident, however; less than 20% of these extra shares were ever taken up, and no additional ships were built.

Even with only the JESSIE SUMMERFIELD trading, results at the end of 1920 showed a profit of almost £5,000. They were to be the only profits the company ever made. Freight rates had slumped during 1920, and at the end of 1921 with three ships in service there was a loss of £10,000. Such losses continued in subsequent years, leading the company into increasing indebtedness, with bank overdrafts secured by the ships, and a personal loan of £2,500 from Captain Samuel Summerfield.

The company's trading account for 1924 shows why the company, and others like them which had invested in expensive ships, could not show an overall profit. Trading costs came to £19,398, of which the largest items were:

Port and cargo charges	£6365
Coal bunkers	£4652
Crew wages	£4537
Insurance	£1501
Repairs	£582
Commission	£533
Tonnage payments to captains	£282
Ships stores	£259
Brokerage	£248

Against this, earnings came to £19,897, giving a trading surplus of just £499. When interest on the loans and overdrafts were taken into account, and depreciation of the three ships at a modest 2%, this became a loss of £2,675. And this was one of the company's better years.

Economies were made: in July 1922 the Liverpool office was given up and the company traded from Robert Henshall's shop in Warrington. But with no sign of freight rates returning to their immediately post-war high, the inevitable had to be faced. In October 1926, buyers were found for the MARY SUMMERFIELD: Dublin merchants who entrusted her management to the Mersey Steamship Co. Ltd. which had been fixing freights for the Summerfield ships. In January 1927, however, a meeting in Warrington decided to wind up the Summerfield Steamship Co. Ltd. Two months later both remaining ships were sold to the Zillah Shipping and Carrying Co. Ltd. Having been based on a design originally prepared for this company, they were clearly well suited to Zillah's requirements. Nevertheless, the JESSIE SUMMERFIELD was sold within a week. She was to spend much of her subsequent career in the Dublin coal trade for which she had been built. The AMY SUMMERFIELD served Zillah well, and retaining her original name lasted until 1951 when she was a rare casualty of the stone trade, the needs of which was a consideration in her design.

The sale of the ships probably did little more than cover the loans and overdrafts on them, and shareholders undoubtedly made a considerable loss on their investment in the Summerfield Steamship Co. Ltd. Aiming at trades in which its principal had extensive experience, and with purpose-built ships to a tried and trusted design, the company might well have succeeded had it not encountered a combination of high start-up costs and disastrously low freight rates.

Fleet list

1. JESSIE SUMMERFIELD 1919-1927

O.N.143608 440g 168n 143.2 x 25.1 x 12.0 feet
C. 2-cyl. by the Ailsa Shipbuilding Co. Ltd., Troon; 10 knots.

4.12.1919: Launched by the Ailsa Shipbuilding Co. Ltd., Troon (Yard No. 372) for the Summerfield Steamship Co. Ltd., Liverpool as JESSIE SUMMERFIELD. *29.12.1919:* Completed. *14.3.1927:* Sold to the Zillah Shipping and Carrying Co. Ltd. (William A. Savage Ltd., manager), Liverpool. *19.3.1927:* Sold to William Robertson Ltd., Glasgow. *21.4.1927:* Renamed MORION. *21.11.1939:* Sold to the Mohochang Exploration Co. Ltd., Manchester (J. Galbraith of Stephenson, Clarke and Associated Companies, Glasgow, manager). *8.12.1939:* Renamed GLENBRIDE. *27.5.1942:* Sold to Chatterley Whitfield Collieries Ltd., Stoke-on-Trent (J. Galbraith of Stephenson, Clarke and Associated Companies, Glasgow, manager). *18.2.1946:* Sold to the Polgarth Steamship Co. Ltd. (James Macmillan, manager), London. *20.10.1949:* Sold to the Alliance and Dublin Consumers' Gas Co., Dublin. *31.9.1963:* Arrived at Passage West, Cork for breaking up by Haulbowline Industries Ltd. *10.4.1963:* Work commenced.

Jessie Summerfield as William Robertson's **Morion**. *W.S.P.L. Cochrane collection*

2. MARY SUMMERFIELD 1921-1926

O.N. 143711 407g 159n 143.0 x 25.1 x 11.6 feet
C. 2-cyl. by Day, Summers and Co. Ltd., Southampton; 9 knots.

17.11.1920: Launched by Day, Summers and Co. Ltd., Southampton (Yard No. 186) for the Summerfield Steamship Co. Ltd., Liverpool as MARY SUMMERFIELD. *1.2.1921:* Completed. *8.10.1926:* Sold to Wallace Brothers Ltd., Dublin (Mersey Steamship Co. Ltd., Liverpool, managers). *16.10.1928:* Renamed RINGWALL. *4.10.1932:* Owners became Wallace Brothers Ltd., Dublin. *27.1.1941:* Mined and sunk south of the Isle of Man whilst on a voyage from Dublin to Silloth in ballast. Her crew of eight was lost. *7.4.1941:* Register closed.

Mary Summerfield *John Clarkson*

3. AMY SUMMERFIELD 1921-1927

O.N. 143718 407g 159n 143.2 x 25.1 x 11.6 feet
C.2-cyl. by Day, Summers and Co. Ltd., Southampton; 9 knots.

11.1.1921: Launched by Day, Summers and Co. Ltd., Southampton (Yard No. 187) for the Summerfield Steamship Co. Ltd., Liverpool as AMY SUMMERFIELD. *7.3.1921:* Completed. *14.3.1927:* Sold to the Zillah Shipping and Carrying Co. Ltd. (William A. Savage Ltd., manager), Liverpool. *2.8.1949:* Owners became the Zillah Shipping Co. Ltd. (William A. Savage Ltd., manager), Liverpool. *23.3.1951:* Wrecked at Llighfaen Pier, Port Rivals, having arrived from Liverpool in ballast. *2.8.1951:* Register closed.

Amy Summerfield *A. Duncan*

THOMAS BROTHERS SHIPPING CO. LTD.
THOMAS COASTERS LTD.
Liverpool

Few of the companies in this book set out with such high hopes and aspirations as Thomas Brothers Shipping Co. Ltd., and few were brought so low, so quickly.

All three Thomas brothers were nephews of the successful Anglesey-born Liverpool shipowner William Thomas (see next chapter). Owen Henry Thomas became joint owner of the coaster NETTA in July 1909, and traded her around the Irish Sea; she visited several South Wales ports before being lost in 1916. William Glynne Thomas was a ship broker, and is first encountered in 1915 managing the HERCULES on behalf of the third brother, Robert Thomas, who was also a ship broker. In 1917, when coasters were in short supply, William, Robert and Owen formed the Hercules Steam Shipping Co. Ltd. to own the HERCULES, which was a converted Trinity House vessel and cost just under £2,000.

In April 1920 in conjunction with their cousin Sir Robert J. Thomas - the son of William Thomas - the three Thomas brothers floated the Thomas Brothers Shipping Co. Ltd. with an ambitious nominal capital of £250,000. The company's prospectus was also written on the grand scale, and it is worth quoting from it extensively.

> 'The company has been formed for the purpose of acquiring and working a fleet of new or recently build steamers, suitable as regards size and type for the coasting trade.
>
> The demand for steamers of this class is greatly in excess of the supply, and the importance of the coasting trade to the community is universally recognized. Coastwise freights are high, and it is believed that if shipping were released from Government control, still higher rates would rule. The recent advance in Railway rates will, it is anticipated, increase coastwise traffic in which case freights will naturally rise, and the Managers are confident that the prosperity of the home trade is assured for a considerable time to come.
>
> The Managers have already acquired a new steamer to be called "Lady Thomas", of 340 tons deadweight capacity and classed 100 A1 at Lloyds for £34,500. She is now in the water and ought to be working in a few days. The nett earnings of this Steamer, calculated at the controlled rates of freight, are estimated at about £12,500 per annum. A freight of 85/- to 90/- per ton d.w. per month could be obtained for her on time charter and allowing for stoppages, it is estimated she would, if thus engaged, earn a nett profit of £11,000 or £12,000 per annum, but the Managers consider that they can work her to better advantage on the open market.
>
> In addition to the "Lady Thomas", the Managers have taken over a contract for a steamer of 500 tons d.w., which is being built by Colby Brothers Limited, Lowestoft, and engined by the Shields Engineering Co. Ltd. The purchase price of this steamer is £43,500 and she is expected to be ready for work in two or three months.
>
> Both of these vessels will be turned over to the company at cost price, and such price will be payable in cash.
>
> It is intended to acquire further tonnage of the same class from time to time, as suitable opportunities offer until the Company has a fleet of 8 or 10 vessels, and it is estimated that with a fleet of this size the Company would make a nett profit of £90,000 to £100,000 per annum. Such a sum after making ample provision for depreciation and reserves, should enable the Company to pay a substantial Dividend.
>
> Sir Robert Thomas, the Chairman of the Directors, has had over 25 years experience of the management of ships, first as a partner in William Thomas and Co., Liverpool, and subsequently as the Director of William Thomas, Sons and Co. Ltd., of London and Liverpool, and he is now Governing

Director of R.J. Thomas and Co. Ltd., the Managers of the William Thomas Shipping Co. Ltd. There is probably no Shipowner in the country with a better record of success as a Ship Manager. Mr. Robert Thomas has carried on business as a Ship Broker and Ship Owner in Liverpool for many years under the style of Thomas Brothers and Co., and he and the other two Directors, who have been associated with him in his business, are well and favourably known in the Mersey District and out ports, and particularly to Shippers in the home trade.'

The cynical may well think that Sir Robert J. Thomas had been brought in because of the reverence with which his father's name was held in shipping circles. Despite the glowing terms of the prospectus, Sir Robert did not have his father's skill as a ship manager, as investors in his deep-sea steamer venture, the William Thomas Shipping Co. Ltd., were to find to their cost. In any case, he had minimal experience in the coasting trade and, resident as he was in Anglesey, could have had little to do with the day-to-day running of the Liverpool office of Thomas Brothers Shipping Co. Ltd.

The two steamers were transferred to the company within days of its formation in April, having been acquired by the Thomases in February and March, respectively. The LADY THOMAS, which had been ordered by Mann, MacNeal of Glasgow, was delivered in April but the MIRIAM THOMAS did not arrive from Lowestoft until November. Did this reflect Colby's slower building rate, or the fact that Thomas Brothers Shipping Co. Ltd. took overlong to raise the cash to make the final payment? The managers took up far less of the shares than they promised in their prospectus, and although the minimum subscription for allotment was reached, by June 1920 only £73,000 had been subscribed – insufficient to meet the cost of both steamers.

Profits nowhere near met the promoters' expectations, with a massive slump hitting trade in 1920. Trading figures for the first year are not known, but a loss of £1,701 was recorded for the year to April 1922. A smaller loss of £396 was reported for the year to April 1923, as there was a slight revival of trade in the last months of 1922, coinciding with the arrival of the ELSIE THOMAS and NANCIE THOMAS, but this upturn was not sustained. As if to justify their acquisition of further ships, the managers claimed that the

Lady Thomas *John Clarkson*

new ships cost £16,000, but could not be built for less than £25,000. The purchase price was less than a half of that paid for the LADY THOMAS two years earlier. The directors were still optimistic, and foresaw 'an increased demand for small boats'. Indeed, things looked up slightly in 1924, with a profit of £800 - but still a far cry from the predicted £100,000. The year also saw the arrival of the DORIS THOMAS, at £8,000 a real bargain, but perhaps reflecting the desperation of her builders, the Manchester Dry Docks Co. Ltd. of Ellesmere Port, to get her off their hands. She was one of a quartet begun during the First World War, but whose completion proceeded at a leisurely pace. Notwithstanding the yard's inexperience of shipbuilding, DORIS THOMAS lasted well, and when withdrawn from service as the BEN AIN in 1963 she was the last single hatch steam coaster on the Irish Sea.

After 1924, however, the financial story of Thomas Brothers Shipping Co. Ltd. was one of continuing and, indeed, deepening losses. In May 1929 it was decided to wind up the company, an operation completed in 1930 when the MIRIAM THOMAS, NANCIE THOMAS and ELSIE THOMAS passed to the National Provincial Bank – a major creditor – for a mere £19,000 for three ships.

With the exception of the bridge-amidships MIRIAM THOMAS, the company's ships were archetypal Irish Sea coasters with single hatches and of a size which allowed them to squeeze into almost any port in Ireland or on the west coasts of England, Wales or Scotland. Those who served on the ships remember their almost invariable cargo as being coal out of the Mersey or Preston to Ireland, from where they would drop back in ballast to the Llŷn to load roadstone for the Mersey. The granite quarries on this peninsula had their heyday in the nineteenth century when there was insatiable demand for setts for roadmaking, and enjoyed a revival in their fortunes in the 1920s with the need for crushed granite for macadamised roads. There was a tendency for coaster companies to form loose alliances with particular quarries, and it was to the exposed jetty of the Yr Eifl Quarry (also known as Caer-Nant or Nant-Gwytheryn) belonging to Croft Granite Brick and Concrete Co. Ltd. that Thomas's coasters gravitated. There they would load stone in any form from dust through chippings to large blocks and deliver it to Mersey ports, of which the West Bank Dock at Widnes was favoured by Croft Granite - at least when the tide served. It was not unknown for all five of the coasters of Thomas Brothers to be in this dock at once. In later years, stone was brought to the West Float, Birkenhead for the construction of a new road along the Wirral Peninsula, the New Chester Road.

Occasionally this trading pattern would be broken, with coal shipped from the Mersey to St. Ives, Appledore or another West Country port with a return cargo of china clay lifted for Runcorn. Photographs also show that the ships were not strangers to Bristol and the Avon, and the ELSIE THOMAS visited Dublin and Belfast.

Many of the crews of Thomas's coasters came from Amlwch, and indeed whole families from the Anglesey port served on the ships. The brothers Sam and Hugh Evans were masters of the LADY THOMAS and MIRIAM THOMAS, the former having two of his sons as mate and able seaman. William Jones, also of Amlwch, was master of the NANCIE THOMAS, later transferring to the J.F.V. In the years between the wars when jobs were by no means easy to find, the crews rarely changed. One trend that became apparent, however, was the gradual arrival of Arklow seamen after Jim Tyrell replaced Evans as mate of the LADY THOMAS.

Owen Thomas and William G. Thomas have to be credited with perseverance, as after the liquidation of their first venture they began in business again, as Thomas Coasters Ltd., buying back all five ships of the original company. In place of the high ambition of Thomas Brothers Shipping Co. Ltd., austerity was now the order of the day, and offices were taken at Wellington Buildings, Litherland Alley, off South Castle Street, which are remembered as being Dickensian in their pokiness. Life in the coastal trade was now more a matter of survival than prosperity, and Thomas Coasters Ltd. is recalled as being a very poor company indeed. Even relatively routine repairs seemed to put an insuperable burden on it. In 1934 the DORIS THOMAS was loading at the Yr Eifl jetty when one of the big swells which made any jetty on the north coast of the Llŷn an unpopular place for ships to linger caught her so that her forecastle windlass was pulled

Doris Thomas
John Clarkson

out. This event, too trivial to merit an entry in the Weekly Casualty Returns, led to her being laid up in Stanley Dock when she arrived at Liverpool, and to her eventual sale.

Trade did not improve during the early thirties, and Thomas Coasters Ltd. was wound up in 1936, with the two brothers going their own shipowning ways. DORIS THOMAS and ELSIE THOMAS were sold (NANCIE THOMAS had gone the previous year) and William G. Thomas took the LADY THOMAS under his own name, operating her from his home.

Owen Thomas took the company's largest ship, the MIRIAM THOMAS, bought from the National Provincial Bank who had mortgaged her to Thomas Coasters Ltd, and she was initially registered under his own name. He then fell back on his old association with Croft Granite, as his ship was registered under the ownership of a consortium consisting of a member of his own family, Mrs Annie Thomas, L.F. Briggs (a civil engineering contractor) and John J. Griffiths of Widnes who was manager of the granite company. The two last-named gentlemen also bought another elderly steamer, the J.F.V., which was also placed under Owen Thomas's management. The final change was to register the MIRIAM THOMAS in the ownership of the Carriers Shipping Co. Ltd. With two respectably-sized coasters, and freights showing vague signs of recovery with the approach of war, prospects should have been brighter for Owen Thomas. But his little company does not seem to have thrived: the J.F.V. was sold in 1939 and the MIRIAM THOMAS was lost in collision in 1942 and never replaced.

Brother William G. Thomas fared better. The LADY THOMAS came through the war unscathed and lasted long enough to see William form a new limited company, the Glynwood Navigation Co. Ltd. This company then sold the LADY THOMAS and bought the VICTOR, which was renamed LADY WOOD. An older steamer, the LADY WOOD was considerably larger than LADY THOMAS, allowing the company to make the most of the improved trading conditions which followed the Second World War. William G. Thomas died in July 1951, and the management of his solitary ship passed to his son Peter. LADY WOOD herself gave a further two years' service before she was fit only for scrap and the days of the steam coaster, it seemed, were over.

Or were they? The Glynwood Navigation Co. Ltd. reappeared in Lloyds Register almost two years after the LADY WOOD had gone, but it now hailed from Hull, where it shared an office with the Holderness Steamship Co. Ltd. Over the next two years it was to own three steamers, two named CUPHOLDER (the second beginning life as Richard Hughes' DORRIEN ROSE) and one LOGHOLDER (already encountered in this book as CELIA MARY in the fleet of Mersey Ports Stevedoring Co. Ltd.). The -HOLDER names help to confirm that the company had been bought by Thomas E. Kettlewell, and was used to register some of his large fleet of ageing and life-expired coasters, most of which he bought at scrap prices, and traded them for as long as he could. In 1958 the second CUPHOLDER was transferred to the Holderness Steamship Co. Ltd. and the name Glynwood Navigation Co. Ltd. disappeared a second and final time.

Perhaps we should not be too hard on the Thomas brothers. It was their misfortune to experience one of the longest and deepest recessions the shipping industry had suffered. That at least one of the brothers survived in the coastal shipping business for 35 years speaks of a tenacity that belies the get-rich-quick promises of the prospectus put out by Thomas Brothers Shipping Co. Ltd.

In the fleet list the convention has again been used of listing all ships owned by the Thomas brothers in chronological order, regardless of their actual ownership.

Fleet list

1. NETTA 1909-1915

O.N. 125788 370g 177n 135.0 x 22.9 x 12.2 feet
C. 2-cyl. by Allan, Anderson and Co., Glasgow; 10 knots.

1908: Launched by the Montrose Shipbuilding Co., Montrose (Yard No. 33) for Joseph Constant, London as MONTROSE ONE. *15.5.1909:* Completed. *20.7.1909:* Renamed NETTA. *26.7.1909:* Acquired by Owen H. Thomas and Edward J. Hughes, Liverpool. *28.2.1912:* Owner became Owen H. Thomas, Liverpool. *23.4.1915:* Sold to Cheviot Coasters Ltd. (George T. Gillie and Co., managers), Newcastle-upon-Tyne. *3.9.1916:* Captured by the German submarine UB 18 and sunk 35 miles north east by half north of Cape Antifer, whilst on a voyage from Rouen to Newcastle-upon-Tyne in ballast. *13.9.1916:* Register closed.

2. HERCULES 1915-1923 Iron twin screw

O.N. 63575 199g 99n 120.5 x 20.2 x 10.6 feet
C. 2-cyl. by David Rowan and Co., Glasgow.

1870: Launched by T.B. Seath and Co., Rutherglen for the Corporation of Trinity House, London as HERCULES. *11.1888:* Sold to William Williams, Holyhead. *26.4.1915:* Sold to Robert Thomas (W. Glynne Thomas, manager), Liverpool. *23.4.1917:* Owners became the Hercules Steam Ship Co. Ltd. (W. Glynne Thomas, manager), Liverpool. *15.1.1923:* Sold to William Cooper and Son Ltd., Widnes. *6.11.1925:* Re-registered as a dumb barge. *26.4.1950:* Register closed after being broken up.

3. LADY THOMAS 1920-1948

O.N. 143633 294g 108n 123.8 x 23.6 x 10.2 feet
C. 2-cyl. by Shields Engineering and Dry Dock Co. Ltd., North Shields.

22.1.1920: Launched by the Ardrossan Dry Dock and Shipbuilding Co. Ltd., Ardrossan (Yard No. 274) for Mann, MacNeal and Co. Ltd., Glasgow as HURLFORD. She had been laid down for Cullen, Allen and Co. Ltd., Belfast. *4.1920:* Completed for Thomas Brothers Shipping Co. Ltd., Liverpool as LADY THOMAS. *1929:* Owners became Thomas Coasters Ltd., Liverpool. *1935:* Owner became W. Glynne Thomas, Liverpool. *1948:* Sold to the Glynwood Navigation Co. Ltd. (William G. Thomas, manager), Liverpool. *1948:* Sold to Falconer Coasters Ltd., London. *1949:* Renamed GRAHAM F. *1953:* Sold to the Warren Shipping Co. Ltd., London and renamed WARREN COURT. *5.6.1957:* Arrived at Haren, Belgium for breaking up by B.J. Nijkerk S.A.

4. MIRIAM THOMAS 1920-1942

O.N. 143680 430g 179n 142.4 x 24.1 x 10.6 feet
C.2-cyl. by Shields Engineering and Dry Dock Co. Ltd., North Shields; 10 knots.

12.10.1920: Completed by Colby Brothers Ltd., Lowestoft (Yard No. 19) for Thomas Brothers Shipping Co. Ltd., Liverpool as MIRIAM THOMAS. She had been laid down for Stewart Line Ltd., Belfast. *14.10.1930:* Owners became Thomas Coasters Ltd., Liverpool. *30.4.1936:* Owner became Owen H. Thomas, Liverpool. *26.10.1937:* Owners became Mrs. Annie Thomas, L.F. Briggs and John J. Griffiths (Owen H. Thomas, manager), Liverpool. *26.10.1937:* Owners became the Carriers Shipping Co. Ltd. (Owen H. Thomas, manager), Liverpool. *15/16.3.1942:* Sank following a collision with the steamer VASNA (4,820/1917) in St. George's Channel whilst on a voyage from Weston Point to Newry. *6.9.1943:* Register closed.

Miriam Thomas *E.N. Taylor*

5. **ELSIE THOMAS 1922-1936**

O.N.140824 305g 114n 130.8 x 22.6 x 9.8 feet
C. 2-cyl. by Gauldie and Gillespie, Glasgow.

20.10.1921: Launched by Ritchie, Graham and Milne, Glasgow (Yard No. 375) for the Moffat Steamship Co. Ltd. (Moffat and Nickerson, managers), Grimsby as ELIZABETH MOFFAT. *1.1922:* Completed. *20.11.1922:* Acquired by the Thomas Brothers Shipping Co. Ltd., Liverpool. *27.11.1922:* Renamed ELSIE THOMAS. *28.10.1930:* Owners became Thomas Coasters Ltd., Liverpool. *13.1.1936:* Sold to Alexander M. Massie, Aberdeen. *11.3.1936:* Renamed GROSVENOR. *7.1.1937:* Sold to W.N. Lindsay Ltd., Leith. *12.7.1940:* Sold to Mrs. E.M.M.G. Cubbin (R.A. Colby Cubbin, manager), Douglas, Isle of Man. *6.12.1946:* Sold to the Estuary Shipping Co. Ltd., Leith. *10.4.1948:* Renamed CRAIG. *27.7.1948:* Sold to Norman Stewart, Leith. *7.1952:* Arrived at Gateshead for breaking up by C.W. Dorkin and Co. *23.4.1953:* Register closed.

Elsie Thomas *E.N. Taylor*

6. NANCIE THOMAS 1922-1935

O.N. 145976 311g 116n 130.3 x 22.6 x 9.8 feet
C. 2-cyl. by Gauldie, Gillespie and Co.Ltd., Glasgow.

29.8.1922: Launched by Rennie, Ritchie and Newport Shipbuilding Co. Ltd., Whiteinch, Glasgow (Yard No. 376) for the Thomas Brothers Shipping Co. Ltd., Liverpool as NANCIE THOMAS. *21.9.1922:* Completed. *28.10.1930:* Owners became Thomas Coasters Ltd., Liverpool. *15.1.1935:* Sold to Andrew T. Lamont (Shipbuilder), Greenock. *6.9.1935:* Sold to Robert Cameron and Co., Glasgow. *20.9.1935:* Renamed KYLE SKYE. *25.10.1940:* Wrecked at Cleats, at the south end of the Isle of Arran, whilst on a voyage from Campbeltown to Workington in ballast. *20.9.1935:* Register closed.

Nancie Thomas *John Clarkson*

7. DORIS THOMAS 1924-1936

O.N. 147521 274g 102n 120.0 x 22.1 x 9.0 feet
C. 2-cyl. by Manchester Dry Docks Co. Ltd., Ellesmere Port; 9 knots.

5.3.1924: Launched by the Manchester Dry Docks Co. Ltd., Ellesmere Port (Yard No. 73) for the Thomas Brothers Shipping Co. Ltd., Liverpool as DORIS THOMAS. She had been laid down for the builder's own account in 1919. *4.1924:* Completed. *1930:* Owners became Thomas Coasters Ltd., Liverpool. *1936:* Sold to A.F. Henry and MacGregor Ltd., Leith and renamed DENNIS HEAD. *1938:* Sold to the Ramsey Steamship Co. Ltd., Ramsey. *1939:* Renamed BEN AIN. *5.6.1963:* Arrived at Passage West, Cork for breaking up by Haulbowline Industries Ltd.

8. J.F.V. 1936-1939

O.N. 128494 515g 197n 162.5 x 26.7 x 11.9 feet
C. 2-cyl. by George T. Grey, South Shields.

5.5.1909: Launched by J.T. Eltringham and Co., South Shields (Yard No. 271) for Spillers and Bakers Ltd., Cardiff as WHEATFIELD. *6.1909:* Completed. *1913:* Owners became the Spillers Steamship Co. Ltd., Cardiff. *1926:* Sold to J.J. Stafford and Sons Ltd., Wexford and renamed J.F.V. *1931:* Owners became Wexford Steamships Ltd. (Joseph J. Stafford, manager), Wexford. *1934:* Sold to Alfred H. Smith, London. *1936:* Acquired by L.F. Briggs and John J. Griffith (Owen H. Thomas, manager), Liverpool. *1939:* Sold to William J. Ireland, Liverpool. *1942:* Sold to Geo. Tom and Co. Ltd., London. *1947:* Renamed FENCHURCH. *1948:* Sold to H. Harrison (Shipping) Ltd. (William J. Ireland, manager), Liverpool. *1949:* Renamed BANNQUEEN and managers became S. William Coe and Co. Ltd., Liverpool. *1951:* Owners became the Thorn Line Ltd. (S. William Coe and Co. Ltd., managers), Liverpool. *16.1.1957:* Arrived at Troon for breaking up by the West of Scotland Shipbreaking Co. Ltd.

J.F.V. *John Clarkson*

9. LADY WOOD 1948-1953

O.N. 124200 437g 165n 150.0 x 25.1 x 9.3 feet
C. 2-cyl. by Hutson and Sons Ltd., Glasgow.

17.6.1907: Launched by J. Shearer and Sons Ltd., Glasgow (Yard No. 46) for the Glasgow Steam Coasters Co. Ltd. (John M. Paton and Peter D. Hendry, managers), Glasgow as VICTOR. *8.7.1907:* Completed. *17.4.1914:* Sold to the North Eastern Shipping Co. Ltd. (G. Elsmie and Son, managers), Aberdeen. *11.9.1917:* Sold to the South Wales and Liverpool Steam Ship Co. Ltd. (Robert Gilchrist and Co., managers), Liverpool. *27.4.1943:* Owners became Coast Lines Ltd., Liverpool. *22.11.1943:* Sold to the Ribble Shipping Co. Ltd. (William J. Ireland, manager), Liverpool. *17.10.1947:* Owners became H. Harrison (Shipping) Co. Ltd. (William J. Ireland, manager), Liverpool. *30.8.1948:* Acquired by the Glynwood Navigation Co. Ltd. (William G. Thomas, manager), Liverpool. *19.11.1948:* Renamed LADY WOOD. *28.4.1953:* Arrived at Llanelli for breaking up by the Rees Shipbreaking Co. Ltd. *11.11.1953:* Register closed.

Lady Wood *John Clarkson*

WILLIAM THOMAS
Liverpool

By dint of his extensive fleet of deep-sea sailing and steam vessels, William Thomas is probably the largest and most powerful shipowner in this book. His coasting fleet was both numerically and dimensionally small, however, although its provenance owed a lot to Thomas's origin.

William Thomas came from Llanrhuddlad in Anglesey and needs to be distinguished from William Thomas of Amlwch, especially as the two enjoyed a close business relationship. Both made good early, William Thomas of Llanrhuddlad giving up the idea of a teaching career to enter the business as a clerk in a Liverpool shipping office. In 1860, at the age of 23, he set up on his own, as a ship insurance broker and ship manager. Through the strong Welsh methodist community in Liverpool he maintained his connection with his native island and its shipping notables, including William Thomas of Amlwch. In 1869 the two Thomases jointly acquired the barque WILLIAM MELLHUISH (681/1859), and even managed to find yet another William Thomas on Anglesey, this time from Newborough, to command her. The conjunction of the three William Thomases was considered propitious, as the first voyage of this ship became something of a local legend, and it is said that its profits repaid the investment fivefold. The money was ploughed back into shipowning, the Thomas of Llanrhuddlad investing in the Amlwch Thomas's schooners, and also those of other West Coast schooner fleets – Ashburner, Fisher and Postlethwaite. He also began to have ocean sailing ships and later steamers built, to be owned by single-ship companies whose shares were avidly taken up by his fellow Welshmen.

Thomas took immense trouble over the design of his sailing ships, so that they were both well-found and highly profitable. His four-masted barques such as the PRINCIPALITY (1,785/1885) and METROPOLIS (1,811/1887) represented the really big cargo carriers of the 1880s and might well have been mere floating warehouses, but were regarded as ships of considerable beauty. Thomas is remembered as a shrewd and single-minded businessman, with a singular knack of having his ships in the right place at the right time to earn a good profit. Although not a sailor himself, he placed great reliance on the skills and knowledge of his masters, and paid heed to their reports of trading conditions in the ports they visited. Apart from managing what became a considerable fleet, Thomas also found time for civic duties and was twice mayor of Bootle.

His association with the Amlwch Thomases was a most cordial one, and he undertook to help market the shares in the small iron steamers which the Amlwch yard began building in the 1880s. Conservative Welsh investors seemed rather wary of taking shares in steamers, and the Liverpool Thomas ended up buying many of the shares himself. Indeed, by the mid-eighties the W.S.CAINE and EXCHANGE were owned by single-ship companies under his management – the only coastal steamers in a large fleet. Amongst the numerous naming schemes he adopted were names with a monetary theme, such as CONSOLS and TREASURY, so perhaps his influence at Amlwch went as far as the name chosen for the EXCHANGE.

The Steamship W.S. Caine Co. Ltd. and the Steamship Exchange Co. Ltd. were registered on the same day in January 1885. Their capitalisation – £4,500 and £5,800 respectively – reflected the higher price of the larger and new EXCHANGE. The capital was divided up into £20 shares, the Liverpool Thomas taking the larger share in the Steamship W.S. Caine Co. Ltd. and the Amlwch Thomas a greater holding in the Steamship Exchange Co. Ltd. Robert Thomas, son of the Liverpool Thomas and who shared the management of the ships, took smaller shareholdings. W.S. CAINE and EXCHANGE seem to have been largely confined to the Irish Sea, the former also visiting Penzance on one occasion.

William Thomas died in 1915, the company which bore his name being wound up and his ships sold in 1916. His name was enlisted by his son Robert – obviously for the prestige that went with it – for the William Thomas Shipping Co. Ltd., a venture in deep-sea steamers which was as ill-starred and unprofitable as his father's had been brilliant.

Fleet list

1. W.S. CAINE 1886-1895 Iron

O.N. 87232 183g 79n 122.4 x 21.1 x 7.9 feet
C. 2-cyl. by De Winton and Co., Caernarfon.

4.1883: Launched by William Thomas and Sons, Amlwch (Yard No. 15) for William Thomas and Co., Amlwch as W.S. CAINE. *2.5.1883:* Completed. *12.3.1886:* Acquired by the Steamship W.S. Caine Co. Ltd. (William Thomas and Co., managers), Liverpool. *9.3.1895:* Sold to John P. Jones-Parry, Liverpool. *18.6.1895:* Owners became the Manchester, Liverpool and North Wales Steamship Co. Ltd. (John P. Jones-Parry, manager), Liverpool. *28.3.1904:* Manager became Robert R. Clark. *28.3.1911:* Sold to William Rouse and Sons, Neyland, Pembrokeshire. *27.12.1918:* Sold to John W. Robertson, Lerwick. *20.2.1920:* Sold to John Johnston, Glasgow. *11.4.1922:* Sold to William Cubbin Ltd., Liverpool for demolition. *5.1922:* Broken up at Birkenhead. *17.6.1922:* Register closed.

2. EXCHANGE 1885-1901 Iron

O.N. 87965 295g 93n 135.0 x 22.3 x 9.9 feet
C. 2-cyl. by De Winton and Co., Caernarfon.

2.1884: Launched by William Thomas and Sons, Amlwch (Yard No. 16) for William Thomas junior, Amlwch as EXCHANGE. *9.5.1884:* Completed. *1885:* Acquired by the Steamship Exchange Co. Ltd. (William Thomas and Co., managers), Liverpool. *10.12.1901:* Sold to the Manchester, Liverpool and North Wales Steamship Co. Ltd. (John P. Jones-Parry, manager), Liverpool. *28.3.1904:* Manager became Robert R. Clark. *23.3.1917:* Sunk by gunfire from the German submarine UB 39 thirty miles north west of Cayeux whilst on a voyage from St. Valery-sur-Somme to Newhaven in ballast. *20.4.1917:* Register closed.

Exchange after her sale to the Manchester, Liverpool and North Wales Steampship Co. Ltd. *John Clarkson*

EDWARD W. TURNER AND SONS
Garston and Liverpool

Of the many small shipbroker-shipowners in the Mersey ports, Edward W. Turner is probably the best chronicled, and we know about the company's activities both from its own written history and the reminiscences of those who worked on their ships.

Captain Owen Spargo described its founder as "...a very widely experienced old sea dog, and if he could not make a ship pay, then there was not much hope for anyone else." Edward Wrake Turner was born in 1840 at Queenborough in Kent and began his seagoing career in the Royal Navy. By 1858 he was an ordinary seaman in H.M. Sloop ARGUS, serving with the Mediterranean fleet. On deciding to leave in favour of the merchant service in 1861, he was told that he would have an excellent future in the Royal Navy. In reply, Turner predicted that he would have his own ship before his commander had one. He was probably right: Turner obtained his master's ticket at the age of 24 and in September 1866 took command of the barque MERTOLA (392/1866).

This was undoubtedly a good appointment. MERTOLA had just been built at Pugwash, Nova Scotia for London owners and established a very regular trading pattern. She also introduced Turner to his wife Annie, of Amherst, Nova Scotia whom he married in November 1867, and to his future home port of Garston, to where he moved his family in 1871. MERTOLA made a number of voyages to Nova Scotia, but her main trade was copper ore from Pomaron in Portugal to Garston, ore which was destined for the copper refiners of St. Helens and Widnes. In 16 years as master of MERTOLA, Turner made 68 round trips to Pomaron and at least five to Nova Scotia. He also acquired shares in the MERTOLA: a common practice which was encouraged as it gave the master an incentive to keep his vessel working and earning money. By 1882 he had acquired all 64 shares in the MERTOLA, but having achieved one ambition, he needed fresh fields to conquer.

Captain Turner came ashore at Garston in 1883, and set up in business as a marine surveyor and shipbroker with an office on Dock Road. He pursued this new career with the same determination as he had put into seafaring, and business steadily built up, helped by Turner's reputation for straight dealing. He took on agencies of a number of insurance companies and had a telephone as early as 1884.

MERTOLA had been chartered back to her previous owners, and with her former mate in command continued trading to Pomaron. She was sold to Liverpool owners in 1885, and entered the South American trade, being lost in the Atlantic in 1890.

Captain Turner soon added shipowning and later ship management to his portfolio. In 1889 the small iron steamer TELEPHONE was bought, but was quickly sold to begin a career running between Liverpool and Welsh ports that has been described in *Cambrian Coasters.* Ship management began in 1899 with the DERWENT and the IBIS and proved a better long-term business proposition than shipowning. DERWENT was managed on behalf of William Standing of Garston, a civil engineering contractor, and she was sold after a few years. However, management of the IBIS began a relationship which was to last for over thirty years.

Owners of the IBIS, Wilson Brothers Bobbin Co. Ltd., had a factory in King Street, Garston which made bobbins for the textile industry and other wooden articles, including soles for clogs. The works was named Cornholme Mills after the company's original home near Todmorden, Yorkshire where Lawrence Wilson had set up in business as a bobbin maker in 1823. Wilson's business required beech logs, and in 1860 he opened a saw mill at Athlone in Ireland which was eventually exporting 7,000 tons of beech timber to England each year. This timber mainly came through Garston – although some also came from Canada – and Wilson Brothers, as the company had become, took the logical step of moving their business, rather than their logs, and opened the Garston works in 1892. It became the company's headquarters in 1902, by when the title Wilson Brothers Bobbin Co. (1900) Ltd. had been adopted. Acquisition of their own ships, which began with the IBIS in 1899, had several benefits. Logs were imported not only from Ireland, but also from around sea lochs in Western Scotland such as Loch Sween and Loch Broom. It was important to use ships which had sufficient cargo gear to handle the logs, and to have crews used to the unusual work. Having their own ships was also attractive because outward cargoes of coal for Irish ports were readily available from Garston. IBIS was quickly followed by CARLINGFORD LOUGH and by at least four wooden sailing ships, which were managed not by Turners but by J.C. Hornby. Wilson Brothers had no ships between 1912 and 1916, but then bought the HELEN, probably to guarantee deliveries of beech when the war meant charters were hard to arrange. Undeterred by the loss of HELEN in 1917 the company replaced her, and built up their fleet to three ships by 1921.

Helen *E.N. Taylor*

GLEN-HELEN was bought in 1920, and renamed in memory of the company's first loss. Owen Spargo joined her as ordinary seaman in March 1921 and in *Old Time Steam Coasting* set down his vivid memories of the beech log trade. GLEN-HELEN would load coal in Garston for ports such as Bray, Dundalk, Drogheda, Waterford, Wexford or Wicklow – no doubt Edward Turner's connections were instrumental in fixing these cargoes. A particularly adventurous aspect of the trade was anchoring offshore to load beech logs which were being felled close to the water, possibly in a Hebridean sea loch. GLEN-HELEN would let go both anchors and mooring lines were run from the stern and fastened to tree stumps on the shore. The felled trees were rolled into the water and towed out to the ship's side using her boat. One of the ship's two derricks was guyed out over the side at about 90° whilst the other was positioned above the hold. The wires from both derricks were attached to slings called snotters which were put around the log. The log was lifted from the water by the derrick over the side, and as soon as it was above the rail the other derrick would take the strain and pull until the log was over the hold. It was then lowered into the hold, where the tree fellers would assist the crew in stowing the logs. The ship's derricks and winches could lift two tons each, but some logs were much heavier and required both derricks working together to lift them over the side.

Loading would begin at dawn and continue until dark, with two hour-long breaks for meals, and would often take two to three days. Probably on account of the cargo work involved, GLEN-HELEN had a relatively large crew of nine, including master, mate, first

Glen-Helen *John Clarkson*

and second engineers, two firemen, two able seamen and one ordinary seaman. The captain and mate were from Runcorn, and like many seamen brought up on Mersey sailing flats, ensured their ship was kept spotless, despite the regular coal cargoes.

Wilsons' steamers survived the dangers of loading offshore, but were not so fortunate in the open sea. HELEN's disappearance in August 1917 may have been due to a mine, or even to sinking by a U-boat which was itself lost before it could report back. In February 1926 GLENCONA, her replacement, was outward bound off Anglesey when a malfunctioning oil lamp set her engine room on fire. The crew took to her boats and claimed that they lost sight of her after a few hours and believed that she had sunk. However, the hulk was later reported off Blackpool on an even keel, and eventually sank off the mouth of the River Lune. GLEN-MARY, the only ship built specially for the company and designed and strengthened for log carrying, was sold in 1929, leaving the GLEN-HELEN to trade until 1932. Her sale left Turners without ships to manage.

Although the Wilson Brothers' ships provided Edward Turner's steadiest income as a manager, the Garston Steamship Co. Ltd. was a more personal venture. The company was floated in 1901, with Edward Turner taking the largest shareholding, but a number of business associates also took shares, including some of the bobbin-making Wilsons, ship repairer Matthew Clover, and two Liverpool tug owners, Adolphe Gottschalk and Joseph Stuart. The Garston Steamship Co. Ltd. acquired a most unusual steamer. The KYNOCH had been built 35 years earlier as a yacht for the engineer George Stephenson, and had been converted to a cargo ship when she was already 30 years old. She was purchased from the proprietor of the Channel Dry Docks, Shipbuilding and Engineering Co., of Passage West, County Cork, who had presumably been repairing or rebuilding her. Turner's company history comments on her notably high horsepower, but this would go hand-in-hand with a high coal consumption, hardly contributing to the economics of a vessel not intended to be a cargo carrier. KYNOCH did not survive long, sinking in November 1902 when even her cargo of empty fish boxes failed to keep her afloat. The company history attributes her loss to the mate taking her inside the Longships

Edward Turner & Sons archives

Kynoch: her origins as a yacht are apparent.

Lighthouse. KYNOCH was replaced by the more conventional, if still elderly, steamer WHIMBREL. She traded widely, and is known to have visited Cardiff, Dundalk, Middlesbrough and Rochester. The Garston Steamship Co. Ltd. was initially profitable, but by 1908 had started to make a loss, such that the WHIMBREL had to be mortgaged in that year. The company was wound up in 1910 and the WHIMBREL sold to Portugese owners.

The losses incurred by the Garston Steamship Co. Ltd. seem to have had far reaching consequences. His bankers pressured Edward Turner, who was now 70, to give up running the business in favour of a younger member of the family. The founder responded by resigning as an alderman of Liverpool - a post he had held since Garston had been included in the borough - and admitting his son Cecil to partnership in August 1911, although the company title was not changed to E. W. Turner and Son until 1916. In the event, Edward Turner survived to the age of 96. The losses seem also to have deterred the company from further ventures into shipowning for many years.

There was shipbroking, agency and other work to be had, however, not only at Garston but at Liverpool - where Turner had opened an office about 1902 but which did not become profitable for almost a decade - and at Manchester where business commenced in 1907. Perhaps the steadiest of this work was check-weighing of manganese and iron ore imported through Garston, a trade which became particularly important during the First World War. At various times the company also became involved in agency work for a group of ten United States ships which were working out of the Mersey in the latter stages of the First World War, importation of U.S. coal during a coal strike, a strike-breaking liner service on the Irish Sea during the industrial troubles of the 1920s, and sale of both cruise ship and airline tickets. From the 1920s Turners also ran a service with chartered ships from Garston to Antwerp, return cargoes being mainly steel and silver sand, the latter for glass-making at St. Helens. This service was taken over by the British and Continental Steamship Co. Ltd. late in 1937.

Turner's motor coaster **Mertola**. *W.S.P.L.*

A return to shipowning came in 1960, when Turners bought a Dutch motor coaster and, in a happy gesture, gave her the name MERTOLA after Edward Turner's first command. The company history remarks that the motor ship's deadweight tonnage differed by just one ton from that of Turner's first ship, and that it was acquired 80 years to the day after the barque MERTOLA was last sighted in the Atlantic. The new MERTOLA was used in connection with a timber importing business Turners had set up in the 1950s, spending the rest of her time tramping within home trade limits. She lasted until 1968. Explaining the decision to sell her, the company cited the increase in wages for seagoing personnel. In 1960 they could employ a master for £24 per week, but in 1968 were having to pay ordinary seamen £45 per week. Yet, they maintained, freight rates had remained the same. The company history is silent on how much the directors' salaries had also increased during this period. MERTOLA was sold to Captain John Matthews, who got round the problem of high wage rates by employing a Spanish crew. Turners remained as managers until 1972 when the ship was sold to Greece.

Captain Matthews of Holywell in Flintshire had gone to sea in the Connah's Quay-owned auxiliary USEFUL (99/1879) in 1944, and his first command had been Coppack's motorship INDORITA (201/1920). He painted a Welsh flag, complete with red dragon, on the funnel of the MERTOLA whilst she was in his ownership, and he was not adverse to flying this as a "national" flag. The MERTOLA was only a start in shipowning, and Captain Matthews had ambitions to own a fleet of ships, and succeeded in this for a few months in 1973. The story of this Welsh fleet, which was unravelled too late to appear in *Cambrian Coasters,* is told here because Turners ended by picking up the pieces.

The four ships involved were completed in Budapest, Hungary in the early sixties, part of a large series of which many went to the U.S.S.R. Einar Hövding, a Norwegian owner, took delivery of six and intended to take at least two more, which were launched with his SAGA- names but were left in Hungarian ownership. Although of relatively modest size, the ships could and did trade worldwide, but became familiar in North European ports. Hövding sold two of them in 1968 and unloaded the other four in 1971, the latter going to Cyprus-based companies owned by Constantin Xenos. The ships do not seem to have prospered even under flag-of-convenience ownership, and they began to appear in lay-up in various ports. ANDREA was idle at Garston from November 1972, running up dock dues which her owner could not pay. When she was auctioned by the Admiralty Marshall in March 1973, John Matthews bought her, along with her three sisters for a

Hövding's **Sagahorn** became Matthew's **Garorm**. *W.S.P.L.*

Lady Mostyn as **Acacea**. *W.S.P.L.*

price which was reputed to be half a million pounds. ANDREA sailed from Liverpool with a cargo of scrap for Spain in March, and was soon renamed LADY MOSTYN, her sisters becoming MARIAM (under arrest at Southampton), GYRAM (at Immingham) and GARORM. Although managed by John Matthews Shipping Co. Ltd. of Holywell the ships and their owning companies remained registered in Cyprus, and perhaps in deference to this the red dragon was not added to the white over green flag on their red, black-topped funnels.

Matthews was no more successful than the previous owners with these coasters, and by October 1973 the Norwegian merchant bank Norinvest A/S - to whom the ships were mortgaged - was looking for someone to run them and approached Edward W. Turner and Co. As their recent management experience was limited, Turners were not an obvious choice, but it is probable that the company had fixed cargoes for the ships whilst they were running for Matthews, with whom they had had business connections through the MERTOLA.

Turner's history helps explain why other owners failed to make the ships pay. When they took over only one of the ships was actually in service. MARIAM was lying at Portsmouth with a flooded engine room and a Spanish and Portugese crew which had not been paid; two were in port with generator problems, including LADY MOSTYN at Penzance. The generators were the ships' Achille's heel. The ships relied on electric power more than most contemporary ships, and were designed to have generators running off their main shaft, but these had never been fitted. As a result, the auxiliary generators had to be run continuously in port and at sea. Having already suffered from neglect, these generators were tired and constantly broke down. Spares for the generators and other machinery had to come from Eastern Europe, and could not be obtained quickly.

There were other problems. In February 1974 MARIAM was towed from Plymouth to Rotterdam for repairs, where a survey found bottom damage as well as work needed in the engine room. She did not actually carry a cargo under Turner's management, and when she finally sailed from Rotterdam in May she had been renamed FLEUR. LADY MOSTYN left Penzance in February 1974 to continue her interrupted voyage from Runcorn to Eleusis, but had to put into Lisbon for repairs to her main engine, not leaving again until April. Then, her cooling water pumps failed and, as her master decided not to stop the engines because of weather conditions, considerable damage was done through overheating and she needed a new crankshaft. In March 1974 GARORM was on a voyage from Savona to Leixoes with coke when her engine broke down leaving her in danger of drifting ashore. After sending out a Mayday, she was towed into Leixoes by a passing German coaster. GYRAM also figured in the casualty reports, having to put back into port with engine problems in December 1973 and suffering heavy weather damage during a voyage from Swansea to Tonnay Charente in January 1974.

Turner's agency department worked all hours to try to keep the ships running, whilst their chartering department was equally vexed, not only with trying to fix cargoes but also with having to make excuses for the ships' failure to deliver them. The company considered taking on extra staff, but concluded that the cost of putting the ships into a reliable condition would be more than the owners were likely to recoup. The Norwegians were advised of this and were asked to relieve Turners of the management, which was duly put in the hands of H.F. Cordes of Hamburg in May 1974. The subsequent history of these ships shows that other managers have not had a long, or profitable, relationship with them; although re-engining and lengthening in 1976 considerably extended their lives and all but one is still afloat in 1996.

After this experience there is no record of Turners venturing again into the hectic world of ship management. In the last two decades, however, they have managed two liner services: the Britain Benelux Line, serving Liverpool, Antwerp and Rotterdam; and the North Delta Line which had a service from the Mersey to Nigeria. Edward W. Turner and Son was sold by the family in 1988, and as part of the Vogt and Maguire group continue as one of the North West's major ship brokers and agents, with offices in almost all major and minor ports on Merseyside and Lancashire.

Fleet lists

1. TELEPHONE 1889-1890 Iron

O.N. 68289 165g 63n 110.6 x 18.2 x 8.8 feet
C. 2-cyl. by Muir and Houston, Glasgow.

20.2.1878: Launched by H. McIntyre and Co., Paisley (Yard No. 17) for David J. McGowan and Henry Lane, Londonderry as TELEPHONE. *18.3.1878:* Completed. *10.1880:* Sold to the Dublin, Belfast and Londonderry Steam Ship Co. Ltd., Londonderry. *3.1882:* Sold to Donald MacDonald, Larne. *15.11.1883:* Sold to Peter Barr, Stranraer. *24.8.1889:* Acquired by William Newall and Edward W. Turner, Garston. *10.10.1890:* Sold to Robert Owen, Liverpool and Owen Griffith, Portmadog. *2.6.1892:* Sold to the Aberdovey and Barmouth Steamship Co. Ltd. (John D. Penney, manager), Liverpool. *22.8.1900:* Sold to William T. Roberts, Liverpool. *2.11.1900:* Sold to the Liverpool and Cardigan Bay Steamship Co. Ltd. (Robert Owen and Co., managers), Liverpool. *3.4.1905:* Owners became the Liverpool and Menai Straits Steamship Co. Ltd. (John D. Penney, manager), Liverpool. *9.3.1915:* Sold to Thomas M. Collier, Bray. *1.11.1916:* Renamed BRAEBEG. *6.1.1917:* Sold to William O. Roberts, Henry M. Grayson, Griffith Davies and John S. Jones, Liverpool. *30.4.1917:* Sold to John J. Murphy, Waterford. *11.12.1922:* Sold to Samuel Gray (Thomas J. Wilson, manager), Belfast. *17.5.1923:* Sold to Harry J. Wright, Llanbedr, Merionethshire. *16.9.1924:* Sold to the Fox Shipping Co. Ltd. (Walter R.S. Smith, manager), Norwich. *20.12.1927:* Demolition began at Grays, Essex by T.W. Ward Ltd. *12.6.1928:* Register closed.

2. KYNOCH 1901-1902 Iron

O.N. 56052 264g 121n 145.1 x 25.3 x 12.9 feet
2-cyl. by Day, Summers and Co. Ltd., Southampton.
1879: Engines compounded.

31.5.1866: Launched by C. Mitchell and Co., Newcastle (Yard No. 145) for George R. Stephenson, Wimbledon as the yacht NORTHUMBRIA. *22.7.1866:* Completed. *1876:* Sold to the Earl of Lonsdale, Penrith. *1879:* Engines compounded. *1882:* Sold to the Duke of Bedford, Woburn Abbey, Bedford. *18.7.1893:* Sold to George H. Marvin, West Cowes. *7.9.1896:* Sold to G. Kynoch and Co. Ltd., Birmingham (Thomas J. Troy, Arklow, manager) and converted to a cargo ship. *6.3.1897:* Renamed KYNOCH. *29.6.1897:* Owners became Kynoch Ltd., Birmingham. *22.10.1900:* Sold to Oliver S.S. Piper, Cork. *7.2.1901:* Acquired by Edward R. Turner, Garston and Joseph Stuart, Seacombe. *19.4.1901:* Owners became the Garston Steamship Co. Ltd. (Edward W. Turner, manager), Garston. *11.5.1902:* Foundered off the Hats and Barrels Rocks, St. George's Channel whilst on a voyage from Neyland to Kinsale with a cargo of empty fish boxes. *15.7.1902:* Register closed.

3. WHIMBREL 1902-1910 Iron

O.N. 80202 649g 393n 180.0 x 28.1 x 13.9 feet
C. 2-cyl. by J. Jack and Co., Liverpool.

4.1879: Launched by William H. Potter, Liverpool (Yard No. 86) for the Cork Steamship Co. Ltd., Cork as WHIMBREL. *3.6.1879:* Completed. *17.12.1896:* Sold to Sollas and Sons, London. *28.10.1902:* Acquired by the Garston Steamship Co. Ltd. (Edward W. Turner, manager), Garston. *2.1910:* Sold to Glama and Marinho, Oporto, Portugal and renamed CYSNE. *29.5.1915:* Sunk by explosive charges set by the German submarine U 41 at the entrance to the English Channel. Her crew landed at Brest.

4. MERTOLA 1960-1968

O.N. 301330 497g 265n 172.0 x 28.0 x 11.2 feet
Oil engine 6-cyl. 4S.C.S.A. by Klockner-Humboldt-Deutz; Koln-Deutz, West Germany; 9 knots.

23.9.1950: Launched by N.V. Scheepwerf Gebroeders van der Werf, Deest, Holland (Yard No. 238) for Soetermeer Fekkes' Cargadoors Kantoor N.V., Rotterdam, Holland as POORTVLIET. *2.12.1950:* Completed. *13.1.1960:* Acquired by Edward W. Turner and Son, Garston and later renamed MERTOLA. *19.5.1968:* Sold to John Matthews, Liverpool (Edward W. Turner and Son, Garston, managers). *1972:* Sold to A. Mamas, L. Mamas, P. Kritikos, and M. Dokas, Piraeus, Greece and renamed ARION. *1974:* Sold to P. Kritikos, Piraeus and renamed MAGDA. *1976:* Sold to Maria Leontos Hajigianni (Intercon Management S.A.), Piraeus and renamed MARIA ELENA. *1977:* Renamed ADELAIS. *1978:* Renamed PANAGIOTISTA. *1979:* Sold to A.G. Nikolaos, Puerto Cortes, Honduras and renamed A.G. NIKOLAOS. *7.1980:* Demolition completed by Capuano Pasquale at Baia, Italy.

Managed for William A. Standing

DERWENT 1899-1903 Steel and iron

O.N. 79124 267g 111n 144.2 x 23.0 x 10.4 feet
C. 2-cyl. by J. and T. Young, Ayr.

12.1883: Launched by R. Williamson and Son, Workington (Yard No. 80) for the Derwent Steam Ship Co. (J. Cassons and Co., managers), Workington as DERWENT. *22.2.1884:* Completed. *1885:* Managers became Gibson and Grenop. *1887:* Managers became W.S. Kennaugh and Co. *1888:* Management reverted to Gibson and Grenop. *31.12.1895:* Sold to William Postlethwaite, Millom. *23.3.1899:* Acquired by William A. Standing (Edward W. Turner, manager), Garston. *2.12.1903:* Sold to George Pile, Penarth. *22.3.1909:* Sold to James Burnie and Richard B. Tinsley, Bootle. *5.1913:* Sold to A/S Dampskip Brugge, Nordby, Denmark and renamed BRUGGE. *1914:* Sold to A/S Marguerite (H. Hansen, manager), Brevik, Norway and renamed MARGUERITE. *15.4.1917:* Sold to Louis Hermans, Bruges, Belgium. *1932:* Owners became Armement Louis Hermans, Antwerp, Belgium. *15.2.1941:* Sunk in collision with the steamer ROBERT (1,272/1924) off Buoy 62, Flamborough Head in position 53.51 N by 00.25 E whilst on a voyage from South Shields to Gillingham with a cargo of coal. Two of the crew were lost.

Derwent *E.N. Taylor*

Managed for Wilson Brothers Bobbin Co. Ltd.

1. IBIS 1899-1912 Iron

O.N. 82554 171g 64n 110.2 x 20.1 x 9.0 feet
C. 2-cyl. by John Payne, Bristol.
1890: C. 2-cyl. by Muir and Houston, Glasgow.

1881: Launched by John Payne, Bristol for Henry Burton, Newport as IBIS. *15.6.1881:* Completed. *2.1888:* Sold to William E. Davies, London. *4.8.1893:* Sold to the Carnarvon and Liverpool Steam Ship Co. Ltd., Liverpool. *15.11.1895:* Beached after collision with the steamer ALARM in the River Mersey. *12.12.1895:* Register closed. Later refloated and repaired. *15.4.1896:* Reregistered in the ownership of John J. Marks, Liverpool. *6.7.1896:* Sold to William Rowland, Liverpool. *27.1.1899:* Acquired by the Wilson Brothers Bobbin Co. Ltd. (Edward W. Turner, manager), Garston. *4.10.1912:* Sold to the Ribble Shipping Co. Ltd. (John S. Sellers, manager), Liverpool. *16.11.1923:* Wrecked on Taylor's Bank Revetment, Crosby Channel, River Mersey whilst on a voyage from Liverpool to Dublin with general cargo. *1.12.1923:* Register closed.

2. CARLINGFORD LOUGH 1901-1910

O.N. 98271 245g 63n 135.7 x 20.1 x 9.4 feet
C. 2-cyl. by Ross and Duncan, Govan; 10 knots.

23.7.1891: Launched by John Fullerton and Co., Paisley (Yard No. 98) for the Carlingford Lough Steamship Co. Ltd. (Joseph Fisher and Sons, managers), Newry as CARLINGFORD LOUGH. *18.8.1891:* Completed. *19.1.1901:* Acquired by the Wilson Brothers Bobbin Co. (1900) Ltd. (Edward W. Turner, manager), Garston. *13.10.1904:* Owners became the Wilson Brothers Bobbin Co. Ltd. (Edward W. Turner, manager), Garston. *7.10.1910:* Sold to John T. Staples, Liverpool. *23.9.1911:* Sold to the Ribble Shipping Co. Ltd. (John S. Sellers, manager), Liverpool. *12.5.1913:* Wrecked on the north side of Curachan Island off Barra whilst on a voyage from Weston Point to Castlebay, Barra with a cargo of salt. *23.7.1913:* Register closed.

Carlingford Lough *E.N. Taylor*

3. HELEN 1916-1917

O.N. 111239 235g 91n 124.0 x 22.1 x 9.0 feet
C. 2-cyl. by Muir and Houston Ltd., Glasgow; 9 knots.

14.12.1899: Launched by J. Shearer and Son, Kelvinhaugh, Glasgow (Yard No. 28) for James Cameron, Glasgow as HELEN. *2.1.1900:* Completed. *13.3.1914:* Sold to Thomas R. Evans (Francis J. Evans, manager), Burry Port. *16.3.1915:* Sold to the Ferrum Steamship Co. Ltd. (G.T. Gillie and Co., managers), Newcastle-upon-Tyne. *23.3.1916:* Acquired by the Wilson Brothers Bobbin Co. Ltd. (Edward W. Turner, manager), Garston. *23.8.1917:* Left Dublin for Garston with a cargo of timber and disappeared with her crew of eight. *22.9.1917:* Register closed.

4. GLENCONA 1917-1926

O.N. 125436 282g 100n 125.5 x 22.6 x 8.9 feet
C. 2-cyl. by Hepple and Co. Ltd., South Shields; 9 knots.

9.10.1907: Launched by Hepple and Co. Ltd., South Shields (Yard No. 577) for Glen Coasters Ltd. (Matthew Worth, manager), Newcastle-upon-Tyne as GLENCONA. *20.12.1907:* Completed. *23.7.1914:* Sold to 'T' Steam Coasters Ltd. (Robinson, Brown and Co., managers), Newcastle-upon-Tyne. *8.6.1917:* Acquired by the Wilson Brothers Bobbin Co. Ltd. (Edward W. Turner, manager), Garston. *28.2.1926:* Abandoned by her crew on fire fifteen miles north west by west of the Skerries whilst on a voyage from Garston to Dublin with a cargo of coal. The crew were picked up by the steamer THE SULTAN (646/1904) and landed at Holyhead. The hulk of GLENCONA drifted some sixty miles and sank near the Lune Light Vessel. *4.6.1926:* Register closed.

Glencona in Glen Coaster's colours. *E.N. Taylor*

5. GLEN-HELEN 1920-1932

O.N. 138873 315g 131n 130.5 x 23.2 x 9.5 feet
C. 2-cyl. by Crabtree and Co. Ltd., Great Yarmouth.

7.1918: Completed by Crabtree and Co. Ltd., Great Yarmouth (Yard No. 165) for Captain W. Aiston, Scarborough as MARY AISTON. *1.1920:* Acquired by the Wilson Brothers Bobbin Co. Ltd. (Edward W. Turner, manager), Garston and renamed GLEN-HELEN. *12.11.1932:* Sold to the South Wales Sand and Gravel Co. Ltd. (Randolph A. Bevan, manager), Swansea. *1960:* Sold to Mrs. J.M. McLennan, Dundee. *1961:* Owners became the Tay Sand Co. Ltd., Dundee. *1962:* Manager became David Davidson. *2.12.1966:* Breaking up began by James A. White and Co. Ltd., Inverkeithing.

Glen-Helen as a suction dredger. *W.S.P.L.*

6. GLEN-MARY 1921-1929

O.N. 145864 394g 148n 143.2 x 24.6 x 10.5 feet.
T. 3-cyl. by Crabtree and Co. Ltd., Great Yarmouth $10^{1}/_{2}$ knots.

11.5.1921: Launched by Crabtree and Co. Ltd., Great Yarmouth (Yard No. 183) for the Wilson Brothers Bobbin Co. Ltd. (Edward W. Turner, manager), Garston as GLEN-MARY. *1921:* Completed. *1929:* Sold to F.T. Everard and Sons Ltd., London. *1940:* Sold to George Couper and Co. Ltd., Helmsdale. *1947:* Sold to J. and A. Gardner and Co. Ltd., Glasgow and renamed SAINT KEARAN. *30.12.1951:* Stranded at Ardmore Point. *27.2.1952:* Refloated and towed to Irvine for reconditioning. *6.4.1957:* Arrived at Port Glasgow for breaking up by Smith and Houston Ltd.

Glen-Mary moored at Newlyn during her Everard ownership. *National Maritime Museum P10512*

Managed for John Matthews, Holywell

MERTOLA 1968-1972
[see Edward W. Turner no. 4 above]

Managed for A/S Norinvest, Oslo, Norway

1. **LADY MOSTYN 1973-1974**

1,199g 575n 244.3 x 37.2 x 15.4 feet
1976: 1,596g 945n 84.44 x 11.28 x 4.9 metres
Oil engine 4S.C.S.A. 8-cyl. by Lang Gepgyar Engine Works, Budapest, Hungary; 11 knots.
1976: Oil engine 4S.C.S.A. 8-cyl. by VEB Schwermasch. Karl Liebknecht, Magdeburg, East Germany; 12 knots.

12.3.1964: Launched by Angyalfold Shipyard, Budapest, Hungary (Yard No. 1989) for Hövdings Skipsopphuging (Einar Hövding, manager), Oslo, Norway as SAGATIND. *1970:* Owners became Saga Shipping A/S (Hövdings Skipsopphuging, managers), Oslo. *1971:* Sold to Skiathos Shipping Co. Ltd. (Mark Scufalos, manager), Nicosia, Cyprus and renamed CHRISTIANA. *1972:* Owners became Patmos Shipping Co. Ltd., Cyprus (G. Dalacouras and J. Alexiou, Piraeus, Greece, managers), and renamed ANDREA. *3.1973:* Sold by the Admiralty Marshall whilst under arrest at Garston to Troodos Shipping Co. Ltd., Cyprus (John Matthews Shipping Co. Ltd., Holywell) and renamed LADY MOSTYN. *10.1973:* Owners became Norinvest A/S, Oslo, Norway (Edward W. Turner and Sons, Garston, managers). *1974:* Renamed ACACEA. *5.1974:* Manager became H.F. Cordes and Co., Hamburg, West Germany. *1976:* Sold to Phestos Shipping Co. Ltd., Limassol, Cyprus (Otto A. Müller, Hamburg, West Germany, managers). *1977:* Managers became Parley Augustsson A/S, Oslo, Norway. *1978:* Managers became Skips A/S King (Sigvald Maarten-Moe), Oslo. *1979:* Manager became Gunther Schulz Schulauer Schiffahrtskontor, Hamburg, West Germany. *1980:* Renamed BULK CARRIER. *12.10.1980:* Foundered after springing a leak in position 54.24.06 N by 16.12.13 E whilst on a voyage from Gdansk to Brest with a cargo of sulphur.

Hövding's **Sagatind** in the Manchester Ship Canal in September 1968: she later became **Lady Mostyn**. *Author*

2. **MARIAM 1973-1974**

1,199g 575n 244.3 x 37.2 x 15.4 feet
1976: 1,599g 944n 84.44 x 11.28 x 4.9 metres
Oil engine 4S.C.S.A. 8-cyl. by Lang Gepgyar Engine Works, Budapest, Hungary; 11 knots.
1976: Oil engine 4S.C.S.A. 8-cyl. by VEB Schwermasch. Karl Liebknecht, Magdeburg, East Germany; 12 knots.

4.3.1964: Launched by Angyalfold Shipyard, Budapest, Hungary (Yard No. 1988) for Hövdings Skipsopphuging (Einar Hövding, manager), Oslo, Norway as SAGALAND. *1970:* Owners became Saga Shipping A/S (Hövdings Skipsopphuging, managers), Oslo. *1971:* Sold to Skopelos Shipping Co. Ltd. (Constantia Xenos) (Mark Scufalos, manager), Nicosia, Cyprus and renamed GEORGE X. *1972:* Managers became G. Dalacouras and J. Alexiou, Piraeus, Greece and renamed FOFO. *1973:* Sold by the Admiralty Marshall whilst under arrest at Southampton to Sporades Shipping Co. Ltd., Limassol, Cyprus (John Matthews Shipping Co. Ltd., Holywell) and renamed MARIAM. *10.1973:* Owners became Norinvest A/S, Oslo, Norway (Edward W. Turner and Sons, Garston, managers). *4.1974:* Renamed FLEUR. *5.1974:* Manager became H.F. Cordes and Co., Hamburg, West Germany. *1976:* Managers became Otto A. Müller, Hamburg, West Germany. *1976:* Lengthened and re-engined. *1977:* Managers became Parley Augustsson A/S, Oslo, Norway. *1978:* Managers became Skips A/S King (Sigvald Maarten-Moe), Oslo. *1979:* Managers became Gunther Schulz Schulauer Schiffahrtskontor, Hamburg, West Germany. *1980:* Renamed BULK MERCHANT. *1983:* Managers became Schulz und Clemmesen Schulauer Befrachtungskantor, Hamburg. *1983:* Sold to Christian Klein G.m.b.H., Vienna, Austria and renamed ISELTAL. *1986:* Renamed NORTHTAL. *1986:* Sold to Northbound Shipping Co. Ltd., Limassol, Cyprus (Cobline International, Drammen, Norway, managers) and renamed SAGALAND. *1987:* Managers became Sealift Linienagenturen G.m.b.H., Hamburg, West Germany. *1989:* Sold to Bulkmar Shipping Ltd., Valletta, Malta (Lueder Bischoff G.m.b.H. and Co., Bremen, West Germany) and renamed WESERKANT. *1993:* Sold to Khaled Toumeh, Muhieddine and Partners (Alamal Transport), Tartous, Syria and renamed MUHIEDDINE IV. *1994:* Sold to Mohammad Fadel Manzali, Bassam Abdul Salam Al Mahmoud and Ahmad Abdul Rahman Markabi (Al Salam Shipping and Trading Co.), Tartous and renamed YASSMIN M. Still in existence (April 1997).

3. GARORM 1973-1974

1,199g 575n 244.3 x 37.2 x 15.4 feet
1976: 1,599g 945n 84.44 x 11.28 x 4.9 metres
Oil engine 4S.C.S.A. 8-cyl. by Lang Gepgyar Engine Works, Budapest, Hungary; 11 knots.
1976: Oil engine 4S.C.S.A. 8-cyl. by VEB Schwermasch. Karl Liebknecht, Magdeburg, East Germany; 12 knots.

20.5.1964: Launched by Angyalfold Shipyard, Budapest, Hungary (Yard No. 1991) for Hövdings Skipsopphuging (Einar Hövding, manager), Oslo, Norway as SAGAHORN. *1970:* Owners became Saga Shipping A/S (Hövdings Skipsopphuging, managers), Oslo. *1971:* Sold to Serifos Shipping Co. Ltd. (Constantia Xenos) (Mark Scufalos, manager), Nicosia, Cyprus and renamed NICHOLAS X. *1972:* Managers became Tidal Marine International Corporation (Harry Amanatides and Ion Livas), New York, U.S.A. and renamed IRENE. *1973:* Sold by the Admiralty Marshall to Phoicis Shipping Co. Ltd., Limassol (John Matthews Shipping Co. Ltd., Holywell) and renamed GARORM. *10.1973:* Owners became Norinvest A/S, Oslo, Norway (Edward W. Turner and Sons, Garston, managers). *4.1974:* Renamed IXIA. *5.1974:* Manager became H.F. Cordes and Co., Hamburg, West Germany. *1976:* Managers became Otto A. Müller, Hamburg, West Germany. *1976:* Lengthened and re-engined. *1977:* Managers became Parley Augustsson A/S, Oslo, Norway. *1978:* Managers became Skips A/S King (Sigvald Maarten-Moe), Oslo. *1979:* Managers became Gunther Schulz Schulauer Schiffahrtskontor, Hamburg, West Germany. *1980:* Renamed BULK PIONEER. *1983:* Managers became Schulz und Clemmesen Schulauer Befrachtungskantor, Hamburg. *1983:* Sold to Christian Klein G.m.b.H., Vienna, Austria and renamed OETZTAL. *1986:* Renamed EASTTAL. *1986:* Sold to Eastbound Shipping Co. Ltd., Limassol, Cyprus (Cobline International, Drammen, Norway, managers) and renamed EASTLAND. *1990:* Sold to Searobin Shipping Ltd. (Marlow Navigation Co. Ltd., managers), Limassol, Cyprus and renamed WESERLAND. *1991:* Managers became Lueder Bischoff G.m.b.H. and Co., Bremen, West Germany. *1992:* Sold to Ahmad Abdulkader Fahl, Tartous, Syria (Ali Samin Shipping Co., Limassol, Cyprus, manager) and renamed HIBAT ALLAH. Still in existence (April 1997).

4. GYRAM 1973-1974

1,199g 575n 244.3 x 37.2 x 15.4 feet
1976: 1,599g 945n 84.44 x 11.28 x 4.9 metres
Oil engine 4S.C.S.A. 8-cyl. by Lang Gepgyar Engine Works, Budapest, Hungary; 11 knots.
1976: Oil engine 4S.C.S.A. 8-cyl. by VEB Schwermasch. Karl Liebknecht, Magdeburg, East Germany; 12 knots.

21.4.1964: Launched by Angyalfold Shipyard, Budapest, Hungary (Yard No. 1990) for Hövdings Skipsopphuging (Einar Hövding, manager), Oslo, Norway as SAGAFJELL. *1970:* Owners became Saga Shipping A/S (Hövdings Skipsopphuging, managers), Oslo. *1971:* Sold to Skiathos Shipping Co. Ltd. (Constantia Xenos) (Mark Scufalos, manager), Nicosia, Cyprus and renamed PATRICIA X. *1972:* Managers became G. Dalacouras and J. Alexiou, Piraeus, Greece and renamed PAULINE. *1973:* Sold by the Admiralty Marshall whilst under arrest at Immingham to Phestos Shipping Co. Ltd., Limassol, Cyprus (John Matthews Shipping Co. Ltd., Holywell) and renamed GYRAM. *10.1973:* Owners became Norinvest A/S, Oslo, Norway (Edward W. Turner and Sons, Garston, managers). *1974:* Renamed PRIMROSE. *5.1974:* Manager became H.F. Cordes and Co., Hamburg, West Germany. *1976:* Managers became Otto A. Müller, Hamburg, West Germany. *1976:* Lengthened and re-engined. *1977:* Managers became Parley Augustsson A/S, Oslo, Norway. *1978:* Managers became Skips A/S King (Sigvald Maarten-Moe), Oslo. *1979:* Managers became Gunther Schulz Schulauer Schiffahrtskontor, Hamburg, West Germany. *1980:* Renamed BULK TRADER. *1983:* Managers became Schulz und Clemmesen Schulauer Befrachtungskantor, Hamburg. *1983:* Sold to Christian Klein G.m.b.H., Vienna, Austria and renamed ZILLERTAL. *1986:* Renamed WESTTAL. *1986:* Sold to Eastbound Shipping Co. Ltd., Limassol, Cyprus (Cobline International, Drammen, Norway, managers) and renamed WESTLAND. *1989:* Sold to Olerama Shipping Co. Ltd., Limassol, Cyprus (Lueder Bischoff G.m.b.H. and Co., Bremen, West Germany, managers) and renamed WESERBERG. *1993:* Owners became Herkules Intermodal Lines G.m.b.H. and Co. (Lueder Bischoff G.m.b.H. and Co., Bremen, managers). *1993:* Sold to Anme Khalil Shipping Co., Tartous, Syria, renamed AL KHALIL II and converted to a livestock carrier. *1994:* Sold to Ahmad Khalil Shouwehni (Shouwehni Co. for International Trade and Transportation, managers), Aleppo, Syria and renamed RAHMO, KONKORD and finally BARAAH. Still in existence (April 1997).

UNITED ALKALI CO. LTD.
IMPERIAL CHEMICAL INDUSTRIES LTD.
Liverpool

This is the major example in this book of a business running coasters which was not primarily in shipping. Although United Alkali had its offices in Liverpool, its coasters were less familiar in the Mersey than in North Wales or Lancashire ports and harbours. However, its river craft certainly were familiar on local waterways, although they are beyond the scope of this work.

United Alkali Co. Ltd. was an amalgamation of most of the British companies which were making alkali by the Leblanc process. A short digression into industrial chemistry is necessary at this point to explain why the company was formed.

Chemically, alkali is sodium hydroxide or potassium hydroxide. It is widely used in industry, particularly in the production of soap, textiles, paper and glass. There are some natural sources, including burning kelp to obtain an ash which yields sodium hydroxide or burning wood to give potash which provides potassium hydroxide, but in quality and quantity these could not keep pace with the needs of industry.

In 1789 the Frenchman Nicholas Leblanc devised an industrial method which involved heating salt (sodium chloride) with sulphuric acid to produce sodium sulphate (known as salt cake, and used as such in glass making) and hydrogen chloride. The saltcake was then roasted with coal or coke and limestone (calcium carbonate) to produce black ash. Amongst other largely useless and noxious products, black ash contained sodium carbonate, which was obtained by dissolving the ash in hot water and allowing the sodium carbonate to crystallise out - the resulting product being referred to as soda ash. Sodium carbonate was useful in its own right - as washing soda, for instance - but could be turned into sodium hydroxide by treating it with lime (calcium hydroxide). Sodium hydroxide, or caustic soda, is the strongest alkali and is the basis of soap making.

Works using the Leblanc process were established in the United Kingdom at Newcastle, at Glasgow by Charles Tennant (an associate of William Sloan, later to become a shipowner) and at Liverpool by James Muspratt in 1823. Liverpool was chosen for the first large-scale application of the process as being close to sources of salt, coal and limestone and to the Lancashire textile industry.

But the Leblanc process had serious disadvantages. The hydrogen chloride formed in the first stage of the process was actually emitted into the atmosphere where it was rained out as hydrochloric acid. This acid rain caused enormous damage to plants, farm animals and people. The major waste product from the second stage, calcium sulphide, was solid and could be tipped, but reacted with rain water to produce the toxic and nasally offensive gas hydrogen sulphide which smells of rotten eggs. Pressure from those concerned about Liverpool's environment led Muspratts to move their works to Newton-le-Willows and Widnes. Worse, at least from the manufacturers' viewpoint, the sulphur tied up in the waste calcium sulphide was potentially valuable.

Recognising the wastefulness of the Leblanc process, there was a search for a better method of producing alkali, and by the 1870s the Belgian Solvay brothers had perfected the ammonia-soda process. Sodium chloride was reacted with lime (calcium hydroxide) to give sodium hydroxide and calcium chloride. The latter was the only waste product, and was harmless. In the U.K. Ludwig Mond acquired the rights to Solvay's process and in partnership with John Brunner established a works at Winnington near Northwich in 1873. Exploiting the new process, and investing heavily in research and development, Brunner, Mond and Co. Ltd. succeeded brilliantly in competing with the Leblanc manufacturers and captured a large share of the market. By 1889, almost a third of the U.K.'s 700,000 tons of soda was produced by the ammonia-soda process. With trade depressed in the late 1880s, the response of the 40 major Leblanc manufacturers was to amalgamate to form the United Alkali Co. Ltd. Formed in February 1891, its aim was to rationalise production to leave a few, efficient works, and to adopt new technology not just for soda production but for the growing variety of other chemicals which were valuable by-products of the Leblanc process. Many old Leblanc works were closed, including Muspratt's and several at Runcorn and Widnes.

Amongst the new plants developed by United Alkali was the Fleetwood Ammonia Soda Works, which began production in 1893 at Burn Naze on the River Wyre near Fleetwood. Salt had been discovered here about twenty years earlier and was exploited by the Fleetwood Salt Co. This new salt field was seen by the alkali industry as a way of breaking the virtual monopoly of the Salt Union in the Cheshire salt field. The Solvay process was adopted at the Fleetwood works - in direct competition with Brunner, Mond - and by 1911 it was producing 100,000 tons of soda each year.

With the chemistry lesson over it is time to return to maritime history. The United Alkali Co. Ltd. acquired its first steam coaster, the aptly-named SODIUM, in 1892 - probably with the business of its former owner Wilton Allhusen. This little steamer was sold in 1906. The company had many other craft, however, including sailing flats, lighters, steam barges and at least one early motor vessel which were used on the waterways connecting with the Mersey. These little craft ventured from the Mersey as far as the Deeside ports and North Wales for limestone and ran between Chester Basin at Liverpool and Fleetwood. However, it was not until the First World War that the United Alkali Co. Ltd. became serious owners of coasters. In 1917 and 1918 they took delivery of two medium-sized and two large steamers, the LITHIUM and HELIUM of 135 feet, and the BARIUM and CALCIUM of 180 feet. The latter pair were not only unusually large, but also had distinctive goalpost foremasts at a time when these were rare on coasters. Another atypical feature was that for at least part of their careers the hulls of these coasters were painted grey.

The ships were built to carry limestone from quarries at Llanddulas on the North Wales coast – especially Raynes' Quarry – to the alkali works at Burn Naze. A jetty had been built contemporaneously with the soda works, and the company originally relied on other owners' ships: those of Zillah and Kennaugh are reported to have been employed carrying limestone. The decision by United Alkali to buy its own ships in 1917 must have reflected the difficulty of fixing ships at a reasonable price when freight rates were inflated by the war.

Calcium (1) *John Clarkson*

Indium *John Clarkson*

A further 180-foot steamer, the SODIUM, was delivered in 1923 by Rennoldsons who had built three of the earlier ships, but was distinguished by a conventional pole fore mast. Rennoldson also built a much smaller steamer, the INDIUM of 110 feet, and her size suggests she was built for trading on the Upper Mersey and the Weaver, although she also served Burn Naze. Reflecting the expansion of the United Alkali fleet, the facilities at Burn Naze had been extended in 1924 when a southern arm had been added to the work's jetty.

The United Alkali Co. Ltd. was the largest manufacturing concern in the United Kingdom, and at its formation had been the world's largest chemical company, but it was hardly the most efficient. The result of a defensive merger of companies whose fortunes were declining, it relied on old and inefficient processes, and had loaded itself with much obsolete plant charged at high prices. The board members, too, were ageing and the company was not adept at the up and coming arts of selling and marketing its goods. In a rather gruesome way, it was spared by the First World War, as one of the products which was in demand was chlorine gas for use on the battlefields. Once peace returned, and the subsequent depression, the United Alkali's deficiencies became obvious. It could not compete with Brunner, Mond on price for soda ash, but had the important advantage of producing chlorine which the Solvay process could not. However, from the 1890s the process of electrolysis of brine was slowly developed. By passing an electric current through salt in solution it was possible to make both sodium hydroxide and chlorine, and this marked the beginning of the end for the Leblanc process. The United Alkali Company became an "industrial pauper".

Events in the wider chemical industry were to bring an answer to United Alkali's woes. In November 1925, several large German chemical and dyestuffs companies merged to form IG Farbenindustrie, partly as a reaction to difficulties imposed on German industry by the Treaty of Versailles. Only in the U.S.A. was the chemical industry organised on such a scale. The industrial and technological might of IG Farben persuaded - or perhaps frightened - the major British chemical companies to come together in a merger. The moving spirits were the cash-rich Nobel Industries Ltd. and the technically competent Brunner, Mond; their heads concluded an agreement whilst returning from the U.S.A. on the AQUITANIA in October 1926. United Alkali Company were dragged in rather reluctantly, whilst the British government agreed to the inclusion of the British Dyestuffs Corporation Ltd. which they partly controlled. These were the four largest companies in the British chemical industry and, on the basis that the British Empire was to be their major field of operations, chose the title Imperial Chemical Industries Ltd. Two other components of I.C.I. are worth recording for their Merseyside connections, both being included because Brunner, Mond held a financial stake: Castner-Kellner who in 1897 had begun producing sodium hydroxide electrolytically at Weston Point, and the Salt Union Ltd. - result of a disastrous merger of most British salt producers in 1888 - which became a wholly-owned subsidiary of I.C.I. in 1937.

To return from global industrial politics to coasters, what change did the merger bring? Outwardly, there was only a new funnel incorporating I.C.I.'s enduring roundel, and even this may not have been applied immediately as not until August 1932 were the ships officially transferred to the ownership of Imperial Chemical Industries (General Chemicals) Ltd. In April 1935 the owning division became the Alkali Division. Amalgamation also brought the coasters to the Mersey and Weaver, where they occasionally served Wallerscote and Winnington works, but essentially they continued carrying limestone to the River Wyre, a routine broken only by cargoes of finished products to other ports, including Glasgow, Bristol, Dublin, Belfast and Liverpool. A round trip from North Wales to Fleetwood could be accomplished in 24 hours, and to encourage the crew a bonus was paid if 28 trips were completed in a month.

Not even the outbreak of war made much difference to the coasters' typical routine of plodding back and forth between Fleetwood and the quarry at Llanddulas. Degaussing gear was fitted as some protection against magnetic mines and a Lewis gun gave at least psychological support in the not-unlikely event of air attack. It was a mine, possibly of the contact variety, which caused the company's first loss. CALCIUM left Fleetwood about 9.15 p.m. on the evening of Sunday, 29th December 1940, sailing for Llanddulas at about six knots. At 4.30 a.m. when she was off the Welsh Coast there was an explosion beneath the stokehold, stopping the engines and extinguishing the lights. Escaping steam enveloped the ship and made it impossible to see anything in the stokehold, where fireman James Morris was the only member of the crew not accounted for. As the CALCIUM settled by the stern the master and chief engineer went below, found his body and brought it up on deck. They also discovered that the explosion had blown the donkey engine across the engine room. The SODIUM had sailed in company with the CALCIUM and on hearing the explosion she came to her sister's assistance. The eight surviving members of the crew and the body of the fireman were taken on to the SODIUM and she attempted to tow the CALCIUM. However, the disabled ship was sinking, and she went down at about 8.20 a.m. off the Little Orme.

Although Captain Atkinson of the CALCIUM claimed that his degaussing gear was switched on and in working order, a naval report disputed that the CALCIUM was fitted with degaussing gear, and also maintained that she was not using a channel which had been checked for mines. The latter is probably correct: channels to small ports would not have been swept frequently. Captain Atkinson and the chief engineer were awarded George Medals for their attempted rescue of the fireman.

As a replacement for CALCIUM, I.C.I. acquired its first sea-going motor vessel, the eccentrically-named JOLLY DAYS, a name which must have caused her crew both amusement and embarrassment. Wartime strengthening of the fleet also involved the purchase of the BEESTON and WESTON on the break-up of Richard Clark's fleet, and - much more notably - the arrival of a new motor coaster, CERIUM. That I.C.I. were allowed to build a coaster for themselves when shipbuilding was strictly controlled speaks of the importance of the chemical industry to modern warfare. Amongst the companies in this book, CERIUM had another claim to fame: she was the first motor vessel built by a Merseyside-based owner for the coastal bulk trades, although Coast Lines Ltd. had considerable experience with motor ships in the short-sea liner trade. In the use of oil engines, local owners were lagging well behind London and Glasgow owners, the latter including William Robertson who was in the same trades as the Mersey companies. The usual reason given for shunning oil engines was their unreliability, but by 1943 the Dutch had over twenty year's successful experience with

German- and Dutch-built engines, and British manufacturers were also building thoroughly reliable units.

Despite the importance of the I.C.I. coasters' work, several took part in the all-out effort of Operation Neptune, the naval part of the invasion of Normandy. WESTON and BEESTON were involved, the latter not returning. JOLLY DAYS also had an adventurous time. She was damaged by fire in Liverpool's Alexandra Dock during the heavy bombing the port received on 7/8th May 1941: the night Brocklebank's MALAKAND (7,649/1919) and her cargo of ammunition blew up. Later in the war, JOLLY DAYS sighted a ditched seaplane in what was suspected to be a minefield. The JOLLY DAYS approached and all the seamen manned her boat and rescued the survivors. Although remaining on the ship, the captain received a award in the form of an M.B.E. LITHIUM took part in a far more spectacular rescue, when she witnessed an aircraft carrier explode: this was presumably the escort carrier H.M.S. DASHER which blew up and sank on the Clyde on 27th March 1943. The LITHIUM rescued some 60 of the crew, the only survivors of a major but little-publicised naval disaster.

After the war, I.C.I. gradually disposed of its older steamers, and slowly added further motorships. The practice of naming them after elements continued with THORIUM of 1947 and CALCIUM of 1959, but an exception was made in the case of POLYTHENE of 1949. The discovery of polyethylene – a name contracted to polythene - in the 1930s was I.C.I.'s largest contribution to the plastics industry. This discovery was made at the Alkali Division's Winnington Works, and was made possible only by a group of scientists working out-of-hours as laboratory management had banned high-pressure experiments because they were inclined to result in explosions. Alkali Division guarded their new, world-beating product very closely and refused to allow other, better-qualified, divisions to become involved. Was the decision to use the name on one of the Division's ships a piece of one-upmanship? The name polythene was not a trade mark, or its use on a ship would not have been sanctioned by the company.

Apart from the loss of the CALCIUM during the war, the fleet went about its business with few untoward incidents. The major peacetime accident occurred on 11th January 1951 when the THORIUM capsized two miles off Fleetwood when inward bound with limestone. Somewhat surprisingly for a relatively new vessel, the cause was found to be water entering through cracks in her deck. After the THORIUM's cargo was transferred to barges she was salvaged in May 1951 and repaired at Ardrossan, not returning to service until September 1952.

Polythene *M. Napier*

By 1957, only three vessels were based at Fleetwood. THORIUM was normally used to carry limestone; SODIUM carried finished product mostly to Glasgow but also to Dublin, Belfast and Irvine; and CERIUM ran with both as supply and demand dictated. On delivery, CALCIUM went into the limestone trade and allowed the last of the steamers, SODIUM, to be retired after over 35 years' creditable service. THORIUM took the steamer's place carrying finished product. Even with this reduced fleet there were occasional slack periods at Fleetwood when ships were chartered out. For instance, CERIUM ran between the U.K. and Scandinavia during the summer of 1960. Her predecessor SODIUM had been on charter to the Belfast Steamship Co. Ltd. for two months in 1949.

I.C.I.'s works at Winnington on the River Weaver received its limestone by rail from Derbyshire, but did use coasters to export its finished product. The vessels used out of Fleetwood were too large to navigate the Weaver, and smaller vessels were bought or built: the JOLLY DAYS which was succeeded by POLYTHENE. The latter also helped out occasionally on the Fleetwood limestone run.

Supply of limestone to Fleetwood ceased in 1964 when the Burn Naze factory closed and the jetty was demolished. The CALCIUM, CERIUM and THORIUM were soon sold, leaving only the POLYTHENE trading out of the Weaver, and she too was sold in 1972 although she retained her name until lost in 1979.

The coasters listed below represent only a small proportion of the total watercraft fleets of either United Alkali or I.C.I. The former had a number of smaller vessels operating on the Mersey and its connecting waterways and elsewhere. Brunner, Mond – United Alkali's competitor until the two merged in 1932 – also had a considerable river and estuarial fleet, which passed into I.C.I. ownership, although they continued to be referred to as "Brunners" until they ceased trading in 1980. Acquisition of the Salt Union brought further river craft into the empire, and the Nobel Division and its predecessors have a long tradition of owning coasters to move explosives, although these were based on the Firth of Clyde.

Sodium (2) *John Clarkson*

Fleet list

1. SODIUM (1) 1891-1906

O.N. 92861 146g 78n 100.0 x 20.1 x 8.1 feet
C. 2-cyl. by the Wallsend Slipway and Engineering Co., Wallsend-on-Tyne.

27.4.1887: Launched by Wood, Skinner and Co., Bill Quay-on-Tyne (Yard No. 5) for Wilton Allhusen, Newcastle-upon-Tyne as SODIUM. *23.5.1887:* Completed. *13.3.1891:* Acquired by the United Alkali Co. Ltd. (Eustace Carey, manager), Liverpool. *2.3.1906:* Sold to Thomas Thompson and Son, Newcastle-upon-Tyne. *18.10.1906:* Owners became 'T' Steam Coasters Ltd. (Robinson, Brown and Co., managers), Newcastle-upon-Tyne. *7.5.1917:* Sold to John Harrison Ltd., London. *24.12.1917:* Sold to William Darlington, Garston. *8.8.1921:* Sold to Alfred H. Connell, Liverpool. *20.9.1921:* Sold to the Solway Shipping Co. Ltd. (T. Wilson and Co., managers), Whitehaven. *1.11.1923:* Managers became Lowden, Connell and Co., Liverpool. *6.3.1923:* Renamed PENTON. *16.6.1927:* Sold to James D. Ormiston, Leith. *22.7.1927:* Sold to Alexander Hannah, Leith. *4.9.1930:* Sold to the Sandwich Hoy Company (Ernest A. Fagg, manager), Sandwich. *18.1.1937:* Stranded one mile south of Gorleston Coast Guard Station whilst on a voyage from Great Yarmouth to London in ballast. Her crew was rescued. *10.1937:* Refloated and sold for breaking up. *13.11.1937:* Whilst in tow of QUEENS CROSS (286/1921) for Whitby the tow parted off Skinningrove during heavy weather and she went aground at Kettleness, north of Whitby, and became a total loss. *22.1.1941:* Register closed.

Lithium *John Clarkson*

2. LITHIUM 1917-1950

O.N. 137540 301g 113n 135.2 x 23.1 x 9.4 feet
T. 3-cyl. by the Shields Engineering and Dry Dock Co. Ltd. North Shields; 9 knots.

15.3.1917: Completed by Cochrane and Sons Ltd., Selby (Yard No. 729) for the United Alkali Co. Ltd., Liverpool as LITHIUM. *23.8.1932:* Owners became Imperial Chemical Industries (General Chemicals) Ltd., Liverpool. *28.3.1935:* Owners became Imperial Chemical Industries (Alkali Division) Ltd., Liverpool. *11.6.1945:* Owners became Imperial Chemical Industries Ltd., London. *31.3.1950:* Sold to T.G. Irving Ltd. (T.G. Irving, manager), Sunderland. *27.4.1950:* Renamed MAYDENE. *14.1.1955:* Arrived at Dunston-on-Tyne to be broken up by Clayton and Davie Ltd. *23.7.1955:* Register closed.

Helium *John Clarkson*

3. HELIUM 1917-1948

O.N. 137548 301g 113n 135.2 x 23. x 9.4 feet
T. 3-cyl. by the Shields Engineering and Dry Dock Co. Ltd., North Shields.

10.5.1917: Completed by Cochrane and Sons Ltd., Selby (Yard No. 730) for the United Alkali Co. Ltd., Liverpool as HELIUM. *23.8.1932:* Owners became Imperial Chemical Industries (General Chemicals) Ltd., Liverpool. *28.3.1935:* Owners became Imperial Chemical Industries (Alkali Division) Ltd., Liverpool. *11.6.1945:* Owners became Imperial Chemical Industries Ltd., London. *1948:* Sold to J. Johnson and Sons (Shipping) Ltd. (Joseph Johnson, manager), Liverpool. *1949:* Renamed HOLLYLEAF. *1952:* Manager became Peter B. Johnson. *1953:* Owners became Johnson, Bretland Ltd. *1954:* Sold to Kendall Brothers (Portsmouth) Ltd., Portsmouth. *1955:* Renamed HOLLYBRANCH. *1957:* Sold to Henry G. Pounds, Portsmouth. *1957:* Sold to Stolk's Handelsonderneming, Hendrik ido Ambacht, Holland for breaking up.

4. CALCIUM (1) 1918-1940

O.N. 140563 613g 280n 180.4 x 28.1 x 10.8 feet
T. 3-cyl. by McKie and Baxter, Glasgow; 10 knots.

11.12.1917: Launched by George Brown and Co., Greenock (Yard No. 102) for the United Alkali Co. Ltd., Liverpool as CALCIUM. *11.3.1918:* Completed. *23.8.1932:* Owners became Imperial Chemical Industries (General Chemicals) Ltd., Liverpool. *28.3.1935:* Owners became Imperial Chemical Industries (Alkali Division) Ltd., Liverpool. *30.12.1940:* Mined and sunk five miles north of the Little Orme in position 53.25 N by 03.30 W whilst on a voyage from Fleetwood to Llanddulas in ballast. One of her crew of nine was lost. *8.4.1941:* Register closed.

Barium *John Clarkson*

5. BARIUM 1918-1952

O.N. 140577 601g 291n 180.6 x 28.1 x 10.7 feet
T. 3-cyl. by the Shields Engineering and Dry Dock Co. Ltd., North Shields; 10 knots.

3.5.1918: Completed by Charles Rennoldson and Co., South Shields (Yard No. 183) for the United Alkali Co. Ltd., Liverpool as BARIUM. *23.8.1932:* Owners became Imperial Chemical Industries (General Chemicals) Ltd., Liverpool. *28.3.1935:* Owners became Imperial Chemical Industries (Alkali Division) Ltd., Liverpool. *11.6.1945:* Owners became Imperial Chemical Industries Ltd., London. *10.10.1952:* Sold to William Cooper and Sons Ltd. (William Cooper, manager), Widnes. *9.2.1953:* Renamed P.M. COOPER. *2.8.1960:* Arrived at Barrow-in-Furness in tow of the JAMES LAMEY (262/1928) to be broken up by T.W. Ward Ltd. *5.1961:* Demolition began. *10.7.1961:* Register closed.

Sodium (2) wearing an ICI roundel on her funnel. *Keith Byass*

6. SODIUM (2) 1923-1959

O.N. 147225 608g 287n 180.2 x 28.2 x 10.7 feet
T. 3-cyl. by MacColl and Pollock Ltd., Sunderland.

15.5.1923: Launched by Charles Rennoldson and Co., South Shields (Yard No. 209) for the United Alkali Co. Ltd., Liverpool as SODIUM. *6.1923:* Completed. *23.8.1932:* Owners became Imperial Chemical Industries (General Chemicals) Ltd., Liverpool. *28.3.1935:* Owners became Imperial Chemical Industries (Alkali Division) Ltd., Liverpool. *11.6.1945:* Owners became Imperial Chemical Industries Ltd., London. *9.9.1959:* Arrived at Barrow-in-Furness for breaking up by T.W. Ward Ltd.

Indium in later life as a suction dredger.
W.S.P.L. Brownell collection

7. INDIUM 1923-1939

O.N. 147269 207g 75n 110.0 x 22.1 x 9.0 feet
T. 3-cyl. by MacColl and Pollock Ltd. Sunderland.

6.1923: Completed by Charles Rennoldson and Co., South Shields (Yard No. 212) for the United Alkali Co. Ltd., Liverpool as INDIUM. *23.8.1932:* Owners became Imperial Chemical Industries (General Chemicals) Ltd., Liverpool. *28.3.1935:* Owners became Imperial Chemical Industries (Alkali Division) Ltd., Liverpool. *1939:* Sold to the Shannon Steam Ship Co. Ltd., Kilrush, County Clare. *1947:* Sold to J. and R. Griffiths Ltd., Cardiff and converted to a sand pump dredger. *1961:* Sold to William France, Fenwick and Co. Ltd., London. *7.1963:* Reported sold to C.W. Dorkin and Co. for breaking up at Gateshead-on-Tyne.

Weston
John Clarkson

8. WESTON 1942-1947

O.N. 143670 485g 210n 152.0 x 25.2 x 10.8 feet
T. 3-cyl. by Charles D. Holmes and Co. Ltd., Hull; 9½ knots.

17.6.1920: Launched by Cochrane and Sons Ltd., Selby (Yard No. 743) for the Overton Steamship Co. Ltd. (Richard R. Clark, manager), Liverpool as WESTON. *16.9.1920:* Completed. *1942:* Acquired by Imperial Chemical Industries (Alkali Division) Ltd., Liverpool. *11.6.1945:* Owners became Imperial Chemical Industries Ltd., Liverpool. *1947:* Sold to the Coe Line Ltd., London and renamed COE-PAM. *1952:* Sold to W.N. Lindsay, Leith and renamed MISTLEY. *19.6.1957:* Sank after striking Reefdyke Rocks off North Ronaldsay whilst on a voyage from North Ronaldsay to Fair isle with a cargo of coal.

9. BEESTON 1942-1946

O.N. 143714 466g 192n 152.0 x 25.2 x 10.8 feet
T. 3-cyl. by Charles D. Holmes and Co. Ltd., Hull; 9½ knots.

15.9.1920: Launched by Cochrane and Sons Ltd., Selby (Yard No. 749) for the Overton Steamship Co. Ltd. (Richard R. Clark, manager), Liverpool as BEESTON. *22.2.1921:* Completed. *20.4.1942:* Acquired by Imperial Chemical Industries (Alkali Division) Ltd., Liverpool. *11.6.1945:* Owners became Imperial Chemical Industries Ltd., London. *9.7.1946:* Sold to the Deeside Shipping Co. Ltd. (Thomas Rose and Co., managers), Sunderland. *21.9.1946:* Renamed DEENESS. *16.2.1951:* Wrecked in heavy weather on the Cotentin Peninsula, France in position 49.38.20 N by 01.51.20 W whilst on a voyage from Guernsey to London with a cargo of granite. *5.4.1951:* Register closed.

10. JOLLY DAYS 1940-1950

O.N. 163011 351g 182n 130.7 x 25.1 x 8.8 feet
Oil engine 4-cyl. 2S.C.S.A. by Petters Ltd., Yeovil.
1.1951: Oil engine 6-cyl. 4S.C.S.A. by MAK Maschinenbau Kiel A.G., Kiel, West Germany.
1962: Oil engine 6-cyl. 4S.C.S.A. by Maschinenbau Augsburg-Nurnberg A.G., Augsburg-Nurnberg, West Germany.

7.3.1935: Launched by John Lewis and Sons Ltd., Aberdeen (Yard No. 132) for Frederick W. Horlock, Mistley as JOLLY DAYS. *4.1935:* Completed. *1935:* Owners became F.W. Horlock's Ocean Transport Co. Ltd., Harwich. *4.7.1940:* Acquired by Imperial Chemical Industries (Alkali Division) Ltd., Liverpool. *11.6.1945:* Owners became Imperial Chemical Industries Ltd., London. *1950:* Sold to the Plym Shipping Co. Ltd., Plymouth and renamed JANET PLYM. *1.1951:* Fitted with a new engine. *1952:* Sold to Instone Lines Ltd., London and renamed SEAHORSE. *1962:* Sold to Angelos Venetsianos, Piraeus, Greece, renamed IRENE and fitted with a new engine. *1967:* Sold to C. Gavrill and Co., Piraeus. *1971:* Sold to G.K. Gavriel, P.G. Gavriel and M. Ch. Tsouba, Piraeus and renamed PANAGIS G. *1975:* Sold to A. Athanassopoulos, S. Loudaros, D. Papadimitriou and S. Athanassiou, Piraeus and renamed AGIOS IOANNIS ROUSSOS. *1979:* Renamed GEORGIOS A. *1980:* Sold to the Naheda Shipping Co. Ltd. and renamed NAHEDA H under the Cyprus flag. *28.2.1980:* Foundered 125 miles off the coast of Israel during heavy weather whilst on a voyage from Alexandria to Beirut with a cargo of potatoes.

Cerium *John Clarkson*

11. CERIUM 1943-1965

O.N. 168870 532g 248n 181.2 x 27.2 x 10.0 feet
Oil engine 5-cyl. 2S.C.S.A. by British Auxiliaries Ltd., Glasgow.

16.10.1943: Launched by the Goole Shipbuilding and Repairing Co. Ltd., Goole (Yard No. 396) for Imperial Chemical Industries (Alkali Division) Ltd., Liverpool as CERIUM. *12.1943:* Completed. *11.6.1945:* Owners became Imperial Chemical Industries Ltd., London. *1965:* Owners became Continental Explosives Ltd., Vancouver, Canada. *1967:* Renamed G.R. VELIE. *1974:* Sold to Westof Marine Ltd., North Vancouver, Canada. *1976:* Sold to W.B. Church (Centennial Towing Ltd., managers), Surrey, British Columbia, Canada and renamed G.B. CHURCH. *1980:* Owners became Centennial Towing Ltd., Gaspe Nord, Quebec, Canada. *1983:* Sold to Commander Leasing Ltd., New Westminster, British Columbia, Canada. *1988:* Sold to 267866 British Columbia Ltd., Vancouver, British Columbia. *1991:* Sold to the Government of Canada (Ministry of Lands and Parks), British Columbia. *10.8.1991:* Scuttled in position 48.43.19 N by 123.21.16 W.

Thorium *John Clarkson*

12. THORIUM 1947-1964

O.N. 181077 604g 288n 196.8 x 28.4 x 9.6 feet
Oil engine 7-cyl. 2S.C.S.A. by British Polar Engines Ltd., Glasgow.

27.10.1946: Launched by the Burntisland Shipbuilding Co. Ltd., Burntisland (Yard No. 312) for Imperial Chemical Industries Ltd., Liverpool as THORIUM. *3.1947:* Completed. *1964:* Sold to W.N. Lindsay Ltd., Leith and renamed ROSEBURN. *1967:* Owners became W.N. Lindsay (Shipowners) Ltd., Leith. *1973:* Sold to Storm Compania Naviera S.A. (Sachinis Shipping Agency Co. Ltd.), Piraeus, Greece and renamed STAVROS EMMANUEL under the Honduras flag. *1976:* Renamed SALVAGER. *1985:* Sold to Ahmet Tahsin Diker Kardesler Kollektif Sirketi, Istanbul, Turkey and renamed L. MEHMET DIKER. *1995:* Sold to Ayanoglu Denizcilik ve Ticaret A.S., Istanbul and renamed DENIZ 4. Still in existence (April 1997).

Polythene with the upper part of her hull painted orange. *John Clarkson*

13. POLYTHENE 1949-1972

O.N. 183740 330g 153n 139.6 x 25.1 x 7.9 feet
Oil engine 6-cyl. 2S.C.S.A. by Crossley Brothers Ltd., Manchester; 9 knots.

8.1949: Completed by the Goole Shipbuilding and Repairing Co. Ltd., Goole (Yard No. 471) for Imperial Chemical Industries Ltd., Liverpool as POLYTHENE. *1972:* Sold to A.C. Stewart and W.G. Stewart, Dartford, Kent. *1972:* Owners became Stewart Brothers (Shipping) Ltd., Dartford. *1972:* Sold to F.A.G. and J. Kennedy, Rochester. *1974:* Sold to W.F. Thompson, Ipswich. *1976:* Sold to W.S. and A.A. Banks (Pentland Ferries Ltd., managers), St. Margaret's Hope, Orkney. *1977:* Owners became Hurst Shipping Ltd. (Pentland Ferries Ltd., managers), St. Margaret's Hope, Orkney. *29.8.1979:* Driven ashore and wrecked in Prince Rupert Bay, Dominica in position 15.34.40 N by 61.28.10 W when her anchor chain broke after having been ordered out of harbour to ride out Hurricane David. She was on a voyage from Roseau to St. Vincent with the motor vessel reported to be the LITTLE STEPHEN in tow for repairs.

Calcium (2) *John Clarkson*

14. CALCIUM (2) 1959-1965

O.N. 301305 643g 292n 183.0 x 31.8 x 12.2 feet
Oil engine 7-cyl. 2S.C.S.A. by British Polar Engines Ltd., Glasgow.

26.3.1959: Launched by the Goole Shipbuilding and Repairing Co. Ltd., Goole (Yard No. 517) for Imperial Chemical Industries Ltd., Liverpool as CALCIUM. *5.1959:* Completed. *1965:* Sold to Shamrock Shipping Co. Ltd. (C.S. Brown, manager), Larne and renamed CLONLEE. *1973:* Sold to Lee Shipping Ltd. (Normandie Dredging and Shipping Co. Ltd., managers), Southampton, converted to a suction dredger and renamed HUMBER LEE. *1976:* Sold to Redland Purle Ltd., Rayleigh, Essex. *1982:* Owners became Cleanaway Ltd., Rayleigh, Essex and later Bristol and used as an effluent carrier. *28.12.1984:* Delivered at Birkenhead to Stretford Shipbreakers Ltd., Manchester. *1.1985:* Demolition commenced.

Nomenclature

Most of the fleet's coasters and some inland craft were named after chemical elements, not all of which were relevant to the company or its business.

BARIUM — A metal related chemically to calcium and found in barytes.

CALCIUM — A common element found in limestone and chalk.

CERIUM — A heavy metal, named after the asteroid Ceres which was discovered in 1801, two years ealier than cerium.

HELIUM — An inert gas, used as an alternative to hydrogen in lighter-than-air craft.

INDIUM — A rare metallic element, named after the characteristic indigo-coloured lines in its spectrum.

LITHIUM — A light and highly reactive metal chemically related to sodium and whose major use is in nuclear bombs.

POLYTHENE — A polymer of ethylene (polyethylene) discovered by I.C.I. Alkali Division chemists.

SODIUM — The metallic constituent of salt and the basis of the alkali industry. Compounds of sodium include soda (sodium carbonate) and caustic soda (sodium hydroxide)

THORIUM — A rare, radioactive heavy metal named after the Norse god of thunder, Thor.

ZILLAH SHIPPING AND CARRYING CO. LTD.
ZILLAH SHIPPING CO. LTD.
Warrington and Liverpool

During its fifty-four years of independent existence, the Zillah Shipping and Carrying Co. Ltd. demonstrated a remarkable constancy in its activities. Its ships showed a slow but deliberate evolution, paralleled by the company's allegiance to a small number of core trades. Until its take-over by Coast Lines Ltd. in 1949 the company's ownership and direction was in the hands of a small number of families. This was a period when change was relatively slow, but with an acceleration of both transportation and business methods in the 1950s and 1960s, the company's business altered considerably, so much so that its independent existence became irrelevant to its new owners. However, in its dog days Zillah was in the front rank of Mersey coastal tramping companies, and any lack of boardroom excitements in this period is more than compensated for by interest in the evolution of its ships: no other local coaster owner followed such a consistent building policy for over half a century.

The Zillah company had its origins in the Warrington area, where in the mid-nineteenth century George Savage, born at Sankey Bridges in 1829, was master of one of the Mersey flats which were equally at home on river, canal or the coasts of North Wales and Lancashire. In 1864 he took eight shares in the flat DERWENT of 50 tons and built at Northwich in 1860. The major shareholder was William Hughes of St. Helens, suggesting that one of the objectives of buying the DERWENT was to carry coal down the Sankey Canal. Savage, who probably commanded her, increased his shareholding to thirty-two in 1868, by when he had recently moved to Widnes. By 1874, Savage still had an interest in the DERWENT but was also the major shareholder in the Northwich-built flat REFUGE (60/1864).

George's son, William Alfred Savage, was born at Sankey Bridges in 1856 and was to follow the same profession as his father. Reports of his early career suggest that he packed a lot in to it. Leaving school at 14, he worked for a ships' fender maker and at a chemical works before joining his father at sea. He is said to have become master and part owner of the sailing vessel MURIEL at the extraordinarily early age of 17, but his first venture into shipowning for which records can be found was the REFUGE. This flat was transferred from his father's ownership around 1883, but was wrecked on the North Wales coast on 23rd April 1885 when carrying a cargo of Llanddulas limestone to Widnes. Undeterred by this mishap, William Savage replaced her that year with the OBADIAH (59/1858). A nice story, but which cannot be substantiated from registration records, is that Savage bought the wooden steamer GEORGE DEAKIN (105/1866) in the late 1880s. The previous owner, whose name the steamer carried, is said to have helped the young Savage by including a number of spare parts not mentioned in the purchase contract.

William Savage was commercially ambitious: whilst he was at sea in the 1890s his wife Priscilla ran a drapery and grocery shop at their home in Liverpool Road, Warrington. Here their next-door neighbour was Joseph Monks, another flatman who was to become a significant Liverpool coaster owner.

In 1890 Savage expanded his fleet with the sailing flat MARY FOXLEY (53/1840), and in 1891 took the bold step of ordering from James Harland and Co. of Tranmere a wooden steam flat. This was launched in 1891 by Mrs. William Savage, and christened ZILLAH. She was completed at the end of August, and within days Savage sold 52 of her 64 shares. Amongst the subscribers were his father George Savage (11 shares and now evidently retired, as he described himself as a gentleman), shipowner William Rowland of Runcorn (6 shares) and Walter Brough, a Warrington baker (12 shares). The Brough family were to be intimately involved with Savage's fleet for over seventy years.

Under William Savage's command the first ZILLAH was to trade between Liverpool (where she was registered), the West Bank Dock at Widnes and North Wales, and along the new Manchester Ship Canal. Her success was such that within four years Savage had sold his sailing flats, returned to the Tranmere yard to place an order for a similar steamer, and had the confidence to float a company to own both the ZILLAH and the newbuilding. The Zillah Shipping and Carrying Co. Ltd. was registered on 29th May 1895 with a capital of £10,000 in £5 shares, which are reported to have been quickly taken up. Amongst the initial subscribers were William and George Savage, Walter Brough, and several councillors and worthies from Warrington and Widnes.

The new steamer was launched simultaneously with the company, and was christened MERLIN. Unusually, she was launched by a man, Captain William Summerfield, who was approaching his eightieth birthday. The name Summerfield was to be associated with the Zillah company for many years, and Captain Samuel Summerfield was to take over as master of the ZILLAH from William Savage, who took command of the MERLIN. Savage had an flair for public relations, and besides inviting many subscribers and influential visitors to the launching party also entertained well over a hundred guests on the trial trip of the MERLIN, with a return sailing from Tranmere to Latchford Locks on the Manchester Ship Canal on 1st August 1895. The guests included representatives of Kneeshaw, Lupton and Co., and in view of the amount of stone that Zillah ships were to carry away from Penmaenmawr during the next sixty years, this suggests that good relations were already being cemented with the quarrying company.

Priscilla *John Clarkson*

By the 1890s wood was an outmoded material for steamers, even the English oak from which ZILLAH and MERLIN were built. However, Savage did not wait long to invest in steel steamers, and in October 1896 took delivery of the Clyde-built PRISCILLA. She was to begin a relationship with the Ailsa Shipbuilding Company which over the next decade was to see nine ships delivered and one acquired second-hand. In size these grew from the 120 foot PRISCILLA to the 157 foot E. HAYWARD. With the exception of the first two Ailsa ships, PRISCILLA and SARAH BROUGH, their appearances were remarkably uniform. A feature they shared with other coasters intended for carrying stone or slate was the small hatch immediately abaft the forecastle, and which gave them a distinctive appearance with the mainmast set back a few feet. Most coasters had just one hold, but two hatches were fitted for a number of reasons. A typical steam coaster derrick would be fifty feet in length, and having a single hatch longer than this would be difficult to work. Safety was also a consideration, as with a single large hatch there was a danger that, when the hull flexed in a seaway, the wooden hatch covers might fall into the hold putting the ship in danger.

The run of Ailsa-built ships was broken by an apparent anachronism, the wooden ketch WINIFRED which was built on the Dee by Ferguson and Baird. She returned to her builder's yard in 1907 to be rebuilt with a paraffin motor, but in spite of this (or perhaps because of it, in view of the notorious unreliability of early marine internal combustion engines) she was a relatively early departure from the fleet. The first ZILLAH had been sold after only eight years' service, although she was to survive for another forty years on the Norwegian coast, and the MERLIN after twelve. This should be contrasted with the longevity of the steel steamers: the hull of the PRISCILLA was considered suitable for conversion to a barge after thirty-six years in the fleet, and the E. HAYWARD served the company for a full half century.

Alongside the newbuildings from Ailsa the fleet acquired a number of secondhand, albeit similar, steamers. In most cases some connection between Zillah and the original owner can be traced. In 1909, for instance, the remaining Brundrit steamers, the CECIL and the Ailsa-built PUFFIN were bought, along with their sailing vessels BERTIE (61/1859) and SWALLOW (67/1868). Under their new owners these ships would continue to trade between Penmaenmawr and the Mersey and Preston. The BERTIE and SWALLOW were sold to an owner in Hoylake in 1913. The LITTLE ORME acquired in 1909 was rather smaller than the fleet's purpose-built ships. Her former manager John R. Lord was – or was to become – a director of Zillah and was probably a shareholder. The name adopted in 1907 was shared with a quarry near Llandudno and suggested that she too was trading from the North Wales coast. Another associate was Summersgill Snoddy, who attended the launch of several Zillah ships, and whose ALYN was acquired in 1911. Very much of a size with other company vessels, ALYN's appearance was distinctive, with a raised quarter deck and derricks at the outer ends of the two holds. When Zillah themselves adopted a similar hull form a quarter of a century later they followed the usual pattern of placing the masts forward of each hold.

The last of this flurry of second-hand purchases, like the first, came from a quarry owner, the ELEANOR of James Raynes of Llysfaen. Perhaps, like Brundrits, this owner (who was closely associated with Kneeshaw, Lupton) decided to concentrate his efforts on extracting stone, and leave it to a specialist company to arrange transportation.

Newbuilding resumed in 1912, although the link with Ailsa had been permanently severed. The short-lived ZELIA came from George Brown and Co. of Greenock, and was similar in dimensions to this yard's ALYN which had been recently acquired by Zillah, and it is possible that she had been laid down for the ALYN's original owners. The Dublin-

Zelia on trials. *Glasgow University Archives DC101/1655*

built SUMMERFIELD of 1913 represented an even more dramatic break with tradition, and at 188 feet was the largest ship owned by the company during its independent existence.

Having tried a Leith yard for the THORNFIELD of 1913, Zillah then settled down to another long-term relationship with a builder, the Lytham Shipbuilding and Engineering Co. Ltd. whose ASHFIELD of 1914 was to be followed by thirteen other ships up to 1948 including SILVERFIELD. Half of this number were built to a length of 142 feet. This was smaller than the last of the Ailsa ships, the E. HAYWARD having scaled 157 feet, but a deciding factor was the growing importance to the company of the coal trade from Garston, other Mersey ports and Preston to the Ringsend Basin, Dublin where the entrance lock restricted ships to this size. Despite being shorter than their predecessors, this group of ships had their bridges placed amidships.

Silverfield *W.S.P.L. Cochrane collection*

The formation of the Zillah Shipping and Carrying Co. Ltd. in 1895 had given Savage a firm foundation on which to expand his shipowning business, but over the next two decades he made some organisational and financial changes to ensure the prosperity of his small empire. Most significant to our story was the transfer of operations from Warrington to an office at 7 Chapel Street, Liverpool. This is believed to have occurred about 1906, but the company's registered office was not officially moved until 1918. In 1909 Savage formed the Zillah Engineering Co. Ltd. to carry out surveys and repairs to his fleet, and around 1911 registered William A. Savage Ltd. to take over the formal management of the company and ships, which had previously been his personal responsibility. In 1915 Savage acquired an interest in the Pwllheli Granite Co. Ltd., undoubtedly to ensure stone cargoes for his ships from the quarries at Minfford and Gimlet Rock, Pwllheli.

On 7th July 1918 William Savage died at his Warrington home, also named Zillah, at the age of 62. He is remembered as a cheery and – as a devoted Wesleyan – unostentatious man. He was always willing to give advice and even financial assistance to those he thought worthy of it, and was deeply loyal to the friends who had helped his business venture and who had been rewarded in turn with directorships. These qualities were reflected in his leaving much of his considerably estate in the form of a charitable trust. The main beneficiaries were intended to be the directors and staff of his companies, but as this was 1918 the charity was extended to our gallant soldiers and sailors, and next in line were the deserving poor of Warrington. What was extraordinary, however, was the specific exclusion of "sailors or firemen or other persons employed by the Companies below the rating of sailors or firemen . . ." For all his openness and generosity, Savage had forgotten his own origins and the men whose labour had earned him so much.

William Savage had no sons or daughters to take his place, and his shipping business was to be run for many years by Joseph Chadwick in conjunction with company secretary Henry Brough, who had joined the company in 1904 after an apprenticeship with Elder, Dempster. Priscilla Savage's interests in the company were taken over by the Savage Trust Ltd.

As a short digression, the ships of the Zillah fleet were to have relatively few managers, or ship's husbands. This term was defined by the Merchant Shipping Act as the person responsible for the ship, and the ship's husband's name appears in every ship's registration papers. This practice differs from that of *Lloyd's Register* in describing managers. Whereas the latter publication will often cite a company such as W. A. Savage Ltd. as managers, registration documents demand the names of an individual or individuals as managers. In practice this is an officer of the managing or owning company, often the company secretary. Hence William Savage is officially listed as manager of all Zillah ships until just after his death in 1918, when Joseph Chadwick takes over. Despite Chadwick's long service with the company, in December 1921 he was succeeded as manager by Robert Wakefield. Longest-serving manager was Joseph Ashton, whose name appears on registration papers from July 1928 until February 1950, after the company lost its independence.

Even before Savage took an interest in the Pwllheli quarry, Zillah were closely associated with the shipment of stone from North Wales. Much was shipped as roadstone (usually described as "macadam") from the Penmaen jetty at Penmaenmawr, serving quarries owned by Brundrits and later by the Penmaenmawr and Welsh Granite Quarries Ltd. Zillah ships could also be found loading at the jetties serving the Port Nant and Port Rivals granite quarries on the Llŷn and limestone quarries at Llanddulas. Limestone carrying was the trade Savage grew up in, and was particularly important to small craft which could enter West Bank Dock at Widnes. Limestone was a vital ingredient of the Leblanc process for making alkali from salt, as described in the United Alkali chapter, and carried on extensively (and offensively) at Widnes. Much of the limestone was shipped on behalf of the Widnes Limestone Co.

A painstaking study of trade at Preston by Peter Kenyon indicates that up until the First World War about half the Zillah arrivals at the port brought stone, many of the ships returning immediately to North Wales for a further cargo. The only outward cargoes from Preston were coal or coke to Dublin. In the autumn months some cargoes of grain were brought in from Liverpool or Birkenhead and an occasional cargo of pig iron from the west of Scotland. Besides the Mersey, other ports visited included Fleetwood, Maryport, Barrow and Newry where the second ZILLAH loaded a cargo of granite setts for Preston in August 1906. Few voyages were beyond the Irish Sea; one notable exception being a trip to Par by the ALYN soon after her acquisition.

It speaks highly of Savage's and his employees' skills that despite the hazards of the trade to the Welsh jetties losses were few. Savage's first loss came only after twenty-one years trading when the almost-new ZELIA foundered not far from Dublin in 1912. The coming of war inevitably spoilt this record, but of the six losses sustained four were definitely and one probably due to enemy action. Accounts of the loss of the CECIL are slightly contradictory, and she may have been a victim of a collision with a larger ship off the mouth of the Somme, although she was only trading to this river in order to carry war materials to the front. Losses fell heaviest on the newest ships, and in just four days in August 1915 the 1913-built SUMMERFIELD and THORNFIELD fell victim to mines and submarine gunfire respectively. By a strange coincidence, both ships were carrying cargoes of wooden huts to the Isle of Man, and some of the Germans interned as aliens on the island may well have been deprived of shelter by the actions of the U-boats involved.

When lost, SUMMERFIELD and THORNFIELD were under requisition as Expeditionary Force Transports, but their trips to the Isle of Man suggest that the government took a broad view on the work required to support British forces in France. Several other Zillah ships were similarly designated: CECIL briefly in 1915, PUFFIN which was specifically assigned to carrying supplies from London to France from November 1915 to December 1918, and AQUILLA for part of 1915 and from 1916 to 1918 when she ran from Dover and Rochester to France, carrying road and railway materials among other cargoes. Around the end of 1915, AQUILLA was in a service which only a starched military mind could name: Timber Transport (Collier). One is left to wonder whether she carried wood to supplement coal supplies, or timber for use as pit props. Another misleading description was that of Fleet Messenger (Commissioned). The vision this conjures up of a fast craft dashing to overtake battlecruisers with vital dispatches is dispelled by its application to AQUILLA and to SILVERFIELD, neither of which were credited with more than 10 knots on a good day. AQUILLA served in this capacity between April 1918 and January 1920. SILVERFIELD was commissioned in the role in August 1915, not long after her completion, and served continuously until June 1920. She had the most adventurous war of any Zillah ship, and was assigned to the Principal Naval Transport Officer, Eastern Mediterranean; duties which would take her to Mudros and the Dardanelles.

As a post-script to the war-time requisition of the company's ships, in 1919 W.A. Savage Ltd. briefly managed two coasters built for the government. This management was probably limited to supervising the building of the WAR TAMAR, as the second steamer, WAR AVON, was sold to Belgian owners before completion.

Delivery of 142 foot steamers from Lytham had continued up until 1916 and resumed in 1920 so that by 1926 six were in service, plus the 175 foot GORSEFIELD. There were also 11 survivors from the pre-war fleet. After 1926 there was a prolonged lull in new-buildings, although as in previous recessions the fleet was strengthened by suitable second-hand acquisitions. The first of these was taken over on the stocks, one of the group of coasters laid down during the war by the Manchester Dry Docks Co. Ltd. at Ellesmere Port. The fourth of these, yard number 74, was started in 1919 and was on the stocks practically completed in 1921, but was not delivered as PENSTONE until December 1926.

Amy Summerfield *John Clarkson*

The prolonged depression which prompted Zillah to forsake newbuilding led to further acquisitions in 1927 when the two remaining ships of the liquidated Summerfield Steamship Co. Ltd. were bought. The AMY SUMMERFIELD and JESSIE SUMMERFIELD were Ailsa-built steamers very much of similar size and appearance to Zillah's ships from this yard. The former was to serve Zillah well for many years, but the JESSIE SUMMERFIELD was sold after being officially owned for only four days and so does not merit a place in the fleet list.

In 1929 four coasters were acquired from William Cooper of Widnes. The APPLIANCE, ASSISTANCE, ACCORDANCE and ADHERANCE kept their distinctive names, and although they were the smallest of the Zillah fleet they worked alongside its other ships for the next decade, mainly in the stone trade.

Assistance *W.S.P.L.*

Evidence from the Preston records suggests that the trading patterns throughout the inter-war period differed little from those established by 1914. A month such as April 1936 saw thirteen arrivals by Zillah ships from Penmaenmawr, all of which returned light. A pattern can be seen emerging, with the smaller ships PENSTONE, APPLIANCE, ASSISTANCE, ACCORDANCE and ADHERANCE serving this trade, and the larger ships carrying coal to Dublin and on a few occasions to Belfast, Drogheda and Waterford. There were occasional grain cargoes from the Mersey, whilst to add variety in October 1935 ADHERANCE took bricks to Douglas. There were china clay cargoes too, for example the THELMA's arrival from Padstow on 20th February 1936. She sailed with coal for Belfast two days later. The pattern of trade to and from the Mersey largely paralleled that from Preston, although it was an order of magnitude bigger, so that on any one day as many as eight Zillah ships might be seen on the river, bringing stone from Penmaenmawr to Liverpool, and taking coal out to Ireland from Liverpool, Garston or Acton Grange on the Manchester Ship Canal.

The major reliance on the Penmaenmawr stone and Dublin coal trades seems to have given Zillah a measure of stability during the uncertain years of the thirties, but it also made them distinctly vulnerable if either trade should be lost. As a alternative the managing company W.A. Savage Ltd. investigated and in the early 1940s bought into the Piel and Walney Grave Co. Ltd. This was a somewhat ramshackle and under-capitalised affair, exploiting an excellent source of gravel but relying on customers such as the Mersey Docks and Harbour Board to take its output in aggregate rather than bothering to install expensive plant to crush and grind the gravel to a regular size. The gravel company was eventually acquired completely by W.A. Savage Ltd., but was to afford poor earnings in return for moderate investment and much worry. Its value lay in providing a guaranteed source of cargoes for the Zillah fleet, but in this it did not come into its own until the post-war reconstruction of Liverpool docks.

The Zillah fleet reached its peak with two dozen ships in 1930, thereafter there was a slow but steady reduction as the Ailsa-built ships were disposed of, being reduced to barges in the case of the PRISCILLA, scrapped (PUFFIN), sold (LITTLE ORME) or in the solitary case of the Lytham-built HEATHERFIELD, lost. As in the case of the SUMMERFIELD over twenty years earlier, their occasional voyages on the East Coast seemed unfortunate for Zillah ships, and the wreck of the HEATHERFIELD near Robin

Hood's Bay blighted the fleet's enviable record of being almost free from major peacetime accidents.

Perhaps this loss encouraged the owners to begin building again, and they returned to Lytham for a modified version of the GORSEFIELD of 1922. The BRACKENFIELD emerged in 1937 and set the pattern for most of the company's further newbuildings: the identical BROOMFIELD, the Ringsend-sized ROWANFIELD, MAPLEFIELD and LARCHFIELD. With bridge set aft, a cruiser stern and improvements to her machinery including a forced draught fan and the relatively high boiler pressure of 200 p.s.i., BRACKENFIELD was regarded as a quite advanced design, with all her seamen and firemen being accommodated in the poop. It is interesting to note, however, that even at this late date her general arrangement drawings show her to be fitted with a full suit of sails.

Delivery of this batch of steamers extended well into the Second World War, the LARCHFIELD not being completed until October 1941. In contrast to the First World War, merchant ship and indeed coaster production had been given a high priority, and it was somewhat unusual to find the Lytham yard being allowed to build a non-standard ship. Exceptions were made only for ships built to existing designs, and the MAPLEFIELD and LARCHFIELD just qualified here, as they were slightly lengthened versions of the ROWANFIELD of 1938.

Larchfield was one of the second generation of Lytham-built steamers with bridge aft. *W.S.P.L.*

Late in 1940 W.A. Savage Ltd. were given the management of a Dutch steamer which had been taken over by the Ministry of Shipping (later the Ministry of War Transport), the EMPIRE TULIP. Strangely, she was the only vessel managed during the conflict, and as a motorship did not match the rest of the fleet. She was soon transferred elsewhere, however, her management going to the Clyde, where she was needed to service the large number of extra ships which were using the river. Despite the newbuildings, wartime saw a decline in the size of the fleet. There was only one loss, albeit a serious one, through war causes, when the BRACKENFIELD was torpedoed during the Normandy Invasion in June 1944. However, wartime conditions contributed to two other losses. In March 1940 the ALYN was wrecked at Langness near Castletown, Isle of Man during an overnight voyage from Preston to Belfast. As a blackout precaution, the lights at both Langness Point and Chicken Rock had been extinguished, and in the rain and total darkness a small error in reckoning the ship's position resulted in disaster. Despite the relatively calm conditions, two of the crew of nine died and one was injured before reaching the shore,

A composite photograph taken about 23rd March 1940 a week after **Alyn** was wrecked at Derbyhaven, Isle of Man. The lifeboat davits were bent during abandonment. Note the damage to the propellor and sternpost, and the forward hold failure. Shortly afterwards the bow section broke away.
William A. Sleigh

and the ALYN herself became a total wreck. In February 1945 the MAPLEFIELD came off worst in an encounter with a United States steamer whose crew must have been less familiar with navigation in the Irish Sea than that of the coaster. This accident does not seem to have harmed the career of the master of the MAPLEFIELD, J. Hughes, who was later to become the company's marine superintendent.

Wartime inevitably meant some decline in Zillah's main trades. North Wales stone was still moved to the Mersey and to Preston, but in smaller quantities than pre-war. In the early years of the war, fewer coal cargoes were shipped to neutral Eire although from 1942 onwards this trade revived. However, Government requisition of the ships was soon to take up any slack, and of the ships left to Zillah at the end of the war, only the AMY SUMMERFIELD, APPLIANCE, ELMFIELD, MAYFLOWER, OATFIELD and SILVERFIELD escaped official service. The greatest requirement for coasters occurred during the invasion of Europe and from about April 1944 the pace of requisition increased markedly. Older ships were not spared, and the E. HAYWARD of 1908 served the United States Navy during May and June 1944. Two other veterans, AQUILLA and OPHIR, worked as cable loop-layers between June 1941 and October 1945, the latter - which is said to have been given the extraordinary name H.M.S. ELDORADO - then requiring ten months for reconditioning.

As ships were called up in this way, demand for those remaining unrequisitioned grew, and Zillah took advantage of this by selling six ships during the war. The oldest of the fleet, SARAH BROUGH, was retired to the Mersey to work in the sand and gravel trade. Three of the small ships acquired from Coopers – ASSISTANCE, ACCORDANCE and ADHERANCE – went to assist in salvage work.

At the very end of 1945, W.A. Savage Ltd. were allocated two vessels to manage. Initially these were to be the EMPIRE MAYLAND and MAYMORN, which were completing at Bristol. The former was actually allocated to the services of Coast Lines Ltd. Even though the war had ended, there seems to have been official indecisiveness about how these vessels were to be used, and within a month the still incomplete EMPIRE MAYLAND was transferred to the management of Elder, Dempster for service abroad. In her place the identical EMPIRE MAYROVER was to be managed by Savages. This class of steamer was designed and laid down before the fall of Japan for operation in eastern waters and their use in home waters was merely an interim measure. The vessels were soon sold and left Savage's management during 1946 and 1947.

There is a point at which the management of any company, if its directorate and management have not been refreshed by the addition of younger men with fresh horizons, moves from the prudent through the conservative to the unenterprising. There were signs of this happening to the Zillah and Savage companies in the years following the war. Perhaps the most obvious symptom was the continued reliance on steam, and Zillah had the dubious distinction of being the last owners to take delivery of a conventional steam coaster, with the completion of the HAZELFIELD at Lytham in April 1948. At 184 feet she was the second biggest ship the company had owned, and whilst retaining the hull form of the pre-war Lytham ships, she reverted to the bridge-amidships layout of the 1920s and earlier. Her main technological advance was oil firing.

Not long after the delivery of the HAZELFIELD the company suffered one of its worst peacetime casualties, and one which tended to highlight its problems – ageing ships and practices, often with ageing crews, in a period when the maritime world was moving ahead at full speed.

Whilst bound from Penmaenmawr to Preston with some 220 tons of granite chippings the PENSTONE sank following a collision with Westfal-Larsen's motor vessel VILLANGER soon after 10.00 on the morning of 31st July 1948. The coaster was virtually cut in two by the Norwegian, which was outward bound in ballast from Liverpool for Los Angeles, and sank within half a minute, taking with her the chief engineer, another member of the crew and – despite the mate's attempts to save them by pushing them through the wheelhouse window – the master and his five-year-old son.

The exact details of the collision differ depending on whose account is read. In the action brought by the mate and the other survivor, it was alleged that the VILLANGER was travelling too fast in the dense fog that prevailed, that she had not sounded any fog

Hazelfield: the last steamer built for Zillah. *W.S.P.L.*

signals and failed to take avoiding action. The mate's evidence that the VILLANGER could only be seen when she was a cable's length away, however, suggests that there was little time for such action. On behalf of the VILLANGER it was claimed that there was no fog only "some haze" and that the PENSTONE was sighted when she was all of a mile away. In spite of their insistence that visibility was good, the cargo-liner's people asserted that the little coaster came on too fast and herself failed to give fog signals. The VILLANGER is said to have given a short blast on her whistle, and when the PENSTONE failed to respond stopped her engines and turned hard to starboard. When the coaster finally reacted, it was to turn to port, in breach of the collision rules and putting herself under the bigger ship's maierform bow, which rode over her and healed her over so that – as the coaster's hatch covers were off – she quickly filled and sank.

As the VILLANGER had on board a "first class Mersey pilot" and the master and mate of the PENSTONE were – like most of their coastal contemporaries – uncertificated, it is perhaps not surprising that the coaster was found two thirds to blame. The court criticised her for a "shocking" lookout, and for being in breach of the collision regulations. The Norwegian was not completely exonerated, however, and was held one third responsible because she did not slow down – a consulting engineer who assessed the damage to her bow considered that she must have been travelling at about 10 knots at the time of impact.

It was not just the company's ships which were getting old. At a meeting of the board of W.A. Savage Ltd. in October 1946 it was suggested that two younger men be appointed, and J.W. Dodd and W.P.M. Brough were duly admitted, although there were no resignations. The former gentleman might have been younger than the other board members, but he could still look back on over thirty years' service with the company.

Against this background it is not surprising that around the end of 1948 a take-over bid for what came to be called the Zillah Group was accepted. The bidder was none other than Coast Lines Ltd., the major British coastal shipping group, and which was at the height of its powers, having recovered largely by its own efforts from its entanglements with the troubled Kylsant Group. Coast Lines were a predominantly liner operation, but amongst their many subsidiaries they did have a coastal trampship operation based on London, Queenship Navigation Ltd. They are rumoured to have approached other Liverpool-based coaster owners, but perhaps Zillah were one of the most attractive, and were sympathetic to their overtures.

The acquisition of Zillah gave the Coast Lines Group a pool of Liverpool-based ships to draw on to meet the needs of their extensive liner operations for additional or spare ships. A fleet of coasters which were operating largely on the voyage charter market was ideal for this purpose, as they could be quickly and economically diverted to liner services as the need arose. Initially, at least, the Group made heavy use of this facility. In 1954, for instance, Zillah ships spent a total of 810 days on hire to Group companies, although the frequency of such hiring then declined.

The first outward sign of the takeover was the appointment of Coast Lines' Chairman, Arnet Robinson, to the boards of W.A. Savage Ltd. and the Zillah Shipping and Carrying Co. Ltd. in March 1949, with the subsequent resignation of J.R. Lord and Robert Ashton. The opportunity was taken to alter the company's title, and a change to the less awkward Zillah Shipping Co. Ltd. was registered on 2nd August 1949. The fleet of steamers continued as before, and was augmented by transfer of similar vessels from other Coast Lines companies, often liner companies where steamers were becoming less competitive. Thus in the years 1949 to 1952 Zillah became the last operator of a number of ageing coasters which, in retrospect, it may have been better off without: the DRANSFIELD (28 years old), FAIRFIELD (25 years), CALDYFIELD (31 years), NORTHFIELD (20 years) and WESTFIELD (17 years). Note how the -FIELD naming scheme had been retained but subtly altered away from the use of a tree name as a preface. As a postscript, it may be noted that the name ZILLAH was the only one used twice during the entire history of the company.

The fleet in 1952 almost equalled its numerical peak of pre-war years, as departures were few and were restricted to the older ships. The most dramatic of these was the stranding and total loss of the AMY SUMMERFIELD at Port Rivals, the fleet's only serious casualty of the trade to exposed jetties in which the steamers were habitually engaged.

Northfield *John Clarkson*

Freshfield: the first motor ship built for Zillah. *A. Duncan*

Although no major British coaster owner had taken the diesel engine very seriously until the 1930s, Coast Lines were amongst the first to wake up to the economies it offered, with the completion of the FIFE COAST in 1933. Ironically in view of Lord Kylsant's early championship of the motorship, this decision came only after the company achieved its independence from the Kylsant Group. The new owners of Zillah were surprisingly slow to apply this new form of propulsion to the fleet, but when they decided to do so fleet renewal proceeded very briskly. The first motorship completed was the FRESHFIELD of 1954 but within six years thirteen motor vessels were either acquired almost new or built for the company in British or Dutch yards.

For almost a decade after the war Zillah's trade had continued largely unchanged, consisting mainly of stone from North Welsh quarries, export of coal to Ireland, and gravel shipped to the Mersey from the now wholly-owned Piel and Walney Gravel Co. Ltd. But two of these three traditional pillars of the company's business were to be all but knocked away, presenting the company with the challenge of finding new trades in order to survive.

The first blow fell in 1954 with the loss of Zillah's near-monopoly in the Penmaenmawr granite trade, with which the company had been involved for sixty years. The reason was almost certainly the quarry owner's desire for lower rates, which they could probably obtain by chartering vessels on a single voyage basis. Zillah's participation in this trade was henceforth only occasional. Some voyages were made from Trevor to London, at least until 1960 when sources of granite nearer to the capital made the business uneconomic. In an attempt to maintain their interest in the trade, Zillah ships lifted some cargoes from Jersey's Ronez and other quarries in the south, but these were not found to be profitable. An echo of the quarry owner's intransigence over rates was heard in 1962, when they stood alone in refusing to pay a 7.5% increase in freight rates. On the advice of the Chamber of Shipping, Zillah declined what few stone cargoes they were offered.

The year 1955 was almost the last in which the company could count on another of its staple trades, shipment of coal to Ireland. One of the reasons for the decline of this trade was the 1955 coal strike which meant that the National Coal Board had to divert to Ireland some coal which was to be imported into the United Kingdom. With the price of

British coal continually rising, the Irish importers were not slow to learn a lesson from this action, and United States and later Polish coal began to take over what had once been a safe market, with an inevitable effect on British coaster owners. In 1958, for instance, over six months went by without a Zillah vessel lifting an Irish coal cargo.

With the sharp decline in these trade, it was well that gravel shipments from Piel had become a major part of Zillah's business in post-war years. As demand increased after the war, and labour became more freely available, production increased steadily. Almost 40,000 tons were shipped in 1948, but this was far below capacity, and it was estimated that 3,000 tons could be shipped each week. The announcement of the Mersey Docks and Harbour Board's Canada Dock improvement scheme brought hope that shipments at such levels could be achieved. These hopes were never fully realised, partly because there was reluctance to invest in the up-to-date equipment needed for extracting and grading the gravel. Board minutes of W.A. Savage Ltd. were chiefly a recital of decisions to acquire second-hand or unsuitable equipment for the works. In addition, the Liverpool dock improvement scheme suffered delays which meant that the flow of gravel was not as brisk as was hoped, and large scale use of reinforced concrete by the Harbour Board's engineers reduced the requirement for gravel. The best year was 1960, with 80,000 tons of gravel shipped, and even this might have been exceeded if a strike on Merseyside had not held up work. With the end of the Mersey Docks and Harbour Board's contract in sight and the consequent loss of the seaborne trade, efforts were made to find other outlets. But neither land sales of 20,000 tons of gravel nor the manufacture of concrete blocks could keep the operation profitable, and with much of the equipment antiquated and virtually beyond repair it was decided at the end of 1962 to cease operations and sell the assets.

From 1955 onwards, the minutes of Zillah's Directors' Meetings are available, forming part of the Coast Lines archives lodged at the National Maritime Museum thanks to the good offices of the P. & O. Group, who took over the parent company. These minutes give a great deal of fascinating information on the company's operations, but it is obvious that they are written mainly for consumption by the main board of Coast Lines. Whilst leaving day to day operations in the hands of the Zillah directors and managers, this board reserved to itself the more important decisions, especially the acquisition of new tonnage. The Zillah minutes are at pains to show that the company was doing well, but could do even better if it was given more of the right ships. The Coast Lines board behave rather like benevolent parents, handing down rewards in the shape of new ships, and also putting matters right when, as was soon to happen, Zillah made a rather expensive mistake.

By October 1955 Zillah had four motor vessels, and already their advantages over the steamers were painfully apparent, leading the board to spend much of its time denouncing the very type of ship they had been happily building until quite recently. Conveniently forgetting that 75% of their own fleet consisted of steamers, the board claimed that uneconomic coal-burners were forcing up freight rates in the Irish coal trade to a point where saturation was soon to be reached. In 1955 the motor ships were earning an average daily profit of £54, compared to a measly £4 for the steamers: a differential in profitability which had recently been considerably widened by a rise in both freight rates and in the price of bunker coal. As a result, the dock and rail strikes during that summer saw four of the coal-burning steamers idle, whilst the motor ships were gainfully employed. Decline in the Irish coal trade was a further nail in the coffin of Zillah's steamers, which were concentrated on the shorter voyages on which they spent proportionately less time at sea, so that their heavier fuel bills were not such a disadvantage.

A certain lack of enthusiasm can be discerned for ships which were not ordered by Zillah. The FAIRFIELD – at 30 years of age by no means the oldest unit of the fleet - was singled out for criticism on account of her wide beam and deep draft, which restricted the trades in which she could be used. She was the first ship to be laid up when the coal trade had its annual downturn in the summer months. Interestingly, however, the FAIRFIELD – although unable to pay her way whilst tramping - proved highly profitable when hired to other members of the Coast Lines Group, which suggests that "internal"

Fairfield *R.M. Parsons*

hire charges were artificially inflated. The Zillah board noted, somewhat unhappily, a downward trend in such hire, and the FAIRFIELD was one of three steamers to be broken up in the autumn of 1955.

The one non-Zillah-built vessel which was considered a useful asset was the WESTFIELD, which had unusually long hatches. In 1955 she was chartered to the British and Irish Steam Packet Co. Ltd. to carry diesel locomotives engined by Crossley Brothers from Manchester to Dublin. She was also used to carry 60 foot rails from Workington for trans-shipment at other West Coast ports. This prolonged her life, and she was the last of the Coast Line steamer transfers to be broken up, in June 1956.

Helped by its new motor vessels, Zillah did have considerable success in opening up new trades during the latter part of the 1950s. Pig iron from Millom to the Bristol Channel proved profitable, and the company could not handle all the cargoes offered during 1955. This trade proved very useful in providing a return cargo for ships carrying coal to northern Irish ports, and positioned them well for export coal cargoes from South Wales. The economy of the motor ships suited them to such longer passages, and considerable quantities of grain and fertilisers were being moved from France to West Coast ports. The OATFIELD spent three months in 1955 carrying fruit and vegetables from France to the South of England, although her size suited her better for the short distance trades out of the Mersey, including grain to Silloth for biscuit makers Carrs of Carlisle and Quaker Oats to Whitehaven; these being very useful return cargoes to balance gravel shipments from Walney to the Mersey. Basic slag was being moved from Partington and Immingham to Continental ports, and this positioned the ships to carry silver sand from Antwerp to Garston for glass-making, and potash from Holland and Belgium to Ireland and West Coast United Kingdom ports. The company were also making a fresh assault on the china clay trade from Fowey and Par, initially to Preston, where there were frequent delays in unloading owing to labour shortages, and later to Runcorn and Ellesmere Port. Another coastal trade beyond Zillah's traditional trading pattern was ammonium sulphate for I.C.I. from the Tyne or the Tees to Avonmouth for Fisons' fertiliser plant. As some compensation for the decline of the Irish coal trade, Zillah picked up some business from the South Wales ports, including carriage from Swansea to Liverpool of "duff coal" – washed anthracite dust for use in tin smelting.

One of the pleasing results of these new trades was the avoidance of the dead period in the summer, when coal exports tailed off due to slack demand and colliery holidays.

On the basis of the new business, a Zillah board meeting in 1955 reported that the company could profitably employ twelve motor ships. This theme was returned to year after year: "even one motor vessel being infinitely more useful to the company than two steamers" said the board in 1957, and to prove their point sold the ROWANFIELD and LARCHFIELD to provide the capital to buy the HOLMFIELD.

Although not getting quite all that it asked for, Zillah did have its fleet of motor coasters considerably enhanced in the next five years, largely by the acquisition of almost-new Dutch-built coasters. The newer ships fell into four bands in terms of size: 600 tons deadweight for the OATFIELD and HOLMFIELD; 700 tons for the GREENFIELD and GRANGEFIELD; 800 tons for the FOXFIELD, FRESHFIELD, FALLOWFIELD, FERNFIELD and FORDFIELD; and 900 tons for EARLSFIELD and EDGEFIELD. In general, these coasters traded successfully and profitably, although some modifications were necessary to the hatchways of the EDGEFIELD to ease trimming and discharging.

The ease or otherwise of trimming coal cargoes in a given ship was always a matter of concern to owners and charterers, as any coal trimmers necessary were often employed at the ship's expense. This was not helped by differences from port to port in the way ships were classified. When FRESHFIELD was loaded at Partington in January 1960, the trimmers called for measurements of the ends and wings of her hold to be taken which revealed that in total they were long enough to merit a higher rate for trimming. On the Bristol Channel, just the ends of the holds were considered in the classification, which made the FRESHFIELD cheaper to load.

The notable exceptions to the trends in size and success referred to above were Zillah's two most ambitious newbuildings, the 1,350-ton BRENTFIELD and BIRCHFIELD from Greenock and Ardrossan, respectively. The entry into service of the former was hardly propitious. She left Glasgow with coal for Dublin on her maiden voyage on 24th October 1955, but just eight days later whilst bound from Dublin to Glasgow with a cargo of gypsum she suffered a major engine breakdown. She had to be towed in, and required a complete new engine. This detained her for six weeks and, to add to their woes, the builders had to pay £1,500 to Zillah to compensate for her loss of earnings.

Brentfield converted for unit load carrying and renamed **Spaniel**. *A. Duncan*

The company's initial enthusiasm for these larger ships was quick to evaporate. When the shipment of gypsum was shifted from Dublin to Drogheda, this port was considered unsafe for the larger ships, and Zillah withdrew from the trade. With a decline in coal shipments, a general worsening of trade and increasing foreign competition, it proved more and more difficult to find profitable employment for the BRENTFIELD and BIRCHFIELD. On one voyage from Partington to Emden in 1957 the latter earned a profit of just £29 for over a week's work. The board complained that there was a glut of similar-sized vessels chasing too few cargoes, and that a number of these had been laid up for lack of work. Quite clearly, a major mistake had been made in ordering these large ships, and the Zillah board turned to its parent to help bail it out of what was becoming an acute problem, requesting employment to be found for the BRENTFIELD and BIRCHFIELD elsewhere in the group. This request was granted in November 1958 when the ships returned to their birthplace for conversion to Coast Lines' first container ships.

But as always there was a price to pay. The transfer of the 18-year old CHANNEL COAST to the fleet was less welcome than the arrival of new Dutch coasters: the Zillah Board merely remarking that as the GLENFIELD she "added to the numerical strength of the fleet". This coolness did not prevent the parent company transferring to Zillah the even older LAIRDSOAK which became the GARTHFIELD in 1960.

It is noteworthy that the arrival of the final additions to the Zillah fleet in 1960 coincided with the disposal of its last steamer. Surprisingly, this survivor was not the most recent steamer, but the E. HAYWARD built in 1908: forty years before the HAZELFIELD. The old ship owed her longevity to her suitability for most of Zillah's local trades, and her length which made her especially suitable for loading railway rails at Workington. When sold in 1958 she was still fit for a couple of years use as a sand carrier, a second career which she shared with AQUILLA, BROOMFIELD and MAYFLOWER.

The HAZELFIELD, in contrast, caused the board recurrent worries. In 1957 her future was debated at length, and conversion to a motor ship was seriously considered. However, it was felt that this expense was not justified, as she was too big for the Walney gravel and Silloth grain trades and too deep for Millom. Two voyages with china clay for Preston had not endeared her to the charterers on account of her depth, and she was really suited only to the Irish coal trade, which was fast falling away. Pleas to have her transferred to another Group company at the end of 1957 fell on deaf ears, and it was decided to put her on the market. She spent seven months laid up in 1958, and was eventually sold to other Liverpool owners only in June 1959: she was just over eleven years old. Later in her career she was indeed converted to a motor ship, as was the ROWANFIELD which had been sold to Danish owners in 1957. Both conversions dramatically extended the lives of the ships, but Zillah should not be chastised too heavily for failing to follow this course. It is claimed that Board of Trade regulations made such conversions very expensive for owners using the British flag, and after much expense the company would have been left with deep-drafted ships not well suited to its new patterns of trade.

Even though they were well equipped with a fleet consisting largely of modern motor ships, Zillah did not find the latter half of the fifties easy. Board meetings heard of one problem after another: grain was being shipped direct to Silloth rather than being transhipped; bad weather had adversely affected the French grain harvest; warm weather had reduced the demand for coal; cold weather in the winter of 1956/57 meant that continental canals were frozen delaying cargoes; ice in the Baltic brought a premature end to the season's Scandinavian timber trade and threw a number of Dutch coasters on to the spot market. The little Dutchmen were a continual cause of complaint for taking cargoes at unrealistic rates, especially in the Irish coal trade.

Behind these complaints can be detected a general change in the pattern of trade. In the early fifties, with more cargoes available than ships to move them, shippers were keen to enter into contracts with shipowners to assure them of having a ship on hand when they needed it. Zillah could offer the flexibility of a relatively large fleet, and benefited from the stability a number of such contracts provided. As the long post-war boom slowly gave way to recession in the late fifties, the position changed and shippers took advantage of the glut of tonnage and relied more and more on spot chartering for their needs.

A further worrying development was reported in the china clay trade: the increasing use of road transport. The board heard in 1959 that English China Clays had acquired a fleet of lorries, resulting in the loss of 40,000 tons a year to coastal shipping. In truth, the world was changing rather too quickly for a company like Zillah, with a management team rooted in traditional trades and business methods. There was talk in 1959 of a likely decline in coal shipments from South Wales to France because of Britain's non-membership of the European Economic Community. Early in 1961 a series of strikes at home and abroad affected the company badly. The worst from the company's point of view was the Merseyside shiprepairers' strike, which for five months completely immobilised the EARLSFIELD which was undergoing her special survey at Birkenhead at the time. Another favourite target at Board meetings was the spread of the five-day week throughout Western Europe. This meant that a ship which berthed on a Friday usually could not complete loading before Monday.

By the early sixties two of the three trades which Zillah had traditionally made its own could no longer be relied upon: only the captive trade in gravel from Walney Island gave the company's ships regular employment and the future of this was clouded. New trades had been energetically sought and won, but none proved as dependable as the old; for instance, I.C.I. lost the contract to supply ammonium sulphate to fertiliser-makers Fisons in 1959, whilst weather and political changes made the coal and grain trades to and from France fitful. The financial consequence was inevitable: Zillah made a loss in 1959, and deficits were recorded in every subsequent year except 1963. As part of the Coast Lines group, the company was cushioned from the effect of these losses, and the deficits were made up by subvention payments by other group companies, including the Belfast Steamship Co. Ltd. and Thomas Allen Ltd., with the promise that this arrangement would be reciprocated if necessary.

All tramp companies are keenly aware of the cyclical nature of their business, and the Zillah board managed to keep their heads during most of this troubled period, although partly for the benefit of the main board they gave long and serious consideration to the state of trade. Their conclusion was that heavy increases in wages, port charges and repair costs had not been reflected in increased freight rates. They pointed out that none of their ships had been idle through lack of cargoes: clearly they were saying that the recurring deficits were not through want of their trying. They maintained that the situation was serious but not hopeless, and if expenses could be controlled and economies effected, then even a small improvement in rates would bring the company back into profitability.

In 1962 an economy was instituted when the rather unwieldy Zillah Group of four companies was reduced to one. The Zillah Engineering Co. Ltd. was solely concerned with repairs and surveys to Zillah ships and, having been under a cloud since the prolonged Mersey shiprepairers' strike in 1961, it was wound up and its staff transferred to Coast Lines Superintendent's Depot. As already related, with little prospect of improving its position without costly investments, the Piel and Walney Gravel Co. Ltd. was also liquidated. The management company W.A. Savage Ltd. and the shipowning company Zillah Shipping Co. Ltd. were merged under the latter title on 1st January 1964. The rationalisation was reported to save £7,000 a year in staff and accommodation costs. Even greater economies were effected by putting the repair work out to tender, W. Holman and Sons of Penzance winning much of it. For instance, dry-docking the FERNFIELD at Penzance cost £4,000 compared to an estimated £7,500 on the Mersey.

The company's position was not helped by casualties and other problems affecting its ships. The pioneer motorship FRESHFIELD was sunk in collision with the Guinness ship THE LADY GWENDOLEN in the Mersey in November 1961. At the time the FRESHFIELD was anchored in fog, yet - although he admitted that visibility was so bad that he could not see the forecastle from the bridge - the master of the Guinness boat was proceeding at his full speed of about ten knots. As justification, he claimed he had his radar set on, but it emerged that only he and the helmsman were on the bridge and that he was paying the radar scant attention. It seems THE LADY GWENDOLEN's master was in the habit of using full speed in fog in order to keep to his tight schedule. His owners were judged negligent for neither impressing on the master the proper procedures for safe navigation in fog, nor for checking that he was following these by comparing deck logs which would record that conditions were foggy, with engine room records which would indicate the speed at the time. Clearly, Zillah and their employees were not responsible for the loss of the FRESHFIELD, but this accident was followed less than two months later by the capsize of the company's last acquisition, FORDFIELD, in the English Channel.

The condition of the GARTHFIELD caused concern as she approached her special survey in 1962. She was very much the old lady of the fleet, approaching 24 years in a company whose average age was just over eight years. She was described as a remarkable vessel for her age, and since her take-over in February 1960 had been an outstanding success from the carrying point of view, with an exceptionally long and deep after hold. This had allowed her to carry outsize pieces of machinery to Portmadog for the building of Trawsfynydd nuclear power station, voyages which had been made every spring tide for eighteen months. But her original Swedish engine could now only manage eight to nine knots and its crankcase was cracked. Her tank top plating was poor, and a number of shell plates almost certainly needed renewing. On top of this her crew accommodation was well below modern standards. With a certain amount of regret she was sold for £12,500 early in 1962; her new Greek owners clearly did not have such scruples about her condition, as over a dozen years later she was still trading, apparently with the same engine.

Holmfield *John Clarkson*

In 1963 the HOLMFIELD was found to have a cracked engine bedplate, necessitating a period of eight weeks in drydock. She had not long been repaired when she ran on to rocks in Bantry Bay, requiring another five weeks of repairs. In 1964 the FOXFIELD had a less serious accident whilst on a similar voyage to the FORDFIELD when an explosion in her anthracite cargo is said to have blown her forecastle twenty feet into the air. She was towed into Dover stern first by two tugs and cost £5,000 to repair.

After a modest revival in trading results in 1963, a further loss was recorded in 1964, followed by a most serious deterioration in trade in 1965 with rates at their lowest for six years, and the company sending vessels to the Continent in ballast. Two mild winters in Europe had meant coal shipments were at a low level, and it was noted that "without a healthy market in coal it is difficult to see how any improvement in tramp rates can be sustained". This pessimism was obviously shared by the British Transport Docks Board, who had cancelled their plans to build a high speed coal loader at Swansea. The only bright spot was the long-term charter of FALLOWFIELD and FERNFIELD to Coast Lines' subsidiary Anglo-Irish Transport Ltd. for unit load services from Preston to Londonderry and to Portrush; the ships lost their cargo gear in the process but gained raised, steel hatches. In spring 1965, EARLSFIELD and GREENFIELD were also chartered to Group companies and converted for similar work. Another victim of the renewed recession was the EDGEFIELD, sold to Irish buyers for £65,000. Despite remedial work soon after purchase, she had always been something of a problem vessel with structural peculiarities making her difficult to trim and reducing her capacity.

Fernfield modified for carrying unit loads. *A. Duncan*

The gloom over future prospects apparent in 1965 resulted in the directors hearing about "proposals to the board [of Coast Lines] regarding the company's future activities". Although these activities were not specified in the minutes, it is clear that Coast Lines felt that coastal tramping had little future, and that the future activities of Zillah's ships were to be purely in support of its parent's liner operations. This decision seems to have been reached by 1966, and there is little further effort to minute the meetings of Zillah directors. It was not until November 1968, however, that a formal resolution was passed to sell the business, assets and goodwill to Coast Lines Ltd. at the book value of the fleet. This sale actually took place on 31st December 1967, so the Zillah directors were merely rubber-stamping a decision of the parent board.

Of the eight ships left, six were transferred to Coast Lines Ltd. or other companies in the group, including the four converted for unit load work, and in this way Zillah's traditional FIELD names lingered on in the Coast Lines fleet until 1971. The FOXFIELD and GREENFIELD were allocated to Burns and Laird Lines Ltd. and had their holds and hatches modified for the carriage of steel between Ardrossan and Belfast, much of it for Harland and Wolff's shipyard. The two smallest units, OATFIELD and HOLMFIELD, were sold to Greek owners. The OATFIELD fetched £30,000, slightly more than her modest book value, but HOLMFIELD made less than half hers, which was almost £56,000. The sales to the Coast Lines Group were made at slightly lower book values, but probably represented more than the ships were worth on the open market. Even in its liquidation, Zillah was benefiting from the protection of its parent.

In contrast to other British coaster companies which succumbed at this time, Zillah had been able to call on the resources of Coast Lines to help it modernise its fleet. But, like too many other coastal shipowners, it had not modernised its management team. It is hardly surprising that directors who had cut their teeth in the days of steam and coal in the twenties and thirties found it hard to adapt to the social, business and technological changes which characterised the Brave New World of the sixties.

Zillah's parent must take some of the blame for this problem, although at the time it had enormous problems of its own, most of which it failed to resolve. Coast Lines' extensive liner services were cut drastically and by no means completely replaced by roll-on roll-off or unit-load operations. In an environment where the group seemed to be desperately seeking to hold on to some vestige of its traditional core business, there was little commitment to investing money or management resources in the peripheral activity of tramping. Nor, with the truncation of liner routes, was there a continuing need for a reserve of ships.

However, Zillah's achievements over six decades must be regarded as very considerable, and rank them as the most consistently successful of the Mersey coaster companies. By concentrating on a few staple trades they weathered wars and depressions, and built up a fine fleet whose numbers remained remarkably constant over half a century. How many companies could boast of keeping a ship employed for fifty years and then finding a buyer for her, as Zillah did with the E. HAYWARD? With the exception of Richard Hughes, they were the only Mersey coaster company to pursue a consistent new-building policy and unlike the Hughes' fleet this newbuilding was never reckless. But in the end what Zillah needed was not just new ships, but new management too.

Fleet list

1. ZILLAH (1) 1891-1900 Wooden screw flat

O.N. 99309 139g 69n 92.0 x 22.2 x 9.9 feet
C. 2-cyl. by Cochrane and Co., Birkenhead; 9 knots.

28.8.1891: Completed by James Harland and Co., Tranmere (Yard No. 14) for William A. Savage, Warrington as ZILLAH. *25.7.1895:* Owners became the Zillah Shipping and Carrying Co. Ltd. (William A. Savage, manager), Warrington. *5.1900:* Sold to Actieselskab Jadar (E. Anda, manager), Stavanger, Norway, converted to a salvage steamer and renamed ERLING SKJALGSON. *1912:* Sold to Actieselskab Tjrve (Einar Meling, manager), Stavanger. *1914:* Manager became Einar Meling junior. *1917:* Sold to Norsk Bjergningskompagni Actieselskab (Morten Beyer, manager), Christiania, Norway. *1932:* Sold to Ole Naesheim, Stavanger. *19.12.1940:* Foundered off Jaeren on the south coast of Norway whilst on a voyage from Stavanger to Fredrikstad. Her crew of six was saved.

2. MERLIN 1895-1907 Wooden screw flat

O.N. 105322 134g 63n 96.3 x 22.0 x 9.6 feet
C. 2-cyl. by Cochrane and Co., Birkenhead; 9 knots.

22.7.1895: Completed by James Harland and Co., Tranmere (Yard No. 15) for William A. Savage, Warrington as MERLIN. *26.7.1895:* Owners became the Zillah Shipping and Carrying Co. Ltd. (William A. Savage, manager), Warrington. *5.3.1907:* Sold to Charles M. Cradock, trading as the Merlin Carrying and Salvage Co. Ltd., Stockton-on-Tees. *24.10.1910:* Stranded north of Craster, Northumberland whilst on a voyage from Craster to Grimsby with a cargo of broken stone, and became a constructive total loss. *10.6.1911:* Register closed.

3. PRISCILLA 1896-1932

O.N. 88914 243g 69n 120.0 x 22.5 x 10.3 feet
C. 2-cyl. by Muir and Houston, Glasgow; 10 knots.

9.9.1896: Launched by the Ailsa Shipbuilding Co., Troon (Yard No. 61) for the Zillah Shipping and Carrying Co. Ltd. (William A. Savage, manager), Warrington and later Liverpool as PRISCILLA. *3.10.1896:* Completed. *31.3.1932:* Sold to Arthur Smith, Birkenhead. *17.6.1933:* Sold to Kelly's Barges Ltd., Birkenhead. *26.9.1939:* Re-registered after being converted to a dumb barge. *25.3.1943:* Sold to Wadsworth Lighterage and Coaling Co. Ltd., Liverpool. *5.1.1959:* Register closed after she had being broken up.

4. SARAH BROUGH 1898-1940

O.N. 88915 299g 66n 132.0 x 23.2 x 10.7 feet
C. 2-cyl. by Ross and Duncan, Govan; 10 knots.

27.1.1898: Launched by the Ailsa Shipbuilding Co., Troon (Yard No. 71) for the Zillah Shipping and Carrying Co. Ltd. (William A. Savage, manager), Warrington and later Liverpool as SARAH BROUGH. *13.4.1898:* Completed. *30.12.1940:* Sold to Abel Barges Ltd., Liverpool. *2.6.1947:* Renamed STOCKDALE. *13.6.1952:* Arrived at Barrow-in-Furness for breaking up by T.W. Ward Ltd. *1.8.1952:* Register closed.

Sarah Brough *W.S.P.L. Cochrane collection*

G.A. Savage *E.N. Taylor*

5. WINIFRED 1898-1912 Wooden auxiliary ketch

O.N. 104472 89g 75n 80.0 x 20.8 x 8.5 feet
1907: 89g 69n 81.7 x 20.8 x 8.5 feet
1907: 1-cyl paraffin motor by Goedkoop Junior, Amsterdam, Holland.

26.5.1898: Completed by Ferguson and Baird, Connah's Quay for the Zillah Shipping and Carrying Co. Ltd. (William A. Savage, manager), Warrington and later Liverpool as the ketch WINIFRED. *17.8.1907:* Re-registered after being lengthened and fitted with an auxiliary engine by A. Ferguson and Sons, Connah's Quay. *11.12.1912:* Sold to the United Alkali Co. Ltd., Liverpool. *12.9.1947:* Owners became Imperial Chemical Industries Ltd., Liverpool. *11.3.1949:* Sold to the Steamship Pelter Co. Ltd., Liverpool. *23.9.1952:* Register closed after she had been broken up.

6. G.A. SAVAGE 1901-1917

O.N. 111362 357g 68n 143.3 x 24.1 x 11.1 feet
C. 2-cyl. by Ross and Duncan, Govan; 10 knots.

18.1.1900: Launched by the Ailsa Shipbuilding Co., Troon (Yard No. 86) for the Zillah Shipping and Carrying Co. Ltd. (William A. Savage, manager), Warrington and later Liverpool as G.A. SAVAGE. *24.2.1901:* Completed. *10.3.1917:* Left Workington for Swansea with a cargo of pitch and disappeared. It is assumed that she was sunk by a German submarine. *28.4.1917:* Register closed.

7. ZILLAH (2) 1901-1943

O.N. 111365 373g 77n 143.0 x 24.1 x 11.5 feet
C. 2-cyl. by Ross and Duncan, Govan.

30.5.1901: Launched by the Ailsa Shipbuilding Co., Troon (Yard No. 98) for the Zillah Shipping and Carrying Co. Ltd. (William A. Savage, manager), Warrington and later Liverpool as ZILLAH. *1.7.1901:* Completed. *8.6.1943:* Sold to Ohlson and Co. Ltd. (Sir Eric Ohlson, manager), Hull. *10.10.1946:* Sold to John Stevanou Livanos, Chios, Greece and renamed KATERINA. *1957:* Deleted from Lloyds Register, no owners having been reported since 1955.

Zillah (2) *John Clarkson*

8. MARGARITA 1902-1917

O.N. 115336 375g 79n 143.6 x 24.1 x 11.6 feet
C. 2-cyl. by Ross and Duncan, Govan; 11 knots.

21.10.1902: Launched by the Ailsa Shipbuilding Co. Ltd., Troon (Yard No. 110) for the Zillah Shipping and Carrying Co. Ltd. (William A. Savage, manager), Warrington and later Liverpool as MARGARITA. *24.11.1902:* Completed. *14.2.1917:* Captured by the German submarine UC 65 and sunk by bombs twenty miles south west by south of Bardsey Island whilst on a voyage from Liverpool to Swansea with a cargo of wheat.

Margarita flying her name pennant. *E.N. Taylor*

9. THELMA 1903-1943

O.N. 118065 400g 75n 143.3 x 25.0 x 11.6 feet
C. 2-cyl. by Ross and Duncan, Govan; 11 knots.

9.11.1903: Launched by the Ailsa Shipbuilding Co. Ltd., Ayr (Yard No. 122) for the Zillah Shipping and Carrying Co. Ltd. (William A. Savage, manager), Warrington and later Liverpool as THELMA. *14.12.1903:* Completed. *15.4.1943:* Sold to S. William Coe and Co. Ltd. (William J. Ireland, manager), Liverpool. *12.7.1943:* Stranded at west end of Doolough Point, Blacksod Bay, whilst on a voyage from Ayr to Galway in ballast. *5.11.1943:* Register closed. *7.12.1943:* Refloated but subsequently sank.

10. MAYFLOWER 1905-1953

O.N. 120889 396g 74n 143.5 x 25.6 x 10.3 feet
C. 2-cyl. by Ross and Duncan, Govan; 10 knots.

16.9.1905: Launched by the Ailsa Shipbuilding Co. Ltd., Troon (Yard No. 139) for the Zillah Shipping and Carrying Co. Ltd. (William A. Savage, manager), Warrington and later Liverpool as MAYFLOWER. *16.10.1905:* Completed. *2.8.1949:* Owners became the Zillah Shipping Co. Ltd. (William A. Savage Ltd., manager), Liverpool. *21.12.1953:* Sold to Richard Abel and Sons Ltd., Liverpool. *28.5.1954:* Renamed MALLOWDALE. *13.11.1956:* Arrived at Troon for breaking up by the West of Scotland Shipbreaking Co. Ltd. *7.11.1957:* Register closed.

Thelma *John Clarkson*

Mayflower *John Clarkson*

Aquilla *W.S.P.L. Cochrane collection*

Ophir *W.S.P.L. Cochrane collection*

11. AQUILLA 1907-1953

O.N. 124059 450g 82n 155.0 x 26.1 x 10.8 feet
C. 2-cyl. by Ross and Duncan, Govan; 10 knots.

2.3.1907: Launched by the Ailsa Shipbuilding Co. Ltd., Troon (Yard No. 171) for the Zillah Shipping and Carrying Co. Ltd. (William A. Savage, manager), Warrington and later Liverpool as AQUILLA. *13.4.1907:* Completed. *2.8.1949:* Owners became the Zillah Shipping Co. Ltd. (William A. Savage Ltd., manager), Liverpool. *27.11.1953:* Sold to Richard Abel and Sons Ltd., Liverpool. *18.12.1953:* Renamed ALLADALE. *31.12.1956:* Owners became the Fleetwood Sand and Gravel Co. Ltd., Fleetwood. *9.1967:* Demolition commenced by C. and J. Davies, Fleetwood. *1.6.1972:* Register closed.

12. OPHIR 1907-1954

O.N. 124102 469g 99n 155.1 x 26.2 x 10.5 feet
C. 2-cyl. by Ross and Duncan, Govan; 10 knots.

9.11.1907: Launched by the Ailsa Shipbuilding Co. Ltd., Ayr (Yard No. 194) for the Zillah Shipping and Carrying Co. Ltd. (William A. Savage, manager), Warrington and later Liverpool as OPHIR. *12.12.1907:* Completed. *2.8.1949:* Owners became the Zillah Shipping Co. Ltd. (William A. Savage Ltd., manager), Liverpool. *30.7.1954:* Arrived at Llanelli for breaking up by the Rees Shipbreaking Co. Ltd. *1.4.1955:* Register closed.

E. Hayward. *E.N. Taylor*

13. E. HAYWARD 1908-1957

O.N. 127944 444g 161n 157.0 x 26.2 x 12.9 feet
C. 2-cyl. by the Ailsa Shipbuilding Co. Ltd., Troon; 10 knots.

10.10.1908: Launched by the Ailsa Shipbuilding Co. Ltd., Ayr (Yard No. 211) for the Zillah Shipping and Carrying Co. Ltd. (William A. Savage, manager), Liverpool as E. HAYWARD. It was originally intended to name her ALETHEA. *7.11.1908:* Completed. *2.8.1949:* Owners became the Zillah Shipping Co. Ltd. (William A. Savage Ltd., manager), Liverpool. *7.12.1957:* Sold to Richard Abel and Sons Ltd., Liverpool. *22.9.1959:* Renamed ENNISDALE. *8.10.1960:* Arrived at Passage West near Cork to be broken up by Haulbowline Industries Ltd. *9.8.1961:* Register closed.

Cecil *John Clarkson*

Puffin *John Clarkson*

14. CECIL 1909-1915 Iron

O.N. 97227 235g 96n 130.2 x 21.1 x 9.5 feet
C. 2-cyl. by Clayton, Goodfellow and Co., Blackburn; 10 knots.

7.10.1890: Completed by R. Smith and Co., Lytham (Yard No. 149) for John Brundrit, Runcorn as CECIL. *7.11.1890:* Owners became the Cecil Steamship Co. Ltd. (Brundrit and Co., managers), Runcorn. *7.11.1898:* Manager became George W. Hayes, Liverpool. *19.3.1909:* Acquired by the Zillah Shipping and Carrying Co. Ltd. (William A. Savage, manager), Liverpool. *24.12.1915:* Stranded at the entrance to the River Somme whilst on a voyage from London to St. Valery-sur-Somme, France with a cargo of Government stores. One account suggests she had been in collision with the steamer LADY IVEAGH (2,268/92) in the River Somme off Le Crotoy. *11.1.1917:* Register closed.

15. PUFFIN 1909-1933

O.N. 111363 404g 59n 150.0 x 25.0 x 9.9 feet
C. 2-cyl. by Dunsmuir and Jackson, Govan; 11 knots.

15.3.1900: Launched by the Ailsa Shipbuilding Co., Troon (Yard No. 87) for the Puffin Steamship Co. Ltd. (Brundrit and Co. Ltd., managers), Liverpool as PUFFIN. *5.5.1900:* Completed. *19.3.1909:* Acquired by the Zillah Shipping and Carrying Co. Ltd. (William A. Savage, manager), Liverpool. *1933:* Broken up during the fourth quarter. *16.7.1936:* Register closed.

Alyn *W.S.P.L. Brownell collection*

16. ALYN 1911-1940

O.N. 127980 350g 133n 142.1 x 23.6 x 9.8 feet
C. 2-cyl. by Gauldie, Gillespie and Co., Glasgow; 9 knots.

1.5.1909: Launched by George Brown and Co., Greenock (Yard No. 53) for the Hamilton Shipping Co. Ltd. (Summersgill Snoddy, manager), Liverpool as ALYN. *25.5.1909:* Completed. *20.2.1911:* Acquired by the Zillah Shipping and Carrying Co. Ltd. (William A. Savage, manager), Liverpool. *17.3.1940:* Wrecked on Fort Island, Derbyhaven, near Castletown, Isle of Man whilst on a voyage from Preston to Belfast with a cargo of coal. *25.4.1940:* Register closed.

17. LITTLE ORME 1909-1934

O.N. 118662 203g 72n 112.0 x 20.5 x 8.4 feet
C. 2-cyl. by Alex Shanks and Son Ltd., Arbroath; 10 knots.

8.6.1906: Launched by the Montrose Shipbuilding Co., Montrose (Yard No. 26) for Alexander W. Watt, Liverpool as E.L. LAWSON. *7.1906:* Completed. *16.5.1907:* Sold to the Orme Shipping Co. Ltd. (John R. Lord, manager), Bacup, Lancashire and later renamed LITTLE ORME. *9.10.1909:* Acquired by the Zillah Shipping and Carrying Co. Ltd. (William A. Savage, manager), Liverpool. *15.11.1934:* Sold to John Campbell, Irvine. *12.11.1936:* Stranded about one mile south of the Point of Ayre, Isle of Man whilst on a voyage from Irvine to Douglas with a cargo of bricks. *24.11.1936:* Refloated and proceeded to Irvine. Although declared a constructive total loss she was repaired. *2.1937:* Re-registered. *1939:* Sold to the Irvine Shipping and Trading Co. Ltd. (Wiliam K. Inglis, manager), Irvine. *1951:* Sold to Barlow and Co. (Dundee) Ltd. (Joseph Barlow, manager), Dundee. *2.1963:* Sold to James A. White and Co. Ltd. for breaking up at St. David's-on-Forth. *18.8.1964:* Register closed.

Little Orme *W.S.P.L.*

18. ZELIA 1912

O.N. 131446 387g 147n 142.3 x 24.6 x 11.0 feet
C. 2-cyl. by Gauldie, Gillespie and Co., Glasgow; 9 knots.

15.6.1912: Launched by George Brown and Co., Greenock (Yard No. 74) for the Zillah Shipping and Carrying Co. Ltd. (William A. Savage, manager), Liverpool as ZELIA. *11.7.1912:* Completed. *13.11.1912:* Foundered off the Bailey Light, about fifteen miles off Howth Head, Dublin whilst on a voyage from Garston to Dublin with a cargo of coal. *19.11.1912:* Register closed.

19. SUMMERFIELD 1913-1915

O.N. 135446 687g 270n 188.2 x 28.7 x 11.0 feet
T. 3-cyl. by Ross and Duncan, Govan; 10 knots.

7.3.1913: Completed by the Dublin Dockyard Co. Ltd., Dublin (Yard No. 79) for the Zillah Shipping and Carrying Co. Ltd. (William A. Savage, manager), Liverpool as SUMMERFIELD. *13.8.1915:* Sunk two miles east of Lowestoft by a mine laid by the German submarine UC 5 whilst on a voyage from Yarmouth to Douglas with a cargo of wooden huts. Three of her crew were lost. *17.8.1915:* Register closed.

20. ELEANOR 1913-1915

O.N. 111214 490g 196n 165.0 x 25.1 x 10.2 feet
C. 2-cyl. by J. Cran and Co., Leith; 10 knots.

7.1.1897: Launched by Cumming and Ellis, Inverkeithing (Yard No. 24) for Compagnie Depeaux, Rouen, France as MARGUERITE DEPEAUX. *7.1897:* Completed. *8.1899:* Sold to James W. Raynes, Llysfaen and renamed ELEANOR. *19.5.1913:* Acquired by the Zillah Shipping and Carrying Co. Ltd. (William A. Savage, manager), Liverpool. *27.1.1915:* Sold to the Antrim Iron Ore Co. Ltd., Belfast. *26.2.1915:* Renamed GLENARIFF. *30.12.1915:* Left Newport, Monmouthshire for Belfast with a cargo of coal and disappeared. *25.1.1916:* Register closed. *9.2.1916:* Posted missing.

21. THORNFIELD 1913-1915

O.N. 135483 488g 197n 160.0 x 26.1 x 9.8 feet
C. 2-cyl. by Ramage and Ferguson Ltd., Leith; 10 knots.

22.6.1913: Launched by Ramage and Ferguson Ltd., Leith (Yard No. 236) for the Zillah Shipping and Carrying Co. Ltd. (William A. Savage, manager), Liverpool as THORNFIELD. *15.7.1913:* Completed. *17.8.1915:* Captured by the German submarine U 38 and sunk by gunfire in the Irish Sea twenty five miles north north east of the Smalls whilst on a voyage from London to Peel with a cargo of wooden huts. *31.8.1915:* Register closed.

22. ASHFIELD 1914-1954

O.N. 137401 436g 167n 142.5 x 26.0 x 11.5 feet
T. 3-cyl. by the Lytham Shipbuilding and Engineering Co. Ltd., Lytham; 10 knots.

25.7.1914: Launched by the Lytham Shipbuilding and Engineering Co. Ltd., Lytham (Yard No. 490) for the Zillah Shipping and Carrying Co. Ltd. (William A. Savage, manager), Liverpool as ASHFIELD. *3.10.1914:* Completed. *2.8.1949:* Owners became the Zillah Shipping Co. Ltd. (William A. Savage Ltd., manager), Liverpool. *3.4.1954:* Arrived at Llanelli for breaking up by the Rees Shipbreaking Co. Ltd. *23.7.1954:* Register closed.

Ashfield
John Clarkson

23. SILVERFIELD 1915-1954

O.N. 137436 436g 165n 142.5 x 26.0 x 11.5 feet
T. 3-cyl. by the Lytham Shipbuilding and Engineering Co. Ltd., Lytham; 10 knots.

2.2.1915: Launched by the Lytham Shipbuilding and Engineering Co. Ltd., Lytham (Yard No. 508) for the Zillah Shipping and Carrying Co. Ltd. (William A. Savage, manager), Liverpool as SILVERFIELD. *30.3.1915:* Completed. *2.8.1949:* Owners became the Zillah Shipping Co. Ltd. (William A. Savage Ltd., manager), Liverpool. *4.5.1954:* Arrived at Preston for breaking up by T.W. Ward Ltd. *18.7.1954:* Register closed.

24. LIMESFIELD 1916-1918

O.N. 137523 427g 160n 142.2 x 26.0 x 11.5 feet
T. 3-cyl. by the Lytham Shipbuilding and Engineering Co. Ltd., Lytham; 10 knots.

4.3.1916: Launched by the Lytham Shipbuilding and Engineering Co. Ltd., Lytham (Yard No. 518) for the Zillah Shipping and Carrying Co. Ltd. (William A. Savage, manager), Liverpool as LIMESFIELD. *28.10.1916:* Completed. *7.2.1918:* Captured by the German submarine UB 57 and sunk by gunfire twenty four miles south east by east from Douglas whilst on a voyage from Belfast to Preston with a cargo of cotton waste. *22.2.1918:* Register closed.

25. BRIARFIELD 1920-1955

O.N. 143669 446g 172n 142.2 x 26.0 x 11.5 feet
T. 3-cyl. by the Lytham Shipbuilding and Engineering Co. Ltd., Lytham; 10 knots.

20.5.1920: Launched by the Lytham Shipbuilding and Engineering Co. Ltd., Lytham (Yard No. 579) for the Zillah Shipping and Carrying Co. Ltd. (William A. Savage Ltd., manager), Liverpool as BRIARFIELD. *9.1920:* Completed. *2.8.1949:* Owners became the Zillah Shipping Co. Ltd. (William A. Savage Ltd., manager), Liverpool. *11.6.1955:* Arrived at Troon for breaking up by the West of Scotland Shipbreaking Co. Ltd.

Briarfield *W.S.P.L. Cochrane collection*

26. BEECHFIELD 1922-1955

O.N. 145912 449g 175n 142.0 x 25.9 x 11.4 feet
T. 3-cyl. by the Lytham Shipbuilding and Engineering Co. Ltd., Lytham.

17.11.1921: Launched by the Lytham Shipbuilding and Engineering Co. Ltd., Lytham (Yard No. 590) for the Zillah Shipping and Carrying Co. Ltd. (William A. Savage Ltd., managers), Liverpool as BEECHFIELD. *30.1.1922:* Completed. It was originally intended to name her OAKFIELD. *2.8.1949:* Owners became the Zillah Shipping Co. Ltd. (William A. Savage Ltd., manager), Liverpool. *16.12.1955:* Arrived at Troon for breaking up by the West of Scotland Shipbreaking Co. Ltd.

Beechfield *E.N. Taylor*

27. GORSEFIELD 1922-1958

O.N. 147177 628g 250n 175.0 x 28.2 x 11.2 feet
T. 3-cyl. by the Lytham Shipbuilding and Engineering Co. Ltd., Lytham.

21.10.1922: Launched by the Lytham Shipbuilding and Engineering Co. Ltd., Lytham (Yard No. 605) for the Zillah Shipping and Carrying Co. Ltd. (William A. Savage Ltd., managers), Liverpool as GORSEFIELD. *20.12.1922:* Completed. It was originally intended to name her ELMFIELD. *2.8.1949:* Owners became the Zillah Shipping Co. Ltd. (William A. Savage Ltd., manager), Liverpool. *14.6.1958:* Arrived at Preston for breaking up by T.W. Ward Ltd.

Gorsefield *Fotoflite incorporating Skyfotos*

Heatherfield *John Clarkson*

Elmfield *John Clarkson*

28. HEATHERFIELD 1924-1936

O.N. 147261 447g 174n 142.4 x 26.0 x 11.5 feet
T. 3-cyl. by the Lytham Shipbuilding and Engineering Co. Ltd., Lytham, 9 knots.

22.4.1924: Launched by the Lytham Shipbuilding and Engineering Co. Ltd., Lytham (Yard No. 644) for the Zillah Shipping and Carrying Co. Ltd. (William A. Savage Ltd., managers), Liverpool as HEATHERFIELD. *17.6.1924:* Completed. *25.1.1936:* Wrecked during fog one mile north of Robin Hood's Bay, Yorkshire whilst on a voyage from London to the Tees with a cargo of scrap iron. *16.4.1937:* Register closed.

29. ELMFIELD 1925-1955

O.N. 147331 450g 175n 142.5 x 25.9 x 11.5 feet
T. 3-cyl. by the Lytham Shipbuilding and Engineering Co. Ltd., Lytham.

8.7.1925: Launched by the Lytham Shipbuilding and Engineering Co. Ltd., Lytham (Yard No. 674) for the Zillah Shipping and Carrying Co. Ltd. (William A. Savage Ltd., managers), Liverpool as ELMFIELD. *3.10.1925:* Completed. *2.8.1949:* Owners became the Zillah Shipping Co. Ltd. (William A. Savage Ltd., manager), Liverpool. *15.2.1955:* Arrived at Preston for breaking up by T.W. Ward Ltd.

Penstone *John Clarkson*

30. PENSTONE 1926-1948

O.N. 149598 267g 100n 120.0 x 22.1 x 9.1 feet
C. 2-cyl. by the Manchester Dry Docks Co. Ltd., Ellesmere Port; 9 knots.

8.6.1925: Launched by the Manchester Dry Docks Co. Ltd., Ellesmere Port (Yard No. 74). She had been laid down for the builder's own account in 1919. *27.8.1926:* Completed for the Zillah Shipping and Carrying Co. Ltd. (William A. Savage Ltd., managers), Liverpool as PENSTONE. *31.7.1948:* Sunk in collision with the Norwegian motor vessel VILLANGER (4,884/29) about three miles south of the Northwest Light Vessel, Liverpool Bay whilst on a voyage from Penmaenmawr to Preston with a cargo of stone. *28.8.1948:* Register closed.

31. AMY SUMMERFIELD 1927-1951

O.N. 143718 407g 159n 143.2 x 25.1 x 11.6 feet
C. 2-cyl. by Day, Summers and Co. Ltd., Southampton; 9 knots.

11.1.1921: Launched by Day, Summers and Co. Ltd., Southampton (Yard No. 187) for the Summerfield Steamship Co. Ltd., Liverpool as AMY SUMMERFIELD. *7.3.1921:* Completed. *14.3.1927:* Acquired by the Zillah Shipping and Carrying Co. Ltd. (William A. Savage Ltd., manager), Liverpool. *2.8.1949:* Owners became the Zillah Shipping Co. Ltd. (William A. Savage Ltd., manager), Liverpool. *23.3.1951:* Wrecked at Llighfaen Pier, Port Rivals, having arrived from Liverpool in ballast. *2.8.1951:* Register closed.

32. APPLIANCE 1929-1949

O.N. 143741 200g 95n 97.4 x 23.0 x 9.7 feet
C. 2-cyl. by W.J. Yarwood and Sons Ltd., Northwich.

23.12.1920: Launched by W.J. Yarwood and Sons Ltd., Northwich (Yard No. 279) for the Woodend Steamship Co. Ltd. (James H. Cooper, manager), Widnes as APPLIANCE. *2.8.1921:* Completed. *5.6.1929:* Acquired by the Zillah Shipping and Carrying Co. Ltd. (William A. Savage Ltd., manager), Liverpool. *7.1949:* Sold to the Liverpool Derricking and Carrying Co. Ltd., Liverpool. *1963:* Deleted from Lloyds Register; believed to have been broken up.

33. ASSISTANCE 1929-1940

O.N. 118004 221g 86n 100.4 x 23.2 x 10.6 feet
C. 2-cyl. by Fisher and Co., Paisley.

31.1.1903: Launched by Scott and Sons, Bowling (Yard No. 160) for Joseph Monks and Co. Ltd., Liverpool as JENNIE. *20.2.1903:* Completed. *27.1.1920:* Sold to the Monroe Shipping Co. Ltd., Cardiff. *17.9.1925:* Owners became the Rena Shipping Co. Ltd. (Kenneth R. Monroe, manager), Liverpool. *20.12.1926:* Manager became Robert Monroe. *26.1.1928:* Capsized and sank after colliding with the Birkenhead Ferries' Landing Stage whilst on a voyage from Liverpool to Dumfries with general cargo. Her crew jumped clear but both the ship and the stage were damaged. *2.2.1928:* Refloated. Later declared a constructive total loss. *19.3.1928:* Register closed. *4.1928:* Sold to William Cooper and Sons Ltd., Widnes and repaired. *29.6.1928:* Re-registered as ASSISTANCE. *5.6.1929:* Acquired by the Zillah Shipping and Carrying Co. Ltd. (William A. Savage Ltd., manager), Liverpool. *14.11.1940:* Sold to the British Iron and Steel Corporation (Salvage) Ltd. (Arthur H. Turner, manager), Glasgow. *27.10.1949:* Sold to the Ministry of Transport (Arthur H. Turner, manager), London. *5.11.1949:* Sold to the Aiden Shipping Co. Ltd., Glasgow. *3.1951:* Broken up at Troon by the West of Scotland Shipbreaking Co. Ltd. *10.4.1951:* Register closed.

Adherance *W.S.P.L. Cochrane collection*

34. ACCORDANCE 1929-1941

O.N. 147234 259g 97n 100.8 x 23.0 x 10.0 feet
C. 2-cyl. by W.J. Yarwood and Sons Ltd., Northwich; 8 knots.

23.7.1920: Launched by W.J. Yarwood and Sons Ltd., Northwich (Yard No. 284) for the Accordance Shipping Co. Ltd., Liverpool (William Cooper, Widnes, manager) as ACCORDANCE. *24.9.1923:* Completed. *5.6.1929:* Acquired by the Zillah Shipping and Carrying Co. Ltd. (William A. Savage Ltd., manager), Liverpool. *22.2.1941:* Sold to the British Iron and Steel Corporation (Salvage) Ltd. (Arthur H. Turner, manager), Glasgow. *27.10.1949:* Sold to the Ministry of Transport (Arthur H. Turner, manager), London. *5.11.1949:* Sold to the Aiden Shipping Co. Ltd., Glasgow. *15.2.1951:* Breaking up commenced at Dalmuir by W.H. Arnott, Young Ltd.

35. ADHERANCE 1929-1940

O.N. 137387 218g 89n 99.8 x 22.3 x 10.0 feet
C. 2-cyl. by W.J. Yarwood and Sons Ltd., Northwich; 8 knots.

21.12.1913: Launched by W.J. Yarwood and Sons Ltd., Northwich (Yard No. 206) for James H. Cooper, Widnes as ADHERANCE. *17.7.1914:* Completed. *29.4.1915:* Owners became the Adherance Shipping Co. Ltd. (James H. Cooper, manager), Widnes. *5.6.1929:* Acquired by the Zillah Shipping and Carrying Co. Ltd. (William A. Savage Ltd., manager), Liverpool. *14.3.1940:* Sold to the Norwest Construction Co. Ltd. (J.S. Baucher, manager), Liverpool. *1.11.1941:* Sold to the British Iron and Steel Corporation (Salvage) Ltd. (Arthur H. Turner, manager), Glasgow. *10.12.1946:* Sold to John Lee (Isaac Stewart, manager), Belfast. *1951:* Sold to D.V. Howells and Sons Ltd., Milford Haven. *1963:* Sold to the Liverpool Derricking and Carrying Co. Ltd., Liverpool. *10.7.1963:* Arrived at Preston for breaking up by T.W. Ward Ltd. in tow of HAZELGARTH (230/1963).

Brackenfield *John Clarkson*

36. BRACKENFIELD 1937-1944

O.N. 164347 660g 253n 171.0 x 28.8 x 11.2 feet
T. 3-cyl. by the Lytham Shipbuilding and Engineering Co. Ltd., Lytham; 10 knots.

14.4.1937: Launched by the Lytham Shipbuilding and Engineering Co. Ltd., Lytham (Yard No. 840) for the Zillah Shipping and Carrying Co. Ltd. (William A. Savage Ltd., manager), Liverpool as BRACKENFIELD. *20.11.1937:* Completed. *10.6.1944:* Torpedoed and sunk by a German E-boat fifty miles south of the Nab Light Vessel whilst on a voyage from the Isle of Wight Convoy Assembly Point to 'Juno' Beach, opposite Courseulles, Normandy, with a cargo of ammunition and case oil. Of the 19 on board, only two were saved. *13.3.1945:* Register closed.

Broomfield *John Clarkson*

37. BROOMFIELD 1938-1955

O.N. 166230 660g 274n 176.7 x 28.8 x 11.2 feet
T. 3-cyl. by the Lytham Shipbuilding and Engineering Co. Ltd., Lytham; 10 knots.

18.11.1937: Launched by the Lytham Shipbuilding and Engineering Co. Ltd., Lytham (Yard No. 841) for the Zillah Shipping and Carrying Co. Ltd. (William A. Savage Ltd., manager), Liverpool as BROOMFIELD. *8.4.1938:*

Rowanfield *W.S.P.L. Cochrane collection*

Completed. *2.8.1949:* Owners became the Zillah Shipping Co. Ltd. (William A. Savage Ltd., manager), Liverpool. *23.6.1955:* Sold to William Cooper and Sons Ltd., Liverpool. *20.7.1944:* Renamed S.E. COOPER. *15.9.1965:* Arrived at Silloth in tow from Liverpool for breaking up by Ardmore Steel of Cumberland Ltd. *19.7.1966:* Register closed.

38. ROWANFIELD 1938-1957

O.N. 166248 495g 197n 142.5 x 27.2 x 11.4 feet
T. 3-cyl. by the Lytham Shipbuilding and Engineering Co. Ltd., Lytham; 10 knots.
1957: 6-cyl. 4S.C.S.A. oil engine by A/S Volund, Copenhagen, Denmark.

2.6.1938: Launched by the Lytham Shipbuilding and Engineering Co. Ltd., Lytham (Yard No. 849) for the Zillah Shipping and Carrying Co. Ltd. (William A. Savage Ltd., manager), Liverpool as ROWANFIELD. *24.8.1938:* Completed. *2.8.1949:* Owners became the Zillah Shipping Co. Ltd. (William A. Savage Ltd., manager), Liverpool. *2.1957:* Sold to Rederiet Kystfart A/S (O.E.F. Rasmussen, manager), Copenhagen, Denmark, re-engined and renamed ROWAN. 1959: Owners became Rederiet Rowan I/S. *1963:* Manager became Jens C. Hansen, Copenhagen. *1964:* Sold to Clementino Benoliel de Carvalho, Panama and renamed ANTONIO MIGUEL. *1976:* Sold to Nikon Shipping Enterprises Ltd., Greece and renamed NICOLA. *1977:* Sold to Compania Naviera Sollube S.A. (Leros Island Hellas Co. Ltd., managers), Piraeus, Greece and renamed LEROS 1. *1981:* Renamed CAP CHRISTOS. *10.1983:* Reported to be in course of demolition by LA.RE.SUB. at Messina, Italy.

39. MAPLEFIELD 1941-1945

O.N. 166322 495g 205n 142.5 x 27.2 x 11.4 feet
T. 3-cyl. by the Lytham Shipbuilding and Engineering Co. Ltd., Lytham; 9 knots.

12.6.1941: Completed by the Lytham Shipbuilding and Engineering Co. Ltd., Lytham (Yard No. 864) for the Zillah Shipping and Carrying Co. Ltd. (William A. Savage Ltd., manager), Liverpool as MAPLEFIELD. *23.2.1945:* Sank in collision with the United States steamer GATEWAY CITY (5,432/1920) four miles east of St. Govan's Light, Pembrokeshire whilst on a voyage from Penmaenmawr and Holyhead to Swansea with a cargo of stone. *2.3.1945:* Register closed.

Larchfield *John Clarkson*

40. LARCHFIELD 1941-1957

O.N. 168803 493g 215n 142.5 x 27.2 x 11.4 feet
T. 3-cyl. by the Lytham Shipbuilding and Engineering Co. Ltd., Lytham; 9 knots.

11.6.1941: Launched by the Lytham Shipbuilding and Engineering Co. Ltd., Lytham (Yard No. 865) for the Zillah Shipping and Carrying Co. Ltd. (William A. Savage Ltd., manager), Liverpool as LARCHFIELD. *15.10.1941:* Completed. *2.8.1949:* Owners became the Zillah Shipping Co. Ltd. (William A. Savage Ltd., manager), Liverpool. *20.2.1957:* Arrived at Barrow-in-Furness for breaking up by T.W. Ward Ltd. *30.5.1957:* Register closed.

Hazelfield. *Welsh Industrial and Maritime Museum 2427/2476*

41. HAZELFIELD 1948-1959

O.N. 182412 692g 324n 183.8 x 28.9 x 11.4 feet
T. 3-cyl. by the Lytham Shipbuilding and Engineering Co. Ltd., Lytham.
1968: Fitted with oil engine 6-cyl. 4S.C.S.A. by Maschinenbau Kiel G.m.b.H., Kiel, West Germany.

18.8.1947: Launched by the Lytham Shipbuilding and Engineering Co. Ltd., Lytham (Yard No. 889) for the Zillah Shipping and Carrying Co. Ltd. (William A. Savage Ltd., manager), Liverpool as HAZELFIELD. *4.1948:* Completed. *2.8.1949:* Owners became the Zillah Shipping Co. Ltd. (William A. Savage Ltd., manager), Liverpool. *1959:* Sold to John S. Monks and Co. Ltd., Liverpool and renamed SPRAYVILLE. *1963:* Sold to Adamandia D. Kopsafti, Piraeus, Greece and renamed FOULI. *1964:* Sold to C., G. and A. Potamianos, Piraeus and renamed AGHIOS GERASSIMOS. *1968:* Fitted with oil engine. *1976:* Sold to S. Efstathiou and others, Piraeus and renamed AGIOS GERASSIMOS. *1976:* Sold to Anas Shipping Co. Ltd., Piraeus. *1978:* Sold to Mak Lines Co. Ltd., Piraeus. *1979:* Sold to Kymi Shipping Co. Ltd. (M. Michailides and Co., managers), Piraeus. *10.1979:* Foundered in heavy weather off Palmorola Island, west of Naples whilst carrying a cargo of contraband cigarettes.

Dransfield *Keith Byass*

42. DRANSFIELD 1949-1955

O.N. 145595 650g 249n 175.2 x 28.2 x 11.2 feet
T. 3-cyl. by the Ailsa Shipbuilding Co. Ltd., Troon.

20.5.1921: Launched by the Ailsa Shipbuilding Co. Ltd., Troon (Yard No. 381) for the Light Shipping Co. Ltd. (Ross and Marshall Ltd., managers), Greenock as ARCLIGHT. *10.1921:* Completed. *1933:* Sold to Gilchrists Traders (Steamships) Ltd. (F.B. Johnston, managers), Liverpool and renamed FIRE QUEEN. *1936:* Managers became Robert Gilchrist and Co. *1943:* Owners became Coast Lines Ltd., Liverpool. *1945:* Renamed ORKNEY COAST. *1949:* Acquired by the Zillah Shipping Co. Ltd. (William A. Savage Ltd., manager), Liverpool and renamed DRANSFIELD. *10.11.1955:* Arrived at Troon for breaking up by the West of Scotland Shipbreaking Co. Ltd.

43. FAIRFIELD 1950-1955

O.N. 147311 801g 313n 190.5 x 32.1 x 11.7 feet
T. 3-cyl. by A. Hall and Co. Ltd., Glasgow.

24.2.1925: Launched by the John Duthie Torry Shipbuilding Co., Aberdeen (Yard No. 464) for the South Wales and Liverpool Steamship Co. Ltd. (Robert Gilchrist and Co., managers), Liverpool as PORTIA. *4.1925:* Completed. *1943:* Owners became Coast Lines Ltd., Liverpool. *1945:* Renamed SHETLAND COAST. *1946:* Owners became Michael Murphy (1937) Ltd., Dublin and renamed PORTIA. *1950:* Acquired by the Zillah Shipping Co. Ltd. (William A. Savage Ltd., manager), Liverpool and renamed FAIRFIELD. *13.11.1955:* Arrived at Troon for breaking up by the West of Scotland Shipbreaking Co. Ltd.

Caldyfield *John Clarkson*

44. CALDYFIELD 1952-1955

O.N. 143533 879g 374n 200.0 x 30.8 x 13.2 feet
T. 3-cyl. by Ross and Duncan, Govan; 10 3/4 knots.

27.11.1920: Launched by the Dublin Dockyard Co. Ltd., Dublin (Yard No. 105) for Michael Murphy Ltd. (Joseph O'Dowd, manager), Dublin as FINOLA. *3.2.1921:* Completed. *1931:* Manager became Sir Alfred H. Read. *1937:* Owner became the British and Irish Steam Packet Co. (1936) Ltd., Dublin. *5.1939:* Owners became Coast Lines Ltd., Liverpool. *3.6.1939:* Renamed GLAMORGAN COAST. *20.2.1947:* Owners became British Channel Traders Ltd., London and renamed STUART QUEEN. *1947:* Owners became Queenship Navigation Ltd., London. *1952:* Acquired by the Zillah Shipping Co. Ltd. (William A. Savage Ltd., manager), Liverpool and renamed CALDYFIELD. *14.9.1955:* Arrived at Preston for breaking up by T.W. Ward Ltd.

45. WESTFIELD 1952-1956

O.N. 149158 496g 223n 161.2 x 27.6 x 10.0 feet
T. 3-cyl. by the North Eastern Marine Engineering Co. Ltd., Sunderland.

30.4.1935: Launched by the Furness Shipbuilding Co. Ltd., Haverton Hill-on-Tees (Yard No. 245) for the Tyne-Tees Steam Shipping Co. Ltd., Newcastle-upon-Tyne as CRAGSIDE. *1946:* Renamed ELYSIAN COAST. *1952:* Acquired by the Zillah Shipping Co. Ltd. (William A. Savage Ltd., manager), Liverpool and renamed WESTFIELD. *30.6.1956:* Arrived at Preston for breaking up by T.W. Ward Ltd.

Seen passing under Irlam Viaduct on the Manchester Ship Canal, **Westfield** had long hatches which made her particularly useful for carrying locomotives from Manchester to Dublin for Coras Iompar Eireann. The structure aft was added during the war to house D.E.M.S. gunners. *K. Cunnington*

Northfield *Keith Byass*

46. NORTHFIELD 1953-1956

O.N. 163319 781g 429n 195.0 x 30.7 x 12.4 feet
T. 3-cyl. by David Rowan and Co. Ltd., Glasgow.

26.1.1933: Launched by the Burntisland Shipbuilding Co. Ltd., Burntisland (Yard No. 174) for the London and Channel Islands Steamship Co. Ltd. (Cheeswright and Ford, managers), London as LONDON QUEEN. *2.1933:* Completed. *1938:* Owners became the British Channel Islands Shipping Co. Ltd., London. *1947:* Owners became British Channel Traders Ltd., London. *1947:* Owners became the Queenship Navigation Ltd., London. *1948:* Owners became the Belfast, Mersey and Manchester Steamship Co. Ltd., Liverpool and renamed STORMONT. *1950:* Renamed CAVAN. *1953:* Acquired by the Zillah Shipping Co. Ltd. (William A. Savage Ltd., manager), Liverpool and renamed NORTHFIELD. *31.3.1956:* Arrived at Preston for breaking up by T.W. Ward Ltd.

47. FRESHFIELD 1954-1961

O.N. 185488 518g 316n 186.5 x 28.8 x 11.7 feet
Oil engine 8-cyl. 4S.C.S.A. by Klöckner-Humboldt-Deutz A.G., Koln-Deutz, West Germany.
12.1969: Oil engine 7-cyl. 2S.C.S.A. by A/S Wichmann, Rubbestadneset, Norway; 10 knots.

4.3.1954: Launched by Ijsselwerf Scheepswerf en Machinefabriek N.V., Rotterdam, Holland (Yard No. 103) for the Zillah Shipping Co. Ltd. (William A. Savage Ltd., manager), Liverpool as FRESHFIELD. She had been ordered by N.V. Scheepvaart Maatschappij Rotterdam, Rotterdam. *28.5.1954:* Completed. *10.11.1961:* Whilst at anchor in thick fog, run down and sunk by the motor vessel THE LADY GWENDOLEN (1,166/1953) near the C19 buoy in the Crosby Channel, River Mersey whilst on a voyage from Par to Runcorn with a cargo of china clay. *19.11.1961:* Raised and beached near Egremont. *8.12.1961:* Refloated and drydocked. Later declared a constructive total loss. *12.5.1962:* Wreck sold to Lars Rej Johansen, Oslo, Norway. *24.7.1962:* Left Liverpool in tow for Haugesund where she was repaired. *8.1962:* Renamed JOIKA. *26.6.1963:* Entered service after repairs. *1964:* Owners became Joika I/S (Lars Rej Johansen and Knut A. Knutsen, managers), Oslo. *1965:* Sold to Lorentz Storesund and Sønner, Haugesund, Norway and renamed ARNHOLT. *1968:* Owners became Sameie L. Storesund and Sønner and Farnes and Tangen (Lorentz Storesund and Sønner, managers), Haugesund. *12.1969:* Fitted with new engine. *1971:* Sold to Monrad Saetre Partrederi, Mastrevik, Norway and renamed BYRDING. *1977:* Sold to Haeroy-Haukenes Partrederi, Fedje, Norway. *1980:* Sold to A/S Fiskernes Bank Kystens Bank, Bergen, Norway. *1981:* Sold to Speed Shipping Ltd., London and registered at Georgetown, Cayman Islands. *1989:* Sold to Byron Shipping Ltd. (Rederi A/B Hasting, managers), Malmo, Sweden, registered at Kingstown, St. Vincent and the Grenadines and renamed MALY. *1991:* Sold to Star Shipping Co. Ltd., Kingstown, St. Vincent and the Grenadines and renamed BIRD. *1993:* Sold to Niusset Maritime Inc., Panama and renamed SEABEC. *1.10.1993:* Foundered in position 36.35 N by 02.46 W after her cargo of containers shifted whilst on a voyage from Barcelona to Genoa.

Oatfield *John Clarkson*

48. OATFIELD 1954-1966

O.N. 185496 538g 360n 175.4 x 27.2 x 10.7 feet
Oil engine 8-cyl. 4S.C.S.A. by Maschinenbau Kiel A.G., Kiel, West Germany; 10 knots.

10.4.1952: Launched by N.V. Scheepswerf 'De Waal' N.V., Zaltbommel, Holland (Yard No. 647) for N.V. Rederij E. en H. van der Kamp, Zwolle, Holland as PIETER HUBERT. *16.7.1952:* Completed. *6.1954:* Acquired by the Zillah Shipping Co. Ltd. (William A. Savage Ltd., manager), Liverpool and renamed OATFIELD. *19.7.1966:* Sold to Y.N. and G.N. Vamvounis, Milos, Greece and renamed SOPHIA. *1974:* Sold to Kaglis Brothers and Stelios Afentakis, Piraeus, Greece and renamed PAVLINA. *1975:* Sold to Thalis Shipping Co., Piraeus and renamed THALIS. *1977:* Renamed LINTA. *1977:* Sold to Madih A. Chami, Tripoli, Lebanon and renamed SARAA. *1984:* Sold to Mohamed K. Moushrit, Tripoli, Lebanon, renamed TAREK M, and subsequently AMANI and FAWAZ. *1985:* Renamed GLORIA under the Cyprus flag. *10.8.1985:* Foundered after springing a leak in the engine room nine miles north west of Beirut whilst on a voyage from Beirut to Limassol with general cargo.

49. FOXFIELD 1954-1966

O.N. 185508 546g 260n 180.2 x 30.4 x 10.8 feet
Oil engine 6-cyl. 4S.C.S.A. by N.V. Werkspoor, Amsterdam, Holland; 10 knots.

13.10.1951: Launched by N.V. Ferus Smit v/h Firma J. Smit and Zoon, Foxhol, Holland (Yard No. 112) for N.V. Scheepvaart Onderneming Kustverkeer (W.H. James and Co's Scheepvaart en Handelmaats N.V., managers), Rotterdam, Holland as LEEMANS. *19.1.1952:* Completed. *11.1954:* Acquired by the Zillah Shipping Co. Ltd. (William A. Savage Ltd., manager), Liverpool and renamed FOXFIELD. *6.4.1966:* Owners became Burns and Laird Lines Ltd., Glasgow and later renamed LAIRDSFOX. *1.10.1971:* Managers became P. and O. Short Sea Shipping Ltd., Liverpool. *28.9.1973:* Owners became the Belfast Steamship Co. Ltd. (Coast Lines Ltd., managers), Belfast. *31.3.1975:* Managers became P. & O. Ferries. *15.11.1977:* Sold to James Henry Ramagge, Panama and renamed LILAIDA. *1978:* Owners became Naviera Lilaida S.A., Panama. *24.8.1989:* Left Gibraltar where she had been laid up since 15.7.1988 in tow for Cadiz. *27.8.1989:* Arrived at Cadiz. *9.1988:* Broken up by Sauvementos y Desquaoles S.A. at Puerto de Santa Maria.

Foxfield *Fotoflite incorporating Skyfotos*

50. FALLOWFIELD 1954-1967

O.N. 185509 566g 265n 189.8 x 29.6 x 10.5 feet
Oil engine 8-cyl. 4S.C.S.A. by Appingedammer Brons Motorenfabriek N.V., Appingedam, Holland; 11 knots.

15.8.1953: Launched by Scheepswerven Gebroeder van Diepen N.V., Waterhuizen, Holland (Yard No. 927) for Rederij Poseidon (A. Kunst and J. Pekelder, managers), Groningen, Holland as MEDUSA. *6.10.1953:* Completed. *11.1954:* Acquired by the Zillah Shipping Co. Ltd. (William A. Savage Ltd., manager), Liverpool and renamed FALLOWFIELD. *31.12.1967:* Owners became Coast Lines Ltd., Liverpool. *1971:* Sold to Arklow Shipping Ltd. (James Tyrell), Arklow, Irish Republic and renamed ARKLOW BAY. *1971:* Owners became Bay Shipping Ltd., Arklow. *22.9.1973:* Foundered forty miles south west of St. Ann's Head, Pembrokeshire whilst making for Milford Haven after taking in water during a storm. Her cargo consisted of potash and other chemicals. Her crew was rescued.

Fallowfield *W.S.P.L.*

51. GREENFIELD 1955-1966

O.N. 185518 504g 256n 174.8 x 27.3 x 11.8 feet
Oil engine 8-cyl. 4S.C.S.A. by Motorenfabriek D. en J. Boot 'De Industrie', Alphen a/d Rijn, Holland; 11 knots.

4.4.1953: Launched by N.V. Scheepswerf Gebroeder van der Werf, Deest, Holland (Yard No. 249) for 'INVOTRA', Invoer-en Transport-Onderneming N.V., Rotterdam, Holland as COOLSINGEL. She was originally to have been named PIETER MAARTEN. *3.6.1953:* Completed. *1955:* Acquired by the Zillah Shipping Co. Ltd. (William A. Savage Ltd., manager), Liverpool and renamed GREENFIELD. *8.7.1966:* Owners became Burns and Laird Lines Ltd., Glasgow and renamed LAIRDSFIELD. *6.2.1970:* Capsized and sank one mile east of the Tees Fairway Buoy whilst on a voyage from Middlesbrough to Cork with a cargo of steel. Her crew of ten was lost. *24.2.1970:* Refloated by Risdon, Beazley Ltd., subsequently drydocked, sold to Cramlington and District Metals Ltd. and resold to Michael Baum and Co. Ltd. for whom she was broken up at Middlesbrough by Tees Marine Services Ltd.

Greenfield *Real Photographs 4212*

Brentfield *W.S.P.L. Brownell collection*

52. BRENTFIELD 1955-1958

O.N. 187114 1,263g 613n 223.8 x 37.6 x 15.0 feet
Oil engine 7-cyl. 2S.C.S.A. by George Clark and North Eastern Marine (Sunderland) Ltd., Sunderland; 11 knots.

21.6.1955: Launched by George Brown and Co. (Marine) Ltd., Greenock (Yard No. 262) for the Zillah Shipping Co. Ltd. (William A. Savage Ltd., manager), Liverpool as BRENTFIELD. *10.1955:* Completed. *4.12.1958:* Owners

Grangefield *A. Duncan*

became Coast Lines Ltd., Liverpool. *1.1959:* Renamed SPANIEL. *1.1.1965:* Owners became Burns and Laird Lines Ltd., Glasgow. *9.9.1968:* Owners became Coast Lines Ltd., Liverpool. *1970:* Owners became Coast Lines (Services) Ltd., Liverpool. *1.10.1971:* Managers became P. & O. Short Sea Shipping Ltd. *1.6.1972:* Owners became the Belfast Steamship Co. Ltd. (Coast Lines Ltd., managers), Belfast. *29.10.1973:* Sold to the Isle of Man Steam Packet Co. Ltd., Douglas and later renamed CONISTER. *1981:* Sold to Asturamerican Shipping Co. Inc., Panama. *29.9.1981:* Arrived at Aviles, Spain en route to San Juan de Nieva where she was broken up by Desguaces y Salvamentos S.A.

53. GRANGEFIELD 1955-1967

O.N. 187101 504g 226n 174.8 x 27.3 x 11.8 feet
Oil engine 8-cyl. 4S.C.S.A. by Motorenfabriek 'De Industrie', Alphen a/d Rijn, Holland.

22.5.1954: Launched by N.V. Scheepswerf Gebroeder van der Werf, Deest, Holland (Yard No. 251) for 'INVOTRA', Invoer-en Transport-Onderneming N.V., Rotterdam, Holland as STATENSINGEL. *3.1955:* Acquired by the Zillah Shipping Co. Ltd. (William A. Savage Ltd., manager), Liverpool and renamed GRANGEFIELD. *31.12.1967:* Owners became Coast Lines Ltd., Liverpool. *4.1968:* Owners became the Tyne-Tees Steam Shipping Co. Ltd., Newcastle-upon-Tyne. *1969:* Sold to the Transen Shipping Corporation, Panama. *1973:* Sold to the Trans Sea Shipping Corporation, Panama and renamed SEA GOBLIN. *1978:* Sold to Terra Investment and Trading Co., Panama (Henry Corrales General Shipping, Tampa, Florida, U.S.A.). *1979:* Sold to the Julianna Shipping Co. S.A., Panama and renamed JULIANNA. Still listed in Lloyds Register (April 1997).

Edgefield *W.S.P.L.*

54. EDGEFIELD 1956-1965

O.N. 187129 573g 293n 202.8 x 30.6 x 11.6 feet
Oil engine 6-cyl. 4S.C.S.A. by N.V. Werkspoor, Amsterdam, Holland.

26.11.1955: Launched by N.V. Noord-Nederlandsche Scheepswerven N.V., Groningen, Holland (Yard No. 278) for N.V. Spoorhout, 'sGravenhage, Holland as SPOLESTO. *18.1.1956:* Completed. *3.1956:* Acquired by the Zillah Shipping Co. Ltd. (William A. Savage Ltd., manager), Liverpool and renamed EDGEFIELD. *1.1965:* Sold to Marine Transport Services Ltd., Cobh, Irish Republic and renamed SARSFIELD. *6.1970:* Sold to Chesham Shipping Ltd. (Briggs Shipbrokers and Agents Ltd., managers), London and renamed VALERIE B. *1971:* Owners became Windridge Ltd. (Briggs Shipbrokers and Agents Ltd., managers), London. *1973:* Sold to Georges Dupenois, Ashburton, Devon and renamed ROSEMARY D. *1974:* Sold to Silloth Shipping Ltd., Annan, Dumfries-shire and renamed SILLOTH TRADER. *1980:* Sold to Evan Thomas Radcliffe, Cardiff and renamed RADCLIFFE TRADER. *11.1983:* Sold to Richard Spencer West, Goes, Holland and renamed MIRABELLE under the Panama flag. *2.3.1984:* Grounded after striking a submerged object at Guajira, Columbia in position 12.08 N by 71.08 W whilst on a voyage from Aruba to Cartagena. *6.3.1984:* Declared a constructive total loss and subsequently broken up.

Earlsfield leaving Jersey on 2nd September 1956.
Dave Hocquard

55. EARLSFIELD 1956-1967

O.N. 169238 635g 333n 199.8 x 30.2 x 12.1 feet
Oil engine 6-cyl. 4S.C.S.A. by N.V. Werkspoor, Amsterdam, Holland.

28.6.1952: Launched by Bodewes Scheepswerven N.V., Martenshoek, Holland (Yard No. 396) for the Coquet Shipping Co. Ltd. (Anthony and Bainbridge Ltd., managers), Newcastle-upon-Tyne as COQUETDYKE. *8.1952:* Completed. *1956:* Acquired by the Zillah Shipping Co. Ltd. (William A. Savage Ltd., manager), Liverpool and renamed EARLSFIELD. *31.12.1967:* Owners became Coast Lines Ltd., Liverpool. *1969:* Sold to R.S. Briggs and Co. (Shipping) Ltd., London and renamed KATIE H. *1971:* Owners became Seabright Shipping Ltd. (Briggs Shipbrokers and Agents Ltd., managers), London. *7.3.1972:* Sank about eight miles north of the Noord Hinder Lightvessel in position 51.48 N by 02.43 E after colliding with the Belgian motor fishing vessel ZEEPAREL whilst on a voyage from Rotterdam to London with a cargo of fertiliser. One member of her crew was lost.

Birchfield *W.S.P.L.*

56. BIRCHFIELD 1956-1958

O.N. 187140 1,265g 611n 223.8 x 37.4 x 15.0 feet
Oil engine 7-cyl. 2S.C.S.A. by George Clark and North Eastern Marine (Sunderland) Ltd., Sunderland; 10 knots.

2.2.1956: Launched by the Ardrossan Dockyard Ltd., Ardrossan (Yard No. 422) for the Zillah Shipping Co. Ltd. (William A. Savage Ltd., manager), Liverpool as BIRCHFIELD. *7.1956:* Completed. *4.12.1958:* Owners became Coast Lines Ltd., Liverpool. *1.1959:* Renamed POINTER. *1.1.1965:* Owners became Burns and Laird Lines Ltd., Glasgow. *9.9.1968:* Owners became Coast Lines Ltd., Liverpool. *1970:* Owners became Coast Lines (Services) Ltd., Liverpool. *1.10.1971:* Managers became P. & O. Short Sea Shipping Ltd. *1.6.1972:* Owners became the Belfast Steamship Co. Ltd. (Coast Lines Ltd., managers), Belfast. *31.3.1975:* Managers became P. & O. Ferries. *6.8.1975:* Sold to the Isthmian Navigation Co. Ltd., Limassol, Cyprus (Hellenic Mediterranean Lines Co. Ltd., Piraeus, Greece, managers) and renamed TAURUS III. *1984:* Sold to Phalarope Shipping Ltd., Valletta, Malta. *1984:* Sold to Larnaca Project S. de R.L., Honduras and renamed LARNACA TOWN. *1985:* Renamed MINA. *16.5.1986:* At Perama, Greece for breaking up.

57. HOLMFIELD 1957-1967

O.N. 187157 488g 250n 169.2 x 27.6 x 10.5 feet
Oil engine 6-cyl. 4S.C.S.A. by Appingedammer Brons Motorenfabriek N.V., Appingedam, Holland; 9 knots.

8.12.1956: Launched by Haarlemsche Scheepsbouw. Maatschappij N.V., Haarlem, Holland (Yard No. 546) for N.V. Scheepvaart en Exploitatie Bedrijfmaats C. Bos, Schiedam, Holland as OOSTER EEMS. *28.2.1957:* Completed for the Zillah Shipping Co. Ltd. (William A. Savage Ltd., manager), Liverpool as HOLMFIELD. *1967:* Sold to Alexios G. Alexiades and Prodromos Iliadis, Volos, Greece and renamed PRODROMOS. *1972:* Sold to A. Fappas and A. Saraganidas, Volos. *1974:* Sold to Dimitrios Fappas, Thessaloniki, Greece and renamed DIMITRIOS F. *1974:* Sold to C. Tzamtzis and others, Thessaloniki and renamed CONSTANTINOS TZ. *1974:* Renamed KOSTRAS TZAMTZIS. *1982:* Broken up in Greece.

Fernfield *W.S.P.L.*

58. FERNFIELD 1958-1967

O.N. 301284 561g 266n 200.0 x 29.7 x 12.1 feet
Oil engine 6-cyl. 4S.C.S.A. by N.V. Werkspoor, Amsterdam, Holland; 10 knots.

25.9.1954: Launched by Scheepswerven Gebroeders van Diepen N.V., Waterhuizen, Holland (Yard No. 930) for N.V. Zuid-Hollandsche Scheepvaart Maatschappij, Rotterdam, Holland as HAAKSBERGEN. *20.11.1954:* Completed. *30.9.1958:* Acquired by the Zillah Shipping Co. Ltd. (William A. Savage Ltd., manager), Liverpool and renamed FERNFIELD. *31.12.1967:* Owners became Coast Lines Ltd., Liverpool. *1971:* Owners became Coast Lines (Management) Ltd., Liverpool. *1971:* Sold to James Tyrell Ltd., Arklow, Irish Republic and renamed SHEVRELL. *1972:* Sold to Enterprise de Navigation de l'Isle Incorporated, Iles aux Coudres, Canada and renamed COUDRE DE L'ILE. *15.6.1988:* Sank following a collision in fog with the motorship ALGOWEST (20,309/82) in the St. Lawrence off Pointe au Boisvert in position 48.26 N by 69.12 W whilst on a voyage from Sept Isles to St. Catharines with a cargo of scrap metal. One of her crew of nine was lost.

Glenfield *W.S.P.L. Brownell collection*

59. GLENFIELD 1958-1959

O.N. 167630 567g 257n 176.5 x 28.1 x 11.8 feet
Oil engine 5-cyl. 2S.C.S.A. by British Auxiliaries Ltd., Glasgow.

10.6.1940: Launched by the Burntisland Shipbuilding Co. Ltd., Burntisland (Yard No. 245) for the British Channel Islands Shipping Co. Ltd., London as CHANNEL QUEEN. *9.1940:* Completed. *1947:* Renamed CHANNEL COAST. *1958:* Acquired by the Zillah Shipping Co. Ltd. (William A. Savage Ltd., manager), Liverpool and renamed GLENFIELD. *1959:* Owners became the British Channel Islands Shipping Co. Ltd., London and renamed ALDERNEY COAST. *1966:* Sold to Nicolaos Grigoriou and others, Piraeus, Greece and renamed ASTRONAFTIS. *1972:* Owners became Nicolaos Grigoriou, S. Antoniades and others, Piraeus. *1975:* Renamed SEA HORSE. *1975:* Sold to Namar Shipping Ltd., Piraeus, Greece and renamed MASTRO COSTAS. *21.2.1976:* Arrived at Monrovia in tow after an engine breakdown during a voyage from Greece to Lagos and Apapa, and laid up. Developed leaks and towed out and beached west of Monrovia by the National Ports Authority.

Garthfield on 18th May 1961. *K. Le Scelleur*

60. GARTHFIELD 1960-1962

O.N. 165124 606g 318n 170.0 x 28.8 x 9.6 feet
Oil engine 6-cyl. 2S.C.S.A. by Atlas-Diesel A/B, Stockholm, Sweden; 9 knots.

14.10.1937: Launched by T. van Duivendijk's Scheepswerf N.V., Lekkerkerk, Holland (Yard No. 225) for William A. Wilson, Southampton as NGARUA. *1.1938:* Completed. *1939:* Sold to the Merchants Line Ltd., London. *1940:* Renamed SILVER COAST. *1943:* Owners became British Channel Traders Ltd., London. *1946:* Owners became Burns and Laird Lines Ltd., Glasgow and renamed LAIRDSOAK. *1960:* Acquired by the Zillah Shipping Co. Ltd. (William A. Savage Ltd., manager), Liverpool and renamed GARTHFIELD. *1962:* Sold to the Mediterranean Shipping Co. (Panajotis Vrangos, manager), Trieste, Italy and renamed KRIOS under the Greek flag. *1963:* Owner became Panajotis Vrangos ('Mesco' Mediterranean Shipping Co. Ltd., managers), Piraeus, Greece. *1968:* Owners became Spyrogiannis Kavadas and Co. ('Mesco' Mediterranean Shipping Co. Ltd., managers), Piraeus and renamed KYRIAKOULA K. *1974:* Sold to Georgios Andrias and Co., Thessaloniki, Greece and renamed DIMITRIOS II. *1992:* Deleted from *Lloyd's Register* owing to lack of information.

Fordfield *W.S.P.L. Brownell collection*

61. FORDFIELD 1960-1962

O.N. 301348 561g 267n 200.0 x 29.7 x 12.1 feet
Oil engine 6-cyl. 4S.C.S.A. by N.V. Werkspoor, Amsterdam, Holland.

9.1.1954: Launched by Scheepswerven Gebroeders van Diepen N.V., Waterhuizen, Holland (Yard No. 928) for N.V. Zuid-Hollandsche Scheepvaart Maatschappij, Rotterdam, Holland as EIBERGEN. *26.3.1954:* Completed. *7.1960:* Acquired by the Zillah Shipping Co. Ltd. (William A. Savage Ltd., manager), Liverpool and renamed FORDFIELD. *11.1.1962:* Capsized and sank in the English Channel ten miles south east of the Owers Light Vessel whilst on a voyage from the River Neath to Amsterdam with a cargo of coal.

Managed for The Shipping Controller and the Ministry of Shipping

1. WAR TAMAR 1919

O.N. 143127 469g 250n 157.2 x 26.1 x 11.0 feet
T.3-cyl. by the Shields Engineering and Drydock Co. Ltd., North Shields; 9 knots.

14.3.1919: Launched by Swan, Hunter and Wigham Richardson Ltd., Wallsend-on-Tyne (Yard No. 1115) for The Shipping Controller, London (William A. Savage Ltd., Liverpool, manager) as WAR TAMAR. *15.4.1919:* Completed. *14.6.1919:* Sold to Latus, Linsley and Co. Ltd., Hull. *16.10.1920:* Sold to the Devon Shipping Co. Ltd. (B.C. Ridd, manager), Cardiff. *7.4.1922:* Renamed CHALLACOMBE. *18.7.1923:* Sold to the Border Shipping Co. Ltd. (G.T. Gillie and Blair Ltd., manager), Newcastle-upon-Tyne. *26.9.1923:* Renamed BORDER FIRTH. *10.5.1939:* Sold to British Isles Coasters Ltd., Cardigan. *3.6.1939:* Renamed *EAST* COASTER. *17.7.1946:* Sold to the Barreto Shipping and Trading Co., Singapore and renamed HUNG SING. *28.5.1947:* Sold to Cheng Chiang Shipping Co. Ltd., Singapore. *10.1948:* Sold to the Rua Lumliang Co. Ltd., Bangkok, Siam and renamed CHAMPADAH. *1960:* Sold to P.T. Pelajaran Sinar Segara, Djakarta, Indonesia. *1961:* Renamed SINAR-DJAJA. *7.1989:* Deleted from Lloyds Register, continued existence in doubt.

2. WAR AVON 1919

O.N. 142774 501g 226n 142.4 x 26.1 x 10.9 feet
1937: 548g 274n 161.0 x 26.1 x 10.9 feet
C. 2-cyl. by Aitchison, Blair and Co. Ltd., Clydebank, Glasgow; 9 knots.

27.1.1919: Completed by the Ardrossan Dry Dock and Shipbuilding Co. Ltd., Ardrossan (Yard No. 302) for 'Neptunus' Société d'Armement (M. Smits and Co., managers), Antwerp, Belgium as INDEPENDANCE. She had been laid down for The Shipping Controller, London (William A. Savage Ltd., Liverpool, manager) as WAR AVON. *13.8.1921:* Sold to the General Steam Navigation Co. Ltd., London and renamed MAVIS. *18.4.1929:* Sold to James Fisher and Sons Ltd., Barrow-in-Furness. *1.6.1929:* Renamed SOUND FISHER. *1937:* Lengthened. *2.1939:* Sold to Empreza Internacional de Transportes Ltda., Rio de Janeiro, Brazil and renamed GUAREREMA. *4.3.1949:* Sunk in collision with a vessel reported as BRITANNIA inside Santos Bar, Ilha das Palmas, in position 23.59 S by 46.19 W whilst leaving Santos in ballast. She sank in position 23.59.54 S by 46.19.30 W.

3. EMPIRE TULIP 1940-1941

O.N. 167407 288g 144n 126.4 x 23.5 x 7.3 feet
Oil engine 4-cyl. 2S.C.S.A. by Appingedammer Brons Motorenfabriek N.V., Appingedam, Holland.
11.1964: Oil engine 6-cyl. 4S.C.S.A. by Bergius-Kelvin Co. Ltd., Glasgow.

9.3.1939: Launched by N.V. Scheepswerf Delfzijl N.V., v/h Gebroeders Sander, Delfzijl, Holland (Yard No. 158) for N. Engelsman, Delfzijl, Holland as PALLAS. *14.4.1939:* Completed. *5.12.1940:* Acquired by the Ministry of Shipping, London (Wiliam A. Savage Ltd., Liverpool, manager) and renamed EMPIRE TULIP. *1941:* Owners became the Ministry of War Transport. *1941:* Managers became Ross and Marshall Ltd., Glasgow. *1946:* Owners became the Ministry of Transport. *1947:* Sold to E.J. and W. Goldsmith Ltd., London and renamed GOLDGNOME. *1951:* Sold to Coastal Tankers Ltd. (Springwell Shipping Co. Ltd., managers), London. *1951:* Sold to the London and Rochester Trading Co. Ltd., Rochester and renamed INSISTENCE. *11.1964:* Fitted with new oil engine. *12.12.1970:* Demolition began by Flamecap Ltd., Rochester. Her engine was removed and fitted into the tug DRAGETTE (50/1947).

Empire Tulip at Swansea soon after the war. *National Maritime Museum N50203*

4. EMPIRE MAYMORN 1946-1947

O.N. 169388 390g 122n 144.0 x 27.1 x 7.7 feet
T. 3-cyl. by White's Marine Engineering Co. Ltd., Newcastle-upon-Tyne.

31.12.1945: Launched by Charles Hill and Sons Ltd., Bristol (Yard No. 336) for the Ministry of Transport, London (William A. Savage Ltd., Liverpool, manager) as EMPIRE MAYMORN. *1946:* Completed. *1947:* Sold to the Government of British Guiana, Georgetown, British Guiana and renamed MAZARUNI. *1966:* Owners became the Government of Guyana, Georgetown, Guyana. *1980:* Owners became the Government of the Republic of Guyana. *1989:* Deleted from Lloyds Register, continued existence in doubt.

5. EMPIRE MAYROVER 1946

O.N. 181262 394g 110n 144.0 x 27.1 x 8.0 feet
T. 3-cyl. by Amos and Smith Ltd., Hull.

1946: Completed by Cochrane and Sons Ltd., Selby (Yard No. 1306) for the Ministry of Transport, London (William A. Savage Ltd., Liverpool, manager) as EMPIRE MAYROVER. *1946:* Sold to the Ta Hing Co. (Hong Kong) Ltd. (Moller Line (U.K.) Ltd., managers), Hong Kong. *1949:* Renamed WA HING. *1948:* Sold to the India General Navigation and Railway Co. Ltd., Calcutta, India. *1949:* Renamed MUMTAZ. *1961:* Owners became Pakistan River Steamers Ltd., Dacca and later Narayanganj, East Pakistan. *1972:* Owners became Bangladesh River Steamers Ltd., Narayanganj, Bangladesh. *1975:* Owners became the Bangladesh Inland Water Transport Corporation, Bangladesh and renamed C5-203. *1976:* Broken up at Chittagong.

Nomenclature

Savage began naming his ships in the traditional way of honouring female members of his and shareholder's families. With the exception of MARGARITA and THELMA, these can be identified. There were also some more fanciful names, which sat less well on coal boats. SUMMERFIELD of 1913 inspired a system consisting of a tree name with the suffix FIELD which, with modification, was to see out the company's existence. After the Coast Lines take over, the new management varied this scheme in a way which retained its attractiveness, although the old style name BIRCHFIELD seems to have slipped through. Many of of the names were of real places, and those with an obvious Merseyside connection are listed below.

AQUILLA	Latin for eagle.
CALDYFIELD	Probably named after the old Wirral settlement of Caldy.
E. HAYWARD	Probably the wife or daughter of John W. Hayward J.P., a subscriber to the company.
FAIRFIELD	There are ten places of this name in England, including a hamlet on the Wirral and a district of Liverpool.
FALLOWFIELD	A south eastern district of Manchester
FRESHFIELD	Part of Formby, Lancashire.
G.A. SAVAGE	William Savage's father.
GREENFIELD	A village near Holywell, Flintshire.
OPHIR	An name from the Old Testament of a place where gold was obtained. Standard English would have the name pronounced "Oh-fer", but the crews persisted in referring to her as "Offer".
PENSTONE	An interesting departure from the usual naming practice, and commemorated the company's connection with Penmaenmawr stone.
PRISCILLA	William Savage's wife, née Caldwell.
SARAH BROUGH	Daughter or wife of Walter Brough, a Warrington baker and shareholder in the company.
SUMMERFIELD	The Summerfield family of Sankey Bridges were shareholders in the company and captained some of its ships.
WINIFRED	Daughter of J.W. Hayward who launched the vessel.
ZILLAH	The name is an obscure one, defined by the Shorter Oxford Dictionary as an administrative district in British India. It was chosen for a rather homely reason, however: it was William Savage's pet name for his wife Priscilla.

MISCELLANY

Many individuals and small companies in the Mersey ports became coaster owners, only to fade away without making a lasting mark on the shipping industry. Listing all of these would be a long, difficult and possibly profitless exercise, as in many case they left little trace of their business other than a name in a register. Those mentioned here are the more substantial operators who owned at least two coasters or who had one or more incidentally to other interests, which ranged from the liner trade to sand dredging. Also listed here are other Merseyside-based coastal shipping companies whose full history has not been included in this book, for reasons explained in the introduction.

John Bacon operated liner services from Liverpool and Preston to Wexford and Bristol Channel ports, buying his first steamer in 1865. As **John Bacon Ltd.** his company was acquired by F. H. Powell and Co. in October 1910, an event which presaged the formation in 1913 of **Bacon, Powell and Hough Lines Ltd.** Already large, this company went on to even greater things after 1917 when it became the core of Coast Lines Ltd. (q.v.)

The SNOW QUEEN (308/1921) was a regular sight in the Mersey between 1922 and 1934, when owned by **British Isles Transport Co. Ltd.** Managed by **William Buckley,** the company was associated with the **B.I. Transport Co. Ltd.** of London which owned MILLOCRAT (235/1921) and KENFINCH (113/1920). Both companies were involved in the grain trade of Joseph Rank, and SNOW QUEEN and MILLOCRAT were brand names for this miller's flour.

Snow Queen of British Isles Transport Co. Ltd. *John Clarkson*

Coast Lines Ltd. was formed in 1917 from Bacon, Powell and Hough Lines Ltd. which had been acquired by Owen Philipps' Royal Mail group. Driven by its new owner's aggressive acquisition policy it came to dominate the coastal liner trade, owning a huge fleet under its own name and its many subsidiaries. The only one of the latter to operate tramps out of Liverpool was the Zillah Shipping and Carrying Co. Ltd.

Coastal Motor Ships Ltd. of Wallasey acquired the Dutch-built coaster LORRAINE D (560/1957) in 1971. On 4th March 1973 her engines broke down whilst on a voyage from Warrenpoint to Garston. She was towed into the Mersey and, after being declared a constructive total loss, languished for many years in Birkenhead Docks where she was renamed ZIRCON in 1981 and GLENHAVEN in 1982. In 1984 the company was listed as managers of CAPECREST (746/1972) and MOUNTCREST (770/1972), but *Lloyds Register* was unable to contact the owners, and dropped them in 1986.

S.W. Coe and Co. Ltd. have been reluctantly excluded from this book on the grounds of space, as the company's history is tied up with that of William Ireland and T. J. Metcalf and Co. Ltd. of London, with whom the company was merged to form **Coe Metcalf**

Lorraine D of Coastal Motorships Ltd. laid up at Birkenhead. *Author*

Shipping Ltd., now **James Fisher and Sons (Liverpool) Ltd.**: Liverpool's last coaster owner, and almost its last shipowner. It is intended to devote a full book to the company.

Arthur Cook bought the iron SALISBURY (114/1876) in 1879, adding further steamers, of which several were built or engined locally, including CLYDE (296/1880), MERSEY (319/1882) and SEVERN (357/1883). He used them in the coastal cargo liner trade. In 1890 or 1891 the business became known as Rogers and Bright (q.v.) although the Cook family remained involved.

Joseph Crosfield and Sons Ltd. were soap manufacturers at Bank Quay, Warrington. The business was established in 1815, and depended on waterborne supplies of animal and vegetable oil transhipped in Liverpool, salt from the Weaver, coal from St. Helens, limestone from North Wales and timber to make soapboxes. Crosfields had a considerable fleet of sailing flats and later steam and motor barges which used the Upper Mersey and eventually the Manchester Ship Canal. Only one of these is known to have been a steam coaster, the MARJORIE (179/1903), bought in 1912 and sold in 1922, being lost on a coasting voyage when owned by Edward Nicholson Ltd.

William Darlington was one of many shipbrokers who dabbled in shipowning. He inherited from his father, John, a business in the Dock Road, Garston, which probably dated from the early years of this port. William Darlington bought the GLENMAY (154/1894) from Isle of Man owners in 1914, and continued to run her to the island. When he added the LINCOLNSHIRE (112/1867) in 1915 he took the precaution of forming a single-ship company to own her. The modest £1,000 capital of the **Lincolnshire Steamship Co. Ltd.** – almost all of which Darlington subscribed – reflected the modest cost of a tiny, 48-year old steamer. Having survived the war with his fleet intact, Darlington added the SODIUM (146/1887) in 1917, but unlike many contemporaries did not rush headlong into expensive purchases. LINCOLNSHIRE was probably used within the river and was sold in 1919, but Darlington did not judge the market so well with his other ships. GLENMAY was sold in August 1921 when coaster prices were plummeting, and at the same time SODIUM was unfortunate enough to be repossessed on behalf of her mortgagees, Parrs Bank, who were themselves in liquidation. Darlington then quietly returned to his shipbroking and agency work, handling the majority of coasters which called at Garston for coal during the 1920s.

John Esplen was a substantial shipowner, and after the First World War had some innovative vessels including the pioneering engines-aft bulk carriers BERWINDMOOR (5,232/1910) and BERWINDVALE (5,242/1911). Of steamers in the near-Continental trade he had AVON (534/1892) and MARIE (504/1864). MARIE disappeared in May 1895 with a cargo of flints from St. Valery to Runcorn, and AVON was lost in collision off the Lizard in October 1897 whilst bringing general cargo from Antwerp to Liverpool.

Another coastal shipowner involved exclusively in liner services was **Robert Gilchrist and Co.,** which began in business in Glasgow in 1824, operating a service of fast schooners between that port and Liverpool. The company moved its headquarters to Liverpool in 1862, and built its first steamer for the coastal trade in 1870, given the appropriate name FIRE KING (438/1870). Ownership of the fleet was complex, as vessels were registered in the names of Gilchrists themselves, of their Glasgow agents or of single ship companies. In 1929 the title **Gilchrists Traders (Steamships) Ltd.** was adopted for the Liverpool and Glasgow ships. Services were extended from Liverpool to South Wales in the 1880s, the **South Wales and Liverpool Steamship Co. Ltd.** being formed in 1886 and surviving until Gilchrists themselves were bought by Coast Lines Ltd. in April 1943. The four surviving ships were re-registered in Coast Lines ownership almost immediately and renamed as soon as wartime restrictions were lifted.

As discussed in the chapter on Thomas J. Sharp, **Henry M. Grayson** was a figure of considerable importance and wide interests in the Liverpool shipping industry. He also had short-term interests in a bewildering variety of ships, some bought to be repaired, others to be traded including hopper barges, tugs, wooden schooners and a wooden steam whaling ship, BALAENA (415/1872). The BALAENA and several other smaller craft were purchased from 1916 onwards and transferred to the ownership of the **Kymo Shipping Co. Ltd.** Deriving its name in part from that of its former manager **William B. Kyffin** of Birkenhead, this company engaged in lighterage, salvage and coaling operations around the Merseyside docks. Its considerable fleet was run down until only the BALAENA was left in 1933. Grayson also had financial interests in many small Merseyside shipping companies and a number of coasters passed through his ownership or management. The GROSVENOR (267/1908) was completed by his Garston yard and managed briefly by Graysons before passing to the Aberystwyth and Aberdovey Steam Packet Co. Ltd., another company in which the family had interests. The HOLYHEAD (196/1898) was bought in 1916 and traded until 1925.

Samuel Hough Ltd. was the third and smallest of the coastal liner trade companies whose 1913 amalgamation led eventually to the formation of Coast Lines Ltd. Hough acquired his first steamer in 1868, and ran a service from Liverpool to London calling at intermediate ports, which was worked jointly with F.H. Powell and Co.

William J. Ireland operated coasters under his own name and that of S. W. Coe and Co. Ltd. and it is the intention to describe his career in a book devoted to the latter company.

J. Johnson and Sons (Shipping) Ltd. had the dubious distinction of being one of the last Liverpool companies formed in order to own steam, as opposed to motor, coasters. HOLYHEAD (196/1898) was bought in 1947 and two years later renamed HOLLYHEAD. This was to match the HOLLYLEAF (301/1917) which had been acquired as HELIUM in 1948, and whose former owners, Imperial Chemical Industries Ltd., probably insisted on a change of name. HOLLYHEAD was broken up in 1951, but HOLLYLEAF found new owners in 1954. For its last year the company was known as **Johnson Bretland Ltd.**

W.S. Kennaugh and Co. began shipowning at Whitehaven in 1883, moving to Liverpool in the 1890s. The company is featured in W.S.S. Monograph No. 1: *W.S. Kennaugh & Co. and the West Coast Shipping Co. Ltd.*

Kilgour and Baker lasted just two years as shipowners. POINT LYNAS (460/1889) was acquired by the **Point Lynas Steamship Co. Ltd.** in 1900, but was wrecked off the coast of France whilst delivering South Wales coal to St. Brieuc on 29th December 1901. WESTBURY (403/1884) was bought in April 1900 and registered under the **Point Culver**

Hollyleaf of J. Johnson and Sons (Shipping) Ltd. *John Clarkson*

Steamship Co. Ltd. but sold in January 1902, without renaming, to Spanish owners via Alfred Rowland. In February 1901 Kilgour and Baker took delivery of the POINT CLEAR (507/1901) from Maryport, only to sell her in October to Alfred Read of F.H. Powell and Co. (q.v.).

Founded in 1905, **Kyle Transport Co. Ltd.** of Liverpool initially owned a modest fleet of ocean-going tramp steamers. In 1920, after some nine of these had passed through its ownership, the company suddenly changed direction and began to buy a very odd assortment of craft, some of which could be described as coasters. KILMARNOCK (613/1919) is discussed at length in the chapter on John Edwards, and was definitely converted to a coaster, but NEILSON (838/1903) had begun life as a hopper on the Tees. Three further acquisitions were also conversions, the motor vessels BARRETT (119/1916), DORIT (135/1915) and DYSERTH (119/1916) having being built for the Admiralty as X-lighters and quite possibly Liverpool's first motor coasters. All four were sold in 1923 and 1924, and with the subsequent departure of the last ocean-going tramp, the company ceased trading. Manager from 1913 was **Alexander Bicket,** who was a subscriber to other Liverpool companies in the coastal trade and was involved in the Alexandra Towing Co. Ltd.

Its name suggests that the activities of the **Liverpool Derricking and Carrying Co. Ltd.** were confined to the docks and river. The company did, however, have several small coasters or one-time coasters amongst its wooden and steel lighters: the EDDIE (235/1900) bought in 1938, FAWN (143/1897) in 1940, and in 1951 the ISLE ORNSAY (162/1905) which sank in Langton Dock when the wall of part of a disused dock shed collapsed on to her on 25th July 1958. Coopers' APPLIANCE and ADHERANCE were the company's last vessels, sold to breakers in 1963. Through manager Harold Edwards, the company had links with the Liverpool Screw Towing and Lighterage Co. Ltd.

Joseph Monks was, like neighbour William Savage, a Warrington flatman who made a considerable impact as a Liverpool coaster owner. The story of **Joseph Monks and Co. Ltd.,** together with that of his sons' company **John S. Monks and Co. Ltd.,** appears in W.S.S. Monograph No. 3: *Monks' Navy.*

Monroe Brothers Ltd. can trace its connections with Liverpool back to the acquisition of the fleet and office of Joseph Monks and Co. Ltd. in 1920. The Monroe family's complex shipowning interests are untangled in W.S.S. Monograph No. 5: *Monroe Brothers Shipowners.*

George Nelson and Sons, substantial owners of sailing vessels and steam coasters in the 1880s and 1890s, had offices in Liverpool after they took over management of Hume, Smith's coasters. However, they originated in Whitehaven, and have been considered as belonging to that port.

The **Norwest Construction Co. Ltd.** of Liverpool bought a number of small steam coasters and river steamers in 1940, including FAWN (143/1897) and ADHERANCE (218/1914), in connection with wartime construction or salvage work. All were sold in 1941.

Parry, Jones and Co. owned several large sailing ships and seemed to be planning a fleet of steamers when taking delivery of OWAIN TUDUR (227/1883). However, this remained their only steamer when sold to William Rowland in 1888.

F.H. Powell and Co. originated in 1830 as Cram, Powell and Co. and operated regular services between Liverpool and London and Liverpool and Bristol. Under its ambitious manager, Alfred Read, the company was instrumental in forming Bacon, Powell and Hough Lines Ltd. in 1913, giving the company, and its successor Coast Lines Ltd., its funnel colours and naming scheme.

R. and J.H. Rea are known both for their tugs, and for managing one of Liverpool's few fleets of coastal colliers, **Rea Shipping Co. Ltd.,** formed about 1902. Large vessels, operating mainly out of Cardiff and the North East Coast coal ports to France and elsewhere, they have been reluctantly excluded. The fleet was absorbed by Cory Colliers Ltd. in 1920.

In 1886 **Rogers and Bright** formed the **Volana Shipping Co. Ltd.** to trade between Liverpool and South Wales ports, later absorbing the steamers of Arthur Cook (q.v.). The Volana Shipping Co. Ltd. was itself bought by Owen Philipps' Royal Mail group in February 1917, and was merged with Coast Lines Ltd. on its foundation.

Thomas Ronald managed but one coaster, the RIVER TAY (510/1902), but is interesting for the manner in which he was quickly deprived of this. Early in January 1902 Ronald was instrumental in floating the **Steamship River Tay Co. Ltd.** to own the ship, but exactly a year later he resigned and was replaced as manager by Alfred Read of F.H. Powell and Co. (q.v.). Read and his associates acquired an overall majority of the little company's shares and this may be an example of corporate raiding. Ronald was an agent for the Liverpool and Clyde Steam Navigation Co. Ltd., managed by Charles MacIver and Co., and which operated a service between Glasgow, Greenock and Liverpool. Read was to become the driving force behind the formation of the massive Coast Lines group, and taking over the RIVER TAY may well have been a way of neutralising a rival service to that of his own company, F.H. Powell and Co.

Worth including if only for his marvellous name is **Summersgill Snoddy. James S. Snoddy** – a Warrington school teacher – acquired the steamer TURTLE (146/1893) in July 1907. In 1908 in conjunction with Summersgill Snoddy – a master mariner resident in Birkenhead and probably his father or brother – he formed the **Hamilton Shipping Co. Ltd.** to finance her, a company registered in Widnes. She came with a charter from Paton and Hendry of Glasgow to carry stones from Gourock to Liverpool. In 1909, the Hamilton company also took delivery of the ALYN (350/1909) from Greenock. On 14th January 1911 TURTLE foundered off Annalong having just left for Birkenhead with a cargo of potatoes. This disaster led not only to the winding up of the Hamilton Shipping Co. Ltd. but also to the sale of ALYN to Zillah early in 1911.

The grey-hulled coasters of **Spillers** were familiar on Merseyside, where their owners had flour mills and a number of river craft to support their flour milling activities. Although having offices in Liverpool, the company had been established at Cardiff where, as **Spillers and Bakers Ltd.,** it began shipowning in 1894. Last of its ships was the WHEATCROP (523/1924) which carried grain to Irish Sea ports until 1952, latterly based in Liverpool under the plain title of **Spillers Ltd.**

Henry Tyrer and Co. were well known in Liverpool as shipping agents, but their shipowning activities were centred on Preston, where their ships were mostly involved in importing wood pulp.

Fawn passed through the ownership of several local companies. *John Clarkson*

Spiller's **Wheatcrop**. *John Clarkson*

Pantocrator P of the Cyclades Steamship Co. Ltd., laid up. *John Clarkson*

Vogt and Maguire Ltd. have agencies at Liverpool and other North West ports, and have occasionally become involved with managing ships. Between 1948 and 1950 Vogt and Maguire (Chartering) Ltd. managed the PANTOCRATOR P (234/1917) on behalf of the **Cyclades Steamship Co. Ltd.** The man behind this was **Socrates G. Paleocrassas,** of that rare breed the Liverpool-Greek shipowner. Three more modern ships were owned by Vogt and Maguire's asssociate **Windle Shipping Co. Ltd.** from 1973 to 1976: the motor ships WINDLE SKY (1,511/1973), WINDLE SEA (1,562/1963) and WINDLE SPRAY (423/1965). Managed by Comben Longstaff of London, these are listed in Captain Ken Garrett's book on this company.

Coastal steamers tended to have long lives, and even when their sea-going days were over they were often found roles in sheltered waters. In the 1920s the **Wadsworth Lighterage and Coaling Co. Ltd.** built up a fleet of barges, some equipped with derricks, for coaling ships whilst they were at their berths in the docks. The fleet included several former coasters, including the LADY KATE (234/1917) previously PANTOCRATOR P. She had been built for Larne coal merchants as DROMAINE and photographs show that she was heavily modified for Wadsworth's trade, loosing her forecastle but retaining a derrick for lifting large tubs of coal. By the 1960s the demand for bunker coal was all but extinguished, and the company sold its vessels. In November 1962 LADY KATE made her last voyage to Preston where she was broken up by T.W. Ward Ltd.

Lady Kate in the Mersey. Owners were the Wadsworth Lighterage and Coaling Co. Ltd. *John Clarkson*

ACKNOWLEDGEMENTS

Over many years, a great number of people have helped with the research for this book, and I apologise if anyone's contribution has been overlooked in the list below.

Acknowledgements must start with four people to whom I owe particular debts. Mike Stammers of the Merseyside Maritime Museum read the introductory sections, made a number of constructive suggestions, and was kind enough to suggest that this potted history of the Mersey Basin passed muster. Perhaps an even larger contribution to getting the book published has been his regular but polite enquiries as to when I was going to finish the work. Charles Waine, whose work first led me to research steam coasters, also volunteered to read the individual chapters, and made many helpful comments about coaster design and economics. John Clarkson allowed me full use of his extensive and matchless collection of photographs, and the book would have been much poorer without them. Rowan Hackman has most willingly shared his comprehensive records of launch dates and spared the author enormous labour.

There are many more: Gerald Adderley who was most generous with his researches which helped unravel the story of the Liverpool-Welsh owners; Reg and Lynne Aveyard for arranging Welsh translations; Derek Blackhurst for generously sharing research into Fishers which was intended for his own book; Nigel Bowker for his records of Mersey craft; James Boyd whose books on Welsh narrow gauge railways often provide the only published sources on quarry ownership and operation; Joe Broady for information on Richard Clark; David Burrell for delving in *Lloyd's Register's* records; Craig Carter for help and publishing my queries in *Sea Breezes;* Terry O'Conallain for information on Robert Leeson and Owen Donnelly; Bob and Robin Cowan for taking a deep personal interest in the history of their company Edward Nicholson Ltd.; Mrs G. Vivien Davies for sharing much information on her great-uncle Richard Hughes; Ivor E. Davies who called on memories of half a century with the Penmaenmawr and Welsh Granite Co. Ltd.; Professor A. Douglas Jones for information on Admiral Jones-Parry; Percy Dunbavand for making available his valuable work in Merseyside ship registers; C.H. Elston of the Liverpool Shipowners' Association for information on R. and D. Jones; Christine Evans who made it possible to tell the full story of her grandfather Richard Clark; Ken Garrett for providing contacts in present-day Liverpool shipping and in the Registrar of Shipping; Roy Griffin who first researched Richard Hughes and has joined me as co-author of the chapter on this owner; Clive Guthrie for his knowledge of Yarwoods and his infectious enthusiasm for all aspects of the industrial archaelogy and history of the North West; Don Hayman for sharing his delving into William Savage's history; Douglas Head for kindly supplying information from his researches into Richard Clark, Zillah, and other owners; George Hignett for memories of Richard Clark's ships; Harry Hignett for invaluable contacts amongst the Liverpool Nautical Research Society and his many other friends; Brian Hillsdon for adding yard numbers; Dr. David Jenkins of the Welsh Industrial and Maritime Museum for help and encouragement particularly with the chapter on Richard Hughes; F.N. Jones for remembering his father's time on the Rose boats; Ron Jones for archival material relating to the Best family; Will Jones for memories of serving in Mersey coasters in the 1930s; Peter Kenyon for sharing his diligent work on Preston shipping; William Leathwood who has been the only person found with personal memories of the Rowland family and also helped to tell the Richard Clark story; Keith Lewis who shared his photographs and records; Louis Loughran for confirmation of flag and funnel details; Paul Mack who enthusiastically helped with his family history; Kenneth Monroe who put me on the trail of Richard Hughes' family and gave me something of the inside story of this business and that of R. and D. Jones; Sybil Morgan for information on Admiral Jones-Parry; the late Peter Norton for delving into Warrington newspapers for accounts of William Savage's early launches; Dr. Roger Oliphant for biographies of First World War commanders; Edward Paget-Tomlinson for sharing his knowledge of the inland waterway trading of the Northwich Carrying Co. and Henry Seddon; Stephen Penney of the Salt Museum, Northwich for access to records; Iona Roberts for using her outstanding knowledge of the Llŷn to help trace the Jones-Parrys; J.B. Roberts who remembered sailing with his father on Edward's KEMPOCK; Ivor Rooke for help researching Richard

Hughes; Alan Smith whose patient researches and extensive local knowledge of the Llanddulas area made it possible to unravel the stories of Raynes, Kneeshaw and Lupton; Captain Owen Spargo for his clear memories of the home trade three-quarters of a century ago; Bert Starkey who amplified information on Runcorn owners from his excellent book *Schooner Port;* Captain Viv Thomas for his memories of working for Mountwood Shipping; Jonathon S.E. Turner for reviewing the chapter on his family's shipping business; Bob and Vera Tushingham for lending me their house so that I could work undisturbed in the tranquillity of the Welsh borders; Dennis, Dudley and Maurice Wallace-Jones who took time and trouble to complete the story of their grandfather Richard Hughes and for allowing use of family photographs; David Whiteside for sharing his researches into early shipping movements at Preston; Ian Wilson for help with northern Irish connections; Joseph Wilson for recalling how he founded Mountwood Shipping; Mary Yale for information on Admiral Jones-Parry; and far from least my wife Heather for horticultural consultancy, patience, proof reading, cartography and much practical and moral support.

For help in completing ships' histories I have to thank the World Ship Society's Central Record team, including Harold Appleyard, John Bartlett, Jim Colledge, Bernard Lawley, Kevin O'Donoghue, Graeme Somner and Peter White; Rowan Hackman for launch dates; Robert Blane and Bill Harvey for details of Ailsa-built ships; Fred Hawks; Bill Schell of Holbrook, Massachussets who freely shared information and contacts; the Central Record's country experts – Robert Bohan for Sweden, André Delporte for Belgium, Bernd Langensiepen for Turkey, Jan Oostmeier for the Netherlands, Arne Tandberg for Norway and Soren Thorsoe for Denmark; Barbara Jones, Anne Cowne, Leslie Spurling and their predecessors at Lloyd's Register of Shipping; Jenny Wraight, Declan Barriskill and others at the Guildhall Library; and staff at both the Public Record Office in Kew and the Merseyside Maritime Museum whose labours made it possible to search so many registers.

Lastly, I'm also very grateful to the photographers, collectors and museums credited alongside their photographs, and for help locating photographs to John Bartlett, Derek Blackhurst, Roy Griffin, Clive Guthrie, David Hodge of the N.M.M., Bill Lind of The Ballast Trust, Mike MacDonald and Norman Taylor, to Keith Byass, Cliff Parsons and Tony Smith of the W.S.P.L.; to Ian Jones for supplying the front and Charles Waine for the back cover illustrations, and to Hugh Smallwood for cover design and flags and funnel illustrations.

ALL CONTRACTS OR ENGAGEMENTS WHETHER IN RELATION TO FREIGHT OR OTHERWISE ARE ON THE TERMS CONDITIONS AND EXCEPTIONS OF THE CHAMBER OF SHIPPING COASTING CHARTER PARTY.

W. A. SAVAGE LIMITED.

SHIP BROKERS
GRAVEL MERCHANTS

MANAGERS FOR
ZILLAH SHIPPING COMPANY LTD
SOLE AGENTS FOR
PIEL & WALNEY GRAVEL

RELIANCE HOUSE
WATER STREET
LIVERPOOL, 2.

TELEX: Nº 62-316
TELEGRAMS
"ZILLAH," LIVERPOOL 2. TELEX
TELEPHONES:
CENTRAL 1604 (4 LINES) & 5781

OUR REF

YOUR REF

DATE

BIBLIOGRAPHY

Books

Anderson B.L. and Stoney P.J.M. (eds) *Commerce, Industry and Transport: Studies in Economic Change on Merseyside;* Liverpool University Press, Liverpool 1983

Aughton P. *Liverpool: a People's History;* Carnegie Press, Preston 1990

Boyd J.I.C. *Narrow Gauge Railways in North Caernarvonshire, Volumes 1, 2 and 3;* Oakwood Press, Oxford 1981, 1985 and 1986

Brooks C. *Grayson's of Liverpool;* Henry Young, Liverpool 1956

Burton V. (ed) *Liverpool Shipping, Trade and Industry: Essays on the Maritime History of Merseyside 1780-1860;* National Museums and Galleries on Merseyside, Liverpool 1989

Cottrell P.L. *The Steamship on the Mersey, 1815-80* in *Shipping Trade and Commerce;* eds Cottrell P.L. and Aldcroft D.H., Leicester University Press, Leicester 1981

Davidson A.S. *Marine Art and Liverpool: Painters, Places and Flag Codes 1760-1960;* Waine Research Publications, Albrighton 1986

Eames A. *Ventures in Sail;* Gwynedd Archives and Museums Service, Caernarfon & London, 1987

Farnie D.A. *The Manchester Ship Canal and the Rise of the Port of Manchester 1894-1975;* Manchester University Press, Manchester 1980

Fenton R.S. *Cambrian Coasters;* World Ship Society, Kendal 1989.

Guthrie C. *W.J. Yarwood & Sons Ltd.: Shipbuilders of Northwich 1896-1966;* Northwich Heritage Society, Northwich 1996.

Hadfield C. *The Canals of the West Midlands;* David and Charles, Newton Abbot 1966

Hadfield C. and Biddle G. *The Canals of North West England;* David and Charles, Newton Abbot 1970

Hayman A. *Mersey and Irwell Navigation to Manchester Ship Canal;* Bridgwater Cruising Club, Manchester 1981

Hughes J. *Port in a Storm: the Air Attacks on Liverpool and its Shipping in the Second World War;* National Museums and Galleries on Merseyside, Liverpool 1993

Hyde F.E. *Liverpool and the Mersey: an Economic History of a Port 1700-1970;* David and Charles, Newton Abbot 1971

Jarvis A. *Docks of the Mersey;* Ian Allan, London 1988

Jarvis A. *Ellesmere Port - Canal Town 1795-1921;* Boat Museum, Ellesmere Port 1977

Lubbock B. *Last of the Windjammers;* Brown, Son and Ferguson, Glasgow 1927

Marriner S. *The Economic and Social Development of Merseyside;* Croom Helm, London 1982

McKnight H. *The Shell Book of Inland Waterways;* David and Charles, Newton Abbot 1975

Meneight W.A. *A History of the United Molasses Co. Ltd.;* United Molasses Co. Ltd., Liverpool 1977

Michael C. *The Wrecks of Liverpool Bay;* Liverpool Marine Press, Liverpool 1994

Norton P. *Waterways and Railways to Warrington;* Railway and Canal Historical Society, Caterham 1974

Paget-Tomlinson E. *Mersey and Weaver Flats: the Sailing River and Canal Flats of North-west England;* Robert Wilson, Kettering 1973

Paget-Tomlinson E. *The Illustrated History of Canal and River Navigations;* Sheffield Academic Press, Sheffield 1993

Place G. *The Rise and Fall of Parkgate: Passenger Port for Ireland 1686-1815;* Cheetham Society, Manchester 1994

Pollard S. and Robertson P. *The British Shipbuilding Industry, 1870-1914;* Harvard University Press, Cambridge, Mass. 1979

Read G. and Stammers M. *Guide to the Records of the Merseyside Maritime Museum;* National Museums and Galleries on Merseyside, Liverpool 1995

Reader W.J. *Imperial Chemical Industries: a History* (two vols); Oxford University Press, London, 1970 and 1975

Ritchie-Noakes N. *Liverpool's Historic Waterfront: the World's First Mercantile Dock System;* Royal Commission on Historical Monuments, London 1984
Sinclair R.C. *Across the Irish Sea: Belfast-Liverpool Shipping since 1819;* Conway Maritime Press, London 1990
Spargo O.G. and Thomasson T.H. *Old Time Steam Coasting;* Waine Research Publications, Albrighton 1982
Stammers M. *Liverpool: the Port and its Ships;* Alan Sutton, Stroud 1991
Stammers M. *Mersey Flats and Flatmen;* Terence Dalton, Lavenham 1993
Starkey H.G. *Schooner Port;* G.W. and A. Hesketh, Ormskirk 1983
Tennent A.J. *British Merchant Ships Sunk by U-boats in the 1914-1918 War;* A.J. Tennent, Chipstead 1990.
Tolson J.M. *The St. Helens Railway: its Rivals and Successors;* Oakwood Press, Salisbury 1983
Waine C.V. and Fenton, R.S. *Steam Coasters and Short Sea Traders, 3rd edition;* Waine Research Publications, Albrighton 1994

Lloyd's Confidential Indexes
Lloyd's Registers
Mercantile Navy Lists

Periodicals

Carter C.J.M. Stott's of Liverpool; *Sea Breezes,* 1967, **41,** 686-693
Eccles D.K.C. Kyle Transport Co. Ltd. *Liverpool Nautical Research Society Bulletin,* 1993, **37,** 35-38
Faulkner A. Seddons of Middlewich; *Waterways World,* 1992, **21** (August), 54-59
Griffin T.R. Richard Hughes and Co; *Marine News,* 1955, **9,** 79- 81 and 100-103
Head D. W.A. Savage and the Zillah Shipping and Carrying Co. Ltd.; *Liverpool Nautical Research Society Bulletin,* 1992, **35,** 67-68.
Head D. Wilson Brothers (Garston) Merchants, Manufacturers and Shipowners; *Liverpool Nautical Research Society Bulletin,* 1992, **36,** 16-17.
Head D. Kyle Transport Co. Ltd.; *Liverpool Nautical Research Society Bulletin,* 1993, **37,** 35-38.
Hignett H.M. Navigation on the Upper Mersey; *Liverpool Nautical Research Society Bulletin,* 1992, **36,** 30-33
Kenyon P. Preston Container Trades (parts 1-3); *Liverpool Nautical Research Society Bulletin,* 1996, **39-40,** 85-89, 19-22, 39-46.
Leathwood W.E. Days of Sail on the Upper Mersey; *Sea Breezes,* 1974, **56** (June), 325-331
Terreta E. Diving – A Personal Quest; *Port of Manchester Review* 1976
Wilson I. Rowland's "Rocks"; *Sea Breezes,* 1976, **59** (November), 645-649
Obituaries of William Rowland in the *Runcorn Examiner* for 8th May 1903, the *Runcorn Chronicle* for 9th May 1903, and *Runcorn Guardian* for 9th May 1903.
Runcorn Daily News for October and November 1981 which carried correspondence about Richard Clark and his ships.

Unpublished and other sources

Lloyd's Register Wreck Books
Records of the Registrar General of Shipping (Classes BT108, BT109 and BT110) in the Public Record Office, Kew.
Records of the Registrar of Joint Stock Companies (Class BT31) in the Public Record Office, Kew.
Liverpool and Runcorn Statutory Registers of British Merchant Ships held in the Merseyside Maritime Museum.
Records of E.W. Turner and Co. lodged with the Merseyside Maritime Museum.

INDEX OF SHIPS

Entries in UPPER CASE indicate names carried by ships in the fleet lists whilst in the ownership or management of Mersey companies covered in this book. Page numbers in **bold** refer to fleet list entries.

INDEX OF OWNERS AND MANAGERS

This index lists all the individual owners and managers of Mersey coasters referred to in this book. Page numbers refer to the beginning of the chapter (including Miscellany) in which the company features.

Notes on the fleet lists

The fleet list entries are presented in the World Ship Society's format.

The first line gives the ship's name whilst in the company's ownership, the number in brackets indicates whether this was the first, second or third use of the name. The dates show the period in the company's ownership. Ships are steel unless stated otherwise.

The second line gives the official number (O.N.), gross and net tonnages at the time the ship was acquired by the company, and length, breadth and depth in feet and tenths. In the case of lengthening, new tonnages and dimensions are given on the subsequent line.

The next line gives details of engines and their builder; where a ship has been re-engined, details are given on subsequent lines. C. 2-cyl. indicates a compound, two cylinder steam engine. T. 3-cyl. indicates a three cylinder, triple-expansion steam engine. For oil engines, the number of cylinders is given followed by details of engine type: 2S.C. for two-stroke cycle, 4S.C. for four-stroke cycle; S.A. for single-acting, D.A. for double-acting. Speeds are quoted when available from registration documents.

Subsequent lines give the ship's full history, beginning with details of builder and, when known, yard number. Where possible, launch dates have been quoted. When a day, month and year of completion is quoted this is the date the ship was registered: when a month and year only is quoted, it is taken from *Lloyd's Register.* Only in the case of ships built by Ailsa or Yarwoods has it been possible to discover on which day a ship has actually been delivered to its owners: this is within a few days of the registration date.

Ships' histories were initially compiled from *Lloyd's Registers, Mercantile Navy Lists* and *Lloyd's Confidential Indexes.* These have been checked and extended by referring to the official registration documents of the ships, the Statutory Register of British Merchant Ships, or the Custom's Register as it is often known. Statutory Registers of all British ships closed up to 1955 are held at the Public Record Office, Kew; and those for most Liverpool and Runcorn registered ships up to the 1920s are in the Merseyside Maritime Museum. The sale dates quoted are those on the bill of sale. For renamings, the date is that on which the new name was registered.

Fates have been obtained from *Lloyd's Register* and *Board of Trade Casualty Returns, Lloyd's Register's Wreck Books, Lloyd's Lists'* reports, *Lloyd's War Loss Lists* for the First and Second World Wars, *Lloyd's Confidential Indexes* and the Cemetery Cards in the Guildhall Library, and *Marine News.*

For ships lost or broken up under the British flag the date the Statutory Register was closed is quoted.

FLAGS AND FUNNELS

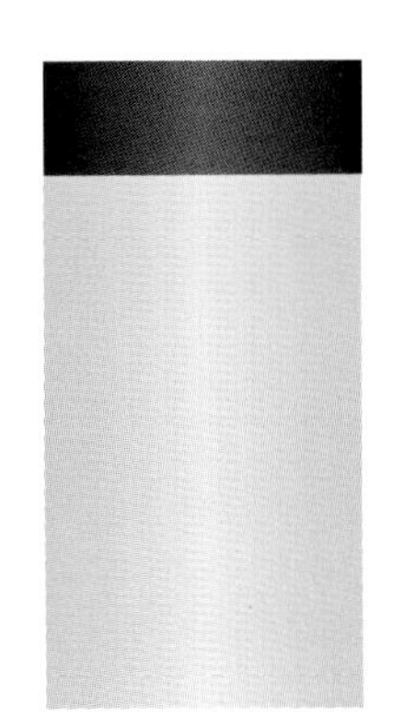

Thomas G. Best

No houseflag is known.

Brundrit and Co. Ltd.

Richard R. Clark
Overton Steamship Co. Ltd.

William Cooper and Sons Ltd.

James H. Cooper

RAYNESTONE had a black 'C' on her funnel from 1974.

John Edwards and Co.

Joseph E. Fisher

Not all the ships used the funnel shown. In some ships the colours of the bands were reversed, whilst CAMBALU had a black funnel with an orange band, to which a black 'F' was added in 1931.

Richard Hughes and Co.

Richard Hughes and Co. (Liverpool) Ltd.

Hughes Holden Shipping Ltd.

Hume, Smith and Co.

The aluminium funnel with the lion emblem was reportedly tried early in the company's existence, but was abandoned after complaints that it was too dazzling! United Alkali's colours were retained until about 1950 when the blue basic funnel and flag were adopted, themselves giving way to the orange funnel and accompanying flag in 1969.

Imperial Chemical Industries Ltd.

R. and D. Jones

The plain black funnel was used until about 1900.

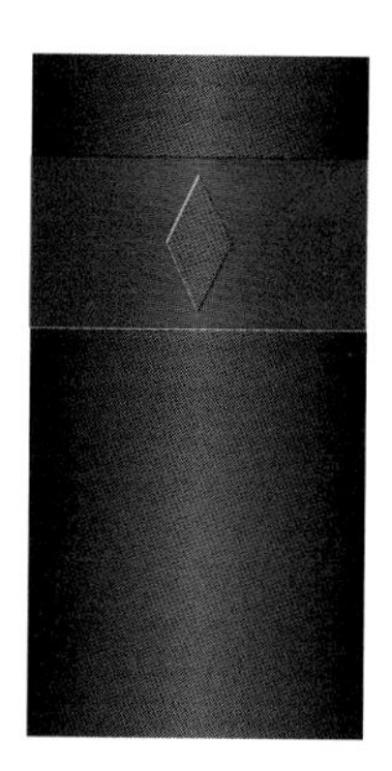

Robert Leeson

KILMARNOCK's funnel was originally red with black top, but because of its tendency to become over-heated it was altered to all-black.

Lowden, Connell and Co.

J.J. Mack and Sons

Associated companies using the same funnel were the Straits Steamship Co. Ltd. (from 1939) and the Liverpool Lighterage Co. Ltd.

Manchester, Liverpool and North Wales Steamship Co. Ltd.

The company appears not to have had a houseflag.

Mersey Ports Stevedoring Co. Ltd.

No houseflag is known.

John K. Morris

Mountwood Shipping Co. Ltd.

Edward Nicholson Ltd.

No houseflag is known.

Northwich Carrying Co. Ltd.

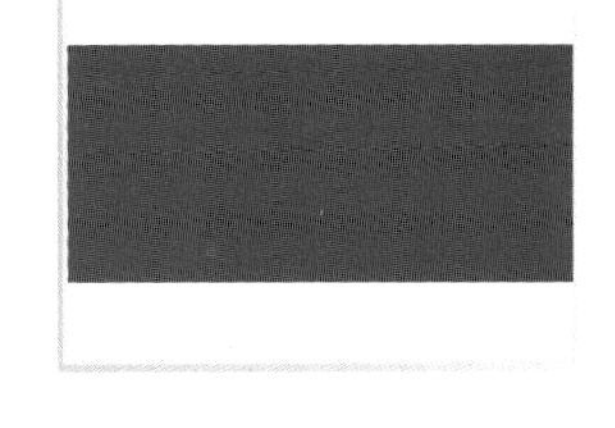

Pollexfen and Co. Ltd.

C.W. Pollexfen used a black funnel with a plain blue band and a plain blue flag.

No houseflag is known.

Antonio M. Ralli and Son

William Rowland

The houseflag is based on that in the trial's photograph of JANE ROWLAND: the red is conjectural.

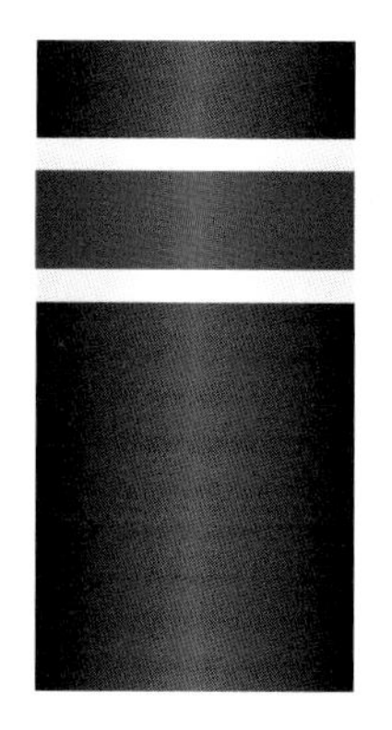

Alfred Rowland

Thomas J. Sharp and Co.

Summerfield Steamship Co. Ltd.

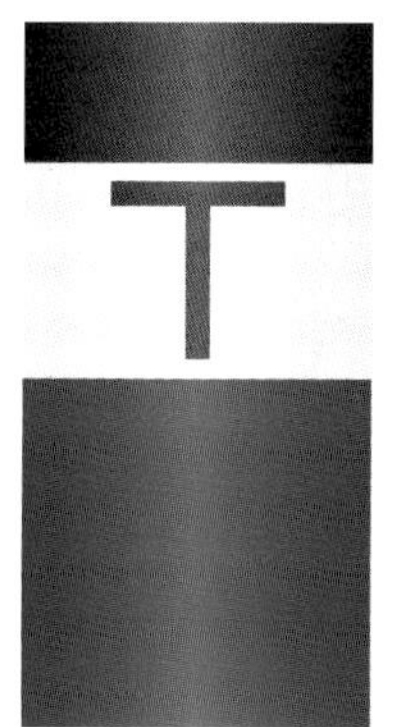

Thomas Brothers Shipping Co. Ltd.

The painting of MIRIAM THOMAS on the cover has a blue flag with white cross and white letters 'TBS Co'. This is believed to be incorrect.

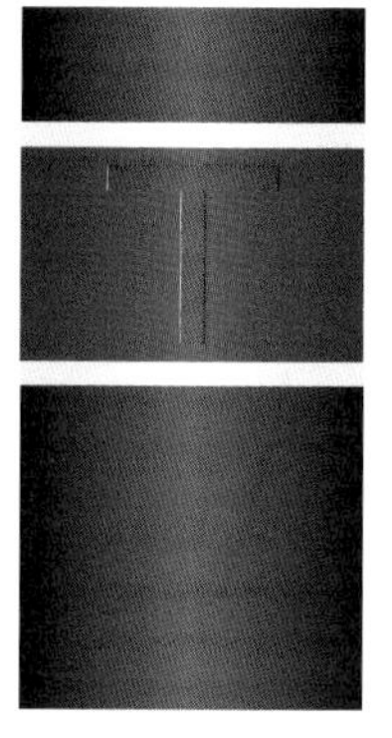

Thomas Coasters Ltd.

Owen H. Thomas

After Thomas Coasters Ltd. was wound up in 1936 Owen H. Thomas continued to use this funnel on the MIRIAM THOMAS.

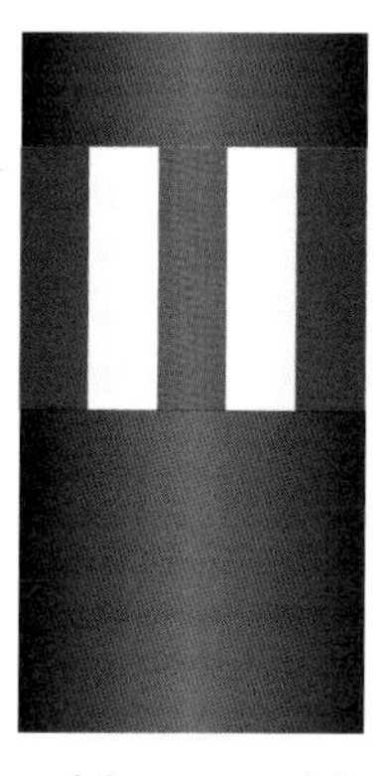

W. Glynne Thomas

Glynwood Navigation Co. Ltd.

Prior to the Second World War the funnel of LADY THOMAS was grey with a black top, separated by a red band with a white letter `T'. In 1946, just before the funnel shown was adopted, she had a black funnel with a plain white band.

William Thomas

The flag changed from rectangular to swallow-tailed about 1900.
The 'L' may stand for Liverpool.

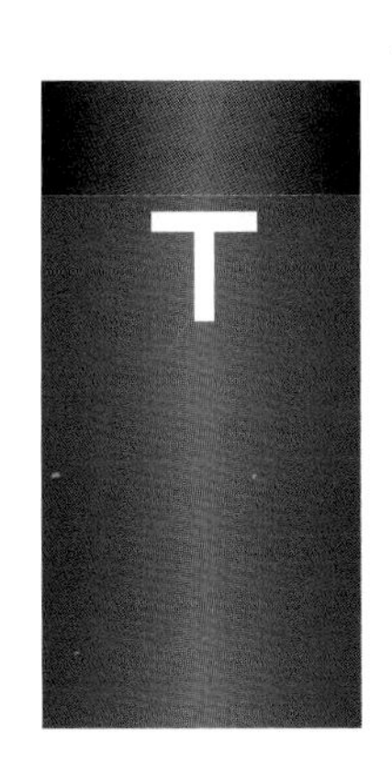

Edward W. Turner

The Garston Steamship Co. Ltd. used the plain red funnel with black top.
The white 'T' was added for the MERTOLA.

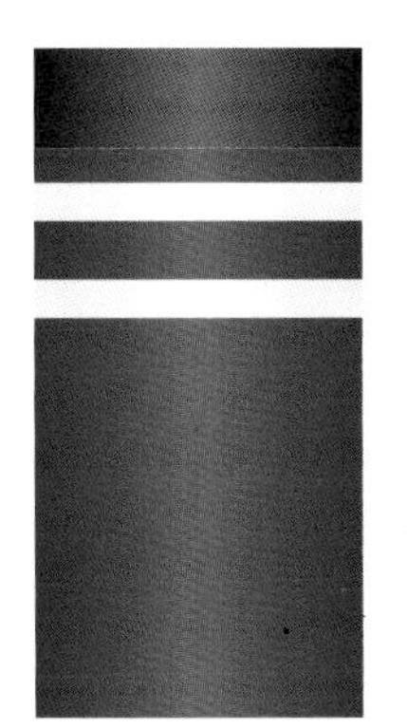

United Alkali Co. Ltd.

Wilson Bros. Bobbin Co. Ltd.

Zillah Shipping Co. Ltd.
Zillah Shipping and Carrying Co. Ltd.

The second houseflag was adopted in 1949 after the company had been acquired by Coast Lines.

Flags and funnels of other companies

Described here are markings of coastal tramp companies covered in the Miscellany section and of larger companies for which evidence is scant.

British Isles Transport Co. Ltd.: yellow funnel with black top.

Coastal Motorships Ltd.: the funnel of the LORRAINE D was painted in a different scheme almost yearly. The two most elaborate schemes were: yellow with black top and bearing either a red band carrying the letters 'CMS' (in 1975 and 1976) or a white scroll with the same letters in red vertically (in 1978 and 1979). CAPECREST simply had a yellow funnel with black top.

Joseph Crosfield and Sons Ltd.: black funnel with yellow band; blue houseflag with yellow St. Andrew's cross.

Cyclades Steamship Co. Ltd.: black funnel with white band.

Kyle Transport Co. Ltd.: black funnel; red houseflag with blue diamond containing white letter 'K'.

Kymo Shipping Co. Ltd.: yellow funnel with black top.

Liverpool Derricking and Carrying Co. Ltd.: yellow funnel with black top.

George Nelson and Sons: black funnel with three red bands; white houseflag with red upper and lower edges and blue letter 'N' on white.

Robert Owen and Co.: some evidence of a black funnel with a green band.

Parry, Jones and Co.: red funnel with black top separated by blue band.

R. and J. H. Rea: red funnel with black top separated by narrow white band, with, on the red, a white-edged blue or black diamond with a white letter 'K'; the diamond device also appears on the red houseflag.

Henry Seddon: funnels were black for river craft but probably buff for coasters.

Wadsworth Lighterage and Coaling Co. Ltd.: black funnel with white band.

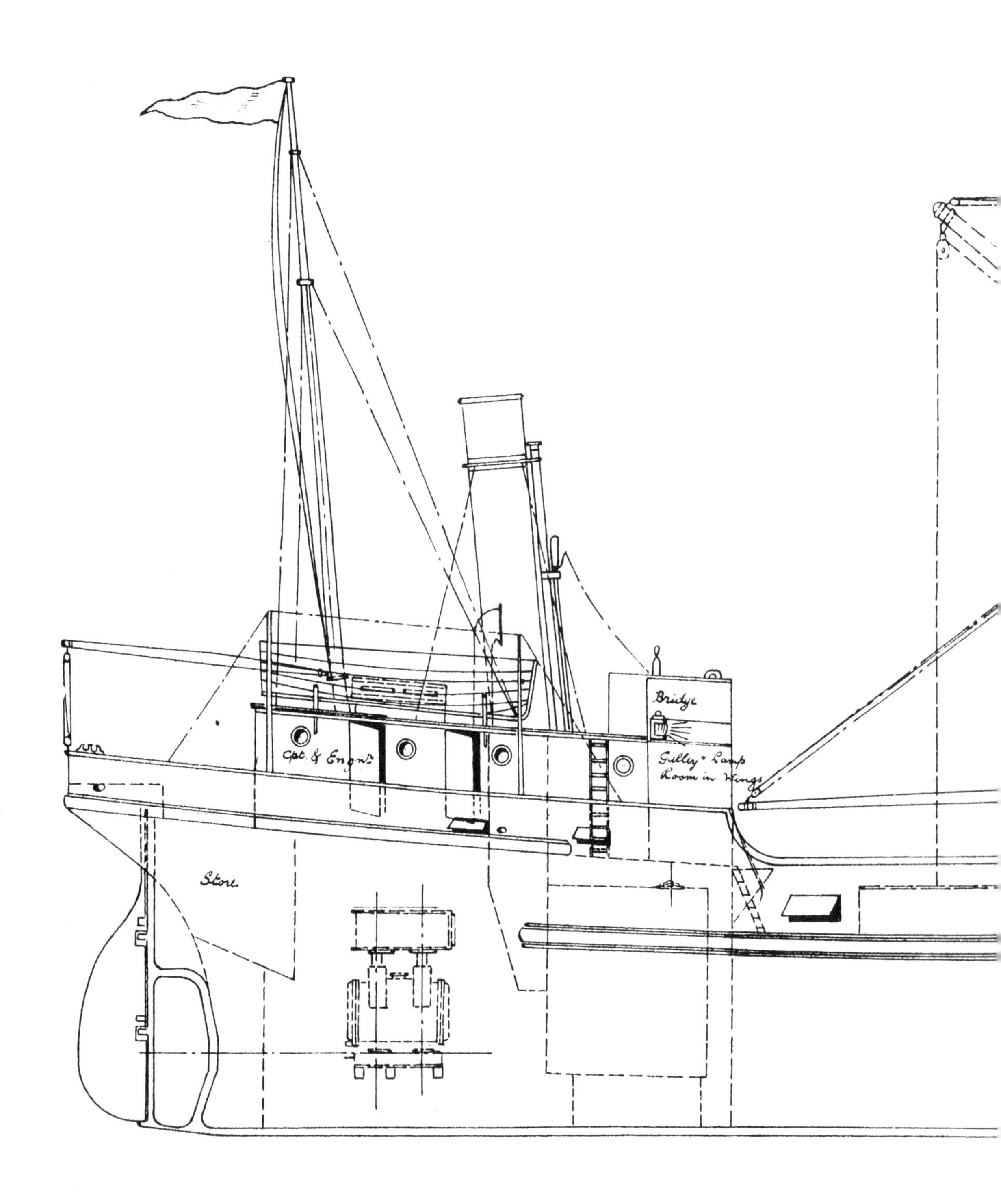
Bridge
Cpt. & Engn.
Galley & Lamp
Room in Wings
Store